THE SINGAPORE LION

"Throughout the turbulent period leading up to Singapore's independence, Rajaratnam played a crucial role as comrade, fighter, thinker, preacher, propagandist. He worked tirelessly to forge a new Singapore identity which transcended race and religion, during his years as Singapore's first Culture Minister and also later, as the country's first Foreign Minister after Separation from Malaysia. Visiting his war-torn ancestral homeland in Jaffna recently, I thought how fortunate we in Singapore are that he came to our shores and made Singapore his home and calling. Irene Ng's book, *The Singapore Lion*, tells the story of a man who altered the course of Singapore's destiny."

George Yeo
Foreign Minister, Singapore

"*The Singapore Lion* is an important book for those who want to understand how Rajaratnam's ideas influenced a generation of Singaporeans and inspired them to believe they could live together in peace despite their troubled past. He was the country's founding father of multi-racialism without which there would have been no independent Singapore. No other book explains better why and how he believed that was the only way it could work. A very well-written and insightful book."

Han Fook Kwang
Editor, The Straits Times

"Irene Ng has authored a must-read book for all Singaporeans and those interested in Singapore. It offers a rare personal insight of the true renaissance man whose creative imagination helped steer Singapore's pioneer years."

Benson Puah
CEO, National Arts Council

"What a delightful book! Irene Ng has done all Singaporeans proud by carefully weaving the rich, sometimes bewildering, life of one of the Lion City's great founding fathers into a tapestry of revelations embracing Mr Rajaratnam's varied and robust personality. Written in clear, crisp and engaging prose, *The Singapore Lion* is a must-read for all who desire an in-depth understanding of a man whose genius shone through both his political and literary life."

Kirpal Singh
Director, Wee Kim Wee Centre
Singapore Management University

"The story of Raja's incisive use of media — a must-read for anyone who needs to communicate ideas effectively and win the hearts and minds of others, be they voters, employees, clients or partners. A brilliant piece of writing."

Shaun Seow
Deputy CEO, Television-Channel NewsAsia,
Radio/Print/Interactive Media,
MediaCorp Pte Ltd

"Irene Ng has fleshed out the Rajaratnam story with lively anecdotes, well-researched materials and well-sourced interviews. They will add to a better understanding of the story of early Singapore, a story that needs to be updated constantly."

P.N. Balji
Director, Asia Journalism Fellowship

The **Institute of Southeast Asian Studies (ISEAS)** was established as an autonomous organization in 1968. It is a regional centre dedicated to the study of socio-political, security and economic trends and developments in Southeast Asia and its wider geostrategic and economic environment. The Institute's research programmes are the Regional Economic Studies (RES, including ASEAN and APEC), Regional Strategic and Political Studies (RSPS), and Regional Social and Cultural Studies (RSCS).

ISEAS Publishing, an established academic press, has issued almost 2,000 books and journals. It is the largest scholarly publisher of research about Southeast Asia from within the region. ISEAS Publishing works with many other academic and trade publishers and distributors to disseminate important research and analyses from and about Southeast Asia to the rest of the world.

THE SINGAPORE LION

A BIOGRAPHY OF S. RAJARATNAM

IRENE NG

INSTITUTE OF SOUTHEAST ASIAN STUDIES

Singapore

First published in Singapore in 2010 by
ISEAS Publishing
Institute of Southeast Asian Studies
30 Heng Mui Keng Terrace
Pasir Panjang
Singapore 119614

E-mail: publish@iseas.edu.sg
Website: <http://bookshop.iseas.edu.sg>

The Institute of Southeast Asian Studies would like to thank the following for their kind donation to the Institute towards the publication of this book: Kampong Glam Constituency Citizens Consultative Committee; Olivia Lum; S. Rajaratnam; Shaw Foundation Pte; Premkumar Pillay; and Ravindran Pillay.

First Reprint 2010

ISEAS Library Cataloguing-in-Publication Data

Ng Irene.
The Singapore Lion : A Biography of S. Rajaratnam.
1. Cabinet officers—Singapore—Biography.
2. Singapore—Politics and government.
I. Title.
DS610.63 R16N57 2010

ISBN 978-981-4279-50-5 (soft cover)
ISBN 978-981-4279-51-2 (hard cover)
ISBN 978-981-4279-52-9 (E-book PDF)

Typeset by Superskill Graphics Pte Ltd
Printed in Singapore by Utopia Press Pte Ltd

To the memory of S. Rajaratnam
and his enduring vision

Contents

Foreword

This biography of S. Rajaratnam is a valuable record of the life of an exceptional man who made a great contribution to Singapore.

Raja was always fighting for the underdog. The first time I met him was in 1952. I was representing the Postal and Telecommunications Uniformed Staff Union; negotiations with the Chief Secretary had failed and the postmen decided to strike.

Raja wrote powerful stories and editorials in the *Singapore Standard* to support the postmen's strike. He felt they were unjustly treated. He acidly highlighted the highly paid expatriate officers who had just given themselves a hefty increase in their expatriate allowance, but were miserly towards these hardworking postmen.

The postmen won public support. After two weeks, the government made concessions. This successful strike changed the course of events in Singapore.

Raja's outstanding quality was his fighting spirit when on a righteous cause. After the pro-communist PAP Assemblymen, all of whom were Chinese-educated, split to form Barisan Sosialis, they pummelled us day after day in press statements and at mass rallies, all reported in full by Chinese-owned newspapers. Many Chinese reporters were their sympathisers. Raja tirelessly rebutted them point by point day after day. I felt weary having to issue rebuttals to absurd accusations. Ever the pamphleteer, Raja never allowed them to go unanswered.

He won the support of the English-educated by his wit in his trenchant dismissals. I still remember him at his typewriter with a cigarette in his mouth, tapping away.

We were close friends bonded by fighting difficult battles together. He always gave me a boost of energy to carry on the ceaseless counter barrage against the Communist United Front whose objective was to weary its opponents and reduce their energy and spirits. His vibrant and indignant response was like a cup of *ginseng* tea for me, reinvigorating me by his infectious optimism. In his affectionate way, he would say, "Harry, they cannot win. We must not allow them to win and ruin Singapore."

He had indomitable courage. When UMNO ultras tried to intimidate us during our two years in Malaysia, he was not cowed. He and Toh Chin Chye, the chairman of the People's Action Party (PAP), proposed the formation of the Malaysian Solidarity Convention, to which the party's Central Executive Committee agreed. They gathered their friends from the states in peninsular Malaysia. Raja persuaded the non-*bumiputra* (Malay) parties in Sabah and Sarawak to join it.

At the Solidarity Convention meetings held at our old open-air theatre at the junction of River Valley Road and Clemenceau Avenue, his booming voice gave confidence to the audience not to be intimidated by the threats of UMNO "ultras". After a few months, the UMNO-led government began to feel the non-Malay ground shifting against them. So Tunku Abdul Rahman, the Prime Minister of Malaysia, wanted Singapore out of Malaysia.

When it came to the crunch, Raja was the most unwilling to sign the Separation Agreement. After hours of contemplation, chain-smoking at the verandah of Sri Temasek, Kuala Lumpur, I decided to tell him that if he did not agree, then he and Toh Chin Chye would have to carry on the fight, and without me. After more agonising, he reluctantly signed it.

His enduring legacy to Singapore is our National Pledge. We had two communal riots in 1964, the first on 21 July, Prophet Mohammad's birthday, and the second in September when I was away in Brussels for the Socialist International Centenary meeting. These were engineered by the UMNO "ultras" to intimidate the Chinese population. In both riots, the police and the army, both under Federal control, were biased, against the Chinese and sympathising with the Malays. In total, 36 people were killed and 563 were injured.

After Separation, he drafted the National Pledge. Given the mood of the people in Singapore at that time, only Raja had the conviction and optimism to express those long-term aspirations in that pledge. He had expressed his ideal of our races becoming one people, all melded into a Singaporean people. I tightened his draft to leave out the more idealistic phrases and to smoothen it.

It was an act of faith to declare: "We, the citizens of Singapore, pledge ourselves as one united people, regardless of race, language or religion, to build a democratic society based on justice and equality, so as to achieve happiness, prosperity and progress for our nation." It was worth aspiring for.

Raja's warm and open personality made him liked even by foreign leaders who were not politically sympathetic. He represented a small country, was able to engage them by his bearing and open friendliness and his broad background knowledge and experience. These he had developed over his long years in Britain when, instead of studying law at King's College, London, he immersed himself in the anti-colonial movements of the Indians and Africans.

He was a good judge of people and talent-spotted men from academia and business to be our ambassadors; Tommy Koh for the United Nations, Ho Rih Hwa for Bangkok, Thailand, and many others. All these successfully represented us. Increasingly, I left the selection of people to Raja as Foreign Minister.

Raja's contribution to Singapore is not in bricks and mortar, or concrete and glass. It was in ideas, sentiments and spirit, captured in words he lovingly typed out. Everyday, when the Pledge is recited in our schools, our children are reminded to live up to our aspirations of a multi-racial society regardless of race, language or religion.

Irene Ng has done thorough and painstaking research over many years to write this biography. She dug into the archival records and the papers that he left behind, and through interviewing relatives, friends and political foes, retraced the path he took.

Lee Kuan Yew
Minister Mentor
Singapore, November 2009

Preface

S. Rajaratnam rarely talked about himself unless probed. He would rather talk about ideas, and the idea he loved most was Singapore. Talk about Singapore and he would be in good form, his eyes alive, his hands gesticulating. Once, over a casual dinner with me in the late 1980s, he became so passionate about his message — the need to stir a love of *meaningful* ideas among the young (as opposed to meaningless) — that he knocked over his glass of red wine on the table. He picked it up, set it upright, and continued talking about the classical tradition of Socrates and Plato.

That is one of the most enduring images of S. Rajaratnam in my memory.

Since that evening, I had become a visitor to his house in Chancery Lane until some months after his death in 2006. When I first met him, I was a senior political correspondent with *The New Paper*, which reached out to younger readers. I believe he saw in me an opportunity to shape young minds, including mine. He was always ready to provide me with quotes for my articles, whatever the topic — from ASEAN, local politics and history to his Saturday nights. Later, in 1998, I rejoined *The Straits Times* — I had started my career as a journalist in *The Straits Times* in 1986 — and continued tapping his brain.

Over the years, as I witnessed how he deteriorated after a series of minor strokes, the visits became more difficult. He began to lose his memory and was visibly alarmed at this. He tried to fight it by writing down all he could remember, such as the name of his wife Piroska on her portrait photographs on the wall, and copying entire passages from the various books in his vast library, by hand, into notebooks. His scrawls reveal his abiding preoccupation with ideas relating to race, religion, national identity and Singapore's future as a united nation, just as it was when he became the country's first Culture Minister in 1959. Then the day came when he could no longer read or write. By this time, in November 2001, I had joined the People's Action Party (PAP) and politics.

In May 2004, I approached Ambassador K. Kesavapany, Director of the Institute of Southeast Asian Studies, with a proposal to write a biography of Raja. His story deserves to be told and remembered. I am grateful that Kesavapany took that leap of faith with me. Without his unflagging support and patient encouragement, it would have been hard for me to undertake and complete this project. I am also thankful to the trustees of Rajaratnam's estate — President S.R. Nathan, Ambassador Tommy Koh and Raja's close relative in Singapore, Dr V. Kanda Pillay — for giving their assistance to this project. Thus began the most ambitious writing project of my life.

I officially started working on the biography in January 2005, while working full-time with the National Trades Union Congress (NTUC). By this time, whenever I popped into Raja's house to sift through his papers, he no longer recognised me. I found that an effective way to elicit a glimmer of life in his eyes was to say anything with the word "Harry" in it. "Can you remember Harry?" "Harry," he would reply, a smile playing on his lips. Minister Mentor Lee Kuan Yew — Harry to Raja — had been a central figure in Raja's life since they met in 1952.

Hence, I am grateful to MM Lee for agreeing to pen the Foreword to this book. I also thank him for the interviews he granted, once in 2005, and another in 2009, with emails in between to address my queries, and for his encouragement throughout.

There were heart-wrenching moments. Going through Raja's papers in his house, I found a speech he wrote in 1990 about ageing and dying. He wrote it when he was 76 and still lucid. In that speech, he spoke about the "Cyborg" problem. "The Cyborg problem arises because modern medicine, surgery, technology and so-called miracle drugs can prolong the process of dying not by just a few weeks or months, but spread over many years during which a human being is transformed into a cyborg — a corpse which simulates life...and a brain drained of its humanity..." He wrote that he had told his wife, when he was about to have a heart bypass in 1984, to do everything she possibly could to enforce his right to die, if he became a cyborg. He wrote about meeting death "as dignified human beings and not as mindless cyborgs which have taken possession of our bodies". Together with that type-written speech, which contained some of his own scribbles, was a sheaf of research materials on dying with dignity.

Sleep eluded me that night. The next day, 10 May 2005, my heart was heavy as I shared this depressing knowledge of his wishes with Professor Tommy Koh. Prof Koh assured me that the next time Raja was rushed to hospital, he would be allowed to pass on without "heroic medical intervention". So it was that, on 22 February 2006, Raja died of heart failure, three days shy of his 91st birthday.

As I stood next to his coffin at his funeral wake in his home, I resolved to do my best to produce a biography which would capture accurately his extraordinary life and all that he stood and fought for. So that people would not forget.

The weight of that vow hung over me for the four years it took me to research and write this book. During this period, I discovered many fresh sides to Raja which provide deeper insights into the man and his role in the history of Singapore and the region. The only way to flesh them out was to do more research, and reflect on what I had found, and then, crucially, to write it up. Raja led a rich, complex and unique life, and it would be an injustice to squeeze it all into one volume. So it will now come in two. The narrative of this book confines itself to Raja's years from his birth in 1915 to the birth of Malaysia in 1963. The second volume of his biography will cover the remaining years until his death in 2006, including how he came to write Singapore's national pledge in 1966 and widened the international space for Singapore as its first Foreign Minister.

This work is a biography. It is not history. Neither is it an academic study of a political leader. Biography focuses on one figure, exploring the significance of his life by examining his actions, relationships, frustrations and achievements over his lifetime. In making him the dominant focus and narrating history with him as the protagonist, there is no intention to play down the contributions of the other PAP leaders or the many individuals who struggled in their own ways to build Singapore. There is a growing body of literature which recounts the contributions of the various national leaders, as well as alternative readings from the perspective of their political opponents. This is not intended to be one of them.

This is also not a PAP book. I wrote it with complete independence; it has not been read or influenced by any PAP leader in all the years it took me to write it. It was good of MM Lee to write the Foreword without asking to read the manuscript.

That said, Raja was a PAP founding leader and its most ferocious propagandist; it must be expected that most of his thoughts and actions relate to the PAP. However, his life and achievements go beyond loyal service to a political party. This book seeks to embed him in a larger history of anti-colonial politics and to explore his role in the shaping of Singapore's conception of itself as an independent entity with its own identity. Singapore's development as a nation might well have turned out differently without Raja driving the process as he did.

After his death, many younger Singaporeans expressed dismay that they had not heard of Raja before or known of his role in Singapore's history. One of them, a 23-year-old student at the Institute of Technical Education, in a letter to *The Straits Times* on 6 March 2006, wrote: "The death of Mr S. Rajaratnam made Singapore's history more personal to me, but it also raised the question: Why had I not known about him earlier?...Mr Rajaratnam is a classic example of someone who has not been given enough importance in our history syllabus." I agree. This book hopes to address this.

I write this book with the general reader in mind. My fundamental job, after poring over all the research material gathered, is to be true to the facts as I found them, interpret their significance in relation to Raja, and write a narrative based on them. Towards that end, I have done so many revisions that I have lost count.

In all, I ploughed through thousands of declassified British and Australian records, Culture Ministry files, Cabinet papers, oral history interviews, newspaper clippings and speeches. Also, boxes and boxes of Raja's private papers. At times, I felt like a detective, piecing together clues from personal fragments he left behind — letters, receipts, income tax slips, photographs, notebooks, tattered pieces of paper. I spent hours watching video footage of Raja at work, observing his body language, listening to his voice, imagining the emotion of the moment. His strong voice accompanied me in my car, as I played and re-played CDs of his speeches flowing with his spirited ideas.

I am aware of the need for the biographer to distance herself from her subject and I have attempted to do so. This biography does not ignore his contradictions or shortcomings. After all, they reflect the complexity of the man. I have strived to be objective and fair, although my admiration for him and his work grew as I learnt more about him. As historian C.M. Turnbull put it, it is the accustomed lot of biographers to come to identify with their subjects.

Raja was a man unique to himself and an original thinker in many ways. One of his most precious contributions to Singapore in that period was to put forth his view that a new common national identity can be created, transcending all communal loyalties, and with that, a new people and a new future. As it has been almost 12 years since I studied the subject of nations and nationalism at the London School of Economics and Political Science, it was interesting to revisit the much-contested concepts and discover how Raja had relied on certain thinkers, in particular French philosopher Ernest Renan and British philosopher John Stuart Mill, to form his own views on the making of a Malayan and later, a Singaporean, nation.

But what made him tick? What made him fight so hard for what he believed in? As I moved from his oral history recordings to contemporary sources, I realised that I had underestimated the scale of my task. His oral history was recorded many years after the events related and was therefore susceptible to lapse of memory and to the wisdom of hindsight. Where I have been able to check facts from contemporary records, I have used these.

I have spent much time at the National Archives of Singapore (NAS) and at the Public Records Office in Kew in the United Kingdom. My sincere thanks especially to Pitt Kuan Wah and Ng Yoke Lin from NAS, for their resourcefulness and ready assistance. I have also visited King's College in London to retrieve Raja's university records, and thank the College for tracking down his details. I was also given access to Special Branch files and Cabinet papers. For this, I am grateful to the Internal Security Department and the Cabinet Office.

In this book, I reveal previously unpublished details of letters, declassified records and transcripts of interviews.

A wide range of people, including his one-time political opponents such as Fong Swee Suan, Dominic Puthucheary and Low Por Tuck, have also been interviewed for this book. To provide a rounded picture of Raja, a standard question posed was what they thought were his weaknesses, as well as his strengths. Their replies are weaved into this book. I thank Sonny Yap, Leong Weng Kam and Lau Ping Sum for helping with some contacts and useful information.

Raja's relatives in Singapore, Seremban and Jaffna were invaluable in helping me reconstruct his childhood and family life. They include Dr Pillay, Mrs S. Seevaratnam, Jothiratnam and Anushia Lingam. There are many others — too numerous to name here, but they are listed at the end of the book.

My research was helped by the fact that Raja left a large corpus of his writings as a journalist. I would not have been able to track them all down, had it not been for my research assistant, Teo Kah Beng, who also met my numerous other requests with ability and equanimity. I thank the excellent librarians from the Parliament Library, especially Mrs Yang Soh Bee and Mrs Cheah-Khoo Sait Poh, the ISEAS Library, the National Library and the Singapore Press Holdings (SPH) library for their generous assistance. A special thanks to SPH and NAS for allowing us to reproduce their photographs.

Some of Raja's notebooks on his passions — ideas on books and photography — and other materials are in my temporary possession. These will be donated to the NAS, ISEAS Library or the National Library for preservation and public reference after this biography is completed. I have also benefited from his private papers in the ISEAS Library, donated by Raja's family.

I would like to thank Prime Minister Lee Hsien Loong for his encouragement, and for officiating the launch of this book. I express my great debt to my NTUC bosses, Lim Boon Heng and Lim Swee Say, for their support while I was working with NTUC until February 2009.

I wrote my first five chapters while on a three-month Honorary Professorial Fellowship in the University of Edinburgh in 2006. For providing an environment that enabled me to focus on writing, I thank the Edinburgh University's Vice-Principal, Prof Geoffrey Boulton, and Grierson Professor of English Literature and Director of the Institute for Advanced Studies in the Humanities, Susan Manning.

The understanding and support of my Tampines GRC MPs and grassroots leaders gave me the peace of mind and courage to persevere with this project. My good friend, Alwyn Lim, was unstinting with his encouragement and practical help. My personal assistant, Emily Ng, helped me to balance the competing demands on my time. I am grateful to them all.

Several people took the time to read the drafts and comment on them. My sincere thanks to Kirpal Singh, Warren Fernandez, Philip Holden, Janadas Devan and P.N. Balji, as well as to the ISEAS peer review committee. All errors are my own. I would also like to acknowledge the work of Triena Ong, managing editor and head of ISEAS Publishing, in ensuring that this biography finally sees light of day.

Last but not least, my loving gratitude to my family who put up with my long hours at my various jobs with unstinting support, even if that meant their seeing less of me. Even when I was present with them, my thoughts were often on Raja. Hardly a day went by when I was not thinking about Raja, reflecting on his actions and decisions, pondering on what that revealed about him and his role in shaping the country he loved so dearly.

My husband Graham, the first to hear me think aloud on any interpretation or finding about Raja and to read all my rough drafts, was my rock during this period. In more ways than one, writing Raja's book has been a profound learning experience for me. If I convince the reader of the historical importance and enduring significance of this singular personality, this book, and the effort of all those involved in its making, will not be in vain.

Author's Note

A word about the narrative style. In reading through the many interviews with Raja and his substantial body of writings, I weaved together his thoughts and reactions to events and recreated scenes to animate them while staying true to the facts. To describe expressions, I relied on available video footage and photographs at the National Archives of Singapore (NAS). Where possible, I tried to preserve the authentic voice of Raja. I have also tried not to intrude on the reconstruction with the usual scholarly apparatus, and relied on my journalism training to tell a story as best I could.

Supporting material is provided in the form of selected bibliography. I have tried to avoid overloading these pages with notes and reduced them as far as I could to essential references which would point interested readers to the relevant sources. Most of his speeches can be found in the ISEAS Library and the National Archives of Singapore (NAS). Where footnotes are not provided for Raja's quotes, these come largely from his oral history recordings with the NAS.

On names: Since there are so many people with similar surnames, which can confuse the reader — for example, Lim Hong Bee, Lim Kean Chye, Lim Yew Hock, Lim Chin Siong — I have used their Chinese names, Hong Bee, Kean Chye, Yew Hock, etc. As for Tamil names, an examination of Raja's family tree provided by his family reveals that there can be different spellings to the same name — for example, Pillay/Pillai, Sabapathy/Sabapathi, and Annammah/Annamah — which arose from romanising Sanskrit/Tamil names at different times. Where official records are unavailable, I use the version confirmed by Raja's family. It is also important to note that the names follow the patronymic tradition, with the father's name prefixed to the personal name. Hence, in Sinnathamby Rajaratnam, the first name — Sinnathamby — is that of the father. Rajaratnam is the given name. It is common for the patronymic name to be reduced to an initial as in S. Rajaratnam. For easier reading, wherever possible, I have also opted for names which would be used more readily in conversation, after a proper introduction; hence it is Raja throughout the book, and not Rajaratnam. No disrespect is intended.

The narrative of this book covers the period 1915 to 1963. For compatibility with quotations, many usages current at that time have been retained, particularly with regard to place-names. Hence, for example, Ceylon is used, and not Sri Lanka, and Peking, not Beijing.

1

Beginnings

The Pessimist and the Optimist were arguing about what it took to make a nation. The Pessimist said: "All we have are Malays, Chinese, Indians, Eurasians, Arabs, Ceylonese and the rest. They have one reason for living in the same place…They come to trade — and when their purpose here is served, they retreat each into their own exclusive world. How can such a hotchpotch of races become a nation?"

The Optimist was upbeat. He quoted a poem from Daniel Defoe which drew attention in an irreverent manner to the mixed ancestry of the British people. The Optimist emphasised: "Saxons — Celts — Romans — Normans — Danes. And the French who today consider themselves Cimbri, Gauls, Iberians, Latins and Germans. And the Germans — for all the screaming of Hitler about racial purity — are composed of Lapps and Finns, Slavs and Mongols. There's no such thing as a pure race. So all this talk of racial purity is nonsense."

This conversation was part of a series of broadcast plays titled *Nation in the Making* written by Sinnathamby Rajaratnam, then a newspaper journalist and a freelance radio scriptwriter. It was aired over *Radio Malaya* in 1957, two years before the People's Action Party came into power in 1959.

It was a conversation that he had played and replayed in his mind for years since he was a young adult, and which he would conduct with the country for the rest of his life. Strains of it continue to echo in Singapore and many other multicultural societies seeking to forge a nation.

Raja personified the Optimist in Singapore. He believed in the ability of Singapore to create a nation out of its disparate peoples. For him, it was an act of will and of faith. A man of towering vision, he was one of the most inspiring political leaders ever to walk on this island. Without him, Singapore's pledge would not be the imaginative leap that it was, written in 1966 during one of the country's darkest periods after the trauma of two racial riots in 1964. Defying the evidence before his eyes, he imagined a nation pulsating as one united people, regardless of race, language or religion, and embedded this vision into the national pledge.

On the surface, Raja was all cool charm and affability, but delve a little deeper — into racial politics, national identity, Singapore's survival — and you would see those trademark flashes of passion and intensity.

He belonged to that rare species — the cultivated man of action. He was a polymath who loved books and ideas. As a writer, he was a reporter, a short-story author, an essayist, critic, historian, and philosopher.

As a political leader, he imagined what Singapore could be and breathed into it a transcendental sense of national consciousness. He was one of the handful, alongside Lee Kuan Yew, Goh Keng Swee, Toh Chin Chye and a few others, who changed the course of history in Singapore. They were responsible for creating the country's political order and shaping the development of the tiny, resource-poor island situated in a turbulent region. Going through his speeches and writings, one is struck by his resilience, his wit, his convictions, his prescience. And his sheer audacity.

As the first culture minister in self-governing Singapore in 1959, Raja rallied the people to pledge allegiance, not to the distant lands they had come from, but to a new political identity and an imagined Malayan culture. Convinced that Singapore would not survive on its own, he worked hard to bring about its merger with Malaysia. Like the other PAP leaders, Raja did not believe that Singapore could stand as an independent state on its own, being all of 500 sq km, and without any natural resources to sustain its 1.6 million people.

Upon merger in 1963, Raja was a prime architect of the vision of a Malaysian Malaysia, a country where people of all races and religion were equal and enjoyed similar rights and opportunities as citizens. He never lowered his sights, despite the ensuing problems which tested his resolve.

He could not predict that, barely two years later in 1965, Singapore would be expelled from Malaysia and left to fend for itself. He never imagined that it was in such agonising circumstances that he would one day be one of the founding fathers of independent Singapore and be among the intrepid band of leaders responsible for its survival.

In that hour of utter despair, Raja summoned the will to charge on. He had spent most of his life fighting for his vision of a just and equal society and reflecting on certain central human problems, especially questions of human identity and value, the politics of race and nation, and political theory and practice.

Raja's ideas on national ideology were rooted deep in his personal value system. They were not based on partisan political advantage. He had been full of ardour on behalf of secular nationalism and equality even in his student days in London in the early 40s, and even before he met Lee Kuan Yew and the other PAP co-founders. He did not dream then that he would one day become a national leader in a position to hold high his vision for the country.

His most honest thoughts on this vision were penned by hand in his notebook in 1990: "We are the first generation of Singaporeans who have been confused about our identity — first as temporary boarders, then British subjects or pro-Kuomintang or pro-Communist China, Indian nationals proud of Nehru and Gandhi…out to be a Malayan, then a Malaysian, and finally, we had, in 1965, to settle for Singaporean Singapore."[1]

He conceded that Singapore lacked "ancient palaces, magnificent temples, crumbling great walls" or a "great past" to be proud of. "But frankly, I have not lost much sleep over this absence, because there is something I am genuinely and sincerely proud of — present-day Singapore." He could look any leader from so-called ancient countries in the eye without blinking — "and they would blink in a staring match".

He wrote: "This is not bravado or jingoism. This is what I really feel. Maybe I am a Singaporean tree which can sink deep roots fast. Maybe the time has come to give more attention to get the coming generations of Singaporeans to sink deep roots fast. Many of the old civilisations took thousands of years before their civilisation reached their peak and declined. But they all had to start with Year 1."

Year 1 for Raja saw a collision of allegiances. Born on 25 February 1915 in Jaffna, Ceylon, Raja was a child of the colonial period, when Ceylon, India, Malaya and large swathes of the world were part of the British Empire.

At the age of six months, his mother brought him to join his father in Seremban, Malaya. This was the wild frontier where his father, Sabapathypillay Sinnathamby, worked as a conductor (supervisor) in a rubber estate. His origins were to leave him with three allegiances — Ceylonese, Malayan, British.

His mother, Annammah, had taken the precaution of giving birth to Raja in Jaffna because of her traumatic experience at the hospital in the rubber estate a few years earlier.[2] The hospital was basic, with backward medical facilities. There in that shabby building, unassisted by a midwife, she had given birth to her first son prematurely — and he had died.

When Annammah, a traditional child bride who had married when she was 14, became pregnant with Raja at the age of 19, she was adamant about returning to her village in Jaffna, called Vattukottai, to deliver her second baby. In her village, she would be tended to by an experienced midwife trusted by her family. When he was born, he was named Rajendram (which can mean God among Kings in Sanskrit) by his maternal grandfather, C. Nagalingam, who registered his birth about two weeks later. His birth certificate, written in Tamil script, duly recorded his name as Rajendram, which was also a name of Yudhisthira, the eldest Pandava prince in the Sanskrit epic *Mahabharata*. In this way, Jaffna, with its ancient myths and legends, claimed Raja as its native son. Its hold on him, however, proved transient and slippery.

After the infant returned to Seremban, his father asserted his paternal rights and renamed him Rajaratnam (Jewel among Kings) after consulting the family priest and the family astrologer in Seremban. As could be expected, this home renaming would require much explaining whenever his birth certificate was needed to verify his identity for official purposes. This was resolved administratively 15 years later, when his father made a statutory declaration on 18 June 1930 that his eldest son, known as Rajaratnam, was the same person whose birth was registered under the name of Rajendram.

For Raja, Jaffna was to be a place far removed, in distance and in his dreams, from what was later to be his own conception of home.

His home was to be Seremban in Malaya. By all accounts, Seremban, the capital of the agricultural state Negri Sembilan, was a non-descript rural village on the western coast of Malaya. The entire expanse of the state, as seen from the main roads and railway lines, was distinguished only by the monotony of miles and miles of rubber trees.

Home for Raja in his first six years of life was in the rubber estate of Jemima, which was about 16 kms from Seremban town. Here, his family lived in an attap-roof building made of wood, raised five feet from the ground, at the end of a jungle track. They shared their rustic quarters with other relatives from Jaffna, also there to work on the rubber estate.

Further down, there was a separate settlement, even more cramped and basic, for Tamil labourers who came from South India. Cows, goats and chickens ambled about freely. Life was primitive. There was no electricity; they lived by the flickering light of the kerosene lamp. There was no piped water. They drew water from the well for their daily needs. Near the well, women whacked wet clothes on a stone to wash their clothes.

When Raja turned two in 1917, a pregnant Annammah returned to Jaffna again to give birth to another son, Seevaratnam. The younger son would grow up to be the more flamboyant and fun-loving child. In sharp contrast, Raja was described by relatives as a serious-minded and quiet boy. He lived in his own world, his soft eyes watchful as they absorbed events around him in the rubber estate.

At the first crack of dawn, the labourers would be out, clearing the virgin forest for planting and tapping the milky latex from rubber trees. The job of Raja's father, Sinnathamby, was to supervise the hundreds of Tamil rubber tappers in the estate. The European planters had recruited these low-caste Tamils by the shiploads from South India — mainly Tamilnadu — as indentured labour.

Life in the estate was full of caution. From his father, Raja was to learn that they faced grave dangers at work. The plantations bordered virgin forests. The tropical jungle was seething with vicious animals, hiding behind the tall *lalang* (grass), beneath the dense undergrowth, or in muddy swamps. Tigers, crocodiles and snakes — especially the hooded cobras and the giant pythons — were only some of the predators his father said to look out for.

When the labourers wanted to cycle on their rickety bicycles from the estate to the Seremban town, his father would holler after them to remind them to travel in groups.

At dawn, there would be a roll call for the Tamil coolies before they headed out for work. At the end of the day, there would be another headcount. "It was not rare for a tapper to be found missing — either bitten by a snake or dragged away by a tiger or a crocodile," Raja recalled. He had witnessed occasions when his father would leave their house and go out in pitch darkness to look for a missing worker.

Then there were the mosquitoes. Many labourers shivered with malaria in their tiny hovels. Many more died.

The unkindest cut of all was that, having risked their lives and exhausted themselves working on the estates, they did not sit back to enjoy the better life in Malaya, but remitted most of their savings back to their distant homeland.

So much hardship endured, for so little.

Raja the boy was also intrigued by the Chinese mine workers. He hardly had any contact with people of other races, but had seen these shadowy figures cycling by the side of the dusty tracks, wearing enormous straw hats and dressed in black from head to toe. They were hardy people, working in tin mines and sieving tin ore in large trays from the mining sites.

Curious and eager to learn, he had asked his relatives about them. He was told that, like the Ceylonese and Indians who came to Malaya, these people came from China to earn a living in the Malay peninsula. Before rubber dominated the Malayan economy, its chief export was tin. A long time before the arrival of the British, the Chinese had sailed down in their junk boats from China to search for this precious metal; they were pioneers with their pick and shovel. Enterprising and hard-working, some eventually rose to become rich *towkays* (bosses).

Raja would eventually come to meet some of them when he moved out of the estate to stay with his uncle in the Seremban town when he started school. The uncle, Thamotharam Pillay, was his father's elder brother.

On weekends, Raja would return to his home in the rubber estate. This arrangement was to continue until Raja's parents were able to afford their own house in town later.

It was these formative years in town that opened Raja's eyes to the life of other races. He saw for the first time how the Chinese would celebrate their festivals. He was entranced by their lion dances, with martial-arts experts prancing to the beat of cymbals and drums, swaying beneath a slice of cloth sewn to look like the sinuous skin of a lion.

He also caught glimpses of Chinese opera performances outside the Taoist temples. As he recollected later, he did not understand their cultures and customs, but found them interesting and colourful. Through his Malay classmates in school, he also had the opportunity to visit the Malay *kampungs* (villages) and observe their way of life.

This was all quite novel for him, as under the British, the different races were largely segregated from one another, with most Malays in villages, Chinese in towns, and Indians in plantations. In their enclaves, they practised their own religions, rituals and ways of life.

The British had encouraged these ethnic divisions as an instrument of colonial rule. The Malay *sultans* retained their symbolic status at the apex of an aristocratic social system, although they lost some of their political authority and independence. The British encouraged the Malay peasants to maintain their farming life in the under-developed *kampungs*, believing that they should be protected from economic and cultural change. Hence, most economic development was left to Chinese and Indian immigrants, as long as it served long-term colonial interests.

But it was these immigrants who were to suffer most during the Great Depression from 1929 to 1933. Raja remembered the scene. Then in his teens, he saw how labourers at the rubber estates lost their jobs *en masse* as many plantations were either closed down or functioned only on a care-and-maintenance basis.

Tens of thousands of Ceylon Tamils, South Indians and also Chinese were repatriated. Those who stayed received starvation wages during the slump and lived hand-to-mouth. The Jemima rubber estate was not spared. Raja's family suffered too, but, being relatively better off, they stretched their resources to help their jobless relatives with food and shelter.

Later in his life, Raja was to return to these themes and to try to make sense of them. He began to think about nationalism in general and about these early migrants from China, India and Ceylon in particular. Their work made possible the development of Malaya, but they were alien minorities in it. In the course of time, those who settled in Malaya continued to be deprived of the same status accorded to the Malays. Years later, Raja was to draw on these observations when he fought for equality for the different races as Malayans.

Raja's father, Sinnathamby, was among the vanguard of rubber planters from Ceylon who came to Malaya in 1910.

His own intrepid father, Sabapathypillay, had earlier led the way. He arrived in Malaya in the late 19th century to clear the virgin jungles for plantations and mines.

This was highly dangerous and gruelling work. But his pioneering work with the *parang* (long knife), which earned him a pittance, was to reap a small fortune later for several generations of his extended family.

Sinnathamby was only 16 when he left the arid agricultural land of Jaffna for the sweltering rubber town of Seremban in Malaya. He did not know that Malaya was on the brink of an economic boom that was to transform his life so completely.

His marriage to Annammah, a mere 14, was formalised just before they left Ceylon. It was an arranged marriage, as was the custom among Ceylon Tamils of the time. Theirs was considered a good match. Ceylon Tamils placed great weight on their customary laws and practices, and were particularly strict about caste and marriage.

Both came from the powerful landowning Vellalar caste in Jaffna. The Vellalars, which dominated in numbers, formed the peak of the Ceylonese hierarchy. They outranked the Brahmins who were ritually the highest caste. Traditionally, the Vellalars were landlords, independent farmers and holders of political office under the colonial powers.

Sinnathamby's family owned small plots of plantation land in their home village — padi fields, coconut, and palm oil plantations — although the yield had dwindled to unsustainable levels over the years; so dry was the weather. He was not highly-educated but could speak a smattering of English, picked up from the village school.

Annammah was his first cousin. Marrying within the extended family was commonplace in the caste-conscious society. Indeed, intermarriages were actively encouraged to keep the blood line pure, as well as to retain property inheritances within the clan.

Aside from caste, Annammah came from a respectable background with uncles who worked as teachers. She herself had received her secondary education in Tamil, considered a privilege for women in those days.

Like most Jaffna Tamils who migrated to Malaya, Sinnathamby and his wife brought these class distinctions to their new land. Although friendly, they kept themselves largely apart from the Tamils from South India who worked on the same estate. Instead, they applied themselves assiduously to keeping up their family ties across the oceans.

Once Sinnathamby and his new bride were more settled in the estate, they ushered more relatives from Jaffna into Seremban. Enticed by the jobs available in the estates, waves of relatives soon joined the young family. Depending on their level of education, some also found jobs as clerks or conductors at estates, as station masters in the railway line, or as clerks in government departments.

Sinnathamby's only brother, Nadarajah, came with his own brood to work in the Jemima estate and was nicknamed "Jemima Nadarajah" for his role as chief clerk.

Annammah's five brothers and their large families also joined the exodus from Jaffna to work in the rubber estate. All stayed in Sinnathamby's home until they could afford their own, or until they were married off.

In all, about 200 relatives from the extended family in Jaffna eventually came to Malaya during the 1910–30 period.

Theirs was a typical story of Jaffna Tamil families — once established in the estates, they used their connections to bring in many more Jaffnese. Nepotism was rife. Indeed, supervisory and clerical work at the rubber estates became effectively the monopoly of Jaffna Tamils until the 1930s when the Malayalees came in.

The Jaffna Tamils owed their dominant position to their ability to act as useful intermediaries for their masters, the European planters. The Jaffna Tamils could speak elementary English and also deal with the Tamil-speaking Indian labourers.

Outside work, however, social barriers between Jaffna Tamil supervisors and Tamil labourers in an estate remained clearly drawn, as was the case in Ceylon.

As a result, until Raja went to school in the Seremban town, his circle of childhood contacts was restricted mainly to his family and relatives living in his home.

He was deeply devoted to his stoic and self-effacing mother. He once described her as possessing a cool and even temperament, and being always courteous to others.[3] On several later occasions, Raja remarked that he owed much of the equanimity that he possessed as a public figure to his mother's example.

Annammah was socially conservative, clothed in the traditional *saree* with a *pottu* on her forehead, and spoke only Tamil at home. She was frugal and sought to keep the family as self-sufficient as possible, growing vegetables in the garden, and rearing cows and chickens.

Deeply religious, she managed the family's domestic rituals and planned for the Hindu festivals, especially Deepavali. On her regular visits to the temple, she would take her sons along, with the loose end of her *saree* draped over her head. The Sri Balathandayuthapani temple would become a regular feature of Raja's life in Seremban until she died in 1977.

Dutifully, he would trail his mother to the temple for prayers and ceremonies. He went not because he believed in Hinduism or indeed in any particular god — he was on his way towards agnosticism by his teens — but because, as he confessed, he wanted to please his mother. He would sit by to watch the devotees praying and wait for her patiently. One of Raja's observations during these moments was that his mother's religiosity was revealed in the practice of Hindu rituals, rather than rooted in the philosophy of the religion. He never offered any prayers himself. His faith was not in any god, but in the love of a mother who must have anguished over his untraditional choices in life.

For Raja, it was a poignant moment when, just after he became Singapore's cabinet minister in 1959, his mother had asked him to accompany her to the Hindu temple. "I was only too glad to keep her company at the temple. She did not say anything, but I knew that she was offering her thanks to God," said Raja.

While both Raja and his brother were close to their mother, they were terrified of their father. Sinnathamby, who sat on the temple's management committee, was strict and strong-willed. Sporting a bristly handlebar moustache, he was a tall, muscular man of stern countenance. As Raja described his father, "he cut a most imposing figure and could instil both fear and respect in people".[4]

His children did not get to see much of him at home, but when they did, they stayed clear. "My father was a quick-tempered man and so, we took no liberties with him," Raja recalled.

Sinnathamby spent most of his time outdoors. As a conductor, he was held largely responsible for the welfare of the labourers, including making sure they were adequately fed and received medical attention when needed.

An astute man, he soon picked up the rudiments of the rubber industry from the European owners, and years later, was able to set up a rubber plantation of his own. This was considered a rare achievement among Ceylon Tamils at the time — by 1940, Europeans owned 75 per cent of the estates, Chinese 18 to 20 per cent, and Indians (including Ceylon Tamils) only 5 per cent.[5]

Sinnathamby also tapped on a lucrative sideline. The first object of a conductor, he knew, was to keep his labourers contented; minor riots among labourers in other estates were not uncommon. One of the ways that he satisfied his men was to provide a ready supply of *toddy*, a harsh liquor derived from palm sap.

He flourished as a *toddy* contractor, and shared this growing business with several relatives who also took up *toddy* contracts. By the time Raja attended secondary school, Sinnathamby was wealthy enough to buy a large bungalow in the Seremban town for the extended family to live in.

After moving to the town, Sinnathamby turned to business and opened a provision shop in town, which sold *toddy* among other products. He also invested in several properties and sold them for a quick profit.

A self-made man, he established a respected place for himself in the community, being in a position to dispense favours and to help those in need. His relatives often turned to him to settle disputes and to arrange marriages.

To Raja, however, his father remained a remote figure.

Life was simple in the wilderness of the rubber estate. During his early years, Raja's major source of entertainment came in the form of his loquacious uncles[6] who lived in the same house or nearby. Night after night, they fed his imagination with tales rich with references to the traditional way of life and philosophy in Jaffna. He was so transfixed by these stories, crafted from experiences of everyday life and passed down through the generations, that the images became etched in his memory and provided the landscape for his imagination.

Visits to the local barber in the village were also events to look forward to. As soon as he settled himself onto the rough-hewn wooden stool, the barber, who was well versed in Hindu scriptures and fables, would launch into the most amazing literary journeys. While the barber snipped the boy's hair, he filled his head with stories from *Ramayana* and *Mahabharata* and other Hindu epics.

These storytelling sessions, so much a part of his growing-up years, gave him a perceptive ear for dialogue and a passion for rendering experience into evocative language. His love for words and stories would remain with him throughout his life. When he tried his hand at writing short stories in London later in his 30s, he was able to evoke the texture, atmosphere and feel of the daily life and dialogue of farmers in a rural Indian village, although he had never lived in one for any length of time before.

In Seremban, Raja grew up in an environment in which blood relations, tradition and class defined life's obligations and possibilities. This was illustrated most vividly by his parents' preoccupation with arranging marriages for their swarm of relatives in Seremban and negotiating dowries, usually involving property, jewellery and cash.

In some cases, Sinnathamby would himself put down the dowry for the prospective bride, although it was traditionally the duty of the family to do so for their own daughters.

Marriage within the Jaffnese community was essentially a matching of status and wealth; the amount of dowry given and the caste rank were the most important criteria in these marriages.

Cross-cousin marriages were the most favoured as the background of both parties would be known, and properties would be kept and consolidated within the extended family. When weddings took place, they would entail elaborate ceremonies with the Brahmin temple priest presiding. The Jaffnese took seriously rules such as obtaining the consent of the parents, and the performance of necessary wedding ceremonies.

This was to be a notion that Raja would rebel against in dramatic fashion when he turned 28 in 1943. Unlike his younger brother who submitted to an arranged marriage with a Jaffna Tamil woman, Raja eventually married someone not only outside his caste, but also outside his race — a Hungarian Roman Catholic named Piroska Feher. No dowry, no ceremony, and certainly, no temple priest.

Raja also flew in the face of the caste's most conservative faction by not even consulting the family before marrying Piroska, and worse, registering the civil marriage while supposedly studying in London, far from the family's prying eyes.

But Raja's sceptical questioning of the complex concepts of culture, tradition and religion was important in several ways. While he developed a profound respect for their place and their power, he was opposed to a blind commitment to ancient dogmas and prejudices with their unexamined assumptions.

His earlier experiences in Seremban laid the foundation for his deeper exploration later into the larger question of identity, which he grappled with all his life — that of the individual and of the cultural community within the context of a modern nation.

Like Raja, almost all the Jaffnese in Malaya before 1920 were born in Ceylon. At that time, most saw themselves as sojourners in Malaya. Their motherland was Ceylon. So strong was their homing instinct that almost all of them returned with their families to Ceylon on retirement.

Ceylon Tamils began thinking of settling down in Malaya only in the mid-1920s, as a result of a change in official policy to recruit local-born candidates for government service. However, even by 1931, there were only 1,667 Ceylonese who had been born in Malaya.[7] Over time, however, some began to sink roots in Seremban. For Raja's parents and relatives, the decision to stay on in Seremban was eased tremendously by the fact that it had become, as Raja would describe it, an "extended, overgrown village" of relatives. They formed their own tightly-knit community, bound by blood, language, culture and religion, in Seremban.

For all his radicalism and his religious agnosticism, Raja recognised the value of culture in providing an anchor to identity, particularly for migrants exiled from their ancestral homeland and traditional moorings. In a speech in 1975, he said: "Probably our forefathers, the ones who left India or Ceylon, were not always the successful people. If they were successful, they would have stayed in their country. It was because they were not successful that they came here to try their fortunes...They probably came with a bag or just enough for a change of clothes. But one thing they brought was their concept of culture. They needed that culture. They had left their country behind...They did not want to go back, but they knew too that they were nobodies without their cultures."[8]

The place that they left behind — Jaffna — was an arid land on which they relied almost entirely for their livelihood. Many, such as Raja's grandfather, owned small plots of land, and tilled them with the aid of their families. They used to grow betel leaves, padi and vegetables.

They reaped the bitter fruits of economic transformation when, by the middle of the 19th century, the population grew beyond what the agricultural economy could sustain. Farmers found it hard to feed their families; youths could not find jobs.

Their condition became more depressed with the encroachment of large tea and rubber plantations owned by European planters. As the British turned Ceylon into a large-scale plantation economy, the villagers lost their rights to raise subsidiary crops and to pasture cattle in what used to be common land.

Stiffened by social prejudice, most Jaffna Tamils stilled their hands from ploughing the land of these white planters. They had their own land, however small, and their own crops to produce. Why should they give up their way of life for the doubtful benefit of uncertain wages? The European planters neatly got around the labour problem by importing large numbers of unskilled workers from India, a pattern that was to be repeated later in British Malaya. Soon, plantations were overrun with Tamil coolies, living in tiny dung huts.

Adding to the Ceylon villagers' distress, the cost of living rose by 100 per cent between 1874 and 1905 in Ceylon. According to the 1911 Census of Ceylon, the prices of land doubled over just two decades. It was difficult to buy land and equally difficult to make it yield because of the lack of rain.

Scenes of the hardship faced by farmers, evoked by the countless tales he had heard from his relatives as a boy, would later find their way into one of Raja's short stories. As he wrote in the story "Famine", first published in 1941:[9]

"After the drought, came the famine, so that it was like walking out of one nightmare into another still more fearful. In the rice-fields, where the harvest should have rustled, heavy and golden, was only the half-burnt stubble of their crops. The farmers stared at the dust and ruin in their fields, and searched one another's faces for an answer, their eyes becoming deep and dull as the days passed by."

For Sinnathamby, the answer was Malaya when his eyes alighted on the glinting rubber industry. He came at an opportune time in 1910, when the price of rubber was rocketing. Until about 1908, the bulk of the world's rubber came from Brazil and the Congo, with only 5 per cent from Malaya. Then came the great demand for rubber which produced the boom of 1909. Rubber trees thrived in the soil and climate of Malaya, and at once, vast areas were brought under cultivation. Negri Sembilan was among the states gripped by the fever.

By 1920, Malaya was producing more than half the world's supply of rubber. The frenetic economic activity transformed the face of Malaya with railway lines crossing the land to transport the raw materials and telegraph offices dotting the landscape.

Politically, it was also a time of ferment. Between 1910 and 1914, the pattern of British rule in Malaya was being put in place. Britain, driven by its hunger to establish a trading base in the Far East for its East India Company, had brought under its control nine sultanates of the Malay Peninsula, together with Port Singapore.

When in 1914, the Johor sultanate agreed to accept a British "General Adviser", it marked the culmination of more than a century of British involvement in the Malay archipelago, which started with the East India Company's takeover of the small island of Penang in 1786.[10] Malaya, as the world's greatest exporter of rubber and tin, produced the bulk of colonial tax revenue and was to be one of the most important economic and strategic territories in the British Empire.

It was a heady era of pioneers and progress, fuelled by waves of immigrants. The expanding economy and the burgeoning government administration with departments for such matters as public works, agriculture, mines and lands required English-educated Asians to staff them.

The job opportunities, the better wages and the low cost of living in Malaya attracted many Ceylon Tamils. In 1911, there were about 8,000 Ceylonese in Malaya. Within the next 10 years, the number rose to 11,600 and, by 1931, almost 17,000 Ceylonese had moved to Malaya.

As a young adult later, Raja was to record this phenomenon in a column he wrote in 1942: "As Malaya developed, it became an Eldorado for ambitious men from India and Ceylon. From these two countries, English-educated youths came by the hundreds, and later the thousands, to enter the clerical and other services in the government for wages far higher than obtained in their own countries."[11]

Drawing from his personal observations, he could add: "I know for a fact that the prosperity of Jaffna, in northern Ceylon, depends to a great extent on the fortunes made and pensions acquired by her shrewd and hard-working sons in Malaya." He had himself witnessed how his family and relatives remitted large amounts of money back to their kin in Jaffna.

Sinnathamby was a classic example of migrant upward movement in the colonial era. Within two decades, he rose from a conductor in a rubber estate to become a rubber planter and a businessman with various properties to his name. He was able to upgrade his lifestyle from a hut in the rubber estate to a mansion in town.

As a beneficiary of the system, he never questioned the British rule or its values. Like many Ceylon Tamils with government jobs, he did not entertain any interest in political activities which might jeopardise one's job status and future.

Sinnathamby felt that his first duty was to serve the interest of his colonial masters and to perpetuate the system. Raja was to observe later: "If at all he had political views, it was to accept the British system as the best of all possible worlds."

This was a view that Raja was to imbibe at first as he went through the revolving doors of various schools, until he developed his own power of analysis and decided, in grand fashion, to rebel against his colonial masters.

2

Becoming Secular

Raja's education was distinguished not so much by what he learnt in school, but what he learnt, in spite of it. At the age of eight, his parents sent him to the Convent of the Holy Infant Jesus in Seremban. His mother believed that nuns were gentler teachers than Brothers who believed that "sparing the rod spoiled a male child".[1]

Six months later, however, the Mother Superior wrote to his parents to ask that Raja be transferred to St Paul's Institution, a missionary boys' school run by the La Salle Christian Brothers. That was how the scrappy-looking boy with the unruly hair ended up at St Paul's in Paul Street on 6 June 1923. Raja was to spend about 10 years of his most formative years at this leading mission school.

In the school, amidst its Gothic arcades, Raja the schoolboy revelled in the newfound freedom to explore new beliefs and practices, different from the natal religious tradition of his family's. The ideas which first absorbed him came from the Biblical texts which he studied as part of his religious knowledge subject in his secondary years. "I was fascinated by the Bible," he said.[2] Its teachings were novel to him. They had structure, lyrical beauty, and most of all, Enlightenment values which appealed to his budding moral sensitivities — all men are equal; all men, whatever their station, can be saved.

He spent many joyful hours reading the King James version of the Bible and committing the stories to memory. Among his favourite ones were those that concerned Moses, who led the Israelites for 40 years in the desert to reach the Promised Land, and little David who beat the giant Goliath with a sling and a pebble. He read and reread them so many times that, years later, he could recite whole passages and entire stories from memory.

The young Raja proceeded to excel in religious knowledge. It turned out to be his highest-scoring subject in both the Junior Cambridge and Senior Cambridge exams. He also discovered he had a flair for the English language. His teachers encouraged him by giving him public commendations for his essays.

He was otherwise an indifferent student throughout his school years. Years later, he described his schoolboy self as "not a particularly bright student, too lazy, playful, never exerted myself". He was precocious and got into a few fights with some of the boys. Once, it was because he stuck chewing gum on another boy's hair. He lost most of the fights because — as he said years later — from his scripture studies, he had learnt to subscribe to the New Testament ethics of "forgive your enemies" in the first instance. "This I invariably did, unless my adversary happened to be considerably smaller and less pugnacious than me," he added tongue-in-cheek.[3] Despite the fears of his mother, the impish boy had never run into enough trouble to warrant being caned by the Brothers.

The teacher who most influenced him during his years at St Paul's was the Brother Director, Lewis Edwards. Beneath his sombre black robes, the Irish Brother was "one of the most jovial and kindly beings I had ever known", Raja recalled.[4] Brother Edwards guided Raja in his education and never lost hope in him despite his average grades.

His mother, who placed great importance on education, supervised his studies after dinner. The Brothers also put in extra effort. Raja recalled their dedication as they stayed behind after school to make sure that lackadaisical boys like him pulled up their socks. They took a personal interest in the holistic development of the boys and treated each of them, as Raja described it later, as "a different human being". The general spirit they passed on to the boys was egalitarian, without care to their social background or race.

Recognising Raja's roving intellect, the Christian brothers encouraged him to read widely. They could see that he was a sensitive boy, with deeper inner cravings. In this nurturing environment, his mind opened up.

During this period, one uncle, who was a Theosophist, made a deep impression on Raja by demonstrating his superior knowledge on the different religions. Theosophy was a movement which held that each religion has a portion of the truth. Seeking universal brotherhood, this mystical religion drew heavily from Hindu and Buddhist teachings, and influenced many Indians during that time. The Nehrus — Motilal and his son, Jawaharlal — were briefly members of the Theosophical Society. At various times, their names were invoked reverently in Raja's home, as was Mahatma Gandhi's for his ascetism. But for Raja, this was decidedly peripheral. Indian politics — or any kind of politics, for that matter — did not pique his interest. World events did not intrude on his aesthetic contemplation.

When not digesting books on religion or philosophy, Raja was devouring books on science fiction. He enjoyed in particular H. G. Well's *Time Machine*, which saw a future with giant crabs as the only inhabitants under a bloated red sun. He also fell under the spell of fairy tales and fantasy, stories pulsing with dragons, witches and phantoms. His imagination came alive, and even after the last page of the book was turned, the characters in the book would continue to play out their tale in his mind for days. Through literature, he was able to transcend his surroundings and explore vast new worlds.

At the rubber plantation, where manual labour was essential for survival, Raja's penchant for reading was regarded as odd and idle. Nor would his parents understand the thoughts and emotions stirred by his extensive reading. They did not approve of his habit of reading well beyond his 10 pm bedtime.

His father would fly into a rage whenever he caught Raja reading in bed way past the witching hour. Such occasions would be frequent. Aggravated by Raja's lack of remorse, his father would occasionally give him a few tight slaps to drum some discipline into him. The effort was futile. His passion for books still clung to him like an addiction.

Later in life, he would say that, if he were stranded on a desert island and could choose only one thing to keep him company, he would opt for a "nice bit of library". All of the other obvious things and persons had their limitations, he said, "which must eventually end in boredom and suicide".[5]

Relatives remember the bespectacled boy as bookish, introspective and reserved, even shy; reading a lot but not often sharing his opinions freely. He was also known for scouring the town to get hold of more books to read. His predilection for browsing in bookshops for long, dreamy minutes spring from these forays which to others was a waste of time.

Perhaps the best evidence of his exceptional nature, as well as the genesis for his lifelong love for books, is manifest in the eagerness with which he built his own library — something that few adults, let alone children, did at the time. He also shared his precious collection with others, including his younger brother, Seeva, and his friends.

Yong Nyuk Lin, who was in Seeva's school cohort, recalled visiting Raja's home often to borrow his books and magazines as a boy. Yong, who would later be Raja's colleague in the first Singapore cabinet of self-governing Singapore in 1959, admired Raja at a distance, finding him a "learned chap" and more serious than most other boys.[6]

Seeva was Raja's polar opposite in temperament. He was a playful extrovert full of pranks. Raja's mother was fond of telling this childhood story: Once, their father gave both boys new toys. Raja allowed Seeva to play with his toys. To his horror, Seeva took them apart. Raja ran to his mother crying. That was the total sum of his protest. He was the mild-mannered and gentle one. This was his natural temperament. His mother would be surprised years later to discover how her sweet son could transform into a tough political pugilist.

At a tender age, Raja began a life committed to the mind and a rich inner world. He was sensitive that this made him different from the many other boys around him. Already, his inability to believe in traditional Hindu strictures was putting him at odds with his family's world, and making him feel as if he lived a life set apart in a different galaxy in the mind.

He was also sublimely detached from material pursuits and displayed a singular lack of interest in practical or financial matters. His father's profitable businesses held no appeal for him. When Raja was spotted at his father's provision shop, he would be in a corner, his aquiline nose buried deep in a book.

At school, Raja also began to explore different cultural worlds. For the first time, people of another race touched his life.

Years later, Raja was to single out two classmates as his bosom buddies. One was a Japanese with the surname Tomanaga, from Tokyo; the other, an Indonesian Chinese, Tan Meng San, from Surabaya. Their fathers owned rubber estates in Seremban.

With his Japanese friend, he swapped comics and talked literature. Later, as the physical self-consciousness of gangling teenagers set in, they took to working out with dumb-bells and chest expanders.

They also flexed their literary muscles and competed with each other in writing compositions in class. Tomanaga would often beat him, rising ever higher in Raja's esteem. When Meng San came into the picture later, all three would go cycling, sometimes up to Port Dickson, about 32 kms from Seremban town. At the Port Dickson beach, they would strip down to their trunks and swim.

It is revealing that Raja did not become as close with the other local boys born in Malaya or those from his own race, but rather with contemporaries who, given their foreign backgrounds, must have felt like the odd ones out in the rubber estate. At some level, Raja probably felt an affinity with their sense of being different.

Raja was also learning to stand apart as a leader. He was mature for his age. His relatives of his own age group noticed it and nicknamed him *penghulu* (Malay for "headman"). In school, he was active as a boy scout and became the scout leader. His abiding memory of his time in the scouts was leading students of different races, and going camping together.

Like the other scouts, he saluted the Union Jack and sang *God Save the King* with suitable pomp and ceremony. Nothing stirred within him at these moments; he felt no allegiance to the King or the Empire. At that stage, he was on a different quest, a search for identity and meaning. He could not accept the inherited notion that people's identities were somehow imposed on them, based on birth, class or circumstance, or revealed to them as passive subjects. This would create a sense of inevitability, of powerlessness that, to him, would make life meaningless.

Meanwhile, as existential questions continued to stir beneath Raja's placid surface, one of his better-educated uncles caused a major ripple by introducing him to paperbacks from the Thinkers' Library series published by the Rationalist Press Association in Britain. The series consisted of essays and extracts from works by various classical and contemporary humanists and rationalists, continuing in the tradition of the Renaissance. The Rationalists promoted the view that the world can be understood by the use of reason.

It was the first time that Raja had laid eyes on books of this sort, with iconoclastic authors such as Herbert Spencer and Bertrand Russell blasting away preconceived ideas. While his young mind did not fully grasp the complex ideas buried within the pages, his hearty intellectual appetite was whetted. Spencer, for example, argued that theism cannot be adopted because, as there is no means to acquire knowledge of the divine, there is no way of testing it. But while we cannot know whether religious beliefs are true, neither can we know that they are false.

For Raja, such arguments provided his first stimulus to radical thought. He was learning to be an intellectual, a thinker who struggled with moral issues and abstract ideas. Such ideas, however, were not very useful in his religious knowledge class in school, as he soon found out. Like Eve tempted by the forbidden fruit, Raja bit hungrily into these radical books and also invited other classmates at St Paul's to try them. He passed the books furtively to other boys in the religious knowledge class, whispering: "Have you read this? It's very interesting. There is no such thing as God."

This frisson of excitement fizzled out when the Brother caught him red-handed. According to Raja, the Brother told him: "I can't stop you from reading this book, but you must not bring it to school." It seemed a gentle enough rebuke. However, Raja harboured the uneasy suspicion that, since that day, he had fallen into the bad books of the Brother.

In one religious knowledge class after that incident, Raja was made to memorise not only the text of the Bible, but also the footnotes. It seemed to him a perverse waste of time. Raja protested: Memorising footnotes was not in the syllabus for the Senior Cambridge exam. He just needed to understand the contents. The Brother held firm and warned: "If you don't want to memorise the footnotes, then don't come to my class." Raja left the class.

It was his first act of rebellion against authority. He was about 15, and with just months to go before he sat for the Senior Cambridge exams. His defiance was a defining event in the evolution of his personality. He felt unjustly treated and had stood up for himself. His family was aghast at the gravity of the situation, but he stuck to his guns.

On 6 February 1930, Raja switched to another school, the King George V School, a government school. To his dismay, it did not teach religious knowledge. Thrown off balance, he began to flounder in his studies. On 5 December 1930, he left school. The ostensible reason, as recorded by his school in his leaving certificate, was that "he intends to proceed to Ceylon". This option, which seemed rather drastic, reflected the father's desperation with his dreamy son.

In the end, Raja was saved from being shipped off to Ceylon when his father sorted things out with the brother director of St Paul's. Raja believed his father made a contribution to the school, but this could not be confirmed. However it happened, Raja demurred to his father's wishes and, in early 1931, returned to St Paul's.

When he left the school on 30 January 1933, armed with his Senior Cambridge certificate, he was gratified that his leaving certificate bore no hint of his struggles with authority or with his studies. Instead, the then Brother Director Dominic John gave Raja a "good" for conduct and a "very good" for applying himself to his studies.

While Raja was struggling with philosophical questions, Sinnathamby was laying out grand plans for his elder son. Now a successful man of standing, Sinnathamby saw high educational qualifications as the means for upward mobility and the marker of social status for his sons.

He was acutely conscious of the need to send his boys to prestigious schools. In those days, Ceylon Tamils with financial means in Malaya focused their children's attention on acquiring a professional qualification either in the fields of law or medicine, both highly esteemed careers.

Raja was indifferent to both. Seeva was keen on medicine. That settled it: Raja would do law. Sinnathamby then made plans to send Raja to the University of London. The acquisition of a law degree from this well-known university was the passport to virtually guaranteed employment and a bright future in British Malaya. Raja acquiesced to his father's decision with a shrug of his shoulders. He recalled his reaction: "To be a lawyer fell on my shoulders, so I accepted it with no great interest in it."

To qualify for entry into the University of London, Raja had to first pass his matriculation exams. He took the one-year course at Victoria Institution in Kuala Lumpur in 1933. It was a leading school, distinguished for producing several outstanding Queen's scholars. In KL, Raya stayed with a relative in Petaling Street.

On joining the school, Raja could not resist writing for the school literary magazine, *The Victorian*, on his favourite subject. He used his initials S.R. but his literary style was evident. The article headlined "The Riddle of Life", published in 1933, lamented that "thy learning has made thee foolish" and that "we know not, in spite of all our profound knowledge, the beginning and the end of Life". He continued: "Though God is conceived in different aspects by each nation yet all believe in a God or Gods. But there are as many who bring convincing and almost better proof for the denial of God than the theist brings to prove his existence."

His existential angst did not help his academic performance. He failed the exams. The next year, his father directed him to Raffles Institution in Singapore to resit the exams.

Raffles was the top-ranking school in Singapore and highly prestigious. In Singapore, Raja stayed in a boarding house in Bencoolen Street. At Raffles, Raja shone at Latin, which he enjoyed. This boosted his confidence. Encouraged by his teacher, he passed the exams.

Looking back years later, Raja described this early period of questioning as good intellectual training as it gave him a broad philosophical outlook. This process also laid the foundation for his ability to join the dots on the big ideas and the broad pictures.

Regretfully, this did not extend to the minutiae of life. As he put it: "I can see the woods but never the trees, never the details. It must be due to this — to start off with religion, philosophy which is a macro approach to life, instead of, say, the scientific mind which starts with details and then builds up into a bigger picture."

The catholicity of cultural sympathy and lack of religious conviction in his school days fed into his nascent political vision. He left school believing in religious freedom and tolerance. For him, this meant more than the freedom to choose one's faith and to tolerate another's. It meant that one should be free to question, challenge and evaluate one's own beliefs, to be open to the merits of another's faith, and to decide, through an act of human will, to live together in peace. We have the freedom to determine our priorities, our identities and our way of life.

There is little doubt that, for him, his ability to make "imaginative leaps" was one he gained only after much practice at performing intellectual somersaults as a schoolboy. His growing-up years were marked by self-discovery and imagination. He also grew in self-confidence as he learnt to rely on his own ability to teach himself from reading a wide range of books and mulling over their ideas. He was compulsively inquisitive about how the world worked and about human nature. Raja was ingraining habits of thought which would remain with him throughout his life.

In his reminiscences later in his life, Raja credited the mission school system for giving him a holistic education that allowed him to think beyond his inherited categories of race and religion. But knowledge was only one aspect of his education. A more profound influence on his development was his personal experiences of having close friends of different races. It was these childhood experiences, he said, which formed the unshakeable core of his subsequent conviction in multiracialism and its ideals.

After leaving St Paul's, Raja and his closest friend, Tomanaga, kept in touch with each other. They could not have predicted how differently life would turn out for each other.

In 1935,[7] at the age of 20, Raja sailed on the P&O liner *Rawalpindi* in first class to England to pursue law in King's College, also the careful choice of his father. The family was oblivious to the impending dangers of World War II, which would consume England and cut off all communications to Raja for several years.

Neither Raja nor the other passengers on the 17,000-tonne ship had any inkling that, barely four years later, the *Rawalpindi* — by then turned into an armed merchant cruiser — would be sunk during the war as it engaged two German battleships south-east of Iceland.

When Raja boarded the steamship, he felt he was departing not so much from a country, as from a close-knit community of relatives. The entire clan had given him a lavish send-off with a farewell tea party in Seremban. So notable was the event that it made the news. *The Straits Times* reported on 6 August 1935 that over 200 people gathered earlier that month at the King George V School hall to honour Raja who was leaving for King's College in London, and described his parents as "well-known residents of Seremban". Speeches were made by various local luminaries and relatives. Later that night, a dinner party was thrown at the residence of a relative, Mr and Mrs K Poopalan.

Clearly, much hope was invested in Raja to do the community and the family proud. Their expectations weighed heavily on his young shoulders. On his way to London, Raja made a special stop at Vattukottai, the village of his birth, in Jaffna. This visit, his first since birth, was at the instruction of his parents, who wanted to make sure he touched base with his "roots" before landing in cosmopolitan London.

Raja's nephew, C. Sivapragasapillai, who lived in Jaffna, recalled the visit which reinforced how central religion was to the cultural life of Jaffna Tamils. Siva, then aged about 17, tagged along as his mother, related to Annammah's side of the family, took Raja on a tour of the many Hindu temples and religious festivals in the village.

According to Siva, the highlight was the Chariot festival where the idols of the Hindu gods were placed in chariots and paraded along the streets drawn by devotees. Raja appeared interested in the intense religious event as they travelled from one temple to another on a bullock cart. Keeping his agnosticism to himself, Raja won over the affection of his relatives with his unassuming ways. After he left, his relatives in Jaffna reported back to his parents what a good son they had.[8]

As Raja continued his way to London, his good friend Tomanaga left Malaya for Japan to do military service and to study Japanese. Later in London, Raja received a letter from his Japanese friend, saying that he was already posted to Manchuria to work as an interpreter in the army.

In his last letter, just before the outbreak of World War II, Tomanaga enclosed a book translated from Japanese, titled *Wheat and Soldier*, with a note to say he would be interested to read it. The book by Hino Ashihei, which was published in 1938, depicted the joys and travails of the noble and self-sacrificing Japanese soldier on the battlefield to liberate Asia.

Unable to picture his Japanese friend as an aggressor, Raja gave it the best interpretation: The book must be a coded message from Tomanaga on how he hated the war, without being able to say so in black and white. Decades later, after Raja became Singapore's foreign minister in 1965, he sought to find Tomanaga through the Foreign Office, but could not trace his friend. Sadly, Raja concluded that he must have died during the war.

For Raja, his life in London through the war years took him down a different road with far-reaching consequences.

3
Turning Left

Raja arrived in London on 29 August 1935, and became homesick immediately. He felt he was in "a strange land with strangers all around you". His boarding house at Steele's Road was basic and cold. Outside, the trees were almost bare. People hurried along the streets with their heads down and their hands in their pockets. The pensive mood in the city matched his own.

Raja longed for the familiar warmth and flurry of his relatives around him. Cast adrift from all that was dear, he drew solace from the presence of some students from Malaya who shared the same lodgings. "That mitigated the loneliness," he recalled later. His misery would have deepened had he been surrounded by non-Malayans. The proximity of his cousin, A. P. Rajah, then reading for the Bar in Oxford,[1] also helped. He represented "some kind of link to the homeland", as Raja put it.

When they met up, the older Rajah proceeded to give the newcomer some advice on how to fit in and reportedly said: "You must wear a pin-striped suit and bowler hat and carry a brolly."[2] This fashion tip was ostensibly to transform the Malayan country bumpkin into an exquisite city gent, conjuring up an instant image of Englishness. Raja ignored this piece of advice and instead donned apparel that identified him with the intellectual class. In photos of that period, Raja cut an elegant figure in typical Oxford trousers, loose fitting with pleats, a smart coat over a V-necked jersey, and a shirt with a tie.

The two relatives would have many more serious disagreements in their later years. Neither of them could know that, after their return to Singapore, they would join politics and face off against each other on opposite sides of the bench in the Legislative Assembly. Rajah would join the pro-colonial Progressive Party, while the younger Raja would help form the anti-colonial People's Action Party. Certainly, no one could have predicted such a radical role for Raja in 1935 when he turned up in King's College at the Strand looking like a lost waif.

In October that year, Raja registered at the college for his three-year law course. His apprehension deepened when he found out that his days henceforth would involve flitting from one college to another for lectures and tutorials. This was because the law classes were arranged by an intercollegiate scheme with University College, located at Bloomsbury, and the London School of Economics (LSE), near Aldwych. Raja found it hard to adjust.

In a bid to put his new life on a more even keel, he headed for what appeared to be more familiar ground and joined the college's literary and philosophical clubs. Here, he thought, he could pursue his abiding interests in philosophy and literature. In a brave moment, he dipped his toes into the waters of drama. He gave the political clubs a wide berth, however, deciding that politics was not his cup of tea. But he was to discover that there was no escaping politics in the intellectual ferment that was sweeping London.

The universities, especially the LSE, were at the centre of raging economic and political controversies. Europe was in the throes of a depression, caused by a catastrophic collapse of the entire Western economy. Almost every scholar seemed to have an opinion on the problems and a remedy at hand.

In the lectures he attended, in the pages of newspapers, over the radio, he was exposed to debates which addressed the social and political events that were on everyone's mind. He heard the conflicting views of various illustrious thinkers such as John Maynard Keynes, who favoured state spending programmes, and Friedrich Hayek, who was suspicious of government intervention in the economy.

Even the discussions at the literary and philosophical clubs were dominated by politics, politics and politics. No meeting was complete without stentorian calls to action. "Things were accelerating and politics was in the air," he recalled. "You began to wonder what this was all about. Your curiosity was aroused."

This cacophonous environment in London was in complete contrast to Malaya where, as Raja noted, "there was a total absence of a political atmosphere". In London, "right from the start, you were plunged into an atmosphere full of politics", he said. This was an eye-opener for the sheltered Malayan village boy. His loneliness fell away and he began to enjoy his new freedom.

He was fascinated by the explosion of ideas and attended as many controversial lectures as he could, such as those by Harold Laski, the voice of Fabian socialism. Laski, who taught at the LSE from 1920 to 1950, influenced many students with his neo-Marxist democratic socialism which called for a full socialist transformation of the economic system. Raja was no exception. Of all of Laski's beliefs, the one that gripped Raja's imagination was his advocacy of equality and liberty.

Every day, Raja was exposed to new ways of thinking, debating and writing. He also met new friends. They were invariably the radical left-wing set. "At that time, the interesting people I met and moved around with were socialists, communists and anti-imperialists," he recalled later. He found them and their views stimulating as they challenged his assumptions on life and the world. They were obsessed with political issues. Even as his circle of friends multiplied, so did his vocabulary. Loaded words entered his lexicon: Marxism. Fascism. Nazism. Leninism. Trotskyism. Socialism.

Raja thought deeply about the ideas being debated, reflected on the problems of race, class and unemployment, and worried about the threat of war. The Franco revolution in Spain in 1936 set off stormy debates in Britain when Neville Chamberlain took the stance of non-intervention while Fascist Italy and Nazi Germany lent Franco their support. In 1935, Mussolini attacked Abyssinia; in 1936, Hitler's forces occupied Rhineland, then, Austria and Czechoslovakia, one toppling after the other. As crisis succeeded crisis, the British intelligentsia produced thesis after thesis on how war could be prevented. "I listened to students arguing politics. Then, suddenly, I found that's what I was really interested in," he said. It was a major turning point for the young man who was still living haphazardly.

His outlook on the world around him took another sharp turn when he joined the Left Book Club after it was formed in May 1936. An avid reader, he was delighted at the access it gave him to cheap books.

Every month, the club issued to members a book, wrapped in a distinctive tangerine cover, for half a crown. This was between a third and a half of the normal cost. Although he professed later that it was the cheap books which he was after, he must have known that the group was more than a reading club. It was a potent political movement which championed socialism and anti-fascism.

Through its books, meetings and rallies, it galvanized mass support for various national and international causes, such as Soviet communism and the Spanish Republic.[3] The club's influence was pervasive, especially in the universities. In every part of England, Left Book Club groups sprang up. About 1,500 local study groups met every week, with membership shooting to nearly 60,000 by 1939.

Raja was posted to the club's study group at the Hampstead area. It turned out to be one of the most important groups, which featured a variety of outside speakers and a vigorous progressive policy. He fervently attended the meetings. The atmosphere of the meetings was often akin to a religious revival. Radical speakers railed against fascism and capitalism, preached the socialist ideal of a classless society, and eulogised Stalin's Russia as the bastion of anti-fascism and the embodiment of socialist potential.

Raja approached the meetings with great intellectual curiosity. The club covered "a whole spectrum from Communism to Democratic Socialism", Raja recalled. It was his university. The Left Book Club rooted him not only in the English linguistic analytical tradition, but also in Marxism. It also initiated him into a whole new way of life.

The club organised an endless round of social and political activities — meetings, public lectures, rallies, book readings — which engrossed him. With his radical cast of mind and elegant feel for literature, Raja would have been welcomed as a talented addition in these intellectual circles. He cut a personable figure with soft, thoughtful eyes and an engaging smile.

Raja came into contact with so much and so many in this period. He knew all the leading members of the club, rubbed shoulders with a range of Fabian socialists, Labour Party politicians, as well as leaders from the British Communist Party. Among those he came to know well were Stafford Cripps, Kingsley Martin of the *New Statesman* and his wife Dorothy Woodman. He also became friends with Labour MPs Aneurin Bevan and Michael Foot, both of whom were involved in the left-wing newspaper *Tribune*. Through them, he forged a link to the purposeful world of journalism.

He embraced those who struck him as "principled, straightforward and honest", such as Cripps and Bevan, but kept detached from the British Communist Party leaders. "They struck me as too servile, everything Russian. Very few of them were really attractive in personalities. They were intolerant, intense...Everything was black and white." From that time, he learnt to be suspicious of anyone who was blindly dogmatic and could not see the multiple shades of grey.

Within months of joining the Left Book Club, the Malayan outsider found himself at the centre of the socialist movement. He took part in the protest marches against Mussolini's invasion of Abyssinia, which lasted seven months from 1935 to1936, as well as in the campaign to support the Spanish Republic.

Like the thousands of members of the Left Book Club, Raja had received a letter from its leader, Victor Gollancz, urging each of them to do everything possible to promote the cause of the Spanish Republic. Spain erupted into civil war in 1936 after an armed revolt led by General Franco to overthrow the elected government. Britain, under the leadership of Stanley Baldwin, declared itself neutral and signed an agreement with other European countries not to intervene in the war. Both fascist Italy, under Mussolini, and Nazi Germany, under Hitler, broke the embargo, sending troops, aircraft, and weapons to support Franco. The Spanish Civil War became international, and Spain became the ideological battlefield of Europe. The debacle awakened Raja to the messy and amoral world of international politics.

Raja followed the ricocheting debate with growing fervour. Many in the right, including Tory MPs, expressed their admiration for the "new spirit" which Hitler gave Germany. The Left was divided, but overwhelmingly affected by Marxist thought.

Many of the left-wing intellectuals leading the debate, such as Kingsley Martin and John Strachey, a Marxist theoretician, believed that international anarchy was the root cause of war and that the object of policy should be to create a World State or some form of international government. They had lost their faith in the League of Nations, set up after the First World War to prevent another war from taking place again. The Left Book Club preached the doctrine that capitalism created war, that fascism was the last, most dangerous form of imperialism, and that the motives for war would disappear when socialism was achieved.

Raja found the left-wing ideas heady and provocative. He sampled the varieties of socialism then available, flirted with Soviet communism, and leaned towards Marxism. When he first encountered Marxism, with its key overarching idea that the mode of economic production determined all the other political, social, cultural and moral structures of a society, he was blown away. "It made a powerful impression on me," he said.[4]

The principal attraction of Marxism for Raja was essentially its usefulness as a system of analysis and interpretation. He was drawn to Marx's idea that justice could only be brought about by revolution in society because, only by getting to the root cause for social ills and addressing the root, could the cause of our problems be eliminated. Based on this intellectual foundation, Raja believed that capitalism was doomed to failure. Marxism, with its grasp on dialectics, convinced him that "in the end, there will be another revolution. Socialism will take over". Over the years, he would collect about eight books on Marx, including his writings and biography.

Theories aside, he also found the Marxist crowd in London the most appealing — they were the ones, he observed, who were consistently anti-imperialist, as opposed to the right-wing capitalists who advocated the continuance of imperialism or defended imperialism.

He broadened his intellectual horizons further by reading widely well beyond his college's reading lists and the Left Book Club's. He studied many other books, such as Thomas Moore's *Utopia*, Plato's *Republic*, John Hobson's *Imperialism*, and Samuel Butler's *Erewhon*. He also read Locke and Hobbes, philosophers who gave contrasting views of politics and society.

Raja had a genuine love for complex ideas which straddled the multiple facets of the human experience. His mind was often ruminating on books as much as on life. His interest in history, literature and the arts, in politics and social life spanned the entire range of human civilisations. Curious about the human experience past and present, he studied the Greeks, the Chinese, the Romans, the Africans.

Books transported him to new worlds and acquainted him with the great minds of generations past. He called the experience the "miracle" of books. "The moment a person reads a book by Plato or Tolstoy or Tagore or Shaw, then Plato, Shaw and all the other great minds of the past come to life," he would later say. They talk to a living person across the centuries and decades — intimately and directly to stimulate and inspire the living reader into thinking new thoughts."[5] The diversity of philosophies he studied added layers to his understanding of the world. From this eclectic foundation, he would eventually build up his own structure of ideas.

To get his hands on an even greater variety of books, he joined the non-political book club, the Readers Union, which was the first general literature book club in London. Founded in 1937, it offered members a gamut of titles, usually non-fiction, at big savings. Raja enjoyed receiving its monthly book selections and poring over its sales pamphlet *Readers News* for its latest books. The experience that the club afforded him — sweet anticipation of new books followed by a rush of pleasure at their arrival — became a part of his life. He remained a loyal member of the club even decades after leaving London, ordering an assortment of books that became the dear companions of his life in Singapore.

While his thirst for knowledge for its own sake was unquenchable, he was not one to swallow everything he read. Raja approached books in the same manner he approached friends: with an open but questioning mind. He challenged assertions made and questioned conclusions.

This is manifested in his thoughtful scribbles in the margins of some books. Besides annotating the books he read, he also had a habit of underlining portions which struck him as noteworthy. Another technique he developed for flagging a critical passage was to write "VIP" (for "Very Important Point") next to it, sometimes with the embellishment of several exclamation marks.

Among the most underlined books found in his home library was *Power, A New Social Analysis* by Bertrand Russell. Raja bought the 323-page book in November 1938, when it was first published. Obviously reading it with a Marxist lens, he disagreed with Russell's assertion that "the orthodox economists, as well as Marx …, were mistaken in supposing that economic self-interest could be taken as the fundamental motive in the social sciences. The desire for commodities, when separated from power and glory, is finite, and can be fully satisfied by a moderate competence".

Raja's riposte as scribbled in pencil: "Not in a capitalist world where insecurity preys on one's mind, and power is conditioned by 'economic interests'." To Russell's observation that "those whose love of power is not strong are unlikely to have much influence in the course of events", Raja rejoined: "But these men are restricted by the social, economic material they act on." Although Raja might critique the comments that Russell makes in this book, there is little doubt that he was an ardent admirer of Russell. Over his lifetime, he would collect more than a dozen of the British philosopher's books alone.[6]

Raja's Marxist outlook would continue to colour his views when he later became a high-profile journalist in Singapore. In his writings, he would be diligent in etching the tombstone for capitalism in Asia while hailing a socialist birth. His Marxism, however, was not a straightforward one. While Marxism was often associated with communism in the 1930s and 1940s, Raja was never a communist. He had many good friends in London, however, who were. Some would have a lasting influence on him.

As he explored the kaleidoscopic ideas in this intellectual wonderland, Raja grew to appreciate the importance of political education and debate. The intellectuals were not only fine thinkers, but also great explainers and compelled their readers and hearers to think for themselves.

The ambience of the discussions held even deeper significance for Raja. It instilled in him the conviction that reason, rational discourse and tolerance of other people's points of view were cherished ideals. Raja admired the openness of the intellectuals to different ideas, and also to him, a young man struggling to find his own path.

Influenced by those around him, he picked up new habits fashionable at the time. He started smoking cigarettes. He also learnt to enjoy social drinking, developing a particular taste for single malt Scotch whisky. He also became more open and secular in his outlook.

Cerebral and autonomous in his own identity, he experienced little conflict in embracing the various cultural and nationalist groups around him, from the Chinese and Indians to the Africans, and sympathising with their causes. This open-mindedness towards the different cultures and ideas was later to distinguish him as a secular intellectual in Singapore.

Kingsley Martin and others in the Left Book Club widened his contacts further, putting him in touch with people whose orbit he otherwise would not have entered. They included the literary circle, with writers such as Louis MacNeice and Dylan Thomas who voiced the troubled spirit of the decade. His exposure to the literary world provided him the opportunity to discover and develop his own gift for words.

He was zealous in attending book launches, where he could meet and hear authors speak about their books. One of them — the launch of the *Half Caste* by Cedric Dover in 1937 — was to leave a powerful, lifelong impression. Dover, a biologist, used a rational, scientific approach to expose popular racial prejudices and to condemn the belief in eugenics which was ascendant during that period. This belief supposed that pure Northern Europeans were superior in civilisation to other races such as Indians and people of mixed races.

Raja was fascinated by Dover's own background — he was born in Calcutta to mixed parentage, defined himself as a Eurasian, rather than the authorised "Anglo-Indian". Dover also had a Malayan link — after studying biology in India and in Edinburgh, he spent some years in research in Malaya. Later, he moved to London where he took up the cause of the "coloured people" as president of the Colored Writers' Association, and of anti-colonialism in India and Africa.

Raja was struck by Dover's opening remarks at the event: "We are all half-castes. There have never been pure races despite the shrill voice of Hitler's Aryanism." For the first time, Raja, young and impressionable at 22, was introduced to the profound complexities of "the politics of nationalism and the politics of race". As he recounted years later: "Until then, I had accepted the problem of race and nationalism as simply a natural relationship between god-like white men on the one hand and inferior Asiatics on the other."[7]

He bought the book, and also many of its key ideas targeting misconceptions and superstitions regarding race. Hungry to explore the ideas further, he also spent hours discussing them with the author Dover himself, and soon struck up a long-lasting friendship with Dover and his wife, Maureen. The Dovers, as well as Kingsley Martin, would be among the people in London with whom Raja would correspond long after he returned to Malaya.

In 1937, very few Asians dared to openly challenge the colonial paradigm. To be anti-Western would be heretical. "Practically all Malayans and Singaporeans like me who went to study in London were loyal British subjects whose dream it was to return home to Singapore and Malaya, as financially well-off coloured sahibs," he recalled.[8]

The left-wing intellectuals he met brought the question of race and politics into the forefront. Raja witnessed how the Indian intellectuals he knew were standing up to the British powers and asserting their equal right to self-determination and freedom.

In his daily life in London, Raja was made conscious not only of colonial racist stereotypes of Asians that were prevalent among some British intellectuals, but also their parochialism. Many who had never visited the East harboured a sense of superiority and held the notion that the people under British colonial rule should leave the politics of governance to the British.

In London, many "coloured" people had felt the sting of racial slights and snubs, turned away as they were from lodgings and restaurants for their skin colour. Raja had his own humiliating experience. He was once refused a room in a London hotel, "for no reason than because I was what is known as a 'coloured' person", as he would describe later.

To him, it was like "the lash of a whip across my face — and, as it were, while my hands were tied behind my back".[9] He tried to dismiss that incident from his mind as he comforted himself that it was not the only hotel in London. "But for days, I could not get rid of the feeling of terrible humiliation brought about for no other reason than that I had the wrong complexion. One kept licking the wound hoping to heal it, but it became more inflamed," he wrote.

Repulsed by the sheer injustice of racial discrimination, he read up extensively on the issues regarding race and politics. He began to form the view that racial distinctions were artificial, that they were, in fact, evolving human constructions and were thus not immutable. It is a fallacy to believe that one racial group is superior to another. Indeed, it is no more than superstition. Given this rational worldview, all humans, regardless of their skin colour, should be treated equally.

By the time he matured into adulthood, his thoughts on these fundamental issues had hardened into convictions, his dreams set in stone. Most young people would pass through this idealistic phase and then leave it as rude realities intrude. But for Raja, it was not a phase. He nurtured his vision of a race-blind and just society through his 30s and 40s, and pursued it all his life, despite severe setbacks.

Just as the university environment in London was bubbling with intellectual excitement when Raja turned up as a student, so the Indian and West Indian immigrant communities were brimming with political vitality. These groups living in London were at the time in the midst of organising their nationalist movements and building up their strength.

Among those with whom Raja spent a lot of time were leading personalities from the India League, a radical pro-independence movement for India which was associated with the Labour left wing. They included its maverick leader Krishna Menon, a socialist who was once an ace student of Laski at the LSE, and radical writer Mulk Raj Anand.

Raja also became close to leaders from an African-Caribbean group which was agitating for Africa's independence. Most prominent among them were George Padmore, an avowed Marxist and pan-African activist who had been involved in the Communist International.[10]

As his friendships with these people developed, Raja was drawn into their work. Of all his political activities during that period, his involvement in the India League had the greatest impact in stirring his anti-colonial sentiments. Even though he was from Malaya, the group took him in because, he said, "as far as the Indians were concerned, I was Indian".

The Indian students startled him with their hostility towards colonialism. Raja recounted: "Most of these Indian students were violently anti-imperialist, which was an eye-opener to me because I took the British in Malaya for granted, that they were part of the scenery. They were never regarded as enemies. But here was a group of people who felt very intensely about British imperialism." At the time, there was no similar anti-imperialist movement for Malayan students in Britain.[11] Indeed, the Malayan students he knew were largely apolitical.

Seized by the vital cause of anti-imperialism, Raja spent much time at the India League's headquarters at The Strand, just a stone's throw from King's College. It became a centre of high-powered propaganda as it poured out pamphlets, periodicals, speeches and appeals. It also organised meetings with distinguished speakers.

Whenever needed, Raja would drop in at the India League office and help out in their activities. "Sometimes, they wanted volunteers to address envelopes, carry placards. So I used to participate," he revealed later.

Raja observed keenly how the Indian nationalists lobbied support from various quarters, particularly the British and the Africans. They also rallied influential British intellectuals to their cause, such as the key movers of the Left Book Club, including Laski, Strachey and Kingsley Martin.

Menon, who would later become India's foreign minister in Nehru's government, particularly impressed Raja with his passion and talent. Menon was a pioneer of the paperback revolution, editing low-priced serious political books at the firm of Bodley Head. In 1935, he set up a new firm under the name of Penguin with another Bodley Head editor, Allen Lane. Menon took charge of the radical non-fiction paperbacks called Pelicans, while Lane edited paperback works of fiction. Menon gave up this enterprise when the cause of Indian independence consumed him.

The connection of the League to Jawaharlal Nehru and Mahatma Gandhi — names Raja had heard mentioned at home as a boy — gave the Indian cause a larger-than-life feel. "All these things, which were in the fringe of my consciousness as a boy — Gandhi and so on — all came back," Raja recalled. He was presented, for the first time, real-life political heroes to look up to.

But his personal gurus, he said, were radical Indian writer Mulk Raj Anand, who did his PhD in philosophy at University College, and another intellectual and writer K.S. Shelvankar, who had studied under Laski at LSE. Shelvankar was to join the *Hindu*, southern India's best-established paper, in 1942 as their London correspondent, retiring 26 years later. Anand was in the Left Book Club's Readers and Writers group, which gathered progressive literary personalities of the time to discuss their novels and poems.

Knowledgeable and thoughtful, Raja blended well with the group of Indian writers who would meet in people's living rooms to recite poems and short stories, and above all, to discuss the struggle in India and the international crisis with the forward march of fascism in Europe. He was inspired by their Gandhian identification with the marginalised and the Marxist principle of the struggle for class justice.

Raja looked up to Anand, a staunch Marxist who was 10 years his senior. At the time, Anand was just emerging as a powerful and controversial writer. For the Indian nationalist, the written word was a weapon of social protest and a means of exposing injustice and exploitation. He had struggled to get his first novel, *Untouchable*, published in London because its central character was a latrine cleaner, a subject considered beneath many European writers.

After 19 rejections, the novel was finally put to print by the 20th publisher in 1935, followed by another book, *Coolie* (1936). These books won acclaim for their sensitive exploration of the lower stratum of Indian society and today are regarded as classics.

In his writings and talks, Anand, a Gandhi devotee, was open about his disgust for religious sectarianism and the oppressive caste system. As a humanist and a believer in the Enlightenment rational method, Raja was sympathetic to the desire to sweep away theology and superstition and to defy blind allegiance to tradition and authority.

Among the books Raja studied at the time was *The Psychology of a Suppressed People*, by Rev J.C. Heinrich, published in 1937. We know he bought the book in 1937 as he had a habit of writing down the year of purchase on the flyleaf of the book. It dealt with the removal of untouchability and raised questions such as whether it was possible to produce leaders of ability from this group. His earlier reading of the Hindu caste system as simply a form of class oppression and religious dogma was dropped for a subtler inquiry into the relationship between ideology and psychology.

Raja also showed himself familiar with the writings of Indian philosopher and poet Rabindranath Tagore, who put India on the world literary map with the Nobel Prize for literature in 1913. In 1936, Raja had bought Tagore's *Collected Poems and Plays*, an anthology translated from Bengali, when it was first published. This immediately put him in good company, for Tagore was a hero to the Indian nationalists in London. Raja, even in his wildest dreams, would never have imagined that, some years down the road, his name would sit alongside Tagore's in a book celebrating the best stories from around the world. Yet it would, but that is for the next chapter.

Anand, who would later be regarded as "India's Dickens" and one of the founding fathers of the Indian English novel, took a shine to the young aspiring Malayan writer. Raja cut quite an exotic figure — born in Jaffna, raised in Malaya and schooled in Singapore. His temperament was restless and sharply inquisitive. He was one of the rare creatures who could pick up a book and commit its key ideas to memory with seemingly little effort. His knack of producing a well-turned quip also made him entertaining company.

Before long, Anand had inducted the Malayan as an honorary Indian and a member of his new pan-Indian literary group, the Progressive Writers' Association. Anand had formed this group in 1935 with other socialist-oriented Indian writers in London, such as Munshi Prem Chand and Sajjad Zaheer. This movement, which spread throughout India, became known as the All-Indian

Progressive Writers' Association when launched in Lucknow in April 1936. It represented all the major linguistic regions of India and spawned a strong movement among progressive writers. At its height, it probably had over 30,000 members writing literature in all the Indian vernaculars.

The new group's interests were openly social and political: to construct a "united front" of Indian writers against imperialism and reactionary social forces. Aligned closely with the Communist Party of India, the association was viewed with deep suspicion by the British government as a communist front. Raja's involvement aroused the interest of the British intelligence, which in 1942 reported his "nationalist sympathies" and his membership of this Communist-dominated Indian literary association.[12]

This association opened more doors for Raja, and he found himself in the company of high-profile radical Indian writers, such as Iqbal Singh and Ahmed Ali. Together with Anand, they co-edited the association's journal *Indian Writing*, a quarterly publication popular among Indians in England. They were to open doors for him to emerge as a promising short-story writer and to establish useful ties with a wide range of prominent writers.

"Many of the Indians were Marxists, but Asian-oriented Marxists, not the European," said Raja. His constant interaction with the left-wing radicals was noticed by the British authorities, who eventually hauled him up for questioning. He was relieved when it led to nothing more than a ticking off. "When they saw that my activities were harmless, they sent me off with a warning," related Raja.[13]

Padmore, a West Indian journalist, was another political agitator who influenced Raja's political trajectory in London. Raja described him affectionately as "an interesting character" and a "wonderful man". Padmore, who was 14 years his senior, was a sophisticated thinker with an easy humour, often seen with a cigarette jutting from his lips, a habit that Raja also took to. They first got to know each other through the Left Book Club and India League circles.[14]

Over time, as they became closer, Raja was a regular visitor to Padmore's house, which in the late 1930s and 1940s was a key node of anti-colonial struggle in London. Padmore, a disillusioned communist who was to emerge as one of the architects of African decolonisation and African socialism, was active in conducting political study classes for colonial students, including those from Ceylon. Besides Raja, the assortment of personalities streaming in and out of his home included Padmore's childhood Caribbean friend C.L.R. James, who was an active Trotskyist, and British Guyana-born T.R. Makonnen, who later became general secretary of the Pan-African Federation in Britain, with Padmore as chairman.

Helping Padmore to host the countless visitors was his co-worker and wife, Dorothy Pizer, ex-member of the London Communist Party. Padmore articulated his anti-colonialism on behalf of all colonial people from a humanist and universalistic standpoint, one opposed to ethnic or racial nationalism. By temperament and reading, Raja was already inclined towards this philosophy, but Padmore reinforced this at every point.

In the midst of this formative period, it was Padmore, more than anyone else, who helped Raja think through the problems with communism, at a time when the influence of communism was overpowering, particularly in the Left Book Club. Padmore also put him in touch, for the first time, with black militants from all the English-speaking countries, and initiated him into the world of the Pan-African struggle.

In their discussions, Padmore shared freely his life experiences with Raja. Before London, Padmore in 1929 was a leading figure in the Communist Party in the Soviet Union, heading the Negro Bureau of the Communist Trade Union International. The Negro Bureau mutated into the International Trade Union Committee of Negro Workers (ITUC-NW), with Padmore still in charge in 1930. A prolific writer for the communist press, he was a powerful figure in the increasingly Stalinized Communist International (Comintern). In 1933, however, he broke ranks with the Communist Party over Russia's colonial policies, which he felt betrayed the black struggle for freedom.

That year, the Soviet Union had issued a new directive to the Comintern to mobilise action to meet Hitler's Nazi threat and to put a brake on all anti-imperialist work. Russia was seeking rapprochement with the Western European powers, and as part of this move, disbanded Padmore's outfit in 1933.

As the Comintern toed the Moscow line, Padmore, who had long believed that anti-imperialism in Africa was part of the revolutionary communist struggle,[15] lost all trust in the communists. As he told Raja, "the Communists were Europeans who were using black men as instruments to further the European Communist cause and not because they believed in the African cause as such".

Padmore moved to London in 1935. There, he relaunched his fight against colonialism. He lived a hard life as a writer, journalist and campaigner, always poor, but never losing sight of his larger cause.[16] In London, the British Communist Party subjected Padmore to the kind of character assassination that, as Padmore later observed, "has always been one of the most deadly weapons employed by the Communists".[17]

As with the Indian nationalists, Raja was impressed by the prodigious output of Padmore's political writing and his aggressive networking. The radical pamphleteer produced a seemingly unending series of polemical anti-colonial books, pamphlets and articles to highlight the plight of black people to the world. He also worked closely with the Independent Labour Party (ILP) and wrote often for its journals, edited by Fenner Brockway.[18] From Padmore and others like him, Raja picked up the art of political pamphleteing.

More profoundly, Raja also learnt to distinguish the international practice of communism from its ideology and, with his precise intellect, cultivated a more mature and nuanced understanding of the movement.

Padmore, whose views on colonialism were avowedly Leninist, was considered a heretic at the time for questioning the Eurocentric bias of international socialism and labour movements in the world, but Raja, who also knew his Lenin,[19] saw sense in his arguments. Padmore's cautionary insights into the work of international communists had a bracing effect on Raja's view of them.

Raja recalled Padmore's advice: "He said he doesn't trust them, that the anti-colonialists or the colonial people must fight their own struggle." Padmore's experience caused him to be more critical about the communist movement and its motives. "He made me aware that they were really working for their own interest — and the British Communist Party was working for British interests," said Raja.

His own encounters with the British Communist leaders confirmed this. "The British Communist Party was European first. Their approach to Asian problems was patronising. I could sense it that they were using the Indians, the Africans, to booster up the prestige and the status of the British Communist Party," Raja recounted.

Padmore, a strong proponent of the Pan-African movement, later became the ideological mentor to figures such as Ghana's future ruler, Kwame Nkrumah, and Kenya's Jomo Kenyatta and Tom Mboya. Raja would find himself drawing extensively from the Pan-African and Indian experiences when mounting his own anti-colonial campaign after he returned to Malaya.

Raja's interest in international affairs was further sharpened by his exposure to the tireless work of Dorothy Woodman, who headed the left-wing campaign and propaganda group United Democratic Control (UDC). Woodman was a ball of fire in the fight for colonial freedom for many Asian and African countries and worked closely with groups such as the India League.

The UDC, which occupied a tiny attic office in Victoria Street in London, was a power-house for anti-fascist and anti-colonial campaigns, churning out pamphlets and organising meetings all over the country. Woodman's numerous causes extended to China, as she spearheaded the China Campaign Committee against the Japanese occupation in China. She also became deeply involved in the resistance movements of Burma, Indonesia and Vietnam. She was a useful resource person and would open doors for Raja when he himself became a commentator on Asian affairs later.

While he was drawn to the Indian independence movement and the cause of freedom in other parts of the world, Malaya was never far from his mind. Throughout the period, Raja continued to keep up his contacts with some Malayan students in Britain, in the hope of discussing Malayan politics.

Among them was Lim Hong Bee, a Queen's scholar studying law at Cambridge. He arrived in 1937. After Japan invaded China, he formed a China Relief Committee at the university, which earned him the ire of the Cambridge authorities. He was also deeply involved in the British Communist Party's activities, to the extent of losing all interest in his studies.

When these communist activities took place in London, Hong Bee would travel to the city and put up at Raja's boarding house. They both shared a love for books. In November 1937, when the book *Red Star over China* by Edgar Snow was a rage in London, Raja sent a copy of it to Hong Bee.

Raja would occasionally visit Cambridge for tea parties with Hong Bee's varied circle of friends. At one of these picnics by River Cam, Raja met Lim Chong Eu, a Queen's scholar from Penang who would eventually lead several political parties at different times in Malaya.[20] Years later, Chong Eu recalled the languid hours spent discussing books and ideas during their student days in Britain, with nary a thought given to the politics in Malaya.

They sprawled along the grassy river bank on lazy summer days and chatted desultorily about "the pleasant things in life", Chong Eu recalled. When the mood struck them, they punted on the river. There was an unspoken hankering for the genteel life of the English upper class.[21]

Such activities did not seem to anticipate the later course of events — when, in 1964 with Singapore a part of Malaysia, Chong Eu would work frantically with Raja and others to steer through the cross-currents of Malaysian politics to reach their joint destination of a multiracial Malaysian Malaysia. Their efforts would lead them into a seething political cauldron.

During the pre-war years in London, however, Malaya was not on the forefront of discussions among the Malayan students. They were caught up in the political movements of the times. As events unfolded, Hong Bee's interest, for instance, became focused on China — the Japanese attack on China, and China's communist movement.

Through Hong Bee, who would years later become the Malayan Communist Party's unofficial representative in London, Raja came to later attend some activities organised by the China Institute at Gordon Square. The institute was open to all ethnic Chinese students.

Raja sympathised with the Chinese communist students in their campaign against the Japanese occupation in China, and was happy to accept Hong Bee's invitation to attend a convention of Chinese revolutionary students in Welwyn Garden City, a town in Hertfordshire in the east of England.

The ostensible purpose of the trip was to campaign for China, but for Raja, it was really the opportunity to visit a new interesting place at a pittance. At the time, Welwyn Garden City was held up as a radical sort of urban utopia in social and town planning, marrying the best of both country and city living.

Throughout this intense period of political fervour, Raja did not lose his sense of humour. This was illustrated vividly at breakfast on the first morning, when he was seated with his friend at a table consisting wholly of Chinese students. One of them could not contain his curiosity and asked: "And what part of China do you come from?"

Raja had often wondered at the way people would ascribe identities according to skin colour and physical features, and thought the opportunity to take the mickey out of such a conception was too good to pass up.

So Raja replied, with a straight face, that he was a China Jew from Turkestan. To his horror, they took him seriously and asked a flurry of earnest questions about his lineage. He realised that "unless I stopped forthwith there was going to be a lot of lost faces all around", he would recount years later.[22] He did not make much of what he learnt from the Chinese convention, but he left with a few more revolutionary Chinese friends and at least one more anecdote on the absurd notion of racial stereotype.

Aware of his Marxist sympathies, some of his communist friends made overtures to Raja to join their ranks. He was reluctant to be drawn in. As he explained later, "I was drawn to Marxism, but I was not a Communist because I met Padmore who told me what Russian Marxism was about." He added: "At that time, Communism was pro-Soviet, because China at that time was still not Communist." Indeed, Mao was then an apostle of Russian policy.

Raja's views on China and communism were influenced by another friend he made at the time, Xiao Qian, a translater, writer and journalist from China. Xiao Qian, who arrived in Britain in 1939, continued his job as a journalist for a Chinese newspaper, *Takung Pao*, while teaching modern Chinese language at the School of Oriental and African Studies (SOAS). He gave regular talks for the Dorothy Woodman's China Campaign Committee.

Keen to learn more about China, Raja began to read up on Chinese literature and philosophy, and discussed them with his Chinese friends. He bought translated works by Arthur Waley. They include *Three Ways of Thought in Ancient China* (1939), which are mainly extracts of Zhuangzi, Mencius and Han Feizi, and *One Hundred and Seventy Chinese Poems* (1939).

His appetite whetted, Raja would continue to collect books on Chinese literature and culture, especially those translated or written by Waley, over the decades. They ranged from Wu Cheng'en's *Monkey* (1942), *The Poetry and Career of Li Po, 701–762 A.D, Yuan Mei:*

Eighteenth Century Chinese Poet (1956), and *The Opium War Through Chinese Eyes* (1960), to *The Analects of Confucius* (1988). These books added considerably to his appreciation of Chinese culture and history.

When the Second World War broke out, Xiao Qian became the only Chinese war correspondent in Western Europe from China. Raja's knowledge of China and its nationalist movement was nurtured, in part, through his friendship with Xiao Qian. Xiao Qian returned to China in 1949 on the eve of the communist victory. He had hoped to resume his career as a creative writer. Instead, for two decades, he was branded a rightist, and twice sent to the countryside to do heavy manual labour. The vindictive turmoil of the Cultural Revolution ate into him, and, in despair, he attempted suicide in 1966.

After Raja became Singapore's foreign minister, he visited Xiao Qian when leading an official mission to China in March 1975, the first Singapore minister to visit the PRC. It was a warm reunion of two old friends, even as their respective countries kept each other cautiously at arm's length. Bilateral ties were normalised only in 1979. Raja's benevolence and sincerity endeared him to people he met in Britain, and he was to return to Malaya with strong transatlantic friendships that would endure for many years.

This phase of Raja's politicisation and maturing was critical in sharpening his political instincts. He had a ringside view of how anti-imperialist and socialist movements operated and how propaganda was effectively exploited to further their political ends. He learnt the art of producing pamphlets and organising campaigns. He brought these lessons to bear later when he joined the PAP and became its propaganda chief.

The sheer breadth of his involvement with distinct cultural and nationalistic groups from different countries suggests that Raja was trying to get at some of the universal verities of life which cut across the artificial barriers of race and nations.

In his interviews on his days in London, Raja tended to portray himself as a tentative student of politics, responding to the vicissitudes of contemporary politics. But his range of political activities and radical friends suggests that he was no bobbing flotsam. He was contributing as an interested participant, seeking out different activist groups, giving his own views, and directing his energy towards the social and political causes which moved him.

While he was busy making a place for himself in the radical world, he was rapidly losing interest in his university course. Indeed, by that time, he had almost all but given up his pursuit of law — his records at King's College suggest that he left the course in 1938 and did not sit his exams for that year. There were many distractions.

Besides the whirl of political and literary activities, there was romance. The woman who stole his heart was Piroska Feher, a blonde-haired Hungarian whom he met in 1938 at a Left Book Club meeting through Woodman. It was a love that was not only to endure severe hardships, but also give him the strength to pursue his own idiosyncratic path in life.

Over time, just as Raja's attitude towards politics went through a seismic shift in London, so did his views on romantic love and marriage. He was affected by the Western notion of equal partnerships and the society's openness to racially-mixed marriages. The latter — taboo in his Ceylon Tamil community — was not uncommon in London.

Several of his Indian and African friends then, such as Padmore and Anand, had married European women. He was also drawn to poetry and literature that spoke of love and the longings of the human heart. Clearly, Raja, this acolyte of reason and logic, was a sentimental and romantic man.

When Raja began to court Piroska seriously, it was with the full knowledge that, if he returned to Seremban a bachelor, an arranged marriage with a traditional Ceylon Tamil woman would be waiting for him. His parents would select the woman, based on her caste and family background, to carry on the pure blood line. This family duty was one that Raja had no intention of honouring. He would marry the woman he loved.

4

Love and War

Piroska was born on 23 October 1911 in Békéscsaba, a city in south-east Hungary. She developed an independent streak early in life. From the age of about 14, she had travelled regularly to Switzerland to study and practise languages — German and English — and to make new friends.

She had also suffered from a lung ailment since childhood and found, as had many others before, that the pure Swiss mountain air improved her condition. In early 1938, she demonstrated her verve when she decided to leave Hungary for London, leaving behind her upper middle-class family.

She wanted to learn English and to train to become a teacher. She was fearful of the rising tide of fascism in her homeland and resented the increasing intolerance against Jews in Hungary. In May 1938, Hungary restricted to 20 per cent the number of Jews allowed in certain professions. A year later, Hungary passed laws which prevented any Hungarian Jew from being a schoolteacher, judge, lawyer, or member of the government.

Piroska was not Jewish, as assumed by many and speculated later by some Western diplomats in Singapore. Her hatred of fascism was motivated less by direct personal experience than by her own sense of human morality and compassion. Hence, while the Australian High Commission in Singapore was mistaken when, in a diplomatic despatch in 1959,[1] it described Piroska as "possibly a Hungarian

Jewess", it was spot on when it added that she "certainly detested both the pre-war Hungarian regime and anything that could be associated with German fascism". She remained fiercely anti-fascist and anti-racist all through her life.

In Hungary, Piroska's parents, who were Roman Catholics, were fortunate to have the means to fund her escape to London. Her father, Karoly (or Charles, in English) Feher, was a managing director of an electrical company; her mother ran a business producing home linen — towels, napkins, bed covers — adorned with handmade embroidery.

Piroska had a younger sister, Klara, six years her junior. Later, she married a lawyer, Dr Kiss Istvan, and became a full-time housewife. They had one son, Istvan, born in 1949.

During World War Two, Piroska's family suffered bitterly in Békéscsaba. In 1944, three tragic events shook the town. Between 24 and 26 June, more than 3,000 Jews were sent to their fate in Auschwitz, and on 21 September, the British and American Air Force bombed the railway station and its surroundings, killing more than 100 people. On 6 October, the Nazis occupied Békéscsaba.

Klara's husband, a Lutheran, joined the military and fought against the Soviet army. He was captured and forced to suffer hard labour as a prisoner of war in a copper mine near Siberia for two years, from 1945 to 1946.

During all those years when Piroska was away in London, no one breathed her name at home in Békéscsaba. Her parents were anxious that the authorities might get wind of her whereabouts and raise questions which might jeopardise the family's safety. They kept their heads down and lived a quiet, cautious life.

The family had few friends. The young Istvan, who had once caught sight of a family photo with Piroska in it, wondered for years who that woman was. Nobody at home would shed any light, and he began to regard her as a mere photographic apparition.[2]

But Piroska was very much alive in London. She kept going by working as an *au pair*. This was not unusual for foreigners then who wished to study the English language and culture by living with an English-speaking family. Life changed for her when she met Woodman, who had a soft spot for visitors or refugees — the line was often blurred — fleeing fascist countries.

Fiercely anti-fascist, Woodman had made it her job to find out about the anti-Nazi movements in various European countries, including Hungary, and had published numerous pamphlets giving the facts about their resistance movements. Piroska became interested in her work and through that, found the man who would become the love of her life.

Piroska, fair with beautiful brown eyes, captivated Raja with her independent spirit, directness and her zest for life. She had journeyed to London to study English and education. She was pretty, slim and petite, standing at 5 feet 2 inches, five inches shorter than him. Raja was initially inhibited by his natural reserve and diffidence, but Piroska, who was three years older, drew him out of his shell.

Before Piroska came into the picture, Raja had, as expected of most men his age, friends of the opposite sex. One of them was a certain Nelly Domeni, a slim and attractive European with dark, curly hair. Keen on exploring the world, Raja had set off in 1937 with Nelly and some friends on a European tour, a luxury which was beyond the means of many at the time.

He drew from the money which his father had transferred to a bank in London for him to see through his law studies. Over three months in 1937, the group explored Europe and embarked on a leisurely Mediterranean cruise.

During this extended "grand tour", Raja, an avid photographer, put his Kodak camera to good use. He took several pictures of the fashionably dressed Domeni with her dimpled smile — on a scenic bridge at Champery in the Swiss Alps in July 1937, and yet another on the glacier of the Mer de Glace at Chamonix in France, dated September 1937.

In photos of that period, Raja looked quite dashing with his dark, sharp features and wavy hair. It is not clear whether Raja's feelings for

Nelly were platonic or romantic, but Nelly's affection for Raja apparently ran deep. At the back of a photo of herself in a swimsuit sent to Raja, Nelly scribbled: "Always Yours". It was dated 9 November 1939, Zurich.

There was another European woman, Cecile Vidal, with a warm spot in her heart for Raja at this time. A photo of Cecile found in Raja's possession, dated 7 April 1937, bore her handwritten inscription: "To my Raja darling with love". They would part as good friends. Cecile, who lived in Switzerland, would maintain her links with Raja even after he returned to Singapore, exchanging platonic letters and reminiscences of their friendship until their old age. But it was clear from all his letters that Raja was completely loyal and faithful to Piroska, even after her death in 1989.

In his bachelor days, despite suffering no lack of female attention, Raja had obviously fallen for Piroska as he began to see more of her. In his photos with Piroska in the late 1930s and early 40s, Raja looked relaxed, happy, and quite besotted. His courtship of Piroska swirled with romance. On clear spring days, they took walks in the park, stopping now and then to lie down on a patch of grass and revel in each other's company. On warm summer days, they had picnics on beaches, rowed a boat, and swam.

One photo captured a happy moment with both smiling in their swimwear on a sandy cove, looking very much in love. Piroska cut a fetching figure in her halter-neck two-piece suit. In many photos of that period, the adoring couple would often have arms entwined around each other. Those were happy days. That was the end of an era, the final year before world war exploded the illusions of plenty and exposed them to the perils of war.

After Britain declared war on Germany on 3 September 1939, Raja shared with the people in London a sense of foreboding. As the people waited for bombs to fall on British soil, they groped through the blackout imposed on the city, clutching their gas masks and hiding in shelters. It was a long wait during what became known as the phoney war, as Hitler saved his air power for the Polish campaign.

Postal communication ceased altogether in June and July 1940. The break of connection with his family in Seremban forced Raja to make his own living. It also led him to strike out in his own direction in life without the pressure of meeting family expectations.

He decided he was not going to waste any more of his time pursuing his law studies, something he had no interest in. After missing his exams in 1938, Raja retook them in 1939 and 1940. He failed both times.[3] He did not graduate.

Despite not completing the course, he owed much to his days in King's College, perhaps more than he was aware. The intellectual training that he received as a law student would put him in good stead later as a formidable debater.

When King's College was evacuated to Bristol that year, with classes conducted in the University of Bristol buildings and students housed in hostels there, Raja chose to stay behind in London and take his chances. A powerful reason for staying behind was Piroska.

Then the blitz began. In September 1940, German bombers began their terrifying raids on London. Raja and Piroska became sensitive to the overture: an eerie rise and fall of the sirens, followed by the dull drone of bomber engines, and then a chilling shriek.

Almost daily, they hurried down together to the underground stations that sheltered as many as 177,000 people during the night. The racket was deafening with German bombers dropping hundreds of tons of bombs on the capital. There were also often dogfights between the German and British fighters.

Raja recounted that because he and Piroska were apart during the day, their first thought at the wail of the air raid siren was often of each other. "When the enemy planes came for the air raids, we had to take refuge in different air raid shelters. When the German planes left, we would be very worried for each other's safety."[4] They often emerged from their separate shelters to find fires consuming the city and bodies strewn among the rubble. The uncertainties of life drew the couple closer. They felt the acute sense of vulnerability that was linked to the wartime prevalence of death.

The anxieties of war also brought home to Raja the reality of raw politics. Ideologies and politics mattered. They were more than topics for intellectual discourse; they were vehicles for belief and action. They could drive countries to war and people to turn against one another; they could sunder human ties, destroy homes and communities; they could take away everything he held dear. "Politics became something practical, something immediate, something which I found myself involved in," said Raja.

Raja and Piroska found in each other a solid love that helped them to cope with the trauma of war and their life's decisions. Caught in a war that cut them off from their families, the uncertainty of their world was a potent backdrop to their relationship.

Stranded without financial support from his family, Raja took the job of a clerk in the Ministry of Supply to support himself and Piroska. It was based at Shell Mex House on London's Strand, not far from where he lived. At the time, the Ministry of Supply, which coordinated the supply of equipment to the British armed forces, was rapidly expanding its manpower to support the rising demands of the country's war effort. It was not Raja's dream job, but the nightmare of war put a different perspective on just being able to get up and go to work. It gave him a sense of purpose.

Food was rationed. Ration books effectively tied people to one butcher and one grocer. Because Raja had to work, Piroska collected his ration coupons and joined the inevitable long queues outside local shops when supplies came in.

Raja recalled: "Because of food rations, we could only get one egg a week each. Even less meat. Piroska suffered a lot waiting in the long queues."[5] To supplement their income, Piroska found a job as a finisher in a clothing factory. Life for the couple was reduced to its most basic: the struggle to keep body and soul together.

Like everyone else in London, the couple had to take pains to ensure their flat was totally sealed from light during the enforced blackout, drawing their dark curtains tightly at night so that, as the theory went, enemy aircraft could not pick out landmarks. For about five years, from 1 Sept 1939 to 14 Sept 1944, their lives were wrapped in darkness. To add to the gloom, they had to cope with an unusually cold and bleak winter — 1940 provided the coldest January and February for 45 years. Heavy snow falls added a new dimension to the perils of the blackout.

In the political world, a cold air also descended on Chamberlain's administration. Germany's invasion of Norway in April and Britain's failures in the campaign had caused the people to lose faith in Chamberlain. They now clamoured for a national leader with military stature. In May 1940, the mood ushered in Winston Churchill's all-party coalition.

Raja kept track of news through the radio, the key source of information and entertainment during the war. The news from the front in 1940 was a series of cataclysmic disasters: the landings and withdrawals of British forces in Norway by May; German conquest of the Low Countries in May and of France by mid-June; British retreat from the beaches of Dunkirk by 4 June.

In the midst of these disasters, Raja heard the soaring prose of Churchill who asserted that "whatever happens at Dunkirk, the British will fight on" and lifted the spirit of a tired nation to give, in return, eventual victory.

While Raja had little sympathy for Churchill's conservative politics, he admired the British leader for being able to inspire a demoralised people to stand up against Hitler in that crucial summer of 1940, when circumstances pointed to an almost certain British defeat. In his resoluteness to confront and defeat the country's enemies, Churchill was able to turn the tide of war, Raja observed. "I never saw such a transformation of a people quite determined to overcome facts or the logic of facts," he said years later.

This leavening experience made a deep impact on him. It demonstrated to him the critical importance of inspirational leadership during frightening times. He would have cause to draw on this lesson when faced with his own Dunkirk moments in politics later.

As the war dragged on, year after interminable year, Raja learnt to depend on the strength of the human spirit to survive and overcome one's fears. The random raids meant that any day could be one's last.

In December 1940, amidst the devastation of the Blitz, Piroska expressed her love for Raja in a book she gave him as a Christmas present. It was the *Book of Songs*, the earliest collection of Chinese poems translated into English by Arthur Waley, first published in 1937. In the book, which contained love odes, she inscribed, "To Raja, my dearest and nearest. From Piroska."

They shared a fragile sort of happiness. In February 1941, the Blitz intensified with up to 700 German aircraft attacking British cities in simultaneous raids night after night. In central London, where Raja and Piroska lived, only one house in 10 escaped damage. Almost half of the nearly 61,000 dead were killed in the London region. If they were not killed by the bomb blasts, they were slain by lacerating fragments, fire, or falling buildings.

The resilience of the people in London came to the fore in the face of this nightly onslaught. Raja and Piroska, like the people around them, showed sustained courage by carrying on with their daily lives in spite of the Blitz.

Raja plunged deeper into London's radical literary world and immersed himself in the bohemian effusion which flourished in the pubs of London during the austere conditions of the Blitz. He relaxed in the company of his opinionated and eccentric friends which allowed a reserved and introspective personality to blossom. They shared with him a love for the written word and an obsession with ideas and ideals. He found pleasure in being surrounded by people bearing the gift of different and complex views, and took delight in unwrapping the many layers of their contending arguments, and getting to the core issues.

When he faced the new troubled decade as a young man of 25 in 1940, he had already made some choices that were directing him towards writing and politics. The first was his decision not to pursue his law degree, the second was his alliance with the Africans and Indian writers who used their art to further the cause of socialism and independence in their homelands, and anti-fascism and anti-imperialism abroad.

He assimilated more and more, not into the mild and apolitical Southeast Asian groups, but into the radical milieus that offered the raucous politics of anti-colonialism. His interest in anti-colonial politics grew in tandem. He related: "It's not an interest in Malayan politics or Singapore politics, but anti-colonial politics. That meant Chinese, Indians, Africans. It all sort of came together, haphazard, unplanned."

He matured in a left-wing Indian and Afro-Caribbean nationalistic environment in Britain, imbibing dreams of freedom and learning from the feisty men fighting British rule in their home countries. Without realising it, he was serving his apprenticeship as a Malayan anti-colonialist at the feet of prominent Indian and African nationalists at the forefront of their country's independence movements.

At the same time, he was also developing a growing confidence in his own powers of analysis. It was obvious that Raja was regarded highly in these circles and respected for his insights. When Padmore and his wife Pizer started working on a book on Russia in the early 1940s, they sought Raja's help with it.

When the book, *How Russia Transformed Her Colonial Empire: A Challenge to the Imperialist Powers*, was published in 1946, Padmore thanked Pizer for her help, and also "our mutual friends" who gave helpful criticisms and suggestions — four names were mentioned, one of them Raja's. The others were Makonnen, Ceylonese T.B. Subasingha, a leading light of the newly-formed Marxist Lanka Sama Samaja Party, and P.P.V. de Silva, another Ceylonese disciple of Trotsky. In the audacious book, Padmore challenged the political parties in Britain to follow Lenin's example with respect to Tsarist empire and give up its colonies.

As expected, Raja's close association with the radical types provoked more than a little discomfort in British official circles. But the danger which he posed during the war may have been exaggerated when, in its report in 1940, the Special Branch categorised Raja as "pro-Hitler", a charge often levelled at communists and socialists for opposing the war with Germany.[6] Like many of his left-wing friends, Raja abhorred war, but there was little doubt that he detested Hitler even more.

All his debates with his friends on the evils of war, fascism and imperialism took on frantic exclamation marks when, in June 1941, Germany attacked Russia, and in December, the Japanese bombed the United States at Pearl Harbor. With the world's two greatest neutral powers dragged into the fray within six months, what was a European war escalated into a world war.

Germany, aware that their only hope for triumph lay in swift and decisive gains, intensified its attacks on Russia, while Japan trained its sights on French Indochina, Singapore, Malaya, Burma, and Hong Kong, and many strategic Pacific Islands.

For Raja, the horrors of war hit home in a devastatingly personal way when Malaya and, then Singapore, fell to the Japanese in February 1942.

It was an emotional moment when he pondered on the possibility that he might never be able to return to his family in Malaya again.

"I saw that politics means that you can lose your home and cannot go back," he said. With this sudden realisation, something fundamental shifted in Raja's mind. Britain was not his home. Malaya was.

His fear of losing his family and his homeland heightened when, a month after Malaya fell, Rangoon was gone. Soon, the Dutch East Indies and the Dutch fleet in Eastern waters went too.

Raja realised that, while it had been exciting making interesting friends and observing the political changes in Britain, it was not his country. His cause was in Malaya. For the first time, he took a more personal and systematic interest in politics. It was not an abstract subject for discussions, but something raw and real.

While he was stirred to do something about the situation in Malaya, he had no idea what or how. Unlike the Indians or the Africans in London, Raja had no critical mass of radical Malayan students with whom to work. Even if there were, it is doubtful whether he would have had the organisational capacity to form a movement like Menon's India League, or Padmore's Pan-African Federation.

The two years when the Japanese occupied Malaya were anxious ones for Raja. He was cut off from his family, and could neither receive nor send any news. He empathised with the fear and misery of others who had already lost their homes during the war. Almost every week, he met waves of new intellectuals and writers in the *émigré* circles who had fled from Germany and Nazi-occupied Austria and Czechoslovakia and become exiles in London.

These countries were witnessing the persecution of Jews and their extermination in concentration camps, the burning of books, and the complete destruction of their societies. The intensity of their suffering profoundly moved Raja and Piroska, who could speak German and was often their interlocutor in conversations with the English-speaking set. Like Raja and Piroska, these *émigrés* could not reckon on an early return to their homelands.

As news of the gruesome extermination camps trickled in, Raja was sickened by Nazi anti-semitism and the demagogue — Hitler —

who was leading this madness. The horror of it was printed indelibly on his mind. It was such experiences, in the darkness of the war, which led Raja to develop misgivings about the unpredictable and arbitrary nature of politics which could sweep such unscrupulous men to power.

Disturbed by the developments around him, Raja studied books which investigated the causes of war, the ideologies of race, the good, bad, and ugly of political systems, and the character of nations. He was powerfully affected by the book *The Illusion of National Character* by Hamilton Fyfe, which he purchased in April 1940. It argued that national character "is the most dangerous and most potent of the elements making for war". He read the book as a warning on how politicians can subvert nationalist fervour for evil ends. It had haunted him ever since.

In these turbulent years, Piroska became more important to him than ever as a stabilising factor in his life. She, in turn, saw in him a rock on which she could rely. Against the wartime backdrop of catastrophe, Raja and Piroska decided to get married. He was 28; she 31. On 2 January 1943, their union was solemnised in a simple ceremony at the Register Office in the Metropolitan Borough of Hampstead. Outside, war continued to rage.

Observing this poignant moment were two friends, Frances Webb, and Alex D. Duff, who put their names to their marriage certificate as witnesses. The couple returned to Raja's rented flat at 89, Priory Road, West Hampstead, as husband and wife.

The flat in West Hampstead was simply furnished, distinguished by a worn sofa and a threadbare rug on the floor. One of their favourite spots was by the fireplace. Raja's own photographs of their cluttered flat bore ample evidence of their lifestyle — reading, smoking cigarettes, and drinking tea. There were books strewn on the sofa and side tables, with empty tea cups and overflowing ashtrays jostling for space.

They were also deeply preoccupied with each other. Raja snapped several tender shots of Piroska in the flat. Among them was one of her reading in an arm chair, her fair features lit up by the soft light shining in from the window. Another caught her looking radiant as she weaved her wavy hair into a sleek bob in front of a mirror. These are adoring pictures taken by a man in love.

They hosted frequent gatherings in their apartment. Their friends fluttered like multicoloured confetti into their book-strewn living room for long conversations over drinks. They would leave lasting memories of sparkling times amidst the blackness of war. One of their friends, Dr Jal Dubash from Bombay, would write to Piroska in 1989, to reminisce about the "wonderful days" in London — yes, the war was awful, he recalled, but "Priory Road was fun", referring to the street where Raja lived.[7]

Perpetually scraping money together, the couple struggled to pay their rent and were often a week or two late. When Raja first became a subtenant of the apartment in 1941, the rent was 21 pounds, 17 shillings, and sixpence per quarter. In 1943, after Piroska moved in, it was raised to 22 pounds, 14 shillings, and two pence. The careful jots in their dog-eared rent books, kept by Raja till his death, charted their fluctuating fortunes and their resilience.

5
Writing Fiction

With Piroska by his side, Raja showed a readiness to engage imaginatively with the new realities and exigencies of life. He was by now beginning to look for openings to supplement his income through freelance writing and sale of short stories to the literary magazines that were so popular at the time.

While he was still hazy about his calling, he was greatly attracted to the purposeful world of political writing. His friends already active in the field were more than willing to provide the contacts and opportunities.

Chief among them was his charismatic journalist-cum-politician friend, Michael Foot. According to Raja, it was this crusading left-wing journalist who first encouraged him to write for several publications in London.

Foot, who first contested the election under the Labour Party in 1935 at the age of 22, wrote for various leftist publications — the *New Statesman*, the *Daily Herald*, and *Tribune* — and achieved notoriety in 1940 by co-writing the bestseller, *Guilty Men* attacking the appeasement policies of the Chamberlain government. He became even more controversial as the protege of the right-wing press baron and politician Lord Beaverbrook when he worked for his newspapers, the *Evening Standard* and the *Daily Express*, turning them into the voice of intellectual populism.

Raja cut his teeth in journalism by working for Beaverbrook's flagship newspaper, the *Daily Express*. Beaverbrook, who was minister for aircraft production (1940–41), minister of supply (1941–42), minister of war production (1942), believed in the power of the press and used it mightily to flay his political foes.

Eager for more action, Raja also freelanced for the left-wing cooperative paper *Reynolds News*, which was highly politicised as part of the labour press. He also wrote for some of Padmore's publications, which pleaded the cause of socialism and liberty. The experience and contacts he gained through his stints gave him a feel of the seductive power of political journalism.

The rudderless trajectory of his professional development took another decisive turn when he ventured into the literary world of fiction. It was a new and challenging area for him; not every writer could make a success of it.

It required imagination, style, discipline, and vivid prose. Despite its demands, it was to this particular literary form that he dedicated much of his energy and skill over the coming years. The exertion saw a sudden flowering of Raja as a fiction writer. He had found another outlet for his creative spirit and his social conscience.

It has been hard to trace exactly when Raja started writing fiction but we know that at least seven of his stories were published between 1941 and 1948. In all of them, he signed off as S. Raja Ratnam, breaking off his given name Rajaratnam into two. This was mainly for convenience.

Most of his stories were set in rural villages reminiscent of daily life in Malaya, India, or Jaffna. The exceptions were "The Terrorist", which was set on a train heading to a fictional place called Midnapore — a subtle combination of Malaya, India and Singapore — and "The Tiger", in which the backdrop was a village in the Malayan jungle, not unlike his own rubber estate in Seremban. This imaginative process of migrating from an Indian landscape to a Malayan one mirrored his later concerns as he pondered on the political fate of Malaya and Singapore.

His style was closer to the Indian short story with its raw imagery and unresolved endings than to the Western with its subtleties and neatness of plot. The heavy rhythm and polemical patterning of his sentences anticipate the characteristic cadences of his later political writing.

His form and technique caused him to be identified by English editors and reviewers as an "Indian" writer, which in itself was not a bad thing given the pioneering work of Mulk Raj Anand in internationalising the work of Indian writers in London at the time. It was easier for editors to promote Raja as an Indian writer than a Malayan one — there was scarcely any alternative Malayan literary movement in London with which Raja could work.

In a conscious effort to strike his own path, Raja used his characters to convey universal metaphors, rather than Indian ones. He turned his sensitive artist's eye again and again to commonplace characters — the farmer, the pregnant woman, the college student — and peeled away their layers to reveal the powerful beliefs which guided their responses to life's events.

All his stories feature a rich mixture of realism, a strong humanist sentiment, and ironic twists, often addressing the irrational side of the human condition and the injustices of mankind. There is no neat solution, no satisfying denouement. He wrote to open up thought and, in the process, brought to bear his own unique perspective.

He made his debut in the August 1941 edition of the journal *Indian Writing*, a quarterly popular among Indians in England. The story, titled "Famine", concerns a rural community which was being starved by famine and must choose between the rules of its religion and its survival — which ultimately depends on eating cattle, considered sacred to Hindus.

The ending was a swipe at the blind irrationality of a man who obeyed the dictates of religion with morally questionable results — he preferred to see his fellow villagers die of starvation than slaughter his sacred cow, only to see the precious animal die from natural causes and being fed on by rats and a swarm of flies.[1]

It was a powerful story. So powerful that E. M. Forster, best known for his novels, *A Passage to India* and *Howards End*, highlighted this story in his British Broadcasting Corporation (BBC) broadcast on 29 April 1942. In that broadcast, Forster described Raja's work as a "touching and well-constructed story" and praised it alongside his remarks on Anand's trilogy of Sikh peasant life.[2] Like several English left-wing intellectuals, Forster was an advocate for Indian independence and allied to the Indian radical writers based in London.

Forster had evidently got hold of the proofs of that edition of *Indian Writing*, and used his radio programme to promote the Indian writers who impressed him.[3] The journal was edited by Iqbal Singh, K.S Shelvankar, Ahmed Ali, and A. Subramaniam, all prominent writers.

Ahmed Ali, for instance, was one of Pakistan's most distinguished writers. A co-founder of the All India Progressive Writers Association, his novel *Twilight in Delhi* (1940) was a major success and led reviewers to rank him alongside Mulk Raj Anand and R.K. Narayan.

In that issue of *Indian Writing*, Raja's story was sandwiched between commentaries by Indian luminaries such as Rabindranath Tagore and Krishna Menon, and book reviews by Mulk Raj Anand, Iqbal Singh, and Shelvankar. There were also other radical writers, such as Marxist thinker, writer and journalist Sajjad Saheer, who later became the first secretary general of the Communist Party of Pakistan when it was established in 1948, and British Communist and writer Clement Dutts, who served as a member of the Communist Party of India in exile.

Certainly, Raja's literary friends were of the controversial and subversive variety. Equally, when it came to their literary stature, he was in distinguished company.

The experience marked the first stirrings of his writer's voice. Forster's public praise for his work encouraged the creative spirit in Raja, who was still coming to terms with how he had failed his Malayan family by abandoning his law studies. Now he had another expectation to fulfil — the burden of promise as a writer.

He rose to the challenge with a quick succession of stories. Two of them — "The Locusts", and "What Has to Be" — appeared in the

August 1941 issue of the *Life and Letters and the London Mercury*, edited by Robert Herring. It was striking that Raja was the only author with two of his stories published in that single edition — most uncommon for a first-time contributor to the monthly periodical.[4] The particular edition has a focus on Indian writers — the only other short story was Mulk Raj Anand's "A Pair of Moustachios". The other six articles were cultural or political commentaries, with authors such as Nancy Cunard and Iqbal Singh.

As Raja blossomed as a writer, he found other outlets for his stories beyond the Anglo-Indian world. Journals edited by the established Euro-American literati welcomed his contributions, allowing him to reach out to a wider audience.

His first story set in Malaya, titled "The Tiger" appeared in 1942 in *Modern Reading*,[5] which published some of the foremost short story writers in Britain. His stories were well received. "The Tiger" was reprinted in 1948 in the *Mirror*, a monthly international review, and was presented as "an example of modern Malayan writing".[6]

The literary journal, *Little Reviews Anthology*, which selected the best of that year's output from Britain's many literary magazines, reprinted "Famine" in its 1943 edition.

Astonishingly, Raja's stories also made their way across the Atlantic. His story, "Drought", emerged in the September 1941 edition of the magazine *Asia*, which was later renamed *Asia and the Americas*. Its publisher was Richard Walsh, the second husband of Pearl S. Buck who won a Pulitzer Prize (1935) and then a Nobel Prize for literature (1938) for her book, *The Good Earth*. Raja's literary reputation was growing day by day.

Simply by depicting the features and life of a rural village in India or Malaya through his characters, he described a world still largely unknown to the majority of his English and American readers. His stories raised awareness of cultural and social issues, and subtly revealed differences and prejudices.

As their titles indicate, Raja was concerned with the mundane lives of rural folk set against bewildering forces beyond their control.

His stories tell us that poverty and exploitation are intrinsic to this world, but such obvious causes of misery are mirrored by a critique of human greed, manipulation, and folly. The overwhelming sense one is left with is a bleak one. There are no easy answers.

In the story "The Tiger", Raja evoked the sounds, sights and smells of a Malay kampong in the evening — the "cry of a waterfowl or the sinister flap-flap of night birds", the gentle splash of a rat diving into the river, the rustle of animals in the tall grass and creepers. "The air was full of the scent of wild flowers and mud and rotting grass." A pregnant woman, Fatima, bathing waist-deep in the river, saw a tiger looming in the dense *lalang* (tall grass) some 20 yards away. After its initial ferocious snarl, its expression turned from threatening growls, to sullen caution to "a surprising gentleness". Fatima returned to the village to tell her mother about the tiger.

The news caused alarm for the village, and, based on an exaggerated account that Fatima was attacked, the headman called for the animal to be hunted down and killed. Fatima pleaded against the hunt — the tiger did not harm her although it could have sprung on her easily. "There was nothing fierce or murderous about it," she insisted to her mother. She was all but ignored as the mob went after the tiger and shot it.

The hunters returned to report that the tiger had put up a good fight — they had to spear it after it was shot twice — and later found out why: there were "three of the tiniest tiger cubs" hidden nearby. At that moment, Fatima moaned in pain as her own contractions began.

Raja's talent as a writer is there on every page, and it is juxtapositions like these that elevate his stories into a timeless portrait of human folly. The tiger meant no harm to humans — it was merely a wary mother protecting her own cubs in the jungle. Fatima knew, from her own personal encounter with the tiger, that it was not murderous. Yet, despite her protestations, the tiger was beset on and killed by aggressive men who ignored the facts and ascribed the worst traits to the tiger, because it was born a tiger.

In "The Locusts",[7] he focused on a labourer in a farm, Thulasi, who was confronted with circumstances — the weather, winged insects, socio-economic class — beyond his control. The labourer believed: "The earth is rich, and when men sweat, it will pour its riches into their laps." The unpredictable weather turned out to be kind, the harvest was splendid — and then the locusts came.

Miraculously, however, they passed without alighting on the crops. The people whooped with joy. Then came the ironic twist at the end of the story: What fed on the labourers in the end were the rich landlords who came knocking to collect their dues, the moneylenders, the tax collectors, and the Brahmin priest. People of a higher caste and born to privilege.

Another story, "What Has To Be", could be read as a commentary on the harm that cruel stereotypes and wrong beliefs inflict on people. A pregnant woman was happy and looking forward to her newborn until reminded that her first baby was born sickly and had died, and that it would happen again. "Suddenly, she was conscious of the sick emaciated body of hers, and of the child struggling to live within. She groped her way towards the mat, aware of a looming dread for her unborn child."

In the "Drought", the reader is brought face to face with the exploitative nature of man and the folly of blind ideology. The setting was again of suffering village folk, with their fields dried up by the drought, and now, their cattle were dying from thirst. The two public village tanks were empty.

Only one man, Mudaliar, had a private tank of water and "saw in their present plight an opportunity to enrich himself". He made an unscrupulous offer to buy their cattle for a "ridiculously low" price, in exchange for water. Out of desperation, most villagers went along with this, except for one man, Suriar.

One can catch glimpses of Raja in his character Suriar, a "taciturn and moody" man who loved to read books, and talked about ideas with passion and vigour. But there the similarity ends.

Dogmatic and stubborn, Suriar refused to allow his ailing father to sell his cow for water. "His ideas as they emerged frightened most of the farmers, for he flouted and ridiculed their traditional beliefs with a mocking logic they could not answer. He talked about rights and justice for the oppressed." His newfound knowledge and rigid ideology, coupled with hatred in his heart for men such as Mudaliar, led to neither a better society nor a fairer world — but a tragic end for his own father.

The story "Drought" proved enduring enough to warrant reprinting in the 1947 book, *A World of Great Stories: 115 Stories, The Best of Modern Literature*, which claimed to select "at least one first-rate story from every country in the world".[8] In the 950-page tome published in New York, Raja's name appeared alongside great writers such as Ernest Hemingway, William Faulkner, F. Scott Fitzgerald, Thomas Wolfe, John Steinbeck, Somerset Maugham, James Joyce, D.H. Lawrence, Jean-Paul Sartre, and Franz Kafka.

It was significant that the book, which grouped writers according to their country, listed Raja under India. While 12 other Asian countries, including Thailand and the Philippines, vied for space for its writers, there was no "Malaya" category. Perhaps even more significant: Besides Raja, the only other writer featured from India was the Nobel prize laureate Rabindranath Tagore.

By the mid-1940s, Raja had been billed as "one of the leading Indian short story writers" in an anthology, *Modern International Short Stories*, edited by Denys Val Baker. Some of his stories have been translated into various other languages — for example, "The Tiger" has been translated into French, and "Famine" into German. "The Tiger" has also been reprinted in the anthology *Short Story International* which features 12 stories from around the world.[9]

Implicit in Raja's stories is the desire to make readers reflect on their own condition and perceptions. His approach to his stories is essentially questioning: he was concerned with what was responsible for prejudice, poverty, injustice, oppression, moral blindness, cruelty, greed, despair. And conversely, he wished to discover what would bring about the opposite.

One of his most powerful ideas, which challenged the prevailing orthodoxy of class and caste, was that people can take control of their own destinies, and that they can determine the kind of future they desire for themselves if they only believe. The idea is powerful even at this distance in time.

This theme was made most stark in his story titled "The Stars", published in 1946 in the book, *Indian Short Stories*, edited by Anand and Iqbal. The story revolved around astrology — a quasi-mystical cosmic science that was taken seriously by many generations of the traditional Ceylon Tamil community, including some of his own relatives in Seremban. In fact, few at that time would get married without first consulting an astrologer to seek an auspicious date.

In his story, Raja spun a satirical tale around "Uncle Ram" whose life — and even the timing of death — were dictated by his reading of astrology. He believed that "there was no event or activity of life without the stars having a hand in it". Tired of her husband's stargazing, Uncle Ram's wife castigated her "good-for-nothing husband" by shouting: "If only you would work harder in the fields instead of wasting your time on such rubbish, life might be easier for us." Uncle Ram's "logic" was that "we are destined to be what we are, and however much we may try, we cannot defeat the will of the stars". He believed it was their lot to be poor and live in a dirty hut.

The tale was a critique not only of astrology, but also of closed minds which could not think beyond their boundary of beliefs. This rigid attitude was dangerous, not least because it left no room for progress. In challenging convention, Raja was not rejecting the value of cultures and religions. Instead, his view was that individuals should make their own choices about their beliefs, identities and lives by giving priority to reason.

Raja's stories received a good review in the magazine *Spectator* in 1947. The reviewer contrasted the work of the younger writers — of which Raja was named as one — with that of Mulk Raj Anand whose characters, according to the reviewer, were "too simple to hold the attention for long; their misery too constant for art".[10] It added that "younger writers of imaginative power", such as Raja Ratnam, "are showing that they cannot be confined by convention to the social tract, but must revert to familiar worlds where complexities of character whet the imagination".

It is remarkable that, despite the enthusiastic reception which greeted his stories by the literary set in London, little is known in Malaya and Singapore about Raja's early fiction. Few today remember Raja for his literary breakthroughs although, in 1964, writer T. Wignesan, who later published three of Raja's stories[11] in an anthology of contemporary Malayan literature, concluded that, "we must accept his place in our literary history as the very first conscious artist of the short story".[12]

It must be put on record: More than 60 years ago, Raja had pioneered the writing of Malayan literature which was accessible to the English-speaking world, at a time when "Malayan literature" as a genre was hardly heard of in the West.

His stories are probably among the first Malayan literature in English to attempt to imagine a Malayan consciousness.[13] He wrote as a Jaffna Tamil growing up in a rural village of Malaya. While he was heavily influenced by the Indian writers at the time, his artistic landscapes were drawn from his mixed provenance and experiences. They reflected the fertility of his imagination as well as his complex view of the world that he lived in.

This is amply illustrated in his story "The Terrorist".[14] It relates the tale of a college student, who despite his intelligence, became an ideological fanatic. He believed in the "cold steely voice" which told him to do great things for the country and to kill for their cause. The twist — moments before he pulled the trigger, the young man began to doubt his revolutionary cause. He felt as if he had stumbled into an unreal world, a dream in which he was "a bloodless puppet dancing to the dreamer's desire". It would turn out to be a nightmare.

In a sense, the story is a paradoxical tale of intellectually proficient and deeply idealistic youngsters being driven to extremism and violence for a cause they did not even fully understand. Raja wanted to challenge the conception that humans were playthings of fate, caught inescapably by the impersonal and random forces of history. The young student had the choice to pull or not pull the trigger, or didn't he? To believe in determinism would entail a shattering loss in the concept of morality, of human choice and will.

In another sense, it illustrates Raja's moral universe where life was not always black and white, but often, shades of grey. The young terrorist had done an evil thing not because he was an evil man, but because he allowed himself to be manipulated by others.

Like all good literature, his multilayered stories can be interpreted in many ways. Space does not permit an adequate analysis of his short stories here, but they deserve to be published in a separate anthology and studied further, perhaps even as part of a school text. The subjects Raja investigated more than 60 years ago, such as moral choices in a changing society, are still relevant today.

It is striking that, in all the years since his return from London, Raja hardly mentioned his literary successes, such as the appearance of his stories alongside some of the best and most distinguished writers in the world. He would have had many opportunities to, especially after he became Singapore's first culture minister.

He made no attempt to compile his fictional short stories into a book. Indeed, it was not without effort that his short stories were located and even then, one cannot be completely sure if all were found.[15]

This much is almost certain — Raja stopped writing short stories of this quality after he returned to Malaya. One reason was that Raja became completely obsessed with championing the death of colonialism and the growth of indigenous leadership through serious journalism and political activism. He directed all his literary powers towards this cause. He excelled in political commentary and satire.

Another deeper reason was that short stories live on an appreciative readership of the genre. In London, fiction writers were respected. The literary journals paid for contributions and welcomed budding writers from Asia. In Malaya, including Singapore, there was hardly any market for English short stories written by Malayans during that period. Writing stories was not considered a worthwhile pursuit.

For the same reason, he must have decided, especially after he joined politics, that he would be taken more seriously with a public persona built around his illustrious record as a newspaper journalist, rather than as a one-time fiction writer in London.

In this sense, London was good to Raja. It developed his creative self in a lively literary environment and gave him the space in various prominent journals and the active readership that Singapore or Malaya could not have been able to provide him.

One of the high points of his fiction writing days must have been when his work was noticed by no less than British writer George Orwell. Orwell, who worked in the Indian Section of the BBC's Eastern Service based in London, subsequently opened the door for him to write scripts and do some part-time broadcasting on Asia for the BBC.

This *ad hoc* arrangement gave Raja an opportunity to learn the technique of writing radio scripts from one of the best in the field. He also appreciated more keenly the value of radio in propaganda. Radio played a significant role in information and propaganda during the war. The BBC, like the print media, came under the supervision of the Ministry of Information, housed in the University of London Senate House. Besides Raja, Orwell also roped in Anand to write scripts for the BBC. The Indian Section broadcast to its subcontinental listeners news bulletins written by Orwell and read aloud by Asian speakers, and some cultural broadcasts written by Asian contributors. The experience would prove useful to Raja when he returned to Malaya and sought to use the radio to propagate his political views.

Orwell, who became literary editor of the *Tribune* in 1943, also set the standard for effective column-writing, churning out for the next three years a series of widely read columns under the title *As I Please*. Raja obviously admired Orwell's irreverent style, and would use a variation of this title for his own series of columns later in the 1950s, called *I Write As I Please*.

Raja himself also wrote news commentaries for the *Tribune*, which by now was roused by the appearance of America as a new imperialist power, especially in Asia. In a column, Raja highlighted the dangers when Americans hunted down the anti-Japanese guerrilla army, the *Hukbalahap*, in the Philippine jungles in 1945, installed a puppet government, and set up what he called "America's New Banana Republic".[16]

Given his extensive network of friends in the business and his growing literary stature, Raja found new opportunities coming his way. In 1946, Raja joined the staff of the London office of the Indian nationalist news agency, *Free Press of India*. This put him at the epicentre of groundbreaking news as he collected cables from international news agencies, wrote articles, and disseminated them to India and beyond. The *Free Press of India* was avowedly a world news service primarily for India, and secondly for the world press.[17]

Raja also wrote for the American journal, *Asia*. Indeed, his earliest piece on Malaya, published in *Asia* in August 1942, was a sharply analytical piece triggered by the Japanese occupation in Malaya. He was aghast at the different reactions of the diverse communities in Malaya to the retreat of the Allied Forces: The Chinese and, to a certain extent, the Indians, showed some militancy. The Malays, however, were "passive, timid and apathetic" and "bewilderment was perhaps the emotion uppermost in their minds", he wrote, quoting the *London Evening Standard*.

Raja commented: "Bewilderment! When one contrasts this picture with that of Russia, China, and Britain where ordinary people have shown a determination and a power to fight to the death, the deficiences of a moribund and hoary colonial system stand out glaringly." He held the British responsible for the state of the Malays: "The Malay, like every other human being, is a product of his history and environment, including his social and economic surroundings." This statement articulates his historical and anthropological approach to understanding individuals and their response to events, which would guide him for the rest of his life.

In the article, he traced the separate development of the different racial communities under colonial rule, demonstrating his grasp of Malayan history, and blamed colonial policy squarely for their divisive state in Malaya.

"The existence in Malaya of 'plural' communities, distinct and isolated from one another, and pursuing their selfish, communal interests, can be pointed to as the factor responsible for the recent tragedy of Malaya" he wrote. He anticipates that at the conclusion of this war, when a settlement is made in Malaya, the question will arise: "Malaya for whom?" For the Chinese? For the Indians? For the Malays? He dismissed each in turn, on grounds of principle and practicality For example, in rejecting the last "Malaya for Malays", he noted that the Chinese "more than any other race, by hard work and enterprise have been responsible for the development of Malaya". To force the Chinese out of Malaya, or to compel them "to be a subservient majority without political power in Malaya" would not solve the future of Malaya and would be "extremely unpractical politics".

He enunciated his own vision and hope of the shape of post-war Malaya: "Under a sane political and economic order such as we hope will prevail after the war, the emphasis must be not on privilege for this or that race, but on justice and equality for all." He would carry this vision, articulated in 1942 long before there was even an independent Malaya, close to his heart all his life. He regarded

Singapore as part as Malaya; the two coalesced into one country in his mind. The central question "Malaya for whom?" was to hover over him for many years.

If writing provided an important outlet for Raja's intellectual and creative evolution in the 1930s and 40s, it also enabled him to secure a new professional identity: A writer, a journalist. There was no indication that Piroska participated actively in Raja's literary endeavours. What she did in fact was far more precious: she made it possible for him to think and write, creating an oasis of calm amidst the chaos of war.

After the war in Britain ended in May 1945, life in London continued to be austere. Rationing not only dragged on, but was gripped even tighter. Some foodstuff, such as bread and potatoes, were rationed for the first time. Houses lay in ruins. "We suffered the hardship and fears brought by the war. But Piroska never complained," Raja recalled many years later.

The Left Book Club had also lost its dynamism — its membership plunged to 15,000 during the war, and after it ended, fell again to 7,000. By 1948, the club was all but moribund.

For Raja, there was another reason for the hollow feel to the VE Day celebrations. Blood was still being spilled in Malaya as the vicious war continued in the Far East. It was only four months later, in September, that Malaya was freed from the terror of the Japanese occupation. The circumstances of Japanese surrender had the most momentous consequences of all for the future shape of war — the American dropping of atomic bombs first on Hiroshima and then Nagasaki in August. Days later, Japan surrendered. Within the following month, Japanese forces everywhere in Asia and the Pacific surrendered.

After the war, the British returned to Singapore with a policy of maintaining it as a free port. It was geared up for spearheading an aggressive British export drive in the East. At the same time, the British worked to keep economic stability in Malaya, the dollar arsenal of the British Empire which depended on the earnings from Malayan tin and rubber. Britain was intent on keeping the income streaming in from Malaya to help it recover from its post-war doldrums.

Meanwhile, British defence strategy also came to be focused on Malaya, especially Singapore. This would become more pronounced after the decolonisation of India and Pakistan in 1947, followed by Burma and Ceylon a year later, which shifted British defence strategy from the Indian subcontinent to Southeast Asia. These economic and strategic calculations were to have an important bearing on the question of Malaya's political future.

In post-war Britain, there was a national mood for change, a desire for fuller social justice and greater security and peace. This mood favoured a Labour government. Despite his heroic status during the war, Churchill lost the 1945 election, to be replaced by Labour's Clement Attlee as prime minister. Raja cheered the change. Some Labour MPs were his friends. The new administration included eight Left Book Club authors, including Strachey, Cripps, and the prime minister himself. As it turned out, Attlee's government would preside over the eventual decolonisation of a large part of the British empire.

As the political landscape transformed in Britain, so did the mood of Raja's African and Indian anti-imperialist friends domiciled in the capital. As the Pan-African Federation — Padmore's vehicle — declared, "to condemn the Imperialism of Germany, Japan and Italy while condoning that of Britain would be more than dishonest". It demanded "for the Colonial peoples the immediate right to self-determination" as an effective step in the process of banishing wars.

The Pan-African Congress in Manchester, which Padmore helped to organise in 1945, marked the turning point in Pan-Africanism. It was attended by Kwame Nkrumah, Jomo Kenyatta, W.E.B. DuBois, Jaja Wachuku, and almost certainly also Raja, given his closeness to Padmore. This conference helped set the agenda for decolonisation in the post-war period.

Because of Raja's closeness with the Trotsky and Marx-Lenin revolutionary crowd, the Special Branch listed him after the war as a

"Trotskyist, for which there are parallels in Ceylon". It was an ominous parallel to draw: A number of Ceylonese students, having become adherents of Trotsky while in the universities of London in the late 1920s and early 1930s, had returned to their homeland to start a Trotskyist movement which became a significant force in its national politics.[18] In 1950, the Malayan Communist Party would also assess Raja to be a Trotskyist,[19] and would attempt to lure him into its cause.

As far as we can tell, Raja had no such political ambition to start a Trotskyist movement or a Communist one in Malaya. What gripped him at this point was a fierce desire to take into his own hands not only his personal future, but also that of his country, Malaya. He had found his cause: He wanted to free Malaya from British rule. It was a dramatic transformation for a young man within a decade. From his vague political wanderings in London, he was to find his own path and emerge in Malaya[20] as a leading voice in its independence movement.

He followed anxiously news of the debilitating post-war situation in Malaya. The initial elation which greeted liberation was soon crushed by a dark mood as the task of rebuilding Malaya heaved fully into view. People struggled with desperate shortages of housing, rice and other food, grossly inflated prices and black markets. Many could not find jobs. Communists, who had emerged from the war as heroes for their bravery in fighting the Japanese, penetrated political organisations and labour unions, agitating them to take up the anti-colonial fight against the British Military Administration (BMA). Strikes and boycotts were rampant.

Raja would observe later: "Japanese conquest and occupation damaged beyond repair not only the myth of European invincibility, but also the elaborate infrastructure of political and economic control Western imperialism had erected painstakingly over near two centuries."[21]

While the seed of Malayan nationalism was sown by the spectre of British surrender in Malaya in 1942, which dispelled the myth of their superiority, it took the post-war introduction of the Malayan Union scheme for it to spring shoots. The scheme, outlined by the British Labour government in the House of Commons on 10 October 1945, was meant as the first step in preparing Malaya for eventual self-government within the British Empire. Under the plan, a peninsular union was to be formed, comprising the nine Malay states and the settlements of Penang and Malacca — but not Singapore. The plan also envisaged opening the civil service to all of Malaya's races, together with common citizenship rights as well as political rights for non-Malays.

The Malayan Union scheme stirred a storm of Malay opposition. The Malays saw it as a threat to Malay privileges and the position of the Malay rulers. Fearful of being marginalised, they closed ranks behind their traditional rulers and the newly-formed United Malay National Organisation (UMNO), set up in March 1946, to protest against the Malayan Union.[22]

In contrast, the non-Malay communities registered only tepid interest in the scheme, although they had the most to gain from it. It was a symptom of their political malaise. The Chinese, weary of turmoil and uncertainty, were largely concerned with rehabilitating their war-ravaged businesses and rebuilding a decent life.

As for the Indians, they were inspired by anti-imperialist leaders such as Gandhi, Nehru, and also Subhas Chandra Bose, who came to Singapore as commander of the Indian National Army. During the war, the INA fought under the aegis of the Japanese against the British for the liberation of India. Just as many Chinese looked to China as their motherland and home, many Indians looked to India, and not Malaya. The prospect of a new China and a new India strengthened these sentiments. But most Indians in colonial Singapore enjoyed one thing that the other immigrants didn't: they could speak English for the most part, and so could adjust to any society under British rule.

During this post-war period, Raja exchanged correspondence with his friend, Lim Hong Bee, to keep in touch with developments back home. Hong Bee had returned to Malaya just before it fell to the Japanese in February 1942. Since then, his life had never been the same. During the war, Hong Bee toiled as a farmer in Endau, near the border between Johore and Pahang, and was believed to have joined the Malayan People's Anti-Japanese Party (MPAJA). There, he met and became good friends with Wu Tian Wang, the Singapore representative of the Malayan Communist Party, who was also active in the MPAJA.

As Raja read Hong Bee's polemical letters on the political situation in Malaya, he was perplexed at the transformation he detected in his friend. Hong Bee was no longer the humorous, carefree man he used to know in London, but a "very intense, obsessive" political animal. In his letters, Hong Bee poured out bitterly his suffering under the Japanese occupation and denounced British imperialism in the most militant terms. He also wrote about the new left-wing political vehicle, the Malayan Democratic Union (MDU), which he had helped form in 1945 with Wu and several others, and told Raja that a representative from the MPAJA would be contacting him in London.[23]

In June that year, the courier, a senior MCP leader, knocked on Raja's door to have tea. He also passed Raja a stack of anti-British pamphlets as well as the MDU manifesto. They chatted about political developments in Malaya. While Raja would claim many years later that he could not remember the courier's name, it was evident that he was a high-ranking communist guerrilla in Malaya. He was in London as part of the special MPAJA contingent to take part in the victory parade in London on 8 June 1946 for their role in fighting the Japanese in Malaya. Raja would not be surprised to discover later that MDU was infiltrated by communists, although it would publicly disavow any association with communism.

In London, Raja became increasingly anxious about the political situation in Malaya. This was fully evident in his column "Malaya in Transition" in September 1946 for the journal *Asia*. In it, he took issue with the Malayan Union plan which excluded Singapore. "The intention to keep Singapore out of the Union cannot be defended except on grounds of imperialist strategy. Singapore is the controlling centre of Malaya's trade and commerce. It is true that the government visualises the eventual entry of Singapore into the Union but why postpone it?" He criticised as "disturbing" the reason given by the Dominion Secretary, Lord Addison, that it was desirable to separate Singapore because the Chinese there outnumbered the Malays.

In this well-researched article, he tracked the new political forces in Malaya. "In general, the temper of these new parties is left-wing, democratic and anti-imperialistic. They include the Malayan Communist Party, the Malayan Democratic Union, the Malay Nationalist Party, the New Democratic Youth league, etc." He observed that, since the beginning of the year, clashes between the government and these political and labour bodies had become increasingly violent. Strikes and demonstrations were countered by shootings and arrests.

He recounted for his international readers: "The showdown came on Feb 15, when the people of Singapore approached the B.M.A. for permission to hold a rally to commemorate the fourth anniversary of the 'Day of Sorrow' when Singapore fell. Permission was refused on grounds that the intention was to celebrate a Japanese victory! But on the morning on Feb 15, British tanks and armoured cards moved about the streets of Singapore." In Singapore, the clashes left six people dead and many injured. Raja was outraged.

To add to his sense of grievance were the profound problems that would remain in Malaya even after the imperialist influences had disappeared. He listed some: "There is the task of mastering the tools of self-government, the use of which has been denied them under imperialism. There is the even more difficult task of establishing rounded economics and creating new political loyalties to conform with the requirements of the 20th century world. But apart from these general problems…is the specific problem of how to integrate two and even three races into a single political community."

He voiced his fear that the advent of nationalism in Malaya had brought to the surface antagonisms based on racial, cultural, and linguistic differences. His reading was astute: The fear was well founded.

As he agonised over the political changes in Malaya, life in London suddenly became a bleak interlude for Raja. He soon began making plans to return home. But first, he had to settle a delicate matter: How to break the news about his marriage to Piroska to his family in Seremban. Their marriage was a *fait accompli* and his family would have no say about the matter.

When he received word from his family in 1946 that his brother Seeva had married a traditional Ceylon Tamil woman, Raja seized the opportunity to mention his own marriage. He shot off a congratulatory telegram to the family in Seremban, and signed off the greeting as Raja and Piroska. This intimation was met with stony silence.

6

The One-Man Band

On 6 February 1947, Raja set off for Malaya with Piroska on a steamship from Southampton. It had been 12 years since he left Malaya. Within that time, the world had changed dramatically. Raja, too, had changed drastically. He was 32, more self-assured, more familiar with life's vagaries. He possessed the self-confidence of a man who had discovered his latent talents and learnt new truths for himself.

Singapore was suffocatingly humid when the couple arrived. At the bustling quay, a gaggle of relatives from Seremban and Singapore were waiting for them. In the midst of them was a young Indian woman in a *saree*, her eyes darting to spot the notorious relative she had heard so much about, but had yet to meet. The woman, Vijayalakshimi Thambiah, had just joined Raja's family a year ago when she married his brother, Seevaratnam, in a traditional Hindu ceremony.

At the sight of Raja, the family rushed to welcome him with hugs and kisses. Their reception cooled appreciably when he introduced them to his new European wife. In their eyes, Piroska, in her crisp skirt suit, appeared aloof and altogether foreign.[1] According to Senathyrajah Kanagasabai, a first cousin to Raja, some relatives left conspicuously to show their disapproval when they saw Piroska. "Some relatives were against him because of Piroska. She was an outsider," he said.[2]

Everyone in the family knew how strict Raja's parents were about marrying within the clan; they matchmade relatives regularly and paid for their wedding expenses if necessary. In fact, earlier on, they had already identified a certain relative to be Raja's bride, and had broadcast this match to some members of the clan. They were heartbroken that their son could not live up to the age-old tradition, and humiliated that he did not attain the prestigious legal qualifications so prized by their community.

Their journey by car to the family home at No. 4, Jalan Dato Klana in Seremban was strained. Over the weeks, the tension continued to hang over the household. Pious relatives huddled to cluck their tongues at the scandal of Raja's marriage to a white woman. When Raja's parents threw a tea party to welcome him home and formally announce his marriage, less than 100 relatives turned up — a small fraction of the entire clan. It was a terse statement of the Jaffna Tamil community's disapproval.

In the confines of their house, Raja had to endure his father's repeated remonstrations to return to London to complete his law studies. In response, Raja said that to continue his studies would be a "complete waste of time". His mind was fixed on journalism. As he would explain later, "I saw journalism as a way to express myself politically."

As the days dragged by, Raja found that the habits and ideas that he had picked up in London did not fit in with the placid environment of his rural hometown. He felt increasingly constrained by the cosy, but parochial environment. As he surveyed the apathetic state of politics around him, he was overcome with a sense of restlessness and frustration. Having witnessed the power of the pen in shaping national movements in other parts of the world, the self-made intellectual was impatient to wield it in similar fashion in Malaya.

Dennis Bloodworth, a close friend of Raja's who came to Singapore as the *Observer*'s chief correspondent for the Far East from 1956 to 1981, put it more lyrically: "For there was within him the swallowed bile of the colonised Asian, and the urge to get it out of his system and on to paper — for a start."[3]

Meanwhile, the communists, who had by then infiltrated many unions, were quick to spot a potential recruit to their cause. The MCP was actively pursuing a "united front" policy which focused on building a powerful labour movement to tap into the discontent of workers.

Lim Hong Bee, who had left for London in early 1947 and was then functioning in the United Kingdom as a representative for the Malayan Communist Party (MCP), did not waste any time in putting Raja in touch with his friends in Malaya.[4] He also asked them to help Raja look for a job in Singapore.

There are conflicting accounts on who exactly followed up on Hong Bee's instruction at this point. In his interviews later in life, Raja would credit Lim Kean Chye, a well-connected lawyer,[5] but Eu Chooi Yip, a reporter with the pro-communist Chinese newspaper *Nan Chiau Jit Pao*, and an underground senior communist leader, insisted that he was the one responsible.[6] What seems clear, however, was that both men, Kean Chye and Chooi Yip, played decisive roles in getting Raja to come to Singapore to work and settle down.

According to Chooi Yip, Hong Bee had written to him from Britain with an introduction letter for Raja when the latter returned to Malaya. Hong Bee had also asked Raja to look for Chooi Yip in Singapore, which he did. "We went by rickshaw when I took him to visit Tan Cheng Lock at his residence to introduce him. Tan Cheng Lock was one of the shareholders of the *Malaya Tribune* and he wrote a memo to hire him as a columnist," Chooi Yip recalled.[7]

Malaya Tribune was the highest circulation paper at one time before the war, billing itself as the "People's Paper". It was a stiff rival to *The Straits Times*, which was too closely wedded with the British establishment for Raja's anti-colonial sensibilities. The *Tribune* was priced at five cents, and was nicknamed the *kerani*'s or clerk's paper for appealing to the popular taste of the broad Asian masses. Like most other newspapers at the time, the *Tribune* was more interested in covering crime, entertainment and sports news, than discussing seriously the political problems of Malaya and the region.

Raja hoped to change all that. And he was impatient to start. Even before the *Tribune* offered him a job, he had begun contributing political commentaries to it. The topics ranged from the power-balancing act of Siam, the French struggle against Vietnam and Asia's overpopulation, to the mounting labour problems in Malaya. They displayed his intellectual heft and sophistication.

His first commentary, published on 9 May 1947, focused on Siam's diplomatic battle to balance the major powers after the war to ensure its sovereignty. This lengthy piece also examined Siam's domestic political troubles and warned of a military takeover. It was prescient. In November that year, a military coup toppled the civilian government.[8]

His next commentary, published a week later, tackled the weighty issue of the new "nightmare threatening to visit Asia — overpopulation". In that well-researched column, citing lessons from India, China and Japan, he suggested that only long-term changes in standards of living, with a society based on new skills, might lead to "more rational breeding habits".[9]

Among his most far-sighted pieces were those on the labour problems in Malaya, which was to foreshadow his deep preoccupation with the subject for several decades. He had a profound belief in the constructive role that the labour movement could play in national politics. It would be a theme that he would elaborate on in many of his columns as a journalist, and would later put in motion himself as a political practitioner.

In his commentary, published on 29 May 1947, he wrote about the tripartite relations between labour, employers, and the government — long before the concept of "tripartism" became a byword for industrial harmony in Singapore's labour scene. In this seminal column, he was unabashedly sympathetic towards the cause of the trade unions. "If Malayan labour has shown itself militant, and at times mule-headed, we must remember that they are striving to raise their standard of living from admittedly low levels to more human levels." He argued that Malayan labour troubles could not be solved by government sanctions and decrees, but by giving them a political voice. "Until effective channels of political expression are afforded labour, the present situation will continue to exist," he wrote.[10]

The government's repressive actions "can no more stop the demand of labour for a greater share in the wealth of the country than one can the stop the march of time". Chiding the colonial government for being biased towards employers during a crisis, Raja warned: "Until government can convince workers to the contrary, mutual suspicion can be the only connecting link between both parties."

At the same time, he chastised the employers — or "capital" as he termed them — for ignoring workers' needs. "To fling at the Chinese and Indian worker the taunt that, in Malaya, he enjoys a far higher standard of living than the starvation diet he enjoyed in his home country does not strike him as very funny." He urged the employers to discard their old attitudes.

As for labour, he had a trenchant message for them too — they should learn from the experience of European trade unionists and avoid their costly mistakes. They must take a national, and not a narrow, sectional view. It must be "filled with a sense of its own responsibility, since its actions affect not only itself, but many others outside the sacred circle".

Written at a time when hostile industrial relations were crippling the country, Raja's exhortations for the three parties to repair their relations and cooperate as a tripartite group were bold and far-sighted. However, like most astute insights ahead of their time, they fell on stony ground. The conditions were not ripe. Raja was to till the field for about two decades before the idea of tripartism was to take root.

As Raja was trying to earn a living as a freelance journalist, Piroska was struggling to fit into the traditional Hindu household in Seremban. Relatives spoke to Raja in their native tongue, ignoring Piroska most of the time. She stoically endured this rebuff, as well as barbs on her suitability to be the mother of Raja's children.

Once, *apropos* of nothing, Raja's mother told Piroska that, while the family could bring themselves to accept her into their fold, they could not accept progeny who were half-caste and did not carry the caste's pure blood line. Relatives who witnessed that hurtful reproof lowered their eyes, but their hearts went out to Piroska. She was visibly wounded by this stricture, delivered in Raja's absence.

Relatives suspect that these comments might have shaped Piroska's decision not to bear children in the earlier years. While she did not care for the concept of preserving a "pure race", she cared very much for Raja; she did not want to upset his close relationship with his family. It was believed that, when she overcame the hurt and felt accepted enough by the family to have children some years later, it was too late, given her age and health. Years later, Piroska confided in her Filipina domestic helper Cecilia Tandoc that she had once suffered from a miscarriage.[11]

What of Raja? Certainly, he loved children and enjoyed entertaining them. He had an arsenal of "magic tricks", which included sleight-of-hand tricks with cards and coins. His nephews and nieces were thrilled by his ability to conjure up coins from behind their ears, among other classic illusions. All these he learnt from books through self-study and experimentation. One of his most thumbed books was John Scarne's *Magic Tricks* (1953), which piqued his interest with its scientific approach to magic.

He had a natural intellectual curiosity about everything, except housework. Tommy Koh, who later became a close friend of the couple, described Raja as being "totally undomesticated",[12] depending on Piroska to look after him and the home. Bloodworth observed that Piroska was often impatient with the impractical side of her husband's nature. "But opposites attract, and there was no doubt about the great love between them," he said.[13] If Raja ever regretted not having children, he never mentioned it.

—✦—

In June, Raja finally received a letter from the *Tribune* in Singapore, offering him the job of an "editorial assistant". In the letter, dated 11 June 1947, Maurice Glover, its English managing editor, wrote that the newspaper's directors had decided at their meeting on 29 May 1947, to offer him this job. Glover added: "I was instructed to offer you the appointment of editorial assistant on three months probation with basic salary of $400 per month plus the cost of living allowance which is at present based on 30 per cent." After probation, Raja's employment would be on a month-to-month basis, but a longer term contract "might well be considered later on", added Glover vaguely.

Without any hesitation, Raja took the job — and never looked back. The *Malaya Tribune* proved a fertile training ground for Malayan journalists. Launched in 1914, the *Tribune* had set itself up to cater to the English-educated local population. It was a path-breaking move as, at that time, the English-language press was tailored to appeal to a European readership, mostly expatriates. English-educated Asians formed only a small sliver of the elites.

The Chinese, Malay, and Tamil communities had their own vernacular papers, which drove another wedge between the different groups with their parochial window to the world. The vernacular papers were interested exclusively in the developments in their motherlands and their own communal issues and grievances. In 1947, ethnic Chinese comprised 44.7 per cent of Malaya's population, while Malays comprised 43.5 per cent. Most of the rest were Indians.

In the English-language press newsrooms, the offices were swarming with a large colony of foreign correspondents who made Singapore their base as they covered events in Malaya and the region. All senior posts in the newspapers were concentrated in expatriate hands. Local journalists were bypassed for promotions even if their reporting skills were as sharp and their shorthand as fast as their European colleagues.

Given this racial discrimination, not many English-educated Malayans sought a career in journalism in those days. Raja was to be among the first emerging group of talented Malayan journalists to break that glass ceiling and to demonstrate that Malayans could think about critical issues of the day for themselves.

—✦—

When Raja arrived in Singapore to take up his new job, the island was not a prepossessing sight. It was an overcrowded swamp dotted with filthy squatter huts. In later years, he evoked vivid images of the environment at the time: "Crumbling cubicles" were everywhere. The hovels and slums covered the face of the island like "festering pimples". "Unidentifiable odours and aggressive stenches" pervaded the place.[14] After much effort, he found his own rented crumbling cubicle in Devonshire Road. The conditions were utterly dispiriting.

Things took a significant turn when Hong Bee's wife, Dr Maggie Lim, who worked in the family planning unit in Singapore, contacted Raja at her husband's behest. Maggie led Raja to the MDU office, housed in the seedy Liberty Cabaret in North Bridge Road, and introduced him to Kean Chye for the first time. It was a decisive encounter which brought Raja into the womb of the left-wing nationalist movement in Malaya.

Kean Chye had just recently taken over Hong Bee's duties as secretary of the MDU, on top of his current post as treasurer, when Hong Bee left for London in early 1947. Kean Chye and Hong Bee went back a long way. In the 1930s, the two men were fellow students at Cambridge University[15] and were caught up in the left-wing student movement there. In 1941, Kean Chye returned to Penang and worked in his father's legal firm. During the Japanese Occupation, he took part in organising an anti-Japanese movement. He was arrested, but released. Within weeks of the Japanese surrender, Hong Bee and Kean Chye began hatching a plan to form the MDU to fight for self-government. The two men, together with Wu Tian Wang, the Singapore representative of the MCP, manage to persuade Philip Hoalim Sr., a Guyanan Chinese lawyer, into lending it respectability by becoming its first chairman in 1945.[16]

By the time Raja met Kean Chye at the MDU office in 1947, the latter had become an outspoken anti-colonialist with a full-bodied taste for communism and ale. Aware of Raja's socialist bent, Kean Chye introduced the potential recruit to MDU's efforts to improve workers' welfare — it ran a consumer cooperative to help poorly-paid workers buy cheap goods in a store, located a floor above the cabaret, and organised the "people's kitchens" to serve meals to the poor.

As they became better acquainted over beer, Kean Chye came to know of Raja's housing woes and offered to show him a place with "more congenial surroundings". That place was an antiquated colonial bungalow at 15, Chancery Lane. The building looked battered and was in a general state of disrepair. Still, it was an improvement over his dingy room.

Attracted by the prospect of some privacy amidst leafy surroundings, Raja and Piroska moved into the roomy building. They promptly found themselves in what would become a seething nest of communists and left-wing sympathisers. One of the tenants was Chooi Yip. Lee Siew Yee, a reporter with *The Straits Times* famed for his coverage of the Thomas Cup matches, was the chief tenant of the house. The scholarly Siew Yee struck Raja as being apolitical — "if he had any political beliefs, they were between him and God," said Raja.[17] He respected the professionalism of Siew Yee, who later rose to become editor-in-chief of the newspaper.

Chooi Yip, a prolific writer who was effectively bilingual in English and Chinese, was another kettle of fish. He was a fervent communist, and his politics were infused into his writings. Raja developed a high regard for the man, finding him sincere and genuine, and completely dedicated to his communist cause. Chooi Yip, who suffered from tuberculosis, cut a pathetic figure. His thin frame was often convulsed with a racking cough. He carried around with him a small tin can for the sputum and blood coughed out. Despite his frail health, Chooi Yip showed no restraint in the energy he poured into his cause. His activities were soon to close in on him as the police declared him a wanted man with a $5,000 reward for his capture.

Raja would later describe Chooi Yip as "very intelligent, very dedicated" and one of the few who, unlike the poseurs, believed in the philosophy of communism with unyielding conviction. Given the need to remain undercover, Chooi Yip found it expedient to lie when he categorically and publicly denied in November 1947 that he was a communist. In his memoirs years later, Chin Peng, secretary-general of the Communist Party of Malaya, revealed that Chooi Yip was, in fact, a senior underground MCP leader in Malaya. The communist chief described Chooi Yip as a "highly-experienced propagandist" who had also secretly run *Freedom News*, the MCP's underground newspaper in Singapore.[18]

Through Chooi Yip, Raja met a host of other pro-communists and communists, such as P. V. Sharma, Gerald de Cruz, and John Eber, all involved in the MDU. Not all activists, however, were mesmerised by communism. Some, such as Raja's childhood friend, Yong Nyuk Lin, who was a general manager of an insurance company at the time, joined the MDU without subscribing to communism. He was in the MDU Executive Committee from 1946 to 1948. Another regular visitor to the Chancery Lane house and the Liberty Cabaret was Goh Keng Swee, then assistant director in the Social Welfare department, who had little patience with ideologies.[19] Goh was to eventually emerge together with Raja as two of the founding leaders of the PAP in 1954, while Yong would join the PAP in 1955.

Raja paid the subscription of 50 cents a month to sign up with the MDU, and, with that, climbed onto the only political vehicle charging against colonialism at the time. Despite their diverse political shades, the men were all bound together by their desire to usher in the demise of colonialism and breathe life into the graveyard of Malayan politics. The injustices and hardship under British rule provided both ammunition and a battleground for these politicised Malayans. The existing right-wing political parties, callow and self-serving, offered neither hope nor vision for change. The men who flitted in and out of 15, Chancery Lane, were "seekers of light", as Raja put it, in this dark political void.[20]

Swept up by the political imperatives of the day, they would talk often into the small hours over beer and cigarettes, discussing the uncertain destinies of Malaya and Singapore. Raja dubbed that old bungalow "a political subversion club".[21] While Raja contributed to the political discussions, he gave the political machinations a wide berth. "I didn't regard myself as cut out to be a politician as such," he said later. Also by then, he was quite alive to the communist infiltration in the MDU, and of the way communists were operating through other organisations, such as the unions and cultural organisations.

For a period, until June 1948, the MDU cooperated with the MCP, regarding it as an ally fighting for national independence. The MCP was then still enjoying public respect for its anti-Japanese resistance movement during the Occupation, and was not yet associated with violence and lawlessness, as it came to be after its armed insurrection in 1948. Sharply observant, Raja could see that the MDU regarded a united front as a tactical necessity in fighting British imperialism. He did not sit in judgment of this tactic; indeed, it would be the same one the PAP would adopt years later.

Raja was frank with his erstwhile collaborators during that period: he did not agree with the idea of a communist system for Malaya, for the simple reason that it would not work.[22] It was impractical. The Malays would not accept communism, which was associated with Communist China.

He was also conscious of the cultural and language barrier. The communists and their supporters were largely Chinese-educated. When they visited to discuss tactics with Kean Chye and Chooi Yip at the Chancery Lane house, Raja preferred to stay aloof. "They were rather mysterious, reticent figures," he recalled. Unlike Raja, who was nursed by the Left Book Club's volumes, the socialism of Laski and European revolutionary Marxism, the Chinese-educated left-wing radicals owed their allegiance more to the writings of Mao Zedong. They were subversive. Little did Raja know that, throughout this period, his movements were carefully monitored by the Special Branch, which had listed him as a "Trotskyist" after the war. Noting this assessment of him, the Australian High Commission in Singapore noted in its report to Canberra that, "in Singapore's official society, this made him suspect to a point although never guilty of subversive activities per se".[23]

His first year as a journalist coincided with an explosion of union strikes, a development Raja would analyse closely in visionary terms. In 1947 alone, there were some 300 strikes. Most of the unions were controlled by the MCP through the Pan-Malayan Federation of Trade Unions (PMFTU). The situation came to a head in 1948 when PMFTU was crushed with tough laws[24] imposed on unions. Many unions shut down. Cast adrift, the communists turned to terrorism.

To retain their grip on workers, the MCP employed intimidation and violence to browbeat employers into meeting their demands and to unnerve any rival, independent unions. Factories were set on fire, hand grenades were thrown, and people killed.

Although Raja recoiled at the violent methods, he was not unsympathetic to the union strikes, which to him were mostly about securing higher wages for the poorly paid workers. He was convinced that the root cause for the workers' agitation was the deteriorating social and economic conditions, and not simply the lure of communist ideology. As he had argued in the case of the political struggle in China and elsewhere in his other columns, as long as these root causes were not addressed, workers would be driven into the arms of the communists. The challenge was to provide solutions.

His reasoning found favour with some influential trade unionists, who reciprocated by feeding him useful material for his columns. Among those who glided in and out of his Chancery Lane home were Sharma, who led the militant Singapore Teachers' Union, as well as Devan Nair, who was also in the union. Raja confessed: "They used to give me points on what I should write in my editorials."

Occasionally, visitors from Burma, Australia, India, Indonesia, and Vietnam would drop in and disappear "like ships in the night", Raja recalled later. The most controversial was the appearance of the influential secretary-general of the Communist Party of Australia, Lawrence Sharkey, who was elected to the executive committee of the Comintern in Moscow in 1935. His visit to Singapore in 1948 was pivotal in inspiring the Malayan communists to take up arms against the British.

In Raja's account, the communists did not pressure him to become one of them. "Their aim was really to make use of me as a journalist to put across certain points of view," he said. He used them too, to further his public crusade against anti-colonialism.

Meanwhile, the MDU, with its vanguard of English-educated intellectuals, kept itself at the forefront, issuing statements and attacking the colonial government on controversial issues such as education and income tax. Raja took umbrage with some of the MDU's positions and communist policies, which he believed harmed Malayan interests.

The debate would spill from his columns in the *Tribune* pages to the dining room of his Chancery home. Despite their obvious intelligence, Raja found his housemates Kean Chye and Chooi Yip increasingly difficult to reason with. When he criticised any communist actions in Malaya, especially their violent methods, he was astonished at their strong and sharp reaction. "All this made clear to me that they were not really interested in Malayan politics." They were, he decided, plugging communist interests.

For all their hopes and for all his expressions of sympathy, Raja never joined the communists. Samad Ismail, a wily, stick-thin communist who worked as assistant editor of the *Utusan Melayu* in the late 1940s and early 1950s, said: "Raja was a sober fellow, an intellectual, and was too smart to be influenced by the Communists. He knew what we were talking about when we talked to him about Communism. He thought Communism was too rigid," said Samad, who often visited his mentor Chooi Yip at the Chancery Lane house to get directions on the communist line.[25] Samad was detained in 1951 for alleged communist activities together with other pro-communists, and would, in 1954, become a founding member of the People's Action Party, along with Raja.

After he signed on with the *Tribune* as staff, he changed his byline from "S.R. Ratnam" to "S. Raja Ratnam" to ease name recognition. His friends already called him Raja. This new byline soon became a regular fixture in the opinion pages of the *Tribune*.

It was an exciting time for a Malayan journalist keen to make a mark on the changing polity. Constitutional discussions concerning the opposition to the Malayan Union and to replace it with the Federation of Malaya were in full swing. The political forces pushing for self-government were picking up pace. In this revolutionary atmosphere, Raja found his political voice.

The *Tribune*'s newspaper office at Anson Road gave him ample editorial leeway. It was a lean outfit with only eight reporters to fill the pages. While the managing editor, Glover, and the editor, W.A. Harpur, were both Englishmen, the chairman of the paper's Board of Directors was Tan Cheng Lock, a respected Straits Chinese leader. He influenced the newspaper's policy.

Cheng Lock was a prominent leader of the opposition to the Federation proposals, which espoused the policy to restore the position of the Malay rulers and to form a federation without Singapore. His bold stance drew him strange bedfellows, from communists to rightists, who recognised his leadership abilities and appreciated his powerful connections with the Chinese business community. Cheng Lock was chairman of the Pan-Malayan Council of Joint Action (PMCJA), formed in December 1946 with several left-wing organisations such as the MDU and the Communist-dominated Pan-Malayan Federation of Trade Unions (PMFTU).

The Council also linked up with several left-wing Malay organisations, led by the Malay Nationalist Party (MNP). The MNP, inspired by the radical current of Indonesian nationalism, had left UMNO in May 1946 because of ideological differences. These were symbolised in their quarrel over UMNO's slogan. UMNO wanted the slogan *Hidup Melayu* (Long Live the Malays) while MNP wanted *Merdeka* (Independence).

With the split, the rivalry between the MNP and UMNO was now concentrated on the Federation proposals. The MNP feared that the Federation proposals would entrench Malay aristocracy and the British, thus choking the growth of an egalitarian nationalist movement of the sort that was fighting the Dutch in Indonesia. Raja followed the contest between UMNO and MNP for the leadership of the Malay community with keen interest.

He gravitated towards the Council's campaign — it fought for key ideas he believed in. They included: for Singapore to be included in a united Malaya, for self-government through a fully elected Central Legislature for the entire Malaya, and for equal citizenship rights to those who made Malaya their permanent home and the object of their undivided loyalty.[26]

The *Tribune* was stridently pro-PMCJA in its coverage. It gave wide publicity to the mass demonstrations organised by the PMCJA all over Malaya. Months of rabble-rousing culminated in a one-day hartal — inspired by Gandhi's historic shutdown in India — in October 1947. The newspaper also lobbied against the proposed pro-Malay policy when it was to be introduced in the peninsula in December 1947, on grounds that it ignored Chinese opinion.

Raja thrived in this politically charged newspaper environment. Having been away from Malaya for a decade, he was initially more comfortable tackling international issues than local politics. But he always found a way to draw lessons for Malaya. Before long, he was pronouncing on the domestic situation with authority.

Through his articles, he set out to educate readers on world developments and the complex dynamics surrounding the fight for freedom in various parts of the world. That was his unique contribution to the political discourse, at a time when local politics was largely about which group would get a larger slice of the pie under the colonial system. He cast the high-wattage beam from his intellectual lighthouse, illuminating the larger forces at work in the nationalist movements abroad and the roles of mass movements, in particular, that of labour. His beam shone over the swathe of the Antarctic, the Pacific, Russia, the Middle East, China, Siam, Indonesia, and the Philippines, and reflected their relevance to Malaya.

Raja's first bylined piece as *Tribune* staff was on the independence of the Philippines from the United States in 1946 and the lesson it held for the other countries in Asia aspiring towards independence. In his 4 July 1947 article, headlined "Filipino Freedom — Shadow and Substance", he pointed out that, although the Philippines was politically free, it was on economic crutches furnished by the United States and functioned as a "military pawn in America's power strategy in the Pacific". "Political independence, as long as it is not reinforced by a certain measure of economic independence and inner political stability, will remain a myth. The resulting weakness will assure them of a no more honourable role than that of being pawns in the power game of their more powerful colleagues," he asserted. It was early convictions such as this that would lead Raja to insist later that small

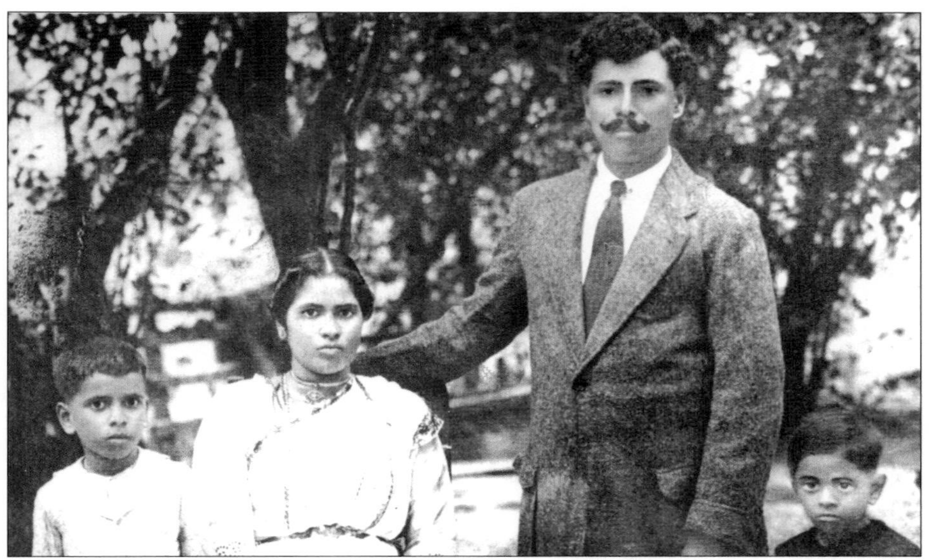

Childhood: Raja (extreme left) with his parents and younger brother, Seeva.

Above Raja at age 21 in 1936, a year after he arrived in London.

Left Outside his flat at 12, Steele Road, London. *(NAS)*

Top left Whirl of activities: Learning to punt. *(NAS)*

Above Taking photos of street protests organised by the Left Book Club. *(NAS)*

Left Enjoying a picnic with friends at Champery, Switzerland, during his Europe tour, 29 July 1937. *(NAS)*

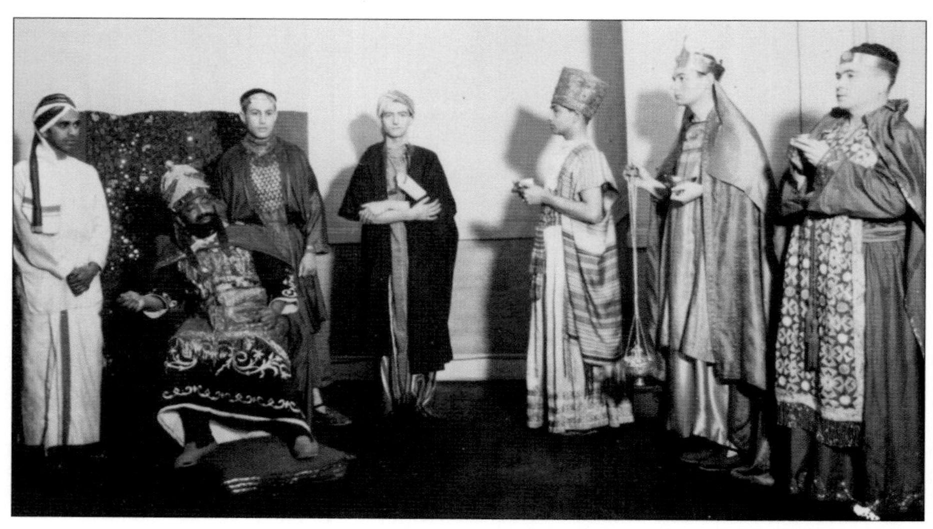

Raja (extreme left) dabbles with drama as part of his literary adventures in King's College. *(NAS)*

Spring dates: Raja relaxing with Piroska and a friend. *(NAS)*

In love: Raja and Piroska. *(NAS)*

Homeward: Returning to Malaya with his new wife, Piroska. *(NAS)*

Carefree days: Raja (extreme left), with good friends. *(NAS)*

Left Home: Apartment at 89, Priory Road in West Hampstead, London. *(NAS)*

Above Tea cups, cigarette ashtrays and books reflect the couple's lifestyle. *(NAS)*

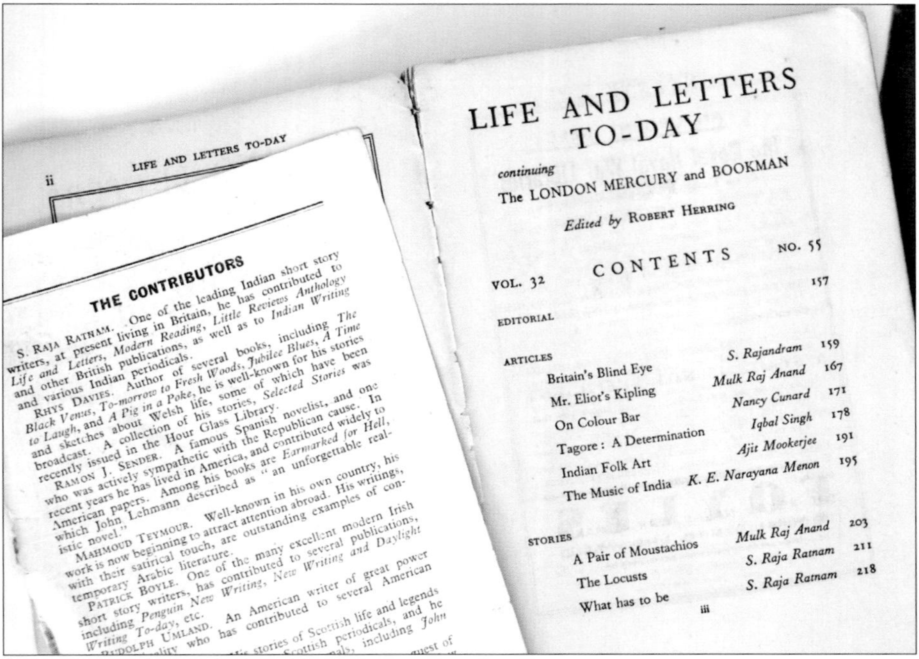

ii LIFE AND LETTERS TO-DAY

THE CONTRIBUTORS

S. RAJA RATNAM. One of the leading Indian short story writers, at present living in Britain, he has contributed to *Life and Letters*, *Modern Reading*, *Little Reviews Anthology* and other British publications, as well as to *Indian Writing* and various Indian periodicals.

RHYS DAVIES. Author of several books, including *The Black Venus*, *To-morrow to Fresh Woods*, *Jubilee Blues*, *A Time to Laugh*, and *A Pig in a Poke*, he is well-known for his stories and sketches about Welsh life, some of which have been broadcast. A collection of his stories, *Selected Stories* was recently issued in the Hour Glass Library.

RAMON J. SENDER. A famous Spanish novelist, and one who was actively sympathetic with the Republican cause. In recent years he has lived in America, and contributed widely to American papers. Among his books are *Earmarked for Hell*, which John Lehmann described as "an unforgettable realistic novel."

MAHMOUD TEYMOUR. Well-known in his own country, his work is now beginning to attract attention abroad. His writings, with their satirical touch, are outstanding examples of contemporary Arabic literature.

PATRICK BOYLE. One of the many excellent modern Irish short story writers, has contributed to several publications, including *Penguin New Writing*, *New Writing and Daylight*, *Writing To-day*, etc.

RUDOLPH UMLAND. An American writer of great power ... lity who has contributed to several American ...

... His stories of Scottish life and legends ... Scottish periodicals, and he ... nals, including *John* ... guest of ...

LIFE AND LETTERS TO-DAY

continuing The LONDON MERCURY and BOOKMAN

Edited by ROBERT HERRING

VOL. 32 CONTENTS NO. 55

iii

Writing between air raids in London: Described as a "leading short story writer" in *Modern International Short Stories*, 1947 (left), Raja's stories also appear in the August 1941 issues of the *Life and Letters*, among others.

Wartime 1941: Raja and Piroska display a spirited attitude to life as British friends go to war. Their friends also include Asian students, and Jewish refugees from Nazi Europe. *(NAS)*

Famous journalist: Raja (centre, standing with arms folded) with the *Singapore Standard* staff. *(NAS)*

Raja reading proofs in the newsroom.

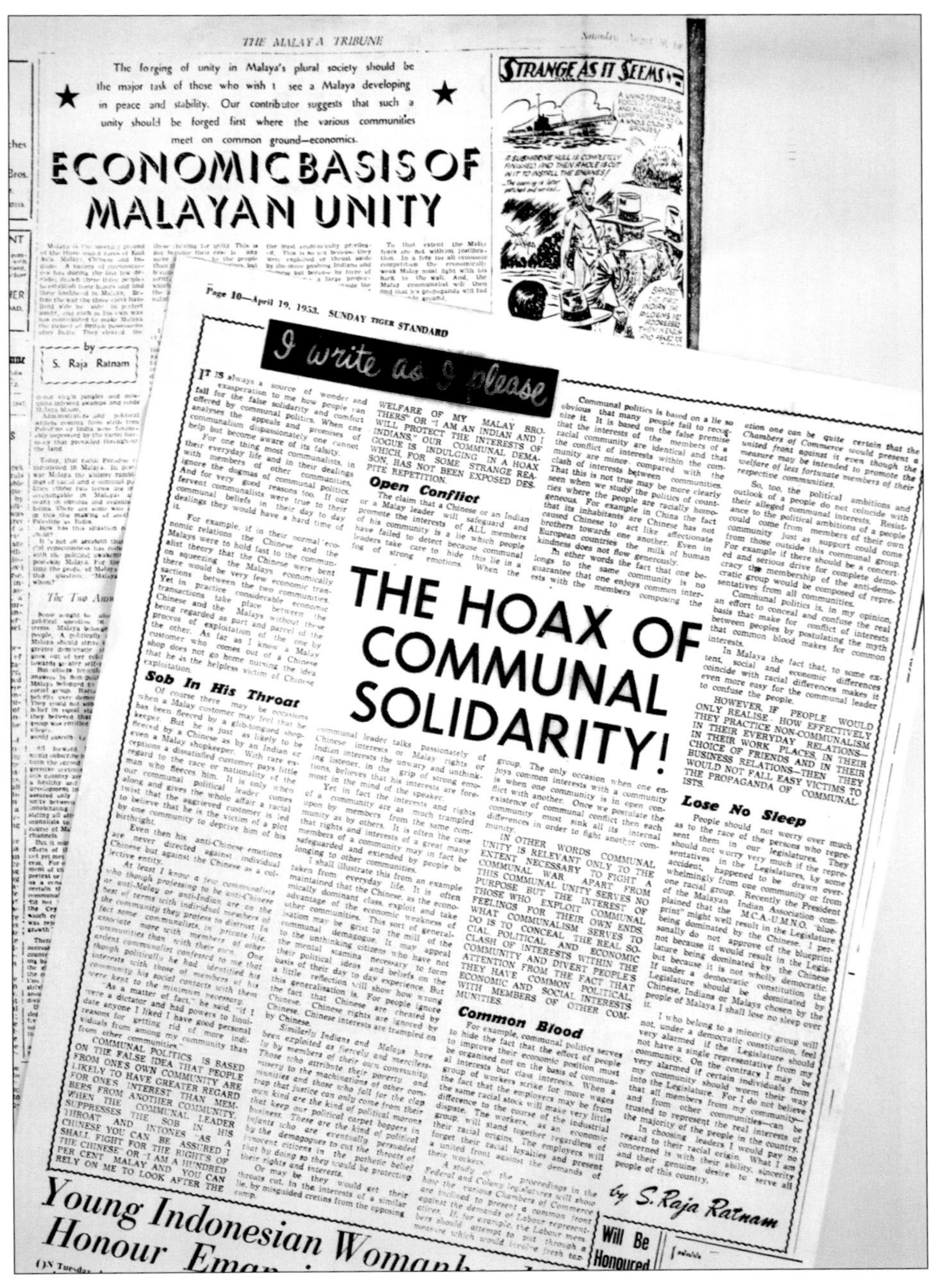

THE MALAYA TRIBUNE

The forging of unity in Malaya's plural society should be the major task of those who wish to see a Malaya developing in peace and stability. Our contributor suggests that such a unity should be forged first where the various communities meet on common ground—economics.

ECONOMIC BASIS OF MALAYAN UNITY

by S. Raja Ratnam

STRANGE AS IT SEEMS

Page 10—April 19, 1953. SUNDAY TIGER STANDARD

I write as I please

THE HOAX OF COMMUNAL SOLIDARITY!

IT IS always a source of wonder and exasperation to me how people can fall for the false solidarity and comfort offered by communal politics. When one analyses the appeals and promises of communalism dispassionately one cannot help but become aware of its falsity.

For one thing most communalists, in their everyday life and in their dealings with members of other communities, ignore the dogmas of communal politics. And for very good reasons too. If our fervent communalists were true to their communal beliefs in their day to day dealings they would have a hard time of it.

For example, if in their normal economic relations the Chinese and the Malays were to hold fast to the communalist theory that the Chinese were bent on squeezing the Malays economically there would be very few economic transactions between the two communities. Yet in practice considerable economic transactions take place between the Chinese and the Malays without these being regarded as part and parcel of the process of exploitation of the one by the other. As far as I know a Malay customer who comes out of a Chinese shop does not go home nursing the idea that he is the helpless victim of Chinese exploitation.

Sob In His Throat

Of course there may be occasions when a Malay customer may feel that he has been fleeced by a glib-tongued shopkeeper. But he is just as likely to be fleeced by a Chinese as by an Indian or even a Malay shopkeeper. With rare exceptions a dissatisfied customer pays little regard to the race or nationality of the man who fleeces him. It is only when our communal political leader comes along and gives the whole affair a racial twist that the aggrieved customer is led to believe that he is the victim of a plot by one community to deprive him of his birthright.

Even then his anti-Chinese emotions are never directed against individual Chinese but against the Chinese as a collective entity.

At least I know a few communalists who though professing to be anti-Chinese or anti-Malay or anti-Indian are on the best of terms with individual members of the community they profess to distrust. In fact some communalists, in private life, associate more with members of other communities than with their own. One ardent communalist confessed to me that though politically he had identified his interests with those of members of his community his social contacts with them were kept to the minimum necessary.

"As a matter of fact," he said, "if I were a dictator and had powers to liquidate anyone I liked I have good personal reasons for getting rid of more individuals from among my community than from other communities."

COMMUNAL POLITICS IS BASED ON THE FALSE IDEA THAT PEOPLE FROM ONE'S OWN COMMUNITY ARE LIKELY TO HAVE GREATER REGARD FOR ONE'S INTEREST THAN MEMBERS FROM ANOTHER COMMUNITY. WHEN THE COMMUNAL LEADER SUPPRESSES THE SOB IN HIS THROAT AND INTONES "AS A CHINESE YOU CAN BE ASSURED I SHALL FIGHT FOR THE RIGHTS OF THE CHINESE" OR "I AM A HUNDRED PER CENT MALAY AND YOU CAN RELY ON ME TO LOOK AFTER THE WELFARE OF MY MALAY BROTHERS" OR "I AM AN INDIAN AND I WILL PROTECT THE INTERESTS OF INDIANS," OUR COMMUNAL DEMAGOGUE IS INDULGING IN A HOAX WHICH, FOR SOME STRANGE REASON, HAS NOT BEEN EXPOSED DESPITE REPETITION.

Open Conflict

The claim that a Chinese or an Indian or a Malay leader will safeguard and promote the interests of ALL members of his community is a lie which people have failed to detect because communal leaders take care to hide this lie in a fog of strong emotions. When the communal leader talks passionately of Chinese interests or Malay rights or Indian interests the unwary and unthinking listener, in the grip of strong emotions, believes that his interests are foremost in the mind of the speaker.

Yet in fact the interests and rights of a community are as much trampled upon by members from the same community as by others. It is often the case that rights and interests of a great many members of a community may in fact be safeguarded and extended by people belonging to other communities.

I shall illustrate this from an example taken from everyday life. It is often maintained that the Chinese, as the economically dominant class, exploit and take advantage of the economic weakness of other communities. This sort of generalisation may be grist to the mill of the communal demagogue. It may appeal to the unthinking citizens who have not the mental stamina necessary to form their political ideas and beliefs on the basis of their day to day experience. But a little reflection will show how wrong this generalisation is. For people ignore the fact that Chinese are cheated by Chinese. Chinese rights are ignored by Chinese. Chinese interests are trampled on by Chinese.

Similarly Indians and Malays have been exploited as fiercely and mercilessly by members of their own community. Those who attribute their poverty and misery to the machinations of other communities and those who fall for the clap trap that justice can only come from their own kind are the kind of political morons that keep our political carpet baggers in business. These are the kind of political infants who are eventually persuaded by the demagogues to cut the throats of innocent citizens in the pathetic belief that by doing so they would be protecting their rights and interests.

Or may be they would get their throats cut, in the interests of a similar lie, by misguided cretins from the opposing camp.

Communal politics is based on a lie so obvious that many people fail to recognize it. It is based on the false premise that the interests of the members of a racial community are identical and that the conflict of interests within the community are minor compared with the clash of interests between communities. That this is not true may be more clearly seen when we study the politics of countries where the people are racially homogeneous. For example in China the fact that its inhabitants are Chinese has not caused Chinese to act like affectionate brothers towards one another. Even in European countries the milk of human kindness does not flow generously.

In other words the fact that one belongs to the same community is no guarantee that one enjoys common interests with the members composing the group. The only occasion when one enjoys common interests with a community is when one community is in open conflict with another. Once we postulate the existence of communal conflict then each community must sink all its internal differences in order to fight another community.

IN OTHER WORDS COMMUNAL UNITY IS RELEVANT ONLY TO THE EXTENT NECESSARY TO FIGHT A COMMUNAL WAR. APART FROM THIS COMMUNAL UNITY SERVES NO PURPOSE BUT THE INTEREST OF THOSE WHO EXPLOIT COMMUNAL FEELINGS FOR THEIR OWN ENDS. WHAT COMMUNALISM SERVES TO DO IS TO CONCEAL THE REAL SOCIAL, POLITICAL AND ECONOMIC CLASH OF INTERESTS WITHIN THE COMMUNITY AND DIVERT PEOPLE'S ATTENTION FROM THE FACT THAT THEY HAVE COMMON POLITICAL, ECONOMIC AND SOCIAL INTERESTS WITH MEMBERS OF OTHER COMMUNITIES.

Common Blood

For example, communal politics serves to hide the fact that the effort of people to improve their economic position must be organised not on the basis of communal interests but class interests. When a group of workers strike for more wages the fact that the employers may be from the same racial stock will make very little difference to the course of the industrial dispute. The workers, as an economic group, will stand together regardless of their racial origins. The employers will forget their racial loyalties and present a united front against the demands of their workers.

A study of the proceedings in the Federal and Colony legislatures will show how the various Chambers of Commerce are inclined to present a common front against the demands of Labour representatives. If, for example, the Labour members should attempt to put through a measure which would involve fresh taxation one can be quite certain that the Chambers of Commerce would present a united front against it even though the measure may be intended to promote the welfare of less fortunate members of their respective communities.

So, too, the political ambitions and outlook of a people do not coincide with their alleged communal interests. Resistance to the political ambitions of a people could come from members of their own community just as support could come from those outside this communal group. For example if there should be a concerted and serious drive for complete democracy the membership of the anti-democratic group would be composed of representatives from all communities.

Communal politics is, in my opinion, an effort to conceal and confuse the real basis that make for conflict of interests between peoples by postulating the myth that common blood makes for common interests.

In Malaya the fact that, to some extent, social and economic differences coincide with racial differences makes it even more easy for the communal leader to confuse the people.

HOWEVER, IF PEOPLE WOULD ONLY REALISE HOW EFFECTIVELY THEY PRACTICE NON-COMMUNALISM IN THEIR EVERYDAY RELATIONS—IN THEIR WORK PLACES, IN THEIR CHOICE OF FRIENDS AND IN THEIR BUSINESS RELATIONS—THEN THEY WOULD NOT FALL EASY VICTIMS TO THE PROPAGANDA OF COMMUNALISTS.

Lose No Sleep

People should not worry over much as to the race of the persons who represent them in our legislatures. They should not worry very much if the representatives in the Legislatures, by some accident, happened to be drawn overwhelmingly from one community or from one racial group. Recently the President of the Malayan Indian Association complained that the M.C.A.-U.M.N.O. "blueprint" might well result in the Legislature being dominated by the Chinese. I personally do not approve of the blueprint not because it would result in the Legislature being dominated by the Chinese but because it is not wholly democratic. If under a democratic constitution the Legislature should be dominated by Chinese, Indians or Malays chosen by the people of Malaya I shall lose no sleep over it.

I who belong to a minority group will not, under a democratic constitution, feel very alarmed if the Legislature should not have a single representative from my community. On the contrary I may be very alarmed if certain individuals from my community should worm their way into the Legislature. For I do not believe that all members from my community—and from other communities—can be trusted to represent the real interests of the majority of the people in the country.

In choosing leaders I would pay no regard to their racial origin. What I am concerned is with their ability, sincerity and their genuine desire to serve all people of this country.

by S. Raja Ratnam

Young Indonesian Woman ...

Will Be Honoured

Raja stimulates thinking about controversial issues in his columns in the *Malaya Tribune* and, later, the *Singapore Standard*.

Dinner parties: Entertaining friends and contacts at his home in Chancery Lane in his younger days. *(NAS)*

Above He continues to host friends in his house right up to his old age, as in this party in 1984.

Left Cover of the first issue of *Raayat*, 13 December 1954.

Singapore could not survive as an independent state on its own in an era of great powers, and hence, needed merger with Malaya.

Displaying his knowledge of China, he also wrote several incisive pieces on the civil war wracking the country. His main contention was that the civil war was not about a conflict of ideologies, but of social forces. The issue, he wrote, was not whether Kuomintang (KMT) could secure military victory over the communists, but whether it could offer social and economic reforms as attractive to China's common man, the peasant.[27] He pointed out how the communists had understood the nature and extent of the pent-up agrarian discontent, and had, unlike the KMT, dovetailed this into their military strategy. Raja's key message was that people would throw their lot in with the communists, not because they subscribed to the Marxist faith, but because their social and economic needs were not met.[28]

It was a cautionary message, coming at a time when Malaya itself was also suffering from massive social and economic convulsions. Malaya's economic plight was fleshed out in ample detail in Raja's columns. People were discontented and frustrated over problems such as the spike in the prices of essential foodstuff, the black market, and racial discrimination in employment. Even among the middle class, "there simmers the fires of discontent originating from economic hardship as well as from racial discrimination in the sphere of employment", he wrote in a column, "If a Crisis Comes" published on 10 July 1947.

In the column, he pointed out the dangers of depending on the traditional tin and rubber industries[29] and lectured the colonial government on the art of economic management. Do a thorough survey of local resources, attract capital towards light industries — such as brick making, paper, tin products — to create new enterprises and more jobs. Diversify the economy. Increase the local supply of rice to tackle the rice shortage, and transform the rice economy from a subsistence economy to a commercial enterprise. He wrote: "To put forward any such programme not only needs imagination and energy on the part of the government, but the latter must be able to create enthusiasm and confidence among the people."[30]

The economic troubles were played out not only in the urban centres, but also at the periphery in the countryside, leading to an agrarian crisis with growing unrest among the Malay peasants. Raja was acutely aware of the political dangers posed by a discontented and backward Malay peasantry, particularly at a time when the contest for control of the Malay heartlands was gaining momentum. UMNO was in ascendance. One of its rivals, the Malay Nationalist Party (MNP), had lost much of its support to UMNO when it joined the MDU-led Pan-Malayan Council of Joint Action to campaign against the Federation proposals.

However, Raja thought that the MNP's fortunes could be reversed when the All-Malayan Peasants' Union was formed in early July 1947, with the support of the MNP and the Pan-Malayan Federation of Trade Unions (PMFTU). Indeed, when the peasants' union was formed, he went so far as hailing it a significant development that would profoundly affect the course of Malayan politics.

In a commentary on 26 July 1947, Raja wrote that, with the peasants' union, the MNP had found for itself "an effective instrument with which to storm the citadels of UMNO power and prestige — the Malay countryside". While UMNO based its propaganda among the Malay peasantry by fanning up religious and racial fears, the peasants' union would appeal to their desire for concrete programmes of agrarian reform to uplift their welfare, he observed.

Raja further argued that UMNO, faced with this new economic tack from the peasants' union, would now have to overhaul its programmes thoroughly if it wished to retain a hold over its peasant followers. "It is true that racial and religious politics can move him into action," he noted, "but when these same discontents are reduced to simple terms, like land, rice and freedom from debts, all other political motivations are rubbed out of his thoughts."[31]

Clearly, Raja was not at all impressed by the tactics of some UMNO politicians which appealed to racial and religious sentiments for support. A socialist at heart, he was also not convinced that capitalism was the answer. He preferred a rational economic approach which involved bringing the Malay peasantry into the mainstream of modernism, so that, whatever their race, "they all feel themselves to be the victims of the same modern capitalist economy".[32] As he argued in another column, the unity of Malaya's plural society should be forged first where the various communities meet on common ground — economics.[33]

To the question "Malaya for whom?" — a question he had been reflecting on since the early 40s — he outlined the two possibilities being considered at the time: One, with sinister overtones, was that Malaya belonged to a particular racial group, entitled to special privileges; the other was that it belonged to all Malayans, regardless of race. Identifying himself with the latter as the "progressive" group, Raja noted the "depressing truth" that the communalists had a decided advantage over those striving for unity, not because of the force of their argument, but because of the economic aspect of the problem.

In Malaya, racial and economic divisions coincided to "an amazing degree". He recognised that the Chinese were, economically, the most powerful group. Rational analysis would reveal that this state of affairs was not due to any special racial characteristics, he argued, but had to do with the economic functions they performed in the economy. The Chinese, for instance, specialised in operating the commercial side of the Malayan economy, which brought higher returns. Raja reminded critics that, by their functions, they were also responsible for the creation of an efficient commercial economy in Malaya. Also, not all Chinese were rich capitalists, as many continued to toil as poor workers.

The Indians and Ceylonese constituted the middle classes and the workers. Again, this was purely because of their economic functions — being on a smaller scale than that of the Chinese, they brought smaller returns. "The Malays are, undoubtedly, the least economically privileged. This is so not because they were exploited or thrust aside by the more pushing Indians and Chinese, but because by force of circumstances, a large proportion has been kept outside the orbit of the modern economy of Malaya," he argued.

The Malays should blame the system of indirect rule for this — which "allegedly created to preserve the mythical Malay way of life" — had in reality erected a wall between the modern Malaya, peopled by non-Malay races, and the Malays' semi-feudal, rural social system.

Raja showed an early understanding of the intricately complex problem when he empathised with the Malays' economic situation, and called on the non-Malay communities to work with the Malays so that they could move into the modern economy. "This does not mean that the Malays should become an object of economic charity," he qualified.

"If the non-Malays can co-operate with the Malays in giving them economic equality, then the Malays would not be averse to political unity. Of course, the welding of Malayan unity will not be as simple as all that, but only along the lines of economic co-operation lies the way to political co-operation between the three peoples of Malaya," he concluded.

There was much more in that vein in his corpus of writings as a journalist. His was a heretical worldview that flew in the face of the dominant opinion of the time, especially among the powerful Malay rulers and politicians in the Federation, who preferred a political answer to the problem, rather than an economic one.

His ardent hope that UMNO would review its communal-based approach would turn out to be wishful thinking. Anxious about the development of Malayan politics, Raja would keep a close watch over UMNO's trajectory, praising its leaders who championed Malayan nationalism, and excoriating those who pursued communal politics.

Despite his best efforts to forge such a social pact among the different races in Malaya, little was to come of it. Raja was to find out by the early 1960s that the question "Malaya for whom" would be decided not by the rational analyses and progressive action he had advocated, but by politically instigated racial clashes.

Not all of Raja's columns were of the political variety. Occasionally, he toyed with light, whimsical topics, such as the 1940 discovery of the prehistoric cave paintings at Lascaux, France. He mused on the power of the cave paintings to move the emotions of people so many centuries later, and related how a woman was so awestruck by the caves that she took off her clothes and finished the visit naked![34]

Generally, Raja's columns, which tended to be pedantic, appealed to the more intellectual crowd. What would become Raja's trademark style — a slashing wit sharp as carving knives — came to full form about a year later, around late 1948. As he gained greater confidence, his distinctive voice thundered through the pages.

With much to comment on, his output was prodigious. The international economic and political order was in a state of upheaval. The Cold War was just starting with the intense rivalry between these two great blocs of power and the political ideologies they represented: democracy and capitalism in the case of the United States and its allies, and communism in the case of the Soviet bloc.

The Soviet Union viewed itself as the leader of history's progressive forces. The West sought to contain the Soviet bloc from expanding. Communists had gained control of Albania and Yugoslavia in 1944 and 1945. In 1946 and 1947, the Soviet Union, with the presence of a victorious Soviet army, helped bring communist governments in Romania, Bulgaria, Hungary, and Poland to power.

The ideological battle was as ferocious, with the Soviet Union and its communist allies committed to destroying the existing world economic order on the grounds that it was a capitalist creation. It was a dogma that found traction particularly in war-ravaged countries, including those of Asia. Against this backdrop, local struggles in Southeast Asia were now viewed as a part of a global chain of conflicts between the two power blocs.

At the same time, nationalism was on the move. The imperial twilight had begun, with countries asserting their independence from their colonial masters. In 1946, the states of French Indochina withdrew from the French Union, leading to the Indochina War (1946–54) against Ho Chi Minh, who had been a founding member of the French Communist Party in 1920. The independence movements in India and Pakistan were spreading social and political ferment against Britain. Closer to home, in Indonesia, the Indonesian independence movement, led by Sukarno, was waging a bitter armed and diplomatic struggle against Dutch colonialism.[35]

Raja was quick to grasp the implications for Malaya and rammed this home in his strident columns. In a column "Europe Over Asia" dated 5 August 1947, he sought to appeal to the conscience of the colonial masters in the form of a passionate letter to a European "friend". He wrote: "You Frenchman and Dutchman have felt the bitter shame and desperate anger that a foreign yoke roused in you. You did not ask whether the German could have ruled you better or whether you were fit to rule yourselves..."

He concluded with a hard-hitting message: "Understand us, sympathise with us, and help us to be free. The question no longer is whether Europe can hold down Asia but whether freedom will come to Asia through a sea of blood or peacefully. We prefer it by peaceful methods."

The British were unmoved by such calls for freedom as they focused on containing the labour unrest and the political foment led by the Council of Joint Action. They were anxious to avoid the situation in the Dutch East Indies, where the locals were engaged in an open armed rebellion against the Dutch. To appease the powerful Malay ground, the British agreed to the demands of the Malay aristocracy and UMNO to restore the position of the Malay rulers and to protect the rights and privileges of the Malays in the new Federation.

On 1 February 1948, the Federation of Malaya came into being, displacing the Malayan Union. Under the Federation, Malay political supremacy was assured, while the non-Malays faced stringent requirements for citizenship. Raja was dismayed by this development, which set in motion the debates that would dominate the years to come.

With the wind taken out of its sails, the Council of Joint Action collapsed. In protest against the new constitution, the MDU decided to boycott Singapore's first partial Legislative Council election to be held on 20 March 1948. With the move, the MDU forfeited its position as the most powerful party political force in Singapore at the time.

Raja disagreed vehemently with MDU's decision to boycott the elections, and argued with Kean Chye and Chooi Yip over this. "They hated the Colonial Constitution," recalled Raja years later. "My position was that, if you want freedom, you should do it the constitutional way, not through armed struggle." He surmised from their explanations that they were dancing to the MCP's tune. "But that never became a source of sharp division between us, only casual disagreements," Raja qualified.

The sharp break came in June 1948 after the MCP decided to wage a guerrilla war against the British in the jungles of Malaya. They dropped grenades. They shot in cold blood white planters and locals who supported the colonialists. Raja, a man of deep moral concern, denounced the violence. The atrocities precipitated events which were to have a powerful influence on Raja's own thinking and on that of many of his contemporaries.

In an editorial on 18 June 1948, Raja accused the MCP and the MDU for their "high-pressure campaign" to foster hatred towards the British, the Europeans, the Kuomintang, and Asian capitalists. Alarmed that the situation had reached a stage in which "murder is the political weapon employed", Raja questioned the colonial government's complacency in Singapore, when the government in the Federation was "at last taking emergency measures which are long overdue".

Emergency came into force in Perak and Johor on 16 June and was extended to the whole of Malaya two days later. Singapore followed suit on 25 June. The Emergency would last 12 years. Under the measures, the MCP and other leftist parties were outlawed, and the police were given the power to imprison, without trial, communists and those suspected of assisting them.

Arrests of MCP personnel started on 21 June. The next day, the MDU, feeling exposed and vulnerable, dissolved itself. The entire communist movement slunk underground. Many of the MDU leaders went into hiding.

The MNP, also infiltrated by communists, was banned in 1950. With that, the Malay peasants' union sunk into oblivion. With communist terror mounting in the countryside, UMNO moved to exploit the British government's fears over the Malay left and strengthened its hold on the Malays.

By the end of 1948, in the Federation of Malaya, about 1,780 people had been detained, and 6,374 banished, together with 3,148 dependents. This was a blow to the communists. In his memoirs, MCP secretary-general Chin Peng confessed that the Communist party had earlier backed the setting up of the MDU and MNP as part of its policy to expand its front operations.[36]

The PMCJA, under Tan Cheng Lock, was also firmly under the MCP's influence. Chin Peng observed: "I am sure it was never in Tan Cheng Lock's mind to become a CPM stooge. But that is exactly what happened."[37] The same fate would befall many other politicians without them knowing it. Such was the talent of the MCP.

With civil and political liberties in a straitjacket, Malaya's march towards *Merdeka* lurched almost to a halt. The exit of MDU had ended the experiment to form Malaya's first anti-colonial political party, leaving the ground to conservative and pro-British political parties. Undeterred by the cautious mood brought about by the Emergency, Raja kept up the pressure against colonialism.

In an editorial titled "BlunderBlitz Goes On", dated 14 March 1949, he railed against the Dutch delegate to the United Nations, J.H. van Royen, for defending Dutch policy in Indonesia. Raja wrote that the Dutch paid scant respect to international morals or world opinion to invade Indonesia. "They murder the Republic. They imprison its leaders. They make their name hated throughout the length and breadth of Indonesia. Having done all these things, the Dutch says that it is impossible to restore the Republican Government...You drive a man out of his home, rob him of his possessions, and then plead that it is unfair to give up the booty because it will mean establishing the status quo."

This column invited an indignant rebuttal from a Dutch soldier, 2nd Lieutenant R.W. Asser, from the Royal Netherlands Navy in Indonesia. In his letter, published on 26 April 1949, the Dutchman accused the *Tribune* of serving politics and not truth. Raja was then unmasked as the writer of this editorial when he responded in full flourish in an article five times longer than the reader's letter.

In his response, published on the same day, Raja unleashed on the unsuspecting reader the full force of his anti-colonial tirade. The Dutch had suffered under Nazi Germany and hailed those who fought against the Germans as "patriots". Yet Indonesians who fought against the Dutch for their own freedom were "criminals and bandits"? "Now that your country has been liberated...you do not seem to have learnt the lesson of your own sufferings."

He reminded the reader that the Dutch had blockaded Republican territory for a long time, especially the rice-producing parts. "You must forgive us if we think that one important reason why the Dutch wants to hold Indonesia is that without it, they cannot enjoy the high standard of living they now do." The enemy that the Dutch was fighting against in Indonesia was not "Communist bandits" as it claimed, but freedom — "freedom in the sense that you would desire for yourself".[38] It was vintage Raja.

Raja soon established himself as one of Malaya's public intellectuals, constantly lecturing the people, trying to awaken them to the anti-colonial imperative, and to teach the politics of democratic socialism to anyone who would listen.

He invested much hope in the labour movement as a democratic force. In his writing about its potential in Japan, his key thrust was that a democratic Japan could be built only on the basis of a strong Japanese labour movement. "What is certain is that, in a country still loaded with the relics of a feudal age, the labour movement remains the spearhead of democracy in Japan," he asserted.[39]

In several other columns, Raja expanded his point, observing how labour had furnished much of the strength of nationalist movements, especially in China and India. As for Malaya, its labour movement had, since its early stages, been political in its orientation. "This was due, in part, to the fact that the early leaders of trade unionism in this country were Communists," he observed.[40]

His most hard-hitting pieces on the labour situation in November 1948 were written in response to the 70-page official report titled, "Labour and Trade Union Organisations", which was presented to the colonial government. Raja's scathing review of the report stretched over an editorial and a three-part series, published from 5 to 9 November 1948. He rapped the British authors, S.S. Awbery and F.W. Dalley, for failing to understand the history of the Malayan labour problems and for viewing them through the eyes of British trade unionists.[41]

Raja's key point was that it was important to understand why the communists and Chinese secret societies had exerted such a "hypnotic influence" on Malayan trade unionism. It was because the communists stepped into the breach to give workers leadership at a time of turmoil. "If in the past a large proportion of workers have turned to communists for political inspiration, it is largely because non-communist elements were either hostile to labour's political aspirations or could not be bothered to give it a lead," he wrote.

It was a bruising indictment on the colonial government, which he punched home with the call for outmoded colonial political institutions to be discarded. Raja asserted that the labour movement was a political movement and it was impossible to divorce politics from trade unionism. The issue then was to see to it that their political aspirations were directed along "more desirable and fruitful channels", Raja argued.

The Special Branch drew its own grim conclusions. In its report on Raja's *Tribune* days, it stated that "Raja is anti-British and anti-Government", and "has been overheard to praise Russia and Russian policy". It added: "He occasionally writes editorials, and when so, they are invariably anti-Government with a left-wing flavour."[42]

Raja was aware that his self-appointed role as a public educator did not make him popular within mainstream newspaper circles. Describing his role as "a one-man teacher, one-man university",[43] he would later reflect: "Some people thought I was a lone ranger in the anti-imperialist movement."[44]

In the office, he was also seen as a lone ranger. His solitary habit of constantly reading and smoking was widely known in the newsroom, as was his maddening tendency to fire off his column only as the newspaper deadline closed in. Not a few times, the entire linotyping pool had to stay back late into the night just to wait for Raja's column. Understandably, M.S. Pereira, then in charge of the linotyping pool, did not think much of Raja's writing discipline and considered him a "lazy" writer.[45]

Clearly, not all could appreciate the way Raja's creative mind worked: It needed to be inspired, and to be inspired, he had to read widely and think deeply. Given this ingrained need to inhale the ideas, writing for him would often be a breathless sprint to make the deadline.

Despite this reputation for reserve, however, Raja was known to be a kind and generous friend to those whose zest for an intellectual and literary life matched his. One of them was Alex Josey, a British radio broadcaster and journalist of bohemian appearance. He was hired by General Harold Briggs to wage psychological warfare against the communists in Singapore.

Shortly after he arrived in 1948, he met *Malaya Tribune* reporter Frank Sullivan who insisted that he must meet Raja. Curious, Josey asked who Raja was. Sullivan, who would later become the press secretary to Malayan Prime Minister Tunku Abdul Rahman, replied: "He is a very important figure. He is going to play a big part in all this", referring to the anti-colonial movement.[46]

When Josey first met Raja, the Malayan journalist struck him as being "extreme left". As Josey described him, Raja was a "genuine socialist" who read a lot of left-wing literature and knew prominent left-wing leaders in London. They enjoyed each other's intellectually stimulating company and soon became bosom friends. They expanded their orbit of friends to include famous writers and aspiring politicians.

Josey introduced Raja to David Marshall, a prominent Jewish lawyer who was a fan of Raja's writings. Marshall, who was to take up the office of Singapore's first chief minister in 1955, found Raja a unique and "very unusual" man with his "dispassionate, cold intellect with an eagle's eye view of international relations".[47] As Marshall would say later, "I call him the man with the seven league's boots because of his understanding of international relations, his capacity to go for the quintessence of an issue — the very core — and to find the simple solutions, and to build his case patiently and quietly."[48]

Marshall had his first glimpse of this special quality when Raja brought him and Josey along to meet his friend, the famous and controversial writer Han Suyin, one Saturday morning in August 1953. Han, a Belgian Chinese[49] best-known for her book *A Many-*

Splendoured Thing (1952), shared Raja's deep interest in the cultural and political conflicts between East and West in modern history.

At Han's house in Johore Bahru, they met another controversial and colourful personality, American writer Emily Hahn, who was visiting the region on a journalistic expedition. Hahn had risen to prominence with two books about China, *The Soong Sisters* (1941) and *China to Me* (1944).[50]

Marshall was deeply impressed by the quality of conversation between Raja and the writers, which opened a new political world to him.[51] Despite their frequent interactions over the years, Marshall would find Raja an enigmatic personality. He would later comment: "He has very few friends not because he's not a friendly person, but because he's a very reserved person. You never know what he thinks."[52]

Josey was more than impressed with Raja; he became very fond of the man. Josey, a charming bachelor with a colourful life, stayed with Raja as his house guest in Chancery Lane for no less than nine years. Through Raja's introduction, Josey became Lee Kuan Yew's long-serving press secretary later. "Raja was a very kind man. I admired him very much," said Josey.[53]

Raja shone in the *Tribune* and was rewarded with salary rises and a secure position. From 1 January 1948 to 30 June 1948, his basic salary was raised to $475 plus $142.50 cost of living allowance (30 per cent) — a total of $617.50 per month. He got another raise from 1 July 1948. His basic salary went up to $525 with a proportionate rise in his cost of living allowance — a total of $682.50 a month.[54]

Then in a letter dated 9 November1948, he was offered a three-year contract of service at $900 a month inclusive of all allowances. These new terms started from 1 November 1948, effective retrospectively.

Hungry for greater challenge, Raja prowled for more issues to flex his intellectual muscles, and roamed into the rarefied regions of mass media and culture. On 17 July 1949, he wrote an informative article based on the question earlier posed to readers: "What is wrong with Radio Malaya?" Evidently, a lot. Readers generally felt that *Radio Malaya* was catering to the "low-brow" and the "bobby-soxer", with the winning letter ($20 to the reader, one Godfrey Smith) boiling it down to "no audience, no money, no equipment and no talent".

Raja concluded that readers wanted more high-brow programmes, with more relayed programmes from the BBC. He noted the profound influence that radio exerts on the average listener, who relied on it "for his recreation and for the satisfaction of his artistic and intellectual hunger". This was a medium that he would himself use to good effect a few years later as he broadcast his views on anti-colonialism and international affairs to reach a wider audience.

The *Tribune* gave Raja a broad canvas to experiment with different writing styles and to eventually develop his elegantly caustic brand of political writing, which won him a following. But it was a small ship, and prospects for progress for Malayan reporters were limited. As the Special Branch noted in Raja's file: "Most of the reporters are dissatisfied with their salaries and are waiting for Aw Boon Haw to start his new paper."[55] That new paper was the *Singapore Standard*.[56]

7

Standard Trouble

When the *Singapore Standard* was launched in 1950, Raja joined the stream of journalists who left the *Tribune* to join the new newspaper. The *Standard*'s first editor was T.H. Tan, also from the *Tribune*. He would be a founder member of the Malayan Chinese Association when it was formed in 1949, first as a welfare association, and then as a full-fledged, centrist Malayan Chinese political party. He later became MCA's secretary-general.

It was T.H. Tan who approached Raja to cross over to the new newspaper. The *Standard*'s general manager, Aw Cheng Taik, formalised the offer in a letter dated 5 April 1950: "Further to your discussion with Mr T. H. Tan recently, we take this opportunity to enquire if you are interested in a position as Leader Writer and Features Editor".[1] The salary offered was relatively good — $1,200 a month, rising by $40 a month after each year's service over three years.

Besides the better salary, Raja was also attracted by the prospect of working for a pan-Malayan newspaper run by Asians and staffed by Asians. The paper was started by the Chinese entrepreneur, Aw Boon Haw, otherwise known as the "Tiger Balm King" for his famed medicinal ointment. Aw's family also owned the Chinese-language newspaper, *Sin Chew Jit Poh*, one of the two main Chinese dailies.

Raja knew that Aw's main aims in creating the new paper were to promote his Tiger products to a wider audience, and at the same time, to gain prestige over his rival, the tycoon Lee Kong Chian, who was chancellor of the newly-created University of Malaya. The Burma-born Aw, who was illiterate in English, wanted a powerful newspaper which, as Raja related, "would shake the whole of Singapore". It would be pan-Malayan in its outlook and serve to unite the different communities. It was an appealing prospect for an idealistic journalist seeking to do great things. Raja was only too glad to accept the paper's offer, and started work in June 1950.

Cheered by the brighter prospects, he broke the news to his father in Seremban in a letter dated 12 July. Earlier that year, his father Sinnathamby, taking pity on Raja's parlous state and ramshackle living conditions, had decided to help Raja and Piroska buy a house to live in at 30, Chancery Lane. It was just down the road from their present accommodation at No. 15. Sinnathamby charged them a nominal rent of $200 a month for the new house and furniture.[2] Raja and Piroska were not so proud that they could not accept this timely assistance. The building in which they stayed was in such a terrible condition that one wall reportedly collapsed shortly after they moved out.

Very properly, in a telegram addressed to "Dear Son and Daughter-in-law", dated 14 July 1950, Sinnathamby informed them that he had included the rents in his current year income tax account for that year, which would come up to $2,100 a year. "As regards your Tiger Standard result, after hearing from you, we (are) all happy about it and hope that this will go on very well," he wrote, signing off as "Yours Affectionately".[3]

Raja's move to the *Standard* proved well timed. The *Tribune* found no respite from its financial haemorrhage and finally folded in 1951. The *Standard*, due to its unfettered style of reporting, sprang to become a direct competitor to *The Straits Times*. The *Standard* gave Raja considerable latitude to exercise his talents. His editorials were invariably provocative and punchy. His strongest words during this period were reserved for the MCP for pursuing violence. In one of his censorious anti-MCP editorials, Raja labelled the communists as "arsonists" for setting fire to rubber factories and warehouses[4] and warned of the spectre of the communists stepping up their offensive with matches and joss sticks.[5] "If the primary objective of the communist rebellion is to disrupt the economic life of the country, then the arsonist is doing this more effectively than his pistol-packing comrades," he wrote. He questioned the adequacy of the prevailing security measures and called for more stringent moves.

When rebuked by his communist friends, such as Chooi Yip and Kean Chye, for not backing the "anti-imperialist" action, Raja retorted that they had succeeded only in "killing some poor innocent Asians". He waved away their friendly warnings to tone his columns down. Raja told them: "This is what I believe. And that's that." Their relationship became an uneasy one.

Shortly afterwards, well-briefed militants tried to throw a scare into him by first, sparking off a general fire in the newspaper office. The second time, they poured kerosene on his desk and set it ablaze. As an added measure, letters bearing death threats arrived at his office. These acts of intimidation only served to stiffen Raja's resolve. He would not be muzzled. It was not only the reality of MCP's brutal power, but the malign intent of communists which drove him to speak out against them.

He was outraged when, at the height of the terrorism campaign, the communist killer squad attacked Singapore Governor Franklin Gimson with a hand grenade. It failed to explode, but the aim was to kill. In 1950 alone, 16 buses, 18 taxis, and the $12 million Aik Hoe Rubber Factory and a godown were gutted on the island. Such atrocities were intended to provoke mob violence on the streets. Amidst the terrorist campaign, Raja's greatest concern was that it would build up racial tension and spark off race riots.

In an unexpected way, his worst fears came true in December 1950, when race riots rocked Singapore over three days. The violence left 18 people dead and 173 injured. It was triggered not by communist violence, as Raja had feared, but a child custody case concerning a 13-year-old girl, Maria Bertha Hertogh.

Maria, the daughter of a Dutch army sergeant and a Eurasian mother, was baptised a Roman Catholic. When the Japanese invaded

Malaya, Maria's mother entrusted her to a family friend, Aminah binte Mohamed. Maria's parents were interned and subsequently lost touch with Maria — until 1949 when they discovered she was living in Terengganu, where she had been renamed Nadra and brought up as a Muslim.

Her parents sought legal custody. Aminah successfully contested the court order and married Maria off a few days later to a Muslim man. On 2 December 1950, the judge ruled the marriage invalid, on grounds that Maria was only 13, and instructed that she be handed over to her mother. Maria was then moved to the Convent of the Good Shepherd where she was reunited with her natural mother.

The press, including the *Standard*, played up the dramatic story. On 5 December, the front page of the *Standard* showed a smiling Maria holding hands with the Mother Superior under the headline "Bertha Knelt Before Virgin Mary Statue".[6] Such coverage provoked anger among the Muslims who regarded Maria as a Muslim, and fanned hatred against the Europeans. To counter the happy images of Maria printed in the English press, the Malay vernacular newspaper *Utusan Melayu* published photos of Maria weeping as well as reports of the girl begging the *Utusan*'s reporter for help. Radical politicians, such as Abdul Karim Ghani, president of the Singapore Muslim League and editor-in-chief of two Muslim newspapers, whipped up passions further by forming a Nadra Action committee and making inflammatory speeches. What started off as a legal case escalated quickly into a religious issue between Islam and Christianity.

On 11 December, riots broke out, with mobs roaming the streets and beating up Europeans and Eurasians. The Sultan Mosque in North Bridge Road acted as a sanctuary for the rioters and stored their weapons, such as a rifle, steel spikes, bottles, and large stones. Four days later, the *Standard* editorialised soberly that "the events of the last few days showed what a mob, drunk with race hatred, could do", and how religion, with its hold on emotions, could be "prostituted for baser ends". The editorial, most likely written by Raja as the paper's leader writer, called for efforts to be directed towards avoiding doing anything which would give free play to the "irrational impulses of the mob".[7]

While Raja's leader did not apportion blame on any single party, it pointed out the role of some people in accentuating the religious and racial aspects of Maria's case and the colonial government's lack of political sensitivity to the racial and religious overtones of the custody case. It concluded: "Had the Government recognised the strong racial and religious tinge that had been given to the Maria case and taken a serious view of it, the Government might have taken measures to counter such feelings."[8] The removal of Maria to a convent was a "blunder". While there was truth in that analysis, there was no denying the culpability of the press itself in inflaming passions.

In the Legislative Assembly, Progressive Party leader C.C. Tan placed the blame squarely on the newspapers as he chastised them for trying to outdo each other in sensational news and for behaving irresponsibly "with utter disregard of the hatred and passions which they were helping to inflame".[9] A commission of inquiry, appointed by the governor, followed. It attributed the first cause of riots to the passions raised by putting Maria in a convent and the coverage of the English- and Malay-language newspapers.

The entire episode tormented Raja. Although he did not oversee the coverage of the Hertogh case in the *Standard*, he could not disclaim responsibility; he was a senior member of the maligned press. He had consistently spoken out against divisive racial and religious propaganda of any kind but, as a lone voice, could not control the excesses of the press, not even that of his own newspaper.

The mass hysteria over the case confirmed in his mind how easily racial and religious passions could boil over and mutilate the social fabric. He also drew a lesson on the art of governing a divided society: The government must be alive to subterranean racial and religious sentiments and have the wherewithal to defuse tensions early. Even more important, it must possess the vision to unite the society. It was perhaps the most fundamental point, which Raja never forgot.

Throughout this grim and perplexing period, the MCP was building up its base. Since the Emergency, the MCP operated fully underground, organising Anti-British League (ABL) and other clandestine cells to rouse anti-government sentiments and recruit more members into the party. The ABL sought to engage in sabotage and terrorist activities on the island to support armed struggle on the mainland, and divert troops that might otherwise be sent to Malaya to suppress it.

Many members of the defunct MDU were active in the ABL, such as Chooi Yip, Kean Chye and John Eber. Samad Ismail was also an influential cell leader. Despite the threats Raja received from the communists for his anti-MCP columns, he remained good friends with these men. He would continue to visit Kean Chye and his family regularly at their house in Wilkinson Road, and have dinner with them about two to three times a month.

Throughout this period, Raja had gone from naive and trusting to knowing and discerning. It was a time of great education. He understood that, as for so many people in those days, it was difficult to be completely clear about where people stood on the ideological spectrum.

He learned that there was no gain in taking easy offence. Often, it was not personal; it was politics. In a time of malice, Raja was not malicious. In a time of disingenuousness, he was clear about what he stood for and why. It was such open traits of fairness and integrity that would continue to win him the trust and friendship of communists and pro-communists, despite his deep disagreements with them.

His character was fully revealed in the drama of the lightning police raid in January 1951, which rounded up about 30 personalities, mostly ABL members including Samad, Devan Nair, Sharma, and John Eber. Raja was in his office when the news of the ongoing arrests broke.

One of Raja's first instincts was to warn Kean Chye and check on the welfare of his wife and children. That evening, Raja and his wife drove to Kean Chye's house and were relieved to find out that Kean Chye had escaped.[10]

Raja himself, however, was not so lucky. He was promptly picked up by the police and taken to the Criminal Investigation Department for interrogation. They demanded to know what he was doing in the vicinity. Raja got off the hook by replying that he was there as a journalist.[11] A day later, Chooi Yip, who had also eluded arrest, turned up at Raja's house, cutting a thin, sorry figure with his blood-shot eyes and racking cough. He was clad only in a pair of tattered shorts. In his haste to escape the police, Chooi Yip had dashed out of his house without time for anything else.

Furtively, in this state of undress, one of Singapore's most wanted men knocked on Raja's door, only to find that both Raja and Piroska were out. To his relief, their domestic maid, who answered the door, recognised him.[12] From the maid, he borrowed a pair of slippers, a hooded raincoat, and continued fleeing.

Chooi Yip then escaped to Indonesia, where he continued his communist operations with direct lines to the communist chiefs in Malaya.[13] However, his health soon deteriorated rapidly. Needing urgent medical treatment, he sought to find a safe way to see his doctor friend in Singapore. Years later, Chooi Yip recounted that he had asked a mutual friend — a former ABL member — to seek Raja's permission for him to be treated in Raja's house. Chooi Yip told his communist friends that there was only one friend he trusted and that was Raja. He believed that Raja would not let him down. Chooi Yip was right.

Despite the threat of arrest, Raja took the fugitive in and allowed him to stay about a week for treatment. Conscious that he was under

British surveillance, he told Chooi Yip to desist from telling him anything about his escape. Raja rightly feared that, if he were caught, he might be forced to talk, and others could be implicated.

Thus Raja did not know then that, after Chooi Yip slipped into Singapore by boat, the person who brought him to Raja's home was communist leader Fang Chuang Pi himself. Fang, better known as the Plen (short for plenipotentiary), had gone underground in 1950, but wielded great influence over MCP members in Singapore through the 1950s and 1960s. Fang, who was Chooi Yip's close colleague when they worked in the pro-communist *Nan Chiau Jit Pao*, said later that, ever since Raja opened his door to Chooi Yip that night, he, Fang, had regarded Raja as someone who was "a loyal friend in the most critical of times".[14]

Why would Raja put his own safety on the line for Chooi Yip? Raja himself provided the answer: He knew Chooi Yip well, both being anti-colonialists, and had a high regard for the communist for his sharp mind and sincerity. As he said: "I would do it for anyone who is sincere with me. Similarly, I wouldn't lift a finger to help someone, even a PAP member, if that person is not sincere with me."[15]

That harrowing episode dramatised Raja's own values: Personal loyalty and sincere friendship above avowed political affiliation. He might attack communist dogma and flay their politics in withering prose, but he took gentle care of his friends.

As Raja's long-time friend, Dennis Bloodworth, observed: "To Raja, friendship was no light matter. He struck no poses, made no melodramatic protestations, for he used words to express ideas, not emotions."[16] His friendship was deep, calm, and tacit. Journalist Samad Ismail, a card-carrying communist close to Chooi Yip, said that Chooi Yip respected Raja for his strength of character. "He knew Raja for a long time and admired him for his principles."[17]

For a long time, Raja held the view that Kean Chye, Chooi Yip, as well as the "Plen", Fang Chuang Pi, must have escaped the police dragnet because of a timely tip-off. Later, it was confirmed to be so. The MCP secretary-general Chin Peng wrote in his 2003 biography that these key figures were evacuated and instructed to lie low in exile until the political situation turned favourable to the communist cause in Singapore.[18]

As for the others who were detained, they pleaded innocence, as would be expected. But given the English-educated background of most detainees, who included the left-wing group active in the University of Malaya, they began to gain wide public sympathy as the arrests came to be cast as an attack on freedom of speech and thought.

The public agitation for their release gained pace with John Eber becoming the *cause célèbre*. Eber, a U.K.-trained lawyer, was prominent as a left-wing anti-colonialist and former MDU leader. He had previously acted as defence counsel for several communists and left-wing trade unionists who were arrested by the police.

During the January sweep, the government accused Eber, among other things, of being an ABL member who helped produce and distribute ABL leaflets, and to have allowed ABL members to hold discussion classes in Kean Chye's house. The government alleged that, if he had the opportunity, he would collaborate with the communists "to undermine law and order".

Claiming innocence, Eber asked repeatedly to be brought to trial to face the charges. Raja, driven as much by his sense of justice as by his affinity to Eber as a fellow anti-colonialist, added his voice to the call and wrote editorials to argue that Eber should either be brought to court, or released. The Special Branch observed: "As chief editor of the Standard, he gave sympathetic support to persons who were involved in the University case in 1951, and in particular to John Eber."[19]

Eventually, in February 1953, Eber was released. Soon after that, he left for London where he re-established contact with Hong Bee and continued his political agitation.[20] Raja maintained close touch with Eber in London, with the Special Branch noting that they corresponded frequently.[21]

Why did Raja continue his friendship with such communist characters who had shown no qualms of resorting to violence and duplicity to achieve their aims? He gave an insight into his personal value system when he spoke about them to a group of students in 1984. "However dangerous and wrong-headed the Communists were, they were also moved by ideals. They manifested unselfish dedication and genuine feelings for the oppressed and the humiliated," he told them.

"Whatever else they were, these men were no jokers out for loot and plunder. In this respect, they towered above many non-Communists who grovelled and snivelled and cheated for no greater ideal than personal enrichment," he said.

Raja admired men of conviction and courage. He had an informed disdain for the cloying and contrived, the political opportunists who pander to their colonial masters and their own self-interest. He believed there were too many of them dominating the Malayan political scene, and he carved them up in his columns in a sort of sorry relish.

Over his years as a journalist, Raja would accumulate as many critics as fans. Of all his critics, among the most powerful was the iron-fisted Lieutenant General Gerald Templer, who at 44 became Britain's youngest general in World War II. The former director of military intelligence, who came to Malaya in February 1952, made it amply clear that he would run the anti-communist campaign like a soldier.

He replaced British High Commissioner Sir Henry Gurney, who was ambushed and killed by the communists in October 1951. One of Templer's first actions was to storm into the town of Tanjong Malim in March to punish its 5,000 residents for failing to warn of the communist guerilla activities in the area. Tanjong Malim, a hotbed of communist action, was a town about 82 kms north of Kuala Lumpur on the Perak-Selangor border. Government intelligence pointed to some 16 guerilla camps in the surrounding jungles.

The litany of atrocities within Tanjong Malim included: Five ambushes, 10 attacks on military and police patrols, five lorries burnt, 6,000 rubber trees slashed, three buses destroyed, one train derailed, eight police officers and seven civilians killed, with more wounded.

Angered by the residents' apparent non-cooperation, Templer shouted at 300 community leaders of the town and announced a 22-hour curfew. No one could leave the area. Shops would be open for only two hours a day. Schools would be shut. No bus services. Rice rations would be slashed to half.

To make his intentions clear, Templer sent a letter to every household to seek intelligence on CPM activities. He urged residents to give "as much information as you can to help my forces catch the communist terrorists in your area".

While Raja understood the uphill task that Templer faced in quelling the communist insurgency, he deplored the draconian collective punishment against the people. He believed it was too severe and would be counter-productive.

As he pointed out in a harsh editorial published on 28 March 1952, the punishment for the atrocities would be borne, not by the perpetrators — the Communists — but by the 5,000 people of Tanjong Malim. This could embitter all the innocent residents against the government. Moreover, only a section of the population would have known about Communist activities, not all of them. Some stayed silent because they supported the communists, but for the rest, their silence was for fear that the authorities could not protect them from the communists.

"The pro-Communist groups who are risking death are not going to be converted by reduced rice rations and the closing of schools. Those who fear for their lives would be prepared to suffer the inconveniences of a curfew rather than a knife in their backs," he wrote.[22]

So what then would this collective punishment achieve? "We will be endorsing the very evils against which we have taken arms. We are subscribing to the principle that it is right to punish the guilty few as well. There is something repugnant about this principle. We cannot plead military necessity and hope to drug our conscience thereby."

Not content to leave it at that, he proceeded to lecture Templer on the art of public communication. Instead of putting through the measures as punishment, he suggested, some should be packaged as a plan to protect the security forces and victims of communist attacks. The spirit and purpose to clean up Tanjong Malim should not have been the punishment of 5,000 people, but to safeguard the town and its surrounding areas from communist attacks. "This may be a matter of emphasis. But it would make all the difference politically and psychologically."

Angered by Raja's audacity, Templer proceeded to make his own political and psychological point and with sharp emphasis, too — he tersely sent for the *Standard*'s editor-in-chief, K.S. Chang, who came from Shanghai, to answer for this piece of perfidy.

Chang knew exactly where he stood as a foreign-born — the threat of expulsion from the country rolled around his feet like unexploded grenade. Raja told Chang to inform Templer that he was the writer of the editorial and would be accountable for it.

When Raja arrived at Templer's office in Kuala Lumpur, he was made to wait for about two hours outside the door, which did nothing for his nerves. When shown into the office finally, he received a stone-cold welcome. There were no niceties, not even a chair to sit on. Templer's hawkish face, with its deep lines and weathered skin, was stern. "His eyes were shining like electric lights. He was so serious that it was frightening," Raja related.[23]

Then Templer, slim and sparsely-built, leaned his back on his chair and rested his right foot on an open desk drawer. The action drew Raja's eyes towards the drawer where a revolver gleamed in plain view. Raja knew that Templer, an old hand at psychological warfare, was trying to intimidate him. Templer then fired him a series of loaded questions: Was he the leader writer who specialised in fanning up sentiments? Was he friendly with the British correspondents who were so fond of criticising his measures?

As Templer barked the questions, he glanced at the revolver in the drawer from time to time. Keeping as cool as possible, Raja sought to explain his stand as a non-communist journalist, and that he wrote the editorial without any malice.

Then unexpectedly, Templer slammed shut the drawer and asked Raja: "Would you like to have whisky or brandy?" Cautiously, Raja replied that it was too early for a hard drink and asked for tea instead. It was served.

This nerve-wracking episode sobered Raja to the cold-blooded and ruthless nature of the fight between the colonial powers and the communist insurgents for control over Malaya.

It also gave Raja a first-hand sense of the General. Raja knew exactly what he was talking about when he wrote, in another anti-colonial column on 29 November 1953, that "General Templer is a man of incisive opinions and he clothes these opinions in words no less incisive. He has never hesitated to call a spade a spade. Thanks to this sort of trenchancy, Templer has never left those who listened to him in doubt as to whether he was talking about cabbages or about kings. There may be disagreement with the views he expresses but never about what he means."[24]

Raja was also clear about his own position.[25] His anti-colonial fervour crackled through his columns, as he remorselessly attacked the colonial establishment's views on various issues. It won him respect from other journalists who knew how dangerous it could be to openly cross the likes of Templer.

James Fu, at the time a reporter-translator with the pro-communist Chinese newspaper *Sin Pao*, observed: "As a leader writer, he had been consistently writing what he believed to be true. He did this without fear and under very adverse conditions. His socialistic ideas and enlightened views contributed to the political development of Singapore."[26]

Unsurprisingly, the Special Branch branded Raja's writing as "anti-British" and described him as "an agitator for self-government in Malaya" who would sympathise with anything which was an attack on the colonial form of government. The intelligence report added: "It is known that his wife shares his political views and ideologies."[27]

In actual fact, Piroska was quite apolitical. Friends observed that she tended to keep out of political discussions, even during private dinner conversations at their home. She was completely loyal to her husband. Raja's public life was his own. Her concern was over Raja's safety and well-being, as well as their ability to pay the household bills.

His breadwinner status was precarious and, on several occasions, hung in the balance as he continued to attack the status quo. Many readers found his defiance breathtaking and wondered how he could get away with it. Eventually, it was to catch up with him, in an unexpected way.

Raja's pugnacious columns continued to land his newspaper and his stoic and long-suffering editor-in-chief, K.S. Chang, in all manner of trouble, and not only with the establishment. Once, Chang was punched in the face by South African sailors, thanks to Raja's scathing editorial on African apartheid.

In that editorial "Witch Doctor Malan", published on 15 September 1950, Raja had branded the members of Dr Daniel Malan's Nationalist Party as "a band of hooligans". The party had just won the elections in South-West Africa.

Raja's inimitable voice was unmistakable as he slammed Dr Malan's brand of democracy as being based on the principle enunciated by George Orwell — "All men are equal. But some men are more equal than others." With Malan and "his colour-conscious boys" dominating the Assembly, the programme of apartheid could be enforced with greater ferocity, he wrote.

Noting that Malan had defied the United Nations, "one cannot help but feel that the democratic world is doing its best to close its eyes to the menace that Malanism presents to the world", he fumed.

The night this editorial appeared, three South African sailors, whose ship was in port, barged into the *Standard* office to beat up the offending writer. They were thwarted by the tall and athletic K.S. Chang. The African seamen hurled abuse at Chang. Punches flew as some night editors rushed to Chang's aid.

The *Standard* reported: "In the free-for-all which ensued, Mr Chang was injured in his face, and the Sports Editor, Mr Larry Carrol, got a punch in his left eye."[28] The saga ended with the three Africans being charged in court the next day for trespassing into the *Singapore Standard* office with intent to cause annoyance. They were fined $50 each or three weeks in jail.

Despite this alarming incident, Raja did not flag in his efforts to educate readers on the controversial concepts of race and nation, in particular, on the dangers they could pose under the manipulative hands of politicians. His worry, as always, lay closer to home. He kept an especially wary eye on any sign of communalism being exploited for political gain in Singapore.

In an editorial "Playing with Fire" on 20 September 1950, he condemned any move by political parties to stoke the "embers of racial antagonisms" in Singapore. Once the "devil of communalism is let loose, it will spread faster than the plague". Writing in his trademark style with a clever use of metaphor, he noted that, while Singapore politics had largely eschewed communalism, there still existed "political carpet-baggers who lurk about the dark alleyways trying to sell communalism, with the furtive air of purveyors of dirty post-cards".

In this context, he expressed concern over the announcement that the United Malay National Organisation (UMNO) was to enter Singapore politics. It would be a "disastrous thing" for Singapore, he wrote, observing that racial jealousies and fears were more far more pronounced in the Federation than in Singapore. He pointed out that in the Federation, the constitution reflected the communal rather than the national aspirations of the people. Because of the strong communal feelings aroused, the Federal Constitution was mainly concerned with preserving a "reassuring balance between the various racial groups", and less with the political rights of the people.

He was not arguing that UMNO should not establish a branch in Singapore, as there were many communal organisations in the colony. The Malayan Chinese Association (MCA), which served the Chinese community's welfare, had also set up a branch in Singapore, but had said it would not take part in local politics, Raja noted. He demanded: "Like other communal organisations in the Colony, UMNO should keep away from its politics." Raja made it plain who would be the losers if communal politics became rife in Singapore: "In a city which is overwhelmingly Chinese, the minority groups which play with the fire of communalism will get their fingers badly burnt."

His reading of the political complexion in the Federation was astute. But UMNO had no intention of staying out of Singapore politics. Neither did the MCA. Raja was naive in this sense. He himself had joined the Singapore branch of the Malayan Indian Congress (MIC) in 1950 and served as its secretary.

The MIC was established after the Second World War to fight along for Indian independence from the British, and later to serve the welfare needs of the Indians. Its name was taken from the Indian National Congress. Raja's association with the MIC was essentially a carry-over from his close links with the Indian nationalists in London. He had kept in touch with his nationalist friends in India and beyond, and had hoped to infuse the same anti-colonial spirit in Malayans.

In the late 1940s and early 1950s, the MIC was leftist and committed to non-communalism. Raja dropped out of MIC in 1954 after it decided to take part in politics, as this move went against his fundamental principles. That year, the MIC joined the National Alliance comprising the UMNO and MCA, with each political party representing its racial group and forming its own popular base along racial lines. Underlying this arrangement was the principle of Malay political supremacy, underpinned by UMNO's hegemonic position to protect the interests of the *bumiputeras* — the "sons of the soil".

For some years now, Raja had been troubled by the impact of racial politics on Malayan nationalism and the course of the country's political evolution. In 1950, he penned a thoughtful, almost scholarly, analysis on Malayan nationalism, scrutinising the development of each racial group and delving into the deep political, economic and social divisions between the groups over the decades. In that 11-page article published in an Asian publication, he noted Malaya's composition of 43 per cent Chinese, 41 per cent Malays, 14 per cent Indians,[29] and observed that, based on population trends since 1921, the proportion of Malays to the rest of the racial groups would decrease.[30] A key reason was immigration.

He recognised, in the existing conditions of "economic rivalry and separatism among the races in Malay", the Malay middle class, which had no roots in the masses, would feel insecure and press the British to increase the sphere for Malay special privileges under the colonial framework. The problem was not the other races, however, but the social, economic and political structure perpetuated by the British, he argued. "By utilising the Chinese and Indians as the instruments of modern economic development in Malaya, the native Malays were isolated from the 20th century world…To this economic isolation must be added the social and cultural segregation induced by the system of indirect rule."

To compound their historical errors, the British were now supporting the aspect of Malay nationalist movement which sought to emphasise the racial dimension of situation and play to the fears of the Malay masses. In his dispassionate analysis which tracked the trajectory of Malay nationalism, he noted that the conservative

Malay politicians could secure support only by appeal to racial exclusiveness. "All the more so, because the Malay conservatives have no real social and economic programmes to offer to their people. They cannot afford to change the present social and economic structure of Malay society because upon it also rests their power and prestige." Yet the prerequisite for racial harmony in Malaya required the removal of such local conservative forces as well as a radical change to the political and economic structure created by imperialism, he argued.[31]

As expected, his trenchant views on racial politics won him few fans among Malay nationalists in the Federation. He was marked by some Malay politicians as a troublemaker and later felt the full force of their fury when he entered the political arena brandishing these same unalloyed views on race and nation.

Real obstacles stood in the path of a rational reception of his views in all their often subversive boldness. To begin with, the overwhelming majority of the people were uncritically in thrall of communal leaders who stood up for their race, religion, or language. Many who could not find jobs harboured the grievance that their situation was caused by racial discrimination. The general climate constituted a major barrier to Raja's views, but no thinker had battled more doggedly against racial politics and prejudices during that period.

In an editorial published on 27 August 1950, the radical writer argued that these concepts of national character, race, and nation are "illusions created by mirrors of ignorance and prejudice".[32] The myth of national character was a convenient weapon for building hatred for a temporary enemy, and for reinforcing many political superstitions, he observed.

He believed that national character, particularly when built around the idea of race, was a deception. "There may be differences deriving from differences in physical environment, education, climate, and historical development. But these external factors can and are being changed. To this extent, national traits are superficial and transitory."

He attacked primordial notions which divide people into fixed categories of race, and used the dominance of a certain race as an argument for determining national character and to justify discrimination. One of the most pernicious myths, he noted, was that the average Asian was contented with a lower standard of living than that of the Occidental — that "a bowl of rice and plenty of sunshine is all the Asian asks for!". Raja rejected these ideas as false and unempirical. His arguments went to the very core of his vision of man: "The basic human qualities are the same everywhere and no group or nation can claim monopoly over human virtues and vices."

Thus, already at this early moment of his career, exposed to the social and political reality in Singapore and Malaya, he had begun battling with the development of communal-based politics in Singapore; it was to become a lifelong battle. He would maintain his position on the frontline, in spite of personal provocations and anguish. He would at times feel desperately alone in his devotion to the cause. That so few seemed to detect the dangers increased his sense of despair over his ability to keep the communal forces at bay.

Even some of his close friends disagreed with him. One of them was Ungku Aziz bin Ungku Abdul Hamid, who described himself in an interview as a "Malay nationalist."[33] He said he had enormous respect for Raja as a "very high-quality intellectual" and "a rare species".

Ungku, who met Raja in 1952 when he worked as an economics lecturer in the University of Malaya in Singapore, held fundamentally different views from Raja on several issues, including race. They sparred regularly. "In a way, he must have handled me with kid's gloves. He handled the left-wing Chinese with boxer gloves," noted the thoughtful intellectual who specialised in poverty issues and rural development. Ungku Aziz himself strongly favoured pro-Malay policies to protect the Malays and uplift their economic lot.

During their exchanges, Raja would prefer to change the subject gently to defuse a potential row with his good friend, rather than to escalate it into a verbal war. He valued personal friendship over personal ego. "He was a very gracious man, not very assertive at all, and struck me as quite a reserved person," Ungku Aziz noted.

Their personal relationship was cemented over regular badminton sessions about two evenings a week outside Ungku Aziz's house at Eng Neo Avenue, followed by social dinners which would often see them tucking into their favourite dish of Peking duck. Alex Josey and Lee Siew Yee would also join them occasionally. As for their badminton skills, Ungku Aziz said: "Raja played because he wanted the exercise. We were not terribly good."

Bloodworth, who met Raja later in 1956, attached symbolic significance to their badminton games at the Badminton Hall, the scene during the 1950s of so many tumultuous political meetings. When they played, it was often at night after work. The hall was dark, except for a pool of light over the court. The only sounds were the squeal of rubber soles and the thwack of racket on shuttle. "They were oblique signals in a wordless interplay of men with a net between them," observed Bloodworth. Raja was indeed a man of few words when it came to his private life and emotions. He showed his feelings in what he did, not what he said. Notwithstanding his reserve, "he was the easiest of companions, natural and simple in manner, without any side or affectation", Bloodworth noted.[34]

He was also a deep thinker with a compulsion to put his thoughts into words on paper. Ungku Aziz noted: "Raja lived in the mind. He thinks on the typewriter. If he had something on his mind, he would put it on the typewriter."

When he wrote, it was often with an informed annoyance, grounded in critical thinking and extensive reading. His columns are rich in irony and show mastery over the use of metaphors. His style on some occasions flashed like a scythe.

To assess first-hand the political developments in the region, Raja toured several countries and interviewed a range of people. In September 1952, he travelled throughout Indo-China to file a series of weekly articles on developments in the region, given its strategic and political importance to the rest of Southeast Asia. His visit was at the invitation of the French government. As Raja explained in his first feature, published on 28 September, Malayan readers could not remain indifferent to events which would eventually shape their own future.

The series of four features, which focused on the war in Vietnam and the prospects for peace, were based on extensive interviews with top French and Vietnamese officials, and comprehensive research. In his almost scholarly articles, Raja argued that French rule must end. However, the Vietnam government could not act as a strong and independent government capable of attracting vigorous non-communist nationalist elements to itself. "A truly independent Vietnam is precluded for the simple reason that the Bao Dai regime is too dependent on France for its survival to be able to do without the French." He pointed out that the Bao Dai government, manned by conservative elements, had failed to rally mass support. He ended the series on a perceptive and pessimistic note, proclaiming the Bao Dai regime a head without a body. Indirectly, the series also served as a sober commentary on the political situation in Malaya.

His columns, written at a rapid gallop, fed a creative intelligence and political drive that swallowed life whole: Sharp sketches of politicians abroad and at home, penetrating analyses of problems on the ground, bold ideas on the way forward.

He was the least superficial of writers; he could not tackle a subject without diving into political history and investigating the complexities below the surface. Leon Comber, who was a Malayan Special Branch officer in the colonial period, observed: "What made him stand out among other local journalists at that time was that he had been 'polished' by his enforced stay in London during World War Two, and was much more savvy about local and foreign politics."[35]

While he might hold forth on myriad concerns that spanned the globe, his overriding preoccupation at this time was to get the British out of Malaya. Given the socialist ideas pounded into him in London, he placed great hope in the trade unions to represent the working class and to form the organised mass base for the anti-colonial struggle. Already, their mood was bitterly anti-colonial. Recognising their potential to further his cause, Raja began developing close ties with them and their leaders. His sympathies for the unions did not escape the attention of the Special Branch which noted that he wrote many editorials to support them.[36]

In 1951, Raja built his credentials with the mercurial trade union movement by founding the Singapore Union of Journalists with several others. In its first election, he was voted as its vice-president. He was to hold the same office for three successive terms, before becoming its president. Othman Wok, then chief reporter of the Malay-language newspaper, *Utusan Melayu*, was among the union members who voted for Raja. "Raja was unanimously elected as union chief because of his personality and of his reputation gained from being an outspoken editorial writer," said Othman,[37] who took over as SUJ vice-president when Raja was promoted to president.

As the union's president, Raja burnished his reputation on the ground as a crusader for workers' welfare and organised labour. Journalists and "very aggressive and excitable" unionists, as he described them, began approaching him with their grievances, seeking his help to wrest better terms and conditions. Other unions also came to him to vent their woes. It was an unlikely role for the mild-mannered writer with the thick horn-rimmed glasses.

From trial and error, Raja learned how to negotiate, how to play tough and how to wait things out, how to take pressure, and how to call a bluff. Although Raja was not the most skilful negotiator in SUJ, "the local journalists within the SUJ looked upon Raja as our leader," said Othman.[38] Through these garrulous sessions, Raja acquired the art of diplomacy — how to smooth ruffled feathers and how to keep volatile relations on an even keel. Raja was clear about his mission in the union: 80 per cent political agitation, 20 per cent union work. "For me, the union was a political weapon against British imperialism and I used that," he said later.[39]

He was vexed that, as long as the Emergency was on, any transfer of political power from London to a reunited Malaya would move at the speed of a pall-bearer. A united political front was needed to force the pace. But how could this be brought about, given the political apathy of workers and the parochial mindset of the unions? He believed that the setting up of a Trade Union Congress, giving a collective voice to all unions, would be one way forward. He sought to dig spurs in the slumbering labour movement with several sharp articles urging the unions to get their act together. In a column on 9 January 1951, he lectured: "Apart from extending trade unionism, a T.U.C. can eventually give the workers the help they need politically." It could also provide the finances, whether directly or indirectly, that working-class parties need. Most importantly, it could provide the education — "the lack of which is partly responsible for the political apathy among workers", he wrote.

He called on all trade unionists to sink "their petty jealousies and fears, give their support to the proposed T.U.C". Then in a hectoring tone, he asserted: "If they don't, they will prove themselves to be smaller-minded than we thought them to be."

In another column on 30 March 1951, he diverted his invective to employers — and employees — who think of trade unions as "simply cudgels for getting better wages and conditions of work". They were taking a narrow view. "The trade union movement has potentialities of greater moment to our national history," he declared, emphasising again his message that organised labour was necessary for the successful functioning of a democracy in a modern economy.

Trade unions, however, had yet to grow out of the wage bargaining stage. Raja called on them to pursue a new objective: They must ensure the conditions which would make increased wages possible. "For example, they must increase the country's economic productivity and ensure conditions of full employment. They cannot reasonably expect to get more wages if there is unemployment or if the total national wealth has not increased." Their interests are fully safeguarded only by changing or repairing the economic system with a view to making it more efficient and more productive, he argued. For that, trade unions must take part in political, social and economic activities.

It was a far-sighted view. Again, Raja was ahead of his time. Trade unions continued to be fixated on their sectional interests. They felt no responsibility towards the progress of the national economy or the advance of political democracy.

Raja's despair with the state of organised labour plunged further in May 1951 when the Singapore Trade Union Congress (STUC) was finally formed. It was hardly the strong anti-colonial movement that Raja had envisaged. The STUC leaders were pro-government and quickly dismissed as "colonial stooges". Mainly white-collar administrative and clerical workers, they had not earned their stripes with the rank and file as champions of labour. Most were also English-educated. They held little sway with non-English-speaking unions, which formed most of labour organisations in the colony. Only 28 of the 107 unions were represented by the STUC.

Raja was thoroughly disenchanted with the feeble state of the labour movement. He knew that, to realise his dream of independence for the country, he needed to find leaders of conviction and vision who could unite the labour movement and ride on its power to oust the British, and shape a fairer society. Until such leaders could be identified, he would continue to prod the unions with his pen.

8

Strike for Power

The time had come for one of those moments in history when people are thrown together and the course of a nation's destiny is changed forever. The first of these events involved Goh Keng Swee, whom Raja knew from the MDU days. While Goh, small-built and wiry, was happy to slug down mugs of beer with the MDU leaders at the Liberty Cabaret, he was detached from their political ideology. He was cerebral and deliberate in his political calculations.

Like Raja, Goh was disillusioned with the moribund politics at home and resented the humiliation of being under colonial rule. His resentment deepened as other countries — India, Pakistan, Burma, and Ceylon — gained their freedom. Unlike Raja who often lived in the realm of ideas and theories, Goh was a down-to-earth pragmatist who chose his allies and his methods carefully.

Goh found his chance when he was released from the civil service to pursue economics in London. In 1949, while studying at the London School of Economics, Goh and several friends set up the Malayan Forum. The aim of the forum, which Goh headed as its founding chairman, was to rouse political consciousness and press for an independent Malaya that would include Singapore.

From Singapore, Raja gave his active support to this Malayan anti-colonial student movement in London. He had felt keenly the absence of such a national consciousness among Malayan students during his 12 years in London, which was in sharp contrast to the upsurge of nationalistic fervour among the Chinese, Indians, and Africans. To help it along, he passed some of his influential British contacts to Goh to follow up.

The Malayan Forum invited speakers from various organisations, including the Fabian Society. Goh realised how well-regarded Raja was in the intellectual left-wing circles when he found personalities such as Lady Hilda Selwyn-Clarke, a leading figure in the China Campaign committee and the Fabian Colonial Bureau, asking after her friend, Raja. She also asked Goh to pass on her contact number to Raja in Singapore.[1] By widening and deepening their political network in Britain and Singapore, Goh and Raja supported one another in their common cause to shape thinking against colonial rule in Malaya.[2]

The Malayan Forum also provided the platform for Goh to exchange political ideas with three like-minded Malayan students — Lee Kuan Yew, Toh Chin Chye and K.M. Byrne — who had known one another since their Raffles College days. After interminable discussions in various pubs, they decided that the "returned students" should play a leadership role in organising a broad-based movement to fight for national independence through constitutional means. The four resolved that, on their return, they would seek out other kindred souls for this mission. One of them would turn out to be Raja, who had long waited for such a group of brave Malayans to emerge.

The circle was closed in April 1952, when Raja received a phone call from Goh after he returned from London. Goh invited him to meet Lee Kuan Yew, a brilliant Cambridge-trained lawyer who was now representing the Postal and Telecommunications Uniformed Staff Union over a pay dispute. Lee had been following his anti-colonial columns in the newspapers. Like them, Lee also wanted independence from Britain. Would he want to meet the lawyer? Raja agreed readily. For the journalist, all anti-colonial issues were grist to the mill.

On that fateful day, Raja turned up to meet Lee at the open-air restaurant of the Chinese Swimming Club in Amber Road. Neither of them knew their meeting would change the political course of Singapore. Against the hubbub of swimmers and background music, Lee briefed him on the background of the strike. The government had failed to meet the union's demand for salary revisions and pensions. Angered, the union had decided to give strike notice. If held, it would be the first since the Emergency was declared in 1948.

Years later, Lee recalled in an interview: "It was a very serious discussion because we were leading the postmen into a fight which was going to cause disruption to a lot of people and their businesses. And we would have done injury to them if they have failed. There would be lost pay. Some would be sacked."[3] The strike could not fail. Lee was astute in trying to get one of the most conspicuously influential journalists of his generation to throw his weight behind the campaign.

During their meeting, Lee told Raja: "We need the publicity to get public opinion on our side and force the Government to make concessions." Could he support the postal union's cause in his articles in the *Standard*? Raja listened intently to Lee's plans, all the while sizing up the man whom he knew only by reputation. Of average height with a good build, Lee cut a charismatic figure, strong and vigorous with piercing eyes and a deep, mesmerising voice. Raja knew of Lee's scholastic achievements — the top student in Singapore and Malaya in the Senior Cambridge examinations, then achieving a rare double first in Law at Cambridge University.

But what impressed Raja more was Lee's work with some unions as legal adviser, which he did without any pay. Here, Raja thought, was a rare English-educated intellectual who cared for the working masses and would toil for them. And here was another opportunity to hammer the colonial government. It was too good to pass up. Lee would later recall: "I found Raja very keen. He was more a campaigner than a journalist, so he was very enthusiastic and said that he would give the full support."[4] When Raja agreed to help Lee, he did not know that the decision would change his life completely.

At that point, Raja was not entirely privy to Lee's larger political plan. Lee's ambition was to build up mass support for the new political party which he wanted to form to advance the cause of independence. Raja had no such ambition to join politics. Never had. All along, he saw himself, first and foremost, as a journalist putting his craft at the service of a cause greater than himself — independence for his country.

In Raja's recollection, the issue of forming a political party never passed their lips — or even crossed his mind — at that first meeting. When they talked politics, it was to share their disdain for the political personalities and parties of the day. But mainly, they were absorbed with the postal strike issue. For Raja, "it was purely getting together to do the right things by the civil servants", as he said later. While that may have been true for the journalist at the start, his perspective would change over the course of the 17-day strike as he worked with Lee to win public support for their cause.

To prepare the ground for the looming battle, Raja fired the first salvo in the *Standard* on 21 April 1952. The article headlined "Postmen's Strike Threat: Give Week's Ultimatum" announced the postmen's decision to go on strike if the government did not meet the five-month-old demands of the 480 uniformed staff of the Postal and Telecommunications Department for wage revision and pension rights. Reporting on the union's extraordinary meeting held a day before, Raja wrote that the union would "appeal to the public for support, pointing out that it was because of their desire not to inconvenience the public that they did not call a strike at Christmas as planned".

Some 20 articles followed in rapid succession. Many made the front page with screaming headlines. They softened public opinion towards the strike and, before long, their hearts were with the union. Through the *Standard*, Raja invited contributions from the public for the strike. Ten days into the strike, which began on 13 May, the public had poured a total of $1,325 into the union's strike fund.

Raja kept up the news bombardment with reports on the protracted union meetings, quoting Lee as the union's legal adviser and official negotiator. Through the reports, Raja helped to build up Lee's image as a responsible and moderate spokesman doing his best first to avert a strike, and later, to end it. At the same time, Raja's reports presented Lee as a tireless champion for the postmen's "fair and reasonable demands".

Ambrose Khaw, who was then a sub-editor at the *Standard*, noticed that Raja would ensure that Lee's press releases, ignored by the pro-British *Straits Times*, would get coverage in the *Standard*. "The Straits Times denied Lee a place in the sun in the media," he noted.[5] Raja's extensive coverage in the *Standard* more than made up for it. As he charged forward with all cylinders firing, pressure on the government mounted.

Unable to ignore the escalating controversy, the other newspapers, such as *The Straits Times*, *Utusan Melayu*, and the Chinese dailies *Nanyang Siang Pau* and *Sin Chew Jit Poh*, began competing to cover news of the strike. Other unions — including the pro-establishment STUC — also came out to support the strike. All these worked to pack a wad of political dynamite for the government. Eventually, it buckled.

The bold headlines in the *Standard* captured the historic drama:

28 April: Unions Decides to Strike. Notice to be served on Govt today;
7 May: Postal Men Not Striking For Fun;
11 May: No March, Police Tells Men Who Decide To Strike
12 May: Mail Delivery To Stop;
13 May: Postal Strike On Today. Last Minute Govt Negotiation with Union Unsuccessful;
14 May: Postal Strike: First day Passes Quietly;
16 May: Postmen Accuse Govt of "Outsiders". It's Improper, They Complain;
18 May: "Govt using Clerks to Break Postal Strike". Federation of Unions to Probe Allegation;

21 May: Nicoll Condemns 2 Singapore Strikes;
22 May: Strikers Decide Today After Talks With Govt;
23 May: Postmen Reject Govt Suggestion To End Strike, Resume Talks;
25 May: Postmen To Suspend Strike For Three Days. Union Meets Today To Vote On C'ttee Decision;
26 May: Postmen Are Back At Work. Will Distribute Fresh Mail Only For 3 Days;
27 May: Postal Talks Progress. 4 of 6 Points Under Dispute Settled; More Negotiations Today;
29 May: Colony Postal Strike Over. Last 2 Points Settled In 3rd Day of Talks;
30 May: A Strike Ends.

While none of the articles carried Raja's byline — merely the uninformative "Standard Staff Reporter" — Raja was the man behind the pen. In his cogent editorials, he portrayed the postmen as the underdogs and the government as the villain. On 13 May, the day of the strike itself, Raja editorialised that the postmen, struggling by with measly salaries, knew that the government had the powers to "snap the strike as if it were a twig", and that "in fighting the wealthiest and most powerful employer in the country, they have placed themselves at the mercy of the Government". But they have struck, he continued, because "they feel that is the only way in which they can place their desperate grievances before the public with a view to rectifying them". Their demands are not excessive. He roared: "Is the Government so hard up that it cannot pay its lower ranks of workers decent wages?"

As Lee recounted in his memoirs, *The Singapore Story*, "Raja was enjoying the fight. This was crusading at its best — fighting for the downtrodden masses against a heartless bunch of white colonial exploiters." Raja was in his element when in battle. It was during this electrifying episode that their great friendship was forged. Their trust in each other deepened as Raja gave Lee the heads-up on his editorial pitch, and Lee relied on Raja to deliver the editorial punches. Raja's polemical style was emphatic, a result of his years hobnobbing with Indian and West Indian anti-imperialists, while Lee, more exposed to the friendly sparring at Cambridge, was partial to the understatement. Lee depicted their partnership as "a duet" — "Raja strong and rigorous, I courteous, if pointed, always more in sorrow than in anger."[6]

Claimed completely by the higher nationalistic cause, Raja broke a long-standing journalism code and passed his galley proofs to Lee at his home in Oxley Road, often past midnight before his paper went to print. For the radical writer, the only rule worth following during that time of oppression was self-rule. It was during this struggle that Lee first saw what a fearless fighter Raja was. "He would stick his neck out. He was not afraid to be sacked by the Singapore Standard," said Lee.[7] Observing Raja's fervour, his newspaper colleague, Khaw, said: "I sometimes wondered if Raja was a politician masquerading as a leader writer."[8]

While Lee found Raja "a very gentle fellow" in person, his writing style was anything but. Lee recalled: "I looked at them to see if they were correct. I just wanted to make sure that he didn't cross the bounds and get people to think we were truculent because I was playing a very understated campaign against the British."[9] A master organiser with a perfectionist eye for detail, Lee took pains to conduct the constitutional mass action completely within the law. From time to time, Lee had to remind Raja — be careful to avoid language that would lose public sympathy and give the British cause to take action against them. Their campaign worked.

As Raja wrote triumphantly in the final column on the postal strike, "the great sympathy shown by the public for the demands of the postal workers, no doubt, had some influence on Government's decision to approach the dispute in a different spirit".[10] Even with the Government writhing on the ground, however, Raja could not resist delivering a kick to its rear — the government should go on and give strike pay to workers, he wrote.

Over the course of the strike campaign, as Lee's larger political intentions became clear to Raja, the journalist was nimble in adjusting his mental gears. Lee related: "Raja knew what was in our minds and was of the same mind — to get the British out. For us — Keng Swee, Raja, Kenny Byrne and Toh Chin Chye — it was the beginning of a political base, to constitutionally force the British out."[11] Lee and his friends were now convinced that, in the unions, they would find the mass base they needed for their political purposes. The postal strike was to set the stage for more militant union action, and would usher in a new phase in the political history of Singapore.

For Lee, the press publicity he received during the campaign, because he had Raja on his side, proved far more important than the case itself. It was the beginning of a partnership of a political lifetime. The postal strike campaign also drew many supporters towards them, forming new networks and energising their left-wing movement. One of their fresh supporters was Sandrasegeram Woodhull, a student activist from the Singapore-based University of Malaya, where Chooi Yip had set up the first ABL cells about five years before.

Woodhull, an ardent student of Marx and Lenin, had supported the postal strike campaign by organising students to raise money for the union's strike fund. He admired Lee for being prepared "to give tongue and utterance to a cause", and Raja for his courage to champion his cause through the newspaper. Woodhull recalled: "We went out of our way to meet up with Rajaratnam and established a getting-together."[12] Raja found Woodhull "intellectually very spry" with a sharp understanding of the theory of Marxism. The chain of events set the course for the liaison between Lee, Raja, Goh and Byrne with Woodhull and his pro-communist coterie, such as Jamit Singh and James Puthucheary.[13]

Meanwhile, Raja kept in touch with his detained unionist friend Devan Nair, who was jailed at St John's Island for his communist activities. During his detention from 8 January 1952 to April 1953, Nair sent letters to Raja through the underground. Raja continued showing his appetite for risk and revolution by publishing Nair's anti-colonial letters in the *Singapore Standard*. Nair regarded Raja as an ally and recalled: "We were working towards a revolution when under detention."[14]

Raja was ready when the next big battle loomed. This time, Goh and Byrne, the two civil servants who stayed in the background at the postal strike, moved to the forefront. The struggle they led was for more pay and better conditions for civil servants. For a long time, the Malayan civil servants had been seething with resentment over the discrepancies in rates of pay between the locals and the expatriates. There also existed a senior hierarchy restricted only to Europeans, with the lower services confined to local officers. To the frustration of many Malayans, British attempts to Malayanise the public service had been feeble and almost farcical.

Raja had been up in arms on the issue of Malayanisation in his columns for some time. Like his friends, Raja saw Malayanisation as a political issue which should ride alongside progress towards self-government and as a necessary step towards self-determination.

In a column as early as 31 January 1951, Raja had slammed the colonial government for not having a clear policy on Malayanising the administration. "It is afraid to make up its mind as to whether it is a Government for transferring power to the local people or a Government anxious to retain power. Unless the Imperial Government shapes a clear policy on this, the whole administration in this country will have about as much purposive direction as a dead dog floating downstream."

Raja gained such a reputation for championing the cause that aggrieved civil servants and unionists streamed forward to feed him with materials to publish. One of them, S.R. Nathan, then a civil servant pursuing a social work course in the University of Malaya, passed to the journalist a satirical cartoon which poked fun at the much-delayed Benham report to review the salaries of civil servants. "The cartoon, drawn by a friend, showed chickens waiting to lay eggs indefinitely," recalled Nathan, who would later become Raja's permanent secretary in the Foreign Ministry.

Things came to a boil when Byrne, an assistant secretary of the establishment office, found out in 1952 that the British were going to pay a new family allowance to expatriate families, but not to local civil servants. Outraged, Byrne and Goh, then a statistician and economist attached to the Social Welfare department, formed the Council of Joint Action in July 1952 to demand a fair deal for all government servants, especially the poorly paid and numerous daily-rated workers. The Council represented all government unions and associations, with more than 10,000 members. The Council's secretary was Lee, with Byrne, Goh and Raja as the main leaders.[15] Their feud with the government was long and bitter.

The four men huddled at the basement of Lee's house in Oxley Road to discuss strategy. They viewed the struggle, as Goh described it, as "the opening battle for the destruction of colonial authority in Singapore".[16] Raja gave his input on how to conduct propaganda and undertook some of it himself in his columns. In a column headlined "The Ugly Word" on 4 July 1952, Raja pronounced that the new expatriate pay scheme was a "means of perpetuating substantial discrimination". He locked horns with federal councillors who supported the scheme, accusing them of being confused and missing the principle involved — that of equal treatment.

The confrontation with the colonial authorities escalated as harsh words were exchanged and the whole administration and the legislative council were politically involved. The government threatened to charge Byrne with "gross insubordination" for deriding the incompetence of his expatriate colleagues to the press. He later escaped with a reprimand. Raja considered Byrne's bull-headedness an asset as their group continued ramming at the rigid colonial system. Long after the anti-colonial battle was over, Raja would remember Byrne, his comrade-in-arms, for his strong character, fierce sense of justice, and an "almost belligerent concern for the underdog".[17]

Despite all their efforts in using the open argument to press their case, the government refused to budge. Six unions then threatened to strike. That did the trick: the governor sent Sir Edward Ritson to draw up a report of recommendations for better pay and conditions of service for local civil servants. In March 1953, Ritson recommended that expatriate family allowances be abolished. Not only that, new salary scales for all government employees should be introduced.

The campaign was a success for Byrne and Goh — and for their fellow rebels, Lee and Raja. It was the first blow delivered by the tenacious band against the colonial authority. It paved the way for the showdown at the Malayanisation Commission, in which Raja was to play a high-profile role when it convened in 1955.

Like all their actions against the colonial government during this period, their hard-line union battles were driven by their determination to oust the British. As Raja later explained, the colonial government and the employers were holding back trade unionism from restricting "the capitalists' right to enrich themselves to the maximum". The working class was docile and disorganised and, for a long time, had accepted injustice, exploitation, and oppression as in the natural order of things. They had to be roused to action. "Given this gang-up between a colonial government and the capitalist class, trade unionism had to be militant," he said. "Since there was no democracy, the workers could bring pressure on the government and employers only by extra-parliamentary methods — by strikes, by violence, by intimidation and even by economic sabotage. In an anti-democratic, colonial atmosphere, the workers could feel no loyalty to the state because it was not their state."[18]

Ironically, he made these comments in 1969, a year after he became Singapore's labour minister. In that landmark speech, he sought to persuade the modern-day unionists to desist from being stuck in the militant mould of the 1950s and to embark on a new course of modernisation, given the vastly changed environment — Singapore was an independent democratic country struggling for its survival after being expelled from Malaysia in 1965, with its situation made worse by the impending British pull-out.

The traumatic events of the post-1965 years could not be foreseen by Raja and his revolutionary friends when they gathered regularly at Lee's house in the early 1950s to work out the path towards self-government. As they explored the hazardous terrain, they widened their circle to include Samad Ismail and Devan Nair, both former detainees, but judged by Lee and his friends to be useful to their mission.

Their deliberations gained urgency when the Rendel Commission was set up in 1953 to review the constitution to move the colony along its transition to independence. Riding on the process, the Council of Joint Action issued a memorandum listing radical demands to the Rendel Commission in November 1953. Besides asking for immediate full internal self-government for Singapore, it also called for a multilingual policy in the legislature.

To pile on the pressure, Raja appeared with his delegation from his Singapore Union of Journalists (SUJ) before the Commission and made similar calls. Raja said that the language barrier ensured that political leaders could be drawn only from the English-speaking elite which made up no more than 15 per cent of the population. This would not make for a truly democratic legislature, he argued.

The Rendel Report, published on 22 February 1954, rejected these demands, considering them a serious threat to stability and liable to make the island more vulnerable to communist subversion and capture. It held that political tutelage was essential in the transition to independence, and retained English as the sole official language.

Nevertheless, the report recommended significant changes: Singapore would be given partial internal self-government, with Britain retaining control of internal security, law, finance, defence, and foreign affairs. It also provided for a Legislative Assembly of 32 members, with 25 elected. The governor accepted the report, which would be implemented at the next election in April 1955.

During this period of political ferment, Raja received an invitation to dinner by the mercurial David Marshall. Marshall asked him to bring Lee, Goh and Byrne along. Marshall, a passionate critic of the colonial regime, laid out for them a lavish spread of food with expensive red wine and champagne in his apartment in North Bridge Road. As they tucked into this largesse, Marshall tried to whet their interest in a new socialist party. He fed them the idea that, by joining forces, they could form a united left-wing party against the conservative Singapore Progressive Party (PP), which at the time was dominating the political scene.

Raja recalled: "First, we were genuinely interested. Marshall was a flamboyant character and intelligent." As their own ideas on forming a new political party were still inchoate, they kept their curious minds open to Marshall's proposed Socialist Party. Moreover, there was some wisdom in not splitting the anti-PP forces.

To Marshall, this was a serious effort at merging the various left-wing groups into a non-communist socialist party — a direction which was encouraged by the British Commissioner General of Southeast Asia, Malcolm MacDonald, to counter the influence of the communists. On 30 December 1953, Marshall had written in his diary that he had met MacDonald and discussed the proposed Socialist Party. He penned: "Agreed to unite with Raja's group". "Exciting," he added.[19]

To his consternation, however, "Raja's group" seemed less than enamoured by his overtures. With the dogged persistence of an ardent suitor, Marshall continued to invite them to his apartment for dinner, each time as lavish, each time as fruitless. Hoping against hope, he persuaded his political allies, such as Francis Thomas and Lim Yew Hock, to delay the formation of the proposed socialist party to give Raja's group more time to come round. The wait was in vain.

Between themselves, Lee, Raja and their group had already discussed Marshall's proposal and concluded, as Raja related, "that this is a crazy party". Raja revealed later that they began to hit the reverse gear when, over the dinners, Marshall introduced them to "all sorts of odd characters" from the wobbly Singapore Labour Party. They did not want to be associated with such politicians. "It would just ruin our own reputation. But Marshall was anxious to launch this party and keen to have some respectable people," Raja related. They surmised that Marshall merely wanted an election machinery, and was not seriously interested in a genuine socialist movement. Their encounters with Marshall also gave them reason to be wary of his combustible and impulsive nature.

Marshall lost his patience with Raja's group when, over one dinner, they continued to hem and haw about joining the proposed Socialist Party. In frustration, Marshall insisted on a definite yes or no on the spot. They asked for more time to think it over. Marshall blew his top and, according to Raja's recollection, shouted: "You people are just playing around with me. You have no intention of joining me." In a fit of fury, he stormed out of his flat. As Raja and the rest waited for Marshall to cool down and return, they heard, to their astonishment, Marshall starting up his car and driving off. According to Raja's account, he and Lee looked at each other, and then at the feast on the table. Shrugging their shoulders, they decided, pragmatically, they might as well stay and enjoy Marshall's hospitality. "Red wine was there, and we got soaked!" recalled Raja.[20]

Marshall's allies ascribed Machiavellian motives to the runaround given by Raja's group. Francis Thomas, who broke away from the Singapore Labour Party in October 1953 and was involved in the early intrigues of the new Socialist Party, believed that the PAP clique's main interest in the meetings with Marshall was to get an idea of the group's effectiveness, and then to reduce its effectiveness by "keeping discussion open as long as possible so as to waste our time and make us later in getting the necessary work done".[21]

But as far as Raja and Lee were concerned, they were exercising prudence in taking the time to probe what Marshall and his group were capable of. They were looking for serious-minded and committed men who could be counted on to be steadfast throughout the hazards of pursuing national independence. They did not find them in the bunch they met at Marshall's apartment.

In April 1954, the Singapore Socialist Party, led by Marshall, was officially born. Later, it absorbed another breakaway group from the Singapore Labour Party and was renamed the Singapore Labour Front. Raja and his friends rolled their eyes at the new party's direction, steered by a motley group whose knowledge of socialism was abysmal. Their main interest, Raja surmised, was public office. "Once the party was formed, we had come to the conclusion that Marshall was not serious about his politics. For him, politics was drama. He was in a play. The party was just a backdrop," said Raja.

At the time, Marshall could not understand why Raja was so disdainful of his advances. It distressed him so much that, on 22 October 1954, he asked their mutual friend, Han Suyin: "Why is he so against us when our aims were the same?" Suyin replied: ""They hate liberals most, these cold unemotional intellectuals." Marshall drew solace from this observation and wrote in his diary: "Gathered impression she identifies him as a genuine Communist!"[22]

This long-drawn charade illustrates how profoundly ideological tensions persisted beneath the façade of bonhomie as new political alliances were broached and rejected, made and broken. It also reflects how intensely Raja, Lee, and their inner circle clung to their own vision of an independent socialist Malaya as they contemplated their place in the shifting political sand.

⸻

Meanwhile, Raja's star was rising at the *Standard*. The newspaper's management recognised the power of his writing, the extraordinary forcefulness which distinguished it from the others. He also had an extensive network of contacts that enabled him to deliver interesting articles that got people talking and buying the paper.

In recognition of his talents, the newspaper expanded his job scope in early 1953. In a letter dated 3 January 1953, Aw Cheng Taik, the newspaper's general manager, informed Raja that, from 1 January, he was authorised to reorganise and supervise the news section of its editorial department, which included the subeditorial and reporting sections of the newspaper, and "you will be held responsible for their efficient functioning".

There was no mention of any pay increase to go with the added responsibilities. To correct this oversight, the newspaper followed up with another letter on 14 January to inform Raja that he would be paid an allowance of $150 a month — by debit note — for supervising the staff of the reporting and subediting departments. Mr Aw wrote: "In view of your supervision, I look forward to a better and wider spread of news in our publications." In addition, Raja's salary would also be raised to $1,450 a month from 1 January that year in recognition of his good work.

Raja, who was not known — to put it mildly — for his administrative skills, wore the new hat with a roguish nonchalance. A late bird, he would often saunter into the office after 11 am, sit hunched over his typewriter with the ubiquitous cigarette in his hand, talk to his top reporters about their stories, and then vanish. He would pop up later in the evening and stay till midnight or even later to see the newspaper to bed. Hugh Savage, who had also moved from the *Tribune* to the *Standard*, once described Raja to his son, Victor, as "a dreamy and lazy guy in the office", presumably because he spent much of his time reading and lost in his own thoughts.[23] Ee Boon Lee, who was a rookie reporter at the *Singapore Standard* in 1953, recalled that Raja was a rare sighting in the office during the day. This apparent absence was not mirrored on the newspaper pages, which was often emblazoned with his bold bylines, to the awe and fascination of many in the office.

Raja's byline became an even more eye-catching fixture when he started a new weekly column, *I Write As I Please*, published in the paper's Sunday edition. As the name — based on George Orwell's *As I Please* column of the left-wing British newspaper *Tribune* — suggests, Raja intended to comment freely on any issue that came to mind.

He wielded his pen like a heroic swashbuckler. He honed a style as unique as his person: engaging, ironic, at once satiric and reflective. He loved the recondite word and the learned allusion. His writing was pungent, wickedly sly, erudite, and sharply metaphoric. His most provocative were, as ever, viscous with nodules of venom against specific politicians and political parties which struck him as regressive and feeble. In his own fashion, Raja did his best writing in his *I Write As I Please* columns, which ran from 8 February 1953 to 31 January 1954.

The series also contained some of his best ideas on politics. Even before there was a glimmer of the PAP, Raja had concrete ideas about what kind of leaders the country needed. In his column headlined "Our parties have no sense of direction" on 11 October 1953, he wrote: "We want leaders who can inspire us with a vision of a better life; who can infuse us with courage and loyalty to a faith that shines brightly and steadily through the confusion that surrounds us and who can make us aware of the great potentialities within us."

Finding Malaya bereft of such leaders, Raja proceeded to whip the existing bunch for being servile to the colonial powers and lacking in both direction and conviction. A political party must draw its strength from mass support and "move forward with the loyalty and fervour of the masses behind it".

Employing the hallmarks of tub-thumping oratory, with repetition and thundering parallel clauses, Raja boomed: "Only a political party of this nature can give its leaders the strength and confidence to undertake the strenuous and complicated task of social and political engineering. Only leaders of such a party can look upon the people without fear in their eyes. Only such leaders will cease to quake in their shoes at the prospect of suddenly being freed from their colonial shackles. Only leaders of such a party will not be intimidated by the hazards that independence must bring."

It was a rousing sermon paving the way for the coming of leaders so anointed. Although this column was penned months before the PAP came into being, no one reading Raja's columns could have doubted that this was a man who believed that it would be unconscionable to stay in the political sidelines.

He expressed only disdain for those who put personal gain or cloistered security before the larger social and national obligations. Unblinking, he stared down communal leaders who preyed on people's fears and prejudices and opportunistic leaders who "can be persuaded to purr like contented cats by the offer of a seat here and an honour there". These are not the kind of leaders this country wants, he declared in his columns.

Beating his breast in despair over the feeble political leaders of the day, he compared them with the "the more vigorous variety" which led the colonial movements in other parts of Asia and Africa. In his column "The Freedom of Whipsnade Zoo", published on 3 April 1953, he mocked Malayan politicians for waffling over target dates for independence.

He accused them of dreading the responsibilities of self-rule because their leadership was not based on the kind of popular national movement that thrust a Gandhi or a Sukarno to power. "National leaders elsewhere were borne on the wave of mass fervour and loyalty. They derived their strength from mass followings...There was no thought of 'sharing power' with the colonial regime. They did not regard themselves as apprentices to a colonial government but as political rivals."

The only party which could command an effective following so far was the MCP, he observed. Were the British to quit tomorrow, the vacuum would be filled by the Communist Party, he asserted. "If an independent Malaya is to emerge soon, then it is necessary to create in Malaya a new leadership based on a mass following and therefore unafraid of the responsibilities that go with the transfer of power. And such a leadership must be evolved outside the fold of government patronage and as a rival to it."

Having set this benchmark, Raja whittled down to size the political leaders whom he felt had fallen short. One of those he picked on was Dato Onn bin Jaafar, founder of UMNO who left the party to form the cross-communal Independence of Malaya Party (IMP) in 1951 after failing to persuade UMNO to accept Chinese members. While praising Dato Onn for his "very courageous" attempts to marshall the strengths of the various races to pursue Malayan nationalism, Raja could not hide his deep sense of outrage and betrayal at what he saw as Dato Onn's deviation from the nationalistic path and his radical change of tack regarding independence.

In an open letter to Dato Onn headlined "From National Leader to National Flop" dated 30 August 1953, Raja observed caustically: "Today, we see a new Onn leading a band of effete elements who believe neither in independence nor in democracy." Quoting Dato Onn's declaration that he did not believe in making a short cut for independence, Raja wrote: "Obviously, you feel that you have been chosen by Fate to lead this country to independence by the longest possible route". He was merciless as he pinned Dato Onn's lack of enthusiasm for Federal elections on his fears of the MCA-UMNO Alliance, which enjoyed stronger support than IMP.

Once provoked on his fundamental cause of independence, Raja rarely allowed his subjects a reprieve even after a brutal assault. In another column, he dragged out Dato Onn's IMP for another beating for having leaders "who shy away from independence like a Brahmin before the approaching shadow of an outcaste".[24]

Years later, as he developed a finer feel for the complex dynamics of Malayan politics, Raja came to revise his caustic view of Dato Onn to a more balanced one. In 1989, with the wisdom of hindsight, he said future historians would judge Dato Onn as a far-sighted Malayan statesman in seeking to forge the concept of a multiracial Malayan nationalism by forming a multiracial political party. While his vision was rejected by the people then, "only time will tell who took the wrong turning — Dato Onn or his critics", Raja commented.[25]

Like every rigorous columnist who subjects his writing to subsequent revision in the light of new facts, Raja confessed in 1989 that his criticism of Dato Onn in his early newspaper commentaries was based on his erroneous belief that the IMP was a "creation of British imperialism".[26] Such an admission is revealing: In the 1950s, his reflexive anti-colonialism overshadowed all else. So powerful was his desire to oust the British, so great his desire for independence, that he would pounce on any politician or political group deemed in its way. His judgement on the spot might not always be fair, but it was consistent.

The young and idealistic Raja was equally ruthless on political parties which twisted and turned with the popular tide. What was one to make of the Labour Party which, though committed to the ideals of socialism, drafted a political programme that might well have been licked into shape by a group of liberal-minded businessmen? And what was one to make of the Alliance which accepted two posts in the Federation's cabinet while officially committed to a programme of demanding elections to the Federal Council by 1954?

He observed that Alliance leader Tunku Abdul Rahman, who also headed UMNO, "must be a naive politician indeed if he believes that the appointment of two Alliance members to 'Cabinet' posts is evidence of a sudden realisation on the part of the Government that the Alliance is not a force to be trifled with...The Government has a shrewd and realistic appreciation of the strength of the Alliance — and even more important, of its weaknesses".

In thinly-veiled sarcasm, Raja expressed his inability to understand "by what obscure process of dialectics Tunku Abdul Rahman is able to endorse the cabinet appointments and yet stick to his boycott threat and election demand". He added: "All I can say is that even the most nimble and determined of men cannot hope to ride for long two horses going in opposite directions." Raja's irreverent handling of the Tunku, who was to later become the first prime minister of independent Malaya in 1957, was in kid gloves compared with the bloody blows he dealt the Singapore Labour Party (SLP).

In his column, headlined "For God's sake, call for the Undertaker!" published on 2 August 1953, he wrote an advance obituary of the SLP in ink spiked with poison. He condemned the SLP for failing to follow its socialist creed, either because they did not understand what socialism meant, or because they did not see the creation of a socialist society as its goal.

"The tragedy of the party was that, instead of becoming a rallying point for the reconstruction of a democratic and socialist society, it became a market place for gentlemen wanting to get elected to the Council." He detailed how those who were not nominated by the party had left the party in a huff, thus "demonstrating that loyalty to the party was conditional on the party being loyal to them".

"It has become a comic opera with clowns going through monstrous antics on the stage," he declared, adding, "it would be a great act of mercy and an even greater act of patriotism if the curtain could be rung down now." He lamented that the SLP was ridiculing the political ideals "wrongly associated" with its name by continuing its farce. "Pack and go home in peace to your homes. R.I.P."

Raja's damning verdict was met with a spirited response by C.R. Dasaratha Raj of the SLP in an open letter to Raja. In the letter, published on 12 August, Dasaratha, who was the Member for Rochore Canal in the Legislative Council, accused Raja of bias, of employing "depraved standards of journalism", and having his own dark agenda in pursuing his "vile and treacherous crusade" against the SLP.

Dasaratha noted that, within the brief space of three weeks, Raja had written two leaders and a column to deal with the so-called decline of the SLP. The SLP leader charged: "You were detailed by the sponsors of a new political party of which announcements appeared in the press recently to play the villain and prepare the stage for the contemplated party to make the debut." He portrayed Raja as an accomplice to a group of conspirators pledged to "create a vacuum in the political field by destroying the Labour Party and then later to fill the vacuum by another political party composed of themselves and their stooges".

Stung by Raja's criticism on SLP's socialist pallor, Dasaratha whipped around to tear apart Raja's credibility on this score: Raja himself was "only an impostor whose sympathy for socialism is in fact as low as the riches of your employer are high". "You are peddling socialism in the columns of The Standard with as much conviction as a teetotal bar man about the liquor he serves. Your socialist contact, apart from a couple of pseudo-socialists, is confined to the few mouldy books of bygone socialist authors reposing on your bookshelves. Socialism is your vocation, not your philosophy because you have not gone through the mill," he raged. With theatrical flourish, he challenged Raja to lead off a debate at the Labour Party Conference on 6 September.

True to form, Raja received this tirade with unmistakable relish. In his riposte on 16 August, Raja thanked Dasaratha for calling him "a conspirator, an accomplice, a villain, a peddler of socialism and a stooge".[27] However, being modest, he had to reject these compliments, he added. "Were I possessed of the qualities he attributes to me, I would have lost no time in joining the Labour Party for I know that talents such as these do not go unappreciated or unrewarded in the party."

Raja scoffed at the accusation that he was involved in a diabolical political plot, and laughed at Dasaratha for working himself into "a dreadful sweat with dreams of his own making". Yes, there had been reports of a proposed socialist party. "But as far as I can ascertain, this projected Socialist Party has never got beyond vague talk by certain individuals," Raja averred. Which was true at the time, as Marshall was sending out feelers to various people on forming a socialist party just then. Raja told Dasaratha that, in any case, "a great many people" who had been disillusioned with the SLP would be only too glad to support any vigorous party with more sincere socialist credentials.

On Dasaratha's challenge to a debate, Raja declined it, viewing it as a political tactic to get a larger number of people for the annual conference than would otherwise be the case. He asked Dasaratha to re-examine his own role in the SLP and concluded with this advice loaded in capital letters: LET THE DEAD BURY THE DEAD. The SLP, which was straggling along on its last legs, never fully recovered from this public onslaught. While still a registered party when elections were called in 1955, the SLP registered no pulse and was politically buried, as Raja had prophesied.

He was particularly merciless on those who manipulated racial sentiments for political gains, a theme he had expounded on as early as 1947. In one of his strongest columns on the subject, headlined "The Hoax of Communal Solidarity", he put forth his fundamental position: Communal politics was based on a lie. "When the communal leader suppresses the sob in his throat and intones 'as a Chinese, you can be assured I shall fight for the rights of the Chinese', or 'I am a hundred per cent Malay and you can rely on me to look after the welfare of my Malay brothers', or 'I am an Indian and I will protect the interests of Indians', our communal demagogue is indulging in a hoax."

Making out his case with depth and clarity, he argued that, in fact, the interests and rights of a community were as much trampled upon by members from the same community as others. He added: "It is often the case that a great many members of a community may in fact be safeguarded and extended by people of other communities, than from their own community."[28]

Raja confronted head-on the potentially sensitive issues, citing examples from everyday life. "It is often maintained that the Chinese as the economically dominant class, exploit and take advantage of the economic weakness of others." A moment's reflection would show how wrong this generalisation was. The Chinese were cheated by Chinese, too. Indians and Malays have been exploited as fiercely and mercilessly by members of their own community. "Those who attribute their poverty and misery to the machinations of other communities and those who fall for the claptrap that justice can only come from their own kind are the kind of political morons that keep our political carpet baggers in business. These are the kind of political infants who are eventually persuaded by the demagogues to cut the throats of innocent citizens in the pathetic belief that by doing so, they would be protecting their rights and interests. Or maybe they would get their throats cut, in the interests of a similar lie, by misguided cretins from the opposing camp."

Raja acknowledged that in Malaya, the fact that, to some extent, social and economic differences coincided with racial differences made it even easier for the communal leader to confuse the people. "However if people would only realise how effectively they practise non-communalism in their everyday life, at work, in their choice of friends, and business relations, they then would not fall easy victims to the propagandas of communalists."

In a statement that was to be his political credo all his life, he said: "I who belong to a minority group will not, under a democratic constitution, feel very alarmed if the Legislature should not have a single representative from my community. On the contrary, I may be very alarmed if certain individuals from my community should worm their way into the legislature." He stressed: "In choosing leaders, I would pay no regard to their racial origins. What I am concerned is with their ability, sincerity and their genuine desire to serve all people of this country."

This column stands out as a gem shining with moral clarity and is worth careful rereading today. He would continue to use his full command of all the tools of his craft and bring his clear-sighted and nuanced understanding on the complex issue of race to his writings and speeches on the matter.

Given his uncompromising stance on electing leaders based on merit and not race, he was incensed when five Indian Federal Legislative councillors resigned in protest over the refusal of the government to appoint an Indian as a cabinet member.

Raja denounced them in his column, "A Hundred Cabinets Are Not Worth It!" on 18 October 1953, asking: What relevance has the accident of birth to do with the suitability or otherwise of a Member to discharge his duties? "Whether we have an Indian, Chinese, Malay or Patagonian in charge of a department is immaterial, the criterion is whether he can perform his duties well — or serve those who appointed him well...It will accord more with a proper sense of honour if Malayans, whether they be white, black, brown or yellow or a nice shade of green, were to get into a Cabinet which is of their own making and which exists by virtue of the real prestige and influence its members enjoy among the people. There is no dignity in begging for favours."

He then trained his fire on two of the offending Indian councillors, P.P. Narayanan and Rajagopal, who came from the labour movement. Raja believed that one of the strongest forces working for a Malayan nation was the labour movement. "If this movement, through the deceit, irresponsibility and weakness of its members, should become prey to communalism, then the prospects of a Malayan nation will be bleak indeed. If the labour movement is incapable of resisting communalism, then let us and our children prepare for the great tragedy that awaits us," he said darkly.

He excoriated the labour movement for not taking a public stand on this. "The silence of many trade unionists and labourites on this issue is, I consider, moral cowardice." If the members in the trade unions and labour parties were "spineless and gutless", then — to prevent a split along communal lines in the labour movement — Narayanan and Rajagopal should either resign or publicly disavow the communalism to which they have subscribed, asserted Raja.

It was a courageous attack. For not only were the two Indian leaders prominent labour leaders, the trade unions at the time were also dominated by Indians who shared their sense of grievance. Raja was obviously not out to win a popularity contest among the Indians. From his harsh language, it is evident that he considered any political demands based on race a beast of an argument that must be wrestled into submission, wherever it was found.

9

Championing Democracy

While Raja might enjoy stirring a hornet's nest with his columns, he was in turn also vulnerable to stings on several fronts. One was the reproach of preaching a strong socialist ideology, supported only by strong words.

After all, he had been away in London for more than a decade, cut off from Malayan developments and the people's struggles during the tumultuous period, had swanned around Europe with people of a certain class and means, and had himself come from a wealthy, property-owning family. Furthermore, what did a Western-trained intellectual know about the needs of the poor Malayan masses, much less be driven to do something about it? This was the same bourgeoisie charge that would later be levelled against Lee and the inner core of the PAP who were returned students with good, professional jobs. Out on a limb on account of his columns, Raja was the first in line to publicly fend off these potentially debilitating arrows.

This was perhaps why, in his first column in his *I Write As I Please* weekly series on 8 February 1953, he sought to bury the notion that one needed to be poor to be a revolutionary and highlighted the role of the relatively well off in leading a revolt in history. The very poor would be too absorbed in their struggle for food and shelter to have the time to contemplate on their lot. "When a man's being is completely dominated by the thought of bread, he has no hankering for butter." It was those who "have sunk from relative prosperity into abject poverty who are the forces for discontent and revolt". They have known butter, and when they get bread to eat, they see themselves as the disinherited and the injured. "This dispossession of the relatively well-off and their transformation into the 'new poor' is also a symptom that the social order is breaking down." To these revolutionary elements might be added the assistance of the wealthy and the aristocrats, who have often provided the leadership for many revolutions.

To back his argument, he quoted examples from the French, Russian, as well as the Nazi and Fascist revolutions, in which frustrated intellectuals and disinherited urban workers formed the core of the insurrections. "It is only when the well-to-do and the not-so-poor have initiated the revolution that the abjectly poor, startled by the cataclysm of rebellion, come out of their lethargy." In other words, when applied to his own situation, the conclusion became clear: Raja had known butter. He was a frustrated intellectual and a disinherited urban worker. He was core revolutionary material.

He hastened to explain in another column[1] that to foment a revolution did not necessarily mean a violent overthrow of an existing regime. A revolution implied a radical change in the political, economic, social and cultural institutions of a society, brought about because the old order proved intolerable and brittle.

Boldly, he staked out his position that the Asian revolution, ushered in by a vanguard of Asian intellectuals, could not be halted. If the Western democratic powers did not understand the movement and keep up with it, its ideological enemy, Communism, would step up to become an ally of the Asian revolution, but use it for its own dangerous ends.

He noted that, in Asia, Communism still appealed to its intellectuals, although a growing number had veered from it because the Communist Revolution, directed from Russia, had become not a revolutionary vehicle, but a weapon of Soviet power politics. "Communism still attracts the Asian intellectuals to the extent that it is opposed to the Old Regimes in Asia but many intellectuals know too that Soviet Communism is destroying the Old Regimes to fill the vacuum with a more ruthless, but efficient, totalitarianism."

The aim of Asian intellectuals and the masses was to bring about the Asian revolution. For that, they needed allies. The communist powers and the democratic forces, however, were interested only in using the Asian movement for their own agenda — giving rise to a "curious and dangerous situation" where the Asian intellectuals were forced to enter into an "uneasy alliance" with the communists or with the democratic powers, he pointed out.

Hovering over Raja's premonition was the warning that the communists of Moscow and Peking would gain the upper hand, being in closer contact with the Asian revolution than the democratic forces of the West. Prophetic words, for there would come a time when a group of Malayan intellectuals would indeed enter into such an uneasy alliance with the communists — and the intellectuals involved would include Raja himself.

Another charge that Raja had to deal with was that he was anti-British, given his barrage of attacks against the colonial regime. While it might win him points with the left-wing Malayan crowd, especially the communists, it would hurt any credibility he might have with the British. This would weaken his effectiveness in pressing for Malayan self-rule.

Hence, when a reader wrote to accuse him of being anti-British, Raja took the opportunity to explain his own position in a calm, reasoned manner — he was anti-colonial, not anti-British. In fact, he considered himself a friend of Britain in that he believed in the political principles upheld by the British for themselves, such as democracy and freedom.

In his column, he argued that the anti-colonial movement was directed against the colonial structure, not against any specific race or community.[2] To be anti-British was to espouse another dangerous form of communal politics, only directed this time against the nationals of the colonial power. He stated plainly: "I abhor colonialism because it is constitutionally incapable of giving full reign to native democratic forces."

He pointed out that the colonial regime was acting as a brake on the democratic forces in Malaya, given the vested interests that had grown around colonial power. The genuine anti-colonialist "wants the democracy that the West enjoys. He wants the political self-respect which every Westerner believes is the birth-right of a people. He wants to control his national destiny unfettered by the interference of forces which do not enjoy the confidence of the people of the country".

His was a high-wire act as he tried to balance his anti-colonial agenda with his "British-friendly" one. It became even more daredevilish when he felt his way forward for an economic system that would work for Asia, given its largely feudalistic and backward condition. Although capitalism was on the ascendant, he was too deeply rooted in socialism and Marxism for a complete conversion.

He believed that capitalism could not answer Asia's needs, given the region's historical trajectory and existing conditions, and argued that "the swift and relatively inexpensive victories of Communism in Asia can in part, at least, be attributed to a shrewder Communist appreciation of economic trends in the East". Expanding on his thesis, he said: "Capitalism as we have known it is not equal to the task before it. Asia may take to Socialism. If we are short-sighted, it may take to Communism. Or Asia may develop its own brand of economic institutions. But whatever it is, capitalism will hardly answer Asia's needs," he proclaimed.[3]

He envisioned an Asian economic model which allowed Asian countries to direct and control their own industrial process independently — one consciously aimed at increasing the standard of living of their people, as opposed to one geared towards increasing the profits of foreign capitalists and the wealth of industrialised countries.[4] In a ringing phrase that could stand as the emblematic motto of his economic worldview, he wrote: "Social and economic justice must be made the primary aim of the economic system."[5]

Raja's approach to socialism was fundamentally ethical in nature. At its root was a critique of the evils of capitalism, in particular of poverty and inequality endemic in exploitation.

He challenged the dominant view that democracy in Asia must be built on strong capitalist foundations as practised in the West. He favoured state planning, with economic development coordinated and directed by the State, such as in Russia. Government intervention would ensure control over the industrialisation process and enable it to harness capital for the purpose of developing the country's productive capacity, as was happening in Japan, India, and China.

Raja was also not convinced that the economic individualism and free-wheeling capitalism of Europe would be able to meet Asia's needs or lead to its rapid development, particularly in colonial and semi-colonial countries. On the contrary, it would subject Asia, and in particular Malaya, to even greater economic distress as slaves to foreign capital, creating a "colonial economy" dependent on the vicissitudes of industrial countries and "where the extraction of tribute for investors would have prior claims over the welfare of the country receiving the capital".[6] While preferring to keep foreign capital imports as low as possible, he recognised the usefulness of foreign capital in developing backward countries, but with a caveat — that foreign capital dovetailed its interest with the economic needs and problems of the countries.[7]

He was particularly sceptical of capitalism's usefulness in solving the long-term economic problems of Malaya, given its heavy dependence on Britain for capital, and with its racial communities divided along economic lines. He questioned the thinking, propagated among some Malay nationalists, that the economic backwardness and woes of Malays could be solved by turning them into enthusiastic capitalists.

"The attempt to create a capitalist class must fail, because that can be done only by restraining and distorting the normal workings of Malayan capitalism," he asserted.[8] He argued against such a distortion on practical grounds — given that the Malay capitalists would be weak for "a long time to come", it would need legislation to protect and favour the emerging Malay capitalists by discriminating against the non-Malays, and indefinitely. Not only that, non-Malay small businessmen must be displaced to make room for a Malay middle class.

This would "provide a fruitful basis for communal ill-will", he warned. Even assuming that the country succeeds in creating a Malay capitalist class — what would happen when a slump hits, as it inevitably will? The intense competition for survival would force out the weaker ones, regardless of their race. "The elevation of a few Malays to the status of capitalists will do little to solve the economic problems of the Malays as a whole."

Hence, capitalism was not the answer. "There is a search for new economic forms, many of which are still in an experimental stage and many of which are non-capitalistic." He offered no ready solution. His was not an economic argument; it was a philosophical one.

He went for the spirit and heart of an economic system, rather than its muscles and sinews. No doubt, Raja sent shivers up the spine of Malaya's capitalist class and the British regime when he expressed admiration for Stalin's central system of planning for being geared consciously towards social, economic and political objectives of the nation. Raja's appreciation of Stalin's economic achievements arose principally from one revelation: "He has shown that we can control economic forces instead of these forces controlling us."[9]

Raja's views were provocative and unfashionable, to say the least, coming at an intense phase of the Cold War period, when the world was ordering its political and economic life along new and different lines from that of Soviet Russia — which the communists claimed was the forerunner of a political and economic system destined to replace what was termed "capitalist democracy".

Raja was clearly tired of hearing the West dictating pat economic prescriptions for Asia's troubles, without understanding its specific conditions and history. He was particularly outraged by the hypocrisy and double standards of Britain, doing one thing for its home country and something else for its colonies.

Raja reeled off figures to show that British companies operating overseas in the Empire made much more profits than those operating in Britain, on the backs of the low wages of workers in the colonies.[10] The British must satisfy the demand for higher wages and better living in conditions in Malaya by a pruning down its rate of profit, he wrote.

Raja also bristled at the ban slapped on Malaya's rubber to China — as part of the ban to export strategic material to China — when Britain itself was trading with the populous communist giant. He argued that trade with China would ease Malaya's problem of surplus rubber, which was driving its rubber prices down. "Though we may not like the political colour of Mao's regime, the colour of its money is acceptable currency."[11]

Raja's combative style and deep insight earned him a strong following among a band of readers. One of them, Harry Chan, then an assistant secretary in the colonial secretary's office, collected all his columns and kept them in a file. Entranced with the political philosophies they contained, he recalled: "I thought, this was a philosopher journalist."[12] To be sure, Raja also gained his share of detractors and intellectual enemies, whose numbers were also growing.

Like a photograph sharpening in developer solution, his columns over time revealed a complex portrait of Raja: He was a fervent democrat, an anti-colonialist, a socialist, a trade unionist, a humanist, a maverick writer. He was also an intellectual with a profound interest in psychology, sociology, and history; an ideas man who loved freedom, equality, social justice, and who abhorred racist ideologies of any kind and those who peddled them. But above all, he was a bold visionary.

It could be said that the bravest visionary statement he made was this line published in his column on 6 December 1953:[13] "In 10 years' time, granting that we have wise and capable leaders to guide us, the unification of the two territories should come about. And certainly, in 25 years, a United Malaya should be a going concern." He staked out this prediction about a year before the launch of the PAP, at a time when the existing leaders and peoples in both territories were allergic to the idea of even joining hands, much less their destinies. But Raja saw the proposition in terms of a "common destiny" with "the two territories kept apart solely through political expediency". However fantastical it might have sounded in 1953, his prophesy on the merger of the Federation and Singapore did come to pass 10 years later — 1963 — exactly the year he predicted.

He could not foresee the abysmal failure of that union and their separation just two years later. What he did foretell with tortured clarity was the economic and political rivalry which would intensify should both parts exist separately.

He argued that the merger question be tackled quickly and not postponed. As he put it: "Singapore is the commercial heart and the Federation the hinterland which produces the goods which Singapore distributes. As a result of this division, there has been a tendency in the Federation to circumvent Singapore and do its own distribution. If we are not careful, Singapore and the Federation may consider themselves as economic rivals instead of as partners."

And if separation persisted, the two territories would develop so many clashes of economic and political interests that fusion would be a very difficult task indeed, he added. Chiding the political leaders on both sides for their "childish sabre-rattling", he warned that their parochial patriotism was "something which we can afford to laugh off now, but in a few years, it might assume the proportions of a tragedy".[13] To his sorrow, this prognosis turned out right: when the PAP took over in 1959 and pushed for merger, the rivalry had reached an acute level, and the stage for tragedy had indeed been set.

Given his belief in the inevitability of merger, he urged Malaya's political leaders and thinkers to cease cultivating "the infantile patriotism of the parish pump" and to teach their people to "acquire a Pan-Malayan outlook and become aware of their common destiny". He did not believe that Singapore could be free from its colonial status if it remained cut off from the Federation, and rapped the politicians of the day for lacking the imagination to foresee the course of political developments which would lead to a United Malaya.

Raja himself certainly showed no lack of imagination, and indeed, perhaps occasionally suffered from a surfeit of it. His lively imagination was a strength when people's minds needed to be opened and their sights lifted to a better world, but could be a political liability if unable to adjust nimbly to the realities of Malayan politics.

Another of his weaknesses was his tendency to labour his point. Raja's preoccupation with democracy and mass movements, in particular, became almost obsessive, and took on epic proportions. He brought readers on long, systematic, sometimes ponderous, odysseys to examine available models of economic and political systems — capitalist, socialist, totalitarian, oligarchic, democratic — and forced them to traverse oceans of words to arrive at a possible destination.

His ruminations on some themes, such as on the psychology of the masses, and the rise and fall of civilisations, were so dense that, in a thoughtful effort to make them more digestible, he split them into two to five parts, with one published each week. As part of his self-appointed role as an educator, Raja would often strive to place the developments in Malaya in the larger context of 19th century and 20th century development of world history.

His writing was also often interspersed with quotations and passages from the sophisticated array of his reading: Marx, E.H. Carr, Kipling, Bernard Shaw, Byron, Mencius, Nehru, Lord Acton, Joseph Chamberlain, Adam Smith, Malthus, Bentham, Disraeli, Bismarck, and Gladstone, just to name a few.

He was able to do this because, over the years of diligent reading, he had quarried the thoughts and ideas he wanted to remember. When he came across a quote or a passage that struck him, he would write it down on scraps of paper at hand, or in his notebook. When he had the time later, he would reread all that he had gathered, reflect on them, and memorise key ideas. Ideas and quotations from famous thinkers were thus often at his beck and call.

Through his essays, his talents began to define themselves: A mastery of historical knowledge, a gift for language, and a finely-honed ability to pursue an argument to its logical end. Of all the books he expounded on, the one which received the most attention was James Burnham's *Managerial Revolution*. He devoted a three-part series to its ideas as part of his exposition on democracy. Raja regarded Burnham as one of the most penetrating critics of democracy of the day, and believed that the best way to understand democracy was to study the various critics of democracy who, "by pointing out the many imperfections in democracy, help us to make democracy stronger".[14]

Burnham's book, which inspired George Orwell's *1984* and *Animal Farm*, had made a considerable stir in Britain when it was published in 1940 and was much discussed in Raja's intellectual circles when he was in London. One of the contentious arguments in Burham's book was that the left/right ideology would be replaced by a new ruling class of technocrats and social scientists. Intrigued by his ideas, Raja also read two other books by the author, *The Machiavellians: Defenders Of Freedom*, and *Suicide of the West: an Essay on the Meaning and Destiny of Liberalism*. Raja also collected Orwell's books, to be exact nine.

For Raja, intellectual engagement was a moral necessity. Barely a month after dissecting the various democratic theories, on 13 December, Raja launched another five-part series which started with a passage on the power of crowds from French pioneer of social psychology Gustave Le Bon's *The Crowd*, with its ensuing instalments sprinkled with views from sociologist Karl Mannheim's *Man and*

Society in an Age of Destruction, psychologist Robert Lindner's *Prescription for Rebellion*, E.H. Carr's *The New Society*, humanist Lewis Mumford's *The Conduct of Life* to David Spitz's *Patterns of Anti-Democratic Thought*. In this series, he raised ideological questions about the nature of mass democracy and the structure of power.

How does the mob mind work in mass society? What kind of political and economic order would most efficiently satisfy the demands of the masses? What are the problems faced by democracy in a mass society? Are the masses competent enough to choose the best leaders? Will a democracy result in average men running the country, as Malaya's conservative forces feared? Was Malaya ready for democracy? These were the questions which fascinated and seized him. In answering them, he established himself as a walking encyclopaedia on the theories of democracy and became one of the country's strongest advocates for democratic self-rule in Malaya.

In answering them, he also revealed a touching faith in democracy, despite its imperfections, and his hopeful view of the masses, despite their human fallibility. "The democrat is impressed by the fact that the mass of mankind is becoming more intelligent, more capable and more civilised in his behaviour, and that it will continue to do so. To this extent, democracy will become less incompetent. The democrat also believes that a democratic society will considerably assist in making the average man more competent."

Aware that this would open him to the charge of being idealistic, he asserted, in another column[15] that it was, in fact, "a more realistic way of life because it did not rest on the myth of human infallibility". Decades later with personal experience running a democratic system as a government leader, he would, however, not be so convinced. Behind the veil of democracy, he would glimpse a deeper reality where the political arena could be a dangerous place of conflicting passions fuelled by race and religion, or a blind alley of ignorant and irrational debate.

—❧—

Raja's radical socialist views, which took several hair-raising turns in his columns with talk of revolutions, the merits of Stalin's planned economy and such, caused much hand-wringing at the *Standard*. Unsurprisingly, his writings had antagonised many of the newspaper advertisers, which were British companies. Some readers were also up in arms. This was not something that the Aws could ignore.

While the *Standard* had a relatively high circulation of 35,000 in 1954, the Aws feared that this too might be jeopardised. They counselled Raja to tone down his columns. Their warnings fell on deaf ears. He was too caught up in the political fervour of his time, too driven by his overpowering sense of mission. He would write as he pleased.

Unable to control Raja's pen, his bosses soon suggested an end to his column series. The curtain was to come down on 31 January 1954. By then, Raja was also weary with the effort of sustaining a weekly column, tired of the warnings to watch his words, and this showed in his increasingly lugubrious writing and his repetitive themes. His mood was sullen and heavy when he ended his column with a three-part series spun around the obscure tale of a Russian revolutionary of the 1850s — Sergei Nechayev, who believed that the goal of political action was the total destruction of the world.

The series headlined, *The Nechayev Monster*, which started on 17 January 1954, sought to peer into the nature of the nihilist mind through the story of Nechayev, whose life inspired Dostoevsky's *The Possessed*. Nechayev was a vicious, delusional young man who resorted to theft, murder, blackmail, and fraud to build up an image of himself as a courageous revolutionary figure, and to support his aim of seeking the revolution of universal destruction. Power hungry and a systematic liar, he was able to win the blind obedience of many to his cause.

Together with Bakunin, a failed revolutionary, Nechayev penned the Revolutionary Catechism, the blueprint of revolutionary nihilism and modern terrorism. In later years, the Catechism provided the "weapon and the armour" for Lenin's Russian revolution, and for Hitler's campaign of terror. Nechayev was eventually caught, suffered torture with fortitude, and died in prison in 1882 at the age of 35 as a "lonely, fanatical, and eccentric political criminal". Raja believed that Nechayev was driven to his actions by circumstances of his life — the grinding poverty, disease and corruption in Russia.

The moral of the story? It crawled out from the deep shadows in his final piece on 31 January 1954. With the gloom of a doomsday prophet, Raja warned: "Perhaps, it is not only in Russia and Germany that Nechayevism rears its head. Perhaps, the times we are living in are conducive to nihilism. A great many people find living intolerable because our way of life offers them no hope. They are baffled by the frustrations of our society. There wells in their breasts an anger and a hatred which could explode into a revolution of destruction."

With nations possessing weapons of destruction and propaganda techniques which can condition people to hate and fear one another, Nechayev's vision of universal destruction "may not altogether be the dream of a fanatic". It was a forbidding conclusion.

Beneath this bleak ending, Raja tagged on a short, but telling, note to announce that his column had come to a "timely end" after a year. "After a year, a writer soon exhausts his ideas and even his ability to dress up old ideas in new garb," he confessed. "He must be given time to brood over ideas and suggestions by intellects far greater than his, so that he may be able to present them with the assured air of one who has discovered these truths for himself," he concluded.

Raja's decision to end his column with a portrait of the Russian revolutionary is underscored by heavy irony. He shared the dilemmas of the angry social visionary and faced not dissimilar intellectual tensions. For those weary of the alienating grip of colonialism, there was something noble about mounting a revolution.

While Raja did not believe in political violence, he could understand the impulses behind it. And yet, in spite of his apparent outrage, the overall picture of Raja at that time was that of a rebel with a cause, but still unclear as to how to translate that passion into a practical strategy of social and political transformation. His mounting frustration found a vent in the discussions at Lee's basement dining room, and found an answer when the core group came to grips with the question: Should they form a political party?

The mood of the core group — Lee Kuan Yew, Goh Keng Swee, Toh Chin Chye, Kenny Byrne and Raja — was intense and sober as they huddled around Lee's dining table to consider the question. Dominating their concern was the quality of the political parties which would contest the elections under the new constitution. As Raja recalled later, "our comments were generally all negative. We didn't have a high regard for any of the parties which were going to contest in the election".

As he would put the options in more graphic terms later: "There were the Progressive Party and their feeble leaders. There were the clowns of the Labour Party of Singapore."[16] It became clear that the choice before the people — and also them — would be between these parties, which he dubbed as "opportunistic elements", and a militant underground Communist Party. It was a dreadful thought.

Their discussions then shifted to the consequences for the country should these people take over. The scenarios did not bear contemplating. "From there, then the idea began to germinate that we should form a political party, to enter politics ourselves," Raja related. Lee argued that it was no use just talking.[17] They should do something about it and participate in the elections.

This was greeted with an avalanche of questions by those around the table: Was the time opportune to start a new left-wing party? What would be the consequences for socialism if the new party went the way of the other left-wing socialist parties, such as the MDU? The odds seemed stacked against it. Except for the MCP, all the pre-Emergency left-wing groups, such as PUTERA-AMCJA, the MDU, and MNP had either been "forcibly liquidated" by the British, or been "castrated" under Emergency laws, as Raja put it later.

They then became absorbed in the question of whether they should take part in the elections, or stay out. Samad and Nair, who joined the discussions after their release from detention, were for boycotting the elections in protest of the Rendel Constitution. They saw the constitution as undemocratic and pro-colonial.

Raja set out a different view, just as he had when MDU decided to boycott the 1948 elections to register its protest. He forcefully reminded the group of the political suicide committed by the MDU by its inaction. He believed that a party committed to constitutional methods of change would be signing its own death warrant if it stood outside the constitutional arena and merely protested with words.

It was a robust argument that was also propounded by Lee, Goh, and Byrne. They further made the point that, if a genuine left-wing party was not launched before the Rendel Constitution came into effect in 1955, the British would have an open field to consolidate its power through the local right-wing, pro-colonial groups.

Against this backdrop of gloomy foreboding, the group decided to take the plunge and form a new political party, the People's Action Party. In October 1954, they announced the inauguration of the PAP. The date was set for its official launch — 21 November.

The other political parties received this news with equal foreboding. In Marshall's diary entry on 24 October 1954, he noted that the new "socialist-inclined" PAP were formed with Lee and Raja, and added: "I believe they may be Communist-orientated."[18]

The Special Branch kept a close eye on Raja's activities. In early 1954, he became more deeply involved in the socialist clique, including the Socialist Club of the University of Malaya, formed in 1953. Lee, Raja, together with the few in their core political group, nurtured close ties with the club which was to prove useful in mobilising students to their socialist and anti-colonial cause.

Toh, who worked as a physiology tutor in the university after his return from London in 1953, began to visit Raja's house frequently to borrow books on politics from his vast library. "I borrowed them to study. That was an important source of material for me," Toh revealed. "I knew nothing about the theoretical basis of politics, except knowing that Marx existed but I never studied Marx," he confessed.[19]

By September 1954, the Special Branch, in a general comment on the political situation, stated that Lee was the acknowledged leader of the "intelligentsia group", which included Raja, the University Socialist Club, Byrne, Goh, and Toh.[20] Alex Josey recalled that these opinionated men — Lee, Raja, Toh, Goh, Byrne — would gather regularly in different houses to talk politics over drinks. Josey, who sometimes joined them, said: "Lee's charisma was such that he simply outshone everybody else." Amidst the din of voices and tinkling glasses, Lee would be the one to end these parties with a firm "Go on, break it up."[21]

Meanwhile, Raja was also active forging links with the radical left in the region. In February 1954, he visited Indonesia with four other journalists at the invitation of Persari, a group of Indonesian film producers. While in Jakarta, he met with Malay radical nationalist Ibrahim Yaacob, who was arrested for his nationalist activities by the British under the charge of subversion shortly before the fall of Singapore to Japan. Yaacob at one time was the leader of the first politically radical organisation among Peninsular or Singapore Malays, invoking the idea of "Greater Indonesia" and "Greater Malaydom".

In mid-1954, Raja also made contact with the three-man mission of the Asian Socialist Conference (ASC)[22] from Rangoon during its visit to Singapore. The ASC, driven by the socialist parties in India, Burma and Indonesia, emerged in 1953 as an effort to link up socialist political parties in Asia to like-minded parties in Europe, Middle East and Africa, and to influence the shape of international relations. It was seen as the Eastern equivalent of the Socialist International. Raja's interest in these socialist activities outside Singapore was duly noted by the Special Branch.

In Singapore, he was champing at the bit to hit out at the colonial authorities with a headline-grabbing issue. On 28 May 1954, he was presented with one when eight students from the Socialist Club of the University of Malaya were arrested and charged with sedition. They had published an article deemed seditious in *Fajar*, an undergraduate magazine. They approached Lee and Raja for help.

The decision was made to engage the British Queen's Counsel D.N. Pritt, notorious for championing left-wing causes. Raja knew Pritt well from his Left Book Club days in London, as Pritt had also acted for the club to great acclaim. Lee was also familiar with Pritt, having visited him in London to ask him to sign papers sponsoring his call to the Bar in 1950.

Unlike Lee, who shrewdly used Toh's name and address in his correspondence with Pritt to avoid detection by the Special Branch, Raja showed no such qualms. Indeed, Raja played such a brazenly prominent role in this affair that the Special Branch, which evidently intercepted Raja's mail, believed it was his idea to engage Pritt and that he was also "the brain" behind the public appeal fund for the *Fajar* case. As for making the arrangements to bring Pritt out from the United Kingdom, the intelligence had Raja and Toh as being responsible.[23]

During this highly sensitive period, despite the axe hovering over *Fajar*, Raja wrote a sharp article for the controversial publication to rip into the notion that the imperial conquest of Malaya was a peaceful process, as purveyed by school textbooks and a correspondent in a newspaper at the time. Not so, he said. Citing well-researched examples from Penang, Malacca, and Perak, he argued that the occupation of Malaya was "not unaccompanied by the double-dealings, breaches of faith and violence that normally goes with building of empires".[24]

Raja's offensive was provoked by his fear that any softening of the public mood towards imperialism, based on a romantic reading of the colonial past, would weaken their will to fight for independence. He was determined to keep anti-colonial fervour at a high pitch.

It was in such a fearless mood that Raja, together with Lee and hordes of students, greeted Pritt at the airport on 11 August 1954. While he was in Singapore, Pritt visited Raja in his Chancery Lane home several times, demonstrating their cosy relationship which caught the eye of the Special Branch yet again.

During the hearing, Pritt proved why he was a top-notch lawyer. After three days, the students were acquitted, to the cheers of their supporters. Raja made sure the episode, which damaged the government's reputation and built up Lee's, received high-profile coverage in the *Standard*.

By this time, Raja had become *persona non grata* with the colonial government. His buccaneering anti-colonial campaign was also putting his career in the *Standard* at risk. As advertisers continued to pull out, the newspaper's management took an increasingly dim view of Raja's editorial stance. Once the favourite son of the *Standard*, he was now regarded as a renegade.

Anxious to placate the colonial officials and woo the advertisers back, the Aws issued Raja an ultimatum: Change his socialist line or quit. At this juncture, Raja came to a momentous decision: He would quit. He would stand by his convictions. So it was that on 1 August 1954, the *Singapore Standard* announced the "resignation" of Raja as associate editor.

His decision rippled through the newsroom. In protest of the management's treatment of their favourite editor, two of his senior reporters K.S. Vass and P.S. Markandan left with him. Some of his rivals in the paper, long envious of his stellar rise, were no doubt pleased at his fall from grace. They would continue to show a certain mean-spiritedness towards him in their columns when he co-founded a political party and stood for his first elections later.

As for the British authorities, his departure from the newspaper was a welcome reprieve. The Special Branch noted in its report: "It has been known for some time past that Rajaratnam had lost ground and was in disfavour with the management of the Standard organisation because his critical leading articles had been antagonizing advertisers resulting in a heavy financial loss. His departure may bring about a favourable change in the persistent anti-Government policy pursued by this paper."[25]

Raja was deeply affected by his dismissal, but refused to allow this humiliation to lacerate his spirit. He assured Piroska that he would find ways to make a living. They had gone through even greater uncertainty during the war years in London. Personal hardship was not something he feared. His greatest fear, at that point, was his ability to continue to use his pen to stab at the injustices of the colonial system. He would press on. Little did he know that losing his job was only the first of many personal sacrifices that he would be called upon to make for his ideals.

As Raja served out his three-month notice at the *Standard*, he channelled his energies into the preparations to launch the PAP in November. He brought a rare collection of qualities to the seminal discussions at Lee's basement dining room. The first was a voracious appetite for baiting the colonial establishment. He had fire in his belly — and ideas to match — on how to force the issue of national freedom in Malaya.

His years of socialising with the radical left-wing and nationalist crowd in Britain had turned him into an expert on the nationalist struggles for independence at home and in other parts of the world, such as India and Ceylon. Lee recalled Raja's input: "He would say: 'Look, this was the way they did it; these were the issues they raised; this was how they got their independence.'"[26] His observations provided useful reference points for their Malayan campaign.

The core leaders also profited from his deep understanding of the various political ideologies, in particular, socialism. He brought intellectual clarity and philosophical depth into their deliberations. Samad recalled that, during the discussions, Raja was constantly brimming with ideas, in contrast to Lee, who was often the most intense and serious in the room.[27]

Another quality was his mastery of ringing slogans and visionary prose to stir the public imagination. It was a skill that was beyond most of the technocratic-minded men in the English-speaking core group — other than Lee — and that was most needed at that embryonic stage of national political awakening.

Besides his talent for ideas and words, the well-known journalist also brought with him a vast network of contacts and friends who could help further the cause of the fledgling PAP group. They ranged from nationalists abroad, foreign correspondents based in Singapore, political leaders of various hues in Malaya, to the local intelligentsia and, perhaps most importantly, his readers. Over the years through his provocative columns, he had become something of a celebrity and won himself a loyal following. His reputation as a fearless anti-colonial fighter was a political asset.

Among those in the group, Lee valued Raja most as an "ideas man". He was however, as Lee put it, "not an organisations man". The nuts-and-bolts mechanics of organising a party was mostly left to Lee, Goh, and Toh. The members of the team, with their diverse temperaments, largely complemented one another. But they shared one major drawback: They were English-educated.

To present a serious broad-based political party, they knew that they needed to have the support of the Chinese-educated masses. They formed the largest group in Singapore. They were also the most hostile towards the colonial authorities. They had long borne the brunt of the deteriorating economic and social conditions in the colony — the squalid housing, the paucity of jobs, the poor wages.[28] They were burning with anger and resentment at the colonial government's neglect of Chinese education and culture, and its rampant discrimination. Over the years, the MCP had fed on their fury and spread its tentacles to gain control over the Chinese-educated, especially through their schools.

The hostile Chinese-educated world was light years away from that of the largely middle-class and Western-educated PAP core group. In a twist of events, their two worlds crossed when the Chinese-educated students, who had engineered riots in revolt against national service, asked Lee and Pritt to defend them in court after their arrest. The Chinese middle school students were struck by Lee's success in the *Fajar* case.

In turn, they impressed Lee with their determination and organisational skills — they seemed able to rally a swarm of Chinese students at the snap of their fingers. Through them, Lee met two of their leaders — Lim Chin Siong, 21, and Fong Swee Suan, 23.

Both were trade unionists with strong links to the Chinese working class and the Middle Road unions. They had just registered an omnibus union, the Singapore Factory and Shop Workers' Union, which had its headquarters in Middle Road. When formed on 4 April 1954, the union had 200 members. Within 10 months, with Chin Siong as the union's secretary-general, the number shot to 30,000 members, with 30 left-wing trade unions in tow. Fong, a bus conductor, became the general secretary of the powerful Singapore Bus Workers' Union. By 1955, the two men would become the most powerful union leaders in Singapore.

Finding them serious-minded and earnest, Lee invited Chin Siong and Fong into the PAP fold. Both appeared soft-spoken and self-effacing in person. But as the English-educated leaders would find out, when put on stage, in front of a Chinese-educated crowd, Chin Siong and Fong would transform dramatically into charismatic orators full of flaming rhetoric, with the power to whip the crowd into red-hot rage.

Raja appreciated the strategic value of teaming up with the Chinese-educated unionists. In his calculations, the alliance with them was necessary for the PAP if it were to become a nationalist party with mass appeal. As noted earlier, even before he met Lee and discussed forming the PAP, Raja had long argued in his columns that a political party must have mass support to give it the courage and conviction to take on the colonial system and the hazards of independence.

On a more personal level, Raja also felt greater sympathy with the Chinese-educated, who were the underdogs, than the "opportunists", as he was wont to call them, in the Progressive Party or the Labour Party. "We were not going to fight them (the pro-communists) because the fight was against the British, the Progressive Party, and so on," he explained later. "So long as there was a constitutional struggle, we knew that they had considerable influence in the Chinese-speaking world — the cultural organisations, trade unions and even with the Chinese bourgeoisie."

When Fong and Chin Siong met Raja, they had a good impression of him. Fong recalled years later: "There were very few English-educated, less so from the newspapers, when the PAP was being formed. He was very good at theories and ideologies during our discussions and prepared the PAP's manifesto and memorandums."[29]

It was during the discussions over the party's first manifesto that Raja came to have a sense of the Chinese-educated leaders. Tasked by Lee to draft it, Raja had crammed it with many of the polemical ideas he had earlier championed in his *I Write As I Please* columns.

A fundamental call was for the creation of an independent democratic state which recognises the unity of Singapore and the Federation with equal citizenship, regardless of race, religion, or language. Lee had no trouble with his ideas, as "we were on the same wavelength".[30]

But while the party's aims were clear-cut — to end colonialism and to work towards a democratic socialist society — there were disagreements with the Chinese-educated leaders on the means to achieve them.

In particular, Chin Siong and Fong were sceptical of the section endorsing the use of constitutional means for achieving its ends. Raja recounted later: "They were more interested in the parts of the party manifesto which did not preclude Communist involvement." Separately, Fong recalled later that they also had very different views and interpretations of "socialism".[31] Another term they quibbled about was "democracy". When Raja confessed later that "the drawing up of the manifesto for the new party was by no means an easy task",[32] it was surely an understatement.

Whatever their differences at that point, however, they were brushed aside as they pursued their common cause of ending colonial rule. As Raja put it, it was this "willing subordination of all other problems to the immediate task of combating colonialism which helped to conceal the reservations that some individuals had about the ultimate aims and objectives of the party".[33] There would come a time when these differences would widen to an unbridgeable chasm, and eventually split the PAP into two rival factions, one led by Lee, and the other by Chin Siong.

The draft of the manifesto then went through the meticulous hands of Lee. "It was a question of style, that's all. Raja was more colourful in his language," said Lee.[34] The final version, which filled 10 sheets of foolscap paper, bore the hallmarks of both minds — analytical and factual, passionate and ideological, acerbic and vigorous.

It was issued on 27 October 1954, three weeks before the inaugural meeting on 21 November. It was couched in broad terms to give a tolerably clear notion of what the PAP stood for, without being too explicit on the details.

While avoiding the contentious word "socialism", the manifesto made its appeal to workers by pledging to reduce inequalities of wealth, and ensure that workers get the full fruits of their industry and enterprise. The PAP's basic platform was to secure national freedom of Malaya, including Singapore.

Right from the start, Raja was filled with fervour for the union of Malaya and Singapore, based on equal citizenship. He was equally passionate about the PAP's role to help achieve this union as a pan-Malayan party. As Raja made clear in the manifesto, the party would, in its approach, disregard the constitutional division of Singapore and Malaya, and be "as actively interested in the problems of our fellow Malayans in the Federation as we are in those of Singapore".

For Raja, this pan-Malayan approach towards the union of both countries was only logical and natural. His pursuit of it would see him embark on a new phase of his life from which he would find hard to pull back.

10

Publishing and Politics

Eager to usher in a new day for Malayan politics, Raja became a zealous evangelist for the radical left-wing party. As part of his mission, he travelled to Kuala Lumpur to spread news of the party to his friends and contacts in the Malayan capital.

Yap Chin Kwee, then a journalist in the Kuala Lumpur-based newspaper *The Straits Times*, recalled Raja's efforts before the PAP was formed: "Raja was trying to impress on us the path to self-government and that we could kick the British out. He talked about a new anti-colonial movement in Singapore fighting for independence, about how the winds of change were coming."[1]

Raja hit a sensitive nerve in Yap, who would become Tunku's political secretary from 1961 to 1970. Being close to the Malay political elite, Yap was suspicious of the PAP's intentions and their implications for the entrenched parties in Malaya. Yap concluded: "He was trying to get support for the coming of Lee Kuan Yew and Goh Keng Swee and to establish a beachhead for the PAP in the Federation." He would monitor closely Raja's initiatives in Kuala Lumpur over the years. Yap observed disapprovingly: "Before and after PAP was formed, Raja did the groundwork for the PAP in the Federation."

To Raja, however, there was nothing sinister about his message; he was being consistent. He genuinely believed in the union of both territories and in the constructive role that the PAP could play to make this happen, together with the established political parties in the Federation which sought independence for Malaya.

Yap thought Raja lacked a sensitive feel for Malayan politics. "First, he was an Indian," said Yap, "and, second, he didn't understand the Malays". Yap's subsequent remarks revealed another, more visceral, reason for his antipathy. He said: "Raja wanted to talk down to us. You think we want to take it? The Malays did not like this sort of attitude."[2]

The attitude that Yap was referring to was Raja's intellectual and debating style which revelled in robust argument. His erudite allusions and polysyllabic flourishes might have earned him plaudits as a newspaper columnist, but, among some circles in KL, his too clever-by-half attitude smacked of condescension. To feed their political animus further, what Raja was preaching — socialism and equality — was considered hostile to their entrenched interests.

Yap's strong reaction to Raja at this early stage of the PAP's development would give a foretaste of the vicious attacks that Raja had to endure about a decade later for his ideas of a Malaysian Malaysia, as opposed to a Malay Malaysia, based on Malay political dominance. Yap, who later contested the 1964 elections under the Alliance banner, would be among the hardliners in Kuala Lumpur who would press the Tunku to take a tough stand against the PAP during the merger years of 1963 to 1965.

Raja's message found a warmer reception with the foreign correspondents and intellectuals in Singapore. This was mainly because of his personal standing with them. Since his return from London, he had conjured the stimulating environment he had so enjoyed in Britain by gathering an assortment of sparkling personalities at his house in Chancery Lane.

In these early days, his guests included Louis Heren of *The Times* of London who was based in Singapore as its Southeast Asian correspondent in 1950; Anthony Schooling,[3] who worked for *Radio Malaya* (later renamed *Radio Singapore*), Alex Josey, and then later, Dennis Bloodworth from the *Observer*. The foreign correspondents were a crusty and hardbitten lot, having covered war-torn countries such as Korea and Vietnam.

In Singapore, Raja was introduced to them as a prominent Malayan journalist. They drew on his local knowledge and news network, and were gratified by his unassuming generosity and kindness towards them.

When Josey arrived in Singapore in 1948, it was at the behest of the British to wage psychological warfare against the communists. He had worked in a similar capacity in Cairo. He joined *Radio Malaya* in February 1949, but by 1950, the British had ended his contract. They parted ways over the anti-colonial and socialist line which Josey was increasingly taking in his writings and broadcasts.

Raja was no doubt a major influence on Josey's shifting sympathies in Malaya. After losing his British contract, Josey fell back on journalism. Raja arranged for him to write for the *Standard*, where they worked closely together on features that championed the causes of socialism, the labour movement and Malayanisation.

Bloodworth, who came onto the scene in 1956, was another intrepid journalist who had in his career traipsed from one danger zone to another. After being based in Paris, he was sent to Saigon to cover the Indo-China war, then to Hong Kong to report on the riots, and from there, on to Singapore. The island was his base for the next 25 years.

Shortly after Bloodworth arrived, he met up with Raja over a beer in November 1956. Bloodworth's first impression of him was of a "shy, reticent man". At the time, Raja contributed to the *Observer*'s syndication service — the *Observer* Foreign Service — as a "stringer, local expert and contacts man".[4] "He introduced me to everyone I should know, including the founding members of the PAP, and also gave me all the assistance he could," Bloodworth recalled.[5]

The social gatherings at Raja's house were mostly informal. Raja would greet guests in a loose-fitting Hawaii shirt, his feet sheathed in sandals. He would offer them a beer. Not one for small talk, he would start serious conversation at once. The condition of the world, the state of the socialist movement, the political problems of the day, the latest book read, were all fodder for conversation. He was a fount of knowledge on almost every subject under the sun. One subject he rarely dwelt on, however, was himself, leading even bosom friends to find him an intensely private and unrevealing man in some ways.

Sometimes, between sips of beer, his eyes would rest on the garden alight with flowers, especially dendrobium orchids. They were nurtured to full bloom by Piroska. Her flowers were among his choice subjects for photography. Another favourite was Piroska herself. An adoring husband, he would snap many photos of her around the house and garden.

The house, a single-storey, three-room bungalow, would remain his only home for the rest of his days. At heart, Raja was a home-loving man who liked the quiet life when he could enjoy it with his wife and a book.

His house was decorated after his own heart, with walls dotted with photographs and lined with bookshelves. The rows of books ranged from historical treatises and political ideologies to science fiction. His collection also showed a particular taste for wicked humour and comic verse. His favourite humour writer was James Thurber. Over his lifetime, Raja would collect nine of Thurber's books, more than say, those on or by Marx (eight) and Plato (also eight). Raja also applied himself to learning how to tell jokes well, reading up various books on the art and techniques of popular comedy. He was not above risqué humour.

His treasury of books was put together from his regular forays into the second-hand bookshops in London, particularly at Charing Cross Road. Some were more recent hauls from one of his favourite haunts in Singapore — the second-hand bookshops in Bras Basah Road. At his convivial dinners with friends, he was an entertaining host as he updated them on his latest find and regaled them with a witty tale or two.

It was during one such dinner at his home that Raja introduced the foreign correspondents to the other PAP leaders, such as Lee,

Goh, Toh, and Byrne. This introduction was another link in the sequence of events that brought the PAP core group closer to their goal of establishing themselves as serious and credible leaders. In the relaxed atmosphere of Raja's house, the foreign journalists were able to get a measure of the new PAP and its leaders. In turn, the PAP men could impress on them their creed and win their trust, if not their sympathy, for their struggle.

Lee attached crucial importance to these social gatherings with the foreign correspondents at Raja's house. He related later: "We were very keen to meet them, so that they would know we were not communists, because we were embarking on a venture which could easily lead to our detention and arrest without trial, like John Eber and company."[6]

As they exchanged views over various subjects — Vietnam, Russia, Korea, China, India, and of course, Malaya — the foreign correspondents concluded this PAP group could be many things — anti-colonial, nationalists, left-wing Fabian types — but they were not communists. This assessment, which was to colour their reports subsequently, would prove critical to the credibility of the PAP and its survival, especially when its struggle hung in the balance.

Bloodworth recalled how, during these discussions, Lee, Raja, and his "moderate" group portrayed themselves as social democrats who wanted to build a socialist society, while making it clear from the outset that they depended on capitalists for economic development. Said Bloodworth: "I admired the quality of the leadership. I thought they held the future in their hands, and if I have to express the opinion, I wanted to see them win."[7]

At these gatherings, Piroska would supervise the arrangements and was very much the manager of the household. She called everyone to dinner, providing tasty Hungarian food. Raja's favourite was her Hungarian goulash. Guests found her a "nice Hungarian wife", as Heren referred to her,[8] and very practical on these occasions.

With her down-to-earth personality, she provided a good foil to Raja's dreamy-eyed one — or as Bloodworth described him, the "theoriser with his head in the clouds". Every so often, she had to sharply remind a Raja lost in conversation of his duties as host. "Raja, give Dennis a drink," she would command, whereupon Raja, who himself drank Clan Campbell whisky, would simply ask Bloodworth to help himself as he continued with his dissertation.[9]

She obviously did not extend the same warm hospitality to all of Raja's friends, particularly Lee. Piroska, who had a mind of her own, had grave reservations about the brash lawyer. From her perspective, Lee had been a bad influence on Raja. Since he appeared on the scene, Raja had been spending an extravagant amount of time with Lee and championing his hazardous causes. In the process, her husband had lost his steady job at the *Standard*. Not only that, Raja had to stump up the money to fund the PAP's activities, like its other leaders. At that point, there was nothing to give her the confidence that this high-risk political venture would succeed.

Quite sensibly, she was worried whether Raja, with his uncompromising idealism, knew what he was getting into. The political situation was mired in confusion. She was all too aware of the fate that had befallen some of his radical and left-wing friends, who had been interrogated, jailed, or banished from Singapore.

It was a testing time for her, as she vacillated between her fears of her husband's involvement in politics and her respect for his ideals. She knew her husband well enough to know he did not do anything in half measures.

When Raja strode onto the stage when the PAP was launched at the Victoria Memorial Hall on 21 November 1954, the issue was settled. She would support him, even if her doubts about Lee continued to churn.

Raja cut a solemn picture sitting in one of the chairs arranged in a semi-circle on stage as one of the 14 convenors. The famous journalist was one of the older faces, at 36. Of the other 13, seven were left-wing trade unionists. The others were lawyers and teachers. The youngest was Fong, at 23. Raja looked at them and decided that, whatever else could be said about them, the lot were at least serious about what they were saying. Unlike the usual run of political opportunists he so enjoyed cutting down to size, these PAP fellows could see that the existing regime needed to be radically changed.

Surveying the crowd of more than 1,500, made up mostly of unionists, Raja was struck by the air of discipline and purpose that marked the event. This was how the party wanted to present itself, a serious force to be reckoned with.

The presence of Tunku Abdul Rahman and Tan Cheng Lock, both strongly anti-communist and right-wing, added to the significance of the event. It was calculated to be a "sort of storm signal for the colonialists", as Raja put it later, to "warn of the gathering forces against colonialism".[10] He fanned the hope that they would join forces with the PAP in fighting for an independent Malaya — including Singapore. He would hope in vain.

Given the colonial status of both the Federation and Singapore, few at that meeting would have thought that, within three years, the Tunku would be elected prime minister of an independent Malaya — without Singapore. And that Cheng Lock, MCA's president, would link up with the Tunku's UMNO to establish the alliance between the Chinese and the Malays (the UMNO-MCA alliance), which would become the strongest political force in the peninsula.

But that was all in the future. On that day of the PAP launch, as the hall reverberated with cries of "Merdeka!", the ideals of the party seized Raja's imagination. He had long desired independence for Malaya and the creation of a democratic socialist society. He had long dreamed of a political party which would fight bravely for these ideals. Now such a party was born. Now the talking stops; the action begins.

Of all the media, the English-language newspapers were the most sceptical. The pro-British *Sunday Times*, in a column by "Billy Budd" dated 28 November 1954, wrote: "I am acquainted with one or two of the Convenors of the PAP. Charming and clever people, but hardly sinewy toilers." This was in all likelihood a pointed reference to Raja. More criticisms against the PAP would follow.

Raja drew his own conclusions about *The Straits Times*, and its sister paper, *The Sunday Times*, as they openly supported the Progressive Party in the run-up to the 1955 elections. Like most of the business community, these newspapers viewed the Progressive Party as most likely to provide stability and predictability during the transition to internal self-government, and ultimately, to independence.

As he played midwife to the birth of the PAP in such bracing conditions, Raja made a complete transformation from a rootless revolutionary to a loyal party man. He was no longer just an observer commenting on events; he would also be a protagonist directly influencing the course of events. As he resolved to take matters into his own hands, he had to tussle with the dilemma that haunts all radicals: will more be accomplished by working within the system or by striking it from without? He decided to do both.

His weapon of choice for his thrust and parry against the system, and all that was wrong with it, remained his pen. Bereft of a job in a newspaper to brandish it, he embarked on the precarious business of publishing his own serious magazine. His new publication was called *Raayat*.[11]

In the permit, Raja was listed as the sole proprietor, editor, and publisher. Thus began his life as a one-man pamphleteer of a democratic socialist dawning. Unable to find funding for his cause, he financed what he was advocating out of his own savings. Lee said: "It was his own idea with his own money."[12]

It started as a weekly publication circulated every Monday. In its first issue, published on 13 December 1954, Raja set out its mission — to end colonialism and bring about a "united and democratic

Malayan nation". It aimed to instil in the people a fervent desire for democratic ideals, and the confidence to forge the ideas to sustain an independent Malayan nation. It would strive to inculcate a Malayan outlook while discouraging the parochialism which "perverts nationalism into xenophobia".[13]

Central to his thinking was that Malaya's cultural, political, and economic development would be greatly influenced by developments in the rest of Asia. Hence, "Malayans must understand the new Asia and its temper if they are to grasp the nature of their own struggles and discontents."

In this context, he lamented the state of the educational institutions. They were "mainly interested in turning out people who could become good colonial subjects driven by the single-minded idea of finding a comfortable and lucrative niche for themselves in the colonial set-up". He asserted the need for people to be re-educated to regain the self-respect necessary to seek self-rule.

Self-government could not be durable, he argued, "unless national emancipation means also the liberation of the people from poverty, insecurity and other forms of social and economic degradation". He emphasised: "Raayat does not want to end colonialism in order to replace it with the tyranny of native oligarchs perhaps more ruthless than a colonialism which has grown mellow through the centuries." In these sentences, Raja conveyed an urgency to galvanise the people to confront the country's problems and to identify nationalist leaders who could brave the rigours of self-government and independence and take the country forward.

His publication was launched at a time when political apathy and timidity were marked among the English-educated group. Their attitude was reflected through the pages of the English-language newspapers and magazines, which concerned themselves largely with the escapades of Asian personalities, commercial news, the social events of the European community, and various happenings in England. There was little discussion on Malayan issues.

Yet the country was facing tremendous social and political problems, with high unemployment and poor housing, issues which the Malayan Communist Party was already exploiting. Now more than ever, with the PAP in the picture, Raja wanted to shake the English-educated from their political stupor. In this important sense, *Raayat* was a revolutionary attempt in Malaya to introduce a new brand of journalism and provide a new platform for frank, rational, and informed discussion on the fundamental issues facing the country.

The cover of the first issue of *Raayat*, which featured an image of the Universal Declaration of Human Rights, set the tone by billing the magazine slightly portentously as "The English Weekly for Thinking Malayans". That heading took on an expanded meaning when Raja filled its pages with not only political columns, but also cultural and literary essays to educate and stimulate thought, much like the socialist publications which had trained him in their journalistic tradition in London.

He wrote many of the articles himself, lashing out spiritedly against the colonial system, hectoring Malayan leaders for their cowardly attitude towards independence, and taking cheeky digs at politicians of all hues in both the Federation and Singapore. His tone was provocative and authoritative.

He examined the social political developments in the Federation with the same intensity as he did those in Singapore. His basic premise had always been that the fate of the two territories was intertwined. He used *Raayat* to make a personal statement as a stout pan-Malayan nationalist, seeking to shape the post-colonial order to come.

His eye on the future, he tackled the big questions: Which political party could boldly lead Malaya into independence and solve the many problems of the people? What kind of political and economic order would work in post-colonial Malaya?

With these imperatives in mind, he would liberally dispense advice to the Alliance and other political parties. He counselled the Alliance, tipped to win the Federal Elections in 1955, "to reflect on the fate that befell the giant Goliath when a midget called David crossed his path armed with a sling and a pebble". The "David" alluded to was the Party Negara, which Dato Onn Jaafar formed in February 1954 after disbanding his Independence of Malaya Party (IMP). Pointedly, Raja told the Alliance: "If it uses its position in the Legislature to retain the privileges of its representatives in the Legislature, then the leadership of Malayan nationalism would pass into the hands of abler men — and men ranged in opposition to the Alliance."[14]

He also took it upon himself to spell out the dangers of a "communal" economy after he read the White Paper published by the Federation government on improving the economic status of the Malays. He was troubled by the wider implications of its proposal to reserve for Malays 51 per cent of transport licences for services in rural areas. He sympathised with the Pan-Malayan Road Transport Operators' Association which had "quite correctly" believed it to be "discriminatory legislation".

He saw that such a system must involve constant intervention by the state in order to maintain the communal economic divisions which the normal laws of a capitalist economy would upset. "A Malay capitalism molly-coddled by the State will remain feeble and inefficient because the only stimulus to efficiency — threat of being ousted by a stronger competitor — would have been removed," he asserted. Not only that, as most of the major enterprises were held by vested interests, all that this attempt to create Malay capitalists might do, he warned, was to create "capitalists sustained by state favouritism".[15] It took courage for Raja to speak up so bluntly on such sensitive matters.

Remarkably, he also managed to inveigle others to address similarly touchy topics. MCA president Tan Cheng Lock tackled the hot topic on whether there was a case for socialism in Malaya. His answer was no: he did not believe that socialism could assure a society of free men, arguing instead for a "property-owning democracy".

Cheng Lock's son, Tan Siew Sin, then MCA's publicity chief,[16] grappled with an even thornier issue: what guarantees were there that the powerful Sino-Malay alliance would not disregard the rights of the minorities once it came to power? This had been one of Raja's grave misgivings over the communal alliance since it developed as a political force. Siew Sin's pragmatic answer was that, given the grip of communalism in the minds of Malayans, the Alliance was a necessary stage in the growth of Malayan unity. The Malays and Chinese, who together formed nearly 90 per cent of the total population, must first be united before they attempt to unite with the other communities, Siew Sin argued. Despite being fundamentally opposed to the views espoused by the two Tans, Raja published them anyway. His editorial policy reflected his stand that political arguments were won not by violence, but by open and straightforward discussion.

It also seemed to him essential to expose Malayans to perspectives from other parts of the world. He published articles from his British contacts — luminaries such as Kingsley Martin, editor of *New Statesman and Nation*, Aneurin Bevan, leader of the left-wing of the Labour Party, and Creech Jones, who had served in the colonial office in the British Labour government of 1945–50. Bruce Bain, the *Tribune*'s literary editor, also wrote for Raja's publication, as did French historian Raymond Aron, an influential columnist for *Le Figaro* in France at the time.[17]

To reflect the shifting position on colonialism in Britain, he drew on his connections with British politicians from the Labour Party. He broke new ground with a four-part series on the policy of the Labour Party towards the colonies if it came to power.

In the series titled "The Socialists and the Colonies", Jim Griffiths, who was chairman of the Labour Party from 1948 to 1949, and in 1950, became secretary of state for the colonies, declared that "it would be the policy of a British Labour Government to replace colonial rule with democratic freedom".

Another socialist MP, Fenner Brockway, called for a date to end colonial rule. Creech Jones asked for more economic aid to the colonies, while John Hatch, who had worked closely with African nationalist leaders, wrote a well-informed paper on the socialist position on colonial questions.

These men were effective voices on colonial issues in Britain, which was facing demands from the colonies for a precise timetable for decolonisation. They were also active in the Fabian Society. That they would write such thoughtful articles for an obscure Malayan publication across the oceans was a revealing measure of their regard for Raja.

No stranger to controversy, Raja showed a readiness to take a strong position on certain topical issues, which might well be at variance with official PAP policy. Indeed, on some, Raja took a harder line than might be considered prudent by Lee or his other PAP colleagues.

One striking example was his stance on the banishment of P.V. Sharma to India. In January 1951, Sharma, a former president of the Singapore Teachers' Union (STU),[18] was arrested for suspected communist activities. In November 1952, he was released on a Suspension Order, on condition that he left the colony for India where he was born. Upon banishment, he made an appeal to return to Singapore, which the government rejected.

Nair, an STU official, had tried to enlist the PAP's support for Sharma's campaign to return, but Lee, a cautious and subtle politician, was reluctant to take it up as a party issue. Like John Eber, Sharma had pleaded his innocence, but, again like Eber, his protestations may be doubted. Evidence would emerge later that Sharma was, in fact, a card-carrying communist. Not only that, it was Sharma who had converted Nair to communism, and, for a long time, had also mentored Samad as his communist leader.

In a stark departure from Lee's more cautious approach, Raja had no hesitation in helping Nair to campaign for Sharma's return, demonstrating yet again his adventurous and independent streak. Raja, who had known Sharma since their MDU days, was hell-bent on being a gadfly to the colonial regime.

Despite the risks of doing so, Raja worked with Nair to draft the pamphlet for Sharma's public appeal. The Special Branch, which considered Sharma a dangerous character, looked upon Raja's involvement with as much disfavour as it did upon the militants from the far left. He was dancing on thin ice when he wrote a column supporting Sharma's appeal in the *Raayat* on 5 January 1955.

After the campaign failed, Sharma fled to China, where Chooi Yip had also taken refuge. After all that had happened, Raja did not reckon that the time would come when, with the survival of Singapore and merger at stake, the likes of Sharma and Chooi Yip would plot against the PAP to sabotage all that he, Raja, had worked for. The PAP's battle with the communists and their fellow travellers would be brutal.

That would all be water under the bridge when they met again decades later, under calmer conditions. Chooi Yip and Sharma would be allowed back to Singapore in the late 1980s, after they agreed to account for their past activities, renounced communism and severed their links with the MCP. It would be a reunion of old, battle-scarred political warriors.

There is a revealing sequel to this story. After Raja stepped down from politics in 1988, he would continue to make appeals on behalf of Sharma to his own PAP government. In a letter dated 15 October 1991 to S. Jayakumar , then the minister of law and home affairs, Raja put in a word for Sharma's son Ravi Sarma, and daughter Remya Sarma, who were both applying for employment passes to work in Singapore. Raja mentioned that Chooi Yip had told him that they were very proficient in Chinese. Both Ravi and Remya hold a college degree in Chinese language and linguistics from Hunan Normal University.[19]

Raja's efforts on their behalf were in keeping with his humane philosophy that, while the battle to crush political foes could be brutal, grace should be shown to their children who were innocent bystanders in the battle. The PAP government agreed.

His philosophy also stemmed from lessons drawn from his own experience — people's views could change. In the 1950s, Raja was himself stoutly against being anti-communist, although he strongly disapproved of the MCP's tactics. Right up to 1959, when the PAP took power and he began to see otherwise, Raja had maintained that communism was not the real problem facing Malaya. Indeed, in *Raayat*, he argued that it was futile to ask people to fight against communism without addressing the root problem — the oppressive social and economic conditions. Why should they fight against the communists who promised to free them from these? He declared: "We think that Communism is not the cause of the world's unrest today but merely a symptom of an unrest which has its roots in conditions which have nothing to do with the Communists."[20] It would be better to ask the people to fight, not communism, but these acute conditions. "It means rejecting the status quo and fighting those who uphold it. It means fighting to establish a democratic society backed by people who believe in democracy."[21]

The heart of Raja's intellectual argument was that people needed an inspiring faith to fight for — and not just to fight against. According to him, that faith was democracy. Carrying the argument for democracy further, he called for an end to the Emergency.

Exposed to the Fabian ideal of reason and Mill's ideal of liberty, Raja considered the Emergency regulations a stranglehold on genuine political expression and the development of democracy. "The shadow of the Emergency Regulations may have forced a great many of us to resort to what George Orwell called 'double-think'," he declared ominously.[22]

To flesh out the ills of the Emergency, he published an essay by John Eber, his friend exiled in Britain, who described his personal experience of being arrested — coming across more as an injured party than the dangerous communist he really was — while the novelist Han Suyin wrote a moving short story on the suffering of the ordinary villagers under curfew.

Convinced of the chastening effects that democracy would have on the MCP, Raja pressed Lee into having the PAP take up this issue:

Propose a general amnesty for the MCP and allow the MCP to function as a legitimate party. Raja believed that, under such conditions, the MCP would then lay down its arms peacefully and conduct its political struggle using constitutional methods, rather than through armed struggle. Lee went along as it sounded logical and reasonable. Also, he had witnessed the evident popularity of such a call during rallies with the Chinese masses.[23]

So, in January 1955, Raja drafted the PAP statement for amnesty for the MCP and an end to the Emergency, which Lee then issued.[24] Decades later, both were to look back on their raw assumptions regarding the MCP with dismay. In minimising the danger posed by the communists, they were in fact living in a fool's paradise. Lee rued: "Raja and I were Western-educated radicals who had no idea of the dynamics of guerrilla insurgency and revolution by violence."[25]

As Raja continued to draft PAP statements for Lee with zest over the months and years, the journalist became typecast as a partisan polemicist. To a significant extent, this diminished his contributions as an original nationalist voice during this early period. Even when he spoke his own mind and acted on his own accord, he would be pigeon-holed as being the mouthpiece of the PAP.

Had he read the Special Branch report at the time which described *Raayat* as an "unofficial mouthpiece of the PAP",[26] he would have been greatly outraged. The publication was the megaphone for his own voice. The range of its contents amplifies this fact. As Lee confirmed years later, *Raayat* was not a PAP vehicle — it was Raja's one-man show.

Indeed, his character is stamped all over its pages. He was pugnacious politically, so was *Raayat*. He was eclectic in his interests, and so was *Raayat*.

Within the 20 to 28 pages of the magazine, he promoted his love for books with book reviews. He shared his delight about modern science, with articles on how the brain worked and the new field of computers and cybernetics. He sought to raise the level of cultural awareness, with assessments on the Singapore art scene. He showed his solidarity with workers, with updates on their trade union activities. Besides that, he also propagated his personal views on race — one "fact" box stated "there are no superior races". And, given his strong international awareness, the paper had a strong bias towards foreign affairs.

Then there were the whimsical articles, such as "The case against neck-ties", which argued against the practice. This no doubt met Raja's hearty approval. He himself disliked donning stiff, formal attire, preferring casual shirts left untucked and open at the collar. More eccentrically, he published two features on how to kick smoking — a great irony as Raja himself had been a heavy chain-smoker since he was about 24.

On a light day, he would puff about 30 cigarettes. By all accounts, he showed no inclination to kick the habit until he was 67. He spurned the example of Lee, who gave up smoking by the early 1960s. Neither did he stop when Lee later banned tobacco smoke from his office and the cabinet meeting room. For many years, Raja was prepared to suffer the inconvenience of stepping out for a puff during the long meetings. He gave it up only in June 1982, when his addiction seriously impaired his lungs and subjected him to constant coughing fits.

He also used *Raayat* to experiment with a story-writing style to deliver some blistering ironies of colonial rule. One result was the fresh and original piece, "When Malaya ruled Britain", which turned the table on Britain as the colony struggling for freedom, with "rich and powerful" Malaya as the colonial master. It took the form of a fictional speech by "Malaya's Secretary of State for the Colonies" which basically dished out the same arguments used by Britain to withhold Malayan independence — only reversed — to show how hollow and hypocritical they sounded.

This was followed up with "Malaya must free Britain" on the travails of being under Malayan colonial rule. This time, the fictional speech was by a British nationalist, the "President of the British

National Congress, Winston Ah Tee Lee", a somewhat contrived play on the names of British premiers Winston Churchill and Clement Attlee. Some readers enjoyed this satirical style, with one writing in to say: "Never has the case for Malayan independence been put so humorously and yet pertinently."[27]

These readers were obviously a small minority. The intellectual tenor of his magazine held a narrow appeal. Its subscription rate of $30 a year for the weekly was another barrier. The low circulation, coupled with the radical tone of his publication, made it hard to draw advertisers. Lacking a literary network, Raja also faced problems marketing his publication.

As for publicity, the only paper willing to give *Raayat* any airing was *Fajar*, the controversial publication of University of Malaya Socialist Club. In its review of *Raayat*, it recommended the new weekly as a serious Malayan journal and referred to Raja as one of the leading Malayan journalists who was "responsible for the era, now past, of intelligent editorial writing" in the *Singapore Standard*. On a more critical note, it commented that, while several distinguished writers contributed to *Raayat*, it lacked articles on Malaya. Also "there is a danger of trying to cater for too wide a range of intelligences and tastes". There was also difficulty in obtaining *Raayat*, adding that "it is worthwhile, however, going out of your way to get."[28]

Heartened by such feedback, Raja expressed plans for Chinese and Malay editions at a later date. This idea was pie in the sky. Already, the English edition was in its death throes. To keep it alive, he took the tough decision to reduce the weekly to a monthly from the fifth issue, which was published on 10 January 1955. He also revised the subscription rate to $7 a year.

Raja was upfront with his readers. In that 10 January issue to announce the changes, he confessed that the response from the public "had not been sufficient" to support the weekly schedule. To his cost, he remained optimistic. He would press on, he wrote, as "during this important phase in the history of our country, there is a need for a magazine which is prepared to discuss local and foreign affairs in an intelligent and forthright manner". It was in this hope that "we are persisting in a venture which, despite the knowing winks of the pessimists, we feel is worth trying".[29]

But this apparently bold venture could not long hide the harsh reality. While he was determined to put principle and intellectual argument ahead of profit, he could not ignore the fact that his debts were ballooning. Meanwhile, the number of subscribers and advertisers were plummeting.

He was prepared to fight on. His printer Hoong Fatt Press, however, was not. Now beset with production problems as well, Raja agonised over his next step. Piroska advised him to cut his losses and get back to a regular job. Raja pulled the plug: *Raayat* breathed its last breath with its edition in March 1955. In all, *Raayat* ran seven issues. During the three months of production, Raja learnt an awful truth: people in Singapore would rather spend 60 cents a month on entertainment magazines than on serious-minded ones such as *Raayat*. It was a very public failure.

It was also a very expensive lesson. He lost all his savings, easily to the tune of tens of thousands of dollars. But more distressing to him was the realisation that, despite pouring his heart and soul into the publication, week in and week out, it made no discernible impact on the political consciousness of Malayans. With its failure, there was a sense of political impotence, of his talents wasted, of his foolishness being on display. He had rushed headlong into a costly venture with high ideals, but without thinking through each practical step or the consequences.

It illustrates his utopianism; his impulsive, impractical nature. It also reflected his uncompromising standards in journalism. He eschewed the low road, although that might have attracted more readers. As he had told his readers in the debut issue of *Raayat*, "if there is any 'exposure' to be done, it will not be that of the flesh of women".[30]

With hindsight, Lee said years later: "Raja was not a businessman. He was a leader writer and a pamphleteer. Somebody should have told him, don't start this paper."[31] But chances were that, even if anyone did, Raja would have given it a go anyway. Purposeful writing was in his blood.

While *Raayat* itself was short-lived, the ideals embedded in it continued to throb in him. He wanted to continue to write, to express himself, to fight for what he believed in. As he explored his options, Piroska worried for him. They lived frugally, even austerely, and were neither materialistic nor acquisitive. A protective wife, she continued to blame his association with Lee and the PAP for their drastic change of fortunes. Lee recalled: "His wife was angry with us for making him lose his job and his fortune. She made me feel very unwelcome when I visited Chancery Lane."[32]

Coming immediately after his sacking from the *Standard*, the failure of Raayat must count as one of the lowest points in his personal life. There are few experiences in life as demoralising, humiliating, and painful as falling from grace. Where once he was a high-flying columnist/editor of a widely-read newspaper, he was now a penniless and jobless man in the wilderness.

The episode also exposed him to ridicule, particularly by his former newspaper colleagues. In a low blow, it was used to mock him at the height of the election campaign in 1959, in the midst of a public row with his former newspaper, the *Standard*. The paper flung at Raja the taunt that "when he walked out of this office, Mr Rajaratnam tried his hand at being editor-manager-publisher of his own paper", adding caustically that, "after a few issues, he made the painful discovery that he could not collect an intelligent public to endorse the policy of his paper".

More humiliation was yet to come. As the *Standard* reminded everyone in its next sentence: "So he walked a few yards down the street to offer his services to yet another pro-capitalist organ."[33] That pro-capitalist organ was the anti-PAP *Straits Times*.

What a bitter pill that must have been for Raja to swallow. Demoralised and exhausted, he re-entered the lion's den of the Malayan press, which proved so formative of his own attitudes to the media in the years since. In more ways than one, the *Straits Times* was an oppressive place for Raja to eke a living. The newspaper had poor relations with the unions, in particular, the Singapore Union of Journalists.

Indeed, in a union dispute back in February 1954, when Raja was SUJ vice-president, the union had appealed to newspapermen and its service staff to stop helping the production of *The Straits Times*, in support of a strike by printers. This spiralled into a bitter row which became personal when *The Straits Times* pointed out in its editorial that the key union officials, including its president Alex Josey and vice-president Rajaratnam, worked for its rival, the *Standard*.[34]

Despite the colourful history of professional rivalry and Raja's reputation as an outspoken unionist and left-wing activist, *The Straits Times* still offered Raja a job. It recognised his formidable analytical and writing skills. Perhaps more importantly, its senior editor, Lee Siew Yee, knew Raja well enough to vouch for his professionalism. Indeed, Siew Yee, a close, long-time friend of Raja, was instrumental in getting Raja the job.[35]

The Straits Times offered Raja the position of a leader writer at a salary of $1,225 a month — about $300 less than what he used to earn at the *Standard*. It was not unexpected as *The Straits Times* generally paid lower wages to its local staff. Raja was at a low ebb when the offer came. Still, in accepting it, he suffered not a little crisis of conscience.

The Straits Times was ideologically opposed to the ideals that he had been championing all his years as a journalist. Not only was it pro-British, it was a newspaper for big business with a reputation for being against trade unions. To cap it all, it was anti-PAP. How could Raja — a tireless crusader for the underdog, a champion for socialism, an agitator against colonialism and, now, a founder of the PAP — work for *The Straits Times*?

His acceptance suggests a measure of desperation. He was sinking in debt. "Everyone knew he was poor then," said Jean Mary Gray, a social worker who would marry Marshall in 1961.[36] Already laid low by the failure of *Raayat*, Raja swallowed what was left of his pride and took the job at *The Straits Times* with its conditions — everything he wrote must be cleared by the editorial board before seeing print. The board was helmed by Leslie Hoffman, who was editor-in-chief. Raja reported to the paper's associate editor, Arlington Kennard, who told Raja: "You can write what you like, but I decide which editorial goes into *The Straits Times* column."[37]

Other than writing leaders, Raja also helped to select features for the editorial page, reporting to Siew Yee. Lee Kuan Yew believed that *The Straits Times* did not give him any opportunities to progress. "They knew where he came from. They gave him no space. He wrote inconsequential things."[38]

The widespread view, indeed perpetuated by Raja himself in later years, was that only the leaders he wrote on humorous or innocuous subjects were published.[39] However, evidence suggests otherwise. During his time in the paper, he was also given space, although not as much as he was used to, to tackle politically sensitive topics which he had felt strongly about, such as labour and wage issues, as well as press freedom.

For example, at a time of massive labour unrest in 1955, Raja wrote to remind readers that increases in both profits and wages were largely a matter of redivision of a given quantity of product. "The task before the Government, employers and workers was to see that this re-division took place in an orderly and intelligent fashion and without bringing the whole economy to a standstill."

The trade unionist could indulge in his legitimate function of getting for the workers a greater share of the reward, both by re-division of the proceeds where it is unfairly divided, and by increased output. "Unfortunately, there have been occasional instances when demands by workers have been so unreasonable as to make it impossible for employers to continue in business. Closure of that enterprise, in these circumstances, has meant the employees being thrown out of work," he noted.

From the tone, it was clear that Raja's view of militant trade unionism had become more nuanced and balanced. His writing was also tighter. While it might well have been winnowed by the editing hands of Kennard, Raja's clear-eyed reasoning came through. He was so authoritative on the subject that Josey quoted him on this in his seminal book on trade unions.[40]

Respecting Raja for his professionalism, Kennard began giving Raja more weighty issues to flex his editorial muscles, despite the constant aggravation. Peter Lim, who joined *The Straits Times* in April 1957, had eavesdropped on many lively spats between Kennard and Raja in the office as they argued over political developments at home and abroad, and the editorial line to be taken. The arguments continued when Kennard was editing Raja's pieces, with Raja protesting at the changes.

The disagreements were not always over policy; sometimes, they were over the finer points of language. Said Lim, who was to work with *The Straits Times* for the next 33 years and rise to become its editor-in-chief: "Raja, of course, respected the chain of command. The arguments were robust but civil."[41]

When *The Straits Times* took an anti-PAP line in its coverage, Raja kept his emotions in check. As a member of the editorial staff of *The Straits Times*, Raja could not be visibly identified with a political party. This contractual leash around his neck also restrained him from being openly active in the PAP, even though he was the key strategist giving shape and substance to the party's ideology. Peter Lim said that Raja took the situation in his stride. He observed: "Raja carried out his duties professionally, putting forth his point of view and trying to justify his editorial stances."[42]

All said, it was a trying time for Raja. Lee Khoon Choy, a journalist who moved from *Nanyang Siang Pau* to *The Straits Times* in 1957, revealed that pro-PAP staff, himself included, were disillusioned with the paper's blatant bias. Raja felt it even more keenly. Khoon Choy recalled: "Raja could not write anti-colonial views in *The Straits*

Times. Also, *The Straits Times* knew about his relationship with Lee Kuan Yew. He had a tough time in ST which was anti-PAP."[43]

Throughout this bleak period, Raja displayed a depth of emotional strength and profound resilience. His close friends did not once hear him moan about the PAP ruining his career prospects, or wallow in self-pity. Lee said: "Raja was a man who didn't do that. He takes his chances in life and that's that."[44]

His relatives continued to benefit from his life-affirming humour and kindness. When his uncle, Kanda Pillay, was getting married in 1955 and needed to borrow Raja's house to conduct his bride's ceremonial milk bath, Raja did not think twice about opening his doors. A few years later, when Pillay needed money to buy a house, Raja withdrew what little he had and lent it with no questions asked. His generosity to those around him during these testing times was matched with that undimmed strength of will and purpose which guided his choices in life.

Raja was filled with a new vigour when nomination day was called for 28 February and polling for 2 April 1955. The PAP fielded five candidates: Lee for Tanjong Pagar, Lim Chin Siong for Bukit Timah, Devan Nair for Farrer Park, Goh Chew Chua for Punggol-Tampines. It also fielded Ahmad Ibrahim for Sembawang, but as an independent candidate.[45]

While Raja could not be openly involved in organising the campaign, he played a vigorous backroom role. He helped to draft the election manifesto for Lee and also gave some points for his rally speeches. He went to all the PAP election rallies. He noted the voter profile: 70 per cent Chinese-speaking.

Initially, he was quite anxious for Lee, who had no command of Chinese, but was repeatedly challenged to speak in the language by his Chinese-educated opponent from the Democratic Party. When

Lee delivered some lines he had memorised for his first rally, Raja immediately turned to the Chinese journalists around him to check their reaction. He was relieved when they told him that, for someone who knew very little of the Chinese language, it was a creditable performance.

His most eye-opening experience during the campaign was witnessing the hordes which turned up for Chin Siong's rallies. Never before had he seen such crowds — and such fervour! It awakened him to the powerful mobilising machinery of the communists. He recalled later: "We knew that we were brushing up against a very formidable force."

When the polling results were announced, there were shocked faces all round: The Progressive Party was routed. The Labour Front — which had fought the elections largely in the expectation that it would be no more than an opposition group — won 10 out of 17 seats it contested, leading Marshall to become chief minister. The PAP won four seats, except for Nair who lost. Lee won by the largest number of ballots cast for any candidate, and by the widest margin.

Upon Marshall's victory, Raja was quick to analyse the implications, given the Labour Front's radical election platform. In a column in *The Straits Times* on 11 April, he observed: "The Labour Front is in the position of a man who, having set out to catch a mousedeer, finds that he has captured a tiger instead. The unexpected catch has set the hunter the delicate problem of how to co-exist peacefully with a beast which could become unmanageable."[46] The beast which Raja alluded to was the public expectations roused by its controversial election promises.

Raja identified three points which had particularly stirred up public emotion: Repealing the Emergency regulations, implementing multilingualism, and pressing for early self-government. "These were also the issues which raised the laughs and brought forth the cheers under the old apple tree during lunch time," observed Raja, referring to Marshall's popular rallies under a tree outside the government offices in Empress Place. Having been voted in on the popularity of such promises, the party was now called on to implement them.

Scrutinising the Labour Front's predicament, Raja concluded that, to survive, it would most likely drift towards the Right or extreme Left, depending on the extent to which it was prepared to tone down its election programme. In his analysis, Raja showed a rational and almost clinical approach to political strategy, which the ebullient Marshall could not be said to share.

Years later, Raja would remember Marshall as the dramatic politician who, by the sheer force of his personality, shook people out of their political apathy. As Raja put it, "he startled people into taking an interest in politics". The new chief minister would himself be startled by the chain of events which followed his victory. Less than two months after the elections, pro-communists stirred industrial unrest to show their strength and to test Marshall's. The mass discontent and strikes led to the Hock Lee bus riots, which gave Raja his first premonition of the troubles the PAP would face.

11

The Malayan Question

12 May 1955. Black Thursday. Raja was working late in his *Straits Times* office, when all hell broke on the streets outside. A mob was parading around a bleeding Chinese student, strapped onto a wooden door.

The boy had been hit by a stray shot fired by a policeman hours ago during a riot which had turned violent. But instead of rushing him to the nearby hospital, the mob carried his body around town, with stops for the press to take photographs as evidence of police brutality. By the time they took the boy to the hospital late at night, he was dead.

Raja related later: "Our reporters told me that they got the impression the mob wanted the boy to die, because they wanted a martyr." He was shocked at their ruthlessness. He was even more shocked that the street violence arose out of strikes instigated by his fellow PAP founders, Fong Swee Suan and Lim Chin Siong. This was not what the PAP, as he had envisaged it, stood for or wanted to be known for.

While Fong and Chin Siong would later protest that they did not start the riots, that it was the prevailing "social conditions" which led to it, their actions indicated that they were more than ready to use revolutionary methods in their struggle.

Earlier in April, they had instigated strikes of the bus companies, notably the Hock Lee Bus Company. Strikers blocked the entrances to the Hock Lee Depot to stop buses from moving out, bringing the island's transport system to a standstill. The ensuing confrontation in May with the police erupted into a riot with four people killed and 31 injured. In a show of support to their comrades, 20 busloads of Chinese students moved into the area. They overturned vehicles and set them on fire. They clenched their fists and hollered communist slogans. It was amidst such chaos, which continued through the night, that the boy was shot.

Hyped up in a frenzied state, the students and unionists continued to run riot over the ensuing days, sparking off more strikes and sit-ins all over the island. Soon, communist-controlled Chinese cultural organisations also entered the fray. From then on, Singapore was a cauldron of strikes and conflict as the Middle Road group of union leaders incited thousands of workers and students to rage against the government and employers.

In 1955, there were nearly 300 strikes, most of them organised by the Middle Road group. They had a devastating effect on the economy. In that year alone, there were 946,000 man days lost, about seven times the year before.[1] As public panic mounted, the realisation grew in Raja that Marshall was "a man incapable of coping with serious crisis". Marshall's unwillingness to take tough action emboldened the pro-communists further.

The riots rocked his Labour Front government and forced Raja and his moderate PAP group to face the unmasked militancy of the communist united front. Raja said later: "It was this Hock Lee riots which, as far as I was concerned, gave a premonition of the kind of problems the PAP would face." Lee, who was the legal adviser to the Hock Lee bus company as well as to the Chinese Students' Union, called it his "baptism of fire" working with the communist united front.[2]

In an attempt to distance the PAP from the violence, Raja worked with Lee on a press statement to denounce the bloodshed, while sympathising with the workers on strike. At the same time, the PAP leaders protested that it could not be held responsible for the action of every member in the PAP.

Dismissing the PAP statement, Chief Secretary William Goode charged that the PAP, their "covert communist supporters and backseat drivers" wanted violence, bloodshed, and industrial unrest, but then realised too late what horrors they had engineered.[3] Marshall called it as he saw it — the PAP was working with communist forces which it knew were "evil" to destroy colonialism.[4]

The PAP leaders felt the heat. But they needed the radical left-wing masses with them and could not melt into a position which appeared to back the government's handling of the riots. So, they attacked it.

Raja, who was in charge of drafting PAP statements, declared that the government had mishandled an extremely delicate situation arising not only from the bus strike, but also out of the situation in Chinese middle schools. "This mishandling afforded opportunity for extremist political adventurers, communist and otherwise, to convert popular resentment against government into violence," he maintained.[5]

While this might be a politically shrewd counter, it was quite disingenuous. The pro-communist instigators behind the riots were not looking for any settlement with the government; their intention was to turn workers and students into militant participants in a violent revolution directed by the communists.

Raja probably discerned this, but muted this awareness to a considerable extent by viewing the turmoil in Singapore as part of the epochal struggle of political and economic forces that was going on in the world, where the people of Asia were shaking off the humiliating shackles of European domination and exploitation. The fight for independence in Malaya was part of the world struggle for freedom and justice.

Raja was single-minded about the fundamental mission at hand — to achieve independence for Malaya, including Singapore. He understood why the Chinese-educated pro-communists threw in their lot with the PAP. Being literate only in Chinese, they knew they would be handicapped in the fight for independence against the British in the arena of constitutional politics. They also needed the PAP as their fig leaf. "We understood Western politics, how it worked, how it should work. So they needed us. And we needed them," as he said years later.

In the eyes of the Chinese-educated leaders, it was the English-educated group which needed them even more during that period, when the PAP was building up its mass base. As Fong emphasised, no political party or leader could succeed without the support of the Chinese-educated majority at the time. "Unless you can associate with this group, really find something to work together, you won't be successful. The Chinese-educated formed the main group and was the most organised."[6]

Given this context, Raja faced a major disadvantage in his political work. Samad Ismail, who had made it a point himself to pick up Chinese when in prison, thought that this diminished to some extent Raja's ability to relate to the Chinese masses and feel their pulse.[7] Samad, who later confessed he was directed by his communist leaders to penetrate organisations, said he knew Chin Siong as a fellow traveller, and described the latter as "the acting man — he can move a crowd, but he was not a planner or a thinker".[8]

Although Raja had many good Chinese-educated friends to keep him updated, the nuances could sometimes be lost in translation. The information might also not be as timely or comprehensive. Partly because of his language handicap and partly because of his tendency to give people the benefit of the doubt, he might not have fully appreciated the sinister tactics of the pro-communists within the party until later that year, when the power struggle for control over the party became more acute.

But from his interactions with them, he knew this much: "The Chinese-educated had great admiration and respect for Communist

China." He was exceedingly wary about this. He was a socialist, but also a manifestly patriotic one. His anti-colonialism was to free Malaya so that it could decide for itself its own system, not to serve the interests of China and to follow its system blindly.

As the island reeled from the tension, crisis and disruption one after another, Raja was assailed with a sense of despair. Swept by the noise and clamour, few had paused to analyse the causes of the industrial unrest and to offer solutions on issues where emotion and prejudice could so easily prevail. It seemed to him essential to underpin the disturbing developments with a matrix of history to give the public deeper perspectives and to bring rational insight into the charged situation. Throughout his career, both as a journalist and a politician, this ability, perhaps more than anything else, set him apart.

In a three-part series in *The Straits Times* in October 1955, he approached the problem surgically, not unlike an emergency doctor faced with a convulsing patient suffering from multiple illnesses. He clocked the symptoms: Out of the 216 strikes which took place between January and September that year, 134 of them were sympathy strikes, with only about a third of them seeking better pay and working conditions. The sympathy strikes were organised in one case to support the Hock Lee bus strike, and in another, to protest the arrest of five trade unionists. This showed that the waves of strikes were as much political as economic in character.

Drawing from his grasp of history and Marxist theory, Raja pointed out that, in the past, the waves of industrial unrest in Malaya had also been political and economic in nature. He attributed this to the dominant influence of the MCP over the trade unions, given its tenure as the oldest political party in Malaya. "For the average worker, the elaborate dialectics of Marx is understood mainly as an unending struggle between the boss and the worker."[9] Communism had taught the worker to accept the conflict between him and the employer as both natural and inevitable, thus readying the worker for greater aggression against employers.

He discerned new factors in the current industrial unrest, however — nationalist and anti-colonial sentiments. "An added vehemence is given to the dispute because the expatriate employer, in addition to being the boss, is also identified with colonialism which, in the case of the politically unsophisticated worker, is understood largely in racial terms," he noted.

Another salient element was the struggle among trade union leaders for the hearts and minds of workers, given the contest for membership between the many unions. The contest took the form of organising new unions or poaching members from older unions. "In this struggle for power, it may be necessary for the trade union leader to make demands which he knows to be unreasonable in order to establish a reputation as an uncompromising fighter for the workers," he observed. In such a cut-throat environment, the union leaders had to be ready to outbid their rivals lest they should be accused of having sold out to the bosses, he added.

After dissecting the facts and trends in a detached manner, Raja presented his diagnosis: Whatever the faults of the trade union leaders, the motivating factor behind any industrial unrest was primarily economic. "Economic discontent is the fuel which may be sparked off by political and other forces." This had to be confronted.

To reduce the fever of industrial tension, Raja focused on the need to increase national wealth, so that there would be more to distribute to workers. But as long as Singapore's economy was subject to the fluctuating prices of tin and rubber, with workers concentrated in manual jobs, there was very little likelihood of there being a real increase in national wealth. "Increases both in profits and wages would largely be a matter of redivision of a given quantity of product. That attempt to redivide wealth would form the basis of industrial quarrels," he wrote.[10]

He called for the government, employers and trade unionists to work together to ensure that this redivision took place in an "orderly and intelligent fashion and without bringing the whole economy to a standstill". In a veiled warning to the trade unionists, he pointed out that, if too much was extracted from an industry, such as overblown wage demands, it would bring the industry to a halt. "This is true, whether the method of distribution of the product is Socialist, Capitalist or Communist," he asserted.

The call for cooperation between the three parties — labour, capital, and government — was a profound one, and one that he had been making with dogged persistence since the late 1940s. Again, his call was scorned by the unionists, obsessed as they were with slogan shouting and burnishing their anti-employer image.

On the employers' part, they could hardly evince any confidence in the reasonableness of union leaders. As for the grand principle enunciated — that national wealth should be increased so that more could be redistributed to the people — this was Raja at his socialist best. Calling the unionists and the employers to adopt an entirely new mindset towards national wealth, Raja argued: "If the worker or the employer does not accept any responsibility towards the enterprise as a whole, then industrial conflict becomes the prelude to economic chaos." If this happens, everyone loses.

It was a tough call. The trade unionists found no reason to foster economic development or the growth of enterprises, feeling that they had no share in either. They regarded it as a given that workers were exploited victims. Instead of dismissing their grievances, Raja took them into account, and in another commentary, urged the government to look into the wages and employment conditions of workers in the various industries. He also called for a review of the wage structure, pointing out the huge disparity between the unskilled and the skilled. "The differences are too wide and one of the tasks of employers and trade unionists should be to narrow these gaps."[11]

He also pointed out that much of the current industrial unrest had stemmed from the manual workers who formed the most depressed section of the working population. "If labour discontent is to be curbed, improvement must first be made in the conditions of these 120,000 who, with their dependents, constitute a substantial proportion of the Colony's population."[12]

He drilled down into the problem further and dug out the fact that about 70 per cent of the 120,000 manual workers in the colony earned between $80 and $150 a month, and about 40 per cent of them got under $120 a month. They accounted for about a third of the total working population. "Obviously, we have in our midst the fuel for industrial and political explosions. Is the standard of living permitted to this substantial section of the population fair and reasonable? Can they be said to have a 'living wage'?" he asked.[13]

He was also disturbed by the economic structure and the estimate that only about 40 per cent of the total population — about 450,000 people — were employed. This meant that four people were supporting 10 in Singapore. "All attempts to increase the standards of living will be defeated as long as this feature in our economy remains…However much we may juggle about with wages and conditions of work, the overall picture would still be four people slaving away to maintain 10."

Most of all, he lamented the dearth of information on wages and conditions of employment. In frustration, he remarked: "My belief is that such a venture at this present time would be about as rewarding as looking in a dark room for a black hen which has probably gone out for a walk."[14]

He noted that no one — not the government, the employers, or the unions — had attempted an evaluation of what was a fair and reasonable wage for Malaya. "A minimum wage of this kind would at least provide the basis on which to build a fair and logical wage structure. If we are to raise the standards from sub-human levels, then we must know what the wage level should be for a man to live like a human being," he argued.

His call for a comprehensive assessment of wages and working conditions was timely and perceptive. No one knew with any reasonable accuracy what the cost of living in Malaya was, hence no one could estimate reliably what should be a basic living wage. This almost total absence of reliable statistics favoured employers in wage negotiations and confused arbitration. It also allowed unionists to exploit the issue by assuming, without any data to contradict them, that all workers were underpaid in any case.

Rising above the din of strikers chanting communist slogans on the streets, Raja's voice of reason made an impact. Barely a month after his last column on the subject, Marshall wrote him a letter dated 30 November 1955, to appoint him to a new committee to inquire into minimum standards of livelihood and issues related to social security. The committee, chaired by Marshall's economic adviser Sydney Caine,[15] then vice-chancellor of the University of Malaya, would make far-reaching recommendations which would lay the foundation for thinking on the issues of minimum wages and social security for workers. Its findings would also provide a more rational and objective basis for wage negotiation and arbitration.

The seven-man committee produced its report on 27 September 1956 after 34 meetings.[16] It was published as an Assembly Sessional Paper in 1957. The PAP hailed the report as a pioneering effort and recommended that it should be "studied by everyone interested in the well-being of Singapore's working class".[17] Raja, as the only PAP man in a committee packed mainly with academics, rose in public esteem for his key role in representing the workers' voice in the committee.

The committee made big news with its findings: the average wage of workers in regular employment in Singapore was around $150 a month, but the commonest wage was between $100 and $120 a month. It estimated that $120 a month would suffice to maintain a family of a man, his wife, and two children at a minimum standard. One in four people was living in poverty.

The committee calculated that it would cost about $27 million a year to raise all households in poverty up to that minimum level. Could poverty be abolished by giving cash hand-outs to the poor? Should a minimum wage be fixed? Raja listened judiciously to the diverse viewpoints of those appearing before the committee — trade unions, employers, experts — and took part robustly in the deliberations to crystallise the committee's recommendations.

A firm believer in social and economic justice, Raja was outspoken in arguing for a fairer system, although he was fully aware of the limits of operating under colonial rule. Lim Chong Yah, who was then the committee's assistant secretary, knew Raja was radically anti-colonial, but could not recall him taking extreme positions during the discussions. "To me, he was more like a Fabian socialist," said Lim Chong Yah.[18] He also remembered how Raja livened the meetings with his humour and wit.

After much discussion, the committee decided against fixing a minimum wage. Instead, it called for the improvement of the existing Wages Council Ordinance, enacted in 1953, to regulate wages. It decided that the fixing of wages should be left to negotiation between employers and employees, supplemented where appropriate by mutually agreed arbitration.

It reasoned that a minimum wage would have wider repercussions on Singapore's competitiveness and cause many jobs to be lost. Singapore's income depended primarily on trade and services to shipping as well as manufacturing production. Its services to the UK defence establishments in Singapore formed its largest single industry. Its trade was partly bulk handling of produce originating in the mainland of Malaya, or of imports, for example oil, for distribution in the region. Competition between Singapore and its neighbours was intense.

At the same time, with the population increasing at a rate of 4 per cent a year, the major problem likely to arise was unemployment. In these circumstances, a minimum wage would probably mean that, "while a certain number would gain higher wages, it would be at the expense of others who would lose their jobs altogether and the aggregate income of Singapore as a whole would fall", the report noted. As the committee pored over the facts and consulted experts,

Raja could not help but gain a more realistic appraisal of the complex situation and emerged with a keener understanding of Singapore's particular economic vulnerability.

While some of Raja's key concerns were addressed in the committee, one area which remained a black hole was the exact number of the perceived rising ranks of the unemployed. The committee found it "impossible" to provide a definitive figure, as many of the jobless did not register with the Labour Exchange to seek jobs.[19] This lack of information annoyed Raja — how could such an important issue be left hanging in the air by the government?

Hence, he joined the Singapore Unemployment Society when it was formed in July 1956 by some left-wing unions to put the spotlight on the issue. It elected Raja into its ranks "to lend respectability to that society", the Special Branch observed.[20]

The society was active. It launched a campaign to press for a social and economic policy that would bring about full employment in the colony. It also organised a convention of political parties and trade unions to discuss the unemployment problem and the question of relief.

Feeling the pressure, the Labour Front government charged that the society was being used for propaganda purposes by the Middle Road bloc of left-wing unions. That might well be so. But Raja considered rational discourse in the cloistered confines of a convention room a preferred method of airing problems than mindless rabble-rousing on the streets.

Mahmud Awang, a dyed-in-the-wool unionist who was involved in the unemployment society, said: "Raja talked sense."[21] Mahmud, who led the Singapore Traction Company's Employees' Union, added: "Raja had substance, not like some militant union leaders who used powerful language but had no substance." The tough-talking unionist observed that, despite Raja's star profile as an English-educated intellectual, the journalist was humble and related well with the low-educated. This trait appealed to Mahmud, a bus conductor who left school at 13 and lived in a one-room attap hut.

It became a regular affair for Raja to sit and chat with the unionists for hours at coffee shops. Mahmud recalled: "You talk; he listens, he thinks. If he can help, he will help. He kept telling us that we must build a society that is fair and just to everyone." Finding Raja sincere and useful, Mahmud pulled him into the activities of his union. "He gave many ideas on what we should do, such as on unemployment," recalled the fiery unionist who would become the president of the Trade Union Congress in 1960. At Raja's urging, his union organised a mammoth protest meeting at the Victoria Memorial Hall in 1958 against apartheid in South Africa, which served to stir further the anti-colonial mood of workers in Singapore.

Through his incandescent ideas at such forums, Raja gave luminosity to the PAP's image by addressing the concerns of workers while attacking the failure of the colonial system in a credible manner. In his clear-eyed approach, using well-researched and rational arguments, Raja helped, to a certain extent, to differentiate the non-communist faction in the PAP from its voluble militant wing. This was an important service to the credibility of the party at this perilous moment, when it was being battered day in and day out for its close links with the pro-communists.

As Raja emerged as a public intellectual of standing, his heavyweight presence was sought by many quarters. Besides the seminal committee on minimum standards of living, Raja was also appointed by Governor Robert Black to serve on the high-profile Malayanisation Commission, in a letter signed by Chief Secretary W.A. Goode, dated 5 July 1955. On 12 March 1956, the governor appointed him to the staff side panel of the Civil Service Arbitration Tribunal. On 18 June, the minister of labour and welfare wrote to appoint him to the Industrial Court, as a "person representing workmen". He was also made a member of the Further Education Committee for the Singapore Council for Adult Education.

Unions also elevated Raja. In 1956, besides being roped in to the Singapore Unemployment Society, Raja was also elected to become president of the Singapore Union of Journalists. It was a frenetic time as he was stretched on all fronts.

Of all the committees he served on during this period, the most significant and controversial was the Malayanisation Commission. For Raja, it was also an exertion in political philosophy and principle. And it was this exertion which gave the commission its epoch-making flavour.

Its purpose was to examine the schemes of service and the staffing positions in the civil service to recommend measures to ensure a more rapid, systematic and complete Malayanisation of the Public Service, which was staffed at the time by British expatriates, especially at the highest levels. As it noted in its report, self-government would be an empty phrase unless it was run by people of the country.

But the Commission went further: It proceeded to entrench the principles of meritocracy and equal opportunity for Malayans. "It is essential that, apart from statutory requirements, every officer should feel that he can get right to the top if he is sufficiently meritorious and paper qualifications should not be a sine qua non for promotion," noted the report.

The Commission's findings marked a watershed in both politics and history in Malaya. It went through all the key positions held by expatriates and examined how local officers could replace them without affecting efficiency in the shortest time possible. It also called for the entire structure of the civil service to be overhauled and reconstituted to serve, not a colonial system, but a self-governing country.

The 10-man committee was chaired by Dr B.R. Sreenivasan, a respected medical practitioner. Other members included Thio Chan Bee, the first Asian principal of the Anglo-Chinese School, Yusof Ishak, the owner and editor-in-chief of the *Utusan Melayu*, and Percy McNeice, an Irishman who was the colony's first social welfare secretary and served as the president of the City Council, as well as chairman of the Singapore Improvement Trust.

The Assembly House at Empress Place, where the hearings were held, became a theatre of political passion as the commission listened to evidence from a total of 211 people. In all, they held 58 private and public sessions, sitting about twice a week from 6 September 1955 to 20 February 1956. Outside the meetings, they ploughed through volumes of written submissions.

The hearings opened the floodgates of all the repressed anger and bitterness that the local civil servants had been storing up for a long time. Through Kenny Byrne, who spoke with intensity on behalf of the Singapore Senior Officers' Association, the local officers brought out allegations of how advertisements were tailored to suit certain expatriates "fairly snugly" and to exclude Malayans. They highlighted how local officers were not being trained to fill higher posts in the public service because there were "no vacancies" as the expatriate officers were sitting in the positions. At the same time, the expatriate officers at the top refused to make room for qualified Malayans.

As the verbatim notes of the hearings showed, Raja was often at once the high priest of Malayan destiny and a magistrate of its power as he interrogated the expatriate officials. He could hardly keep his indignation in check as he heard the testimonies of discrimination by expatriate administrators against the local people.[22]

Employing prickly quips and pointed questions, Raja skewered the top expatriate officials appearing before the Commission for their supercilious and biased attitudes towards locals. He argued chiefly on matters of principle, in a vein of outrageous paradox. He used their evidence to test the idea of equality and fairness, to see whether they could stand the glare of reality. When they did not, he showed little mercy. Many a time, the expatriate officers were forced to eat their words with Raja feeding them helpfully, word by word.

One such episode was his grilling of Major W.L.P. Sochon, the commissioner of prisons, on 29 September 1955. All its 49 principal officers in the prisons service were expatriates. The major told the commission that it would be a long way before locals could be trained to become principal officers. This was because they lacked the required qualification of an honours degree, or the army first class certificate of education which could not be obtained locally.

The major's position was that, if the locals were recruited without this qualification, it would affect the efficiency of the prisons service. Yet during the questioning, it emerged that not one of the 49 expatriate principal officers had a degree. Raja's hackles were raised when the major defended their recruitment on the basis of their experience and character.

In a querulous tone, Raja questioned the major on why his emphasis on experience and character was not extended to local officers. Raja also confronted him with the advertisements which stipulated that recruits need to have paper qualifications and to reach the rank of warrant officer or its equivalent, and the army first class certificate of education or its equivalent, to qualify as principal officers.

This qualification, however, was not available locally because, unlike Britain which had a standing army to provide such rank or certification, Malaya had no such army. Was it necessary to require that the local officers have this army-related qualification to be recruited? The major replied that it was. Raja cut through the claptrap: "To my knowledge, of the present 64 principal officers, there are only three or four who possess the Army First Class Certificate...Why do you insist on high qualifications for local officers while in the case of expatriate officers, you dispense with them?"

Major Sochon spoke blithely about raising the standards of the prisons, only to be caught out when Raja noted coolly that none of its existing expatriate principal officers had previous experience, and yet the prison service had been fairly efficient. "Would not the same attitude be given to recruit local principal officers without requiring any prison experience and yet be able to have a fairly efficient prison service?"

As the major mouthed feeble replies, Raja pressed on: "As the requirement stand, would it be correct to say that it does discriminate against local officers getting into prison service as principal officers?"

The major stammered a denial, but Raja would have none of it. He persisted: "In view of what has been said this evening, would you consider revising your statement in your reply to our question that we will have to go a long way before local people can be trained as prison officers?" Major Sochon declared that he was stating the ideal. Unconvinced, Raja continued to fire more questions at the hapless major, with a few other members following his lead.

Finally, after his case was clinched, Raja said: "Now, from what you have said this evening, I gather that we could maintain the present level of efficiency by Malayanising at a considerably shorter period than as pointed out in your memorandum." Suitably chastened, the major did not attempt a reply.

Raja was also concerned about the training opportunities provided and their relevance to local conditions. In a closed session on 15 September 1955, the committee perused the required training course for police recruits. According to the minutes, Raja suggested that "the Commission might consider whether it would be possible to run our own training schools in the future". This call illustrated Raja's larger vision for Malayanisation which went beyond just staffing positions with locals, but also making sure that they were trained to serve a self-governing Singapore, as opposed to a British colony.

This concern was starkly expressed during the commission's hearings on broadcasting, when Raja insisted that it was not enough to Malayanise the personnel of the department — it was even more essential to Malayanise the programmes by expanding the vernacular sections and staffing them with qualified people so as to meet the cultural and educational needs of a country on the threshold of independence.

He continued to emphasise this point when dealing with the staffing of the Raffles Library. He pressed L.M. Harrod, who ran the library, to provide a vernacular section, arguing about 80 per cent of the city's population did not read English. At the time, the Raffles Library was a subscription library catering entirely to the English-speaking with about 5,000 members. Harrod replied that he was not familiar with the extent to which the non-English-speaking section of the public read, and admitted that he did not have anybody qualified to deal with Chinese books in the library.

Raja asked Harrod to look into changing this state of affairs. This recommendation was also inserted into the Commission's final report.

Over the course of the lengthy hearings, Raja also sought to make sure that opportunities for promotion did not rest on academic credentials alone, but also on merit — the experience, knowledge and ability of the recruits. He argued for training and opportunity to be extended to local officers without paper qualifications to allow them to rise up the ranks. At issue was the principle of equal opportunity.

He was particularly harsh on expatriate administrators who did not allow for this wider definition of meritocracy in the Malayan civil service. He was even harsher on those who practised double standards — making exceptions for expatriate officers without qualifications, and yet were unwilling to do the same for locals.

The cascade of news stories and headlines arising from the commission hearings and reports captured the imagination of Malayans and thrust Raja to eminence. Lim Chong Yah recalled that Raja became "a bit of a hero". "We needed local people to speak up for us. Raja was an outstanding figure and was a well-known journalist."[23]

There was little doubt that Raja provided the essential impetus in the commission for a more blunt and unforgiving reading of the colonial system.

This emphasis did not go down well with at least two other members, notably McNeice, the colony's first social welfare secretary, who distanced himself from the commission's report, and produced his own Minority Report. Unable to agree on the basic principles in the draft report, McNeice stopped attending meetings from 3 February 1956.

In his minority report, issued in February 1956 together with another member Robert Ho, McNeice argued that a disservice had been done to the British officials, and took exception to the insinuation of a plot to keep local people out of the civil service. In an attempt to provide balance, he noted how the British had made significant constitutional progress amidst tackling complex problems and political disturbance and called this "a major achievement" by those responsible, which far outweighed any criticism on grounds of omission in matters of details.

McNeice's views succeeded only in highlighting the perception gulf separating the expatriates and Malayan nationalists. Nationalists such as Raja saw the dichotomy between what the British were thinking in London and what they were doing in Singapore. At the Colonial Office level in London, the British recognised that it had to speed up the timetable for decolonialisation, and hence the upcoming Constitutional talks in London. But at the colony level in Singapore, careers for British expatriates were at stake. Therefore, there was no eagerness to promote locals or to expose them to higher responsibilities.

After years of venting his frustration over the lip service paid to Malayanisation, Raja now found himself in a position to force the pace. He had eager collaborators: he collected fused charges from his observations in the Commission and passed them on to Lee who ignited them readily in the Legislative Assembly.

On 24 November 1955, Lee accused the Marshall government of weakening on the Malayanisation policy, and attacked the Chief Minister on his "drift" towards expatriate officials which, Lee claimed, had caused people to lose confidence in this policy. Lee told the Assembly that Dr Sreenivasan had received a rude shock in his capacity as chairman of the Malayanisation Commission and "has considerable qualms as to whether he should write his report after his own heart because he might then find it difficult to make it acceptable to the Chief Minister".

Furious at this damaging charge, Marshall summoned Dr Sreenivasan to his office. After he left, Marshall issued a press statement to state that Dr Sreenivasan had not seen Lee for a long time and added that there was no truth to Lee's suggestion that he had lost confidence in the government's intention to Malayanise the civil service.

What Marshall might have forgotten was that, while Dr Sreenivasan might have not seen Lee for a long time, Raja saw both quite often and was privy to the tussle within the commission. If Dr Sreenivasan had struggled over whether he should water down the report to please his political masters, he was now under pressure to do the opposite to show his backbone. For Raja who was arguing for a stronger report, it must have been a happy outcome.

The Commission was working at high pressure to meet Marshall's request for an early interim report, as the public service was one of the topics to be discussed at the first All-Party Constitutional conference in London then scheduled for April/May. It produced its interim report in February 1956 and a final one in May.

The overall effect of the Malayanisation Commission was to quicken the tempo towards self-government. The right was so clear, the wrong so intolerable, the case so convincing, that it seemed to them that the British had lost the moral authority to continue governing Malayans as they demanded their legitimate right to rule themselves. Goh Keng Swee believed: "There was no doubt that their will to govern was destroyed as the result of the exposures which took place during the Malayanisation Commission."[24]

Soon afterwards, the government responded by publishing Command Paper Number 65 of 1956, in which it set out its statement of policy on Malayanisation. It called on the transfer of more positions within the service to local residents to give local leaders in the colonies greater control of the administrative affairs of their country. Harry Chan, then an assistant secretary in the Colonial Secretary's Office and one of the civil servants who had given evidence to the Commission, believed that the hearings were the "tipping point" for colonial rule in Singapore.

When Marshall led the first All-Party Constitutional Mission to London on 14 April 1956, he promised voters — if he failed to secure self-government, he would resign. The negotiations in London turned out to be a fiasco as he shocked the British by demanding full independence and exhibited ill-tempered and erratic behaviour which alienated even his own delegation. The British were prepared to concede on many areas, but not on internal security, given their doubts about Marshall's ability to confront the communist threat. When he returned to Singapore empty-handed, he had little choice but to resign, which he did on 7 June.

Raja was underwhelmed by Marshall's histrionics. Such antics confirmed in his mind that Marshall was not a serious politician who understood the ramifications of politics, but was merely a performer who enjoyed the drama of politics, like "an actor in a Shakespearean play". "He was more interested in presenting himself as an anti-colonial fighter. I don't think he understood the Communist threat," said Raja.

Replacing Marshall as chief minister in 1956 was Lim Yew Hock, who did. Yew Hock, a clerk who rose through the union ranks to become president of the Singapore Trade Union Congress, showed no lack of toughness in dealing with the communists and their front organisations.

In a series of anti-communist purges starting in October 1956, Yew Hock dissolved unions, banned cultural societies, and shut down Chinese schools. He locked up communist open front leaders, unionists, journalists, and student leaders.

Among those detained were some from the PAP — Lim Chin Siong, Fong Swee Suan, Devan Nair, S. Woodhull, and James Puthucheary. The pressures on Raja and the other PAP leaders were immense, as they assessed its impact on the party's organisational strength.

In the eerie aftermath, they were also all too conscious of the danger of the PAP itself being branded as a communist front, and dealt with as such.

Despite the dangers, Raja was propelled into action after the crackdown sparked riots and arson which left 13 dead, 123 injured,

70 cars destroyed, two schools razed, and two police stations smashed. Tear gas and helicopters were brought in to quell the riots, with the police arresting about 1,000 people. All these had the effect of putting Raja in a combative mood. Issuing statements as the PAP's propaganda chief, he decried the violent crackdown and accused Yew Hock of seeking to ensure there was no organised challenge at the next election by weakening the PAP.

Further provoked by what he saw as Yew Hock's indiscriminate arrests, Raja used his position and clout as a long-time SUJ president to pick a direct fight with the chief minister. With extraordinary personal courage, he pressed for the release of several left-wing journalists detained under the Banishment Ordinance.

He marshalled an army of facts and principles to mount his fight. Was the arrest of this or that journalist based on mere suspicion or sound evidence of subversive activity? Were the arrests a clampdown on suspected communists, or on left-wing journalists critical of the government? Was the freedom of the press at stake here? Soon, Raja was winning the admiration of many left-wing journalists for his courage and tenacity as he stood up to the government, at a time when fear and foreboding pervaded the newsrooms.

For a time, Raja focused much of his energy on freeing a *Nanyang Siang Pau* translator named Seah Yong, who chaired the editorial board of the SUJ publication. To gather the facts, Raja, together with SUJ vice-president Lee Khoon Choy and secretary Francis Wong, visited Seah in the Outram jail.

In his solitary cell, Seah was shattered as he pondered on his imminent banishment — he was married just four months ago that June, and his wife was pregnant with their first child. He was anti-colonial like most Chinese-educated journalists at that time, but maintained that he was not involved in subversive activities.

Seah had never met Raja until that day in jail. He was never a PAP member. All he knew of the famous journalist, from reading his articles since the *Singapore Standard* days, was that he was anti-imperialistic. "When he came, I was very touched," Seah related, his eyes brimming with tears. More than 50 years later, he would still be visibly moved at the recollection.[25]

Seah found Raja intelligent and sincere — "a good man with a heart". After several more visits, Raja was convinced of Seah's innocence. He told the tormented man that he would fight for his release. Seah recalled: "I had the confidence that he would fight for me. I saw the sincerity in his eyes."

Aflame with the rightness of his cause, Raja marched into the chief minister's office with the SUJ delegation to plead Seah's case on 18 October. Yew Hock gave Raja's views his careful consideration. This was partly because the SUJ president came with a phalanx of journalists ready to report on what transpired, and partly because no politician wanted unnecessarily to arouse Raja's debating ire.

In a detailed submission, Raja told the chief minister that Seah, a music lover, had neither the inclination nor the time for subversive activities. Seah was completely occupied with his cello and piano practices, his singing rehearsals for a music production, his recent marriage, as well as his work as editor of the SUJ publication, on top of his duties as a translator.

Raja also informed the chief minister that Seah was particularly vulnerable to malicious and vindictive attack — he had acted as the leader of a faction of editorial workers which was in conflict with another group in a recent internal dispute. Would the chief minister concede that it was possible for secret information — because it was immune from the test of the law courts — to sometimes be falsely and maliciously given? Yew Hock acknowledged this possibility and, to the surprise of many, agreed to review Seah's case.

A day later on 19 October, *The Straits Times* reported at length the exchange between the chief minister and Raja, who was quoted as spokesman for SUJ. Its headline "Seah is innocent, Lim told", above a highlighted quote "It is possible police tips are lies", revealed the sympathetic stance of *The Straits Times*. That was another surprise.

That this conservative newspaper would give this specific case such space and treatment was a measure of Raja's persistence and power of argument. He straddled the worlds of politics, trade unions, and journalism, and could hardly be said to be detached. But he persuaded his editors that the fundamental issue was about the freedom of the press. He put up a valiant case that his editors in *The Straits Times*, despite being openly anti-communist and hostile to the PAP, found hard to ignore.

In an editorial headlined, "The Case of Mr Seah" on 19 October, Raja argued cogently: "The arrest of a journalist on political grounds, like the suppression of a newspaper, inevitably raises the suspicion that authority is infringing the freedom of the press." Noting that Seah was accused of subversive activities, Raja wrote: "This is a very broad accusation. Technically, the Straits Times is subversive two or three times a week."

It was "extraordinary and disconcerting" that the government could not say which of Seah's particular activities were subversive. Raja noted that Yew Hock had assured the SUJ that Seah's arrest was not intended to infringe on press freedom. "He must agree, however, that appearances are against him, and he will appreciate the fear which the (SUJ) delegation felt as to the freedom as to which views differing from those of the government of the day can be expressed." Some weeks later, Seah was released.

Seah held Raja in ever higher esteem, and wished that Raja would one day become Singapore's prime minister, a position that Raja himself would never covet. That Raja was Ceylonese and English-educated mattered naught to the Chinese-educated journalist. "We were Chinese-educated, but we accepted him and embraced him because of his heart and sincerity," said Seah.

Despite his public fame, Raja showed an instinct to fight for the underdog, which endeared him to many independents and outsiders. His lifelong struggle, in whatever context he found himself, was to determine what was right and to stand for it, whatever the risks to his person. If you have conviction, it is unconscionable to withhold your body from the battle merely because you might be defeated or destroyed. That was his belief.

Notably, no other newspaper championed the translator's case. Quite the opposite, in fact — the *Singapore Standard* lambasted the SUJ and *The Straits Times* for making representations on behalf of Seah and of press freedom in general. Its columnist, Aster Gunasekara, wrote: "Surely, it is not suggested that journalists, like kings, can do no wrong. That because a person happens to be a journalist, he is at liberty to rape the law with impunity and get away with it," he wrote.[26]

Raja was appalled at the misleading twist put on Seah's case. But he knew that the writer Gunasekara had an axe to grind. All along, Gunasekara had been rabidly anti-PAP, publicly calling for it to be banned alongside the MCP. Raja would later haul him up for dishonourable mention in his attack against the *Singapore Standard* during his election campaign in 1959.

Raja would also be reminded by his former *Straits Times* editors of his own words on freedom of the press during that stormy election campaign. What some of these effusions illustrated all too vividly were the intellectual and moral tangles which Raja would find himself grappling with as he shifted from an abstract thinker to a political practitioner. As newspapers, especially foreign-owned ones, were to find out when Raja became culture minister, his views on freedom of the press would evolve and harden into an iron framework as he forged the art of government and tempered it with experience.

During this perilous period, Raja was one of the trusted few to whom Lee turned for ideas on political strategy and public statements. The others included Goh and Toh. Fong, a member of the PAP's first pro-tem Central Executive Committee (CEC), said: "Eventhough he was not on the CEC, I know he was consulted on all party matters. He played an important role in the PAP's ideology."[27]

Othman Wok, who joined the PAP a few days after its formation, called Raja the party's "think tank".[28]

Raja's role continued to be characteristically intellectual: as a journalist and pamphleteer, an organiser of the circulation of propaganda, and a thinker. When the occasion demanded it, which was often, he would press into service his constant companion, the Remington portable typewriter, to draft statements for the PAP. Lee recalled later: "We would say, Raja, 'you write this out' and he would tap away."[29]

While juggling his varied roles, Raja made time to report for an international audience as a stringer for some foreign publications, such as the *London Observer* and *Jana*, a political magazine covering Asia and Africa. *Jana* was published by the Associated Papers of Ceylon based in Colombo. He wrote on a range of issues, from Marshall's constitutional talks in London and the secret societies in Singapore to the search for technicians in Asia.

Still reeling from his failed *Raayat* venture, Raja no doubt welcomed the additional income. *Jana* paid Raja 75 rupees as retainer and one rupee for every column inch published as its correspondent. *Observer* paid two guineas per 100 words published in the *Observer* and £1.10 per hundred issued by the *Observer Foreign News Service*.

Given the demands of his exigent editors overseas, Raja was often called to write at a moment's notice or to slash his longer features to fit their needs. It was oft times an exasperating experience. In a sympathetic letter on 6 July 1956, Frederick Tomlinson, the *Observer*'s news editor, informed him of a newsprint shortage and advised him to prune his articles to 300 to 350 words. "This effort will save needless cable charges and be less frustrating to you in the end," Tomlinson advised.

Even as he wrote for an international audience to educate them on Malayan developments, he himself was being educated on the art of leadership in Chinese-dominated Singapore. It was a time of great political instruction as he observed Lim Yew Hock being whipped by the Chinese masses for his collaboration with the British on the communist crackdown. Whoever the British embraced would be tagged as the puppet of the colonial master. Against that colonial puppet, one could mobilise the odium of everyone, from the rickshaw puller to the hawker to the student-intellectual.

Astutely opportunistic, Raja drafted PAP statements, issued by Lee, to discredit Yew Hock as a "colonial stooge". Raja observed later: "He could not get rid of the taint that he was the British stooge. He hit too hard and he was not subtle enough." Yew Hock's political destruction at the hands of the Chinese masses served as a lesson to Raja and his non-communist colleagues who sensed that their own showdown with the communists was only a matter of time.

As Raja summarised their analysis later, Yew Hock's problem was that he lacked the "intellectual finesse" to project his fight against the communists as one conducted on behalf of Malayan nationalism, and not on behalf of British colonialism. He had also failed to isolate the communists from the wider Chinese community, leading to what was widely criticised as indiscriminate arrests. Raja and his colleagues would strive to avoid Yew Hock's errors.

In the Legislative Assembly, Yew Hock made great play of the fact that, out of so many arrested, many were connected with the PAP, and as many confessed that they were instructed to penetrate it to use it for communist ends. This was not a blinding revelation to Raja and his PAP colleagues. They were aware that the PAP branches were already dominated by communists, who had also effectively taken control of the party's propaganda channels.

The non-communist leaders also observed closely how the communists penetrated other mass organisations, manipulated them, and orchestrated events. The communists exploited both Chinese nationalism and Marxist-Maoist ideas of egalitarianism which proved so appealing given the political climate. As the communists' revolutionary cry was echoed and re-echoed in the

PAP ranks, Raja could feel the pressure they were exerting for the PAP to bend to their will.

Hence, despite all his huffing and puffing over the arrests and the Emergency regulations, Raja, together with his colleagues, had begun to appreciate the need to keep the Emergency regulations in place. This was a case of familiarity breeding contempt. It was a significant shift for Raja, the expert on the theory of democracy, who had not so long ago argued so strenuously for the end of the Emergency regulations.

Raja's views on the menace posed by the communists would harden further after the election of the third PAP Central Executive Committee (CEC) on 8 July 1956, when pro-communist strength increased to four out of 12 members. Their machinations became obvious when they attempted to change the party constitution to suit their purposes.

Throughout the first half of 1957, an underground struggle was waged in the PAP ranks between the two rival groups. At the next CEC election on 2 August 1957, the pro-communists set out to capture the party, and almost did — they won six of the 12 CEC seats.

Later, Raja and his non-communist colleagues discovered, to their consternation, that the pro-communists had outwitted them by passing admission cards to their supporters so that they could pack the hall to vote. Raja would recall: "It's something new for us. You don't play according to Queensbury Rules with these chaps. They knew all the tricks."

Equally shocked was Goh Keng Swee, who likened their situation to "innocent virgins roaming a brothel area". They had misread the situation and did not understand that the mass base was firmly in the grip of the communists. "We were their prisoners," said Goh.[30]

Immediately, Lee conferred with Raja and the trusted few to devise an escape route. They decided unanimously that the elected non-communist leaders would not take office, so as not to provide cover for the pro-communists and their militant activities. Caught off-guard, the pro-communists were forced to take over the key offices and became exposed. Tan Chong Kin was chairman and T.T. Rajah, a lawyer, its secretary-general.

Raja knew T.T. Rajah quite well — he was, in fact, a distant relative, one of his many far-removed cousins. Before this incident, T.T. had regularly visited Raja's house to borrow his left-wing books, including the works of Lenin. Raja never thought that this relative would join forces with the communists. At least once, Raja had tried to warn T.T. against being manipulated by the communists.

In T.T.'s account, Raja had visited him in his office before the first meeting of the newly-elected CEC. Raja told him that the other five elected members were hard-core communists. He tried to persuade T.T. not to join this group.

Unconvinced, T.T. asked Raja, if the five were hard-core communists, why did the PAP accept them as members? According to T.T., Raja replied: "If the PAP did not use them, some others would use them." Raja was being frank in spelling out the grim reality, but T.T., who was deeply influenced by Mao's revolutionary ideas, was affronted. Years later, T.T. would recollect: "I was deeply dismayed and affected by these words and they sunk deep in my memory."[31]

T.T.'s account reflected the process of Raja's transformation into a political strategist with Machiavellian overtones. This did not happen overnight, but only as he encountered the viciousness with which the pro-communists were plotting to subvert the PAP, and his dreams with it. While his London days exposed him to the power of communism as an ideology, he had not experienced its force as a political opponent on the ground, until now.

The atmosphere of intrigue and duplicity in which the pro-communists operated in the PAP introduced him to the intricacies of political manipulation and subterfuge, and shaped his views on political tactics. Raja, open previously to the ideas of communists, became more guarded. Samad Ismail noticed the change. "Raja started off very left-wing but became more realistic over the years."[32] He also became shrewder.

After the episode, T.T. stopped going to Raja's house. What T.T. had not realised was that it was his own worried father who had approached Raja at his house to plead for his help to advise his son. Raja had done what he could to warn T.T. Raja later said: "He thought that I was a running dog of Lee Kuan Yew and a reactionary and so on." Raja was to weather worse scorn from a wide range of opponents for his visceral loyalty to Lee and their joint mission. Raja was to prove steadfast.

Years later, Raja, a tireless observer of human nature, concluded that T.T. was not so much gripped by the ideology of communism, but by the personal sense of importance which the communists had awarded him as a progressive, socialist fighter. Having been elevated to prominence by the communists, he had to be loyal to that built-up reputation, without realising he was being used by the communists. Raja added a catching observation: "I think this was how they trapped non-communists into becoming servants, whether conscious or unconscious, of their cause."

The communist capture of the PAP prompted another round of government purges. On 22 August, it detained 35 people, including all the pro-communists on the CEC, except T.T. Rajah.[33] Fearful for his own fate, T.T. resigned from the PAP's CEC on 3 September and a month later, also from the party.

Lee and his colleagues reassumed leadership of the party, and amended its constitution so that the CEC would not be such easy prey again.[34] For Raja and his contemporaries, it was their first taste of a new conflict, which would become even more bitter.

12

Moment of Truth

Feeling claustrophobic in the editorial cage of *The Straits Times*, Raja searched for other ways to advance his political ideas to the wider public. Inside him, a philosopher and a political pundit was shrieking to be let out. He found an outlet in radio.

From 1957, he wrote and presented scripts regularly for *Radio Malaya*. Drawing from his experience working part-time for the *BBC* in London, he proved to be adept at it. He used dialogue, music and sound effects to translate what could be sonorous topics, such as nationalism and democracy, into fascinating dramas.

Through the voice box, Raja managed to reach a wider audience than he did with the newspaper. The radio was then a pervasive medium of communication, with people from all walks of life turning on their radio sets in coffee shops, offices and homes. This was before the era of the television, which came to Singapore only in 1963.

Amidst the crackling sounds of radio, Raja started a new relationship with the listening public. He used the intimacy of the microphone to insist on the importance of removing barriers between the different races to build a Malayan nation.

His most ambitious project was to animate his ideas through the conversation of a picaresque group of characters for a six-part drama series "Nation in the Making". The half-hour plays were aired at 7.30 pm every Thursday from 11 July to 15 August 1957. In each programme, listeners were drawn into a discussion between the characters, with explanations of historical developments and past wars. Their attention was paid a thousand fold with the characters asking difficult questions about race, religion and politics, and provoking them to think through the arguments.

The protagonists in this series are the Optimist and the Pessimist. These two characters inform, amuse, outrage, argue through the ebb and flow of dialogue, as they debate what are the essential factors in the making of a nation. Their varied supporting cast includes a "Chinese", "Malay", "Indian", and "student of Malayan history".

The sound effects bracketing their dialogue range from a Chinese funeral march, Christian singing and Indian temple music to the roar of a "Merdeka" crowd. Reading the scripts, one is struck by the clarity with which Raja ticked off systematically, one by one, the arguments against a Malayan nation and laid out the tenets that could form the foundation of a Malayan nation.

To convince his audience, Raja, the connoisseur of books, drew from his extensive reading on nations and nationalism. He interspersed the dialogue with quotes from leading thinkers to show that the idea of a nation was a contested one, with no single definition, and need not rest on the existence of a common race, language, or religion.

Among the thinkers and the ideas they argued for were Ernest Renan: "What constitutes a nation is not speaking the same tongue or belonging to the same race, but having accomplished great things in common in the past and the wish to accomplish them in the future...", and John Stuart Mill: "A portion of mankind may be said to constitute a Nationality if they are united among themselves by common sympathies which do not exist between them and any others — which make them co-operate with each other more willingly than with other people, desire to be under the same government, and desire that it should be government by themselves or a portion of themselves exclusively".

By the end of Part 1, the enlightened discussion between the Optimist and the Pessimist had eliminated common religion and race as being vital for the creation of a Malayan nation. In Part 2, Raja introduced a character "Malayan" who summarised the debate thus far: "So there you have it — the vital stuff which brings a nation to life. What is it? It is a condition of mind, a spiritual possession, a way of thinking, feeling and living. It is sometimes called national consciousness."

To the Pessimist's question of how this national consciousness could be created among the different races with their own separate histories, the Malayan reminded him of H.A.L. Fisher's definition of a nation: "What is essential to the growth of a national spirit is a common history — common sufferings, common triumphs, common achievements, common memories and common aspirations." The discussion became even more fascinating as it shifted to what constituted a common history for Malayans.

A gifted guide, Raja took his listeners through the Hindu-Buddhist empire of Srivijaya which ruled the Malay archipelago from the 5th century to the 14th century, followed by Majapahit empire, and the rise of Malacca as the centre for diffusing Islam in the Malay archipelago in the 15th century. Then the Portuguese captured Malacca, followed by the Dutch, with a British interregnum.

The pretext for this history lesson was the visit of the Optimist and Pessimist to the Timeless Regions to consult the Spirit of History — they wanted to ask how they might discover the binding strands of a Malayan history.

Raja's own views of the start point of modern Malayan history can be detected when the dialogue turned to the hardship faced by labourers from India and China who came to work in Malaya. A character mused that, perhaps one day, someone would write of how the immigrants "came to this country herded like cattle in filthy junks and steamers; of the thousands who die of disease during the journey, of how they were cheated and exploited by labour contractors, and of how they toiled to reclaim land from jungle and swamp..." They had endured common sufferings. The Spirit of History intoned: "You can put down their sweat and sacrifice and their sufferings in your book of the national history of Malaya."

As for the Malays, they were a rural people who earned their living by fishing and agriculture. Though the British developed and modernised Malaya, the British government did nothing to bring them into the new 20th century society. Had schemes been introduced to modernise the economy of the Malay peasants 30 to 40 years ago, said the Optimist, "we would not today be talking about safeguarding the economic position of the Malays".

A riveting exchange follows, which laid out Raja's unassailable and life-long convictions on the making of a Malayan nation:

The Spirit of History:	"All that the people of Malaya need is the will to be a nation...The will to be a nation can come only if the people see themselves not as the product of the history of China, or of India, or of Europe, but as the product of the Malayan history we have been helping you to discover."
Pessimist:	"But how many Malayans will see themselves in this way?
Optimist:	"There may be many of the old generation who will always think of themselves as Chinese or Malays or Indians. They can't help it. It's partly the fault of our educational system. History in school is taught as if it only begins with the coming of the Portuguese or Sir Stamford Raffles or with the founding of the Chinese Emperors or Indian Kingdoms."
Spirit of History:	"Yes, the new generation of Malayans must be made conscious of their common Malayan past."

In this series, he also confronted the danger of the communal demagogue in a controversial fashion — he wrote a part for the Malay communalist to rant in Malay as he blamed rich "foreigners" for the lowly lot of Malay peasants. Given the sensitivities, Raja's use of such unadulterated racial rhetoric on air was shocking. But he wanted to use the dramatic moment to expose the depraved motivations of the communalist and his lies.

Depicting the communal leader as a common rogue, the Optimist said: "He was anxious only to exploit the poverty of the people to get more followers, more votes. He wants to be a leader. And one way of getting people to follow you is to rouse their anger, their fear of the enemy...And since a great many of them have had unpleasant experiences with Chinese shopkeepers or Indian moneylenders or have been envious of the foreigners who ride in big cars and live in big houses, it is only too easy to rouse racial hatred. But our communal leader never bothered to tell them that a great many Chinese live in slums, and are just as poor as the Malays and that there are many undernourished Indians. And there are many rich Malays."

Another gem encrusted in his radio plays was his definition of a real leader. He dismissed the idea of communal demagogues being leaders. In the words of the Optimist: "Don't you agree that a leader is the sort of man who can inspire people for a cause — appeal to the best in people."

Inspire people for a cause; appeal to the best in them. Raja himself sought to do that as the "Malayan" in the play intoned: "It is up to us who care for their country, who really love the people, who believe that our great resources and talents can be used to bring more happiness — it is up to us to teach the people, to explain to the people, to continue to fight with truth and decency against the racialist."

In reply to the Pessimist who believed in "reason, logic, facts", the Malayan appealed to a higher logic: "It is a declaration of belief that people can be made to think, that you can appeal to their reason, and that you can bring out the decent and human qualities in them. We must believe in this or perish. If we believe that our people are essentially reasonable and decent, then we can believe that they will understand us when we say that, unless we become a nation, we will destroy ourselves."[1]

Reading the script some 50 years later, there is a sense that the dialogue regarding race and nation is yet unfinished. Raja's concerns with the contending pulls of race vis-à-vis a common national identity continue to haunt contemporary consciousness. He imagined a nation united by a common will and national consciousness, untethered to the divisive concepts of race, religion, or language, long before its outward shell of independence was formed.

His radio plays, like his short stories, deserve greater study for their contribution to the idea of a Malayan nation and the contested notions of the beginning of Malayan history.

Raja was provoking people to imagine a Malayan nation in their heads and to turn it into reality with their hearts. He was encouraging them to trace their history to the day they came to Malaya and suffered together to build up the country. These views, formed even before he joined politics in 1959, would determine his policy direction when he championed the controversial creation of a "Malayan culture" as culture minister.

Through the radio, Raja reached out to impressionable young minds, who might otherwise never have known his views. In the 1950s, thousands of schools received educational broadcasts, including the Chinese schools. Committed to the task of educating them, Raja regularly wrote scripts on current affairs for secondary classes, aired at 11.35 am.

Foong Choon Hon, who then worked for *Radio Malaya*, would translate Raja's scripts into Chinese to be broadcast to the Chinese schools, expanding his outreach into the intellectual domain of the communists. Foong recalled: "From reading his scripts, I knew he was a very intelligent writer and very anti-colonial, but he didn't approve of violence. He was letting people know what was really happening in the world, how they would affect Malaya and giving his insights into the shape of Malaya's future."[2]

Foong remembered how Raja often emphasised that Singapore was a multicultural society and should develop a Malayan consciousness which transcended their communal loyalties. It was a controversial idea for many Chinese-educated students, exposed almost exclusively to ideas only from China. Wang Gungwu, a historian who specialises in the study of overseas Chinese, noted: "In Singapore, most Chinese schools were still actively promoting Chinese culture and that would contradict anything that defined "Malayan" as any kind of amalgam of different cultures."[3]

In the final programme of a series, *Looking Forward*, broadcast to students during their third term in 1957, Raja focused their minds on the importance of being able to anticipate future problems so that dangers could be averted.[4] Noting that political power was in the hands of mainly the older generation which had not been taught to think of itself as Malayan, he said: "Imagine what would happen if, during elections, people voted for a candidate, not because of the party he belonged to, or because of his individual merits, but because of the community to which he belonged. And if we are not careful, Malaya might well see the kind of communal disturbances which plagued India and which still occasionally are there."

One of the urgent tasks before the government and before Malaya's leaders was to train people to think like Malayans, particularly the older generation. "I would say that this is Malaya's No. 1 problem," he asserted. He said every wise government must anticipate problems intelligently, so that it was prepared to face them when they came.

His efforts at political education continued as he ruminated on the issue of democracy and the role of leaders in programmes such as the *People In The News* series. Among the personalities he featured were those he knew and admired — Indian nationalist and first prime minister Nehru and Pan-African nationalist Kwame Nkrumah.

Showing his breadth of knowledge, Raja also wrote and presented programmes on international issues. They included the series *World Affairs*, aired for a more adult audience at 8 pm. He also wrote and presented talks on topical issues for the programme *Talk of the Week*, aired at 9 pm, and commented regularly on national and international events in the daily programme *In the News*. Besides writing and presenting, he also took part in radio forums on topical issues. His diction was crisp and measured, with a touch of the Indian accent. His voice was gentle and unimposing, yet authoritative.

For each script, he was paid between $20 and $40. The receipts give a good record of his preoccupations during a period of raw, dislocating change. Ideas drove politics at the time, and Raja was at the forefront in a succession of ideas, moulding, changing, kneading people's minds towards a common vision.

As he took to the airwaves to spread his views, he was viewed by the British intelligence with increasing suspicion. This was tested in 1958 when Raja applied for the post of chief editor at the station. Immediately, he came up against security objections by the intelligence agencies. A Special Branch report dated 31 July 1958, noted: "This, in view of his close connection with the PAP, is believed to be another attempt by the PAP to penetrate the government service."[5]

Interestingly, Raja must have got wind of the excitement stirred by his application as he went to see H.H. Beamish, the acting director of broadcasting, to withdraw it. In a letter dated 24 November 1958, Beamish wrote to Raja: "It was very good of you to call round on Saturday to tell me what you had decided. I quite understand your point of view, and may I say, so does the Chief Secretary's Office. I told them you had decided to withdraw your application for the post of Chief Editor, and in very general terms, your reasons for it."

It must have been a sweet moment for Raja when he became culture minister in 1959 and had the run of the radio station. One of his first tasks was to meet the broadcasting staff and set out his priorities. Chief among them was to educate the young. Foong, who was present during that discussion, recalled: "He said it was important to shape the minds of young people because they are our hope for the future."

Meanwhile, Raja's own hopes for a united Malaya were being shattered. The Federation became independent on its own on 31 August 1957.

With this new development, he was forced to revise his basic political assumptions.

He was mistaken to assume that the presence of the Tunku and Cheng Lock at the PAP's inauguration signalled that the anti-colonial struggle in Singapore and the Federation would be conducted in a pan-Malayan context. He also showed a lack of realism in assuming that both territories would automatically become a united Malaya with the end of colonial rule.

The Tunku's opposition to merger with the island, with the concurrence of the British, meant that the two territories would move along different paths in their constitutional development, with the Federation achieving independence first. In his negotiations with the British for independence for the Federation, the Tunku refused to consider Singapore as part of his political equation, as he feared that it would threaten the privileged position of the Malays in Malaya.

With Singapore in Malaya, the Chinese would outnumber the Malays. In 1957, 75 per cent of Singapore's 1.45 million people were Chinese. In the Federation, Malays make up 49.8 per cent, and Chinese 37.2 per cent. In a United Malaya, with Singapore included, Malays would account for 43 per cent of the population, with the Chinese outnumbering them at 44.3 per cent.

As Raja came to terms with the discomfiting realities, he understood that the path to a united Malaya and independence for Singapore lay not in fighting the British, but in convincing the Federation leaders. Ever an optimist, Raja believed that the Tunku's fears could be overcome.

With a new constitution for internal self-government in 1958 for Singapore, he was seized with an urgent need to develop in the people a Malayan consciousness, as opposed to a Chinese consciousness. He believed that the sooner the people in Singapore developed this Malayan consciousness, the sooner Singapore could attain merger and independence. He continued to work furiously towards that day.

With his whole heart, Raja believed in a united Malaya; he did not believe in an independent Singapore all by itself. He was not only intellectually committed to the idea of a united Malaya, but emotionally as well. He crossed the causeway to visit his family in Seremban regularly, particularly for the annual Deepavali celebrations, and considered Seremban as much his home as Singapore. He could not forget that the PAP's *raison d'etre*, as stated in its first manifesto, was to fight for independence of a united Malaya, including Singapore.

Besides print and radio, he reached out to different audiences in various discussion forums in person, such as the gatherings organised by the University of Malaya Socialist Club. One of them, held on 30 March 1957, saw him discussing the importance of a common language for Malaya in a club gathering attended by Han Suyin, Toh Chin Chye, Jamit Singh, and several Chinese-educated students from the Nanyang University.[6]

It was at such university forums that Tommy Koh, then a law student, first met Raja. "I was impressed by his good looks, eloquence and passionate opposition to British colonialism," Koh recalled.

Raja's argument to his disparate audiences was consistent: To end colonialism in Singapore, it must have merger with the Federation. To have merger with the Federation, Singapore, which was predominantly Chinese, must convince the Federation, which was predominantly Malay, that the different races could unite in one common Malayan brotherhood and be loyal to Malaya. Hence, the people must be taught to think in terms of Malaya and Malayans.

The first obstacle to this objective was language. Therefore, it was important for all to learn a national language — and that should be Malay as it was the most widely spoken and understood language in Malaya. Malay was also the national language in the Federation. Raja believed that "only through the use of a national language can the various communities break down the walls that now separate them — walls that are now forcing them to develop communal and distinct cultures".[7]

The cleavage between the races, the violence on the streets and in the neighbourhood, seemed to mock his high eloquence on the merits of democracy and the emergence of a Malayan consciousness. But he knew it was important to rouse not only the English-educated, but also the non-English educated majority to support the democratic system, its ideals, and its institutions. Otherwise, only brute force remained.

At the time, most Chinese-educated students looked to China for inspiration and were affected by developments in their motherland. They were proud of China's emergence as a power and felt that an Asian giant had awoken. They recalled the humiliation and sufferings inflicted on China and the Chinese people by imperialists in the last 100 years since the Opium War and welled up with pride at the triumph of the communists in China.

Chan Chee Seng, a young clerk with Hong Kong and Shanghai Bank, was among them, but his mind was open to Raja's message. He started learning English when he was 15, and reading Raja's columns in the *Standard* was part of his self-tutelage in the language. "When I saw his byline, I would cut it out and try to read and understand it. I would put the article in my pocket and take it out to read carefully when I rode on the bus," Chan related.

He got to meet Raja years later when the famous journalist walked into the bank as a customer. As they became more familiar with each other, Raja would take Chan and a few others to a hawker stall in a back street near the bank and talk about politics over coffee. "Raja paid most of the time, and wouldn't let us pay," he recalled. He found Raja humble and friendly.

Before long, partly because of the conversations with Raja, Chan became attracted to the PAP's cause.[8] He gave Raja's ideas on developing a Malayan consciousness his serious consideration. "This was something new to us. We found it a new way of looking at the world and understanding things. It was very different from our way of thinking," said Chan.[9]

Others, such as Hoe Puay Choo, a Chinese-educated seamstress who became a member of the PAP's central executive committee and the PAP City Councillor for Kampong Glam in 1957, considered his views on a Malayan identity unrealistic, given the emotional bonds of the Chinese-educated to China. But whenever she met Raja, her attitude would soften. Although they could communicate only in bazaar Malay, she was disarmed by his gentle bonhomie and courtesy. Like many of the Chinese-educated workers at the time, she had felt disadvantaged and even despised by the English-educated. "A lot of the English-educated people looked down on us but not Raja," she said.[10]

Mindful that the English-educated and the Malays made up about 40 per cent of the island's population, Raja also made a special effort to reach out to the Malays, to assure them of the PAP's non-communist objectives and its seriousness in setting up a multiracial political party. At that time, not many Malays would join the PAP, as it was seen to be dominated by the Chinese-educated. To bring more Malays into the party ranks, Raja gave talks to the Malay members, most of whom came from the unions.

Othman Wok, who translated Raja's talks into Malay, recalls: "During these sessions, Raja told them about the PAP's political goals, and the role that Malays could play in Singapore's development." More pertinently, he would also explain the benefits of merger with Malaya, on the grounds of economic development for all, including the poor Malays.

Recognising Raja's talent for words and passion for ideas, Lee put Raja in charge of the party's Political Bureau, set up to educate party members on what the party stood for and set out to accomplish. It was a crucial role, given the power of the cadres to elect the CEC.

Lee also freed Raja to operate in areas where his talents shone most and were most needed — and that was to take effective control of the party propaganda. He put Raja in charge of *Petir*, the party newsletter. Raja discharged his role with ease and relish. Lee recalled: "I left him to it. It was not necessary to give him any specific instructions."[11]

Raja understood that one of the greatest challenges for the party was to educate opinion. Hence, cadre classes were organised each month for branch committees, and where possible, a Malay and Indian section would be set up in each of the branches. Raja made sure the classes were conducted in the different languages, using translators. In these classes, Raja would explain in detail the party's ideology and the tasks ahead. At the same time, he emphasised the need to recruit more Malays and Indians into the party to give it a more multiracial complexion.

By then, the political battle had begun to polarise sharply — on one side, the non-communists (also referred to at the time as the moderates) led by Lee, and the pro-communists (sometimes also called "extremists"), led by Chin Siong.[12] Their clash came to be symbolised by the two rival groups' constant demands — Lee's group wanted a non-communist, democratic socialist, united Malaya by peaceful and constitutional methods; Chin Siong's wanted independence for Singapore by itself, complete control over internal security, and a pro-communist Singapore using revolutionary and militant methods.

The balance of power on the ground was with the pro-communists. Although the moderates controlled the levers in the PAP Central Executive Committee, the pro-communists had effectively taken over the running of the PAP machinery in the branches. Raja was realistic about his group's weaker position at this point. As he told Bloodworth during this period, they were up against very disciplined and dedicated people. "It is very difficult for us to rally chaps to work as hard as they will. And they'll take on any job, and work any hours simply to further their cause."[13]

Unlike the non-communist workers, the pro-communists were full-time revolutionaries. They could also count on the ranks of the young unemployed who squatted day and night in the branches. The pro-communists had also commandeered the channels for indoctrinating the branch members on communism through their daily activities.

Raja refused to be daunted. Instead, he lashed out at the pro-communists for their "political infantilism" and "adventurism", noting how they had zig-zagged in their tactics from week to week in their bid to capture power. Their shout for an independent Singapore, as a country all by itself, was evidence of their political immaturity, he asserted. "To base their actions on the naive belief that the party consists of weak and feeble individuals who can be manipulated at all time is evidence of political adventurism," he wrote.[14]

As for those who talked glibly about armed revolution, they should consider carefully the consequences of armed revolution, both to themselves and their compatriots, he warned. "If they are still convinced that the only way out is armed revolution, let them leave our Party, go across the Johore Causeway and take up arms in the Malayan jungle," he said.[15]

Unsurprisingly, this censure fell on deaf ears. But Raja's diatribe against the dissidents, together with statements from several PAP leaders, served to shore up at least an appearance of the PAP's resolve to get its house in order. It was a race against time as the City Council election was scheduled for December that same year, in 1957. To remain standing in the political arena, the PAP must be ready.

As he gave himself up to the cause, Raja became indispensable as the craftsman of the party's ideology. He carved out what the PAP really stood for — "an independent, democratic, non-Communist Socialist Malaya" — and polished all its nuances to a high shine. With his precise exegesis, he gave the party some inner coherence, which was lacking previously when two different voices were speaking to the ground — one non-communist, and the other pro-communist.

Raja explained each term at length in the pages of *Petir* as well as in his political classes. He emphasised that the party did not support armed revolution, and asked those who got into the "wrong train" to get out now. He explained that an independent Malaya meant not only trying to force the British to grant independence to Singapore — "they would probably withhold it" — but of persuading the Federation to take Singapore in. Only by merging with the six million people in Malaya could Singapore hope to be independent.[16]

On the PAP's ideals for a non-communist socialist Malaya, Raja stressed that Singapore, by itself, could not be socialist given its features — small, without natural wealth or large-scale industries. Socialism was possible only for Malaya as a whole. It would not be achieved overnight but, given the multiracial composition of Malaya, it was the only way forward.

The PAP's task, at its broadest and most ambitious, was to unite the different races into one people. That, at least, was how Raja framed the matter: "Our party believes that, while armed revolution cannot unite the three major races of Malaya, a peaceful constitutional struggle based on democratic socialism can."

Aware that pro-communists would be found in every class he conducted, Raja addressed their viewpoint directly as well. He knew that they were inspired by the armed revolution in China.

He explained that the situation in Malaya was different from that in China. The most important difference was that Malaya had three major races, Malays, Indians, and Chinese — and of these, only the Chinese had indicated any inclination for armed revolutionary violence. All that had been achieved in the nine years of armed warfare against the British and three years of armed resistance against the Japanese — 12 years of warfare waged mainly by the Chinese in Malaya — was to isolate the Chinese from the other races, he pointed out. Not only that, it had caused great hardship to the large masses of Chinese in the Federation because of their suspected support for armed rebellion, he reasoned.

Raja never stopped insisting that there were better ways to achieve a socialist society than by armed revolution and never stopped reiterating it. He amplified the message when the pro-communists sought to capitalise on the confusion in the PAP ranks with the Federation's independence on 31 August.

Raja authored a key party document, "The New Phase After Merdeka — Our Task and Policy" to stress that the party's key enduring objective remained unchanged in 1958 — to create an "independent, democratic, non-Communist socialist Malaya (Federation plus Singapore)". In the document, published as a special issue of *Petir* on 22 November 1958, Raja tried to address the fears of Federation Alliance leaders as well as the uncertainty of its own party members.

He made clear the distinction between democratic socialists and communists: Both democratic socialists and communists wanted to create a socialist society "where man can no longer exploit his fellow man by the possession of material wealth". The democratic socialist believed that he could achieve this social revolution peacefully through the democratic system. The communist disagreed with this and espoused militant and military methods of class struggle.

Drawing on his vast knowledge of world movements, he gave a historical world view of the democratic socialist movement. He started with the dawn of civilisation 5,000 years ago with the early farming communities, passing through the feudal system, the industrial revolution, the birth of capitalism, Marxism, and ending with the democratic transformation of the capitalist system.

He examined China's violent road to socialism, and concluded that that "to approach our own problems with the categorical and inflexible attitudes of revolutionary violence is not only unprofitable, but positively disastrous. It is our duty to point out the error of the text book approach and prevent these so-called Marxists from bringing racial tensions, strife and ruin upon Malaya".

It was an onerous task convincing the Chinese ground, influenced as they were by the MCP's propaganda that a merger with a Malay-dominated Federation would bring about an irretrievable loss of Chinese culture and language. Chee Seng, who often helped to translate Raja's points into Chinese, noted that, at the time, many of the branch members believed the pro-communists' line that "merger was bad". "The argument was quite intense. I didn't believe it was bad. Raja helped me understand the reasons for merger."[17]

Undeterred by the government purges, the communists and their sympathisers continued to stream in and infiltrate the PAP branches. They also pumped out recruits to take positions in new unions and societies, especially from among the Chinese-educated students in Chinese middle schools and the Nanyang University (Nantah).

As they graduated from school to university to the workplace, thousands nursed the grievance caused by the government crackdown on their schools and organisations. Many took part in communist-led demonstrations, sit-ins, and strikes. They nurtured a taste for political revolt that would define the politics of the day and beyond.

Through the pounding pressures he faced during this period, day by day, Raja retained an unflagging faith in his party's cause. Faced with the communist threat, his mood was one of confrontation and confidence. They would fight the communists and their supporters, and they would win. His warrior spirit made a perceptible difference to the team. Lee recalled: "He contributed that spirit of 'Let's fight them. Let's get rid of them. Let's fight and do it on our own. We can't be intimidated!' " Lee added: "And he was not intimidated."[18]

From their battles with the pro-communists, which would last six years, they would emerge more streetwise and sinewy. Their approach to their adversaries became more muscular, sometimes bordering on thuggish. They had witnessed how demagoguery and populist slogans could rouse a crowd into irrational action and violence.

Their harrowing experiences forced them to re-examine their assumptions of mass politics and communism. Even with his firm grasp of communist theory, Raja would note wryly later: "The PAP leaders, after such unpleasant experiences, made it a point to re-read the tactical writings of Communism a little more intensively." For Raja, the experience was instrumental in the development of his own political judgment.

Throughout this treacherous period, Raja and the core team perceived themselves as innocent political novices operating on the moral high ground. This was apparent in the first signed account of party history, published in 1964.[19] In his highly partisan account, Raja portrayed the PAP protagonists as raw but valiant and honest political amateurs, forced to do battle against far more powerful, well-organised and experienced communists on the one hand, and the well-established, right-wing pro-colonial forces on the other.

This self-perception is pivotal to understanding their acute sense of vulnerability and their political development and transformation into tough, even ruthless, leaders when they took charge in the new government in 1959. It also allowed them to take risks in the political arena, to work by trial and error, and not recriminate against one another when things went awry. There was no political handbook for them to fall back on. They were writing it for the future generations of Singapore's leaders.

Raja was exultant when, despite being weakened by the treachery within its ranks, the PAP did well in the City Council elections — it won all 14 seats contested except one, and routed the Labour Front and the Liberal Socialist parties. But more importantly, the PAP emerged with the best scores, with the highest number of votes per candidate.[20]

The election also saw the political resurrection of Marshall, who had some eight months earlier announced his "permanent" retirement from politics. He had cobbled together a Workers' Party and put up five candidates. Four won. PAP's showing startled the Liberal Socialists and the Labour Front. Yew Hock withdrew from the Labour Front and formed a new party, the Singapore People's Alliance, together with deserters from the Liberal Socialists.

Raja thought it augured well for the party when a PAP councillor, Ong Eng Guan, a Melbourne-trained accountant, was elected as mayor. Ong was a forceful figure at election rallies and a rousing Hokkien

Left Raja (extreme left) at the third annual conference of the PAP at the Singapore Badminton Hall, 1956. *(SPH)*

Below First election campaign: Raja rails against the English press at a rally in Fullerton Square, 1 April 1959. *(NAS)*

The first PAP Cabinet: (left to right) Yong Nyuk Lin, Ong Eng Guan, S. Rajaratnam, Ahmad Ibrahim, Ong Pang Boon, Goh Keng Swee, Toh Chin Chye, K. M. Byrne, Lee Kuan Yew outside the City Hall after the swearing-in ceremony, 5 June 1959. *(SPH)*

Raja talks to the various cultural groups about promoting a Malayan consciousness, 26 July 1959. *(NAS)*

Left Bringing Christmas cheer to blind children at *Radio Singapore*. With Raja is war heroine Elizabeth Choy, principal of the Singapore School for the Blind, 24 December 1959. *(SPH)*

Below Discussing the problems facing Singapore with civil servants at the Political Study Centre, 22 October 1959. *(NAS)*

Above Promoting photography: Raja at a pan-Malayan photographic exhibition, 31 July 1959. *(NAS)*

Left Books: At the National Library's opening, officiated by the Yang di-Pertuan Negara Yusof Ishak, 12 November 1960. *(SPH)*

Below Multiculturalism: At the *Aneka Ragam Raayat* concert at the City Hall steps, 5 December 1959. *(SPH)*

Grassroots work: Opening the Kampong Glam Community Centre, 4 June 1960. *(NAS)*

Nurturing the young at his Kampong Glam Children Club, 24 February 1963. *(NAS)*

Being welcomed by the lion dance troupe to his community centre, 9 June 1963. *(NAS)*

Bidding farewell to William Goode, the last British Governor in Singapore, 2 December 1959. Raja describes Goode as a politically perceptive man and a "fine example of an upright, intelligent British administrator". *(SPH)*

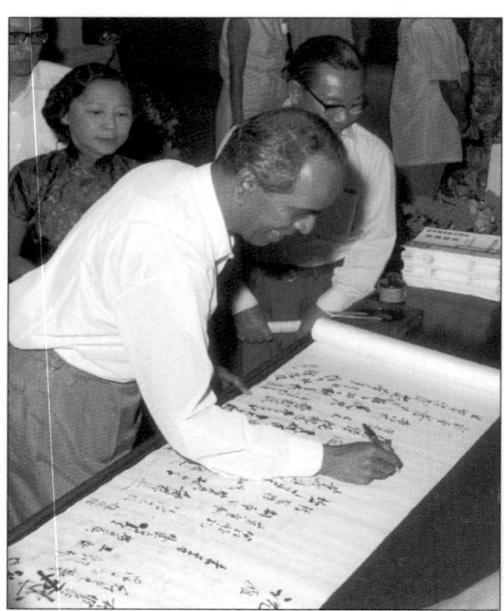

Opening an art exhibition at Victoria Memorial Hall, 18 July 1963. *(NAS)*

Building links with Indonesia through cultural exchange, City Hall steps, 16 August 1959. *(NAS)*

Hong Lim by-election: Raja preps PAP candidate Jek Yuen Thong on nomination day, 11 March 1961. *(NAS)*

Raja (second from right) with Goh Keng Swee (far left) unveiling plans for a new industrial town at Jurong. On Goh's left is Kenny Byrne, 2 July 1960. *(SPH)*

Left Raja speaks at a referendum lunch-time rally at Fullerton Square, 1 September 1962. *(NAS)*

Below Raja attends a Legislative Assembly session, 7 December 1961. *(SPH)*

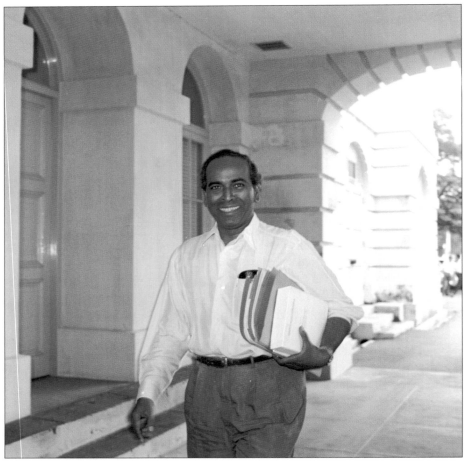

orator comparable to Lim Chin Siong. In fact, it was Raja who had introduced Ong to the PAP when it was being formed. At it happened, the PAP leaders were at the time looking for a suitable person to become the treasurer of its first pro-tem CEC. Toh, who became the party's first chairman, related later: "Since he was an accountant, we invited him to be party treasurer."[21] This decision would haunt them later, as Ong capitalised on his positions to build a personality cult and, in 1960, made a treacherous bid to split the party.

Initially, Raja regarded Ong as an asset to the PAP, given his powerful oratory in Chinese. Then Ong began to indulge in dramatic antics such as destroying the paraphernalia of colonialism like the mace and pictures of Queen Elizabeth II, sacking expatriates, and recruiting Chinese-educated personnel. His actions appealed to the Chinese-educated group, who hailed him as a folk hero, but they alienated the English-educated group from the PAP.

Although other PAP leaders were angry with Ong for his antics, Raja showed more tolerance. Raja rationalised that Ong had to take this "destructive" approach to challenge the status quo and weaken the colonial administration.

Lee had a less charitable assessment of Ong, as did several others in the core group. Lee believed that Ong was doing immense harm to the country and the PAP. He was not at all surprised that Raja held a kindlier view of Ong; it was in character. Raja was inclined to give people the benefit of the doubt and to offer generous interpretations of their actions. Where life bred in Raja a more philosophical and forgiving view of human nature, sometimes verging on naivete, it developed in Lee an instinct for wary deliberation. The two balancing qualities buttressed and strengthened their partnership as they faced the vicissitudes of political life.

Raja came to realise the danger that Ong posed to the party only after the 1959 elections, when he was made national development minister.

The third constitutional talks in April 1958 resulted in an agreement on a constitution for a State of Singapore, with full powers of internal government. Britain retained control over foreign affairs and external defence, while internal security rested in the hands of the Internal Security Council. In August 1958, the British parliament changed the status of Singapore from a colony to a state, and elections for the 51-member Legislative Assembly were scheduled for May 1959.

From November 1958, the PAP began to prepare for the general elections. A major decision that the PAP had to take was whether it should fight to win to form the government, or to constitute a strong opposition bloc in the assembly.

Raja was stoutly against fighting to win. He told the team: "Look, we haven't got an organisation. I think you need a few years as an opposition to build up your reputation and organisation." He knew that the real struggle for the PAP would begin after self-government was achieved, between communists and non-communists.

Raja was uneasy at the prospect that, if the PAP were to field 51 candidates, it would be a Trojan horse for some "hidden communists" and the PAP would not know any better until they were waving their red books in the Legislative Assembly. Once in, they would cause no end of problems. As Raja confided in Bloodworth at the time, "Remember, when the PAP got three seats in the old Assembly, we were able to make a hell of a nuisance of ourselves and to show up the Lim Yew Hock government as a bunch of colonial stooges by talking in public and getting our speeches printed in the newspapers. If they get three chaps in, they'll do the same to us. So we've got to be very careful."[22]

Raja further argued that a government which assumed power under a constitution which did not grant full independence would run into severe difficulties. He listed them: There would be demagogues who would try to cash in with slogans about an independent Singapore and other violent, anti-colonial posturing. Merger with the Federation might be a very slow affair, providing more fuel for advocates of an independent Singapore. There would be, in such circumstances, attempts to brand the government in power as compromising with colonialism. Even more onerous would be the task of trying to resolve the economic and social problems of an isolated Singapore with no natural resources. Added to these was the equally formidable problem of trying to transform a predominantly Chinese Singapore into a Malayan Singapore.

Raja believed that it would be better for the PAP to build up its strength and its experience for another few more years as an opposition party. Let some other party make the mistakes and incur the odium in the course of trying to resolve these difficult problems, he advised.

These were powerful arguments against forming a government. Indeed, until about the beginning of 1959, the trend of thought within the party was against fighting to win. Lee gravitated to this view as he knew the problems facing the next government would be immense. At that time, unemployment was 12 per cent and the birth rate was four per cent a year. Economic prospects were grim, made worse by the militant climate of labour unrest. Lee was not at all confident that they could withstand the communist assaults that would follow.

Lee recalled the arguments: "Raja, ever the idealist and the ideologue, was in favour of our forming a strong opposition."[23] Disagreeing, Goh Keng Swee and Kenny Byrne argued that the PAP had to form the government. They feared that, if it waited another five-year term, the corruption would spread from the ministries into the civil service itself. Towards the end of 1958, Lee began to discuss this question with the principal pro-communist detainees — Lim Chin Siong, Fong Swee Suan, Devan Nair, Woodhull, and James Puthucheary — in their detention centre at Changi.

Lee made plain his deep reservations about setting out to win in the next election, because a PAP government would soon be in trouble with the MCP. Chin Siong and company were alarmed by this position. As Nair said, "We all knew that, if the PAP did not form the next government, we would not be released by the British and Malayan Governments, whose representatives would sit on the Internal Security Council of Singapore."

Lee told them that he and his non-communist colleagues in the PAP would not fight to win, unless he was assured that they would abide by the democratic socialist values of the PAP, respect peaceful constitutional means, and take a clear-cut stand against the armed insurrection led by the MCP.

Lee added that Raja, Goh, Toh and himself were working on a document called "The Tasks Ahead". The first chapter would set out their political platform — independence for Singapore through merger with a democratic, socialist, but non-communist Malaya. Gradually, the detainees offered promises to support the party. Knowing that promises could be broken, Lee asked them to put down in writing the terms on which they would give that support. Nair wrote a draft. By that time, Nair had become disenchanted with his Chinese communist friends' brand of politics, which was distinguished more by their Chinese chauvinism than by their Marxism.

Lee kept his non-communist colleagues informed of his discussions with the detainees. Lee suggested to Raja that, given his grave doubts about fighting to win, he should visit them himself to make his own assessment. Raja did. At the detention centre, he met with Woodhull, Puthucheary and Nair whom he knew quite well, but not with the Chinese-educated members, being less familiar with them.

The trio impressed on Raja that the PAP must fight to win. Raja tested them with this counter: "But we will have trouble with the communists, apart from anything else." They responded with assurances that they would help to curb the communists.

To make sure they were on the same page, Raja launched into a discourse on how communism was not practical for Singapore. He told them that the party manifesto made clear that the political battle in Singapore was only one phase of a bigger battle for merger with Malaya, and the Malays in Malaya would never stand for communism.

During the discussion, Raja noticed that Nair was the most categorical on his stand against communism; the other two prevaricated.

At one point, Raja noticed sores all over the hands of Woodhull and asked him: "What's wrong with you?" According to Raja, Woodhull replied: "Nervous tension. Raja, you people better fight to win because if you don't win, if the PAP doesn't come in, if Yew Hock comes in, we may be here for life. So you must fight to win." Raja told them, if the PAP did that, they must promise to stand by the PAP and take on the communists. Woodhull agreed. While not entirely convinced, Raja took their assurances at face value.

By the beginning of 1959, Nair had his political statement ready for the five principal detainees to sign. It spelt out their commitment to the PAP's fundamental stand. They signed it. Raja nursed some doubts about their sincerity. His reservations were not unfounded. In the end, only Nair would stand by it.

Ultimately, the key factor which clinched the issue for Lee, Raja and the non-communist leaders was this question — which party would take power if the PAP did not. The answer was the SPA, a coalition of the Labour Front and the Liberal Socialists, which Lim Yew Hock had cobbled together the previous November. For Raja, it was a repugnant thought.

As he put it later, "the SPA as then constituted was not only a monstrosity but a party which would have plunged Singapore in chaos and tragedy".[24] He also believed that the SPA would not hesitate to ban the PAP — after all, the SPA had been vocal in its accusation that the PAP was a communist front. This led him to conclude that "the PAP would have about as much chance of building its strength under an SPA government as a mouse would have in a house full of cats".

It was when pondering life as a defenceless rodent that Raja realised that the PAP had to fight to win. This realisation was forced on Raja, but he accepted it with the same stubborn courage with which he accepted all confrontations and challenges. As the PAP firmed up its plans, Lee approached Raja to take part in the elections. To do that, he had to leave his job at *The Straits Times*. Would he do it?

It was a moment of truth for Raja. He knew that the May 1959 elections would decide the destiny of the country on the verge of achieving its independence. To Raja with his keen sense of political consciousness, it must have seemed as if history had speeded up. The centuries of foreign domination dragged by, punctuated by wars and the slow decline of the British empire, then the rush of bewildering events leading up to this moment: To take part in the creation of an independent state which would serve the needs of the people as alien rulers had not done.

While his commitment to the PAP was solid, his self-knowledge gave him cause for pause. Raja did not think he had the natural disposition or capability to be a politician. He was reserved and scholarly. He loved the written word more than the spoken. All along, he had felt that his forte was as a journalist and a publicist, and that was how he could best contribute to the PAP.

He confessed to Lee that he didn't see himself fitting into the life of politics. First, he felt disjointed when surrounded by a sea of unfamiliar faces. He told Lee: "It's difficult for me to get on with anonymous people." He could get on with friends, people he knew with faces he recognised. "But in politics, you are really dealing with people who are anonymous, the masses. And you got to be nice to them, understand them, respond to them." It was not his temperament.

Another problem was language. A politician must feel the beat of the people he hopes to lead and have that personal touch. But he could only communicate in English and marginally, in Tamil, or through an interpreter. "So there is no intimacy that a politician must have with his voters. If Singapore were 70 per cent English-speaking, then I would have no difficulty," he said. But Singapore was 70 per cent Chinese-speaking.

Lee told Raja that he could learn politics, that he needed capable, English-educated people on his team, and asked him to think about it.

Raja took several months.

Lacking worldly vanities and enjoying the pleasures of life simply, power did not tempt Raja. Neither did money. Although the issue was never broached with Lee, Raja was fully alive to the real possibility that joining politics would see him having little income, if any at all. That was a gamble that Raja could not take without first consulting Piroska.

As usual, she was worried for his personal well-being. Nobody knew if the PAP would win the election, but everyone could see the troubles ahead. And if the SPA were to win the election, what would happen to Raja?

During this period, while Raja was pondering over the matter, Piroska became even frostier to Lee whenever he visited their home. From her stand-offish behaviour, Lee formed his own conclusions: "She thought I was leading him astray. She wished I would not turn up, and leave Raja alone and to work in The Straits Times."

Lee was not the only PAP man who had to suffer Piroska's fierce disapproval. Arguably, Kenny Byrne had a worse time. Once, Piroska threw him out of the house during a dinner. Nalini Nair, a close neighbour, witnessed the scene: Byrne, who had been drinking, was railing against Marshall, a Jew. Byrne said that only Jews could behave the way he did, and he could understand why Hitler did what he did to Jews. Nalini recalled: "Piroska was white with anger. She said, "Kenny, you will now leave my house and don't come back."[25] Raja and others tried to placate her, but she would have none of it. Shaking with fury, the pint-sized woman said: "No, I will not have such a man in my house." Byrne, burly and barrel-chested, left with tail tucked between his legs.

Piroska could be as obstinate as Raja on matters of principle, but close friends also knew her to be a supportive wife who was devoted in looking after Raja. Not wanting to burden him with her own fears, she made it simple for Raja; she told him to do what he thought was right.

Raja decided to go with his deep convictions. Close to his heart lay the principles and ideals of his party to which he had helped give shape and clarity. He was also imbued with a strong sense of loyalty, not only to the cause and to the party, but also to his fellow PAP founders. Above all, he honestly believed the PAP was the best chance to bring Singapore to independence, and to realise the hopes of its people. As he would say years later: "I never wanted to join politics. I was persuaded, and quite rightly, too, that if I didn't take to politics, irresponsible groups would take over."[26]

A dutiful son, Raja then visited his family in Seremban to inform them of his life-changing decision. It was met with a storm of disapproval from his father.

Unable to accept the prospect of a jobless son, he asked Raja to resume his law studies in London and become a lawyer. How could he disappoint the family? Look at his brother, Seeva — a successful doctor. But Raja, who wanted to follow in no one's footsteps, knew he wanted a different life. His mother was more understanding. Raja recalled: "My mother knew that I had already made up my mind and did not stop me. After several arguments, my father had to agree reluctantly."

His parents' earlier unhappiness over Raja's choice of wife had meanwhile melted away. Over the years, Raja's parents had grown to appreciate Piroska's complete devotion to Raja. Relatives related that, in her later years, Raja's mother confessed to them that no Ceylonese Tamil girl from their own clan could measure up to Piroska's standard as a life partner for Raja. It was a complete change of heart.

As for Raja's decision to join politics, it would also take time before his parents trusted his judgement. Before he left Seremban, his father told him something he would never forget: If he really wanted to join politics, he must always bear in mind integrity. He must not do things that would put the whole Ceylonese Tamil community to shame.

It was advice that he received with a tinge of disappointment although he appreciated the intention. Raja said: "My father's character remained the same. He still paid much attention to public opinion and the opinion of the community. I knew the intention of my parents. They regarded the honour of the community as being very important, but they perhaps did not know that, when I took up politics, it was not for the honour of the ethnic community but for the national community."

He drew assurance, however, from the thought that, if anything were to happen to him after he joined politics, his family would be alright.

"I knew that at least I had a doctor brother who would be able to look after my parents in their old age. I knew that should I get into difficulties with my politics, then my parents would also look after my wife," said Raja. That he contemplated such a scenario showed the amount of forethought and agonising that went into his decision, and the courage that it demanded from him. It also reflected his conscious preparedness to do battle until the bitter end. There was no half-heartedness about this decision.

His decision to hurl himself into the political vortex was a tale of how solitary men rise above the flow of events only when thrust up by the forces beneath the surface. Years later, Raja would say: "It is an instance where events change the life of a man rather than the man taking control of his own history. I happened to be born at a time when the whole of Southeast Asia, specifically Singapore, had entered a transitional phase."

While that may be so, the fact remained that it was the reaction of such men to the great pressures on them that shapes history and lives. His life was of his own making. Since his days in London, he had sought to determine his own fate. He had chosen journalism, when his father wanted him to pursue law. He had chosen a Hungarian Roman Catholic for his wife, when family tradition dictated a Ceylonese Tamil woman of Hindu belief. His choices had been a bid for freedom. Now, he chose the murky world of politics, when most around him sought the security of a stable professional career. This was a bid for freedom writ large, freedom for the country.

In March, Raja, the thinker and the theorist, left his familiar world of journalism and strode into the maelstrom of mass politics. On 29 March 1959, *The Straits Times* reported blandly his entry into politics in a snippet, leading with: "The president of the Singapore Union of Journalists, Mr S Rajaratnam, has resigned from his job at The Straits Times to do 'full-time' work for the People's Action Party."[27]

Raja would not be a typical politician. In later years, his good friend Bloodworth observed: "Some people were good enough to say that he was not made of the stuff of politicians at all. He might prepare the most witty and perceptive speeches made in South-east Asia, working late into the night to do so, writing by hand, but he did not have the smooth tongue that was the mark of the professional baby-kisser. When he first stood for election in 1959, Singapore may have lost its most outstanding author."

For Raja, there was a bigger, and more important, story for him to work on. With his ambitious idealism and passion for the country, he eyed Singapore as an open-ended narrative, the plot as yet to be written.

13
Taking Power

For the historic 1959 election campaign, Raja helped to provide the conceptual framework for the ideas in the PAP manifesto. From his 10 years as a journalist writing strident columns, he had thought his way through most issues and knew how to carve through a dozen arguments at a time and present policy solutions in his polemical way.

He worked closely with Lee Kuan Yew, Goh Keng Swee and Toh Chin Chye to finalise the ideas. Goh was a brusque, hard-nosed man who would emerge as Singapore's economic architect and chief mandarin. Toh, the party chairman since 1954, was a sharp political analyst with a good grasp of organisational details. In shaping the manifesto, Lee was pragmatic and realistic, keenly aware that, if the PAP was elected, it would have to implement what it promised.

Lee listened to the views from the trusted few and had occasion to change his mind as a result. Raja had seen this happen many times. But once Lee was convinced of a certain position, he would ram it through. Raja would say of the original team later: "Lee Kuan Yew was really the leader. He's number one. So he was leading the group as a whole. Keng Swee was more of the civil servant, and I, the ideas man."[1]

Raja had little problem with Lee's firm leadership style; at core, he believed that Singapore, particularly at that transfiguring moment, needed a dominant leader, a strong man standing at the pinnacle to confront the forces of history, just like Nehru did in India. Raja also more than appreciated the need for the PAP to speak in one coherent voice. He had long been sickened by politicians who ducked and dithered, who quarrelled among themselves, and operated without clear policies and principles. He resolved that the PAP would be different.

Raja was not a natural follower who submitted to authority easily or gave his allegiance lightly, but he saw in Lee an exceptional leader who shared his deep convictions and his vision for Singapore. He found a ready ear in Lee, who relied heavily on him for ideas on strategy and policy. Since their collaboration with the postal strike in 1952, he had developed a close relationship with Lee; it was one of mutual respect.

He knew that Lee could sometimes be abrasive and make his assessments based on a grim view of man and circumstance. But here was a man who was pummelled unmercifully in the political arena and still held his head up and fought on. Raja recognised in Lee an inner toughness and an obstinate will to succeed, and believed that the new prime minister of a vulnerable island needed that to lead the country.

As they prepared for nomination day on 25 April, they bounced ideas off each other on the party's election platform. The concentrated process allowed them to clarify their thinking, and to be reasonably confident that their programmes were well considered, coherent, and persuasive. They decided to focus on their key message of providing an "honest and efficient government" that would give priority to tackling employment, housing, and education — issues that appeal to the recently enfranchised working class.

Raja's passion for the historic necessity of merger and a Malayan culture coursed through every chapter of the manifesto like veins through a body. Even in the section on women's rights, next to the promise to outlaw polygamy, Raja inserted the recurring refrain: "We must develop the culture of various races, and fuse the cream of the cultures of all races into a unified Malayan culture."

Another common thread running through all the proposals was the need to be realistic, given the island's limitations, and that it would take time to achieve a socialist society, which was possible only in the wider framework of a union between the Federation and Singapore. Another striking feature of the manifesto was its injunction to the people to play their part in building the nation and solving its severe problems. In essence, the manifesto was a comprehensive blueprint for achieving independence and building a new nation.

At the same time, the PAP leaders set out to identify 51 candidates for the elections. Raja, Lee and Goh selected the candidates in a process that was as secretive as it was haphazard. They struggled to recruit suitable English-educated candidates; many rejected their advances. As for the Chinese-educated, the problem was of a different order. The numbers surging forward were legion, but the problem was in sifting out the pro-communists, an almost impossible task.

Raja focused on recruiting those he knew. One of them was *Straits Times* journalist Lee Khoon Choy, whom he approached in, of all places, the office car park. Raja's pitch was simple: He should stand for elections because "the PAP is the right political party for Singapore". It took several attempts before Khoon Choy was persuaded to come forward. He turned out to be a good choice — he would become Raja's reliable parliamentary secretary in the culture ministry after the elections.

As for Goh, he too approached several people, mainly professionals. Among them was Dr Lee Siew Choh. Goh had thought that "reasoning people like doctors could not possibly be pro-communist". He would live to regret that error of judgement. Lee Siew Choh would lead the pack to break away and defect from the PAP in 1961.

Looking back years later, Raja considered it a triumph that they were able to persuade 51 people to take on the uncertainties of politics. They formed a motley group, ranging from professionals, barbers, butchers, and seamstresses to shop assistants. Many were in their 20s without even their "O" levels or the Chinese Junior Middle School certificate. All were told to read "The New Phase after Merdeka

— Our Task and Policy", which set out the fundamental policy of the party. The candidates were required to sign a pledge that they would uphold the policy and constitution of the party. Sixteen of them would dishonour that pledge in 1960 and 1961.

Raja felt the rush of adrenalin when he stood before enthusiastic crowds at the PAP weekly pre-election rallies. At these events, which began on 25 February, the PAP leaders systematically unveiled the policies and programmes in the manifesto in a series of speeches. Thousands of people swarmed the grounds. Raja had never spoken at a mass rally before, and did not particularly look forward to his turn.

He was thrown in at the deep end and learnt to swim while battling the currents against the PAP. The PAP was up against some 160 candidates from 11 other political parties, plus 34 independent candidates. The PAP's main rival, however, was the SPA led by Lim Yew Hock.

The election campaign established Raja as a fighter. Raja was a veritable propaganda machine as he fired off policy statements and press releases one after another during the election campaign. He was fundamentally a good-willed man, but in that political furnace, other qualities were called for — tenacity, guts, loyal leadership. Their political foes treated them badly, and Raja, for one, gave back as good as he got. It was a performance calculated to keep the PAP in control of the election campaign.

In the campaign, the PAP set out to court the largest roll of voters ever to head to the polls. There were about 590,000 eligible voters, half of whom were first-time voters.[2] The introduction of compulsory voting also brought in a fresh group of English-educated voters.

Many among them, particularly the civil servants, were cold towards the PAP, turned off by the party's revolutionary slogan shouting and, in particular, Ong Eng Guan's terror-filled version of PAP administration. The English-language press fuelled their fears.

The PAP started by campaigning as political outsiders — optimistic radicals, initially sneered at as communists, patronised and despised by the right-wing parties and the English-language press. The PAP leaders, all self-taught politicians, needed one another, encouraged one another, and validated one another. Amid mounting pressure to prove themselves, they had to fend off criticisms from within the party, while dealing with broadsides from the right-wing political groups and press.

Raja was outraged at the wilful distortions of the PAP's stand and the intimidating tactics employed by the SPA with "secret society thugs" to canvas support and intimidate PAP activists.

The campaign was, in some ways, a grand circus, and its repercussions are still felt in Singapore politics. Over the years, steps have been taken to reshape the political environment into a more serious and rational one, given the stakes involved. The 1959 campaign was also the crucible that transformed Raja from a thinker-writer into a feisty political orator. It cemented his political philosophy and commitment to attack and counter-attack, which drove the politics of the 1960s and beyond.

The pace was set at the PAP's first rally on 15 February, when Toh revealed that the SPA had received political funds from the Americans through Education Minister Chew Swee Kee to defeat the PAP. This was held as proof that the incumbent government was incurably corrupt. The disclosure led to a commission of inquiry, the resignation of Chew, and the accelerating decline of the SPA's credibility.

Throughout the campaign, the PAP leaders, including Raja, bludgeoned the SPA with this issue. In one rally, Raja said he heard that the SPA wanted to give out free balloons, but after the Chew Swee Kee case, they had no one to blow the balloons. He added: "There were only two kinds of political parties — the PAP which was honest and sincere — and all the others which had gangsters, racketeers and wealthy men".[3]

Amidst the frenetic campaign trail, Raja found the time to pen a series of satirical fictitious letters in *Petir* to criticise the platform of the rival political parties in a light-hearted way. The "letters" were ostensibly between a father, "Koh Song O" (Malay for "zero" or "nothing"), and his "dear empty headed son", sometimes addressed with the endearment "my little imbecile".

While no names of persons or political parties were mentioned, Raja poked fun at them in a not-so-subtle manner by using the party symbols, calling them the Lion, Orchid, and Torch parties. The PAP was, of course, the Lightning Party. "Koh Song O" is in charge of the "bamboozle department" (B.D. for short) from the "Rojak Party", a clear reference to the SPA. In one of the "letters", Koh Song O informed his son that a safe party slogan was: "We will double whatever the Lightning Party promises".[4] These pieces provided light relief to an otherwise punishing campaign.

But Raja drew a serious lesson from the Chew Swee Kee episode. He woke to the realisation this would not be the last time that foreign powers would try to subvert the PAP. The foreigners' strategic objective, as Raja saw it, was to command an influence in this part of the region. Raja said years later: "Singapore by itself is not important. It becomes important when it is aligned with a super power, then we become important not only to the 'controlling power', but more so to the other competing powers."[5]

The 1959 election was taking place against the context of not just decolonisation, but also the Cold War. Raja, always a man for the bigger picture, grasped that some foreign countries — such as America and Kuomintang Taiwan — feared a PAP victory as they believed it would mean a victory not only for the Malayan Communist Party, but also for the PRC-Soviet alliance. Southeast Asia featured prominently in the calculations of the Western powers, concerned about the march of communism in the region.

It did not take much for Raja to figure out that some powers wanted the SPA to defeat the PAP. Kuala Lumpur also favoured the SPA. The Federation leaders understood that the party which would win the election would be the one which would in future negotiate with Kuala Lumpur on the question of merger. They did not relish dealing with the PAP on this issue, given its radical image.

Predictably, the PAP manifesto was roundly thrashed in the English-language newspapers. The *Standard*, for example, scoffed at the party's five-year plan as "castles in the air" and laughed at its plan to set up an Economic Development Board. "Already, some business organisations in the island have moved or are planning to move across the Causeway because of the economic insecurity created by the prospect of a PAP government."[6] The tone of English newspapers' coverage of the pre-election rallies was often scathing, with reports depicting the PAP leaders as communists or extremists. The Chinese and the Malay press were more supportive. The Indian press was the friendliest towards Raja, playing up his comments as an Indian candidate.

Given the political undercurrents involved, the PAP leaders were furious at the English media's distortion and campaign to isolate an important group of voters — the English-educated — from the party. They thought that the English newspapers' attitude was all the more unjustified because they had been careful in presenting themselves and their policies as credible, realistic and honest.

Raja lent considerable weight to this view. He knew the power of the pen and recognised a newspaper crusade when he saw one, having mounted many in his career as a journalist. He had observed first-hand how the credibility of politicians could be weakened by just a headline or a slant. In an election campaign, the public judgement forms in a matter of weeks and, once formed, calcifies.

As the PAP leaders set out to win to form the next government, they were determined to show who was boss, because the English press was behaving as if it was another power centre, unelected and unrepresentative. It was also acting as a political adversary, attempting to influence the electorate against the PAP.

To out-shout the English press, they took their own megaphone and message to town, literally, directly to the English-educated at regular rallies at Fullerton Square, which was in the centre of the city. For the strategic attack on the press, Lee sent out Raja. He emerged battle ready with a full pack of heavy ammunition drawn from his experience working in both the *Standard* and *The Straits Times.*

Many regard Raja as a cerebral creature. But even intellectuals have to draw blood when they do battle in politics. In the temper of the times, the political culture was "you are either with me or against me". To the PAP, the English press was definitely against.

On 15 April, Raja took to the stage in a mass rally and, together with other PAP leaders, launched a coordinated attack against the English press. For about an hour, Raja and a battalion of PAP speakers, including Lee, Goh, Toh, Byrne and Yong Nyuk Lin, rained their fire on the two English-language newspapers. The English press duly reported their abusive remarks, but not without giving them a snarling twist.

Lee received the most coverage for his threats: he accused the English press of misleading the English-speaking community by distorting the news so as to present the PAP as "extremists and wild men". Referring to the tendentious reporting in *The Straits Times* on the PAP's stand on merger, Lee threatened to apply the public security law to any newspaper man who tried to sour up or strain relations between the Federation and Singapore after 30 May.

Raja followed up with a defiant cry: "Our party has grown despite distortions, propaganda and accusations of very powerful political parties bought over by racketeers and wealthy men and attacks by the Press which is controlled by wealthy men."[7]

Goh played his part, picking on the *Standard* in his monotone. He said he hoped the newspaper would "come to its senses or face the consequences" when it came to power. Other speakers reinforced the onslaught colourfully in the different languages, including Malay and Chinese. With every volley lobbed at the English press, the workers in the crowd cheered. The Chinese-educated were especially euphoric. They equated the English newspapers with colonial interests, and felt a sense of *schadenfreude* at seeing them toppled from their perch.

Peter Lim, then a *Straits Times* journalist, noted: "Attacking the English-language press was powerful stuff to consolidate credentials with the so-called vernacular ground."[8]

A venomous fury seized the English press. In its sulphurous front-page editorial on 19 April, the *Standard* mocked the PAP leaders for being "very angry men". The newspaper dared the PAP to do its worst to them. "We certainly will not bow to 'smart-alec' politicians." As for *The Straits Times*, it accused the PAP of being hostile to a free press and lamented that, not for a 100 years had the freedom of the press in Singapore been in such a danger. It charged the PAP leaders of deploying threats "no doubt because they believe threats sometimes work but also because a strong section of their following expect it from them". It observed that there was occasionally a conscious "bold, bad boy" pose about PAP leaders, as noticeable as their undress uniform of tieless white shirt and trousers.[9]

Raja was not about to let all these accusations pass. Two days later on 22 April, at a lunchtime rally at Fullerton Square, he took the centre stage and devoted his entire speech to pulverising the English press. He put to use his insider's knowledge of the newspapers and gave the gory details as he "exposed" his former employers for their hypocrisy. He noted that, since the last PAP rally, two Singapore newspapers had become very interested in the freedom of the press. He said he would deal with the *Standard* first because it was "the less intelligent" and sometimes "indulged in 'mental foolery' ", and would leave *The Straits Times* for another rally a week later.

He told the crowd of several thousand that the *Standard* changed its policy in 1954 from the creed with which it was founded in 1950. As associate editor at the time, he had been told to change his policy or quit. He had quit. He said that during his time as an editorial writer in the paper, he pursued a policy which would create a socialist Malaya. "But the management was against it and I had to quit."

From 1950 to 1954, he had also pressed forward strongly for the Alliance and Tunku Abdul Rahman when they were fighting for *Merdeka*. But after this, the *Standard* was the only paper in Malaya against *Merdeka*, Malayanisation, trade unions, and the workers. "The Standard talks of the freedom of the Press, yet it stifles the views of those it does not agree with," he said.

He then resurrected the case of Seah Yong, and noted that, when the SUJ protested Seah Yong's innocence in 1957, the *Singapore Standard*'s columnist Aster Gunasekara attacked the union. When *The Straits Times* took up the case, the *Singapore Standard* attacked *The Straits Times*. Raja then turned his attack on Gunasekara, who had been virulently anti-PAP in his columns. He pointed out that Gunasekara had, in his column on 26 August 1957, urged the government to wind up the PAP and put its leaders behind prison bars. "Now, he is afraid the PAP may give him the same medicine which he suggested for us at that time."

Raja asked the crowd not to be misled by the newspapers' claim to serve the people. He said that since 1954, the *Standard* had not championed the cause of anyone except the vested interests in the country. He then challenged the *Standard* to reproduce a letter given to him terminating his services. He said: "This letter will reveal why I had to quit the paper and whose interests this paper looks after."

It was a masterful attack, full of colourful anecdotes and personal revelations. People saw a different Raja. He was fiery and animated, eyes flashing and arms gesticulating. He expressed himself in a vivid, word-coining, muscular English; at times high-flown, at others, colloquial, sometimes downright rude, but always engaged. He also showed a surprising knack for using humour to defuse the PAP's biggest problem during the campaign — people's fear that it was dominated by wild-eyed extremists. He thrilled the crowd with his quick wit, even as he swung his fist at political foes.

Journalists regarded his hard-hitting performance as par for the course in a political battle. Looking back, Peter Lim commented: "The basic cause was political: a nationalist attacking colonial establishment interests as part of the fight for independence. Raja had to say it strongly, because he was brought up in the British newspaper tradition of hard-hitting, no-need-to-be-balanced editorials. It's a tradition that said: have a point of view, the sharper the better, so we expressed it like thunder — loud, cannot be ignored."[10]

The English press was apoplectic. The next day, *The Straits Times* led off with the headline "Ex-journalist leads PAP attack No. 2 on the English Press", while the *Standard* gave it a sensational page one treatment protesting "Again We Are The Target of PAP Fury." It showed an unflattering photograph of Raja holding aloft a copy of the *Sunday Standard*, with the caption quoting him as saying: "This is typical of how the *Standard* twists the news."

A day later, on 23 April, Gunasekara came at Raja with hammer and tongs in his column. "Mr Rajaratnam posed as a champion of the working-class. In other words, an anti-capitalist. He has publicly confessed to having worked for four years on this paper, which he calls pro-capitalist. From here, whatever the reason, he shifted to another pro-capitalist newspaper. He has shown no reluctance to turn to capitalists for his livelihood." Gunasekara had taken over from Raja as SUJ president when Raja resigned to take part in the elections. His frontal personal attack on Raja hinted at a deep-seated hostility which might perhaps have been based on more than professional rivalry.

His belligerent column was followed up by a snide editorial in the *Singapore Standard* on 25 April, headlined "Growls, Barks and Bites". Referring to Raja's disclosure on why he left the *Standard*, the newspaper retorted: "What could be wrong with people who seek to sink their money into a business, wanting to safeguard their interests? Do not politicians do the same? Are not the growls, barks and bites of the PAP one of their methods of safeguarding their interests?" Cuttingly, it reminded Raja that he had tried his hand at being "editor-manager-publisher" of his own paper — referring to *Raayat* — and failed. So he joined yet another pro-capitalist paper, *The Straits Times*. On Raja's peroration that the *Standard* was his first target on the range of English-language papers — being "less intelligent" and sometimes indulging in "mental foolery" — it reminded Raja that he was its first leader writer and remained so for four years.

Unfazed by the counter-attacks, Raja trained his fire on *The Straits Times* a week later as promised. Addressing several thousand people at a PAP lunchtime rally at the Fullerton Building car park, he noted wryly that the paper was very interested in the subject of the freedom of the press. He referred to *The Straits Times*' editorial the previous week headlined "Threat to Freedom" and quoted from it: "The freedom of the press is the freedom of the individual, and the moment the liberty of the press is restricted, freedom vanishes."

He roused the huge crowd with a contemptuous question: "One question they fail to answer — freedom for whom? Does freedom for *The Straits Times* mean freedom for Singapore, for the majority of the people, for a thousand or for a hundred?" More likely, he added, it meant freedom of expression for those who run and control *The Straits Times*. Therefore, if a person wanted to find out for whom *The Straits Times* wanted freedom, he must first find out who controlled *The Straits Times*.

A citizen of Singapore could at least vote out the government he did not want after five years. But *The Straits Times* shareholders could not remove the directors. He said the newspaper was owned by Europeans who controlled the management shares. He named four: R.C. Kendall, W.M. Piercy, K.A. Seth, and A.C. Simmons. The paper was also closely connected with British companies, he charged. "On the whole, it is far easier for a local man to enter the gates of heaven than for him to become a director of the Straits Times," said Raja.

He concluded that, now that he had shown the British vested interests in *The Straits Times*, the people could understand the kind of policy that the newspaper followed. These people wanted to make as much money as they could while they could, and used an influential paper such as *The Straits Times* to get the English-educated to be auxiliaries for their interests. *The Straits Times* thought that the only people they could get to fight their battle were the English-educated. But they had lost this battle and were now preparing to move across the causeway, he said.

He assured the crowd that, as a journalist, he himself believed that there was no division between the English-educated and those educated in the other languages. Any group that tried to split the people was doing wrong. Referring to *The Straits Times*' editorial which had described the PAP men's attire of tieless white shirt and trousers, he charged that *The Straits Times* supported only those who wore "neck ties, top hats and morning coats". "Don't be fooled by *The Straits Times*. When they talk about the freedom of the press, they don't mean freedom for you or for me," Raja told the crowd.

The crowd lapped up his speech. Some *Straits Times* journalists, such as Ee Boon Lee, also cheered inwardly. Raja gave voice to their inchoate anger at being discriminated against in the newsroom, with the European expatriates getting higher wages and promotions while they were passed over. Said Ee: "I was just a junior reporter. I could not criticise my European bosses, but Raja could."[11]

Boon Yoon Chiang, another *Straits Times* journalist covering the elections, thought that Raja's criticisms of *The Straits Times* sounded a tad extreme, but credited Raja for proving to be the party's most effective voice in the attack against the press, given his eloquence and his inside experience at the newspapers. As Ambrose Khaw, then chief subeditor for *The Straits Times*, observed: "Raja was the best and most qualified man for the job."[12]

In a scorching comeback, *The Straits Times* hit out at Raja in its editorial. "It was quite a performance by an imaginative mind released at last from the discipline of newspaper work." The paper asserted that no company, in or out of Singapore, exerted the slightest influence over the newspaper.[13]

Raja stood by his own observations and conclusions from working with the English-language press. His blistering attacks escalated the PAP's long-running battle with the English press and embroiled him in a convulsive public feud with the press. Lee later said that, after

Raja named Simmons at the rally as one of the four white men who ran *The Straits Times*, "Simmons realised that Raja and I were not joking when we said that if we formed the government, we would take them on. They were already making preparations to move the company and key staff to Kuala Lumpur because they feared a PAP victory. I had no doubts that they were determined to fight us from the federal capital."[14]

On 20 May, Lee renewed his warning that any foreign-owned press that attempted to sour up relations between Federation and Singapore would be dealt with under the subversion laws. At the rally, Lee said that, in 1954, Tunku Abdul Rahman attended the PAP inauguration and said on its platform that if Malaya had more people like Raja, Lee, and Toh Chin Chye and so on, "we shall be a united people and we shall be independent". Five years on, and because of a few "unhappy incidents", it was not the British, but the Tunku who was now opposing a merger of the two territories. He warned *The Straits Times* not to be "smart guys" by playing up these little differences between the PAP and the Tunku. Any foreign capital engaged, either wittingly or unwittingly, in fostering bad relations, ill feeling of animosity between the Chinese in Singapore and the Malays in the Federation, was inviting trouble.

He addressed his warning in particular to the "four white men who control the Straits Times — Simmons, Jenkins" — then turning round to Raja on the platform to ask "and who else, Raja?" As Lee checked with Raja in full public view, it became obvious to all that Lee relied heavily on Raja for information on the English newspapers. Foreigner observers also took note. Diplomats filed back despatches noting that Raja "would seem to be the source of Lee Kuan Yew's recent diatribes against its foreign ownership",[15] while *The Times* in London observed: "In the dispute between the party and some newspapers, his counsel must be of great weight."[16]

On 18 May, *The Straits Times*, fearing a PAP victory, moved its head office from Singapore to Kuala Lumpur. On 20 May, Leslie

Hoffman, then the newspaper's editor-in-chief, wrote an editorial arguing that Lee must choose between democracy and totalitarianism. Hoffman then reminded the PAP of Raja's article on free speech in the *Singapore Journalist*, the organ of the SUJ, in October 1955. In the article, Raja had expressed the hope that, when the assemblymen cry "*Merdeka*", they mean also "*Merdeka*" for the press and pressmen.

In response, Lee said the PAP believed in the freedom of the press, but drew a distinction between locally-owned newspapers — which must stay and take the consequences of any policy they might have advocated — and the ones owned and controlled by foreigners or foreign interests, the "birds of passage".[17] In a defiant move, Hoffman took the case to the International Press Institute, then meeting in West Berlin, and told the newspapermen gathered — four days before polling day on 30 May — that the PAP posed a real threat to the freedom of the press in Singapore.

The public dispute was protracted and rancorous. On the surface, the feud seemed no more than the screeching collision of two political agendas. The PAP was out to create a new socialist system in an independent Singapore merged with the Federation; the English press was out to protect the capitalist status quo. The PAP was seeking public support for its policy that the press was not to be owned by foreigners to purvey their line; the English press saw itself as the unelected voice of the people.

But it was more than that. Under the surface, it was a struggle for the control of the power centre and the battle for the hearts and minds of the people. The PAP leaders had an acute sense of the country's vulnerability and knew that when they formed the government — and it was looking more certain by the day that they would — they would have to rally the people to surmount the grave challenges facing the island. They would have to carry the masses with them in order to achieve merger with the Federation. It would take all their will, unity of purpose, and determination to succeed.

The PAP leaders could not afford to have the English press agitating the ground against its plans and policies. They were also anxious about the effect that the press attacks would have on the Federation leaders in Kuala Lumpur, which could complicate the prospects for merger.

Apart from this, Raja was also exasperated that the English press, run by Europeans, operated as if they knew what was best for Singapore. They did not seem to appreciate that the colonial era would soon come to an end, and a new era would begin under the PAP — the era of an independent country infused with a Malayan consciousness. The bitter feud during the election campaign was to have a lasting impact on press relations under the PAP and would inform Raja's views on the role of the press in an independent country.

Aware that the attack on the English press was causing a backlash among the English-educated, Raja turned his attention to them towards the end of the campaign. The civil service represented a major proportion of the English-educated community. The PAP needed to win them over to run the government machinery and implement its policies when it came into power. Raja was assiduous in his pursuit, changing his hectoring tone employed for their political adversaries to one of gentle coaxing.

It was a tricky assignment — he had to build up the party's image as a credible and rational party for the English-educated, while attacking its right-wing foes and the English press that were so mercilessly twisting its record. His task was not made any easier when, on 30 April, the *Standard* ran a front page article headlined "Top officials worried over their future" on the fears of senior civil servants of being victimised by the PAP if it gained power. It also reported on how the senior officials had met to discuss steps to safeguard their livelihood and "save" the civil service from political pressure.

Two days before polling day, Raja sought to allay their fears in a party political broadcast. He told the English-educated that the PAP offered the English-educated "the honourable role" of helping to bring about a peaceful and democratic social revolution. They were well equipped to perform this role, he said, because of all the cultural groups, they were the "least communal and therefore, more Malayan in their outlook" and had a better understanding of the spirit and purpose of parliamentary democracy.[18]

In that radio broadcast, Raja refuted the smear of the SPA and Liberal Socialists that a PAP government would push the English-educated out and give their jobs to those educated in other languages. He noted that "they have charged us with being Communists. They have claimed that a PAP government intends to rob you of your provident fund and your jewellery. They have tried to freeze your blood with visions of women and children being herded into PAP communes". The two opponent parties knew very well that nowhere in the PAP policy statements, speeches, or writings had the party ever said that the PAP would do any of the preposterous things. "No falsehood, no distortion has been spared to create the myth that the PAP is a scourge sent to punish the English-educated and eventually exterminate them as a class," said Raja.

He was at his persuasive best. Urging them to look at the facts, Raja pointed out that he was English-educated, and so were Lee, Toh, Goh, Byrne, and many candidates. "What are we doing in a party which, according to the SPA and Lib-Socs, is dedicated to bringing about our own destruction?" he asked. "Now in a self-governing Singapore, we intend to give equality of opportunity to all classes, whether English educated or not. The political adventurers in the SPA and the Lib-Socs have distorted this to mean extinction of the English-educated," Raja declared.

The overtures to the English-educated came too little, too late, however. As the campaign drew to a close, Raja returned his focus to the party's national agenda. While the fight with the English press was fundamental, the PAP leaders knew that the majority of voters were concerned about bread-and-butter issues, such as jobs and housing, not abstract theories. It was a frantic time of rushing from one rally to another. In all, the PAP held six mass rallies and between 60 and 100 street meetings in the 33 days of campaigning.

Journalists covering the campaign were not surprised at Raja's savage attacks on his former employers. A typical view was that voiced by broadcast journalist Foong Choon Hon: "If you want to go into the political arena, you must fight against the people fighting you. The English newspapers which were anti-PAP were an important factor. For him to attack the newspapers attacking the PAP was a logical strategy."

But could his diatribe against the two newspapers be driven also by a personal grudge? After all, the *Standard* had sacked him unceremoniously while *The Straits Times* had denied him any prospect of wage increases or job opportunities. It would be unlikely. Those who had worked with him spurned the notion that Raja nursed a personal grievance. Ambrose Khaw, who had worked with Raja in the *Tribune*, the *Standard* as well as in *The Straits Times*, said that Raja "did not have a rancorous bone in his body".[19]

Besides, Raja enjoyed cordial relations with the editors in *The Straits Times* and at the *Standard*. Indeed, Lee Khoon Choy, who had worked with Raja at *The Straits Times*, described Raja's relationship with Hoffman, as "quite good".[20] The Tiger Balm, owned by the Aw brothers who ran the *Standard*, had also advertised in Raja's ill-fated *Raayat* several times, indicating a congenial relationship between the Aws and Raja.

Peter Lim confirmed this view: "Raja never indicated to me that he held any grudge against anyone. He was always the gentleman, not necessarily the perfect one all the time, though. He could use ungentlemanly language and could fight unfettered by Queensbury Rules."[21] Similarly, Boon Yoon Chiang, a *Straits Times* journalist who later joined the new Culture Ministry under Raja, did not believe that Raja was a vindictive person. "If anything else, he was generous to a fault. But as a politician, he had to follow the party philosophy and ideology."[22]

In retirement, Raja would characterise himself as "among the few who articulate and emphasise the PAP's stand when attacked". He added: "In that sense, you can call me a public relations man or the chap who projects the PAP image."[23] It was a role few could play, not only because of Raja's superior linguistic skills, but because of his special role in giving birth to the party and strengthening its body and spirit at every stage of its vulnerable life. The at-birth experience had fostered in him a fierce protective instinct which could not be easily replicated.

Journalists covering the election campaign found Raja a good orator, a natural on stage. While distinctly polemical, Raja was not above using simplistic slogans for effect; choice ones include "anti-working class", "pro-capitalist". Lee noted: "Raja turned out to be a quick learner, speaking forcefully in English and reducing his editorial style to punchy street language. He also spoke bazaar Malay and got his point across effectively in a strong voice and with expressive body language."[24]

Privately, Raja found it a strain. He confessed later: "I was not used to mass speaking. I won't say I enjoyed it because it was an effort on my part." He found it even more onerous when he spoke at other rallies packed with a non-English speaking crowd. "I knew 80 per cent of those who were listening to me didn't know what the hell I was talking about. Or if I spoke in broken Malay, even then they only partially understood what I was saying." To get through, he would simplify his message. "But when you simplify the language so much, then you can only convey simple childish ideas." It went against his intellectual grain.

Yet, using simple language at his rallies, he was able to put his points across on the complex subject of Malayan nationalism. He matched reason with vision, and expressed himself with a passion and conviction which later generations have rarely matched.

His most significant speech in the entire campaign was on the creation of a Malayan nation, which he delivered on 19 April. In it, he expounded his bold ideas on nation-building, which fell in two parts. The first was to check the forces of communalism. This would entail stamping communal fires before they spread, and to inoculate the new generation in schools against the "communal virus" and imbuing in them an "unshakeable conviction that they are Malayans".

The second was to try, through positive measures, to give the people and, in particular the younger generations of Malayans, "immunity against the blandishments of communal and racial demagogues". There was much idealism in this speech. In a rousing statement, Raja said: "We of the PAP regard ourselves as a vanguard generation. We will ensure to the best of our ability that the new generation of Malayans, when they take over from us, will not inherit a country riven by racial strife and communal hatreds."

He expressed his conviction on the "inevitability of a Malayan nation" with merger, but voiced concern as to how this was to be brought about — painlessly and smoothly, or "attended by tragedy and suffering, bitter communal conflicts and inter-racial carnage". He issued a warning which turned out to be prescient: "If communal conflict ever breaks out in Malaya, then a Malayan nation will come about as a result of the subjugation of other races by a dominant group."

His tone was one of steely determination and optimism. "The fatalist may take the attitude that many nations in the past were born after a long struggle between peoples of many races and cultures…As socialists, we believe that the people, and not the stars, order human affairs. We believe in the rational organisation of our economic, social and political system. Through this rational approach to the problem of nation-building, we believe it possible to build a Malayan nation without first having to pay the terrible price implicit in the fatalist approach," he declared.

His speech, which was a key policy statement, was read at two pre-election rallies in Nee Soon and Kampong Melayu. It was also delivered in Malay by Roslan bin Hassan, a member of the PAP's CEC, and in Chinese by Chan Chee Seng, who was then PAP's city division secretary.

In his historic speech, crackling with passion and intellectual verve, Raja spelt out the immediate task at hand — "to combat and expose communal demagogues and other reactionary forces who in moments of desperation will not hesitate to use communal passions, hatreds and rivalries to obtain their sordid ends". He pointed out that the biggest obstacles on the road towards a Malayan nation were communalism and political parties based on appeals to racial pride and religious exclusiveness.

"The people of the Federation, in particular the Malays, have been frightened into believing that merger means Chinese domination. Some of our political enemies have alleged that PAP is a stumbling block to merger because our so-called 'extremist' attitude has frightened Federation leaders. If what is 'extreme' is our political ideology — that is, the ideology of democratic socialism — then merger is being refused not because there is doubt about our devotion to Malayan nationalism but because of our allegiance to a socialist philosophy. If our right-wing opponents are right in this, then it would be another illustration of our thesis that communalism is often used as a cloak to cover up class interests," he said.

He analysed the communal rivalry as based to a considerable extent on economic discontent and fears. "It is necessary to explain to our Malay people that it is not the non-Malays who are depriving him of economic opportunities, but a colonial-capitalist economy. If there are poor Malays, there are poor Chinese and Indians too in the towns as well as the countryside." One defence against communalism was to stress that, if people wanted to improve their economic lot, they must do so by combining on a class and not a racial basis. To this extent, the PAP's policy on trade unions to help openly in creating powerful and vigorous labour organisations was a major contribution to the defeat of communalism, he said.

"Similarly, our economic policy to provide more economic opportunities should help to blunt the communal weapon. By encouraging Malays, Chinese and Indian workers to fight effectively through non-communal unions and political parties, we would be able to show our brothers in the Federation that class and not race should be the basis for effective political action," he said.

He highlighted the central role of schools to "ensure that the generation now in schools does not become prey to the communal fears and myths of their fathers" and to turn out men and women "completely Malayan in outlook and completely immune to the communal virus".

It was a powerful and stirring speech, which distilled Raja's fundamental ideas on nation-building. He was riding forces larger than most observers guessed. The forces at work would take his effort into an entirely different direction he could not predict or control over the next few years.

On 15 May, the press perfunctorily announced that Raja was the "big name" among the four candidates contesting Kampong Glam, which had 10,991 voters. The other three were a clerk Mahmood Latiff (SPA), sales manager Ong Eng Lian (Liberal Socialist), and a businessman Wu Shiaw (Independent).

Kampong Glam was one of the smallest constituencies with a Chinese-educated majority. The area was pockmarked by pockets of intense poverty. It was also crawling with gangsters. On the bright side for Raja, it had the basic rudiments of a branch machinery, established for the City Council elections. The branch was left behind by Hoe Puay Choo, a seamstress who stood in Kampong Glam at the City Council elections in 1957.

When Raja showed up at his branch, he found strangers dropping in at all hours of the day and night to help him win. He was surrounded by eager young women in pigtails and energetic labourers who "turned up from nowhere". "I didn't know who the hell they were," he recalled.[25]

Many were in fact young seamstresses. Hoe, who had been educated up to secondary school, had headed the Seamstress' Union. Many were also pro-communists or unionists, out to ensure a PAP victory. Raja's first branch secretary was Yap Seong Leong, a Works Brigade camp commandant, who was then courting Hoe and would marry her in 1962.

For the first time in an election campaign, Raja came into contact with the Chinese-educated branch workers on the ground. They ran the entire election campaign for him, from putting up posters and canvassing for votes to speaking at mass rallies.

Raja recalled: "They never told me what they were going to do. They had organised the poster campaign, the canvassing. They just told me: 'Please, Mr Raja, come tomorrow 2 o'clock or 3 o'clock,' or whatever it is. They never discussed it with me." They would also never take "no" for an answer. Raja recounted: "That means they were treating me as a pawn in whatever game they had in mind."

It was symptomatic of the political control exercised by the pro-communists at the grassroots level in almost all PAP branches island-wide. At the time, however, the full significance of the situation did not hit Raja until he lost most of his branch workers, including his branch secretary Yap, during the confrontation with the pro-communists from 1961 to 1963 over merger.

At the local rallies, it was a struggle for him to hold the largely Chinese crowd. He could not compete against the fiery Chinese-speaking orators. His two Chinese-educated opponents hammered away at Raja's weak points. Ong Eng Lian from the Liberal Socialist party took the racial tack and asked the crowd: "What can this Indian do for you? He can't even talk to you." Raja rebuked such appeals to communal sentiments. "Communalism will remain, as in the past, the last refuge of right-wing reactionaries, political rogues and adventurers," he retorted.

Despite his language handicap, however, Raja found his speeches greeted by a rapturous crowd even if they did not understand him. Raja was intelligent enough to know that "people were responding favourably not because of what I said, but to show that they were in favour of the PAP. If somebody clapped, everybody clapped". Despite the odds against him, he hoped to scrape through on the back of the PAP's standing with the masses. Raja also expected a similar close call for the other PAP candidates throughout Singapore, given that most were unknown political greenhorns.

When the results were announced on 30 May, polling day, Raja was stunned. The PAP won a thumping 43 seats out of 51 in the Legislative Assembly with 54 per cent of the votes. Its biggest rival, the SPA, was routed, winning only four seats. The Liberal-Socialist party was completely wiped out.

In his own constituency, Raja romped to victory with 57.5 per cent of the votes, garnering 6,324 votes. His closest rival, Mahmood Latiff from SPA, managed only 1,747 of the votes. While jubilant, Raja had the intellectual honesty and humility to recognise that it was not his charisma or his speeches in English which won him his seat — he owed his triumph to the PAP's standing, as well as to the pro-communist support. The English-educated voters largely spurned the PAP, but their votes were split between the two right-wing parties, the SPA and Lib-Soc, giving the electoral edge to the PAP.

Aware that the party's success would depend on the great mass of Chinese-educated voters, the PAP had pledged during the campaign to secure the release of the eight pro-communist political detainees associated with the PAP, if it was elected. Now that it was, the party had to fulfil its promise.

On 1 June, William Goode, governor of the colony and the first *Yang di-Pertuan Negara* (head of state) of the new Singapore, asked the PAP to form a government. The core group, who had dreamt big dreams in the basement of Lee's house and survived the stresses and strains of political struggle together, stood ready: Lee as prime minister, Toh as his deputy, Goh Keng Swee as finance minister, Raja as culture minister, and Kenny Byrne as minister for labour and law.[26]

But they refused to take office until the PAP political detainees were freed. The pro-communists were duly released from the Changi gaol on 4 June, after signing the document titled "The Ends and Means of Socialism" endorsing the non-communist aims of the PAP. While their supporters cheered and fired crackers, British and Australian diplomats in Singapore sent reports to their respective capitals to highlight the dangers of subversion that these "PAP extremists" posed.

The foreign analysts expected the recently released detainees to reassert their influence in the trade unions, and to use their levers in the industrial field to challenge the government's authority. The Australian commissioner, D.W. McNicol, wrote: "Only time will show whether the present PAP ministers have the courage and the resolution to take effective action to meet such a challenge."[27] William Goode noted another problem, with implications on merger: "The present Federation Government is suspicious of the true character of the PAP and of the ability of its present leaders to maintain their control against the Communist threat."[28]

The night before the release of the political detainees, the PAP leaders held a mass rally in the field in front of the City Hall. Lee introduced his new cabinet of nine, including himself, to the crowd of some 50,000. Lee used his speech to temper their hopes and to prepare the PAP's defences for the attacks which would come from the communists.

When it came to Raja's turn, he extended the barricades against the communists by explaining to the crowd the differences between the communist doctrine and the ideology of the PAP party. While they shared many similarities, such as the belief in economic and social justice, the key difference was that the PAP did not believe in using violence to bring about revolutionary change. It believed in non-communist, democratic socialism.

The recent election showed, he said, that a government could be overthrown without bloodshed. "During the next five years, we hope to convince people that social justice and economic justice can be secured through the methods of democratic socialism." While the task would involve work and sacrifices on the part of the people, it would not be, as in the past, for the benefit of a minority of well-to-do people. "We are also conscious that, if our democratic socialist experiment fails — then the choice will be between right-wing fascism or left-wing Communism," he said sombrely.

He felt the weight of responsibility on his shoulders as he took his place in the first cabinet of self-governing Singapore. He would be at the forefront of the protracted struggle against the communists to lead the country to independence through merger. Now in power, he had to learn the art and craft of government in relation to the country's own circumstance and the wider world; how to transform himself from an opponent of the imperial regime to a legitimate practitioner of government, even while seeking merger with the Federation, and more problematically, how to translate his ideas of a Malayan nation into reality. It was a daunting prospect.

14

Creating National Identity

Raja surveyed his changed world from an office of faded colonial grandeur in City Hall. His window looked over the Padang (field), the stage for many of the country's historic events. It was here that, in 1819, the Malay chiefs signed the treaty with Stamford Raffles, an official of the British East India Company, to cede Singapore to the British Empire. It was here that, in 1945, the Japanese surrendered to the British. And it was here that, just days before on 5 June 1959, Raja and the PAP cabinet were sworn in as the first fully-elected government of self-governing Singapore.

It ushered in a new phase of Singapore's history, an age of experiment, of self-determination. As the country's first culture minister, Raja epitomised that spirit as he imagined a nation united and free.

His office on the third storey of the City Hall, with its grand colonnade of Corinthian columns, was his workshop. It was strewn with books and notes and all the apparatus of a writer. He had easy access to the prime minister, Lee Kuan Yew, and the deputy prime minister, Toh Chin Chye, whose offices were on the second floor.

To a large degree, the prime minister left it up to Raja to define his job and its scope. Even the nomenclature of his ministry came from him. Before the cabinet was officially formed, Lee had initially proposed to Raja that his ministry be called the Ministry for Information. Raja had other ideas. As he told Lee, information was only one part of the job, but the more important part was to confront the communal divisions in the society and to establish a sense of national identity among the various races. Lee had initial misgivings. As he confessed later that year, there was the "natural English-educated reluctance" to talk of a Ministry of Culture "because of its association with ideas and ideals which are supposed to be intolerant and illiberal", said Lee.[1] But, in a move which reflected the weight he gave to Raja's views, Lee went along with his proposal.

Raja was to spend the better part of his six years as culture minister on a quest to define the country's national identity. He worked hard to foster a sense of identification with the new ideals of the state. As he put it, "we must create in our people an awareness that they belong to Singapore and that Singapore belongs to them".[2] He focused on developing state symbols — the flag and the national anthem — which would give a powerful impetus to the growth of national sentiment.

He had other vital priorities: Build up the capabilities of the mass media, change its orientation towards a more national outlook and develop new channels of communications, such as television, to transform the people's understanding of themselves and the country. There were grave challenges facing the island, particularly rising unemployment, and one of his key tasks was to help the people understand them and to confront the realities.

While he was conscious of the communist threat, he was convinced that a purely anti-communist approach would fail to win over the masses. As he said at a rally on 3 June 1959, while anti-communism would appeal to the rich, "to the trishaw rider, the labourer, the underpaid clerk and people like them, communism holds no terror". Together with the other key PAP leaders, Raja had to craft strategies to counter the communist menace, without using the repressive police action which had turned the Chinese ground so savagely against Lim Yew Hock.

Raja and his colleagues decided that the way forward was to win the minds of the people to democratic socialism, to foster loyalty to Singapore and Malaya in the Chinese population, and to show that their democratic socialism offered a better system than communism.

This approach was not without its own dilemmas. William Goode, the country's first *Yang di-Pertuan Negara* and also the first UK Commissioner for Singapore, captured it in his report to London on 30 July 1959: "To succeed, they must retain the support of the Chinese working and student classes. In this lies their weakness, since they will be obliged to indulge in popular gestures which will antagonise the business and commercial class upon whom they depend for economic progress."

Indeed, some investors had already taken flight at PAP's victory at the polls, while others were waiting nervously at the sidelines. To calm them, he toned down his revolutionary rhetoric and his belligerent anti-colonial stance. At the same time, he was only too conscious that the sentiment on the ground remained bitterly anti-colonial.

The statue of Raffles, which stood arms crossed by the Singapore River, was at first earmarked for removal, but Raja and his colleagues decided that this would only give the wrong signal to the world. So it stayed. "To pretend that he did not found Singapore would be the first sign of a dishonest society," Raja said.[3] He understood that this new phase required leaders who build, rather than destroy.

Hence, instead of tearing down the statue of Raffles, he found other ways to signal a break from the past. And that was to rename the Raffles National Library to National Library, and the Raffles Museum to National Museum. Earlier, he had advised the cabinet against renaming all the localities, something which nationalistic leaders of many other post-colonial countries were prone to doing.

As he argued in his paper to the cabinet on 26 October 1960, wholesale renaming "would cause unnecessary confusion in the minds of the public" and, therefore, proposed to rename only those buildings or institutions which had "a bearing on the political and constitutional progress of Singapore". It was significant that, of all the buildings in Singapore, he considered the library and the museum the most worthy to bear this symbolic mantle.

His choices posed their own unique problems — while the Local Government Ordinance gave the local authority the powers to rename any street, there were no such provisions for the renaming of public buildings. As such, Raja had to move two bills in the Legislative Assembly on 29 November 1960 to enact the changes. Giving voice to the symbolism, he said: "When before the dreams and ideals of Raffles were the motivating force of the ruling class, today new ideals and aspirations have replaced those of Raffles."[4]

The energy and passion which he had poured into his anti-colonial fight were now channelled into this crusade to build a nation. In this new phase of self-government, it was no longer about fighting the colonial masters for freedom; it was about fighting the enemies within. It was a matter of urgent necessity, or in his words, of "practical politics", to confront the ever present danger of communal strife.

He warned: "With the transfer of political power from the British, there is the ever present danger of the struggle for political and economic power degenerating into communal rivalry, and, if uncontrolled, into communal conflict."[5] He was convinced that a common Malayan culture was the only effective defence against racial conflict.

He had observed how many newly independent countries, such as India and Ceylon, had unravelled with racial and religious wars, and was determined to shepherd Singapore onto higher ground. The field was strewn with hazards. In the recent elections, of about 600,000 voters, only about 270,000 — less than half — were people born and bred in Singapore. As new migrants with no roots in Singapore, their loyalties and world view were wrapped around their own kin, clan, and motherland.

Even those born in Singapore were bitterly divided, with the English-educated and the vernacular-educated separated by social and economic class.

The obstacles before Raja were even more formidable when viewed against the terrain of widespread unemployment, poverty, illiteracy and squalid living standards. Such conditions provided fertile ground for racial agitation and also for communist penetration. As it would take a long time to solve these massive problems, Raja considered it necessary to create a rational environment in which problems could be discussed sensibly, and to build bonds between the different races in the shortest time possible.

His was a creed that holds that a good and wise government can and should sway public opinion and behaviour; it can and should encourage its citizens to confront difficult options and adjust to evolving realities. He believed that there was nothing pre-ordained in history and, for the country's ideals to be realised, political leadership was essential.

There were many frustrations. Not least was being forced to work on a shoestring budget and a skeletal staff for his ministry. Given the emaciated state of the Treasury, Goh allotted only $2 million to the Culture Ministry in the PAP's first budget in November 1959.

This was a pittance compared with the $27.4 million for the National Development Ministry, the $21.9 million for the Education Ministry, and the $20.5 million to the Finance Ministry.[6] The budget allocation reflected the government's priorities: Housing, education, and jobs. "Culture" trailed far behind. Over the first few years, Raja would be embroiled in a long-running dispute with Goh for more funds and staff for the multiple roles that his ministry played.

The low priority accorded to Raja's ministry at the start was also apparent at the first cabinet meeting on 8 June 1959, when permanent secretaries were assigned to the various ministries. All the ministers — except Raja — were provided with at least one permanent secretary; indeed, Goh had two. In contrast, Raja had to get by with one administrative officer, a Henry Armstrong, who would be transferred to the Culture Ministry after his release from the Prime Minister's Office.

It was only a month later, in July, that Raja had his first permanent secretary, a British expatriate P.R. Lewis. This did not work out. Raja found no rapport with Lewis, who was formerly permanent secretary to Francis Thomas, minister for communications and works. Two months later, in September, Lewis was replaced by Lee Siow Mong, a respected authority on Chinese culture. Siow Mong, who was secretary for the Malayanisation Commission, understood better where Raja was coming from, having tracked his views over the years. Later in his retirement, Raja recalled that it took the best part of three to four months before his ministry found its feet and was operative. "I'm not a great administrator. It was haphazard, you know, building up a ministry as I went along."

To tax his resources further, new departments from other ministries were transferred to him — without any increase in staff or funding. They included the transfer of the museum and library from the Education Ministry, and also the tourism industry from the Finance Ministry. The Culture Ministry also took over two departments — broadcasting and printing — from the Ministry of Home Affairs.

Against this inauspicious background, some of his colleagues and staff arched their eyebrows at Raja's ambitious plans for his ministry. But the stout-hearted Raja, who enjoyed operating at the precipice, was galvanised by the enormity of his mission. Creativity and resourcefulness of a very high order were called for, and he rose to the challenge.

Four days into taking office, on 9 June, he signalled his determination to break down communal barriers and build a Malayan consciousness by announcing a major change in press and broadcasting policy: From then on, *Radio Singapore* would devote more time to serious programmes with a Malayan emphasis, and present news broadcasts and commentaries from a Malayan point of view.

"We want listeners to think as Malayans. It is no use looking at Asian affairs through Western eyes," he said. While the foreign viewpoint would not be excluded entirely, the emphasis would be on giving the Malayan outlook to issues.[7]

He also announced his decision to integrate the Departments of Broadcasting and Information to make them more effective. It was necessary, he said, "to help us win the battle of ideas and maintain a non-communist, socialist democratic Malaya". The programmes would be orientated towards the aim of building national solidarity among the different races, he said.

Two days after the media announcement, on 11 June, Raja gathered his key staff officials for their first policy meeting in his office. They included his parliamentary secretary Lee Khoon Choy, who was his former colleague in *The Straits Times*, and the directors of each department. They were overwhelmed by his grand ideas, which often came with a generous dose of philosophy.

He impressed on them the purpose of the machinery of information services — it was to present government policy and activities to the people in the most effective manner possible. He said the ministry would issue directives periodically. He then proceeded to issue two: To give impetus to the creation of a "truly Malayan consciousness" through the presentation of one cultural group to another in a sustained way, and to stimulate serious thought and discussion on the urgent problems facing Malaya.

He instructed *Radio Singapore* to break down the existing cultural barriers within the station, and to expose its audience to the various cultures through its four channels, each catering to their language group — Malay, Tamil, Chinese, and English channels.

A major concern was reaching out to the Chinese audience. He called for new programmes such as cultural talks to introduce the Chinese to other cultures. He also wanted to increase programming for rural audiences with community listening sets, so that those who did not own a radio could also be informed of public affairs. He wanted more programmes produced particularly for women.

From his first staff meeting, he inaugurated a policy of proactive communication across language streams to educate the public and guide their opinion on national issues. This emphasis manifests his conviction that the common man possesses a rational streak which could be appealed to. He considered political education, with programmes stimulating serious discussion on problems of the day, a crucial plank in the foundation of a functioning democracy.

His senior officials reeled at the long list of demands made by their new Minister, without any additional manpower or budget. They were quick to impress on him that their financial position made it impossible for them to carry out these proposed programmes. While sympathising with their plight, he charged them to make every effort towards realising the objectives and "to demonstrate to the people that there had in fact been a change of policy".[8]

Unfamiliar with the mercurial thinking of their new minister, officials sometimes found themselves second-guessing him and overreacting to policy directions, to Raja's despair. As early as their second weekly policy meeting on 18 June 1959, Raja had to caution his directors "of the need for balance in the interpretation of the new policy". This was after the controller of programmes, Derek Cooper, told him that one request programme had already been dropped "in response to the new policy".[9] It was a perplexing time for all as they groped their way forward in the new political terrain.

Of all the policies Raja announced, the most ambitious was the creation of a Malayan nation and the accompanying ideas on developing a Malayan consciousness and a Malayan culture.

In his first address to the Legislative Assembly on 21 July 1959, he spelt out his basic creed which laid the foundation for Singapore's national ideology: "The shape of a man's nose, the cut of his eyes, the colour or the texture of his hair, are not a sound basis on which to build a political or an economic philosophy. Neither can political and economic problems be solved by reference to something which we just got through the accident of birth — our skin, our colour, and the shape of our eyes".

He continued: "Therefore, a Malayan outlook then initially means acceptance of the truth that, in politics and economics, racial considerations do not enter. More positively, it means acceptance of the fact that, whether we are Malays, Chinese, or Indians, we are committed to living in this country for all time."

The Malayan outlook was "worth fighting for, because even the term of life of political parties is more or less foreordained", he asserted. "They will run out their allotted time. But people, the Malays, Chinese and Indians, will live here for hundreds of years. And we of the present generation can at least help them solve this difficult problem, by removing from their minds what is really superstition — that race and religion are factors which should enter into our political calculations. And not only that, but that they should also become the basis for political conflict. If we can, during our term of office, exorcise this superstition, then perhaps, we would have done a great deal for the future of our country," he said.

This one-hour speech counts as one of his most thoughtful speeches and probably his most utopian, one still well worth reading. It stands out as among the finest expressions of national ideology voiced by a political leader in Singapore at that embryonic stage of its political development.

These sentiments of equality, regardless of race, language, and religion, would form the basis of his struggle for a "Malaysian Malaysia" during the merger years from 1963 to 1965, and for Singapore's national pledge after the country was expelled from Malaysia. His premise strikes a deep chord in Singapore today and retains its appeal. In laying out the fundamental basis for his core belief in equality so evocatively at this formative period, he had added something permanently to Singapore's conception of itself.

He believed that a Malayan nation could be created, and the prelude to it was a Malayan consciousness, which he sometimes used interchangeably with "Malayan outlook". The latter could be brought about "by implanting in the minds of people ideas and sentiments which provide them with a sense of common identity, common purpose, common effort, and common destiny".

He argued it was not an impossible task as detractors might think. He reeled off examples from round the world — people were not born Americans, French, or Japanese. "A man becomes an American, or Frenchman, or Japanese because of mental conditioning he is subjected to. In other words, national consciousness is largely a question of education and upbringing. A child is not born a Frenchman, or a German or a Malayan, or even a Malay or a Chinese. It is through the long process of mental conditioning that he turns out to be a Malay, Chinese or Indian," he contended.

In what had become his constant refrain, he said: "It is not race but the cultural conditioning to which a man is subjected that makes him whatever he is". He pointed to his own experience: He himself thought as a Malayan even though he was a Ceylonese.

"One becomes a Malayan when one ceases to evaluate the character, goodness, and intelligence of a man by the colour of his skin, by the shape of his nose, or the texture of his hair." His conception of a Malayan was a strikingly ethical one. It emphasised moral attributes, as opposed to physical ones. In its essence, he envisaged the Malayan nation as embodying a principle, as a form of morality.

As courageous were his ideas on race and cultural evolution. Unlike some in the cabinet, Raja held the view that racial sentiments were a result of socialisation and politicisation, not something rooted in the blood.

His boldest assertion, given the hold of traditional outlooks at the time, was that race was a prejudice, and an attitude that could be removed by rational analysis. If people responded to racial and communal pulls, it was simply because these were the older and traditional basis for unity. Even culture was artificial "in the sense that it is a creation of man". "Culture, as sociologists will tell you, is the environment created by man to free himself from the cruel dictates of his natural environment," said Raja.[10]

He often reminded his various audiences that a living culture was in a constant state of change. So when a certain community talked about wanting to preserve their culture, they must make clear which elements and from what phase of history. Take Chinese culture. "The Chinese culture of 2000 B.C. is something quite different from the Chinese culture flourishing in 1960 A.D. and will be quite something else in, say, 1970," he said.[11] Chinese culture as practised in China had also been subjected to great changes over the decades — the communist rulers of China had made Marxism the basis of their culture and had also repudiated the philosophies that for centuries had provided the motive power for Chinese culture: the teachings of Confucius and other ancient sages. Chinese culture in the new Malaya, like the other cultures in the country, would evolve as they came under the influence of a common social, political, and economic system.

He was not denying that race might be a factor in Malayan politics. But again, this state of mind was a result of conditioning: "So long as a group of people, however wrongly, believe that the bonds of race are real, then for all practical purposes, race becomes a factor in politics. But racial prejudice is, as any social scientist will tell you, a cultural trait — a part of one's pattern of cultural behaviour." It was a provocative viewpoint.

While his perorations were for the Singapore audience, his use of the term "Malayan culture", rather than "Singapore culture", discomfited some in the Federation. Wang Gungwu, who was teaching at the University of Malaya in Kuala Lumpur during the period, recalled that his Malay colleagues and friends faulted the concept of "Malayan culture", as espoused by Raja, for neglecting the central position of Malay-Muslim culture in the Federation.[12]

Raja was more than aware of the intensifying rivalry between different racial groups for dominance and the dangers this posed to the development of Malayan nationalism. He did not expect his position on race and culture to be popular. As far as he was concerned, he was telling the fundamental truths about life in Malaya, truths that might not be comfortable, but which needed to be understood.

These truths, however, were not easy for the average person to grasp and accept. For one thing, in 1959, about half the population in Singapore were illiterate. But even the literate person would find the complex and abstract nature of "Malayan culture" something of a puzzle.

Understandably, the most frequent questions Raja had to deal with on this topic were: What was this Malayan culture he was trying to develop? How long would it take to create one? To the first, he would reply that it was not for him or anyone to define, but for it to evolve. "No one has the intelligence, the imagination, and the breadth of knowledge to indicate precisely what the nature of Malayan culture should be, and what it would be like."[13] All the government could do was to stimulate a Malayan consciousness to provide the necessary *emotional* base for the creation of a Malayan culture, he replied.

He imagined, however, that its notable feature would be "the emergence of new beliefs and social behaviour which are common to all the communities".[14] As to how long it would take to create this Malayan culture, his riposte was that it was a meaningless question "because a culture is not a statue or a chair".

The central difficulty of explaining what the term "Malayan culture" meant barred the way to easy acceptance and enthusiasm. In addition, the key words did not mean the same thing to all. To cap these troubles, the different communal groups wanted their own culture to form the basis of the Malayan culture. Some, such as several UMNO assemblymen, pressed for Malay culture to form the core, others said it should be Chinese, given their dominance, and yet another group claimed the Peranakan culture as the rightful mother of Malayan culture. This contest for dominance would continue for years.

It was left to Raja, the Ceylonese Tamil, to hold the ring and to stand firm on the principle of equality for all communal groups in the national ideology. As far as he was concerned, this was non-negotiable. He fought tooth and claw against communal groups who tried to dictate the agenda, considering communalism the major obstacle to the creation of a Malayan nation. He had rounds of exhausting dialogues with the various cultural groups over this issue.

Coming from a minority ethnic group — or as he put it once, the "minority of minorities" — Raja demonstrated a stronger commitment than perhaps others to this universalistic conception of national identity.

But his own background could also have worked against him. Wang, a leading authority on Chinese studies today, said: "Being neither Malay nor Chinese — and he was certainly not a traditional Indian — he was seen to represent a minority standpoint and was not credible in the eyes of those who still favoured the protection of communal or ethnic cultures. I don't think there was much more he could have done under the circumstances."[15]

Raja's sense of racial politics sharpened as he contended with similar communal pressures in the process of designing the state flag. Deputy Prime Minister Toh Chin Chye was involved in the earlier stages, delving into the technical rules of heraldry in drawing a flag and a crest, but he was overseas when the time came to finalise the design and provide the interpretations of the symbols.[16] The task fell to Raja. It was an intense experience that left a deep impression on him.

For the flag to be a national symbol, as opposed to a PAP one, Raja consulted all political parties represented in the Legislative Assembly in closed-door sessions. Lee was also closely involved and guided the discussions. They were so fraught with racial and religious controversies that, at one point, the entire project seemed at stake.

A.P. Rajah, a legislator who took part in the discussions, related about a year later: "After three or four days of coming and going, of likely breakdowns, almost certain breakdowns, we eventually got a solution."[17] The process honed Raja's diplomatic skills as he attempted to moderate extreme positions. The result was that the final design, used in the flag today, bore very little resemblance to the first.

In Raja's account, the first draft of the flag design was red as the background with a yellow star in the centre. The Singapore UMNO was up in arms against it, protesting that it was virtually the flag of the Communist Party. Later, someone suggested that the flag should be green in the background with a large white star. This demand was deemed excessive — that would have Islamised the flag. Meanwhile, the pro-communists, influenced by the five yellow stars on the flag of China, were firm on using the red background and the yellow star.

Raja was caught in a quandary. Each group had its own interpretation of symbols. He recalled years later: "After several discussions, arguments and much persuasion, we managed to persuade all, including some people inside the PAP, to use red and white as the background colours of the flag, with five white stars and a crescent moon."[18] The crescent moon also caused some consternation among the non-Muslim community. Some countries were also confused. "They saw the crescent moon as a proclamation of our religious identity," said Raja. This perception, too, had to be cleared up.

To prevent "any too free a translation of the new symbols", Raja provided an "authorised translation" of the symbols when moving the Singapore state arms and flag and national anthem bill on 11 November 1959.

The colour red stands for universal brotherhood and equality of man. "Whatever the colour of our skin, the shape of our nose and eyes, the blood that gives us life is of one colour — even among those who claim to have blue blood," he said. The colour white signifies purity and virtue. The two colours combined signify that "we hope to achieve brotherhood and equality through purity and virtue". As for the crescent moon, it signifies a country eternally young. "This is expressive of one of the essential qualities of our people, for not only are our people physically young but they are also young in spirit and outlook.... The new Singapore, like the new Asia, therefore, finds its inspirations in what it hopes to do in the future rather than what it has done in the past."

The five stars represent the ideals on which the new State of Singapore is founded — democracy, peace, progress, justice, and equality, he said. Reading the lofty meanings he invested in the symbols, few today could have guessed just how ugly the disputes surrounding the realisation of the flag had been.

In the Legislative Assembly, opposition member Thio Chan Bee gave credit to Raja for creating "this new precedent" of consulting the opposition political parties on the design of the flag. "We know that the Government side could unilaterally impose its ideas on the House," he said. Opposition assemblyman Mohd Ali bin Alwi, who spoke in Malay, also praised him for being "very compromising in accepting constructive suggestions" on the design.

For Raja, the entire process was a salutary lesson not only in compromise, but also the sensitive nature of racial and religious discussions. He said years later: "Each time I recall the controversies arising out of the State flag, it would remind me of the special character and complexity of a multi-racial and multi-religious society."[19]

Raja's character as a leader was tested in his first few years as culture minister as he committed himself to championing the idea of a Malayan national identity — a course of action that shaped his own public persona. His colleagues in cabinet discovered that, unlike some others who melted under pressure and only paid lip service to their ideals, Raja would live up to his personal principles.

Throughout the entire time he promoted these ideas — which was his entire life — he was mocked for all sorts of sins. Among the accusations hurled at him was that he was attempting to dilute existing cultures, and to pressure-cook the various cultures into a melting pot acceptable to no one. Others ridiculed him for even trying to deliberately create a Malayan culture — that it was nonsense, idealistic, and a waste of time. Some were mortified by what they thought were monstrous representations of the Malayan culture — Chinese, Malay, and Indian costumes and art forms mixed and matched in a forced and ridiculous way.

The personal attacks were the most vicious, with some Indians criticising him for selling out on his own culture, and some Chinese and Malays telling him to go home to Ceylon. Then there were those who pointed derisively at the European woman he married, as if that disqualified him from speaking about Malayan culture. He did not deign to acknowledge the personal taunts, although they must have hurt. He would not be spared from such spiteful hate-mail even after he retired from politics, as he continued to fight for his vision of a non-communal and secular national identity.

As for the intellectual criticisms, all too often they sprung from a misunderstanding or oversimplification of his ideas. A close reading of his writings and talks from the early 1950s shows that Raja had been more nuanced and sophisticated in his approach to the question of national identity than might have perhaps been understood by his detractors. What he was advocating, first and foremost, was the primacy of loyalty to a national identity over race (a term which he also used interchangeably with "communal group").

The question then was: what was this national identity? It was in the effort to give it some form and substance that he expounded on the need for a Malayan consciousness and a Malayan culture, terms he used loosely. In discussing them, he was often more focused on the subjective elements — will and consciousness, rather than the "objective" elements such as clothing, customs, or food. His key appeal was to the political and moral components of the nation. While he did sprinkle phrases such as "cultural fusion", "melting pot", and "cultural synthesis" in some speeches — which no doubt added to the confusion — it is apparent, when these are read in context, that he did not call for the existing cultures to be dissolved into a uniform brew.

This was why, even as he sought to develop a Malayan culture, he also encouraged the development of the different languages and cultures, as long as they did not threaten Malayan nationalism. That threat would come only, he said, when they strengthened loyalty and submission to foreign countries, and not to Malaya. As long as the first and last loyalty of every Singapore citizen was to Malaya, then the flourishing of other languages and cultures would be a source of strength to Malayan culture, he maintained.[20]

Whether a national identity can be created was thrown open to doubt. But what were the options? He invoked the need for faith: "We must first accept the premise that it is an act of faith; that a Malayan consciousness is desirable, possible and inevitable. We must accept this premise because, if we do not, then the job of creating a Malayan culture becomes difficult and perhaps might even end not in a Malayan culture or Malayan consciousness, but in communal anarchy...We must believe we can do it soon and that we can do it by a deliberate act of will."[21] The combination of tactical and doctrinal concerns entwined in this statement underline the fluidity in Raja's outlook. Some have seen it as a sign of confusion, others, as the opportunistic attempt to make a virtue of necessity by enriching such key notions as "culture" and "nation" in the light of the dangers facing the country. His viewpoint was a complex amalgam of socialism, patriotism, secularism and anti-ethnocentrism.

It is a pity he never pulled the many strands of his thoughts together and systematised his ideas on national identity in a book. His pursuit of ideas was often so hurried and ferocious that it occasionally overran his care in consistency. But perhaps, the attempt to see in him a coherent ideology can be misleading.

He peddled no simple doctrines. His was the political generation that had little choice, but to find its own solutions to the "national question" and break its own path. It is hard for a lone prophet to avoid a certain overassertiveness.

He might have pushed his theories of cultural development a little too far when insisting that its pace could be speeded up: "Since culture is the creation of man, he should not only be able to determine its course, but also its tempo."[22] But on the larger vision, his overkill was justified. He was right about the dangers posed by communalism in a newly post-colonial society, as could be seen from the virulent ethno-religious nationalism that had seized India and Ceylon and torn their societies apart.

He realised that, in creating this Malayan culture, no government could force the people to move faster than they were prepared to. "But what it can legitimately do is to exhort, explain and exhort again why it is necessary to develop a Malayan culture and create a Malayan consciousness as soon as possible," he said.[23]

Exhort, explain and exhort again. Raja was a picture of reasonableness as he appealed to the people's nobler side. His mild and gentle exterior belied the aggression of his imagination which at times seemed almost callous in the fierce and uncompromising demands it made on the people. They must subjugate their communal identity, forged over thousands of years, to a collective Malayan identity yet to be determined. They must sing the state anthem in a tongue they did not understand. They must rid themselves of any belief — what he called "superstition" — in their racial superiority, treat everyone as equals in a democratic state, and educate their children to do the same.

Raja's staff had the unenviable task of setting his ideas into motion. It helped that they were inspired by their dynamic minister. V.T. Arasu, then an assistant supervisor in the ministry's translation unit, was among those who thought that his expositions on the new national ideals were brilliant and well thought-out, although occasionally too philosophical and intellectual for the average person.

Arasu, who served the Culture Ministry from 1959 to 1985, maintained: "I still think nobody and none of the other Ministers have excelled him in writing speeches."[24]

Foong Choon Hon, who worked in *Radio Singapore*, saw political genius in Raja's multicultural policy: "If you are practising Malayan culture, how can you be pro-communist?"[25]

There were, of course, those who had neither the interest nor patience for Raja's lectures on culture, which often reflected his prodigious familiarity with ancient history and anthropology. Gopinath Pillai, who was president of University of Malaya's Socialist Club in 1960, remembered chairing a talk on Malayan culture, with Raja as the speaker. Despite the minister's scintillating performance, the forum attracted only a small crowd. Gopinath said: "The topic was dull."[26]

Raja persisted. He wove his message into every engagement he attended, which were many. He accepted all invitations that came his way — all, that is, except events organised by groups which were exclusively communal in character and intention. He drew a line there, and pronounced it government policy not to support any event and group which did not promote a Malayan outlook. This had a salutary effect on communal groups which coveted his presence at their functions.

In January 1960, at a Tamil festival organised by several Indian groups, Raja made it crystal clear that he came only because the festival's purpose, as stated by the organisers, was to "encourage Tamils to make Malaya their home, owe absolute and undivided loyalty to Malaya…and to help evolve a united Malayan nation".[27] He told the Indians present that, for the new government, the creation of a Malayan nation and Malayan consciousness was not a pious slogan, to be repeated fervently on such occasions and then forgotten.

"For us, the creation of a Malayan nation is a matter of life and death for the people of this country. Of this, we are convinced 100 per cent. We either create a Malayan consciousness very soon — or we end up in bitter and violent racial strife," he warned. Aware of sceptics in his midst, he added: "It is no use our paying lip service to the concept of a Malayan nation, a Malayan consciousness, while quietly going about strengthening communal loyalties and prejudices. If we do that, then disaster is inevitable."

He cautioned that, under conditions of bitter communal rivalry, minority groups would be the ones which suffer. "Communal solidarity is not the answer, for if it is a matter of communal strength deciding the issues, then victory will go to the strongest and most powerful communal faction," he argued.

Raja made a special effort to reach out to the young. Khoon Choy noted: "He believed that, in schools, students from the different races should study the different cultures of other races." Whenever he met youngsters, Raja encouraged them to discard the divisive prejudices of their elders and embrace a Malayan outlook.

He made one of his most direct pleas at a combined school variety show in 1960, where he laid the burden of realising the vision of a national identity on their shoulders. Raja told them that the older adults had never had the benefit of an education which taught them "to be one people". The least that could be done now was to see that, by the efforts of the government and the people, "we can make the future so that, in about 10 or 15 years time, you will not do things in terms of a Malay, Chinese or Indian. Instead, you will say that 'I am a Malayan' and do things for the people of Singapore and Malaya as a whole."[28]

Few displayed as great a confidence that Singapore could create a nation and its own distinctive identity. Even Lee had his doubts. He said later: "I thought it would take a long time."[29] Over the years, in private, they would have frequent arguments about the place of race in identity. Lee later said that they never persuaded each other. But publicly in 1959, Lee went along with Raja's views on creating a Malayan nation and culture in the shortest time possible. Lee said years later: "He believed in it and took that public line. So we acquiesced."[30] It was hard for Lee not to admire Raja for his strong convictions on this issue. In this sense, Raja provided a countervailing influence to Lee, which helped to moderate some policies. Towards the end of 1959, the prime minister was sufficiently moved to pay a public tribute to his culture minister "for the enthusiasm with which he has gone into his job of building up a Malayan consciousness, and his belief that it is possible, desirable and attainable". "That faith has sustained him where lesser souls might well have flagged in their enthusiasm", Lee told the Legislative Assembly.[31] Coming after months of being put through a sort of hell for his efforts, Lee's words must have been as balm to his spirit.

Raja brought both the practical readiness of the journalist and the scholarly traits of the man of letters into his work. His senior staff became accustomed to the sight of their minister pounding the keys of his typewriter and producing reams of pages without pause. Indeed, Raja was often so deeply absorbed in his thoughts and so immersed in his duties that he sometimes overlooked the fact that he had officers. Khoon Choy recalled how, after three months of doing very little on the job, he marched up to Raja to ask if there was anything for him to do. If not, he wanted a transfer. Raja looked at his parliamentary secretary, registered his presence, and decided: "You look after culture."

That was how Khoon Choy found himself involved in this area. Raja was tireless in conjuring up creative ways to bring the different races together. "He was always thinking. He was full of ideas. I was trying to do things to fit with his ideas," he recalled.[32] One of the most successful was the multicultural festivals, called *Aneka Ragam Rakyat* (or People's Cultural Concerts), to showcase the richness and variety of one culture to the others. Through awareness would come appreciation, and through appreciation, a sense of unity. At least, that was Raja's hope.

To bring the shows to people from all walks of life, the open-air concerts were held not only in the town centre, but also in rural areas and on islands. He opened a series of regional theatres all around the island over the next four years. The first such theatre in the heartlands was at Hong Lim Green, which Raja opened on 23 April 1960. The open-air stage served seven constituencies around the park, which spanned the heavily built-up Chinatown area. Arasu recalled: "This was the first time the government supported open-air entertainment, where all the different cultures were brought to the same stage. This was the novelty."[33]

The open-air concerts led to a burst of cultural activity, as artistes and performers were brought together and encouraged to mount joint shows. This boosted the profile of the performing groups which, for the first time, were provided with audiences which ran to the thousands. These regular concerts also served to fulfil Raja's vision of bringing music and culture to the masses, instead of being confined to the elite English-educated minority at Victoria Theatre.

Another of Raja's initiatives, this time less successful, was to promote *Music and the Arts for Everyone*, as the programme was called. Once a month, the Culture Ministry organised indoor events with the aim of encouraging an appreciation of the arts. To help reimburse the performers, an entrance fee of $1 was charged.

This did not take off. The reluctance of people to part with $1 for a concert was a strong indication of the low level of arts appreciation at the time.

Instead of being bowed down, he set his sights higher: To build a national theatre that would symbolise Singapore's new aspirations as a self-governing country. Rather than commemorate the occasion, as some countries do, by erecting statues "extolling the virtues of some great individual" or "some useless structure of bricks and mortar", as Raja put it, Singapore would mark it "by putting up a theatre where our cultural talents could be displayed for all to see".

He envisioned a time when tourists would come to Singapore "to be enthralled by the richness and variety of our culture — a culture rooted in many civilisations".

Like some of his grand ideas, this proposal was initially received with trepidation among some in the cabinet, given the tattered state of the Treasury. To sidestep this obstacle, Raja made public appeals for funds. The initial public response was cold, with some people asking him: In such uncertain economic times, who would give money to build a cultural performing venue?

To add to the negativism, he received a letter from a citizen criticising his ministry for spending so much time and money on the promotion of the arts. The writer demanded: "Which is more important? Houses, schools, jobs and hospitals or music, painting, literature and drama?"[34]

Raja had this searing answer: "This is the sort of question that is asked in societies which are spiritually and intellectually sick. Such a question comes naturally only in a society which has become less human and almost animal in character. It is only in animal societies that its members are preoccupied with the essentials of life — food, shelter, water and propagation. A society which concentrated only on these essentials of life would be no better than a society of monkeys, sheep or ants."[35]

It was a painstaking effort for Raja and his team to turn the public mood towards the National Theatre project. To rouse public interest, Raja played the drum roll to welcome any effort by groups or individuals to raise funds for the theatre. He also urged every citizen to contribute to the theatre fund in a dollar-a-brick campaign.

When people eventually began responding, he was elated. He declared that the theatre would be "a permanent memorial to mark the attainment of self-government by the people of Singapore" and "a symbol affirming our faith in our ability to create a Malayan nation and a Malayan culture through united action".[36]

Despite his brave rhetoric, it would take two more years of hard labour and debate before the theatre, with its iconic design, could finally take shape in 1963. When opened on 8 August 1963 to commemorate Singapore's self-government, the building at the foot of Fort Canning Hill was the first and largest national theatre in

Singapore, with a capacity of 3,420 seats. It cost $2.2 million, with the public giving $786,000 and the government footing the rest.

A chorus of critics also rose up against him when he envisioned cross-cultural productions as a way to bring the different cultural groups together to collaborate.

At the first performance of a Chinese opera, *Princess Kwei Ying* conducted in English on 24 July 1960, Raja welcomed the effort as a contribution towards breaking down the walls that separated the arts of the various communities.[37] At last, non-Chinese could have a chance to understand the spirit of Chinese opera. However, some Chinese purists saw the effort as sacrilegious and a dilution of their culture. Others asked, in horror, if this was the shape that Malayan culture would take.

Chastised but not penitent, Raja stayed the course, carrying the same message to all communal groups. In all his actions, he was careful never to take sides with any community. When he attended a music festival commemorating the 150th birthday of the Indian poet, Sree Swathi Thirunal, he urged the Indians also to create new forms of creative expression which, though rooted in Indian culture, would take on a Malayan hue. "To do this, Indian artists must study, understand and absorb the art, music and drama of other communities as seriously as they do their own," he said.[38]

Similarly, he exhorted musicians to compose contemporary music that expressed the needs and feelings of a 20th century society, and to draw from the four great cultural traditions in Malaya. "Here in Malaya, we have Malay, Indian, Chinese and Western music forms, and it would be a poor composer indeed who confined his interests to only one of these traditions."[39] In a similar vein, he urged dramatists and writers to produce contemporary plays set in Malaya.

In 1959, it was considered a cultural breakthrough just to have the different cultures perform on the same stage. It would take a long time before the concept of contemporary cross-cultural productions would be accepted, let alone celebrated.

But it is a measure of the power of that idea, planted in the dry, infertile soil of 1959, that it should survive to flower more than 40 years later. In recent years, such cross-cultural productions have become not only *de rigeur*, but also a distinctive hallmark of Singapore's efforts to position itself as a global arts city.

To concentrate people's minds on the country's new ideals, Raja masterminded a week-long cultural extravaganza to inaugurate the new state flag, the new anthem, the state crest, and to appoint the country's first Malayan-born head of state. The celebrations, called National Loyalty Week, were launched on 3 December 1959. That week, the people were treated to concerts, dramas, film shows, photographic and art exhibitions, and even a phone number to dial in to listen to the anthem, *Majulah Singapura*.

Raja was pleased to see Yusof Ishak, a former newspaper journalist and editor, installed as Singapore's symbolic head of state. He had known Yusof, the founder editor of the Malay-language newspaper *Utusan Melayu*, since his own journalist days. "He was very open-minded. He did not like feudalistic ideas and customs. He never allowed Malays to kiss his hand," said Raja.[40]

On the day of Yusof's inauguration, the state flag also replaced the Union Jack which for 140 years, from 1819 to 1959, except for the two years under Japanese Occupation, had flown over Singapore. *Majulah Singapura* was sung in place of *God Save the Queen*. It was a moment to savour.

Musician Zubir Said had originally written the tune for the City Council in 1958, but Raja and several others, such as Toh Chin Chye, wanted the march to be adapted for the new anthem. Raja was familiar with Zubir's passion for music and for Singapore — the musician, who came from Indonesia, had given him useful views on promoting multiracial harmony, and had walked the talk by helping the Culture Ministry to organise its *Aneka Ragam* concerts.

For the anthem, Raja told Zubir that the music and lyrics should reflect the spirit of anti-colonialism and the desire for national self-determination and autonomy. At the same time, they should also express the desire of the various races to be united and to forge ahead together. With the prospect of merger with Malaya, he asked for the lyrics to be in Malay. But they must be simple enough for the non-Malays to accept them. Most important, they should stir the people's emotions. After listening to Raja's litany, Zubir could only promise to do his best.

When the proposed anthem was composed, the first thing that Raja did was to ask his political secretary Rahim Ishak for a detailed report of the Malay lyrics. After that, Raja, together with Toh, Rahim and Lee Khoon Choy, went to the *Radio Singapore* station to listen to the different musical arrangements produced by Zubir. They settled on one after making some adjustments. Pleased with the final version, Raja recommended to the Cabinet that the composition be adopted as the national anthem.

At its meeting on 2 November 1959, the Cabinet decided that Raja should be the one to introduce the Singapore State Arms and Flag and National Anthem bill, and to take the bill through all its stages. Raja would also move a motion to adopt the national symbols as described. He duly did both in the Legislative Assembly on 11 November, yet another historic day when the country laid claim to its first national symbols.

Zubir did not ask for any payment. Nevertheless, in a letter dated 23 October 1959, Raja offered him an honorarium of $2,000 in appreciation of his contribution, and to confirm his agreement to the arrangement, particularly to the surrendering of the copyright to the government. Zubir accepted the honorarium, but requested that this payment not be made public. Raja agreed to his request.

As an exceptional item with no precedent, there was, of course, no existing budget heading for this payment. This taxed the accounting control system as evidenced by the various notes passed to and fro between different departments seeking an appropriate budgetary home for this singular item. In the end, the honorarium was provided from savings. As the Culture Ministry had none, the savings came from the chief secretary's establishment budget for "Language Proficiency Bonuses" which was transferred to a new subhead created under Home Affairs, titled "Honorarium to Composer of State Anthem". Such were the exigencies of the day.

In 1960, there was yet another innovation which caused a stir: National Day was declared on 3 June, the date Singapore had its first popularly elected government and achieved its self-governing status. The opposition criticised the celebration as an effort to profile the PAP, and dismissed it as a waste of money. Rejecting their calls to scrap it, Raja returned yet again to his views on identity and explained the purpose of National Day — it was to drive home to the various communities in Singapore "the concept of a common identity, of a common purpose".

The laborious effort to give birth to a collective identity at times brought out an uncharacteristic edginess in Raja. It was manifest in his reaction — or rather, overreaction — to British poet-academic D.J. Enright who had dismissed the government's efforts to create a Malayan culture as "futile" at his inaugural lecture at the University of Malaya on 17 November 1960. Raja's response was visceral and immediate. Enright was summoned swiftly to report to the minister for labour and law, only to face not just the acting minister for labour Ahmad Ibrahim, but also a very stern Raja. The culture minister warned him that if he once more interfered in local politics, he would be deported.[41]

At that meeting, Raja also handed the academic a letter, dated 18 November. It was signed by Ahmad Ibrahim, but the words were notoriously Raja's. In the letter, Enright was told that it was not for "mendicant professors" such as him to enter into the field of local politics reserved for citizens. "We have no time for asinine sneers by passing aliens about the futility of '*sarong* culture complete with *pantun* competitions' particularly when it comes from beatnik professors," it added.

This reprimand provoked an explosive debate on academic freedom and freedom of speech, which has since been memorialised in the Singapore academia's institutional memory as "the Enright affair". The letter itself, couched in strong emotional language, sparked off an entire side debate of its own, with the opposition and journalists querying if such language befitted a government minister in an official letter. Academics and students mounted protests on campus.

Raja addressed the episode bluntly in the Legislative Assembly. The government reprimanded Enright only after the second time he criticised the government's policy on Malayan culture. The first was an interview with an undergraduate journal, the *Malayan Undergrad*. Raja read his criticisms as "sneers" at the government's efforts to try create a Malayan culture, and was concerned about Enright's influence on young minds at the university. He said: "When a professor who has been here for only seven months should suddenly say that not only is the Government wasting its time, but that it is probably wrong in trying to go out of its way to weld the people into a nation, then it is necessary for the Government to make it quite clear that anyone who is not there to take the consequences of his gratuitous advice on an important matter should not give this gratuitous advice."[42]

On the strong language in the letter, Raja was unrepentant. He said: "If anyone were to read the wartime speeches of Sir Winston Churchill, he would find that the honourable gentleman used robust language when he felt it was necessary to do." In Enright's case, "we felt that, because the subject concerned was so vital to us and because we felt so strongly about it, it was necessary to make known our feelings on this matter in no uncertain terms," he said.

What the incident revealed was that there were two sides to Raja — one the brilliant and highly analytical visionary, and the other who felt so passionately about his ideas that, at times, he went overboard, with thoughtful statesmanlike utterances of noble ideals and rational sentiment giving way to shrill and strident denunciations. The Enright affair was one of those seminal events that contributed to the hardline image of the PAP, although Enright himself more than survived the official reprimand — he remained in Singapore for 10 years and became a well-established writer, publishing four novels and six collections of poems.

Over time Raja woke up to the reality that moulding people's attitudes towards a shared culture was a much more difficult proposition than he had imagined. Or rather, the reality was forced on him. He was horrified when he learnt that, in December 1960, a group of Malays was plotting to precipitate a clash with the Chinese by alleging that the PAP government had neglected Malay interests and favoured the Chinese. The group, Angkatan Revolusi Tentera Islam Singapura (Artis) told the Malays to prepare for an alleged attack on them by the Chinese, but the Malays could buy shirts or charms from the *bomoh* (witch doctor) to make them invulnerable. The clash, which was to take place on 6 January, was thwarted only because of swift police action.

Making the case public, a sober Raja told the Legislative Assembly: "There is room in a democratic country for protest over grievances, whether real or imagined. But what is dangerous and unforgiving is the incitement to violence and hatred. Anyone, whether Malay or Chinese or Indian, who, in a multi-racial society, glorifies violence and preaches hatred and used them as political fuels inevitably prepares the ground for racial carnage."[43]

Raja was stricken by how this "handful of desperadoes", without any following or influence, could inculcate in hundreds of people a dangerous mood of anxiety by appealing to the economic discontent of the Malays. The racialist propaganda that the government was favouring the Chinese at the expense of the Malays was completely false, he said, but some unemployed Malay youths might be ready to believe such propaganda. He noted that this danger would persist as long as people have not yet learnt to think and act nationally.

In another move to beat back such dangers, the government banned a locally produced book, *Wind and Rain in Rubber Estates* on 10 January 1961. The book, with its poem about Chinese rubber tappers in the Federation, endorses hatred and violence as justifiable political fuels and bases for political action. Raja told the Legislative Assembly: "The eventual result of poems like this must be to build up an atmosphere of fear and hatred to be consummated in racial violence," he said.

He asked the people to consider what effect such poems, which advocated revolutionary violence of the Malayan Communist Party, would have on relations with the Federation Government and "on our Malay brothers who fear Communism and who are, from time to time, told by Malay communalists that the Chinese are working for the victory of Chinese Communism".

He appealed to everyone to remember this: "We live in a mixed community where old suspicions and fears have not been completely eradicated." As long as this is so, the danger of communalism exists. "It is like a wild and hungry beast pacing impatiently behind the bars of a cage. We, who bear no hatred against races and creeds, intend that this wild beast remains locked in its cage, so that eventually it will waste away and die," he said. He was to encounter this beast and wrestle with it many times as he trekked deeper into the uncharted territory of creating a Malayan nation.

Every single step forward was hard fought. Raja took the strain. He had committed himself on a perilous journey, and could not, would not, give up.

15

Shaping the Good Society

In the cabinet, Raja stood out as an epitome of robust optimism tempered with the grim recognition of the challenges ahead and the resolve to face them squarely. In the first few years, his courage to meet adversaries head-on, his swiftness of mind and clarity in explaining ideas established him as one of the most valued men in the cabinet.

All members of the cabinet, except Ahmad Ibrahim, had higher educational qualifications than Raja, but when it came to intellectual argument, few could equal him. Yong Nyuk Lin, the education minister at the time, called him the "brain". His colleagues also appreciated his calm and unflappable demeanour. Yong recalled later: "Goh Keng Swee would say 'buzz off', but Raja was smiling, easy-going, no matter how trying the circumstances. If Lee Kuan Yew had harsh words, Raja would just smile and smooth things."[1]

Certainly, Raja's standing with the prime minister was not in doubt. Lee said in later years that in the first cabinet, those he considered his intellectual equals were Raja and Goh.[2] Having worked closely with Raja on political strategy since 1952, Lee was the first in the cabinet to appreciate his talent with ideas and their public presentation. As Lee said later, "on political feel, on presentation on how to get people on our side, how to keep a multiracial country together, I couldn't find a better man. He believed firmly in it".[3]

Compared with his colleagues, Raja was the more street-savvy and polished, if also the more disorganised, political operator. In public communications, Raja's advantage, which the other cabinet ministers lacked, was his decade-long experience in journalism, in both print and broadcast.

From the first day, the prime minister and the other ministers turned to him for help to publicise their policies and to personally draft their press statements and sometimes, even speeches. His in-tray was constantly overflowing with such requests.

One typical assignment: In a cabinet meeting on 5 October 1959, Raja was asked to rewrite a draft statement from the minister for home affairs, Ong Pang Boon, "in simple language". Another: In a memo to Raja on 12 June 1961, Goh complained about the draft press statement attempted by his Treasury staff on the upcoming property tax — it was "absolutely no good" — and asked Raja's ideas on "how the subject should be approached and along what lines the press statement should be made".

Yet another: Toh wrote to Raja on 2 August 1961, to lament that the Mass Work Bureau committee had not thought enough about the publicity for the upcoming new government flats and asked for Raja's input. It was a politically sensitive issue, as squatters had to be evicted for the flats to be built. With each such assignment deftly executed, Raja's reputation as the chief public communicator in the cabinet rose.

His journalism background, with its incessant pressures of haste, of dealing with unpredictable issues as they arose, had bred in him a habit to respond swiftly and energetically. He carried his insights into the cabinet. At the second cabinet meeting on 15 June 1959, he presented his colleagues with a three-page memo on "Ministerial press relations", which outlined his general press policy.[4]

Many ministers were new to the business of public communications, and were by instinct wary of reporters. Raja encouraged the ministers to hold weekly press conferences at pre-arranged times to prevent overlapping, and stressed the benefit of establishing good relations with the press by giving "considerate treatment" to their wish for speedy replies and to pursue their own angles, other than the official ones provided.

Knowing the power of radio to move minds, he coaxed his cabinet colleagues to broadcast their policies over radio and, separately, to address questions from the public as well. In the radio's first series, *A Matter of Policy*, which started on 25 April 1960, ministers for the first time answered questions on government policy submitted by listeners over radio.

Following this, Raja also introduced the four-language radio weekly programme *Question Time*, in which residents could put forward their problems to the government and have them answered on air. Through such initiatives, he set the template for political discourse in the broadcast media. The radio was a popular medium. In 1959, more than 70 per cent of the population tuned in daily to the radio broadcasts.

Tapping on its outreach, he continued his own efforts to educate the public on major issues. One of his broadcasts, also translated into Chinese, was on "Democracy in Action", in which he addressed the popular misconception that, as long as people had the right to elect a government, the foundation of democracy was strong. On the contrary, democracy needed other important pillars to work — unity and the willingness of leaders to serve the country; disciplined citizens; and sensible and fair-minded opinions, he lectured.[5]

In simple and crisp language, he explained that in a democracy, citizens had to elect their government from many political parties. They had to compare the various parties' announcement of their economic, political, and social policies. But before they could make a sound choice, they must at least be knowledgeable about current affairs. But some of these were very complex issues. He said: "Many countries have not done much in educating their citizens on political issues. Sometimes this is deliberate, sometimes it is because the political leaders have limited knowledge themselves...After they have elected their government, they may find that their leaders are incompetent and ignorant, or are frauds." Hence, well thought-out and fair-minded opinions were the only weapon against political fraudsters, he said.

He saw it as the responsibility of his ministry to educate the people so that they could vote wisely. "We can use public media to get citizens to improve their understanding of democracy." This included radio, films, pamphlets, and posters.

The new division in the ministry issued press statements explaining government policies and wrote the news for radio. The library and the museum also promoted educational campaigns. If Singapore wanted its democracy to continue to work, he said, effort must be made to help its people better understand the issues that matter. "We cannot make the mistake of handing over the democracy to a group of muddle-headed leaders who are not able to handle such issues," he concluded.

The PAP was a government in a hurry, and Raja tried to make sure, with speech soft and hard, with press statements, radio programmes, pamphlets and films, that the public be kept abreast of the changes. But it turned out to be an unsettling time for all as his ministry struggled to crank up its machinery and gear up its staff to keep pace with the demands.

Raja stayed calm under the incessant pressure. He held the hands of his nervous staff and guided them closely on political propaganda. This was apparent in the minutes of his staff meetings.

In one discussion with his staff to publicise the government's development plans in June 1961, Raja directed that special attention be paid to housing and education, two hot political issues of the day. He also instructed his broadcasting division to focus on the impact of the programme — and not on the length — to draw listeners. For example, short slogans could be more forceful than long ones, he said. Knowing that much depended on intelligent implementation, he arranged to meet the producers to make sure that his ideas were understood and, more importantly, to deal with their doubts.

Eager to create the public impression of a government on top of things, Raja was distressed when the sluggish reaction of some ministries resulted in the press relying more on speculation than facts to report the news. He brought the matter up at the cabinet meeting on 5 October 1959, after another press fiasco involving sensationalised reports of a riot of 200 secret society detainees at Changi prison. The cabinet then decided to give Raja and his parliamentary secretary access to all heads of departments to get to the bottom of matters of public interest, so that "unnecessary sensation and speculation by the press" could be avoided.[6] Information was power, and this decision gave Raja unprecedented power: he could now go over the heads of ministers to ferret out the facts and respond to the press quickly.

This was cold comfort to Raja, however. From very early on, he had been arguing in cabinet for each ministry to build up its own public relations department as "it is not a separate departmental activity but an essential aspect of all government".[7] At the time, the culture ministry acted as the centralised public relations department for the entire government. It took requests from newspapers for all ministries. It was also in charge of issuing all government press statements, as well as notifying newspapers, news agencies, and foreign correspondents about press conferences held by all ministers or heads of departments.

Raja was justifiably worried about a news bottleneck if all queries had to go through his under-staffed ministry. But Goh, who was in charge of the civil service, was adamant that the government could not afford the luxury of having a press relations department in each ministry.

While Goh and Raja shared a genuine friendship, it was obvious that they had vastly different temperaments and priorities. Given his urgent task of reorganising the economy, Goh thrilled only to the swishing of the fiscal axes. In contrast, Raja, the ideologue, believed that fiscal rectitude could wait: The need to win the hearts and minds of the people was urgent.

For the first three years, Raja would engage in several protracted disputes with Goh over more funds and staff to implement his culture ministry's ideas and programmes. Raja once said that both of them usually got on like a house on fire, but when it came to occasions when his ministry asked for funds for its projects, such as the $4 million for television, they were like "two houses on fire".[8]

The persistence of Raja's appeals and the imperviousness of Goh to them were chronicled vividly in a series of written exchanges from 22 October 1959 to 2 March 1960. In his first appeal, Raja asked Goh to unfreeze the staff positions needed as early as possible "because we are really in a fix". No response. Raja chased Goh in another letter on 9 December 1959. This time, the request also included the addition of a librarian to take charge of Raffles National Library. Raja informed Goh that the library was in its "present chaotic state" because it had never had a permanent head. Still no response from Goh.

Raja began to exhibit impatience at what he regarded as Goh's dilatoriness, and shot off yet another memo to Goh on 20 January 1960. The dominant note was one of frustration. Again, Raja reminded Goh that his ministry had taken in extra work from other ministries such as Department of Broadcasting, Raffles Museum, Raffles National Library, and the Printing Office, but with no increase in staff. "Indeed, if there was anything at all, it was decrease in staff due to resignations, retirements and other forms of casualty," he said.

Raja had to send yet another strong missive on 23 February 1960, before Goh finally replied — on 24 February 1960, a good four months after Raja's first written appeal for senior staff. And when he did, he was sympathetic, but unconvinced. This provoked Raja to shoot off a few more letters, but to no avail.

Unsurprisingly, Raja's problems soon snowballed. Some of his key plans had to be dropped or postponed. On 21 March 1961, his senior officials reported that there had been no radio news talks the past two months because of the staff shortage, and "editors, being overworked, getting mentally fatigued". For the same reason, the 11 am news service also had to be dropped. The launch of a new radio service in four languages, *Suara Singapura* (Voice of Singapore), had to be postponed from 1 June 1961, to 24 July.

National campaigns to publicise new policies also suffered as Raja could not summon up the necessary staff to carry them out. As his senior officials put it, the situation had become "most embarrassing".[9]

Whatever the disagreements he might have with any cabinet member, no outsider would know of it from Raja. He was very scrupulous about this. For this reason, his colleagues found him completely trustworthy and discreet.

By the same token, his parliamentary secretary, Khoon Choy, found his boss frustratingly "secretive" — to the point of ordering him to leave the room whenever Raja took a call from the prime minister or a cabinet minister. Foreign correspondent Dennis Bloodworth also found Raja tight-lipped when probed on cabinet discussions. The British correspondent said: "In his 24 years as a government minister, he never once confused his political and personal loyalties by telling me anything that would involve a breach of faith with his colleagues. I learned more from ministers I did not know half as well."

Years later after his retirement from politics, however, Raja did let on that he found Goh "very strict" about politics, emphasising efficiency and discipline. "I was different. I associated politics with ideas. But his idea of politics was how to run the civil service!" said Raja.[10]

The prime minister, of course, was not oblivious to the different outlooks of his two key men. Lee said years later: "Goh's view was that it would be extravagant, better concentrate on infrastructure and spending which would give us revenue, but I had to keep Raja's part going, because if you don't carry the ground with you, you lose the next elections, which puts an end to the whole road show."[11]

The culture minister had to be resourceful, given the budget constraints. Lee appreciated the drive and commitment which Raja had brought to his task, which was "to make sure that the ground kept on moving with us; we should not be too far ahead of the ground".[12] It was an assignment which made full use of his experience and skills.

Where once he used his position as a journalist to bring down the colonial establishment, Raja now courted the vociferous print media to engage them in the new task of nation-building. He set out to do this by appealing to their nobler instincts, influencing their attitudes towards the PAP with his considerable charm and reason, and redefining the mission of journalism in nationalistic terms.

In his first public statement on the print media, published on 15 June 1959, he redefined the business of newspapers to be "valuable instruments in helping to reshape society, to reshape our political structure". He was not saying that newspapers should not make profits, but that their role should be "a public service first and as a money-spinner second".[13]

He gave notice that, in the next five years, the country would be going through momentous and drastic changes. Newspapers should prepare readers to face them. The major responsibility of a newspaper was "to present true, accurate and significant news so that those who read its pages will understand the currents of thought, especially political trends, in the country".[14]

He appealed to the newspapers' self-interest — the fortunes of newspapers were tied to the country's development. He also appealed to their patriotic spirit and professional pride — where once, in the colonial system, journalists played a marginal role in society as "entertainers", in the new Malaya, they would be playing an important one of building a nation.

But before they could do that, journalists must themselves be "well-informed and enlightened," he stressed. He was anxious for them to raise their professional standards and, over the years, would repeatedly call for some form of systematic training and academic grounding for them.

The new role he ascribed to journalists led him to redefine what would make a good journalist. In the old days, the true newspaperman was considered to be one who began as an office boy in the newspaper and, he said, "who has been toughened and prepared for this soul-consuming profession in the hard school of experience, bad liquor and bad language". This conception should change with the times, he argued. In modern society, the journalist must "be a man properly trained for his work, and with sufficiently intellectual discipline and knowledge of the things he has to write about", said Raja.[15]

No doubt from personal experience of receiving such news coverage, he observed that it was because of the ignorance of some journalists about a subject that they missed the significance of an event or a speech, and focused instead on the superficial. This must improve. In the 20th century, the newspaper was not merely a vehicle for passing on news. It also shaped public opinion and attitudes, for better or for worse. "This being so, we cannot remain indifferent to the intellectual and moral qualities of the men and women involved in the newspaper industry," he reasoned.

For a modern democratic society to work, there was a need for a well-informed public. The system was based on the principle of one man, one vote, and on the premise that the average citizen could grasp the complex challenges facing the country and make the right decisions, he said.[16]

His message was generally received with a mixture of scepticism and apprehension by the press. The English-language press, particularly *The Straits Times* and the *Standard*, were still smarting from the PAP's attacks during the election campaign, and the aggressive role that Raja, their former staff, had played in it.

As for the Chinese press, the problem it posed to Raja's aspirations for a more responsible press was even more intractable. They expressed the Chinese point of view, promoted news about China, Chinese language and culture, and found it hard to accept the new government-prescribed role of propagating a Malayan outlook or, even more unsettling, a Malayan culture. Many Chinese journalists were pro-communists, and indeed, some were members of the MCP.

Raja organised several dialogues with their editors, with Lee Kuan Yew presiding, to discuss their policy orientation. Where the senior editors were openly hostile, Raja and Lee worked on winning over younger and more promising journalists in the hope that, over time, they would take on a more Malayan outlook and form the next generation of editors. The combination of soft persuasion and hard tactics was also used on the Malay and Tamil press.

For all his theories of press freedom expounded before he joined politics, Raja showed that he was as hardline and reactionary as any when it came to cracking down on communist propaganda. Lee related later: "He knew that, if we allowed this to continue, especially the Chinese press, we would have the whole society in an uproar. We did not want a Chinese-dominated society."[17] As Raja took in Lee's determination to beat back Chinese chauvinism, his respect for the prime minister increased manifold. It took political courage for a Chinese leader to take such a stand in a Chinese-dominated society.

On his part, Raja was vigilant. To stop communist propaganda from appealing to pro-China sentiments, many books, music, and films were banned, especially from China. Chinese cultural groups performing communist items were also blacklisted and barred from appearing in concerts.

Raja's yardstick was straightforward: "When you find a certain Communist play, poem or music is in conflict with our intention to create a Malayan loyalty and a Malayan consciousness, we have prevented it."[18] According to the policy then, it was the Home Affairs Ministry which decided on the prohibitions, in consultation with the Culture Ministry. In 1959 alone, 23 tabloid papers and 13 magazines were banned.

To track the coverage of the different newspapers, he started a daily digest of newspapers, which summarised the key news points from all the newspapers in Singapore. V.T. Arasu, who did the Tamil translations for the ministry, recalled the drill: Every morning, Raja would meet the editors in the ministry's news division for daily briefings of all the newspapers. He also worked his translators hard.

As he scrutinised the coverage of news under the glare of his press policy, the opposition repeatedly attacked him for intimidating the press and curtailing their freedom to express independent views.

To one such criticism in the Legislative Assembly, Raja replied candidly that it was part of his duty to make contacts with the press. "Very often, as I can quite well remember when I was newspaperman, various politicians ring up the press to plead for a particular cause, or ask the journalists whether they could either play up or play down an item."[19]

In the same way, the government was perfectly entitled to lodge a complaint against any newspaper or to make a plea to any journalist, he said, adding that freedom of speech applied to the government too. "As far as I know, I have pleaded and intervened with the Press on behalf of Government but I have certainly never gone to the extent of intimidating or threatening the Press with direct consequences, unless they have transgressed the law."

That said, Raja would not tolerate fabricated stories prejudicial to the maintenance of public order. He also warned the press that, if they indulged in sedition or subversion, they would fall foul of the government and the law. His job was an onerous one. Occasionally, he also had to caution the editors if their newspapers published sensitive articles which could harm Singapore's relations with other countries.

One of the earliest instances of this was in March 1960 when Indonesia complained angrily about an article published in the Chinese-language newspaper *Sin Chew Jit Poh* which highlighted the evacuation of Chinese businessmen in Indonesia. In early 1960, the Sukarno government had announced a ban on ethnic-Chinese Indonesians from the rural retail trade business.

The *Sin Chew Jit Poh* article, published on 14 February 1960, was highly critical of this ban, implying discrimination against ethnic Chinese. Coming from Chinese-dominated Singapore, this stinging criticism touched a sensitive nerve in Indonesia, which was the largest Muslim country in the region.

In a letter to the newspaper's chief editor, the Indonesian consulate general in Singapore pointed out that the Chinese in Indonesia, which formed a minority, had held a monopolistic position in trade since the days of the Dutch colonial period, "and they continued to exercise it without the slightest regard to the interests of the country, which had given them hospitality as guests and even indulged in exploitation of the masses in the rural areas".

Ominously, the Indonesian consulate general questioned if the Singapore newspaper was championing the cause of the Chinese. He added that, to worsen matters, the abuse was directed "towards a Government with which friendly relations are being sought" and warned that such criticisms could carry "far-reaching consequences".

Raja, who received a copy of this letter, was perturbed by the tone and its implications. At the time, Singapore was making systematic efforts to build up its relations with Indonesia, which accounted for about 20 per cent of Singapore's overall value of trade. In late 1959, Raja had hosted an Indonesian cultural mission, and wined and dined its media. In early 1960, Prime Minister Lee had visited Indonesia.

Raja was acutely conscious that it would not serve Singapore's interest to be viewed as a Chinese state in the predominantly Malay archipelago, given the racial sensitivities in the region. Moreover, in the light of Singapore's political imperative of merger with Malaya, such a Chinese image would only do Singapore harm. Although he had strong opinions about the ethnic policies in other countries, Raja bit his tongue and focused on Singapore's national interest.

Rather than ride the ideological high horse, Raja approached the matter with a pragmatic mien. In a soothing letter to the Indonesian consulate general in March, Raja said he had spoken to the chief editor about the article. "I have told him that it was not right that he should make comments on events in your country the way he did, and especially at a time when both our countries are trying to build up friendly relations. I have asked him to keep off and avoid writing anything that might embarrass you or your government and also this government, and I have no doubt that he will co-operate. In the circumstances, I think it will be good for all concerned if this matter is allowed to rest where it is now," he wrote.

This episode provides a vivid insight into Singapore's pragmatic approach in dealing with its immediate neighbours and Raja's role in managing the Singapore media to play their nation-building role within these geopolitical constraints. Against such an unpredictable landscape, the basic contours of Singapore's media policy were being shaped. It was also against such harsh realities that Raja began to temper his views on freedom of speech and expression, formed when he was a radical student in London. Lee noticed the change in Raja after he became the culture minister. "It was only the reality of what worked and didn't work that slowly changed him," observed Lee.[20]

The government's relations with the media generally fluctuated with the national mood and the editors' attitude towards "responsibility". As Raja kept stressing, freedom of the press and responsibility came together. "Personally, I think the two are inseparable. They are merely aspects of the same question, that if you want to have a free press, then it must also be a press which is aware of its responsibilities."

Over the years, his experiences with the media and their impact on society would serve to congeal his thoughts over a fundamental principle: whether press freedom was an end in itself. Years later, in 1987, he would enunciate his position unapologetically: Freedom of the press was not as an end but a means to an all-embracing end — "the integrity and independence of our country; its security, its prosperity; the eradication of anything that would sow the seeds of social, racial and religious conflicts which is the rule rather than the exception in the world today".[21]

In that speech addressed to foreign correspondents in Singapore, he stressed that Singapore had far more vulnerabilities than most nation states, given its make-up. Nevertheless, Singapore had functioned fairly adequately since 1959 only on the basis of two intangibles — "ideas and the human character shaped by these ideas".

More fundamentally, Raja's views on the virtues of the ideologies of Mill's liberal democracy and Marxian socialism underwent a marked shift after he became culture minister, when the realities of governing a divided country began to sink in.

Raja would rationalise his earlier uncritical acceptance of Liberal democracy and Marxian socialism along these lines: Up till then, the objective was straightforward — to end colonial rule. It was possible to mobilise people of all classes, creeds, and races on the basis of anti-colonial slogans. "Mill's eulogy of liberty and Marx's and Lenin's trenchant indictment of capitalism-imperialism were just the right type of ideological fuel to feed the anti-colonial flame".[22]

It was upon grappling with the complex task of building a Malayan nation that he realised that neither doctrine could provide the answers to problems confronting Singapore and the Federation. The solidarity of pre-*Merdeka* days had given way to "fissiparous trends, which if unchecked would bring political instability and worse for both territories". In particular, he referred to the racial and cultural divisions in society, which he sensed would determine the form of the political struggle in Malaya. This would prove prescient.

Over the years, he continued to ponder on what would make a good society — a question that had occupied philosophers down the centuries — and concluded that: Before a good society could be created, first there must be good citizens. Unlike philosophers who could only pontificate and write reams, however, political leaders could help create this "good society". Put simply, the job of good government, he believed, was to create the kind of society that one could be proud of — "the good society where there will be less injustice, less poverty and less degradation of the human spirit".

The idea that you could shape the values and ideals of a society was one close to his heart. In his first press interview as culture minister, which he gave to the Chinese newspaper *Nanyang Siang Pau*, he launched into the philosophical question of how one's worth should be measured in society. He said that, in the past, one's worth in society was measured by one's wealth and social status — the wealthier one was, the higher one's social status and prestige. This materialistic conception was wrong, he said.

He said that, the new PAP government, founded on socialist principles, would rectify this — one's worth would be measured by how one had contributed to society and benefited the lives of the people. "Even if the individual was just a trishaw rider, as long as he contributed to the society, in the eyes of the PAP government, he would be worth more than a billionaire," said Raja. Character and contribution to society mattered more than material achievements.[23]

While such views might well be articulated to score popular points with the Chinese-educated at the time, Raja was not just mouthing platitudes. He would return to this theme many times over the years. In his retirement, during the economic boom years of the late 1980s, he would bemoan the trend towards materialism in Singapore — he dubbed it "money-theism" — and warned it would undo society. He hankered for a moral world in which character mattered more than material wealth and believed it was within the Government's powers to create such a world.

His personal values and principles acted as a springboard for shrewd, pragmatic, politically astute action. There was, however, a tension at the heart of Raja. He wanted to create a society where ideas flow, where people read widely, think for themselves, decide wisely, and make for a better and fairer world.

But as he learnt how to govern a people with low education and literacy, where racial passions could easily be whipped up and ruthless communists lie in wait, he accepted that certain self-restraints were necessary. He was fundamentally a patriot and a nationalist, ready to adopt new positions to ensure the survival of the nation, or at least, his idea of the nation.

It was a fraught time as Raja and his colleagues tried to balance the concerns of the various communal groups. Given the dominance of the Chinese, the PAP leaders' championing of Malay as the national language, their condemnation of communal attitudes, their promotion of a Malayan culture, and the overriding importance they placed on merger with Malaya, showed "admirable political courage and good sense", noted Goode.[24] On the other hand, the PAP leaders also knew that they needed to retain the support of the Chinese-educated majority, if the PAP were to succeed against the alternative leadership offered by communists.

Towards this end, the government took some measures which appealed to the desire of the Chinese-educated conservatives to sweep away "yellow culture", as represented by the so-called materialist, sex-obsessed West, and to usher in a "healthy culture", as represented by the cultural heritage of the East.

The anti-yellow culture campaign, which included a ban on pornographic materials, striptease dances, pinball machines and juke boxes, was led by Home Affairs Minister Ong Pang Boon — and supported by the very urbane Raja at the forefront. It was an unlikely role for the open-minded intellectual, but the duty of every leader is to accept necessity without cavil, and Raja accepted more than one necessity.

According to a cabinet memorandum from the home affairs minister dated 17 January 1963, Raja had amended and approved the press statement in June 1959 which Ong had issued on the banning of striptease dances and yellow publications. As for Ong's radio broadcast on the policy, aired on 24 June 1959, it stated: "The speech was prepared by the Minister for Culture." The directives formed the basis for the work of the Board of Film Censors and the Committee of Film Appeal.

As the campaign escalated, however, Raja became more than a little uncomfortable with the ardour of the Chinese-educated conservative forces which were influenced by the revolutionary fervour in China. Their increasing demands seemed to him excessive and oppressive. In his view, a strict rejection of "Western values" was too simplistic an approach in the complex process of building a post-colonial society.

In any case, he knew that it was a myth to believe that everything about the East was good, or that everything about the West was bad. His dismay heightened when he saw how the anti-yellow campaign was interpreted and implemented on the ground.

As part of the campaign, Raja had announced on 11 June 1959 that rock-and-roll and sentimental music would be scaled back. "We do not intend to ban rock-n-roll and other light music," he said.[25] While he took care to stress balance and not a total ban, the newspapers disregarded all nuance with their sensational headlines, which screamed "No more rock around the clock" and "Minister of Culture Knocks the 'Rock' ".[26]

Given the mood of regimented social discipline, a total ban was implemented on the ground. Raja also hinted that a clean-up of the cinemas would be launched if it became necessary to prevent the screening of films which were considered detrimental to the morals of the people and which exploited sex. He told the media: "The film censorship policy will reflect this new attitude." Immediately, that statement, together with Ong's, was translated into a stricter film censorship policy, and a nationwide blitz was launched on cinemas.

As minister for culture, Raja found himself playing the role of the guardian of public morality by default. This persona was a great leap from the young intellectual of London days who felt at home with the liberal and cosmopolitan set in the British capital. But to him, the principle of collective responsibility was sacrosanct. In executing the collective will of the cabinet, Raja kept his private reservations on the scale of the prohibitions from public view.

He also kept close to his chest his anxiety for his blonde wife, who could become an easy political target in what was fast becoming an anti-West campaign. Unknown to many, he sent Piroska away during that period to London, where she stayed for several months.[27] Meanwhile at work, he suffered long lectures from the puritanical left on his attire. "I used to wear these colourful shirts...They felt I should be soberly attired, just white shirt and white pants if possible," he recounted later. His reactions to developments, however, occasionally unmasked his own values.

Foong Choon Hon, who was then working in the broadcasting section of *Radio Singapore*, recalled one incident in the early 1960s which revealed Raja's authentic self. The incident involved an African tribal troupe which was in town to perform at a cultural festival. Naturally, their dancers performed in tribal attire — this meant bare-breasted women. At their rehearsal, the attending Culture Ministry official was so mortified at the sight that he ordered them to cover up before they could perform. It became the turn of the Africans to feel insulted.

When their predicament reached Raja's ears, he was livid. He went down to the site, berated the official and promptly reversed the order. Foong recalled: "For the first time, I saw him angry. He asked the official: 'Did you ask them to do this? Don't you know it's their culture?' " He ordered the official to apologise to the African troupe. Their cultural pride restored, the Africans performed as originally planned, in their tribal topless glory.

This incident clarified Raja's approach on censorship — context and intention were important considerations. Scenes of nudity or sex were not necessarily pornographic. In fact, he recognised that sex was a legitimate theme for art, literature, and painting. But as he put it, there was a world of difference between using sex as a theme for literary and artistic purposes and exploiting them for commercial ends.

Hence, he frowned on commercial advertising which used women's flesh to sell products. Not only would such crude advertising coarsen popular tastes and attitudes over time, it also reflected poorly on the product being advertised. If it needed to be associated with a nude woman to get people to buy it, then "it could not be much of a product".[28]

Given his public position on commercial advertisements, it was unfortunate that P. Ramlee, the famous movie actor and director, saw fit to invite Raja to a cultural show which turned out to be a fashion parade advertising Maidenform brassieres. Taking Ramlee's invitation at face value, Raja had sent his political secretary, Rahim Ishak, in his stead. When Rahim attended the show on 20 July 1960, he was accosted by the spectacle of three girls appearing in various sizes of the brassieres. Outraged, Rahim walked out of the show. On receiving Rahim's complaint, which must have privately amused Raja, he got his permanent secretary, Lee Siow Mong, to write in protest to Ramlee.

In the letter, Ramlee was rebuked for misrepresenting the show in his invitation to the culture minister, which turned out to be an "advertising stunt and culturally undesirable". The minister "strongly disapproves of this camouflage of a commercial and culturally undesirable programme under the name of 'culture' in order to induce him to lend support to it". From the wording of the letter, it would appear that, to Raja, the transgression was an ethical one about integrity — Ramlee was wrong to mislead him about the commercially-driven show under the guise of culture — than about the morality or immorality of women parading in brassieres.

Raja's friends knew that he possessed a remarkably open mind, ready to appreciate the beauty of various cultures. He had an eclectic taste in music, but particularly enjoyed the Indian flute and Western ballet music. He also liked sentimental tunes. A favourite was the Frank Sinatra hit, *When I Fall in Love*, which reminded him of his feelings for Piroska.

He also enjoyed watching movies and documentaries. His best-loved film was *The Defiant Ones* (1958), starring Tony Curtis and Sidney Poitier, which tells the story of two escaped prisoners who are shackled together, one white and one black, who must cooperate in order to survive. His nephew S. Vijayaratnam remembered Raja treating him as a schoolboy to the first James Bond movie *Dr No* with the sexy Ursula Andress as the Bond girl in the early 1960s. The anti-yellow culture ultra-conservatives would not have approved.

After retiring from politics, Raja disclosed that he was unimpressed by the demands of some Chinese-educated politicians to clamp down on "so-called yellow culture", such as revealing costumes at beauty contests. He could be unyielding as "I was liberal about what they considered yellow culture". At times, Raja could hardly keep a straight face when dealing with pressure from some Assemblymen on the issue.

During a debate on 13 December 1960, Ong Eng Guan, posing as a champion of the anti-yellow culture drive, protested that he heard the trotting of horses on the radio and "all the Yankee talking which is not very good for the school children". Ong also objected to programmes such as *Tarzan* and *Flash Gordon*. Raja's merry riposte: "I thought the trotting of horses anywhere sounds like trotting of horses. I cannot distinguish between a Yankee horse and a Malayan horse or an Indian horse." As for *Tarzan*, he found nothing offensive about it. "In fact, I read an article in the New Statesman analysing the social and political significance of *Tarzan*…The paper was quite satisfied that *Tarzan* is a very healthy form of comic entertainment."

In 1961, when the PAP set up a review committee to evaluate the work of the government and party, Raja used the opportunity to moderate the anti-yellow culture campaign. He co-chaired the committee with Goh. In their report, published on 27 August 1961, they noted: "What may be immoral and undesirable to one group of people may not be so to others. Such differences of opinion are likely to arise in an even more acute form in a multi-cultural society where sense of values differs."

While the government should be stricter about allowing materials "which exploit sex, crime and immorality for base ends", it did not mean that "any intelligent and frank discussions and portrayals of sexual and criminal themes is yellow". The report noted: "The test lies in the intention behind the film, book or play. We should not impose on the community the particular prejudice or feelings of prudery of individuals."

While some applauded Raja for his learned and cultured views, others continued to revile him for the role he played in the anti-yellow culture campaign. Sivanandan Choy, who became a rock-and-roll legend in Singapore by the 1980s, particularly detested Raja for discouraging rock-and-roll music. While in his teens in the early 1960s, Siva once performed in a school concert in which Raja was the guest-of-honour. According to Siva, the minister sat stone-faced throughout the performance, and when he went backstage, did not shake Siva's hands when he did so with the other performers. The young rocker took it as a deliberate slight. "This incident affected me seriously…so I could not take Raja seriously from then on."[29] It was such "narrow-minded" attitudes at the top, charged Siva, which had held back the country's cultural development.

The reality was that at the time, rock and roll, with its unfortunate association with long-haired hippies and drugs, was hardly regarded by the conservatives in Singapore as central to the country's cultural development.

The general mood was also dictated by the merciless survival politics of the day. Indeed, it was significant that in the same period when Siva felt slighted for performing rock and roll, Raja was being attacked in the Legislative Assembly by the PAP-breakaway group — the Barisan Socialis — for promoting Western culture and undermining the morals of the youth. The relentless swipes at him were part of the campaign by the Barisan to discredit him in the eyes of the Chinese-educated conservative majority.

Given the vicious battle for political survival which defined that early period, the opposition's populist cries against Western influence was an undeniable constraint on Raja's actions. No doubt, stretched in multiple directions, he had also decided that some causes were worth fighting for and dying for — such as a Malayan culture — but he would pass on rock and roll.

Raja had a tough-minded appreciation of the problems facing Singapore and the need to get civil servants on board. To start with, many of the top officials, recruited mainly from middle-class, English-educated families, had little more than a rudimentary grasp of the political realities of the day. Most were also oblivious to the dangers posed by racial divisions and the threat of communism. Some were ceasing to care, with their morale affected by the raft of radical reforms introduced and by the cut in their allowance, imposed as part of the government's austerity drive.

To transform the civil service into an effective instrument of policy, Lee set up the Political Study Centre, housed in a colonial government bungalow in Goodwood Hill, on 15 August 1959, and put Raja in charge of its policies and courses. Its day-to-day running was the job of George Thomson who, prior to this new posting, was the director of information services in the Culture Ministry.

Raja brought a unique mix of strategic skill and formidable knowledge to a stuffy bureaucracy characterised by caution, narrow horizons, and a specific cringe towards things considered "political". His focus was to make sure that civil servants grasped the special problems facing Singapore, be appraised of the priorities and policies of the PAP government, and be convinced of their value to the people.

Addressing the civil servants at the opening of the centre, he impressed upon them that they must make the mental adjustments to serve a popularly elected government. In the past, they might be rewarded for pursuing "safe" options. No longer. Under this new government, they must be prepared to embark on new experiments. He said: "Novelty and experiment are necessary for this country's survival. The civil servant's task is no longer to preserve a disintegrating colonial order but to act as midwives of the new social order that is struggling to be born."

He noted the tendency for bureaucrats to abhor experimentation as it opened them to public criticisms. "Because mistakes may lead to criticism of a bureaucracy, the safest and easiest course is to try and persuade the Minister that the action he contemplates is probably destined to fail," Raja observed. If the minister was a timid man, he could easily be frightened into inaction, especially it was impressed upon him that he had to assume responsibility for the mistakes of his subordinates, he added. "This avoidance of novelty and experiment may be all right in a stable or a stagnant society. But it can be fatal to civil servants, ministers and the country as a whole during periods of great social and political changes," he argued.

Stressing that the country was undergoing great social and political transformation, he said: "Unless the civil servants understand the significance and scope of this transformation, they may find themselves swept aside by men with more imagination and greater flexibility of mind. The disquiet the new Government may have caused among some civil servants may not be so much over its political ideology as over its insistence on experiment and novelty — both of which are essential during periods of great social change."

He told them that the courses at the centre were designed to help them understand "the kind of world that is in the process of being born". He assured them that these were not indoctrination courses. "The object is not to convert you to a particular political creed, but to help you understand the social and political forces that you, as civil servants, must harness for constructive ends," he said.

Raja's role in drawing up the syllabus for the centre came to light only about a year later in August 1960, when Lee had to clarify the role of Thomson, an expatriate officer much reviled by Ong Eng Guan. "The political line, the policies, the programmes of this Political Study Centre were laid down and are still being laid down by a committee under the chairmanship of the Minister for Culture," Lee informed the Legislative Assembly on 11 August.[30] Raja's role was further clarified in 1961 when the opposition members, suspicious of the centre's agenda, demanded to know what was being taught there. At the Legislative Assembly debate, Raja stood up to inform them that the syllabus included the history of the Malayan Communist Party and its methods. "We do not believe in

Communism. To that extent, it is necessary for civil servants … to know the nature of one of the political forces with which they have to contend, and their method of operation."[31]

Raja considered it essential for civil servants to be sensitive to the political currents in the country at a time of rapid change. Hence, he also introduced talks on nationalism, Malayan culture, and what was happening in the wider world, "the causes of revolution in Asia, and the need for a fundamental shift in attitudes and policies to meet the challenges".[32] He personally visited the centre at least once a fortnight to oversee the teaching and to engage the civil servants in discussions.

Beyond political education, there was a broader purpose to the discussions: As he said in an interview later, "they give civil servants an opportunity to discuss things with their Ministers; not only people at higher levels but in the intermediate levels as well. Therefore, they would then feel they are not just dummies carrying out instructions by the Government. They feel they have a sense of participation; that their advice is listened to, and in a number of cases, they have put forward very fruitful suggestions about how political problems should be approached."[33]

The importance of his central idea is hard to exaggerate. He believed that good government depended on the kind of relationship established between the political leaders and the bureaucracy. As he said, "each must match the other in intellectual power, political perception and in the depth of their devotion to the nation's interest".[34]

Raja considered the job of a civil servant as a vocation. "Of course, a civil servant must be reasonably well paid but what should motivate him is a conviction that his role in society is more crucial to the future of a nation than that of the men in the market place."[35] Years later, he took some satisfaction from his observation that, within two years of the establishment of the Political Study Centre, relations between the PAP ministers and the civil servants improved.[36]

His insights on the need for the civil service to experiment and take risks at a time of change continue to ring true today. His conviction of the need for civil servants to be attuned to political currents remains vital. These imperatives have filtered into the ethos of today's bureaucrats.

Raja was popular with the civil servants under his charge. He believed in setting the broad direction for his administration and delegating the detail of policy and its implementation. Once delegated, he gave his trusted officials latitude to experiment on the ground. "He would spell out the priorities and then leave us alone as long as we delivered," said Hedwig Anuar, who worked as a librarian from 1952 until she retired in 1988.

Raja wanted to transform the Raffles Library, which had been transferred from the Education Ministry to the Culture Ministry in 1959, from one that catered mainly to the English-educated middle-class, to one that reached out to the masses across language groups. At the time, the library was a subscription library in a single building. Hedwig, who was then assistant director of the library, recalled: "Raja was interested in expanding the library, and reaching out to as many people as possible with books. He was a great reader himself."[37]

Under his watch, the library moved into new premises in Stamford Road. The new national library, with its distinctive red-brick structure, was opened on 12 November 1960, to the promise that it would serve nation-building and the quest for knowledge. Raja worked hard to obtain the funds for new stocks of books and to increase readership in the library. "Money spent on books for all the people is one of the best investments in the future of our country," Raja declared.[38] He was equally adamant that the national library had to cater to four language groups. Hedwig recalled: "Raja believed it's important to be multicultural in all aspects."

He was passionate about promoting reading in the community — especially among the children. He remembered his own difficulty in searching out good books when he was a boy and resolved to make it easier for that generation's young. Towards that end, mobile libraries were rolled out to the community centres in the neighbourhoods in 1960. More than 2,000 students in 35 rural schools used the mobile library services once a fortnight during term time. By the end of 1960, there were about 45,000 library members. It represented a 43 per cent increase over the 13,500 in 1959, with the fastest rise from the junior membership.

Looking back on her years serving Raja, Hedwig said: "He was one of the best Ministers. He was a real gentleman, polite, affable and approachable." Despite the many distractions and limitations imposed on Raja, it was a credit to him that he managed to rally his overworked staff to achieve significant progress.

Part of this was because of his personality and inspiring values. As Boon Yoon Chiang, who worked at the Culture Ministry from 1960 to 1967, said: "Raja was a good boss. He would defend you to the hilt if he thought you have done your best. But he would not tolerate sloppiness."[39] He would also not hesitate to help his staff out of trouble. In 1959, Foong Choon Hon fell into the bad books of the Special Branch for his broadcasting training stint in London, where he was suspected of consorting with communists. He was suspended on his return, on security grounds. Raja went to considerable effort to help him get reinstated at the Culture Ministry. Foong, who then returned to the station, described Raja as "very kind, friendly and big-hearted".[40]

Raja had some blind spots. Often deep in thought, he sometimes appeared remote to his staff. He was poor at remembering names. He was not noted for his sartorial sharpness, preferring to wear his loose shirts untucked. He did not care for ties or matching socks. He favoured comfort over style. It fell on Piroska to remind him constantly that he was now a cabinet minister and had to look the part.

Raja did not make a virtue of fastidiousness. His life was a perpetual struggle for order, and it showed on his desk. It was not that Raja was an untidy person; it was just that he read several books and magazines at one time and liked to have them within easy reach. It was the same at home, to Piroska's constant annoyance.

Indeed, the only time their live-in Filipina domestic help, Cecilia Tandoc, ever heard them raise their voice at home was over his books in 1986. Raja was reading in the living room when Piroska told him: "I don't like all these books in the living room." Raja kept on reading silently. As she began to tidy them away, Raja said in an irritable voice: "Why don't you just leave me alone with my books." Hurt by his uncharacteristically sharp tone, Piroska locked herself in her room and stayed cooped up there for several hours. Finally, Raja went to the door to call her to join him for tea in the patio, adding gently: "Don't raise the matter anymore. It is over." They had tea. His books stayed.[41] His need to be surrounded by books was a lifelong trait, as was his routine of reading late into the night.

Although Raja no doubt caused grief to the bureaucratic bean counters, the prime minister recognised his standing with his staff: "He was our civil servants' favourite minister, courteous, understanding, considerate and friendly."[42] Raja's stature in the cabinet was also unassailable, despite helming what started out as a low priority ministry. V.T. Arasu noted: "The Ministry of Culture started expanding because of the stature and position of Mr Rajaratnam. It was the most important ministry next to the Prime Minister's Office in terms of public involvement."[43]

Besides civil servants, he also sought to instil this sense of mission among community leaders through the People's Association (PA) formed in 1960. The aim of PA, which ran community centres for the public, was essentially to forge closer bonds between the people and the government.

Together with the Minister for Labour and Law Kenny Byrne, Raja was closely involved in settling the organisations listed under the schedule of the draft People's Association bill. To build up the PA as a secular organisation to provide a common space for all races, he took particular care to remove groups from the list which were communal or religious in nature.

He then drew up a syllabus to train young community leaders in 1961, with a special focus on current affairs and political theory, and was also one of the lecturers.[44] Unlike the English-educated civil servants at the Political Study Centre, however, the people running the PA were mostly Chinese-educated and already under the influence of the communists. It would take at least another three years before the situation could be reversed.

He opened his own community centre in his constituency Kampong Glam on 4 June 1960. During its events, he often urged residents to get involved in community activities. The community centre was regarded primarily as a recreational centre, offering various activities for residents, but he wanted it to also become a source for inculcating a sense of national unity and developing local leaders. Despite his exhortations, he found it hard to enthuse his grassroots leaders with his vision, or to attract more residents to get involved in the centre.

Almost all his grassroots leaders were Chinese-educated, and as he learnt to his cost later, mostly pro-communist. At that point, he was quite oblivious to the depth of the communist penetration. Busy with his multiple ministerial duties at the national level, Raja largely left the community management meetings to his grassroots leaders, who conducted them entirely in Chinese dialects. But he would attend the functions. When he did, he constantly called on residents to get more involved in running the centre and organising its activities. But few came forward. In retrospect years later, Raja saw that residents were unwilling to take part in the community centre activities until they were sure that the PAP had broken with the communists and could assert its primacy over them.

A typical story was that of Ong Kim Leong, a Kampong Glam resident who then worked as a clerk. He was reluctant to help Raja in his constituency until 1964, after the PAP's split with the pro-communists — and then only after much persuasion by Ong Soo Chuan, the political secretary to the Culture Ministry at the time. Being Chinese-educated, Kim Leong communicated with Raja in bazaar Malay. He found Raja "very humble" with no airs, and stayed to become his election agent in 1968 and 1972.[45]

He was most struck by Raja's ability to stay cool under pressure, despite severe provocation. Kim Leong recounted one incident during a constituency meeting: While airing his grievance over a municipal issue, a grassroots leader banged his fist on the table in anger, shocking everyone present. They looked at Raja, expecting him to put the hot-tempered man in his place. Instead, Raja responded in a calm voice, asking the man to speak steadily and not to get angry. "He did not over-react," Kim Leong noted.

Raja's persona at the Legislative Assembly could not be more different. From his first appearance in the Legislative Assembly in July 1959, he had been gladiatorial in the debates, delivering sharp speeches and spunky rebuttals. He developed a distinctive oratorical style — pungent and polemical, yet humorous and engaging with metaphors and parables. Raja proved powerful and nimble in the political boxing ring, and established himself as a formidable heavyweight. Each jab punched home an idea, and he had a lot of ideas.

The exchanges in Parliament were often vicious and hard-hitting. Raja was at his obnoxious best. He was an irascible pest to the opposition, constantly interrupting from the benches with taunts and asides, and rising to make points of clarification, of elucidation, of order.

When he jumped up to rebut the opposition, he often did so emphatically, with his index finger jabbing the air, a habit that earned him repeated rebukes from the Speaker. Ever so often, the Speaker had to ask Raja, in midstream of his verbal attack, to refrain from pointing too much at the opposition. Once, an exasperated Speaker suggested that Raja put his hands in his pocket instead.[46] Taking the rebuke in good humour, Raja said he had tried to overcome the habit by holding on to a pencil, but as that had not quite worked, he would "try to point the right way".

When this resolve dissolved in the passion of the debate yet again, the Speaker advised him to hold his spectacles in his right hand to stop it from pointing at the opposition. Raja replied, with a twinkle in his eyes, that he would not risk his glasses by doing so, and would just try to control his hand.[47] Like his pointing hand, however, Raja was not a person to be easily controlled when in hot pursuit of his political adversaries, or his vision for the country.

16

The First Test

The first major political crisis in government which tested Raja's mettle came not from the pro-communist figures who had given the leadership so much strain earlier, but from an unexpected quarter — his non-communist cabinet colleague Ong Eng Guan.

This was the accountant whom Raja had introduced to the PAP as a promising leader, and later supported as the rabble-rousing PAP mayor of the city council, even when the other top leaders in the PAP disapproved of Ong's melodramatic antics. Raja also put up patiently with Ong's faults when, as minister for national development, he paid more attention to building a personal empire for himself than public housing for the people.

Raja's benevolence towards Ong was in sharp contrast to Goh's reaction to the man. The finance minister had taken such an intense dislike to Ong that they were not even on speaking terms. But, as Ong would find out, there was a limit to Raja's tolerance.

The major breakpoint in Raja's attitude to his friend came when he discovered Ong's conspiracy to take over as prime minister in 1960. He had a robust contempt for Ong's attempts to split the cabinet and play one minister against another in his power grab. Ong regarded Lee and Goh as his chief nemeses, but believed that Raja, being his long-time friend, would be open to his overtures. Ong was mistaken.

In a fragment found among his private papers, Raja observed acidly that Ong "came into conflict with his Ministerial colleagues and the party because of his belief that he had been cheated out of the Prime Ministership. This suspicion was totally unfounded because those of us who knew him intimately never even entertained the idea of him as Prime Minister".[1] They were only too aware of his weaknesses, Raja added contemptuously. In trying to manipulate the culture minister, Ong had underestimated Raja's political acumen as well as his loyalty to the party and to Lee. Beneath Raja's mild and friendly demeanour lurked a tough and shrewd character — much-needed traits in any party leader.

Finding himself isolated in the cabinet, Ong then turned his attention to the parliamentary secretaries and assemblymen. To Raja, nothing more confirmed his low opinion of Ong as when he found out that Ong was planning to table 16 resolutions on behalf of his Hong Lim branch at the party conference on 19 June 1960, a move calculated to openly challenge the political leadership.

In his resolutions, Ong accused the party of, among other things, not being firm in its anti-colonial struggle and demanded talks with Britain to revise the one-year-old constitution for full independence.[2] He also called for the immediate release of detainees, for all expatriate officials to be sent away, and for the anti-yellow culture campaign to be intensified uncompromisingly. He denounced the new trade union laws which circumscribed and deregistered unions.[3] He also proposed that cabinet decisions be vetted by a "party policy committee" on which all 51 branches would be represented.

It was clear to Raja that Ong's resolutions were a siren song to entice the pro-communists and the disaffected PAP members into an alliance with him. On being released from prison, Lim Chin Siong and Fong Swee Suan, who were appointed political secretaries, had slunk into the woodwork of the trade unions to consolidate their hold on workers and penetrate new unions.

Within a year of his release, Chin Siong had boosted the membership of his omnibus union, Singapore General Employees'

Union, from 3,000 to 22,000, with several known communists holding key positions. They had continued to use united front tactics to win power by gaining control of the PAP from within. As long as the British and the Federation had overriding powers in the Internal Security Council, they knew that a direct coup would not be possible.

During this time, Chin Siong and company were also working on S.T. Bani and Woodhull, among others, to join their radical movement and strengthen their hold on workers. Years later, Woodhull, who admired the teachings of Lenin and Mao, confessed he favoured the militant approach espoused by Chin Siong over the non-violent constitutional route treaded by the non-communist PAP leaders. Woodhull disclosed: "Actually, I was in many ways, very critical of things like non-violence. I did feel that a degree of violence was necessary in any national liberation movement."[4]

Raja was deeply troubled by the developments. Ong's aggressive power play — and his call for full independence for Singapore — could not have come at a more testing time for the leadership. Sensitive talks with the Federation on a common market had just begun, which the Singapore government considered critical for creating the industries and jobs needed on the island. The political paroxysm did nothing to soothe the confidence of investors.

The government's difficulties during this period were captured starkly in an article in *The Economist* published on 11 June 1960, eight days before the PAP conference. Aptly headlined "Singapore's Predicament", *The Economist* observed that the PAP government faced a real problem "of providing bread for the swelling ranks of the unemployed (at least 100 new jobs must be found each day), at a time when the entrepot trade is in serious difficulties, when the rival appeal of Kuala Lumpur's new industrial suburb is thought to be growing and when overseas capital for industrialisation is still inhibited by fears about Singapore's political future". It added grimly that, given that the aspirations of the Chinese-speaking masses were not being satisfied, the greatest danger now facing the government was that Chinese chauvinism might get out of hand.

As a member of the cabinet, the Internal Security Council and the party's Central Executive Committee, Ong knew well how precarious the situation was for Singapore and the enormity of the government's problems. In moving the 16 resolutions at this delicate time, he was exploiting the situation. The more Raja contemplated Ong's betrayal, the angrier he became. He resolved to heighten his guard against such political opportunists. He also hardened his heart against them.

At a CEC meeting called by Lee prior to the PAP conference to discuss Ong's challenge, it was Raja who urged that they must put paid to the rebel at once.[5] The decision to oust Ong was unanimous. On the day Ong issued his resolutions, Raja was ready to rip into them. His starring role did not go unnoticed. As the British High Commissioner in Singapore reported in his despatch on the three-day conference, "the attack on the resolutions seems to have been led by Rajaratnam, who was joined by Byrne and by Yaacob bin Mohamed (Ong Eng Guan's parliamentary secretary)".[6]

In his rebuttal, Raja focused on the damaging insinuation that the PAP had given up its anti-colonial struggle. In a withering rebuke, he said: "If by anti-colonialism, he means pressing the British for immediate independence; throwing out all foreign enterprises, seizing all foreign enterprises, then Mr Ong knows that that is not practical."

Raja then rehearsed all the arguments why Singapore must become an integral part of the Federation, with particular emphasis on the economic imperative. He said the government was trying to change the colonial character of the economy by trying to set up industries. "But we find that, in order to do that, we need to co-operate with the Federation. Without access to the six million customers in the Federation, we cannot set up efficient industries." It was too costly to set up modern industries, with heavy capital investment, to cater to the needs of only 1.5 million people, he said.

He called for a sense of political reality: "The fact that we have a right-wing, Malay-dominated government requires that our strategy should be more flexible." He explained how, during the past year, the government had taken steps to allay the fears of the Federation that the people of Singapore were not loyal Malayans, and that Singapore was incapable of having a stable government. If Ong had a concrete strategy to press for independence, "he should tell us". In all the time Ong was a member of the PAP Central Executive Committee or of the government, he never did, said Raja.

At the long-drawn conference, which ended with a vote for Ong's expulsion, the entire exposure was done with a grim thoroughness which, as one foreign correspondent noted, "recalls the purges in the communist world".[7] To make clear the party's position to the wider public, Raja issued a press statement on behalf of the Central Executive Committee which gave a point-by-point reply to the 16 resolutions. The statement also criticised Ong for his personality cult, disloyalty to the party, and his blunders as minister.

Ong remained ever defiant. He crossed over to the opposition benches. Two assemblymen who backed him — S.V. Lingam and Ng Teng Kian — followed. They left in their wake a destructive tailwind. Aware that the debate was viewed by the PAP leadership as a test of loyalties, the pro-communists issued a statement supporting Ong's expulsion.

There was a certain cynicism about their move. No sooner had the ink dried than they cried to the government to take heed of Ong's points — particularly regarding the unconditional release of political detainees and the registration of communist united front unions.

Below the surface, there was also rumbling in the ranks of the non-communist PAP assemblymen. While supporting Ong's expulsion publicly, many had privately nodded their heads at Ong's resolutions. One of them was Lee Siew Choh, parliamentary secretary for Home Affairs and the PAP assemblyman for Queenstown, who was all for Ong's calls for the party to be more democratic and accountable to members.

Since assuming power, the PAP core leaders had found it expedient to involve as few people as possible in policymaking. One reason was the uncertainty they felt about the loyalties of some of their professed supporters. Another was their sense of urgency to introduce laws and implement policies, however unpopular, to address the country's mounting problems.

Their top-down style owed much to their belief that policy should be determined by wise and honest leaders with an eye not only on the short term but also the longer term — and not by grassroots activists or political opportunists who were more fixated with the here and now, weighed down by dogma, or driven by their own political agendas. The issues preoccupying the government were also complex, requiring an agile mind able to scrutinise the contending forces at play in the country as well as in the wider region and beyond.

Perhaps, there was more than a touch of arrogance in their belief that others could not be trusted to analyse the country's problems rationally or to have the country's interest at heart. But their experiences so far — with insidious power struggles and the endless political bickering — had not given them much cause for confidence.

For the PAP leaders, their stated policy of independence through merger was the most pressing. It was also the most delicate, involving secret manoeuvrings with the Federation leaders and the British. The PAP leaders carried a deeply ingrained fear that the island could not survive economically or politically as an independent state on its own. They had also pressed their point with the British, who continued to be anxious about the communist threat.

Despite their separate appeals to the Tunku to open Malaya to Singapore, the Tunku kept his shoulder against the door. Not only that, he would occasionally declare his intention to lock the door and throw away the key, for fear of being stormed by the Chinese chauvinists and communists at the gates.

With the weight of the country's problems on their shoulders, the PAP leaders were more interested in practical solutions than power politics. They had observed how demagogic and corrupt leaders in other Third World countries used populist tactics to win elections only to be plunged into interminable power struggles while they squandered away the country's resources to stay in power.

Raja was struck by the trend in many developing countries: After achieving their freedom, they would be in a worse condition than when they were under imperial rule. The colonialist has been replaced by "indigenous parasites who, through corruption and open extortion, have impoverished their countrymen in order to live lives of splendour and luxury unequalled even by imperial governors and viceroys", as he later pointed out.[8]

His analysis led him to conclude that there was an "in-built tendency" in most social systems towards bad, inefficient, and unjust governments. This was because good government required constant effort and sustained discipline, and people did not want to put up with the hard work and sacrifice that went with it. The PAP leaders were determined to avoid this downward spiral.

They considered it a hallmark of a good government to do what was right and not what would win them praise. They believed that, at the heart of good governance, must be men and women of ability and integrity who were prepared to act in the national interest rather than their own. In the longer term, this model would serve the country better. In the first year of its government, however, there was no evidence as yet that this model worked. It would take several years before a system anchored on these principles was put firmly in place, and many more years before the country could reap the benefits and see the value of such a system.

A consequence of this approach was that, by the end of its first year, the PAP leadership had gained a reputation for being harsh and autocratic, with decisions made by a closed, inner circle. The tightness of the decision-making circle was resented by some in the PAP who felt excluded from the process. Hoe Puay Choo, a Chinese-educated seamstress who was a member of the PAP's central executive committee, said later: "Lee consulted only a few people, Raja and Goh Keng Swee, sometimes Toh Chin Chye."[9]

From her vantage point, Raja was the number two or three on the power hierarchy in terms of influence on party policy. She nursed the grievance that she had not been privy to the policy discussions to merge with Malaya.[10] It was a dire sign that even the PAP's CEC was not united on fundamental issues such as these. The gathering storm was to break later, with Hoe counting among those who left the PAP to join the rival Barisan Sosialis in July 1962.[11]

On the ground, the pro-communists stoked the PAP branches' frustration at being excluded from policy decisions. By now, the branches were under their firm control. This tinderbox atmosphere was the setting to which Ong's resolutions struck some sparks.

There would have been an implosion, had Ong been a more likeable person. But as Lee Siew Choh said, it was fortunate for Lee Kuan Yew that "many of us did not like Ong Eng Guan and his ways". "We thought he was more opportunistic than genuine. And therefore we did not support him. But if you separate the 16 resolutions from the person of Ong Eng Guan, we would have supported them."[12] It was yet another ominous sign of the division in the ranks.

As soon as Ong joined the opposition, the Legislative Assembly turned into a histrionic burlesque. After three years of sparring with Ong over matters great and small, the usually unflappable Raja, in a revealing moment during a Legislative Assembly debate on 14 June 1963, made a rare personal outburst. He recalled how he had met Ong when "time was hanging heavily on his hands in an accountant's office" and had invited him to join the PAP. "Ever since, I have regretted this great error on my part. It was one of the biggest mistakes I have ever made," said Raja.

Ong gave Raja grief from his first appearance in the Assembly. Playing to the packed gallery, Ong resurrected his 16 resolutions once again to press the government on them in the debate on 3 August 1960, on a motion of the Address of the *Yang di-Pertuan Negara*. In his speech, he renewed his efforts to split the leadership. He referred to an article in *Petir* critical of him, which carried Raja's byline.[13] Ong told the assemblymen in the House that he did not think it was Raja who wrote the article. "The Prime Minister knows that Mr S. Rajaratnam and I are good friends. He (Lee) always writes the articles and just gets them out using other people's names."

A day later, Ong intensified his attempts to drive a wedge between Raja on the one side, and Lee and Goh on the other. Ong praised Raja and two other ministers — Toh and Ong Pang Boon — as "reasonable and nice gentlemen". In the same breath, he maligned Lee and Goh, saying that it was these two people who had, in the past year, "steered the present Government along a pro-colonial course".

Faced with Ong's stream of abuse against the government and its leadership, Raja discarded any previous restraint. Before launching into his caustic response, he said in a sorrowful tone that "it is not an easy or pleasant thing to defrock publicly a former party and government colleague, especially also as he is one with whom I have had good personal relations". Then came the "but". "But", he said, knowing very well Ong's political tactics, this relationship would not stop him from what he had to say, "because he has chosen to play a political role which, whatever the consequences for him, will, I am convinced, mean disaster for the country".

Then, in an attack dripping with sarcasm, Raja contended that the 16 resolutions were not the "charm that will ward off evil in the country" as described by Ong, but part of a manoeuvre to reinstate and recoup his declining political fortunes within the party.[14]

Turning to the opposition members in the House, Raja said he hoped that they would realise that Ong was himself "a pawn in a game played by adventurers more skilled, more clever and more agile than he is". These political adventurers who manipulated him knew his weaknesses and, therefore, played on them, he said. In taking this tack, Raja was amplifying the key thrust of Lee Kuan

Yew's attack on Ong in his speech earlier, where Lee drew out how the communists were exploiting the "Ong Eng Guan affair" and trying "to fish in PAP troubled waters". Lee added that he was not saying that Ong and his two associates were "left-wing adventurers". But they were being used.

As for that article in *Petir* which Ong claimed Raja did not write, Raja was scornful of Ong's innuendo: "For something like 15 years, I have earned my living by writing for newspapers, and, that being so, I think I am quite capable of writing my own speeches." In fact, that particular article that Ong referred to was a reproduction of Raja's off-the-cuff speech made before 150 party members. Raja accused Ong of fabricating the story "in the hope of convincing the people outside that the Minister of Culture was really a pro-Ong Eng Guan man, but that he had his arms twisted by the PM to say these things". Raja made clear, in case anyone else was still in doubt, that he was firmly with Lee Kuan Yew.

Over the next few years, as Ong became more outrageous in his abuse of the PAP, Raja ratcheted up the ferocity of his attacks. He particularly deplored Ong's tendency, as Raja said, for "fabricating stories" and making wild allegations. In the debates in the House, he refused to allow Ong to get away with any of them. One of Ong's most headline-grabbing charges was to accuse Lee Kuan Yew and Kenny Byrne of nepotism in the Assembly in December 1960. Ong declined Lee's challenge to repeat his accusations outside the Assembly. He also refused to substantiate his allegations in the House.

Instead, he resigned his seat. The government promptly set up a Commission of Inquiry to investigate his charges. After interviewing witnesses, including Ong himself, the commission found no truth in his accusations and concluded that Ong was "not a person to be believed". Seizing the offensive, Toh then moved a motion to condemn

Ong for dishonourable conduct[15] following the commission's report on 1 March 1961.

Raja again opened the attack. The other three PAP Ministers who spoke over the two-day debate were Ong Pang Boon, Goh Keng Swee and Lee Kuan Yew. Their volleys were well-coordinated and strategic, aimed at destroying Ong's credibility ahead of the upcoming by-election in Hong Lim.

But there was also a larger fundamental principle at stake, and Raja presented it in his speech: It was about the sort of democracy and Assembly that Singapore should strive for. He said: "The issue before us is simple: Did Mr Ong utter reckless falsehoods? If he did utter such falsehoods under the cover of Assembly privilege, was he not being dishonourable? If he had uttered lies, then should he not be compelled to withdraw them and apologise to the House? Would not democracy be brought into contempt and ridicule if Assembly privilege were used as a cloak to utter falsehoods against innocent people?" If the answers to these questions were yes, then the motion to censure Ong — far from being a blow against democracy, as some of Ong's supporters had charged — would make more secure the foundations of democracy, he argued.

Raja lambasted the opposition parties, the SPA and the Workers' Party, for depicting Ong as a champion of democracy and as a heroic fighter for free speech, instead of demanding an immediate investigation into his allegations and pressing Ong to prove them. Raja thought this showed that the opposition politicians did not, in fact, believe Ong's allegations of nepotism and political corruption. If they thought the allegations were true, they would have agitated for a thorough investigation to discredit the PAP in the eyes of the people, just as the PAP did to the SPA in Chew Swee Kee's case.

Raja asked if their stand on free speech involved the freedom to lie recklessly and deliberately. The PAP's view, he said, was that the freedom of speech means "the freedom to tell the truth without fear".

He charged that, had Ong been allowed to get away with his lies, he would have been encouraged to spread new lies under the cloak of Assembly privilege. Ong would have nothing to lose. "By persisting in baseless smears and allegations, he hoped that some of his lies would be believed." The fact that his smears injured innocent people was no concern to Ong, said Raja. "Such conduct is, in our view, dishonourable and in the long run, will bring democracy into contempt and ridicule," he stressed.

SPA's Lim Yew Hock was livid at Raja's direct assault on the opposition, and protested that the minister for culture should be "a little bit more cultured in his attack on the Opposition". He also hit out at Raja for making a pre-election speech.

The next day, Goh Keng Swee defended Raja's position: "I myself consider the clear and dispassionate analysis of the Minister for Culture to be an attempt to bring together the complicated threads of this episode to show a pattern of underlying political forces attempting to make use of Ong Eng Guan to advance their own interests. This was a piece of political analysis, not political electioneering." Goh then sharpened the argument by reinforcing Raja's key thrust: "It is the contention of my colleague, the Minister for Culture, that in the Hong Lim by-election, there is a ganging-up against the PAP." The ganging up was between Ong and the opposition parties, the SPA and the Workers' Party.

In his speech, Lee Kuan Yew pursued the point further: The action of the opposition in adding more dirt and smear to Ong's allegations was not only unprincipled, it was also irresponsible. It was an attempt to not only bring down the government, but also to "wreck the system by misleading the people as to what this Assembly was about, as to what the issues are". Lee laid down his cards: "Let me assure them that it is a positively dangerous line to take with this Government, being of the character and of the temperament that it is. One thing we must be prepared to do — that each and every allegation of malpractice must be investigated, for the fundamental precondition for the successful working of the democratic system is that those who offer themselves as members of the political leadership to implement policies on behalf of the public must be men of some honesty and integrity, in order to make any election pledge and any election programme worth looking into."

The similarities of the stand taken by Raja, Goh and Lee in this debate were striking. Read together, their coordinated speeches crystallised for the first time the PAP government's position on democratic debate in the political arena and on the moral standing of elected representatives. Their fundamental position has been the PAP government's credo ever since. There is freedom to speak and criticise, but every lie that smears the standing of the government or its leaders will be nailed down, and the liars exposed. This is necessary to create a responsible political environment. Those who put themselves up for election must be prepared to be scrutinised and be above moral reproach.

To check against further abuse of privileges in the Assembly, a Committee of Privileges was set up under the Standing Orders of the Assembly to investigate any complaint of breach of privilege. Toh observed: "It reflected how much a new self-governing Parliament had to learn not from precedent but from experience."[16]

For Raja, there was another deeper lesson to be drawn. That was the need to discern who could be trusted to stay the course. In an article which showed his political maturation in assessing friends or foes, he identified three types of characters to watch out for.[17]

First, the "weaklings" — those who lack the moral and intellectual stamina to support the movement through all its setbacks and difficulties. "They whine and bleat and lose their bearings in times of crises and difficulties."

Second, those who develop "megalomaniac delusions of personal grandeur" and ram against the collective will and leadership of the movement. "Such people meet their just desserts when they are unceremoniously thrown out by the scruff of their necks…Surgical excisions of malignant tumours are vitally necessary so that the organism as a whole may preserve its purity and vitality."

The most sinister was the third — enemies disguised as friends. They were those who have from the beginning nursed a "secret hostility and contempt" for the movement which they have publicly espoused, only in order to advance the interest of causes quite extraneous to the movement and to which they owe their real loyalty. "Such people must expect, if and when they are exposed, to face public execration as double-dealing merchants of dishonour," he wrote in the 14 November 1960 issue of *Petir*. The PAP shall not grieve when it comes to the parting of ways with such double-dealers, he asserted. It was a clear warning to the pro-communists in the party of the confrontation to come. It would come sooner than he expected.

In this empoisoned atmosphere, Ong formed the United People's Party, and fought the Hong Lim by-election in a straight fight against the PAP. It was Raja's task to introduce the PAP candidate at a press conference — he was Jek Yuen Thong, a former *Sin Pao* reporter who was now Lee Kuan Yew's political secretary. Raja was familiar with Jek. When he was detained by Lim Yew Hock's government in August 1957, Raja, as president of the Singapore Union of Journalists, had pressed for his release.

In his introduction, Raja began by contrasting the characters of Ong and Jek. Jek was "far cleaner" than Ong. He had worked loyally for the party "not to enhance personal glory but because he honestly believed the principles and aims of the PAP", said Raja. In contrast, Ong was an opportunist who sought to split the party, and who appeared to be interested in promoting his personal glory. He was now in alliance with "bankrupt political elements" such as the SPA, the Workers' Party, and the Singapore Congress, Raja declared.[18]

During the long campaign, from 11 March to 29 April, the PAP made "integrity" the central issue. As part of this strategy, they sought to discredit Ong's character, not sparing personal details such as his illegal private life as a bigamist.

In pungent terms, Raja put to the people the PAP's case: If the elected representatives of the people do not have regard for truth and honesty, "then every rogue in town has as good a claim to represent the people of Singapore". "If a man can lie to his own colleagues in the party and the Government, then he would not hesitate to bamboozle and betray those who elected him when it suited him."[19]

The voters were cold. Most were turned off by what they viewed as a vindictive feud between Lee Kuan Yew and Ong. The more the PAP attacked Ong's character, the more their sympathies went to Ong. Hong Lim was Ong's base, a grotty quarter in Chinatown heaving with poverty. He was popular with the Chinese-educated masses. He spoke their language, Hokkien, squatted with them on the road-side and ate with them.

In contrast, Jek, a Cantonese, spoke very little Hokkien. He could not move the mob at rallies the way Ong could. The PAP leaders worked hard to overcome this by door-to-door canvassing, knocking on doors, giving out flyers. Lee, a Hakka, also started learning Hokkien to counter Ong's attacks.

As propaganda chief, Raja weighed in on political strategy during the intense campaign. Jek often visited Raja's house to discuss tactics with him.[20] Raja also pitched in at the rallies with impassioned speeches of his own.

Bloodworth, who covered the election for the *Observer*, noticed that the PAP leaders were generally reserved about how the vote would go. Of them all, Raja struck him as being the most sanguine and optimistic. "He really believed that Jek Yuen Thong would pull it off," the journalist recalled.[21] Jek did not. Ong won 72 per cent of the votes polled. It was a humiliating defeat for the PAP.

Raja was crushed. The loss delivered him a sharp lesson in democratic politics in Singapore. He was distressed that Ong's campaign had unleashed Chinese chauvinist passions.

The Chinese-educated were angry about unemployment, their poor housing conditions and strict immigration controls, among other things. They wanted instant miracles from the PAP, although it had been in power for only all of 10 months. In this short time, they did not know the PAP, but they knew Ong, having seen how he had built drains and put up street lights.

According to reporters, Ong also used the extraordinary tactics of getting some young Chinese women to fall on their knees in front of the older folk and wail to them to vote for Ong, for the sake of their ancestors. Bloodworth recalled: "Everybody agreed at the time that this was going to be far more effective than, say, Rajaratnam going round saying, "You got to vote PAP!"[22]

The people's verdict was received as a cautionary tale on the vagaries of the democratic system — it rewards charismatic leaders with an oratorical gift for moving a mob and communal sentiments, and not necessarily the most capable and honest one.

Besides Ong's personality cult, there were other forces at work. The pro-communists, while publicly speaking for the PAP candidate, had given Ong their vote. It did not escape the PAP's notice that when Lim Chin Siong spoke during the campaign, he carried a double message. Or as Raja put it, Chin Siong was "wishy washy".

While asking voters to vote for the PAP on the podium, he had added ambiguously that Ong's resolutions appeared to be in the interests of the people, although Ong himself should not be supported. More significantly, Chin Siong had dwelt on the struggle for freedom without any reference to merger, and also spoke at length on the need to eliminate the Internal Security Council.

When the PAP refused to budge on these issues, the pro-communists passed word around to support Ong. While aware that the ground had turned sour against the PAP, Raja believed that the communist underground had exploited the by-election to teach the PAP a lesson for not toeing their line.

The defeat prompted an agonising reappraisal among the PAP leaders. To show that the PAP meant business, they considered the possibility of resigning as a cabinet. In an editorial in *Petir*, which was carried by the mainstream press, the party said that, if the result of the Hong Lim by-election accurately reflected the feelings of the people, it would be both "immoral and impractical" for the PAP government to cling to office.

But if the loss were no more than a protest vote, not against the basic aims of the party, but against the way in which it had tried to realise these aims, then the setback in Hong Lim should be a spur towards rectification. It was necessary for the party to analyse the setback to determine which it was — a mere protest vote, or a repudiation of the PAP's basic aims — and to act accordingly.[23]

According to Raja's account, the PAP's remarks about resigning were greeted with "cries of protest" by the communists and their supporters in the unions, cultural associations, and other open-front organisations. "It was not that they liked the PAP but that they feared that the PAP might be replaced by an anti-Communist group which would not hesitate to embark upon brutal repression of the Communists," Raja later analysed.[24]

Speculation about the PAP's resignation prompted the Federation leaders to take more seriously the idea of merger as they confronted the alternative — a Singapore sliding into communism, controlled by the Malayan Communist Party, and thrown into chaos at its doorstep. As chronicled by the thoughtful analysis contained in the telegrams to London, the British, who were watching the developments unfold in Singapore with increasing dismay, had also put this point across strongly to the Tunku.

The Tunku was sufficiently disturbed by this prospect to make the historic announcement on 27 May 1961, that merger was on the cards. The Tunku said that a plan was needed for the territories of Malaya, Singapore, North Borneo, Brunei and Sarawak to "be brought closer together in political and economic co-operation". "Malaya today as a nation realises that she cannot stand alone and in isolation."[25]

Raja was surprised by the Tunku's volte-face on merger. But he lost no time in working with his PAP colleagues to give immediate public backing to the Tunku's announcement. Raja's initial analysis, which he confirmed with his colleagues later, was that "the Tunku had agreed to merger not because he believed in it, but he saw it as an insurance against a possible collapse of PAP authority". He surmised that the British must have convinced the Tunku of the danger that Singapore's mounting security problems would pose Malaya.

The Tunku's long-standing fear of Singapore's Chinese majority upsetting the racial balance would be addressed with the inclusion of Sabah, Brunei, and Sarawak.[26] With the three Borneo territories, the Chinese would be outnumbered by the Malays and the indigenous peoples.

As Raja reflected on the Tunku's motivations for his proposal, he could not help worrying whether this "Grand Design" or "Greater Malaysia Plan", as it was called, would suffer the dire fate of other similar ideas mooted in the past. Still, it offered a sprig of hope. Raja clung to it tenaciously, as to a branch on a cliff face. Echoing around him were the keening cries of sceptics who doubted the ability of the non-communist leaders to hang on and hold out against the formidable might of the communists.

Reflecting the general assessment of those outside Singapore, Australia's prime minister and minister for external affairs, Robert Menzies, stated that "the present PAP leadership is unlikely to remain in power in Singapore unless demonstrable progress is made toward merger in the near future."[27] And if Singapore were to win independence on its own *without* merger, as the pro-communists had called for, "Singapore would be easily subverted by Communist China. It would in time almost certainly be governed by radical Chinese aiming at close association with Communist China".[28] Such were the stakes.

These security concerns, however, were not uppermost in the minds of the leaders of the Borneo States, who recoiled from Tunku's statement on merger. Their foremost fear was Malay domination by the Federation with merger. Still British colonies, the Borneo states expressed a preference for self-government and independence first before any movement towards Malaysia.

On 9 July 1961, A.M. Azahari, president of the Partai Rakyat Brunei, Ong Kee Hui, chairman of the Sarawak United People's Party (SUPP), and Donald Stephens, leader of the United Pasok-Momogun Kadazan Organisation (UPKO) in Sabah, took a united stand: They said that any merger plan as voiced by Tunku would be "totally unacceptable to the people of the three territories".[29]

For the PAP, the political situation at home was no more encouraging. To add a twist to the fast-moving plot, there was also another by-election to fight. This was triggered by the death of PAP assemblyman for Anson, Baharudin bin Mohd Arif. Beyond this, there was yet another bigger battle to gear up for — against the pro-communists on the historic issue of merger.

One lesson Raja learnt about politics was that, if the ground was not with you, no amount of strategising and organisation could turn the tide. To find out where the PAP went wrong, the party set up a review committee on 18 May 1961 to evaluate the work of the government and party and to recommend measures to correct their errors. Two ministers led the committee, Raja and Goh. They invited memoranda from party branches and members. They received an earful, with 47 submissions in all.

Activists complained about the behaviour of the civil servants — their discourtesy, their rigid interpretation of the rules, and their high-handed manner especially to the poorer people. There was also unhappiness with the way the government had pushed through the reforms without adequate explanation or consultation. The committee also reported the failure in public relations. This was ostensibly Raja's territory. Arguably, that failure was less an indictment on Raja's own abilities, than on the government's overhaste in introducing policies without due regard to public relations.

In the process of the review, Goh began to appreciate more the crucial role that Raja played in explaining policies, and the need to give more support to his ministry to play that role well. As for Raja, it meant he had to reassess his ministry's priorities and programmes. To tackle the problems identified, the review committee proposed, among other things, a national courtesy campaign to foster better relations between the public and the civil service, and the establishment of a Central Complaints Bureau, the forerunner of the government's Feedback Unit.[30] Underlying their recommendations was the somewhat grudging realisation that the PAP leaders needed to give people a hearing. While the PAP leaders did not want to be slaves to opinion, democratic leadership demanded that they listen to the views of the people.

For both Raja and Goh, the consultation exercise was a crash course on how to work a democracy on the ground. Despite the experience of the Hong Lim by-election, where his most ardent efforts at political persuasion made no discernible impact, Raja continued to have faith in people's ability to think rationally. From his viewpoint, if the PAP leaders failed, it was because they did not explain themselves well enough in a period of democratic change.

Not all leaders always shared Raja's equanimity over the people's ability to choose rationally what was right over what was easy, or to make decisions that favoured the greater good over personal interest. Most of the people were poorly educated, if not illiterate. They spoke in different tongues, desired different ends, and held different basic assumptions of the country's interests.

There were many competing political systems and models of governments in the world. During that period, the tension was between communism and capitalism. Western democracies faced a clear adversary, communism. Within Western democracies, there was a further dogmatic division, between the socialist left and the conservative right.

Faced with the array of mind-boggling problems as a political practitioner, the likes of which he had never encountered before, Raja learnt to rely on his own powers of analysis and that of his colleagues. Certainly, no single ideology or theory had all the answers. While Raja was well versed in the doctrines of socialism, he was not doctrinaire in his approach.

That said, he remained ineluctably wedded to the abstract notions of equality and social justice, perhaps to a greater degree than the others. While the PAP leaders called themselves democratic socialists, in the final analysis, they would do what worked for the country. The burden was on the particular system to demonstrate that it could raise standards of living and uphold the people's basic rights.

As Raja and his fellow leaders struggled to govern a divided country and guide it into modern statehood, they adapted what proved successful in other countries and, over time, would evolve their own democratic model according to Singapore's unique conditions. Mistakes would be made as they groped their way forward. Raja, too, would not be spared from committing errors. But as he said once, it was natural to make mistakes; the important thing was to learn from them.

During this period, Raja was also sharpening his instincts for diplomacy and international relations. Although Singapore had no power over its external relations, and hence, had no foreign minister, Raja showed no discomfort speaking and behaving like one when France tested Singapore's nerves — and provoked Raja's anti-imperialist instincts.

At the time, France was waging a six-year war against Algeria's independence fighters. In early 1961, Ferhat Abbas, prime minister of the Provisional Government of Algeria, visited Singapore. Raja made sure Abbas was warmly welcomed the moment he set foot on Singapore. Singapore's embrace of the Algerian nationalist leader angered the French, who promptly made a protest to the British government over this. Singapore stood firm in its support to Algeria's independence cause and refused to be cowed.

In the vanguard was Raja. On 22 February 1961, he moved a motion in the Legislative Assembly to express Singapore's support for the cause of freedom for the Algerian people and to propose a token sum of $10,000 to be contributed by the government to a public subscription in support of the Algerian people's struggle for freedom.

In scathing tones, Raja told the Assembly: "The French, with characteristic obtuseness, appear to have taken a dim view of the welcome accorded by Singapore to Dr Abbas. They thought it necessary to make a protest to the British Government over this. The British, for their part, not only transmitted this silly protest to us but also saw fit, presumably out of deference to French sensitivity, to deprecate the Singapore Government for having accorded the honours to an enemy of French imperialism."

This Western reaction was typical, said Raja, of their insensitivity to "the winds of change in Africa and to the attitude of the Asian peoples to the liberation struggles now erupting from one end of Africa to the other". He lectured France for not having learnt their lessons of their "ignominious defeat" in what used to be known as French Indo-China, and lambasted it for "the savagery of imperialist repression" in Algeria. He gave the Assembly a history lesson on Algerian nationalism, and called on the French to recognise the right of the Algerian people to self-determination.

While Singapore was in no position to "offer massive help to the courageous people of Algeria", it could sustain the spirit of the Algerian nationalists by token sympathy and support, he said. Hence, he proposed an "Aid to Algeria Fund", with $10,000 from the government, and asked the public also to donate to the fund.

On its part, the PAP donated $2,000 to the fund. In total, about $25,000 was collected. On 15 November 1961, Raja presented the cheque to Lakhdar Brahimi, the diplomatic representative in Southeast Asia of the Algerian Provisional Government.

This episode was an early manifestation of Raja's ease and sophistication with world affairs on the public stage. When he spoke on international issues, it was with verve, élan, and confidence. He displayed an uncanny ability to marshal a myriad of details to build a strong case for Singapore's stand on an international issue, and to argue it convincingly. He was taking shape as a leading intellectual light in determining Singapore's foreign policy.

During this time, Singapore was also taking its first tentative steps to set up its trade and cultural representation in Jakarta, Indonesia. The centre, opened on 4 September 1961, was the first overseas establishment by the PAP government. This move was driven primarily by economic considerations. Indonesia accounted for about 20 per cent of Singapore's overall value of trade.

Singapore's overseas diplomatic representation and trade interests were handled by the British embassy, but, as Goh Keng Swee noted in his cabinet paper,[31] "in view of the size of the trade, the extremely difficult methods of exchange, the barter and control by which this trade is conducted and the fact that the first duty of the British Embassy was towards the UK affairs", there was every reason to establish direct trade representation in Jakarta between the Republic of Indonesia and the State of Singapore.

While Goh provided the economic impetus for the mission, it was Raja who helped the staff to get their bearings in Singapore's first overseas mission. This was virgin territory for Singapore. But it helped that, earlier in 1959, Raja had already laid the foundation by building up cultural links with Indonesia, an early example of the benefits of cultural diplomacy. As Singapore had no Foreign Service, staff had to be seconded from other ministries and put under the charge of the Division of Commerce and Industry.

The first senior trade and cultural representative was Abu Bakar bin Pawanchee, while his assistant was Ridzwan Dzafir. A month after Abu Bakar arrived in Jakarta on 20 August 1961, Raja and his wife visited Indonesia to establish better ties with the country and to give his official signature to the new Singapore trade and cultural office.

Raja and Piroska, who came as guests of the Indonesian government, visited the office on 5 October and encouraged the skeletal Singaporean staff to persevere. Given Indonesia's suspicions of Singapore's intentions, it was a tough posting for the staff. They faced numerous problems, from office plumbing to diplomatic access. According to Abu Bakar's discreet report, Raja made helpful suggestions. As it turned out, Abu Bakar would later serve Raja as his first permanent secretary when Singapore set up its Foreign Ministry after separation from Malaysia in 1965.

These developments highlighted the multifarious dimensions of Singapore's challenges — petty and big, domestic and international. Yet it was a struggle to focus the people's minds on them in the din of the noisy, confrontational politics of the day. Raja could hardly hide his despair at the low level of debate in the Legislative Assembly, with opposition members criticising PAP policies without offering any solutions, and being just out to confuse the issue and score political points.

In a flash of frustration, Raja chastised the opposition in a debate in 1960, reminding them that "politics is no longer a game of marbles". He told them: "What we say, what we do or what we do not do, can mean happiness or tragedy for the 1.5 million people whose future is in our hands. This is not a boast; it is a statement of fact. After the first year, the play of social forces has reached a stage where we cannot treat them as matters for academic discussion, but as offering serious problems and calling for serious decisions on which the whole future of 1.5 million people would depend."

To avoid getting stuck in the quagmire of complexity, Raja pursued an approach that brought to bear his powers of analysis — he simplified. To do this, he abandoned the unceasing preoccupation with the immediate and the urgent and, paradoxically, set his mind to the underlying ideas that changed the course of mankind over the centuries.

So it was that, during this period of flux, Raja snatched himself away from the hurly-burly world of politics and retreated to the hallowed world of contemplation. He sat back with his cigarette and reflected on the great ideas throughout the history of mankind that had changed the world.

The very idea of man's ability to develop language, numbers, and abstract thought filled him with a sense of, in his own words, "the wonder of man". He compulsively committed his thoughts to paper. He then published them in the party organ *Petir* over five instalments under a series "Ideas that changed the world", which ran from 4 January to 9 March 1960. In these articles, he revealed himself as a polymath and a philosopher king, pondering ideas that had shaped mankind's progress over centuries, as opposed to dwelling on the petty politics of the day and the ephemeral characters flitting across the stage.

He was powerfully fascinated by how writing came into being only about 6,000 years ago, although man has lived on this planet for about a million years, how language made abstract thought possible; and why prehistoric cave paintings disappeared after the Old Stone Age. He showed a strong rational streak as he analysed the evidence, culled from his vast readings.

Raja started off the series by tracing how ideas, in particular abstract ideas, exerted a powerful influence on man's behaviour and actions. Noting how some countries suppressed ideas deemed dangerous, he wrote: "All this gives substance to the claim that the world had become a battlefield of ideas, though some people tend to back up their ideas with tommy-guns, tanks, submarines and atom bombs."

He added optimistically that, by and large, guns, tanks, planes, and persecution have failed to suppress good ideas, truthful ideas. "The history of the growth of ideas is a history of the conflict between good and bad ideas, between false and true ideas. On balance, victory has gone to the good and true ideas. At least that is my view."

In his second article, he examined the development of language, considering it "the greatest of all ideas conceived by man". Language enabled man to engage in intellectual debate and to develop a sense of history, with the ability to describe events and situations which his audience had never seen or experienced. He marvelled at how language gave life to abstract concepts such goodness, soul, beauty, and love. Through language, people also acquired a new sense of solidarity based on mutual understanding. "That is why, even today, the basis of most societies is a common language."

In another piece, he proceeded to reflect on the prehistoric cave paintings produced by the Old Stone Age hunters some 20,000 years ago, commenting on the lifelike vibrancy of these works. He concluded that the hunter's drive to produce these works was not to satisfy his artistic craving, but to satisfy his hunger. The Stone Age man, who believed in magic and animism, thought that drawing pictures of bisons with arrows stuck in them would ensure success in hunting. But why did such cave paintings then vanish later? His next article, on the birth of writing, picked up this point. As man's thinking became more analytical and abstract, his drawings became less detailed, more symbolic, and looked less and less like the objects they were supposed to represent. The pictures became signs. Thus writing was born.

Writing made it possible for humans to communicate over long distances, to large groups of people, and over great periods of time. It also enabled mankind to accumulate knowledge and to pass it down the generations, leading to a rapid advance in the growth of human knowledge. Stone Age man was able to make the mental leap from direct representation to abstraction, and Raja used this as evidence of man's ability to continue making the necessary mental leaps.

The concluding article continues to analyse the notion of abstraction as he considered the ability of man to conceive and use numbers. Among primitive people, many could not conceive of anything beyond five. Thousands of years had to pass before men thought of numbers in the abstract. He marvelled at how 10 symbols — 1 to 9 plus 0 — allowed men to make calculations which made it possible to build skyscrapers, harness atomic energy, erect electric power plants, or guide rockets to go round the moon and return to the earth.

Given that he was a busy politician beset with the stresses and strains of office, it is astonishing that he had time to pen such articles. It demonstrates vividly how his fertile and restless mind continued to whir and pause on the grand issues of life even as it darted from one issue to another in the strife of his daily political life.

In part, his reflections were driven by an inner need — he craved for the abstract and the philosophic. For Raja, a true intellectual, ideas had an electric vitality that could take on a life of their own: In truth, ideas engaged his passion more than state administration or power politics. He regarded the history of ideas as the gateway to self-knowledge. He needed it to remind himself of the potential within man to transcend the limitations of life, and of the power of good ideas to triumph in the end. Written at a time when his own ideas for the country, such as a common language and a Malayan culture, were under constant siege, these long-ranging reflections must have helped renew his faith in mankind and his pursuit of ideas.

But with the political currents becoming stronger, there was also probably another reason for this series — to persuade the tightly-wound and practical-minded men around him of the power of ideas. Organisation and efficiency are important in running a country, but it is ideas that ultimately possess the transformative power to shape

Singapore and its people. If allied with sufficient energy and force of will — and it must be added, imagination — ideas can transform the outlook of an entire people and generation.

Raja saw PAP's political struggles to find answers for the country as part of that great conversation over the centuries. Based on mankind's historical record, he drew courage from the "wonder of man" to make a revolutionary leap to its next level of progress. This belief in mankind's potential merged in his mind with his natural inclination towards optimism and a Panglossian faith in his ability to achieve what he willed. This faith was to be further tested at the Anson by-election.

17

The Lion's Roar

As Raja set to work preparing for the coming Anson by-election due on 15 July 1961, his name was being bandied about among top communist circles in Peking as a candidate for another sort of campaign — the Communist plot to subvert merger.

Since the first week of June, Chin Peng, secretary-general of the Malayan Communist Party (MCP) had been in Peking to discuss developments with the Communist Party of China (CPC). Deng Xiaoping, the secretary-general of the CPC, was convinced that the Southeast Asian region would soon be ripe for communist domination and pressed Chin Peng, a ruthless guerilla fighter who had spent many years in the jungle, to revert to armed struggle. Deng promised that China would fund the MCP's insurgency. Enthused by the prospect of eventual communist domination in the region and the ready access to funds, Chin Peng fell in line with China's wishes.

It was against this strategic backdrop that Chin Peng summoned Eu Chooi Yip, who controlled MCP operations in Singapore from his base in Indonesia, to Peking. Together with Siao Chang,[1] a senior MCP Politburo member based in Peking for more than six years, they discussed the strength of the Singapore underground and the Tunku's bombshell announcement on merger.

At that critical meeting, they decided to sabotage the merger plan, or at least to delay its implementation for as long as possible.

They were fearful that, once Singapore joined Malaya, the communist network on the island would be smashed. Between the three, a strategy was hatched — exploit the internal weaknesses of the PAP.

Chooi Yip told Chin Peng that the PAP was being split three ways, exposing its political vulnerabilities. According to Chin Peng's account, Chooi Yip argued strongly that "there was an ever widening split between the PAP's right-wing faction, led by Lee Kuan Yew, and a middle-of-the-road group, seemingly headed by Sinnathamby Rajaratnam". The third faction was the "Chinese communal group".[2] Chin Peng was sceptical about the depth of difference between Lee and Raja. But both Chooi Yip, who had kept in close touch with the Singapore underground, and Siao Chang, who had for years been relaying party instructions from his base in Peking to senior communist cadres in Singapore, were convinced that "the rift was present and would worsen".

Chooi Yip could claim to know Raja well, having been his former housemate at Chancery Lane. After escaping the police dragnet in Singapore in 1951, Chooi Yip had then fled to Indonesia's Riau Islands, a key staging point and withdrawal centre for the Singapore communist guerillas.[3] To convince Chin Peng of Raja's radical proclivities, Chooi Yip related how, during the Emergency, Raja had helped him to get medical treatment for his tuberculosis and gave him refuge in Singapore.

Chin Peng, whose words were often backed by elimination squads, related: "We then decided to instruct our Singapore underground to work on winning over the Rajaratnam faction to an anti-Malaysia stand and, at the same time, do everything possible to undermine Lee's determination to press for the formation of the new Federation incorporating Singapore."[4] With that directive, Raja, who had been resisting communist overtures since his salad days in London, became a chief target for the communist plot to sabotage merger.

The analysis of the MCP leaders reflected their perceptions of the differences between Raja and Lee: Raja was seen to be more "left" than Lee in his approach to politics, more radical, more ideological. The communist leaders knew that Raja was powerfully influenced by Marxist thought in his London days and had many communist friends whom he had treated gently and even protectively. In contrast, Lee's approach was less ideological, more political, and entirely pragmatic. As Chin Peng put it, he thought that Lee would use his communist contacts as much as he could and would one day move against the MCP — and the MCP regarded the arrangement "in very much the same light".[5] The communists were adroit at sensing any differences in the PAP ranks and exploiting them to press the communist agenda.

Given that the MCP was illegal in Singapore and Malaya, the communists had to work through their underground operatives in their different guises to turn their targets. Over the past 30 years, they had developed and honed their techniques and psychological warfare. They were particularly skilful at exploiting a man's weaknesses. Their methods would typically involve efforts to create a defeatist state of mind with intimidation and pressure, and then to entice by offering blandishments of power and position, and finally, to weaken and erode the person's attitudes towards what he had previously accepted as absolute moral standards — such as betraying a friend.

No doubt, the communists tried various approaches to win Raja over to their cause. He was obviously well-versed with their arguments, as he would later rehash them to expose their intent after the battle was over. The typical communist line would go: The communists had a network of formidable organisations, with thousands of dedicated people willing to risk all for their cause. They had the moral and material support of China and Soviet Union. The force of history was on their side. What did the non-communist PAP faction have? A bunch of beer-swilling English-educated intellectuals with a support base that would crumble under communist pressure. The non-communist PAP could not win. If they turned against their non-communist leaders in the PAP, they would be rewarded with position and power in the new government under their control.

These bribes and threats would work with many, but not with Raja. His strength of character and conviction was a bulwark against communist intimidation. Years later, Samad Ismail, who later confessed in an interview that he was a high-ranking Malayan communist, confirmed the extensive communist efforts to influence Raja and the futility of it all.[6] Samad, who visited Chooi Yip in Indonesia during that turbulent period, said: "Chooi Yip admired Raja because he was not ambitious, and not easily influenced". Samad said the communists found Raja "too smart" to be manipulated.[7]

Raja himself never spoke about the communists' attempts to turn him against Lee during this period. Perhaps, it was to protect his friends who had tried. In an assessment which summed up the general view held among communist circles, Samad said: "Raja was a decent fellow. You can trust him. He doesn't stab you in the back. You can be quite frank with him in discussions."[8]

Instead, what Raja did disclose years later was his own attempts to dissuade the likes of Woodhull from going along with the pro-communist group. Having had many ideological discussions with Woodhull over the years, Raja was aware that Woodhull had a sharp understanding of Marxist theory. As the communists began working on party stalwarts to join them, Raja confronted Woodhull about working with Chin Siong's group to further the communist cause.

While Woodhull denied that he and his group were working for the MCP, Raja said: "He knew that I knew he was putting it on. He knew that they were working for the MCP cause…Woodhull knew what Communism was all about," Raja related later. He, too, knew what communism was all about, and because of that, was clear-eyed about the MCP's sinister agenda.

Had the communists succeeded in capturing him, the Singapore story might well have turned out differently. The MCP knew that it would have been that much easier to checkmate the embattled prime minister, without the ferocious Raja at his side. When Chin Peng heard the news that his men had failed to turn Raja against Lee and merger, the guerilla fighter was despondent, but not surprised. He observed: "Rajaratnam was, from the very beginning, undoubtedly Lee Kuan Yew's man."[9]

Chin Peng's conclusion missed the larger truth: More than Lee's man, Raja was his own man, with his own convictions. Raja firmly believed in the union of Singapore with Malaya, even before he met Lee in 1952. As his record showed, he was not, by instinct, a rubber stamp for anyone's agenda. Nor was he anyone's puppet.

He was then 46, eight years older than Lee. Raja had not devoted half a lifetime to developing his own ideas and pursuing his own dreams, only to betray them when he finally had the chance to turn them into reality.

While Lee might exert a powerful influence over Raja, he did not have control of Raja or his actions. (This was a point also noted by the British in a classified report in 1964, when Raja favoured a more aggressive political role in Malaysia.) Unlike perhaps some of his colleagues, he was not intimidated by Lee's ruthless intellect and felt little compunction telling Lee the blunt truth about his mistakes.

Years later, Lee said: "In our arguments, he'd win some, I would win some. That was what made us good friends. I never insisted that in everything I was right because I was Prime Minister. He would not concede just because I was Prime Minister."[10] From the day they entwined their fates in a common cause to fight for independence for Singapore, Lee and Raja had been through traumatic times together. The events that tested them could have proven serious enough to weaken their alliance, if not for their exceptionally strong personal and political bond. When the chips were down, they closed ranks. Against their political opponents, they were doughty fighters.

The communists had better success influencing the "Chinese communal group" headed by Lim Chin Siong. The communists exploited the emotions of Chinese chauvinism. As the Anson by-election loomed, Chin Siong and his group started hissing, spitting and striking at the non-communist PAP leaders for championing merger.

On 2 June 1961, Chin Siong and five other prominent trade unionists[11] from the Trade Union Congress (TUC) — dubbed the "Big Six" — issued a statement warning that they might not support the PAP if it pursued a pro-merger course. They alluded to the anger of the people at the PAP "selling out" Singapore to the Federation. This was followed by a list of familiar demands: abolish the Internal Security Council, release all political detainees, grant citizenship to certain individuals close to Lim Chin Siong, and so on. The force of 42 trade unions was with them, they declared.

Raja and his non-communist colleagues dug in their heels and stood firm in their commitment to merger. Despite the pounding pressure, Raja appeared relaxed about the party's fortunes and told Bloodworth, during one of their badminton games at the time, that Chin Siong was provoking a crisis in an opportunistic bid to regain his credibility with the masses. His popularity had taken a battering because of his association with the PAP, which had hitherto resisted his radical demands.[12]

The latest list of demands was an angry attempt, thought Raja, to coerce the PAP into providing a favourable climate for the growth of communist forces. However, given that the British had overriding powers to suspend the constitution if the communists captured power, it struck Raja that the action of Chin Siong's group seemed uncharacteristically reckless.

As Raja brooded on the unexpected development, the editor of an English Sunday newspaper came to see him about the widening rift in the PAP and asked if something could be done about it. Raja replied that it was very difficult because their demands were contrary to the party's policy. The editor then told him, with a half-smile and a knowing look: "Raja, I think you don't know much because these boys have a good pipeline with the UK Commission."[13] Focused on the communist threat, the significance of this remark did not hit Raja until later.

Exploiting the internal squabbles in the PAP, David Marshall from the Workers' Party waded into the by-election pitch. He tapped on the anti-PAP sentiments and echoed the popular demands of the pro-communists — immediate independence for Singapore, and the abolition of the Internal Security Council.

Facing him was the PAP candidate Mahmud bin Awang, president of the Trade Union Congress (TUC). In 1955, he led a strike in the Singapore Traction Company, where he served as the president of the union. A year later, he was detained by the former Lim Yew Hock government for "his firm anti-colonial and nationalist stand", as the PAP put it.[14] In Raja's estimation, Mahmud's revolutionary and trade union credentials should help to win the support of the unionists and the masses.

Since the Hong Lim by-election, however, Raja had been disturbed by the way emotions and chauvinistic sentiments had swayed the vote. Still, he nurtured the hope that greater sense and rationality would prevail in Anson. Unlike Hong Lim with its majority of poor and illiterate Chinese, Anson was more representative of Singapore in terms of its population, race, and social classes. Logically, Anson should reflect the broader national sentiment towards the PAP government, and not sectional or communal interests.

In a bid to foster the conditions for democracy in a country with hardly any democratic tradition or experience, Raja used the campaign to educate the people on the value of the vote. While merger remained the central plank of the PAP campaign, he framed the significance of the by-election as putting "democracy on trial".

In this, he was guided by his conviction that democracy would only deliver responsible government if people understood in the first place what being a responsible government meant in a democracy. And more specifically, what democracy meant given the special constraints of Singapore. In a mission to focus minds on the issue, he wrote an article in *Petir*, published two days before polling day, on the "rules" and essence of democratic government.[15] It laid out the early template for the PAP's approach to democracy, which is still relevant today.

Raja wrote that in a complex society such as Singapore, with conflicting group and individual interests, no government could hope to satisfy everyone. All that a democratic government could do was satisfy the legitimate aspirations of the majority without jeopardising the legitimate interests of the minority. Similarly, a government must preserve a sensible balance between satisfying immediate aspirations of the people and their long-term interests. This involved imposing certain restraints on the natural self-interest of the people.

One of the most difficult tasks in a democracy, he said, was to get people to see this and "to make people realise that the resources of Government are no bigger or smaller than what the community as a whole is prepared to contribute". "An equally difficult task was to get the people to realise that a responsible government must invest now to provide for the welfare and prosperity of the people in the future." This meant making sacrifices in the present.

A dishonest and irresponsible government could dissipate the resources of the community by concentrating only in satisfying the immediate needs of the people. But that might mean misery and poverty for the people down the road. On the other hand, too much of a preoccupation with the future could lead to the "wanton sacrifice of a decent life for the present generation in the interests of the next".

The PAP chose in the by-election to re-emphasise and to stand by its basic principles. It did not come out with popular concessions and promises just to get votes, he stressed. "Our concern is not with the passing and sectional antipathies a Government earns in the course of its life. These are the inevitable concomitants of democracy," he wrote. The PAP's concern was whether people supported its approach to democracy, which involved balancing the needs of the different groups and making sacrifices to create a better future for all.

Having sketched the outlines of democratic government on the broad political canvas, he then returned to the Anson by-election. The by-election, he wrote, was about testing whether people would support a government "which has honestly tried to improve their lot within the limitations of a democratic structure and the constraints of an entrepot economy".[16]

Raja's message was a valiant bid to place the campaign on a higher plane and usher in the sovereignty of reason. However, it was soon drowned out by a dramatic development two days before the polls. Eight PAP assemblymen issued an open letter to declare their support for Chin Siong's demands, and to attack the PAP for the lack of intraparty democracy.[17] The plot thickened.

Polling night was a nail-biting one for the PAP. Ever the optimist, Raja thought that the PAP might just about snatch a narrow victory. As in the Hong Lim by-election, his assessment was based more on hope than fact. With the support of the pro-communists behind him, Marshall won by 546 votes.

The double whammy — first, Hong Lim, now Anson — dealt the PAP a cruel blow. Raja and his colleagues needed no further proof of the lengths the pro-communists would go to defeat the party — even destroy it — to suit their own purposes. This realisation was a major turning point for their uneasy alliance with the pro-communists.

With the PAP's second by-election defeat, Raja's mood shifted from frustration to anger. He fumed that even among gangsters, there was a minimum of honour and a certain code of ethics when they fought against another gang — "one of which is that you do not stab your friend in his back until you have disposed of your common enemy". Even among gangsters, they did not stick a dagger into their own comrade when he called out for help. The decent thing to do, if a person disagreed with the government of which he was a part, was to resign from office before publicly opposing and fighting the government.[18]

It was time to draw a line between those who were prepared to fight on the side of the PAP, which meant fighting for independence through merger, and those who were not. Years later, Fong Swee Suan related that after the Anson by-election, there were several tense meetings between the key leaders of both factions to thrash out their respective positions. On the pro-communist side were Chin Siong, Woodhull, and Fong. On the non-communist side were Lee, Raja, and Toh Chin Chye.

According to Fong, after rounds of discussions which only laid bare the unbridgeable gulf between them, Raja finally told them: "Either you go into Malaysia and swim or sink with us — or we part ways." A stunned silence greeted his stark ultimatum. Fong recalled: "We understood what he meant. It meant that we have to make a decision, whether we go into Malaysia or we go on our own way. We were very impressed. He was a very straightforward man." At the meeting, the pro-communist group uttered no response. They felt there was no need to. "Almost immediately, we made our decision — we decided to split from the PAP," said Fong.[19]

Troubled by the growing rancour dividing the party, Raja and the core leaders decided on their next move: Purge the party of its tormentors. Raja related years later: "After the Anson by-election, we knew that they betrayed us, that they were unreliable. They were going to make things more and more difficult for us. So, we decided to get rid of them."

Meanwhile, Marshall, who was no communist himself, was jubilant at his victory. The Workers' Party chief, who had a personal antipathy towards Lee Kuan Yew, called blithely for the prime minister's resignation. He ignored warnings from the PAP that he was being used by the pro-communists, and refused to believe that his victory was at the command of the communists.

But then this was the same man who, as Singapore's chief minister in December 1955, had met Chin Peng for the Baling peace talks together with the Tunku — and then declared publicly that he didn't believe that Chin Peng was the leader of the communists in Malaya.[20] Marshall would have a different election result in 1963, when the communists decided that he was no longer useful. He would not only lose the election, but also his deposit. In Raja's assessment, Marshall did not grasp the realities of power politics and thus unknowingly lent himself to manipulation by the pro-communists.

Raja himself learnt rapidly that one should be sceptical when individuals who spout pro-communist lines deny being used by communists or being affiliated to them. As he would remark years later, those familiar with communist methods know that the communists were masters in "the technique of manipulating chosen targets without the target being aware of it".[21] Similarly, no communist working in the open front would confess to being a communist. To confess would be to betray the communist cause. Hence, Chin Siong's public denials of being a communist were scorned by the PAP leaders, who countered with evidence to unmask his communist proclivities.

The shadowy and volatile nature of their enemy meant that they had to steel their nerves and keep their wits about them at all times. They saw themselves as living in a situation of grave danger, surrounded by dark recesses where cunning eyes glint and conspiracies are hatched. Their acute sense of siege exacted a cost — at times, their concern with communism seemed to some as bordering on the obsessive. In a letter to *The Straits Times*, one of the rebels, James Puthucheary, reinforced this impression, asserting: "Everybody who disagreed with the PAP leaders was branded Communists, pro-Communists or Communist dupes."[22]

As one of the PAP's strategists, Raja appreciated that simply calling someone a communist or pro-communist, without a credible theory of how they came to be so and the dangers they posed to Singapore, would not be convincing. Together with Lee, Goh and Toh, Raja gathered the evidence and built up the intellectual case against them. In the battle to come, the PAP leaders believed that their strength lay in their knowledge of the methods and psychology of the communists. Raja could recite chapter and verse from literature by Lenin and Marx, and would put that to good use.

The PAP leaders took their fight against the pro-communists into the open and into the Legislative Assembly. On 21 July 1961, Lee moved a motion of confidence in the government in the Assembly. It was a huge gamble. If the motion was not carried, the government would resign and general elections follow. But the PAP leaders knew they had to be careful how the purge was done — if they appeared to be disposing of the pro-communists after making use of them, they would lose the support of the Chinese-speaking ground.

Hence, the PAP leaders sought to make it clear that it was the pro-communists who had betrayed them; that it was the pro-communists who were consorting secretly with the British; that it was the pro-communists who were selling out the people in opposing merger by serving the interests of the communists and not of the country.

Lee kicked off the gruelling debate, which stretched from 2.30 pm until about 4 am the next day. In his speech, he laid out the "plot, counter-plot and sub-plots" which would make "an Oppenheim thriller read like a simple comic strip cartoon". The key thrust of Lee's forceful speech was that the battle with the communists must be won by argument and in the hearts and minds of the people. "It will also be shown that the Communists have not only been duped by the British but duped to the extent that they betrayed their PAP comrades in the nationalist Left united front."[23]

After about 26 ministers and assemblymen had spoken, including Toh and Goh, Raja joined the marathon debate to address the key points at the ungodly hour of 1.35 am. He related a G.K. Chesterton short story in which the detective almost failed to solve the mystery because he had overlooked one suspect — the postman. He said: "The postman is taken so much for granted that no suspicion is aroused by the fact that he visited the murdered man's place. Similarly with the British. We were so pre-occupied with thinking that this was a manoeuvre between the non-Communist PAP and the Communist elements that we forgot that the British too — the postman — were somewhere around."

He reinforced the PAP government's case that the British had met the pro-communists at Eden Hall and given them an assurance that nothing would happen to them if they took over the government. This served to embolden the pro-communists to obliterate the PAP at Anson. "They felt that, after the PAP lost Anson, that defeat could then provide the necessary fuel to oust the present leadership of the PAP government and the party," said Raja.

What was behind the British scheme? According to Lee, the British had hoped that, once the pro-communists revealed themselves openly as enemies as they had done in Anson, the PAP would fight back and carry out a purge similar to the one executed by Lim Yew Hock — "something they (the British) have so far failed in persuading the PAP to do". By drawing the links between the British and the pro-communists, the PAP leaders seized the opportunity to polish their anti-colonial credentials and, at the same time, taint the pro-communists as being duped and manipulated by the British.

UK commissioner Lord Selkirk would later deny that he was trying to trick Chin Siong and company when they met at Eden Hall on 18 July 1961. In an interview in 1982, Selkirk recalled the essence of his reply to their question concerning the British position on a possible leftist takeover of the government: "It's a free constitution, stick to it, and no rioting, you understand?" In other words, the British would not stand in their way to form the government if they won the elections constitutionally, without recourse to violence.

When the PAP leaders learnt of this avowed British line to the pro-communists at the time, they greeted it with complete incredulity. Given Singapore's strategic importance and the pressures exerted by the British on the PAP government to act against the communists, it was extremely hard for the PAP leaders to believe that the British would now open the constitutional door for the communists and their lackeys to sweep into power. Raja maintained: "I don't believe for one moment the British would accept if the leftists won constitutionally".

At the Assembly debate in 1961, Raja said he was not interested in how the pro-communists and the British got on. "What we are interested in is the future of the PAP government and the aims and policies for which it stands, and more important, the establishment of an independent, democratic, non-Communist socialist Malaya. Our primary concern is with the lives and destinies of the 1.5 million people who trusted us, and whatever happens, we are not going to sell them out either to the British plotters or the beer-hall revolutionaries who have been duped by the British," he said.

Warning that the drama was not over, Raja gave notice: "We of the PAP will make our own arrangements and manipulate and manoeuvre as we think fit." This statement, resonant with Machiavellian echoes, marked yet another stage of Raja's development into a tough political operator.

Over the years, he had learned from his street-fighting experience in the hard-knocks school: Political survival required constant manipulation and manoeuvre. Politics was not just about the open argument and the niceties of democratic debate, however much he wished it were so. When faced with opponents out to do you in by fair means or foul, to be sweetness and light would be political suicide.

Raja's position on this would harden over time with the calluses formed as a result of his protracted and bruising battles against an obstreperous opposition. He would reiterate his view 24 years later: "The rules of politics must be, as they always have been, this: If an opposition declares that, instead of being a vehicle of constructive criticism, it will now become a vehicle for bringing down the ruling government, then it is well within Queensbury rules for a prudent government to bring down the opposition first. If the intention of an opposition is to destroy a ruling government, then the latter must destroy the opposition first — all within the rules."[24]

It might sound intolerant. Indeed, Raja was fully aware that such a stance exposed the PAP to the charge of being harsh on the opposition. But given his scorching experience in the 1960s, when politics was a matter of life and death, he would not be impressed.

Raja steeled himself for the worst when the confidence vote was taken in the early hours of 22 July 1961. The PAP needed 26 votes in the 51-member Assembly for a majority to carry the motion. After a headcount, it was certain of only 25. When the vote was called, 13 PAP rebels abstained. In the end, the government was saved by the crucial vote of an ailing PAP assemblywoman Sahorah Ahmat, who had to be carried into the chamber in a stretcher from her hospital bed. It was a nail-biting moment for Raja and his colleagues.

The division of the vote made the split within the PAP official. The repercussions were swift: A few hours after the debate, Lim Chin Siong, Fong Swee Suan, S. Woodhull, and Lee Siew Choh were relieved of their offices and dismissed from the PAP. All those who abstained from the vote on the confidence motion were also expelled. With their expulsion, the PAP was whittled down to 26 members — its majority now hung on just one vote.

In an effort to topple the government, Chin Siong and company tried to persuade the remaining PAP assemblymen to join them. They used threats, harassment and bribes of money, power and position. When that failed, they formed a new opposition party, Barisan Sosialis (Socialist Front), with Chin Siong as its secretary-general and Lee Siew Choh as its chairman. With their own political vehicle, their struggle to oust PAP government intensified and quickly escalated into a campaign to quash merger.

Publicly, Raja greeted their defection with derision. He disparaged them as political opportunists, lacking in principle and conviction. He believed that some of the 13 PAP assemblymen who defected to the Barisan were not so much communists, as "weaklings who believed that, if they took the Communist line, the Communists would bring them mass support and so ensure their political future in any forthcoming elections".[25] The PAP's defeat in two by-elections "only served to increase the opportunism of these weaklings in the PAP", he wrote.[26] Raja expressed only contempt for those who betrayed their colleagues and allowed themselves to be used for communist ends. He maintained that such a party born out of treachery would never succeed.

Privately, however, Raja was anxious about the strength of his opponents. Knowing how dedicated and ruthless the communists were, he expected a brutal fight with sinister twists and turns. Given this grim reality, Raja's strategy, simply put, was to out-tough and outlast the Barisan. As he told Bloodworth during this period, "all we've got to do is to hang on. The pro-communists are pinning their hopes on toppling the government. We shall hold on until merger is an accomplished fact".[27]

He knew it would not be easy for the PAP troops to hold the line against communist assault. Many people were scared stiff of the communists, with their reputation for settling scores, and flinched at their shadow. The battle called for strong nerves.

In his public statements, Raja sought to arouse the people to the dangers posed by the pro-communists, and to prepare them psychologically for an ugly confrontation. Barely a month after the split, he warned that the pro-communists who had failed to capture the party and changed its policy would now try "to do their best to upset all measures and steps towards independence". "We must be patient and calm and watch closely to what extent these people will go to obstruct the road to merger."[28]

The ability of the PAP itself to stay patient and calm was tested severely over the next year, as its majority swung like a pendulum in the Assembly. On 11 August 1962, PAP assemblywoman Hoe Puay Choo crossed over to Barisan, reducing the PAP with 25 votes to 26 in the Assembly. Five days later, on 16 August, Lingam, who had been with Ong Eng Guan's party, returned to the PAP, restoring its majority by one vote to 26. This one vote was to vanish when, on 21 August, PAP minister Ahmad Ibrahim died, leaving the party with 25 votes once more.

Smelling blood, the opposition went into an attacking frenzy in the Assembly, moving motions and calling for divisions at every opportunity. It took all of the PAP leaders' energies and political acuity to prevent the government from collapsing so that they could work out merger details with Malaya and the Borneo territories.[29]

Outside the Assembly, the political battle spread rapidly to the trade unions — the PAP's original mass base — and the PAP branches, the party's organisational muscle. The TUC was dissolved and its army of unions broke up into two opposing sides. The PAP unionists formed the National Trades Union Congress (NTUC), while the pro-communists set up the Singapore Association of Trade Unions (SATU). When the dust settled, no one was left in doubt which was the stronger force. The NTUC had about 12 unions. SATU had 43.

The Barisan rubbed in the PAP's humiliation further by also wresting away the bulk of the PAP's branches — including the PAP's *paid* organising secretaries. Of the 25 who had been selected in 1959 to organise and supervise party activities at the branches, 20 left with the pro-communists. Many members of the 51 PAP branches also defected to the Barisan, with some taking entire branches with them. PAP branches were infiltrated by the extremists and transformed into militant nests. Raja would observe sombrely later: "Their impact on the party had not been unlike that of a visitation of locusts in a rice field. They had eaten up the goodness and strength of the party."[30]

His own Kampong Glam branch was almost entirely wiped out. His branch was previously buzzing with Chinese-speaking members, with many from the Seamstress' Union. Overnight, almost all vanished. His branch was "hanging by the skin of my teeth", Raja recalled.

Years later, Hoe Puay Choo, the one-time president of the Seamstress' Union, related: "They left because of policy differences with PAP, nothing personal with Raja."[31] This was little consolation to Raja, who also lost his branch secretary Yap Seong Leong.

Yap, who was married to Hoe, felt obliged to leave the PAP in 1962, after Hoe crossed over to the Barisan in the Assembly. Hoe disclosed: "He left the PAP and the branch but didn't join Barisan. But he never said a bad thing about Raja."[32] Words now meant little. With the battle joined on merger, it was not words but deeds which would decide, as he said, "who is on which side of the thin red line".[33]

The Barisan's forays left the PAP in shambles. Lee Siew Choh had cause to gloat: "The PAP under Lee Kuan Yew was a mere shell. Hardly anything was left."[34] As the PAP ploughed on despite its gaping wounds, the pro-communists inflicted fresh injuries through the People's Association and the Works Brigade. Raja and the PAP leaders did not see that coming: These were mass organisations which the PAP had designed to reach out to the ground. Instead, these organisations had been infiltrated by the pro-communists and become their tool.

Both the PAP assemblyman in charge of the Works Brigade, Wong Soon Fong, and PM Lee's own parliamentary secretary, Chan Sun Wing, in charge of the People's Association, turned out to be with the communists. Lee related later: "We thought we had non-Communists in charge. We were wrong. They thought that the Communists were in the winning side, so they went with the Communists."[35] Years later, Raja also confessed that, up to that point, he had not realised the full extent of the communist penetration and organisational power.

Things would get considerably worse. The Barisan worked up the Chinese-educated students in the Chinese schools and inflamed all possible grievances on the ground. At the same time, Chin Siong and his unions stirred up the workers and sparked a rash of industrial strikes. Militants of the Works Brigade held street protests. Staff from the People's Association went on strike. Student activists from the Chinese middle schools accused the government of endangering Chinese education, boycotted examinations, and picketed in schools and outside the Ministry of Education. As the political agitation intensified, Singapore wobbled in a state of instability, the preconditions of mass action.

The heat on the PAP leaders was scorching. Every day, they had to contend with some mischief or other, confront distortions, fend off character assassinations. Even as they fought to stave off a political explosion, they had to deal with the blow that one more union, one more branch, one more activist, had switched sides. No respite seemed in sight.

The pressure-cooker politics left the PAP leaders drained both emotionally and physically. It was apparent they were approaching exhaustion and collapse. At his lowest point, Lee Kuan Yew was overcome by an acute sense of dejection. As he surveyed the devastation visited by the Barisan, Lee could not help but be seized by the utter hopelessness of it all. His spirits sank as he took in the disastrous position they were in.

In later years, Lee recalled his mood at this point: "My spirits were very low, because how could we fight them? We went into elections in 1959 with this party machinery and the cadres we had cultivated. Then they absconded and joined the other side and left us with very few. So with this paltry remnant, a minority, how the dickens were we to fight the next elections?"[36] Given the grave situation, even Goh was reduced to just staring at the ceiling fan. They felt battered, even brutalised, by the pro-communists.

The natural reaction in such circumstances was to hunker down and prepare for defeat. In that darkest hour, Raja did not allow the prevailing mood of impotence and gloom to overwhelm him. He looked at his doleful colleagues — and saw not a losing team, but a talented and capable one which represented Singapore's best hope for survival. They could win the fight against the communists.

Defying the overwhelming evidence pointing to the PAP's defeat, Raja radiated confidence as he told Lee: "Don't worry, Harry. To hell with it. We'll fight on."[37] Raja spoke with a deep sense of inner moral purpose, completely convinced of the rightness of their cause. They were not a gang of rulers acting out their own interests, but elected leaders fighting for the survival of a non-communist Singapore. With a ring of absolute conviction, he told Lee: "We must fight and we will win. We'll carry on and rebuild."[38]

With his indomitable fighting spirit, Raja fortified the morale of Lee and his colleagues and charged them up. It was a galvanising moment that transformed the mood of the PAP from despondency to defiance, and changed the trajectory of the battle. Raja gave him, Lee said, the heart to go on fighting. As Lee recalled, "when everything looked bleak and we were in the depths of despair, Raja roared like a lion".[39]

His roar proved not only fearsome, but also steady and strong. Almost every day for three years, from 1961 to 1963, the pro-communists berated and denounced the PAP at mass rallies and in the Chinese language press. They used confusion tactics and worked to erode the people's faith in the PAP leaders. Lee recalled: "At times I felt weary rebutting their accusations, but Raja was tireless."[40]

Raja showed his mettle as he hurtled into battle, firing one salvo after another. Hunched over his Remington typewriter, with his ubiquitous cigarette jutting from his lips, he hit the keys with the rat-a-tat-tat of a machine gun, his quick, darting mind marked by the repeated triumphant ping! of the carriage return. With great gusto, he attacked each and every one of their points. Lee recalled: "They reviled the PAP as turncoats and renegades who had sold out the people; Raja answered in terms as pungent, rebutting and debunking them. He put his pamphleting skills to work, and his robustness stiffened everybody's morale."

In his assault, Raja used vivid language: He called the Barisan Sosialis, among other things, "Barisan Communists". He branded them "bar-room Lenins" with the "mental agility of trained parrots".[41] He quoted several passages from Lenin's writings to show that the Barisan was deliberately instigating strikes and creating distress among workers to carry out communist aims. His Lenin-quoting tactic so irritated the Barisan leaders that one of them, Bani, called Raja "the Fascist who wants to teach me to be a better Communist".[42]

Raja's bare-knuckled attacks and tactics would probably seem overly aggressive to the ears of today's voters, but, in the context of the times, they were the strong stuff needed to break the overpowering communist air of invincibility and mass influence. Many of the PAP assemblymen and supporters were fearful of the ruthlessness of the communists. Even Minister for Law and Labour Kenny Byrne, the burly leader who was so courageous in attacking the British, was timorous before the communists and had suggested cooperating with them.[43]

Raja's statements confronting Barisan's ideology and countering their attacks were a tonic to the morale of those who had resisted Barisan's overtures to defect. One of them, Chan Chee Seng, read the arguments put out by both sides and drew sustenance from the fact that Raja's were more persuasive.[44] Raja's words and attitude made people feel braver in his presence.

He kept on top of the state of play in the Chinese press with the help of translators. One of them was Jek Yuen Thong, who was inspired by Raja's role as the strategist in the fight against the pro-communists. "He was directing us on what to do, how to reply in answer to articles. Whenever the Barisan Sosialis gave a statement attacking the PAP, he was the one who directed us on how to reply and what to say," Jek related.[45]

Raja's feisty spirit during this period left an indelible impression on his colleagues, especially the prime minister. By temperament a placid and soft-spoken man, Raja, by his own self-admission, was "not a person who thrives and lives by publicity". But he did not vacillate before his duty in the fight. "He was a tower of strength," said Lee, who would come to rely on Raja's resolve even more as the attacks intensified over the next two years.

Nothing was more illuminating about Raja at this time than his willingness to put himself in harm's way for the party and the country, and his determination to fight until the final hour. He showed that he had a tough inner core which could be relied upon. Lee observed: "He fought back ferociously, indefatigably, never losing much sleep on the consequences and penalties if we lost."[46]

During this period, Raja also gained a deeper respect for Lee. He saw how Lee, bruised and battered, fighting exhaustion and despair, rose from the ashes phoenix-like with determination to lead the PAP into battle. He also saw how Lee gave his all every single day and how he took the hits without flinching. Raja said later: "He had physical and moral courage."

Despite the appalling pressures, Raja found Lee ready to look realities in the face, however unpleasant, and to deal with the problems objectively. This was a prized leadership quality in Raja's book. By way of contrast, he liked to quote a Chinese sage who said that there were 36 ways of tackling a problem, and the best of these was to run away from it.

Studying Lee's moods during his low moments, Raja again realised that Lee's hard composure was on the surface. He had seen Lee at his most vulnerable, at his most emotional, and recognised that Lee's cross was a heavy and punishing one. It was a cross that Raja would help to bear.

In retrospect, it is clear that he enjoyed a unique relationship with Lee, one which was not easily replicated with the others. Their close bond was sealed as they went through the traumatic battles together and found in each other a courageous and trustworthy friend. Lee said of Raja later: "I cannot count the thousands of hours we spent together over the years, discussing our doubts, our fears and our hopes. Whatever the outcome of an issue we had to resolve, whether it ended in an advance or a setback, we got to know better each other's biases and strengths. We learned to complement each other. Most of all, we trusted each other. He was the older man, but he had an optimistic streak that was infectious."[47]

Together with Goh and Toh, they worked as a close-knit team. Among them, Lee was the master strategist. As Goh recalled, there were several occasions when all seemed lost. "There appeared no answer to the terrifying dominance of the Communist open front organisations in full cry. Yet he (Lee) would come out with some devilish stratagem to spring upon the enemy and confound them."[48]

During this harrowing period, the team displayed an ability to adjust at lightning speed to new, unpredictable events. They showed resilience and a capacity to learn from mistakes as they rebounded from their multiple defeats on various fronts. Their ability to press forward, particularly when viewed against the efforts of their more powerful adversaries, owed much to an emotional strength and their brotherhood forged in the crucible of hardship and defeat.

All the external pressures drove Raja deeper into his own ideological motivation to create a new future — back into his core belief that the fate of the country was not predetermined by the stars, but decided by the force of ideas and human will.

His guiding philosophy was distilled in a statement he made in his later years: "The only thing you can be certain about in this otherwise uncertain world is that the past is unchangeable, the present will disappear in a moment but there will always be a tomorrow to be shaped as you wish." He added: "You can make the tomorrow you want, provided you have the wisdom, the guts and the will to struggle for it."[49]

It was this belief in the human spirit and in the malleability of the future that drove him to seek to loosen the vice-grip of communalism on people's minds. It was this same belief that now spurred him to struggle for the survival of the PAP and its vision for Singapore, against the full arsenal of the communists.

Out of his introspective study of mankind and nations throughout history, Raja understood that the fate of a nation was often determined by how its people responded to crisis. "In a crisis, the weak spend their time wailing and nursing both serious and trivial pains. Others become scavengers feeding on people's misery and discontent in the belief that that is the road to salvation. But the strong wipe away their tears and get down to the grim business of wresting victory out of adversity."[50]

Raja was at his element in a crisis. This was an act of will. Yet another: They could make the tomorrow they wanted. That tomorrow, in Raja's secular bible, hinged on the single issue of merger with Malaya. Convinced of this, he became the chief protagonist in expounding the case for merger in the newspapers, in public talks, and in private discussions, in an effort to deliver more allies and supporters to the PAP's side. He drove the government's "Merger and Malaysia Campaign" as chairman of its committee — a position rich in irony given the MCP's earlier designs on him to lead its anti-merger faction.

As he led the propaganda offensive against the Barisan, he quickly became a target of hate, after Lee and Goh. The pro-communists considered Raja an enemy because, as Lee said, "he was too much of a political protagonist. He was our ideologue. Every argument they put up, he spent time demolishing on radio and television".[51]

Even his political foes could not help but be impressed. Fong Swee Suan said years later: "I admire him. He never had any wavering from the PAP. When it came to defending the stand on merger, he would do whatever within legal means. He was very loyal to the party, very outspoken, very straightforward." Ruthless as well? Fong replied: "Not ruthless. I prefer to use the word 'straightforward'. You know what he meant and where you stood with him."[52]

The PAP's determination to achieve merger did not go unnoticed. The Australian High Commission in Singapore reported to Canberra that Lee and his cabinet colleagues were driven by conviction and were "wholly committed to the Herculean task of ensuring a future for Singapore through merger with the Federation".[53] It added the sharp observation that, "were they primarily interested in the retention of power, they could have compromised with the left-wing on this issue".

Certainly, in all his days in politics, Raja demonstrated no personal ambition towards power. This trait remained very much in evidence all his 28 years in politics. Echoing the views of many familiar with Raja's character, Marshall said: "He had unique qualities, that man, and absolutely no political ambition except for his party."[54] Unlike several other Old Guard leaders who were reluctant to retire from politics, Raja was ready to give way to new blood and return to the life of an ordinary man in 1988. When looking back on the PAP's achievements, Raja preferred to speak in terms of the collective "we", rather than the personal pronoun "I". As many who knew him said, he was an innately humble man.

Raja had also learnt, from studying the fate of other societies, that the most able clutch of politicians could not prevail against the communists without an outstanding leader at the forefront. Recognising this, Raja had all along been diligent in building up the public image of Lee Kuan Yew as a strong leader. This was often at the expense of his own image. As a result, few took the full measure of the man. Yet in retrospect, it is clear that Raja had unique qualities, which during this perilous period helped to keep Lee and the PAP in power. Arguably, without his intellectual input and talent during these critical years, the government would have been less resilient than it was. Without him, it would have found it harder to outwit and out-debate its opponents, and might very well have lost the argument for merger.

Raja fought the battle for merger on various fronts at once: the Barisan Sosialis in Singapore, the socialist parties in the Federation and the Borneo territories, and the Malays in the Federation. At home, for the merger campaign, Raja orchestrated the biggest and most elaborate publicity exercise of the government, stretching from late 1960 to the national referendum on 1 September 1962. This period was one of the most hectic in his life. As Lee described the situation then, "it was a hothouse, being hammered every day".[55]

Raja marshalled all the resources of his Culture Ministry to win the people's consent for merger, as his ministry put it dramatically, "in the face of the most vicious campaign of opposition that had ever been launched by any Communist party in Southeast Asia".[56] In this effort, he made full use of radio, and a year later, the television when it was launched. He thought up the campaign slogan "Malaysia as sure as the sun must rise" and erected 10 giant neon signs to scream the words. All mail was also franked with it.

The campaign began with a series of 12 broadcast talks by the prime minister over *Radio Singapore*, in which Lee explained the issues at stake, the motivations and methods of the communists, and the battle ahead. Lee set out to prove that Barisan, SATU and Partai Rakyat were communist front organisations, and exposed the key people involved, such as Lim Chin Siong, Fong Swee Suan and James Puthucheary. Raja's ministry published the prime minister's radio talks, aired from 13 September to 9 October 1961, in four languages in the book, *The Battle for Merger*.

Meanwhile, the Barisan leaders, such as Siew Choh, continued to deny they were communists or pro-communists. To pin them down, Raja issued them an open invitation: They would be given air time on radio if they would talk about "Why we reject Communism" and "Why we think Communism unsuitable for Singapore". "If any Member of the Barisan Sosialis can say that publicly — come out anywhere. Write in any newspaper, talk over the radio, 'why I reject Communism,' then we will believe him." None took up his offer.

Instead, they took to the streets. On 29 November, as the debate on merger continued to rage in the Assembly, Lee Khoon Choy, now parliamentary secretary to Education, was blocked by 200 Chinese middle school students picketing outside his Education Ministry office, preventing him from attending the Assembly. In a quick-witted move, Raja stood up to immediately introduce a motion for the House to call on the police to ensure that those responsible were dealt with according to the law.

As if with a wave of the magic wand, the students suddenly dispersed outside the Education Ministry and vanished, demonstrating once again the direct link between the Barisan members in the Assembly and the militant students at the picketing line.

During this time, the Barisan leaders found many things annoying about Raja — his mocking interjections, his quick and often wicked attacks, his dogged persistence, his emphatic style. Even his pointing finger was a source of irritation. Indeed, Bani found Raja's pointing finger so distressing that he rose to protest — yet again — that Raja pointed his finger "too often at Members of the Barisan Sosialis". Raja's riposte: "I shall take great care not to intimidate Members opposite with my finger. If they are the stuff of which revolutionaries are made, they should not be too easily intimidated, for after all, it is a very, very small finger that I am pointing."

Besides Raja's offending finger, Barisan was also agitated that he was reaching out across the causeway to other socialist parties in the Federation. This interfered with the Barisan's plans to form its own anti-merger alliance among the socialists and communists in the region. The Barisan had charged that the PAP was turning right-wing. A left-wing government could not risk working with a right-wing government in the Federation. This was an argument that resonated among the disaffected socialists in both Singapore and Malaya.

The PAP was trapped in a political pincer. On the right stood the Federation's right-wing government and its Malay-based system. On its left loomed the communists and radical socialists.

Raja negotiated the treacherous terrain by advancing the view that merger would make it constitutionally feasible for political parties in Singapore to join forces with political parties holding similar socialist views in the Federation. This way, the PAP could influence the course of events throughout Malaysia.

As he wrote in *Petir* in its 22 August 1961 issue, the PAP did not fear merger, even if it involved working with a right-wing government, because it considered that the non-communist, socialist struggle it had set itself to achieve was, in the context of the Malayan historical situation, a long-term struggle.[57]

In an attempt to block the Barisan's advance in the Federation, Raja visited Kuala Lumpur to refresh his ties with his socialist and newspaper contacts. One of them was the editor of the Malay-language newspaper *Utusan Melayu*, Said Zahari, whom he had known since his *Singapore Standard* days. Raja knew that Said Zahari was sympathetic towards the Barisan and sought to convey his anxiety over its dangerous direction.

According to Said Zahari, Raja tried to persuade him that Chin Siong was a Chinese chauvinist. They spent hours chatting in his *Utusan* office, before adjourning for lunch at a Muslim Indian restaurant. Said Zahari wrote in his memoirs: "Raja left KL, obviously disappointed, because I had not bought his Chinese chauvinistic depiction of Chin Siong."[58]

In all probability, Raja was more dismayed than disappointed, his worst fears confirmed. It would be made public later that the Special Branch had listed Said Zahari as a communist. He was linked to A.M. Azahari, leader of the Partai Rakyat Brunei, the anti-merger rebel who mounted a revolt in Brunei in December 1962. Said Zahari, who became the president of Partai Rakyat Singapura, was said to have introduced Azahari to Barisan leaders such as Chin Siong and Puthucheary.

Raja's efforts to seek the support of socialists in the Federation gave the Barisan added cause to hurl more abuse at him. In the

Assembly, Bani said that Raja's attempts to split the Malay and Chinese members of the socialist movement in Malaya failed because "they were able to see through the PAP's mischievous and bankrupt propaganda line".

Undaunted, Raja continued his attempts to woo socialists in Malaya to support merger. On 27 January 1962, knowing full well that they would face a tough crowd, Raja and Devan Nair turned up at the Malayan Socialist Conference in Kuala Lumpur to present the PAP's working paper on merger. Among its key points were that "the true Socialist approach should be based on a realistic appraisal of social and political forces at work in this region", and that the task of socialists was not to halt Malaysia, "but to shape it in such a way as to ensure the growth and victory of Malaysian socialism".[59]

The two PAP leaders arrived forewarned that pro-communist elements inspired by the Barisan were planning to convert the conference, attended by some 300 socialists, into a forum for communist propaganda against Malaysia and merger. Right on cue, the PAP's working paper was thrown out on the first day, without either of them being heard.

When Nair and Raja insisted on being heard, in the name of freedom of speech, the chairman ordered them to sit down. The pair then collected their papers, while Raja shouted: "This is a Communist-dominated conference and not a meeting of Socialists." Amidst shouts and boos from the gallery, the PAP leaders strode towards the exit. Raja then bowed to the chair and said: "Thank you. Thank you very much. We will have nothing to do with a Communist-controlled meeting." Shouts of "get out" and "go back to Singapore" rang out from the gallery, accompanied by a chorus of whistling and booing.

Refusing to be cowed, Raja struck a picture of defiance as he called a press conference that day itself. He declared they would not return to the conference until the credentials of the delegates were examined. He knew there were communists in the conference who wanted to wreck Malaysia. He said: "In Singapore, the Communists have been exposed and they are frustrated. They are looking for new grounds. If the people try hard, they will outwit the Communists but if they fail, they will be swallowed up. The Communists are making very serious attempts to subvert the socialists in Malaya and the Malaysian region."[60]

He charged that the new turn was the result of the Partai Komunis Indonesia (PKI) resolution to sabotage Malaysia. On 30 December 1961, PKI, the third largest communist party in the world, and its secretary-general D.N. Aidit had condemned the formation of Malaysia as a British neo-colonialist ploy. At the Legislative Assembly later, Raja was vehement in denouncing the Barisan Sosialis as "PKI stooges" for toeing its line.

Raja's sharp rhetoric during the merger campaign, punctuated by his constantly jabbing finger, put the PAP's political adversaries on the defensive. Siew Choh accused Raja of employing the "usual blah-blah threats and intimidation".[61] Bani accused Raja of having "Fascist tendencies".[62] Another Barisan assemblyman Low Por Tuck called Raja "the henchman of the Prime Minister", prompting Raja to ask, tongue in cheek, if it was a term of abuse or endearment.[63] His eyes fastened on merger, Raja continued to charge forward even as he bore the brunt of the Barisan's jeers.

18

Wooing North Borneo

Raja pored over the map of the imagined Malaysia as a suitor might gaze at the photograph of his intended beloved. These days, he could think of little else but Malaysia. He traced its contours. The island of Borneo lies to the east of Singapore. The southern section of the island, Kalimantan, was part of Sukarno's Indonesia. Above it sat the states of Sarawak, Brunei, and Sabah — the three North Borneo territories invited to give up their colonial status to join Malaya and Singapore in matrimony to form the union of Malaysia. But as in love, nothing was certain.

Raja was concerned about the reluctance shown by the North Borneo territories to the Malaysia plan. These territories, covered mostly in jungle, were fearful of being subjected to the control of Malaya, which they regarded as a foreign power. Relatively backward in their development, they were particularly apprehensive that their people — especially their indigenous groups — would be subjugated by Malay dominance under the pro-Malay government in Kuala Lumpur. Their suspicions posed more than a hitch: Should they refuse to join Malaysia, Singapore would be left in a lurch. For the Tunku would almost certainly walk away from merger with Singapore on its own.

Unwilling to submit Singapore's fate to the impersonal forces of history, Raja set out to woo North Borneo to embrace Malaysia. The effort would take all his ardour and ingenuity. His opportunity came when Singapore hosted the Commonwealth Parliamentary Association (CPA) on 21 July 1961. As leader of the Singapore delegation, he called on his reservoir of diplomatic charm to persuade the leaders in the Borneo territories to view Malaysia in a more positive light.

He spent much time with the likes of Donald Stephens, a Kadazan Eurasian proprietor and editor of the *Sabah Times* and founding leader of the newly-formed United National Kadazan Organisation (UNKO), and Ong Kee Hui, chairman of the Chinese-dominated Sarawak United People's Party (SUPP). He built a good rapport with them.

Behind closed doors, Raja assured them that Singapore would stand up to any unfair pressure on them, and that they would not be bulldozed into Malaysia. Giving an insight into Raja's proactive role, Lee Kuan Yew disclosed years later: "Raja was a crucial ideas man on how to bring Sabah and Sarawak in. He went out to meet them and assured them that they would not be marginalised, and he believed so."[1]

Raja proved a cogent voice. His reputation as a fearless newspaper columnist had preceded him. He was known for his outspoken anti-colonial views as well as for his strong stance against political dominance by any one racial group. Being a Jaffna Tamil — a minority within a minority — he also presented a more credible face than perhaps Lee in assuaging their fears and suspicions, a point which Lee himself acknowledged years later.

Lee said: "He was our best persuader for this group of native Sabahans and Sarawakians. A Chinese would not be convincing. He was more credible than me, because I am Chinese and joining up with Malaysia — they could do the sums. He was a minority from Singapore and would be a minority in Malaysia, so he carried more weight. And he was very affable. He had a friendly and persuasive style."[2] He was also gently persistent.

At the CPA conference proper, after Lee's opening speech urging the delegates to speak frankly on the question of Malaysia, Raja pressed for talks between representatives of the various countries to examine the problems as well as the benefits associated with forming Malaya.[3] Speaking on 22 July, Raja said he was convinced that, on balance, the benefits to be derived as members of Malaysia would far exceed the limitations on freedom of action which they would enjoy as independent units. "What is important is that Malaysia would not result in the domination of the weaker by the stronger partners or the economic ouster of one by the other," he stressed.

He argued for the territories to form Malaysia in one big step, rather than to opt for an interim period of self-governance first as preferred by some North Borneo leaders. Other than the danger of vested interests growing around the division over time, thus making reintegration harder later, there were also larger geostrategic considerations. They lived in an era of big states and superstates. He said: "This is an age of power politics played, for the most part, with small countries as pawns...The smaller and weaker the political unit, the less its capacity to resist." As part of a bigger unit, Malaysia, "we protect ourselves and consolidate our position by our collective strength", he told the delegates.[4]

This argument also applied to economic development. He spelt out the economic benefits of Malaysia, with its population of 10 million, and its larger area, forming a big economic bloc. "If we go our separate ways, sooner or later, individual units will come under the economic domination of some more powerful units," he warned.[5]

The North Borneo delegates were understandably more concerned about the benefits of Malaysia to their rural and tribal people, many of whom were hardly exposed to external developments. Their lack of political development under British rule was also stark, as was their lack of insight into the power politics in Southeast Asian and beyond.[6] Indeed, when the Tunku announced the Malaysia plan in May 1961, there were only two political parties in Sarawak, one in Brunei, and none in Sabah.[7]

In a renewed attempt to expand their political horizons during their meeting on 26 July, Raja highlighted the trend for even big countries in Europe, Asia, and Africa to find security and prosperity in larger regional groupings. He said: "The urge towards Malaysia is an instinctive groping for such regional security and prosperity…The urge towards Malaysia springs from a fear of loneliness in a hostile and warring world."

With these statements, he was also laying out his early fundamental thoughts on the international relations of small states. His was a classical realist approach, based on a hierarchical system led by the great powers, defined by their size and military capabilities. His world view was firmly grounded on the realities of the Hobbesian world. On such a conception, small states were vulnerable to manipulation, if not conquest, by bigger countries and could become, as he put it, "helpless prey to freebooting nations".[8]

After rounds of talks, the North Borneo leaders took up cautiously Raja's proposal for a conference to discuss the issue of forming Malaysia. Remarkably, Stephens, who was previously stoutly against joining Malaysia, said the time had come for serious thinking and "to sit down together and get down to what we want".[9] At the same time, he could not resist airing suspicions that Borneo might become a colony of the Federation. To this, Raja assured him that within the basic national structure of greater Malaysia, adjustments could be made to suit individual units. Constitutional lawyers were so agile that they could easily meet that demand. "All you have to do is say you want a suit of this shape, size or colour, and they would make it for you — just like a tailor," he said.[10]

With his eloquence and arguments, he managed to soothe somewhat the fears of the politicians from the North Borneo territories towards Malaysia. It was a quietly triumphant moment for Raja when, at the end of the CPA conference on 23 July, the Malaysia Solidarity Consultative Committee (MSCC) was formed to continue discussions on the Malaysia plan.

But for all his expressions of personal conviction, Raja would find that the merger talks between Singapore and Malaya, which started a month later on 23 August, were nothing like the tailor-sharp snip-snip affair that he had envisaged. Instead, they involved much patience, drink, poker, and golf with an aristocratic Tunku who refused to be rushed. As the Tunku's deputy, Abdul Razak, told the British, the Tunku was a man who acted largely out of intuition.[11] This intuition, when brought to bear on external affairs, could yield unpredictable results.

Raja had mixed views about the Tunku. On the one hand, he respected the Tunku for his tolerance and moderate stance on racial and religious issues. In a tribute to the Tunku written on 3 February 1963, before merger with Malaysia, Raja considered the Tunku a source of strength to the cause of Malayan nationalism, contrasting him to the "many second-rate and third-rate Malay leaders in the Federation who, having neither the strength of character or intellect to offer the people anything worthwhile, are openly and recklessly pandering to Malay chauvinism".[12] He noted that, in an age of ideological leadership and revolutionary violence, the Tunku offered "no coherent and complex ideology for his followers to annotate and elaborate into a grand political philosophy". Instead, he was guided by "an earthy common sense" with a philosophic attitude to life, which bred in him a tolerance for other views.[13]

On the other hand, on a more personal level, he could not help but find the Tunku's decision-making process something of a mystery. An intellectual, Raja dealt better with leaders who arrived at decisions through constant reading, historical understanding and rational discussion, than relying on unreliable human senses and superstitions.

The Tunku also had his own doubts about the likes of Raja. According to Yap Chin Kwee, who was the Tunku's political secretary at the time, the Malayan premier was uneasy with Raja's radical and socialist views, particularly when applied to Malaya. "Raja didn't understand Malay politics. He only understood MacDonald's politics," said Yap in a sarcastic reference to Raja's Western-acquired logic.[14]

Yap's allusion to Malcolm MacDonald, who was Britain's Commissioner-General of Southeast Asia, was ironic. The idea of a broader confederation incorporating Malaya, Singapore, Sarawak, and North Borneo was, in fact, originally owed as far back as the early 1950s to MacDonald.[15] It was highly likely that, over the years, the British had intimated to the Tunku the idea of a larger Malaysian federation involving the Borneo states.[16] However, the idea never got off the ground. Now in 1961, spurred by the changed political landscape, the concept of Malaysia was brought down to the practical politics with the Tunku's announcement on 27 May. The nagging question on Raja's mind was: This time, would it be brought to fruition?

The prospects for Malaysia bobbed up and down, like a boat tied short to the dock, with the ebb and flow of the merger negotiations between Singapore and the Federation, and of the sentiments of the North Borneo territories. The tides were real; the sense that the boat was safe to sail was an illusion.

Raja could sense the political undercurrents as he was involved intimately with the merger negotiations at each stage. While the negotiations with Malaya were driven largely by Lee and Goh, they discussed the issues with Raja each step of the way. During this period, the three leaders functioned as a triumvirate on Malaysia, Lee revealed. "Keng Swee would look after the economic side. Raja would look after the racial and political side. I got to balance everything to get it through," he disclosed.[17] Between the three of them, they decided the key strategies.

Their deliberations were also carried over to the cabinet meetings. After each meeting with the Malayan leaders, notes would also be circulated to the cabinet and discussed under "Any Other Business". In this way, the other cabinet ministers were also kept informed and understood the public line to be taken. Lee said: "Raja would give his opinion. It was important that we listened to him and what was the explanation to the public. He was in charge of explaining it to the public."[18]

Raja works a piling machine to officially start the construction of the National Theatre at King George V Park, 26 March 1962. When completed, the building was iconic. *(SPH)*

The National Theatre launches the first-ever Southeast Asia cultural festival. 8 August 1963. *(NAS)*

Raja (fourth from right) persuades chief delegates from the North Borneo territories to join Malaysia, 1962. *(NAS)*

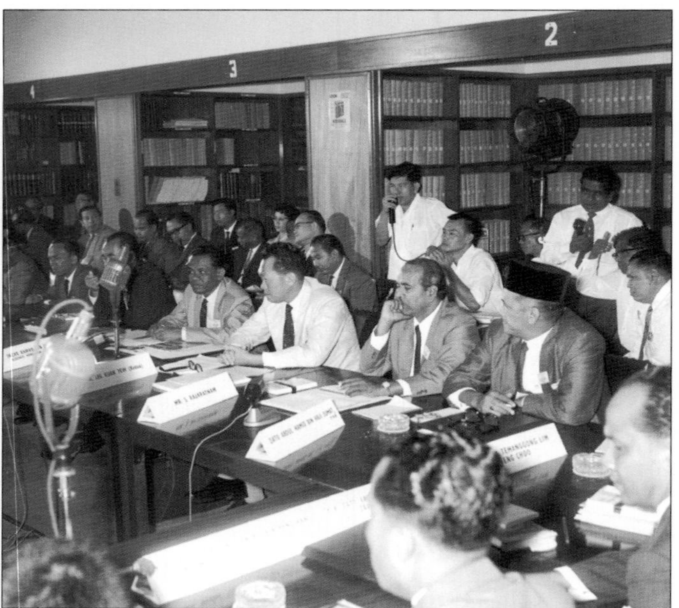

Raja and Lee Kuan Yew at the signing of the "Memorandum for Malaysia" blueprint ceremony at the Singapore Assembly House. Others involved: Yeo Cheng Hoe (Sarawak), Mustapha bin Dato Harun (North Borneo), Pengiran Ali bin Pengiran Haji Mohd Daud (Brunei), Mohd Khir Johari (Malaya) and Donald Stephens (Sabah), 3 February 1962. *(SPH)*

Left Lee Kuan Yew and Raja prepare to debate with opposition members Lee Siew Choh and David Marshall at a radio forum on merger, 16 August 1962. *(SPH)*

Below Lee and Raja meet the press at the Singapore airport after their merger talks with the Tunku in Kuala Lumpur, 21 June 1963. *(SPH)*

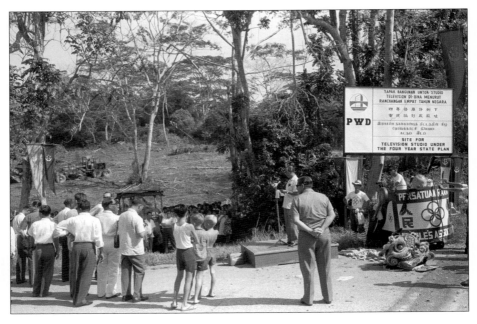

Raja announces plans to build the new *Television Singapura* studio site at Caldecott hill, 8 June 1963. *(NAS)*

Above The first person appearing on the screen at the launch of *Television Singapura* was Raja, 15 February 1963. *(SPH)*

Left Thousands throng the opening of *Television Singapura* at the Victoria Theatre. *(SPH)*

Raja, Piroska and Education Minister Yong Nyuk Lin at a Thaipusam festival, 7 February 1963. *(NAS)*

Raja chats with the Hongkong stars who came for the Southeast Asia cultural festival, 6 August 1963. *(NAS)*

Raja and Toh Chin Chye at a multicultural exhibition during the Malaysia Solidarity Consultative Committee meeting in Singapore, February 1962. *(NAS)*

Cultural diplomacy in Malaya: Raja eats with the Singapore "goodwill cultural troupe" in Kuala Lumpur, 22 April 1963. *(NAS)*

And meets performers backstage in Kuala Lumpur, 23 April 1963. *(NAS)*

Lee Kuan Yew, accompanied by Raja, inspects the guard-of-honour on Malaysia Solidarity Day, 31 August 1963. *(NAS)*

Despite the uncertainty ahead, the two leaders project confidence at the celebrations at the Padang. *(NAS)*

Lee Kuan Yew and Raja on a constituency tour of Kampong Glam, Rochore and Crawford, 20 July 1963. *(NAS)*

Above Raja and Lee with the Malaysian Prime Minister, Tunku Abdul Rahman, 18 August 1964. *(SPH)*

Left Dream come true: Celebrating merger at City Hall, 16 September 1963. *(NAS)*

Perhaps most significant was Raja's involvement in the momentous three-day talks with the Tunku in September 1961 in Kuala Lumpur. In the first round of talks on 23 August during which broad principles were discussed, Singapore was represented by Lee and Goh. But for this following meeting in September, Lee took Raja along. Besides Lee, the Tunku and Raja, also present at the September meeting were the Malayan deputy premier, Razak, and the permanent secretary of the Malayan Foreign Ministry, Ghazali Shafie.[19]

The much-awaited discussions between the two sides took place over hours of eating, drinking, and rounds of golf. Lee found Raja a solid and steady person to have at the negotiating table. He would be bland even if he opposed a point. "He would smile and put it in a non-combative way," said Lee.[20] He was also patient. As Raja did not play golf, he sat on the verandah to smoke a cigarette and ponder the political state of play, as Lee and the Tunku hit golf balls on the course.

On 14 September, their discussions culminated with an "in principle" agreement on the basis for merger. This agreement marked a crucial milestone in the negotiations and gave a powerful impetus towards merger. The principles were spelt out in the White Paper, which laid out the heads of agreements between both countries and was debated in the Assembly in late 1961. Lee would tell the Assembly on 30 July 1963: "The three of us — the Minister for Culture, the Minister for Finance and I — brought the wrath of the Communists on us because we went up there (Kuala Lumpur), played golf, talked over dinner and lunch. They hated us more than others because we forged this thing."[21]

The basis of the deal was that Singapore should have 15 seats in the Federal Parliament — a proportionately smaller representation than it could claim on a population basis. In return, Singapore would join the Federation with rights to determine its own affairs, except on defence, external affairs, and internal security. Singapore would have control over its labour and education policies. As for citizenship, while Singapore citizens could have common status under the Federation, they were not allowed to vote or participate in the Federal elections.

As soon as these terms were announced, the Barisan ripped into them and accused the PAP leaders of selling out Singapore by agreeing to be second-class citizens. This criticism gained strength as it coursed through the ranks of the Chinese-educated and was re-echoed in the unions, coffee shops, and schools.

Not a single day passed by without an exchange of fire between the Barisan and the PAP. Most exhausting were the marathon debates in the Assembly, with sessions ending well past midnight. Two months were spent on the White Paper on merger alone, after it was introduced on 20 November 1961.

Siew Choh spoke for 7½ hours, detailing his objections to merger. Raja's rebuttal on 22 November was relatively more succinct — 2½ hours. Dwelling on Siew Choh's condition for merger — automatic federal citizenship — Raja said that this would be rejected by the Federation or the 11 states within it because that would mean granting more favourable terms to Singapore than were granted to their own citizens.

In addition, there would also be resistance on political grounds. In a sober statement, he said: "Any solution, however fine and reasonable it might sound in theory, which leads the Malays to believe, however wrongly, that it is an attempt to bend them to the will of another community, is bound to fail, certainly to lead to disaster. Similarly, any measure which excites the communal fears of the Chinese and Indians is also doomed to failure." While communal fears and suspicions might be based on "prejudices and illusions", he said, "unfortunately, they are there and it is the duty of any practical politician to take these unjustified fears, prejudices and superstitions, into consideration".

Having taken part in the merger talks, Raja knew that, while not ideal terms, they were the best they could get from the Tunku for now. Determined to preserve Malay dominance in the Federation, the Tunku did not want the Chinese in Singapore to rock the political boat by giving them voting rights in the Federation. In the mainland, the Malays, who made up 55 per cent of Malaya's population, had been able to exert political dominance with an alliance which the dominant UMNO had forged with the Chinese political party MCA and the Indian party MIC.

Raja saw the merger deal as the best chance of political and economic survival for Singapore as a democratic, non-communist country. Taking the longer-term view, he envisaged the stage of limited merger as a transition phase for Singapore and the Federation before full merger took place. He believed that this transition phase was necessary to create mutual trust and confidence in the course of which their differences — inherited from 15 years of separation — would be resolved.

Although the very basis of the communal-based alliance offended his core principles, Raja was realistic in acknowledging that such a political arrangement was perhaps necessary in the Federation as long as large sections of the population continued to think along communal lines. This did not mean, however, that he accepted it or intended to perpetuate it upon merger, or even that he would countenance its intrusion into Singapore politics.

On the contrary, he made no pretence of his hopes that his ideas on equality for all, regardless of race, language, or religion, could spread throughout Malaysia and bring about change over the years.

As the merger talks continued, Raja was busy shuttling to and fro between the capitals of the North Borneo territories to help form a consensus on Malaysia. After the MSCC was formed, it met four times between August 1961 and February 1962. It culminated in a memorandum which largely set out the principles later adopted in the formation of Malaysia.

From the minutes of the meetings and the activities at the sidelines, it is apparent that Singapore drove much of the pace of the MSCC and crystallised the ideas for Malaysia. Its effectiveness owed much to the resourcefulness and persuasiveness of Raja, who led the Singapore delegation to the first MSCC meeting, and also of Lee, who led the delegation to the remaining three meetings.

At that first meeting in Jesselton on 24 August 1961, Singapore was represented by only two leaders — Raja and UMNO assemblyman Abdul Hamid bin Haji Jumat. They formed the tiniest delegation — the other countries sent three to six people each. Signalling Singapore's intent to punch above its weight, Raja announced to the press that his team would do all it could to make the merger plan a reality. He said: "The special interests of the people of Borneo will be fully safeguarded and it will be for the people themselves to decide what they want."[22]

As soon as the meeting opened, Raja revealed his guiding hand in the election of the committee's chairman. Raja, who had been working hard to build a consensus on the choice, proposed Donald Stephens. This was seconded by the other Singapore delegate, Abdul Hamid. There were no other nominations.

In carrying out his role, Stephens came under constant criticism from the other Borneo leaders, as noted by Sabah academic James Ongkili, "for oscillating from being anti-Malaysia to becoming pro-Malaysia in the second half of 1961".[23]

During the discussions, which sometimes inevitably turned inward-looking, Raja's great value was his ability to see the larger picture and to keep the delegates' eyes fastened as far as possible on their common external threats. He sought to impress upon them that, for nearly a century, the Malaysian territories had been administered as a single political and economic unit by the British. When the British pulled out, a vacuum would be created. "We must find some way of ensuring that the central administration is carried on. If we do not do it, someone else will do it for us. Once we leave a vacuum, a vacuum must be filled. If we are not prepared to do it ourselves, sooner or later someone else will follow on as each of the countries disintegrates," he warned.

He highlighted the dangers of "atomisation" — "the breaking up of individual tribal units" — if there was no central political and economic coordination. This was what happened in Africa and many other newly-independent countries, he pointed out. In the same vein, he continued to urge the Borneo states not to pursue the line of "independence first before Malaysia". He warned that such a stance would ensure the Balkanisation of Malaysia for a long time and invite intervention and interference of outside forces that would like to bring these territories under their sphere of influence.

These were not idle musings. The meetings were taking place against a backdrop of mounting tension and instability in the region. The progress of the Malaysia negotiations, with a target date set for 31 August 1963, had driven the Philippines and Indonesia into vigorous opposition. The Indonesians had their vision of *Melayu Raya* (Greater Malay Nation), a greater Malay world of which Indonesia — and not Malaya — reigned over the cultural and political centre. As for the Philippines, it claimed Sabah as part of the territory of the former sultan of Sulu. Later, opposition also came from Brunei. Its powerful Partai Rakyat Brunei dreamed of reviving the ancient glory of Brunei as the centre of a united Borneo.

It was hard not to listen to Raja when he spoke on international politics. He spoke knowledgeably and with authority. To many, he became by default the foreign affairs specialist of Singapore, the visionary strategist who interpreted the shifting balance of power in the region and beyond, the occasional diplomat who intervened in mediating disputes and the ambassador — both inspiring and controversial — of the idea of a common Malaysian heritage and culture.

He was less sure-footed when it came to the shape of the political system that was to come in Malaysia. While he sought to assure the North Borneo delegates that their legitimate special and local interests could be accommodated, he could give no satisfying answer on the dominant political ideology for Malaysia. He could only urge them to put aside their specific political ideologies: "Do not think of Malaysia in terms of unity between governments, unity between political parties, but as an attempt to unite people who are basically alike, who are the same racially, culturally and in every respect."[24] Within Malaysia, there would be a free play of political forces, "ideological and otherwise", he believed.

This presumption, which he repeated openly in the run-up to merger, was never challenged or corrected by the Federation leaders, leading him to pursue it with greater vigour and confidence at each reiteration of the theme. It was a presumption which would be tested upon merger, and found, to his consternation, to be built on quicksand.

Despite his valiant efforts to address the concerns of the North Borneo delegates towards Malaysia, the first meeting failed to make much headway. Many of the fears expressed by the North Borneo leaders — such as of becoming a second-class state of "a colony of Malaya" — could only be addressed in concert with the Malayan leaders. The absence of a representative from the oil-rich sultanate, Brunei, had also dampened the mood. Brunei, disinclined to share its oil wealth, would send only observers to the remaining three meetings of the MSCC, and would eventually pull out of the Malaysia plan.

Raja returned to Singapore with the heavy knowledge that there were still many daunting obstacles to overcome. To pave the way for the second MSCC talks in Kuching, he hit on the idea of using culture and sports to propagate the idea of Malaysia among the ordinary people in the Borneo territories. And so began the plans to send a cultural mission on a nine-day tour of the Borneo territories. In his original conception to the cabinet, Raja included a touring football team to play matches in the main towns of the Borneo territories.[25] In the end, the football team did not materialise, but the cultural tour did, to great fanfare.

Raja told the media that the 48-member goodwill mission, which set off on 24 April 1962, was to show that Singapore was not merely a trading centre interested only in making money. It would also showcase Singapore's efforts to develop its various cultures and to integrate them into a united people, while highlighting the shared cultural heritage of the Malaysian territories.[26] Asked by reporters if the mission was to help make Malaysia attractive to the people of Borneo, Raja found it prudent to deny the connection. He was no duffer: To make explicit such a political link would have doomed the mission to failure.

The value of the cultural exchanges came precisely from the fact that it represented and connected people, rather than necessarily governments or policy positions. To underscore this message, all proceeds from its indoor shows, with tickets costing from $1 to $3, were donated to charities in the three Borneo territories, including the Sarawak Society for the Blind, the North Borneo Anti-Tuberculosis Association, and the Blind Training School.

The $40,000 tour to Kuching, Brunei and Jesselton was Singapore's most ambitious exercise yet in cultural diplomacy. It would have been hard to pull off had it not been for Raja's political stature and his peerless ability to straddle both culture and foreign affairs.

Meanwhile, over the next few months, the Federation also hosted the North Borneo leaders on a series of visits to Malaya, where they had friendly discussions with the Tunku and other Federation leaders. These exchanges served to soften their attitude towards Malaysia.

For the second MSCC meeting, Raja worked closely with his Malayan friend, Ghazali Shafie, who was adviser to the Malayan delegation and permanent secretary of the Malayan Foreign Ministry. On 16 December 1961, Ghazali, who was travelling to Kuching on a Malayan air force plane, stopped in Singapore to pick Raja up. En route, they discussed the speeches for the delegation and made amendments. Ghazali, who was to later become the Malaysian foreign minister, had a high regard for Raja. "The man was so knowledgeable on almost anything that I used to look forward to meeting with him," said Ghazali.[27]

The second meeting continued to tax Raja's diplomatic skills. It was obvious that some North Borneo members, particularly from the

Sarawak United People's Party (SUPP), were seeking to delay the process. It was an open secret that the SUPP was by then already subverted by the communist clandestine organisation. At the end of the discussions on 20 December, Raja helped Ghazali to prepare a communiqué of the meeting. Together, they made sure that issues such as internal security had prominence. Ghazali related: "Rajaratnam and I agreed that we should not distribute the draft to the delegations that night because we did not want the Sarawak delegation to consult their bosses who might think of some mischievous ideas to undo the consensus."[28]

This instructive episode highlighted the distrust between the delegates which continued to bedevil the process. At the last moment, before the North Borneo delegates left Kuching, they made an unsuccessful attempt to amend the communiqué without consulting Stephens, the chairman of the committee, or any representative from Singapore or Malaya.[29]

Despite the attendant problems, at a press conference at the Singapore airport on their return from Kuching, Lee and Raja struck a confident note that Malaysia was inevitable. As Raja said, "all the delegations, including the Singapore delegation, ended up reiterating that they accept Malaysia in principle, and nobody can stop it".

Alarmed by the momentum towards Malaysia, the communists intensified their efforts to do just that — to stop it. Their most flagrant display of defiance came on 30 December 1961 when Partai Komunis Indonesia (PKI) condemned the formation of Malaysia as a British neo-colonialist plot.

The external developments cast a shadow over the MSCC's third consultative meeting in Kuala Lumpur, held from 6–8 January 1962. In a concentrated effort to win the confidence of the North Borneo delegates, Raja deliberately looked out for their interests wherever possible. This came out strong and clear at a radio forum which featured Raja (Singapore), Donald Stephens (Sabah), Ong Kee Hui (Sarawak), and Ong Yoke Lin (Malaya).

The bulk of the forum, recorded by *Radio Malaya*, grappled with the eligibility of local people for entry into the federal civil service. The stress given to this topic by the North Borneo leaders reflected the deep-seated fears of their non-Malay indigenous people about possible racial discrimination in the public service on joining Malaysia. These fears were shared by the non-Malays in Singapore.

Probably speaking beyond his political remit, Raja pronounced that the federal service must not be thought of purely as an avenue for advancement for the inhabitants of any particular state, but should be a two-way traffic. People from all states, including Borneo, would have the right to enter the federal civil service. At the same time, the federal civil service could be a pipe leading to the various states, especially those less advanced, to help in their development.[30] Whether Raja's reply soothed the fears of the North Borneo people on this issue was open to doubt, but it assured their leaders that here was a Singapore leader who was willing to speak up for their interests.

More significantly, at a deeper level, Raja's remarks were immensely revealing. They reflected his understanding of Malaysia as representing the creation of an entirely new sovereign state wherein the many diverse peoples might find equal opportunities. Little did he suspect that such a conception was never shared by the Tunku, who, as demonstrated when he expelled Singapore unilaterally in 1965, saw Malaysia as simply Singapore and the Borneo states being wedded to the Federation wherein Malays enjoyed special rights and privileges.[31] In retrospect, the Malaysia which Raja and his PAP colleagues envisioned and were working towards was completely incompatible with that of the Tunku's.

Singapore's vision of Malaysia was brought into sharp relief at the fourth and final meeting of the MSCC in Singapore from 1 to 3 February 1962. This was Raja's turf and he used it to maximum political advantage.

In conjunction with the MSCC meeting, he organised Malaysia Week to help people imagine what Malaysia was capable of, how the different cultures would live together in harmony as one people, and the course of actions they could take that would make the dream real. Through photo exhibitions and cultural shows, Raja sought to expose their minds to the idea of a common heritage. He was proudest of the cultural extravaganza, *Malam Malaysia* (Malaysia Night), which saw cultural troupes from all over Malaysia, including aboriginal groups, performing together for the first time.

To encapsulate what the people shared in common, his ministry also published a booklet, *Malaysian Heritage*, produced in four languages and distributed in Singapore and the Malaysian territories. No one who attended the events or read the publication could have any doubt that Raja's vision was for a Malaysian Malaysia, even before the slogan was coined in 1964.

On the face of it, the publication looked innocuous enough, with ritual messages from the leaders of the delegations, but on closer scrutiny, it made for profound and controversial reading. It published an article by Raja, headlined "Political Case for Malaysia", which summarised his key arguments for Malaysia.

On the problems posed by their differences in terms of race, he expounded his consistent view that "this is not a material difference but a psychological one". He sought to dispel their fears that their cultures and languages would wither away. Boldly, he wrote: "I suggest that race is not a factor in the building of the Malaysian nation." In a familiar theme, he maintained that "it is a prejudice and an attitude which can be removed by rational analysis and by making ourselves aware that race and religion in a modern state are not things which should divide the people".

He highlighted the need for Malaysia to generate sentiments of kinship, of sharing a common destiny and a sense of belonging. "What we should be aware of is that we have a common political objective, a sense of common destiny and the will to create a common history," he wrote.

To illustrate their common past, another article in the publication, titled "Our Cultural Heritage", traced the cultural evolution of the people in the territories dating back to 40,000 BC, and cited recent advances in archaeological research. It highlighted that Malaya and Borneo were both influenced by the Hoabinhian culture characterised by the use of heavy axe-like tools flaked from stone pebbles, which flourished between 8000 BC and 2000 BC. They were believed to be ancestors of present-day Melanesians.

Its most striking assertion was that the Malays were a migrant group at one point in history, around 1500 BC. They were mainly riverine people. People from the north, from North Annam, came slightly later, bringing with them the Dongsan culture with the use of bronze — their pottery could be found in northern Malaya and Borneo — followed by migrants in the Han period, who introduced the rice culture. The Indian traders probably came to Malaya from AD 200, and to Sarawak as early as the seventh century AD. It was a fascinating article, containing nuggets of information mined from various historical, archaeological and anthropological texts.

With his historical understanding of the diverse ancestry of the people in Malaysia, it is little wonder that Raja was not inclined to submit intellectually to the idea that the Malays were the original "sons of the soil" and, therefore, entitled to a special protected position as was the practice in the Federation. In the Federation, the Malays have special rights and privileges in the public services, commerce, and land holding.

In Singapore, its Constitution recognised "the special position of the Malays" and made it the government's responsibility to "protect, safeguard, support, and promote their political, educational, religions, economic, social and cultural interests and the Malay language". But unlike the Malayan Constitution, it did not provide for special rights and privileges. Raja took some satisfaction in this. In a radio talk on 27 February 1960, he highlighted: "Our Constitution and our political struggle have, by and large, followed a non-communal course."

For Raja, the socialist principles of justice and equality had long been the leitmotif of his ideology. This was reflected in his categorical reply when the Singapore UMNO assemblyman, Mohd Ali, asked him in 1961 to appoint a Malay as the assistant head of the newly established Dewan Bahasa dan Kebudayaan Kebangsaan (Institute of National Language and Culture). Raja was uncompromising: "The Government does not make appointments in terms of whether a person is a Malay, a Chinese or an Indian." The person would be selected based on his qualifications and experience.[32]

He also did not believe that a political leader should be elected based on his race, nor should he see his role as a leader of his particular ethnic community. As he told his own Ceylonese community years later, a member of a minority community should not aspire to be the political leader of his community. Instead, he should project himself as a national leader. "It is one thing taking pride in one's communal culture and heritage and quite another cultivating the communal syndrome — the belief that communal parties and communal leaders representing slightly over 20 per cent of the population can do great things for their people."

He spelt out the logical conclusion if the minority groups cultivated a communal syndrome: It is an invitation to, and permission for, the majority community to go in for communal politics, too. "Once the minorities do this, they would relieve the majority community of the responsibility of being equally responsible for the welfare of the minority communities as they are for the majority community," he said. But while he appealed to their logic with political arithmetic, building a non-communal Singapore was for him, first and foremost, a matter of principle.

Those who sought his assistance knew Raja for his principled approach, as well as for his compassion and generosity. S. M. Vasagar, who headed the Sri Senpaga Vinayagar Temple and the Ceylon Sports Club at various periods, recalled approaching Raja many times for help. To his appeals, Raja's stock response was: "I will help you as long as it is within the law".[33] And he did. Later in the 1980s, when Vasagar asked him for funds to expand the temple at Ceylon Road, Raja gave a personal donation of $50,000. For Raja, who vacillated between agnosticism and atheism, this was not a matter of communal ties, but of social service and friendship. Vasagar knew this: "If anybody reaches out to him, he will help."

Many others from the different races were similarly touched by his sense of service. His anxious letters to Goh Keng Swee in the 1960s record his attempts to find jobs in the public sector for his Chinese-educated volunteers who were out of work.

He was as conscientious in making appeals on behalf of his residents in Kampong Glam, distinctive for its Muslim quarter. One of those he put pressure on was S.R. Nathan, who was a seaman's welfare officer in the early 1960s. Nathan recalled: "There were Malay writers out of work. He sent me notes to ask me to find them jobs and assist as a social worker."[34] M. Subramaniam, a grassroots leader who helped Raja at his weekly Meet-the-People sessions, observed: "Raja had a natural tendency to help, when the requests were reasonable."[35] He applied himself diligently without regard to their race or religion, relentless in his quest to build a non-communal society.

His conviction was based not only on his universal socialist ideals, but also on his specific understanding of the historical development of the different races in Malaya, gained from a careful study into the subject since the 1940s. It offered an index to his fundamental concepts of human nature and the ideal society. It includes a belief in the rationality of man and a conviction to change society. His treasure trove of ideas, collected with care over the years, was the inexhaustible source from which he drew the essential blocks on which his ideal society was built. While he was influenced by thinkers as diverse as Plato, Rabindranath Tagore, Marx, John Stuart Mill and Bertrand Russell, the truth was that Raja was a true eclectic, drawing from aspects of their teachings which appealed to his own sense of beauty, justice, goodness, and reason.

To no small degree, his conviction also owed its origins to his personal experiences and observations from growing up as a sensitive boy in Seremban, and maturing into a rebellious man in London. He knew how alienated the Indians and Jaffna Tamils in the rubber plantations in Seremban felt in the country which they toiled and lived; he also knew how discriminated the "coloured" people felt in the streets of London. He had felt the injustice to the very marrow of his being. While Cedric Dover's book, *Half-Caste*, gave him a convincing argument to reject the idea of racial superiority, Hitler's Aryanism and the horrors it unleashed in the Second World War gave him a reason to hate it. The racial savagery that continued to tear apart many countries, including his once peaceful birthplace Ceylon, impelled him to stand guard against it.

Raja was one of the rare conviction politicians who genuinely believed in the creation of a race-blind society, based on justice and equality, and in the ability of a good government to create such a good society. If his credo, so progressive in the 1950s and 60s in this part of the world, seems more convincing today, it flows from his unalterable faith that has since been encapsulated in the Singapore national pledge. In the first half of the 1960s, however, such a conviction would become a source of personal torment for him as it ran headlong into the fiercest contradictions inherent in Malaysia.

Whatever his misgivings, in the run-up to merger, he portrayed such ideological and political differences as matters that could be resolved after Malaysia was formed. Given that the PAP's political survival hung on merger, the overriding imperative for him and his colleagues was to realise Malaysia against the ferocious efforts of the communists to foil it.

It took Raja months of patient shuttle diplomacy to help ease the anxieties of the Borneo leaders about joining Malaysia, and to stiffen the resolve of the MSCC against its naysayers. His assertive role was dramatised at the final MSCC meeting in Singapore when he rallied the committee to take a united stand against the PKI resolution, which he said was in effect an outside power calling on groups or individuals within Malaysia to break up Malaysia. This was an open challenge, he said.

He further argued that the communiqué should make it clear that the MSCC tolerated no intervention from outside, and that any differences in the MSCC could be resolved amongst themselves. The North Borneo delegates were cautious, worried about offending the Indonesian government. Raja refused to budge. Supporting his proposal, Lee Kuan Yew pointed out that there had been a deliberate and concerted conspiracy by the communists to create trouble everywhere, with mischief-making and lies. Their challenge must be met. The chairman, Stephens, wondered whether Raja's proposal would be in line with the aims of the MSCC, while several other delegates questioned the need to make a stand against the Indonesian communists. In the end, Khir Johari from Malaya broke the impasse by suggesting that the Singapore delegation put up a draft. Raja duly drafted the joint communiqué.

Looking back years later, Raja believed that it was "because of Singapore's presence, that people like Donald Stephens, Ong Kee Hui and a few others, came in". Without Singapore, the two states would have continued to resist the idea of merger with Malaya. "They were quite convinced that, so long as Singapore was there, they could be a counter-balance to any Malay assertion," Raja observed.

Again, in his own accounts, he hardly dwelled on his own specific role in the MSCC. But Lee, who was equally energetic in getting North Borneo on board, saw Raja's role as crucial. Raja was pivotal in the discussions to make sure that "the terms would become palatable and saleable, acceptable to the people in North Borneo", said Lee.[36]

It was a hard slog. As foreign correspondent Denis Warner, noted in 1965 just after separation, "it took two years to sell the concept of Malaysia in Sabah and Sarawak." "Without Singapore," it added, "it is improbable that either would have agreed to join."[37]

The intense period of regional diplomacy leading up to merger cemented the relationship between the PAP leaders, notably Lee and Raja, with the key politicians from North Borneo. They would continue to work closely after merger, and would later join forces to form the controversial Malaysian Solidarity Convention to push for the Singapore-inspired vision of Malaysian Malaysia in 1964.

It is necessary to remember Raja's tireless efforts in coaxing the Sarawak and Sabah leaders into joining Singapore to merge with Malaya, to appreciate how stricken he would later be by guilt and grief when faced with Singapore's expulsion from Malaysia in 1965. It would represent to him not only the abandonment of his dreams, but also of his friends in Sabah and Sarawak who had trusted him and his assurances on Malaysia.

As the date for merger drew nearer, the pro-communist trade unions stirred a witch's brew of industrial mischief to inflict maximum economic damage on the island. In 1962, some 165,000 man days were lost in strikes, compared with 26,500 in 1959 in Singapore. The economic disruption and violence which accompanied some strikes forced the government to draw a line between genuine labour disputes and cynical political agitation.

Keeping his political antennae on high alert, Raja reread carefully Lenin's teachings to trade unions. One of the books he pored over was *Lenin on Trade Unions and Revolution* from which he would quote copiously in the Legislative Assembly later. He came away convinced that the Barisan was using communist agitating techniques to instil revolutionary fervour and hatred among the workers for the state and all instruments associated with the authority of the state, particularly the police.

From their actions, the union leaders showed little interest in settling the disputes. Instead, they sought to prolong the workers' grievances to precipitate clashes between strikers and the police. To expose their tactics, Raja was relentless in his efforts to confront the Barisan with the evidence in and outside the Assembly.

He met the press time and again to explain how the government was dealing with the strikes. He also issued swift press statements to correct distortions by the pro-communist unions. His task was fraught with pitfalls. In one press conference on 1 November 1961, he dealt with the strikers who refused to meet with the minister for labour and commissioner for labour to settle the matter peacefully, but instead resorted to violence and intimidation. Raja told the press: "They have assaulted a number of people, pelted stones on vehicles, attacked nightsoil wagons, with the express purpose of trying to bring the essential services in Singapore to a standstill."[38] Asked by the press about the violence, he replied that the government was quite capable of taking a firm stand in protecting the security and health of the people. At the same time, he said: "We are still prepared to settle the strike peacefully." It was a tense period as the pro-communist unions tried to push the government to fall on its own sword. It had to be careful how it pushed back and how hard. He knew, from bitter experience, that the Barisan would seize every opportunity to accuse the PAP of being "anti-worker".

Right on cue, Lee Siew Choh rose in the Legislative Assembly to accuse the PAP of oppressing workers and of being anti-worker by using police to deal with strikers. He also charged that the PAP was trying to dominate the trade union movement in Singapore.

Referring to his former PAP days, Siew Choh said: "We have been in the PAP for quite some time, and we have learnt the maze of thinking that the triumvirate of the PAP indulged in." He added, in case anyone was left in doubt: "The Prime Minister, the Minister for Finance and the Minister for Culture — the triumvirate of the PAP."[39] In identifying the "triumvirate" of the PAP, Siew Choh was astute in recognising the political dominance of the three leaders during this period. As a political opponent, Siew Choh never underestimated Raja's powerful role alongside Lee and Goh, having experienced its impact and been the worse for wear for it.

In the midst of the potentially explosive situation, Lee and Goh intensified their attempts to finalise the negotiations with Malaya on the financial arrangements and common market. Meanwhile, Raja was busy holding the propaganda fort in Singapore. He scoured every statement from the Barisan for the false note, the double talk, the dangerous line. Every time there was an attack, Raja was out there with a rejoinder and a retort.

He scoffed at the Barisan when it claimed in April 1962 that it had seen through its "powerful binoculars" a "huge rocket base" on the tiny island of Pulau Tekong, to be used to launch "atomic warheads" against China and Russia. In a mocking rebuttal, Raja said that the only military installation on the island was a 400-yard rifle range, and it was difficult to see "even with the aid of powerful binoculars" how it was possible to shoot atomic missiles from a rifle range to Russia and China. He lashed out: "In fabricating this science fiction plot, not only has the Barisan Sosialis displayed the usual disregard for truth but they have also spiced their falsehood with racialist mischief." In claiming that the non-existent missiles were to be used against China, "the intention clearly is to play on the feelings of the Chinese population", he charged.[40]

Coupled with the hard bargaining at the merger talks, the distinctively rambunctious politics on the island made for an increasingly agitated Tunku, who was already prone to regard Singapore as a "headache".[41] In a fit of frustration, the Tunku, in a meeting with UMNO members in Singapore in March, said the Federation looked on Singapore as a little China where many followed what China did and where the extremists wanted a communist regime. He warned that, if Singapore rejected merger and the extremists caused trouble and bloodshed, the Federation would close the Causeway.[42]

Several days later, at a dinner in Singapore hosted by the Singapore Chinese Chamber of Commerce, the Tunku further warned that the outcome of a complete break between Singapore and the Federation of Malaya might be war and bloodshed. War could follow if an isolated Singapore sought solace in the company of powers unfriendly to the Federation, and "we, on the other hand, would be compelled to approach the Western powers for help".[43]

These sudden pronouncements alarmed Raja and the other PAP leaders. Their sense of the innate vulnerability of Singapore was registered acutely during this period. As Raja had articulated earlier, the conventional view was that small independent states, lacking economic and military muscles, would find it hard to survive in a hostile environment. For Singapore, this was reinforced by the island's dependency on Malaya for drinking water.

Singaporeans were also confused and frightened as to what the Tunku's warnings might portend. As *The Straits Times* noted in its editorial, closing the Causeway colourfully described the completely separate development, economic and political, that must follow rejection by Singapore of the Malaysia concept. The newspaper added: "This may be what some opponents of the merger want, a withering of the vine that in the end, would produce the revolutionary explosion which economic depression would engender."[44]

In an effort to calm the ground, Raja, in a statement issued as director of the PAP's political bureau, said that the Causeway would "never be closed" because the people here would ensure that Singapore remained a "source of strength rather than of weakness" to the Federation. Blaming the Barisan Sosialis for the Tunku's warning, he said "it would be fatal if the leader of the Federation formulated policy on the basis that the Barisan Sosialis represented the spirit and temper of the people of Singapore".

In vivid language which expressed his revulsion, he described the Barisan as a "pimple on the face of Singapore". "Once it has burst and the pus has been exposed, Singapore would be free of such a pimple. No party which has been born of betrayal, which sustains itself on political deceit and falsehood, and stoops to exploiting racial fears, can ever have the support of the people of Singapore," he asserted.

He added that the PAP did not believe that the bulk of the people of Singapore were China-minded or that they constituted a little China. To believe that was to believe in a course of despair. "While we cannot hope to transform all the races of Malaya into Malayans overnight, we are convinced with, imagination and determination, we can achieve our goal of welding the various communities into a Malayan nation," he said.

It was an extremely dicey situation. In this highly charged atmosphere, he had to constantly rush around to put out one fire after another. The next crisis was sparked off by the Barisan's racially tinged arguments against merger — that it was a sell-out of Singapore Chinese to Malay feudalists, that Singapore citizens not born in Singapore would be repatriated to India and China, and that shops would be handed over to Malays.

Furious at this dangerous line, Raja said firmly: "Anyone who makes a case against merger in communal or racial terms should be dismissed as a race monger. If racialist propaganda is met with open contempt and hostility, then the chances are that the racialist will abandon this mischievous and dangerous propaganda line."[45]

Meanwhile, the pro-communists were busy igniting the explosive combination of Chinese language, education and culture. They fuelled Chinese chauvinist sentiments among the Chinese-educated at the Nanyang University (Nantah) and fanned anger against the government by portraying it as being anti-Chinese language and education. Lee and the Chinese-educated PAP MPs worked on overdrive to counter their charges.

Unexpectedly, at the height of the tensions, it fell on the Jaffna Tamil minister to speak directly to the Nanyang University. Unlike the Chinese PAP MPs who might perhaps have had to worry about protecting their "Chinese" credentials, Raja was completely unencumbered by such inhibitions.

On 30 March 1962, he appeared at the university's third convocation ceremony in its Jurong campus as acting minister for education to offer an official olive branch. The education minister, Yong Nyuk Lin, was on leave. Raja was not put off by the cold crowd or the pouring rain. Or even that he, and the government's overtures, would very likely be rejected.

Having been fully briefed by Lee and others, Raja was aware that he was dealing with a political time bomb: Nantah, opened in 1956, established itself as a bastion of Chinese education, culture, and language with the financial muscle of Chinese businessmen, such as Tan Lark Sye who became the chairman of Nanyang's executive council. Three years later, however, the Prescott Commission gave a poor report on its academic standards. Despite the grants offered by the government to reform itself, Nantah had spurned its extended hand. Instead, it persisted with its China-oriented curriculum and became a hive of pro-communist activity. This created a stand-off with the government.

At its convocation ceremony in 1962, Raja spoke plainly to the university in a conciliatory tone. As he stood soaking wet, drenched by the downpour, Raja urged the 385 graduates to take their place in the building of a Malayan society and to change their mindset towards the PAP government. It was necessary to realise that Nantah was no longer operating in a social and political environment hostile to its development. It was wrong, he said, to continue to harbour the illusion that the Nantah had to wage an anti-government battle. As long as the problem of Nantah was viewed primarily as a political struggle between government and those who believed themselves to be the exclusive guardians of the Chinese university, "then not only are we working on false premises, but we are also hindering the rapid progress of Nantah", he said.

Stressing the increasing need of Singapore for more highly educated and technically qualified people, Raja said that the problem of Nantah was primarily educational, and not political. "A university is essentially a house of learning and our contributions to the development of the university will be judged ultimately not by the slogans and platitudes we uttered, but by the extent to which we made it a house of learning," he said.[46]

The real problem for Nantah, as for other universities in Malaya, was how best they could supply as quickly as possible highly educated and skilled people which the society needed. "The business of a good university is to help carry forward the educational revolution that is so vital for the modernization and enrichment of our society." Raja assured Nantah that the government wanted to make it an integral part of the Malayan university education. The government had offered parity of treatment with the University of Malaya in Singapore. "The offer is still open to Nantah." Also open was the offer of government aid, he added.

Tan Lark Sye chose to ignore Raja's plea. Instead, in his speech, he dwelt on the theme that Nanyang could "go on forever" on its own, with or without outside aid. *The Straits Times* captured the situation when it commented, in its editorial on 4 April 1962, how "the acting Minister for Education, Mr Rajaratnam, was at pains to emphasise the Government's readiness to give Nanyang full parity treatment with the University of Malaya, coupling with this assurance the anxious plea that Nanyang's problems should be examined strictly in terms of education". Noting that there was no response from Tan Lark Sye, the newspaper concluded: "The gap has widened, and it is not hard to see who must bear the responsibility."[47]

For years, the Nanyang University would continue to be hostile towards the PAP government and its calls for reform. In a vengeful mood, many of its graduates would campaign actively for the Barisan and take part as its candidates in the next elections in September 1963. Lending his influence and funds to their campaign, Tan would appeal to the Chinese to support the Nantah graduates who stood on the Barisan ticket. This would prove his undoing.

After the elections, his citizenship would be revoked for collaborating with the "anti-national group of Communists in Nanyang University", who were former agitators of the communist-controlled Singapore Chinese Middle School Students Union. It would eventually take more than a decade before Nantah gave up its emotive role as a symbol of Chinese language, education and culture, and established itself as a national institute of learning.

These draining battles, coupled by the often irrational politics around him, made Raja crave for some sense and coherence in the world. While he was often ready with a smile and a witty quip, he was not by temperament a carefree man. His nature possessed a dimension of depth, and a corresponding sense of tragic possibilities which often kept him awake at night. Like most inhabitants of richly-ornamented inner worlds, he was given to periods of agonised brooding.

Since he joined politics and experienced it in the raw, he had searched for an approach to politics that would be based more on rational thinking than on unpredictable human passions and prejudices. This obsessive quest led him to reflect on how man, through the ages, had evolved various methods to deal with the problems and uncertainties that had confronted him. As was his wont, he put his musings down on paper. They were published in a two-part series in *Petir* in 1962.[48]

He observed that "international politics, in particular, is based on concepts that are neither rational nor reassuring for the safety of mankind". He was disdainful of the way political arguments had become a matter of finding facts to defend conclusions already reached. He argued for a more rigorous approach, which involved gathering facts systematically, scrutinising them, and verifying the conclusions by experience. He called this the "scientific approach".

The "scientific approach" differs from common sense in that "its method excludes, as far as is humanly possible, human likes and dislikes." He regarded the scientific approach as "the highest and most sophisticated form of human thinking".

In his analysis, a great deal of contemporary political thinking in Asia, Africa, Europe and America was a blend of what he called "the supernatural" and "the common-sense" approaches. His main thesis is that, until politics and economics — which remained at the supernatural and common sense level — are subjected to the scientific discipline, "we shall stumble from one political crisis to another and from one economic stupidity to another".

The supernatural approach regards man as the victim of a capricious world of gods, demons, spirits and witches, and other invisible forces. In this view, there is no question of man controlling events or changing the world. All he can hope to do is to placate these supernatural forces or win them to his side through such devices as prayer, sacrifice, magic rituals, charms, and witchcraft.

The common sense approach relies on the five senses of man — sight, sound, touch, smell, and taste. Common sense, while generally a reliable guide to knowledge and action, can sometimes mislead. When a man looks at a star, his common sense tells him that the star exists at that very moment. But the scientist will tell the man that he is seeing a star whose light might have taken a million or more years to reach the earth, and which might well have exploded into cosmic dust during that time.

Raja argued that the first two methods — supernatural and common sense — were unreliable and could lead to wrong conclusions. As an example, he cited the justification by the whites in Africa for apartheid — this was based on arguments such as the black African was a man of low and savage intelligence and prone to crime, which drew from the supernatural and common sense approaches to politics.

The most reliable method, he said, was the scientific method. The host of new social disciplines — such as sociology, anthropology, statistics, political geography, social psychology, and cultural anthropology — now made it possible to apply the scientific approach to politics, he propounded.

Although he doubted whether politics could be made into an exact science such as physics or astronomy, given the "unpredictable human wills and passions", he believed that a scientific approach could "purge politics of the irrational fears, superstitions, and ignorance on which a great deal of political actions are based". "A science of politics may not acquire the precision of astronomy but I believe that it will at least ensure that politics does not remain at the level of thinking which governs astrology and alchemy". He added: "After all, politics is basically a method of organising human society with a view to ensuring the happiness, security and prosperity of the individuals who comprise that society — whether that society embraces a nation or, as it must eventually, the whole of mankind." A scientific approach, he said, was simply a way of organising large groups of people efficiently for ends that will promote the happiness of all. He concluded: "That, surely, is an end worth striving for."

His reflection on a rational approach to politics took place against a backdrop of unprecedented ferment, with seismic political tremors shaking the very foundations of Singapore politics. The stresses and strains of the merger negotiations, often at the mercy of the leaders from the other states who, more often than not, subscribed to the "common sense" and "supernatural" approach to politics, bore down on him. The relentless pressures from the vicious battles with the Barisan taxed him considerably. He was often sleep-deprived and close to exhaustion. Despite his calm exterior, the toll on him, mentally and physically, was enormous.

On 9 May 1962, after playing his regular game of badminton, Raja collapsed. He had suffered a heart attack.[49] At the time, the prime minister was away on a six-week tour of Afro-Asian countries, mounting an international offensive to win support for Malaysia and to debunk the communists' distorted propaganda that Malaysia was neo-colonialist.

In a telegram on 19 May 1962, Gordon Jockel, the Australian high commissioner in Singapore reported to Canberra the shocking news: Raja was "fairly seriously ill" and had been warded in hospital where he was expected to stay for at least 10 weeks. "That, at any rate, is the first medical verdict. The Government is keeping this development secret for the time being."[50] On the typed telegram was a hastily written scribble in response to the news: Raja's absence would be a "real loss to Cabinet".[51]

19

The Malaysian Dream

Raja's heart problems kept him out of action for more than two months. The heart attack took him and Piroska by surprise. Prior to this, his most serious ailment was acute laryngitis. While recuperating in hospital, he was straining at the leash. Unable to stay quietly on the sidelines during this crucial period, he continued to roll out speeches, which he asked others to deliver in his stead.

One speech at the second anniversary of the Kampong Glam community centre was a scorching diatribe against "reckless and destructive trouble-makers" out to create suspicion and disunity among the various races. He accused them of engaging in "loud talk and irresponsible acts, including hooliganism". While he did not name them, it was clear he was referring to the pro-communists who continued to rage that the Chinese were being sold out to the Malays. He said: "These brainless men are but the tools of more ambitious politicians who, having failed to come to power by constitutional means, hope to come to power in the wake of racial violence."[1]

He called on the people to make sure that its multiracial harmony was maintained, and to make clear to the race-mongers that "we regard them with the aversion we feel for plague-carrying rats". The more the people expressed their contempt for race-mongers, the less inclined would they be to spread their "dangerous and stupid racialist propaganda", he insisted.

Clearly, his harrowing brush with mortality had not mellowed him. As soon as his doctors cleared him for active work in early August, he flung himself back into the last-ditch battle for merger with increased ferocity.

He resumed his attendance at the weekly cabinet meeting on 14 August 1962. The focus was on the referendum for merger on 1 September 1962, and into this campaign, he would concentrate all his energies. The period leading up to merger was a fundamental turning point in the political history of Singapore and marked a crucial milestone in Raja's maturation as a politician.

On that day, the electorate would be asked to choose between three types of merger. First was the one proposed by the PAP government, second, the Barisan Sosialis, and third, the Singapore People's Alliance. The three options were presented as: (A) the White Paper proposals, (B) complete and unconditional merger for Singapore as a state on equal basis with the other 11 states in accordance with the constitutional documents of the Federation of Malaya, and (C) merger on terms no less favourable than those given to the Borneo Territories.

The questions were crafted to present option A as the most attractive. Option B would lead to the disenfranchising of half of Singapore's adult population and the removal of Singapore's autonomy over education and labour, while the terms for option C were yet unconfirmed. There was no option provided to vote against merger, leading the Barisan to campaign for the casting of blank votes.

The referendum was a gamble for the government and for Singapore. The Federation leaders did not think a referendum was a good idea. Based on their own reports, the Federation leaders believed that the political and security situation in Singapore was deteriorating and that the PAP was losing its political grip. Ismail bin Dato Abdul Rahman, the Malayan minister for external affairs, for one, believed that merger would founder on the referendum unless the opposition was first broken up by arrests. The British were alive to the communist campaign against Malaysia, but maintained that it was not possible to carry out the arrests without Singapore's support.

From the start, the Federation had been pressing the British and Singapore governments to undertake wholesale arrests and banishments of the communists in Singapore before merger could take place. The Malayan leaders, especially the Tunku, had been most dissatisfied with the way the British and Singapore had handled the communists since the island received its new constitution in 1959, noted Philip Moore, the deputy UK commissioner in Singapore, in his despatch on 28 April 1962. The Tunku was convinced that communism called for "positive counter-action", rather than the "political manoeuvring" being practised by Lee in Singapore,[2] and pressed for Lim Chin Siong and his colleagues to be arrested before merger could take place.[3]

The truth was that neither Malaya nor Britain wanted to be seen to be initiating the repressive moves, even as they pressured Singapore to act. According to Ghazali Shafie, the permanent secretary of the ministry of external affairs in Malaya and the key official in charge of the merger details, Selkirk told him the British should not do anything which might appear repressive in the view of the British Parliament — and that any arrest in Singapore should be openly done by Lee Kuan Yew.[4]

By now shrewder and tougher politicians, Lee and his colleagues were not so foolish as to fall in easily with the demands. The PAP leaders were adamantly against repressive action until Malaysia was completely settled. They held firm to their view that any arrests at this point would only provide a rallying point to the Barisan against the Malaysia plan. The Barisan would then be able to claim to the people and the world at large that this was an attempt by the PAP to silence legitimate opposition, and stir the ground against the PAP government and merger.

Raja counted among those in the cabinet who urged Lee to hold firm with the Tunku on the issue of arrests, and to stick to their method of using political tactics and open confrontation. The Tunku was so exasperated with Lee's firm stand on this that, in a discussion on 13 March 1962, he said he would have nothing to do with Malaysia or Singapore. Lee's answer was that they would then have to see Singapore gradually routed by communism and eventually become a serious danger to the Federation.

For all his political posturing, however, Lee knew that he had fewer cards to play than the Tunku, and realised that it was important to keep relations with the Federation stable as far as possible for merger to take place. On the other hand, to secure merger from the Federation on stronger terms, the PAP leaders needed to be able to talk to the Tunku from a position of political strength, with the backing of the majority of the people in Singapore.

The merger negotiations between Singapore and the Federation on crucial points — common market and financial arrangements — remained outstanding. With so many crucial details yet to be ironed out, the PAP could not afford to be diminished as a political force in Singapore.

At the same time, Raja was highly nervous about racial violence breaking out in Singapore. As he confided in Bloodworth during this period, "in all probability, the communists would create the biggest possible trouble to prevent merger". "If their constitutional opposition to merger fails," he added, "then they would try to create chaos here so that either the Tunku withdraws in disgust or the British are forced to suspend the Constitution."[5] The result: There would be no government to carry on merger negotiations and the communists would be able to mount an anti-colonial campaign against the British. This would cause mayhem.

Raja also feared that any further delay in merger would lead to the Federation calling off the merger and cutting out Singapore as its principal trading port. That would spell disaster for the island.

It was against this complex backdrop of power politics and problems, often not obvious to the ordinary eye, that Raja launched his bellicose campaign to defeat the Barisan and those opposing merger. With pugnacious vigour, he set out to disabuse the notion, held by the Malayan leaders and fanned by the Barisan, that the PAP was a spent force. Along with the other PAP leaders, Raja intended to make sure, whether the Malayan leaders liked it or not, they had to deal with the PAP on the question of merger.

Back at work, Raja revved up the entire machinery in his ministry for the referendum. His campaign was geared towards building a sense of the inevitability of merger and an understanding of its advantages. He made no effort to conceal his goal of getting people to vote for option A, the PAP's proposals as approved by the Legislative Assembly in a White Paper.

In a meeting with his senior officials on 16 August 1962, he issued these instructions: Two sets of talks should be prepared urgently for the referendum, one for "propaganda", and the other for "instructional purposes". The first would be on the essence of the three options and exhorting people to vote for the first. He stressed that this was the White Paper proposals approved by the Legislative Assembly. The second would be done in consultation with the Elections Department and would be on the procedural aspect of voting.

Raja told his staff that "polemics should be avoided as this will be the business of political parties in the campaign". The three options and the advantages of the first would be presented in simple terms. He also said that it was important to counter the blank vote campaign of some of the opposition groups by emphasising to residents the necessity and responsibility to exercise their vote in the national interests, as well as their own interest.

By now a canny tactician, Raja also gave notice that it would be necessary to make new points as the campaign progressed, in the light of new developments, or to counter moves by the opposition. His was an open call to conduct government propaganda. His key staff did not flinch from it. They understood the political imperatives.

Over the years, through intelligent persuasion and constant interaction, Raja had won them over to his political views and instilled in them an urgent sense of mission.

It was a battle of survival for the country. He made them believe in the national cause for merger and in the menacing threat posed by the communists and the pro-communists. As Boon Yoon Chiang recalled: "One of the things Raja told us: You must always be prepared to defend what is right and what you believe in, against all odds."

Boon, an independent-minded journalist, understood where Raja was coming from. When Raja was a journalist, he could cavalierly write as he pleased, but once he became a government leader, he had the heavy responsibility of safeguarding the security and welfare of the people. Boon said: "He had to do what was necessary to make Singapore survive and work. To us, his ideas were sensible, given the environment we were in. I was never asked to do something I didn't want to."[6]

Of course, not all was sweetness and light. By now, Raja had learnt how insidious communist penetration could be, and took care that they did not infiltrate his Culture Ministry and undermine the merger campaign. He kept his radio broadcasters on a tight leash.

Raja put the government's public relations machine on full throttle with his mastery over the various forms of media, from photo, film and print to radio. He asked his ministry's film unit to produce an explanatory film to be shown in cinemas and through the film units. It should introduce people to the mechanics of voting, with a preference for the first alternative.

He also asked for six documentaries to be produced dealing with citizenship, and suggested that films on merger incorporate footage of PM Lee arriving at the Singapore airport from London on 8 August 1962, after the successful Malaysia talks. In the run-up to the referendum, the ministry's field section screened 747 film shows on merger and Malaysia.

Raja also instructed that the frequency of the multicultural *Aneka Ragam* concerts be stepped up before the referendum and asked whether they could be held at least every other day "in locations where there was maximum impact and where propaganda was most needed". In all, 10 *Aneka Ragam* shows were staged before Referendum Day, at which option A was put across through banners and skits. Raja also made sure that there was a concentration on jingles and slogans related directly to the referendum, and pressed for more slogans to exhort people to vote for the first option.

Radio took centre stage in Raja's propaganda master plan. In all, the campaign for merger involved 36 radio broadcasts in three languages. Anticipating the criticism that the PAP was suppressing the opposition's voices, Raja encouraged free and open discussion and debates with them over the radio, in newspapers, and in the last stages of the campaign, at public mass meetings. In this, Raja was acting in concert with Lee Kuan Yew, who had made the strategic decision to give the opposition maximum latitude.

This was a double-edged sword. It would give the opposition an opportunity to grandstand and sway the crowd, but it would also allow the PAP to nail down every lie and counter every argument. Raja revelled in such an atmosphere.

As part of their strategy to counter the pro-communists, Raja and Goh decided that Lee should put himself in the open to, as Lee described, "draw their fire and destroy their arguments by demonstrating how false they were, all big lies".[7]

To confront the arguments of their opponents openly, Raja arranged a series of three radio forums from 18 to 25 August on the issue of citizenship, which had emerged as the make-or-break point in the merger battle. Raja took part in all of them, together with either Lee or Goh, squaring off with two opposition leaders each time.

The format of the forum was designed to tease out differences; the leaders of each political party had to state their position to a question posed by the local media on the issue at hand. The debates were lively and robust. The radio forums gave Singaporeans a measure of the calibre and the trustworthiness of the leaders who sought to decide their future.

In the first radio forum, Raja appeared together with Lee, and two opposition leaders, Lee Siew Choh and David Marshall. In the forum, the prime minister showed why he was a top lawyer as he sliced open the opposition's arguments layer by layer with intellectual precision. Raja complemented Lee with his waspish wit and pointed jabs.

Zeroing in on the controversial citizenship issue, PM Lee pointed out that he had secured from the Tunku what the opposition wanted, that Singapore citizens would automatically become Malaysian citizens by the special agreement with the Federation. Dismissing the prime minister's assurance, Siew Choh assailed him again for "betraying the people" and continued his tirade of getting only "second class citizenship". Raja cut in to point out the need to distinguish those who were open to merger, and those who did not want merger at any cost — "whatever terms we give".

Raja recalled that when merger was first proposed, Lim Chin Siong had said it was impossible as there were two distinct governments, one left-wing and the other right-wing, pursuing different policies, especially regarding labour and education. "When we gave them merger with autonomy in education and labour, they switched their line and asked for Penang-and-Malacca type merger." Now given common citizenship, they said, no, it's a change in terminology. The plain fact was that Barisan did not want merger, full stop. Raja charged: "We can give them tomorrow complete citizenship — everybody becomes a Malaysian citizen, then they will go round saying: there you are, terrible, we have lost Singapore citizenship."

He picked up on the same theme at the next radio forum, broadcast on 20 August. Raja was joined by Goh Keng Swee and two opposition leaders, Lee Siew Choh again, and Ong Eng Guan.

In retrospect, from the viewpoint of political history, one of the most insightful points Raja made at this forum was on the political role that Singapore could play in Malaysia. This was in response to the opposition's criticism that Singapore would have no influence over Malaysia's policies, as it would have only 15 seats in the Central Legislative Assembly in Malaysia. To this, Raja retorted that it was not the number of seats that counted. Then came his startling comment: "In politics, it is political parties, principles, which control. So, if the PAP party can win elections throughout the Malaysian territories, then it can control the Central Legislative Assembly."

It might appear an audacious position, but to Raja, entirely reasonable. This was an issue that Raja had obviously thought through to its logical conclusion, perhaps more than others. Since the issue of merger was broached, he had been open and consistent about his intention to engage in the politics of the new Malaysia when it was formed, and his belief that this would be constitutional.

Probably without knowing it, Raja was touching on what was an acute fear of the Tunku — losing control over the Central Legislative. Mindful of this, the British had earlier assured the Malayan leader that, even after merger, the Tunku's position was fairly secure, and he was unlikely to find that more than eight of the 15 Singapore representatives in the Central Assembly would vote against him.[8]

Looking back years later, Raja did not think the issue was discussed explicitly between the two countries, but believed it was something understood. The Federation leaders appeared to have a different understanding — that Singapore was to stay out of Malaysian politics and mind its own business. Raja obviously did not share this understanding, even in 1962. With the advantage of hindsight, given such diametrically different starting points, the collision course between the Federation and Singapore was already set, even before Malaysia was born.

On 25 August, in the third and last radio forum before the referendum, Raja, together with Lee Kuan Yew, locked horns again with Marshall and Ong Eng Guan. Siew Choh, who was invited to take part, decided to stay away — a decision which Raja could not resist ridiculing almost *ad nauseam* later. Marshall proved a moving target as he vacillated throughout the course of the debate. When the Chinese-speaking vice-chairman of the Workers' Party subsequently contradicted

Marshall's stand in a Chinese newspaper report, Raja concluded that Marshall was not in control of his party.

At a PAP rally on August 31 at Fullerton Square, Raja told the audience that what Marshall said in English had been misinterpreted mischievously by his Chinese party leaders to the Chinese press, in an attempt to show how Marshall was being "taken for a ride by his party". Shortly after Raja said this at the rally, Marshall appeared dramatically, pipe and all. Raja wrote in a letter to *The Straits Times*: "This set up a medley of catcalls, whistles and boos. But by and large, these sounds were intended to encourage Marshall to get on to the platform."

In an exchange of letters between Raja and Marshall in *The Straits Times* following that incident, Marshall took issue with Raja's recollection of the event. Marshall said, among other things, that it was Raja who had called for him to come up the stage. Raja settled the argument by asking *Radio Singapore* to rebroadcast the portion being contested. "This will give the people an opportunity to judge whether Mr Marshall or the tape-recorder is reporting faithfully," said Raja, thanking Marshall for prompting this rebroadcast.[9]

In the end, Marshall was to discover that Raja was right — his party's vice-president Sum Chong Heng and secretary-general Chua Chin Kiat had indeed been twisting his position to the Chinese press, and the communists had captured the Workers' Party. This led to Marshall's resignation in January 1963. When Marshall stood for elections in September 1963 as an independent, the communists promptly withdrew their support, leading to Marshall's political downfall.

To the watchful Raja, Marshall's experience was yet another salutary lesson in the communists' skill in manipulation and causing confusion on the ground. If you were not alert, you would be used without your being aware of it and cast off at their convenience.

As he navigated the minefield of political traps, Raja became adept at the technique of using radio recordings and press photos to expose falsehoods and pin down the facts. They provided unassailable evidence to confront those who sought to contort the truth. The public could then be the judge.

The decision to use radio forums to engage the opposition turned out to be a masterstroke in the battle for the hearts and minds of the people. The broadcasts were reported in the mainstream print media the next day, with large portions of the debate reproduced almost verbatim. Raja rubbed in the unimpressive performance of the Barisan leaders and scoffed at the "Communists and their front men" for fearing the open encounter. He observed that they accepted the invitation to radio forums with alacrity at first. But the first encounter in which Lee Siew Choh took part was "such a disaster for the Communist cause that subsequent invitations to such forums were very reluctantly accepted, and then finally, consistently rejected", he said.[10]

It was a hectic campaign. Along with other PAP leaders, Raja had to speak at various rallies round the island, sometimes at several separate locations in one evening. Sobered by the shock defeat of the Hong Lim and Anson by-elections, Raja was now more circumspect in his predictions. Perhaps, the PAP could scrape through with 50 per cent of votes for it, and 40 for the opposition, he thought. He based his estimate on the PAP's performance in previous polls, which had hovered around the 51 to 53 per cent mark.

When the referendum results were announced on 1 September, a big smile lit up Raja's face. Tears of relief rushed into Lee's eyes. Over 71 per cent of the poll wanted merger on the lines of the PAP proposals, only 25 per cent cast blank votes. The Australian high commissioner in Singapore reported to Canberra in a cablegram three days later: "Realism and common sense of Chinese community as shown by comparatively small total blank votes, in spite of intense grassroots campaign by Barisan Sosialis is regarded as particularly gratifying."[11]

In a sudden shaft of insight, Raja realised that, "given time and the right approach, PAP could build itself up as a considerable force in Singapore politics". A photograph captured Raja's preoccupation in the immediate aftermath: Arms folded, he was peering intently at what the reporter standing next to him was scribbling in his notebook as Lee made his first public comments on the results. Raja knew that the battle for the hearts and minds of the people was far from over. Now that the PAP had the upper hand, he was not about to let slip the opportunity to poke a pin into the communists' once-terrifying image of invincibility and to deflate it.

He did so in a barrage of speeches and articles, constantly hailing the victory of the "democratic nationalist forces" over the "anti-national and pro-Communist forces" who opposed merger and Malaysia. The most important outcome of the referendum was that it shattered the myth built up by the pro-communists of irresistible mass support, he declared.[12] "This myth of the mass influence of the Communists was often used to neutralise the non-Communists with the threat that, if they openly opposed the Communists, then they would be dealt with when the Communists won the next general election," he said.

Raja observed that, with this myth destroyed, more people were prepared to stand up to the communists. "The power of Communist intimidation has been considerably weakened as a result of the exposure of this myth of Communist mass influence."[13] He clearly regarded the referendum not only as a political triumph, but also a psychological victory for the non-communists.

He proclaimed: "We are proud that we, of the non-Communist Left who, two years ago, when they deserted us, were in a difficult situation, who have been reviled by the Barisan Sosialis as feeble, vacillating and purposeless social democrats, have helped to break the Communist spell of invincibility. If for no other reasons, whatever happens to us, we shall be satisfied that we in the PAP have been able, for the first time in 30 years, to break the myth, the humbug that the Communists are invincible."[14]

So pumped up was he by this apparent breakthrough that he trumpeted it tirelessly until merger was in hand. He took the powerful message to the NTUC, which had for the past year been straining against the organised force of the pro-communist unions. At a rally, organised by the NTUC at the Victoria Memorial Hall, Raja told the unionists that the referendum victory showed that the pro-communists were "in fact dwarfs with feet of clay".[15]

While warning that the pro-communists might try to smash their solidarity, he declared that there was no doubt now that the NTUC would finally emerge victorious "because the NTUC is not a stooge of alien forces; because the NTUC is fighting for what is right and what is of benefit to the people of this country".

He gave Nair, the beleaguered general secretary, a pat on his back. After Raja spoke, union leaders from Afro-Asian countries, who were fraternal delegates at the NTUC conference, pledged their support to the NTUC in its fight for independence.[16] The rally was a great public display of Afro-Asian unity, and boosted the morale of the NTUC.

While he was giving such rah-rah speeches, he was psychologically preparing himself for another showdown with the communists and their supporters. In his public speeches, he often depicted the referendum as a "straight constitutional fight and trial of strength between the Communists and the democratic non-Communists".[17]

For portraying it as a polarised battle, some have later accused Raja of oversimplifying reality. Not all who opposed merger necessarily supported the communists. That might well be true for some, and Raja was too intelligent not to know this. But tactically, they were not the main target.

In the heat of the battle, from his vantage point in the frontline trenches, he could see that the key obstacle to merger was the communists and their front men, abetted by what he called "left-wing adventurers". Given this analysis, the strategic decision was to concentrate all the PAP's bombardment on these prime adversaries. The object was not to win the hard core over, but to neutralise their power. This strategy, if well executed, would also keep the Chinese chauvinists and others who opposed merger from straying into the communist camp.

The referendum campaign was an intense experience for Raja. He learnt the need to respond swiftly and forcefully to accusations. The high road may be honourable, but as he discovered, it did not necessarily lead to political enlightenment. More broadly, the referendum campaign taught Raja that he had to define his political opponents, and not allow them to define the debate. He was no longer a political innocent and did not pretend to assume the pose of one.

He studied the political terrain revealed by the referendum results and identified areas which needed reinforcements. In his analysis, most of those who had cast blank votes at the referendum came from the rural areas. He concluded that one key reason was that, unlike those in urban areas, people in the rural areas did not tune in to the radio or read newspapers.

Hence, they were not exposed to the open argument between the democratic forces and the communists. They were sitting ducks for communist propaganda, spread through their front organisations on the ground such as the Country People's Association and the Rural Dwellers' Association. As Raja observed, "the democratic case did not reach the ears of the rural people as widely as the Communist case."

In the Legislative Assembly, he goaded the Barisan by informing them blandly that, because of this, he would press on with his plans to have more radios and to install TV sets in rural areas. He declared that once this happened, "we can not only begin to nail down every Communist falsehood and rumour but bring home to the rural people the simple truth, that the democratic system can give them a better life".[18]

If Raja sounded belligerent to the point of being galling, it was intentional. All these years, with more menacing methods, the communists and pro-communists had tried to intimidate him, his colleagues and his supporters. They sought to destroy the PAP and very nearly succeeded. They were still trying. After the referendum, the Barisan had defiantly announced that its immediate aim was to overthrow the present PAP government in the next general elections and then win the election for Singapore's 15 seats in the Federal Parliament. This was just the sort of statement which would make Raja's blood boil.

As far as he was concerned, there was nothing inevitable about the survival of either Singapore or its democratic socialist system. He was attentive to the human element, to the difference that a single idea made in shaping history.

As he told the Publicity Club at a luncheon talk on 4 December 1962, the propaganda battle with the anti-democratic elements — communists, communalists, and demagogues — was going to last for a long time and "as far as this Government is concerned, it will ensure that the propaganda arm is as effectively strengthened as our economic, social and industrial sinews".

He added that, if the term "propaganda" had today become a term of abuse, "it is partly because some propagandists and propaganda have indulged in deceit, falsehood and insincerity". He argued: "Propaganda, by itself, is a neutral activity. It may be good or bad; it can be logical or illogical; it can stimulate people to a high level of intelligent behaviour or it can reduce people into a nation of moronic sheep."

Referring to the efforts to engage the opposition in debate over *Radio Singapore*, he said: "Our propaganda is democratic in that, unlike in totalitarian societies, it is not a one-sided monologue." He noted that the Barisan leaders turned up only for the first two sessions of the radio forums on the referendum. "By scooting from the Radio Singapore auditorium, the anti-democratic forces exposed their own lie that they were denied free speech." He said: "If at times, you find our political propaganda a little tiresome — and I admit sometimes it is — please remember that it is but a small price to pay in the defence of democracy."[19]

Younger English-educated people were sometimes put off by what they saw as Raja's cockiness, but the older voters were dazzled by his brilliance and courage. So were his colleagues. Lee observed: "The more you pressure him, the more you put the heat onto him, the more his faculties function. And he hammers away at his typewriter and fires back with gusto! And the communists can give you hell. And he gave them hell back. You know, it's like the band when you are going to battle. Your band collapses — no tune — and your soldiers get demoralised. So when your soldiers read the powerful reports, their spirits soar…Morale is three-quarters the battle."[20]

The Barisan found Raja's missives hard to counter. Dominic Puthucheary, who was the PAP assistant organising secretary before defecting in 1961 to become a leader of the Barisan and SATU, described Raja as a "very effective spin doctor", adept at coining phrases to caricature his opponents in a negative light. The Barisan sought to caricature him, too, belittling him as the "PM's henchman" and "Dr Goebbels" among other derogatory names, but, as Puthucheary complained, "Raja's advantage was his monopoly over the media".[21]

For all their efforts to rubbish Raja publicly as Lee's lackey, the Barisan leaders appeared more than aware of Raja's independence of thought and action. As Puthucheary said, "I don't think a man like Raja, with his independent mind, was a henchman for anybody. But Raja and Lee had a commonality of ideas".[22] In hindsight, Low Por Tuck, another PAP-turned-Barisan assemblyman, detected a strategy in Raja's tough posture — it was not only for the benefit of the Barisan, but also the wider public. Low added: "I think the important thing was that he had to show to Malaya and Indonesia the PAP's stand. It was a pressure for him."[23]

The British reported on 7 September 1962 that the decisive result of the referendum had materially changed the political situation in Singapore. "For the first time in 18 months, Lee Kuan Yew is again in a very strong position, and if he plays his card sensibly, he should certainly be able to hold Singapore until August 1963." The British observed that, by political cunning and resolution, Lee had revealed the weakness of the communist forces.

The Federation leaders did not share this view. Behind closed doors, the Tunku and his top advisers continued to profess a gloomy assessment of Lee's political strength and Singapore's security situation. The British reported that in their meeting on 14 September 1962, both Ghazali and Razak expressed their doubts to them as to whether Lee would last till February 1963.

Raja was no doubt aware of their bleak prognosis. Already, in the last year, there had been increasing signs that the Tunku no longer considered the PAP capable of staying in power. Indications of the Tunku's attitude were the decision the year before to start up the Alliance Party formally in Singapore, and more recently, the efforts of Tan Siew Sin, the Federation minister of commerce and industry and also president of MCA in the Federation, to build up the MCA in Singapore in direct competition to the PAP.[24] The MCA had a deep distrust of the PAP, fearful that the Singapore party would encroach on its Chinese base in Malaya. The distrust was mutual.

Amidst this shifting background of political rivalry, the PAP leaders had evidence to suspect that, if the Alliance government in the Federation had its way, it would prefer to deal with a Singapore government led by the more pliant, right-wing Singapore Alliance (SA) than the aggressive left-wing PAP.

The SA, a new incarnation of the Singapore People's Alliance, was headed by Lim Yew Hock, who was ready to echo the Federation's views and to copy its communal-based political system. Like the Federation Alliance, the SA involved a partnership with communal-based parties, the Singapore UMNO, the Singapore MCA, and the Singapore Malayan Indian Congress (SMIC). It was formalised on 24 June 1963 with a view to contesting the elections as an "integral member of the Grand Alliance of Malaysia",[25] to be inaugurated when Malaysia was formed.

These developments gnawed at Raja, and he was anxious to make sure that the communal politics practised in the Federation did not beat a path into Singapore.

However the Federation leaders felt about the PAP, the referendum cleared the way for the PAP to press on with their merger plans with renewed vigour. The PAP leaders intensified the negotiations over financial details and common market arrangements, which they considered to be the key to the whole question of Singapore's future survival and progress.

The Federation leaders, on their part, remained apprehensive about the capacity of its industrial sector to compete against Singapore, and feared the Chinese dominating its industries at the Malays' expense. Even as the wrangling accelerated, new issues emerged. One of them, which fell squarely on Raja's turf, was over the control of the local media.

As part of the movement towards merger, Raja was involved in efforts to bring together the officials of the information and broadcasting departments in the Malaysian territories. In a conference of Singapore and Malaya officials in Kuala Lumpur on 1 October 1962, Raja was initially assured when the Tunku, who took over the Ministry of Information and Broadcasting, expressed his support of the rights of the different races in the new Malaysia to aspire to form the government, even to become prime minister. "This nation has a Malay King and our States have Malay Rulers but they are all constitutional Rulers. Citizens of the country of whatever race have the right in Malaya, and later Malaysia, to be the Prime Minister and to form the Government and the Governments of the States," said the Tunku.

Raja took this statement at face value. This was not the first time the Tunku had expressed his position on this fundamental issue. In his message in the souvenir publication *Malaysian Heritage*, published by Raja's Culture Ministry in early 1962, the Tunku had written that, "in the Federation of Malaysia, not only will we all become leaders of our nation, but all can be eligible to become the Prime Minister of the Federation of Malaysia". It was such statements which provided the basis for Raja's belief that, in the new Malaysia, the political playing field would be open to all races and all political parties.

The Tunku was more than aware of the power of the media to influence politics in Malaysia, and wanted complete control of it, including Singapore's media. Raja thought it most unwise to relinquish control of the Singapore media to the Federation. As far back as September 1961, Raja had given his views to the cabinet that radio and future television services should not be handed over to the central government upon merger. His argument had been that the media must meet the needs of the local people, whose composition was different from that of the Federation.

This stand proved wise. Already, there were indications that Kuala Lumpur had been giving directions to *The Straits Times* in Malaya to cut down publicity for Lee and the other Singapore ministers. Through his regular visits to his journalist contacts in Kuala Lumpur, Raja kept himself well informed of the Malayan leaders' preoccupations and their line to the Malayan media.

Back in Singapore, Raja discussed with Lee his misgivings over the Tunku's statement. Lee was immediately suspicious of the Federation's anxiousness to take over the control of the Singapore media, although it had been agreed that Singapore would be responsible for administration and day-to-day programmes. He believed this was designed to limit his political influence, particularly during an election. Lee did not intend for one moment to relinquish these powers, and made this clear to the Tunku when they met, adding to their list of disagreements.

On the whole, Raja's relations with the Federation leaders were ambivalent. They admired his sharp mind and eloquence. But, like the communists and many others, they saw him mainly as Lee Kuan Yew's man.

Abdullah Ahmad, who was then political and press secretary to the Malayan deputy premier Razak, recalled an occasion in 1963 when Lee was due to appear in a forum on merger at the University of Malaya in Kuala Lumpur. Instead, Raja was sent as the PAP's representative. UMNO was in a fix. Raja's reputation had preceded him. According to Abdullah, those nominated, including Raja's

Malayan counterpart Khir Johari, withdrew at the prospect of being on the same panel as Raja. In the end, Razak sent his political secretary, Abdullah, to represent UMNO.

Abdullah, who knew of Raja's boldness through his columns in the *Standard*, recounted: "I was 26 years old. I asked Razak: "Why send me? I remembered what Raja was capable of. He said: 'Dollah, are you having an inferiority complex?" I said it's not fair. Anyway, it was an order, so I went."[26] The forum was as lively as he expected.

Years later, Abdullah maintained that the attitude of the Malayan leaders was that it was not Singapore's place to change anything in the Federation, especially its pro-Malay policies. He described the Tunku's position: "You come here, you don't come to try to change the system. You join us as we are." The fundamental problems between the two countries would sharpen into focus as Singapore moved closer to the date of merger, Malaysia Day, scheduled for 31 August.

To strengthen Singapore's propaganda capabilities, Raja worked like a man possessed to get TV off the ground. His major problem was staff with the necessary expertise. He flew to London in November 1962 on a one-man recruitment drive. He returned home with two experienced technicians and two programme assistants from the British Broadcasting Corporation (BBC).

While in London, he also attended a TV course at the BBC, which was recommended by Lee Kuan Yew. While in London in September, Lee had himself spent two hours with Hugh Burnett of the BBC and profited from the lesson on TV technique. Lee immediately thought of Raja and urged him to do the same. In his letter dated 16 September 1962, Lee told Raja: "I think, if you can understand the instruments and the potentials it has for getting over ideas, you will be able to make much more effective use when we get our station going some time in November." Then in a collegial tone, Lee said: "If you agree, tell Chin Chye and Keng Swee so that arrangement can be made for someone to act for you when you are away. I shall be back at the end of September." Raja took up the proposal gladly, and returned from London better equipped to launch a TV revolution in Singapore.

Television Singapura began broadcasting in February 1963 with a pilot service and, in April, it was established as a regular service with one channel. In its first ever transmission at 6 pm on 15 February, the first image people saw flickering on the TV screen was Raja's beaming face. His voice was strong and clear as he said: "Tonight might well mark the start of a social and cultural revolution in our lives."[27]

It was an exceedingly difficult start. In a reflection of the paucity of programmes available, the first transmission lasted a mere 1 hour and 40 minutes, with a feature film on TV, cartoons, a comedy skit, a variety cultural show, and news. Raja sought to bring the new medium into more homes through low licence fees and a multilingual service. Those who could not afford to own sets could watch TV in the community centres which had electricity. Ananda Pereira, who started work in the TV unit as a floor manager in 1963, recalled: "It was a struggle as we were floating in uncharted waters. Unlike the BBC, we had to cater to a multi-lingual and multi-racial audience."[28]

The launch in 1963 took three years of careful planning. In his cabinet paper dated 7 October 1960, Raja had outlined two options for the TV station — one short-term, the other long-term, with their different costings, and had argued for the long-term proposition.

The long-term plan, carried out over three years, involved building more studio room and additional equipment, costing $1 million. The short-term one would cost $440,000. For both options, the transmitting station would be at Bukit Batok, standing at 107 metres. Bukit Timah Hill, the highest point on the island, was not available because the police and the telecommunications department had already sited their stations there. Studios and administrative buildings would be sited at Caldecott Hill as part of *Radio Singapore* and would form a single administrative unit. In its meeting on 14 October, the cabinet approved the more expensive long-term plan for a fuller television service. This decision gave Raja the confidence to push full steam ahead. In the process, he outdid himself and busted the budget — in the end, the introduction of the television service totalled about $3.7 million.

The budget accounting aside, the government could not have had a better person in charge of harnessing the power of new technology than Raja. He had a naturally curious mind and a lifelong fascination with technological innovation. Piroska would often despair at his childlike wonder which would lead him to buy the transistor radio, the quartz watch, the cordless phone, the electric shaver, and vibrating massage chair, among other things, as these were first introduced. He marvelled constantly at the human capacity for innovation, and welcomed invention — the arts and the sciences — as the fruit of the creative powers of man. Keen to learn more about the latest TV technology, he visited TV factories in Japan in May 1960 to observe how TV parts were assembled and tested.

Despite the fear with which some in Singapore first greeted television, Raja approached the new media like a proud father discovering the many hidden talents of his child. Beyond television's functions of instructing and entertaining, he also saw the equalising and transformative power of television as it entered into the everyday life of the masses. Its primary aim was to be nation-building, as Raja sought to marshall its unifying power to unite an essentially migrant, illiterate population, and to imbue in them a national consciousness.

Raja was quick to use the exciting new medium to showcase the country's progress under the PAP. For the first time, through the goggle box, people could see their political leaders opening factories, schools, community centres, visiting constituencies, and speaking at political rallies. This was an eye-opener for the people, an entirely novel experience.

Five weeks after the launch of *Television Singapura*, in March 1963, Raja was confident enough to declare that, with the people's cooperation, "Television Singapura will be one of the best television stations in this part of the world." He was pleased that the station was already able to go $3^1/_2$ hours a day, compared with other countries which had started TV earlier, but managed to transmit only two to three hours a day. He urged TV dealers to make sets more affordable to the masses, adding, "there is not much point in the Government spending millions of dollars to cater for a small section of the people only".[29]

Raja was anxious to broaden the audience for TV and to make it financially sustainable. He buried his initial reservations about commercial advertising, and in 1964, launched a commercial service. As he explained at the launch, "television advertising is the only practical and relatively painless way of financing television without making undue demands on the pockets of either the viewers or the tax-payer." It was a fundamental break with traditional financial arrangements for public broadcasting.

Hitherto, he had held at arm's length anything to do with commercial advertising, concerned that it would lead to lower standards in programmes to please advertisers. For a long while, he was a purist in regarding broadcasting as a community service and a public good, not to be soiled by grubby commercial hands and distracted from its primary mission, which was to instruct and entertain.

This extended even to sponsorship of commercial programmes organised by *Radio Singapore*. In a staff meeting on 3 January 1961, the commercial manager pointedly asked Raja for a policy ruling on making use of the Odeon and Capitol theatres to sponsor commercial programmes organised by *Radio Singapore*. According to the minutes, "the Minister could not agree to this proposition as this would give the impression to the public that the Government was helping the owners of these Theatres to profit from Radio Singapore programmes".

Raja was to expand his notion of public service over time as he realised that commercial advertising and sponsorship were a practical way of shouldering the financial burdens and risks of the expensive business of broadcasting, especially TV. At the same time, he recognised the danger of television subordinating this national objective to the secondary objective of getting advertising revenue. Hence, when launching the TV commercial service, he hastened to assure viewers that there was no danger of this happening over *Television Singapura* because it was not a commercial concern out to make profits for shareholders. "It looks upon advertising revenue merely as an additional source to finance a better television service," said Raja.[30]

In making this significant shift towards commercial sources of funding, Raja displayed an openness and willingness to overturn his own policies with changing circumstances. This pragmatic streak was also evident when, in 1963, he mounted a strong argument in cabinet for a reversal of the government policy to ban the broadcast of horse racing.

The cabinet had earlier decided that no horse racing be broadcast over *Radio Singapore* and *Rediffusion* to curb the activities of bookmakers. In his cabinet memo dated 23 January 1963, Raja observed: "Since the ban and the establishment of betting shops, it does not appear that the amount of betting on horses had decreased." He noted, from the number of people attending the Singapore race course, that horse racing was a popular sport in Singapore. He argued: "It is the policy of Government to encourage as many people as possible to buy a television set and this is a positive means of doing so. Further, television is a most important medium of communication between the Government and the people, and the more sets there are, the more effective is this medium of communication. In the present set up of Singapore, this is a very important consideration."

After hearing Raja out, the cabinet, in its meeting on 30 January 1963, agreed to do a U-turn and permit the televising of horse racing in Singapore — on the condition that not more than three races were televised each day, subject to review from time to time. Given the conservative bent of the cabinet, this decision was quite a triumph for Raja. It reinforced his continuing confidence that this cabinet was a rational and pragmatic one which would respond to reason. It was also a powerful encouragement for him to keep returning with daring ideas.

⁂

Under Raja, the film censorship policy also became more liberal. In the past, it came under the purview of the home affairs minister. Film censorship and the Board of Film Censors' Department were transferred to the portfolio of the culture minister in early 1963. This was essentially prompted by the advent of TV, and the need to make sure that the Board of Film Censors department and the TV service would be working to a common directive policy on censorship.

Attuned to the power of moving images, Raja kept an eye on the types of films shown to the public in Singapore. In one of his earliest policy statements on film censorship, he laid out the general principles: "Scenes which tend to bring the police into general disrepute and contempt; defiance of the police and law and order; anything which tends to excite inter-racial feeling or rivalry; anything that might provoke sedition or cause disturbances of public tranquillity; certain matters which might contravene good taste in regard to public morals; films which tend to depict horror for its own sake."

Beyond these law and order considerations to do with the police, there were also broad political objectives: Films which tended to bring into disrepute the constitution and the ideals on which a state is founded, or to incite the people into political violence, political disorder and unconstitutional acts.[31]

Despite the long list, film censorship was, in fact, more relaxed under Raja than previously. It did not follow, however, that every anti-communist film would get passed. One had to be intelligent about censorship.

This came to light when Raja was asked in the Assembly why certain anti-communist films, such as *Satan Never Sleeps*, were banned in Singapore. After the obligatory dig at the Barisan — Raja quipped that the title reminded him of the Barisan's history — he replied that the film *Satan Never Sleeps* was a "very poorly produced, rather puerile, anti-Communist film". Because it was so badly done, it was banned. "There is no greater disservice you can do to the democratic cause than to put forward a picture which is so puerile that you are likely to win more converts to Communism than anything else". His reasoning was, "if you are going to expose Communism, do it intelligently. But if you do it in such a bad way, you are more likely to rouse the antagonism of people who might otherwise not be interested in Communism."

Intelligent propaganda was hard work. As Raja put it once, before the PAP was elected into office in 1959, the people never saw or heard from their rulers. The PAP changed that. "We try to win the consent of the people not just during election time but all the time. That is why the Government spends a great deal of time talking to the people, explaining to the people, trying to persuade the people to support policies and laws which the Government thinks is good for the country," he said.

On the persistent charge by opposition leaders such as Lim Yew Hock that the government was indulging in propaganda, Raja huffed: "These same people, when they were in charge of the government, were too lazy or bankrupt of ideas or afraid of ideas to talk to the people and explain to the people what they were doing and why they were doing it."[32] More likely, it was because they did not have the likes of Raja in their ranks.

20

Merger At Last

Meanwhile, a gathering storm of external threats was fast looming on the horizon. Failing to halt the momentum in Singapore towards merger, the Barisan had looked abroad for allies, linking up with left-wing opposition parties in Malaya, Sarawak, Brunei, and Indonesia. These parties were opposed to the Malaysia plan, denigrating as a "neo-colonialist plot" for the British to retain power in the region.

Raja made it his duty to track their every statement and analyse their every move, anticipating that the communists and their united front leaders would launch a last-minute effort to sabotage merger and Malaysia. He kept up the pressure on the Barisan, denouncing their actions and banning communist publications, films and performances.

Alarm bells jangled as A.M. Azahari of the Partai Rakyat Brunei led the armed rebellion in Brunei in December 1962. The party's anti-Malaysia aims were backed by the Communist North Borneo National Army (Tentera Nasional Kalimantan Utara or TNKU). In the early hours of 8 December, elements of TNKU launched attacks in Brunei and in nearby areas of Sarawak and North Borneo. From his base in Manila, Azahari proclaimed the Unitary State of Kalimantan Utara, which covered Brunei and areas of Sarawak and North Borneo. British and Gurkha troops from Singapore quickly quelled the uprising, which was declared over on 16 December.

Azahari's political appeal, however, remained potent. Indonesian public support for the rebels' cause swiftly emerged. Demonstrations were staged in Jakarta, with Indonesian President Sukarno publicly declaring Indonesia's sympathy and hopes for the "new emerging forces". A war of words erupted with the Tunku accusing Indonesia of inciting the people of the three Borneo territories to oppose their governments, and warning that this would result in calamity.

Six weeks after Azahari's revolt was stamped out, Sukarno — who saw Malaysia as a rival to his Indonesia-centred vision of a Melayu Raya (Greater Malay nation) — declared Indonesia's open, armed hostility to Malaysia. The Confrontation had begun.

The Indonesian navy received orders to fire upon any Malayan fishing boat trespassing in Indonesian waters. The Confrontation, with its slogan "Crush Malaysia", sharpened the already tense and uncertain situation in Southeast Asia and changed its geopolitical dynamics. As hostilities intensified, Raja's sense of Singapore's vulnerability became even more acute — the tiny island was sandwiched between Malaya and Indonesia, and had no defence of its own to speak of.

In Singapore, the Barisan brazenly took the side of the armed revolutionaries, issuing a statement to support its cause. Lim Chin Siong had recent contacts with Azahari, causing the Singapore Special Branch to suspect them of hatching subversive activities. As days passed, the situation looked increasingly grim for Singapore and the Malaysia plan.

Sensing sinister motives at work, Raja excoriated the Barisan for supporting Azahari and for being "traitors" to Singapore. He referred to various earlier statements by Barisan leaders that they preferred a merger with Indonesia to one with Malaya. He drew links to their association with the Communist Party of Indonesia (in Indonesian: Partai Komunis Indonesia or PKI) headed by D.N. Aidit. It was the strongest communist party outside the Soviet Union and China.

By this time, the Tunku, who was unequivocally anti-communist, had run out of patience with those in Singapore and Britain who counselled restraint and caution in dealing with the communists and their rabble-rousers in Singapore. His own experience with the communists, based on the 12-year Emergency in Malaya, was that stern and decisive action was necessary. The Malayan communists had killed over 5,000 people during their armed insurrection. The Tunku feared there might be another bloodbath if the "communist conspiracy" in Singapore was not dealt with before merger. The UK high commissioner to Malaya, Geofroy Tory, reported to London that "there is a real risk that the Tunku may refuse to take Singapore until the Communist conspiracy has been dealt with".[1]

The Tunku's calls for the arrest of Barisan Sosialis leaders before merger intensified in December 1962.[2] After a series of meetings, a reluctant Lee finally agreed to the security swoop with this proviso — Malaya would include at least one member of the K.L. House of Representatives in the list of simultaneous arrests in the Federation.[3] Lee argued that this inclusion was necessary in order to emphasise the pan-Malaysian nature of the security operation and to justify the arrest of some Barisan assemblymen. The PAP was careful about the public presentation of the arrests; it did not want to be tarred as a British stooge carrying out an "imperialist" move to stifle opposition to Malaysia.

Lee needed his cabinet colleagues behind him on this critical decision. Several, such as Toh and Raja, had earlier expressed strong reservations about any repressive action before merger, unless it was necessary to maintain law and order. Their key concern had been that any such action before merger would play into the hands of the Barisan and give them victory at the next elections. But arguably, the latest series of events linking the Barisan with external revolutionary forces, had changed the complexion of the game.

Sharp analysts, the British had earlier sensed dissension in the PAP cabinet ranks on this issue. In their report in July 1962, Selkirk and Moore had assessed that locking up the Singapore communists might well destroy Lee's government, since "some of his colleagues would strongly disapprove and are likely to desert him on this issue".[4]

At the Internal Security Council meeting in December, Lee had to tread cautiously when pressed again by the Federation to act against the communists. Lee consulted Goh Keng Swee and Ong Pang Boon who were present at the meeting in Kuala Lumpur and also spoke on the telephone to Toh and Raja in Singapore about it. According to the British, they were apparently unanimous in their view that at least one subversive member of the KL House of Representatives must be included in the security swoop.[5] A major operation should not proceed without that undertaking.

Faced with this strong stand from Singapore, the Tunku reluctantly gave his word to Lee on this. On that basis, the security operation was set to take place in the early hours of 16 December. On Lee's instruction, Raja drafted a statement calling for the crushing of the Brunei revolt; this was to prepare public opinion for the arrests. At the last minute, however, the Tunku changed his mind about including subversive members of the Federal parliament. Informed of this, Lee called off the operation at 2.30 am in Singapore. Lansdowne reported to London on 17 December 1962: "Unquestionably, the Tunku has broken his word and I am afraid that the fact that he has done so to a man whom he mistrusts and dislikes will make the relationship between these two men even more difficult than ever."[6]

Despite the roller coaster relationship, the PAP leaders continued to believe that the destiny of Singapore was irrevocably interwoven with that of Malaysia, and tried hard to avoid a collision with the Tunku.

During this period, Raja was focused on safeguarding the peaceful passage of merger and Malaysia. He intensified his bombardment on the Barisan for siding with foreign powers against Malaysia. As he charged later, when the communists and their supporters knew they could no longer rely on the people of Singapore to fight their battle against Malaysia, they turned to "Azahari and foreign volunteers to fight their anti-Malaysia battle for them". He added: "The Brunei revolt fizzled out. After that, they were banking on the fact that relations between Malaysia and Indonesia would worsen so that Confrontation would pass from a passive to an active stage where they hoped foreign volunteers and armies would invade Malaysia and help to break up Malaysia."

Disturbed by the escalating developments, the Tunku warned the British that he would call off Malaysia altogether unless the communists and their united front leaders in Singapore were arrested. Unwilling to risk worsening relations with the Tunku, Lee gave his nod. On 2 February 1963, a security operation, code-named "Cold Store", was carried out. About 115 people, including Lim Chin Siong, Woodhull and Puthucheary, were arrested in Singapore.

It was a surgical strike with targets selected carefully. Because the key Communist United Front (CUF) leaders were detained, the operation, which involved a relatively small group, struck a heavy blow to the giant organisational structure built up by the communists. Years later in his memoirs, Chin Peng admitted sorrowfully: "Operation Cold Store shattered our underground network throughout the island."[7]

With the benefit of hindsight years later, Samad Ismail said of his communist comrades in Singapore: "They exposed themselves too much. They were too pigheaded."[8] He revealed that this was an assessment also shared by communist underground leader Eu Chooi Yip then based in Indonesia: "Chooi Yip admitted the mistakes, the rashness. We allowed ourselves to be dictated by our militant members." They had also underestimated the ability of the non-communist PAP leaders to mount a sustained counter-attack.

But at the time, in 1963, the PAP leaders could not be certain if the operation would break the CUF, or if it would erupt into widespread public resentment and greater support for anti-government agitation.

Raja was not without anxieties. Since his journalist days, he had revealed his preference for rational argument and his reluctance to part with it. The open encounter of ideas was his weapon of first resort. But given the grave security threats against merger and Malaysia, Raja recognised that a pre-emptive strike was necessary for the peace and security of Singapore.

Bloodworth, who reported on the Operation Cold Store arrests for his newspaper, the *Observer*, recalled seeing Raja and Toh just after the security swoop and found them both convinced of the need for it.[9] An ill wind was blowing to break up Malaysia, with an Indonesian vice-chief of army staff stating that its army was awaiting orders to support the fight to "free" Kalimantan Utara. That development, together with the link-up between local communists and those operating outside Singapore, was too ominous to be left to gather strength.

Whatever qualms he might have had, Raja did not duck from the unpleasant responsibility of helping to explain the arrests. He sought to convince the people that it was a nationalist effort conducted on behalf of Malaysia, and not an attack on the opposition. As he emphasised, it was when the Barisan Sosialis and communists not only supported violence, but were also engaged in playing the "treacherous role of supporting the intervention by foreign volunteers that the Internal Security Council decided that the Communists now constituted not anti-colonialists but fifth columnists in our midst".[10]

He added: "These Communists were arrested not because they were our political opponents. We tolerated them for two years. We gave them every opportunity to say or do what they liked." It was only when they became "fifth columnists", selling out Singapore and Malaysia not only to people like Azahari, but worse, becoming "stooges of foreign powers and foreign groups like the Indonesian Communist Party" that they had to be detained.

He was ruthless and relentless in disparaging the Barisan as traitors, "acting as stooges for foreign elements". "They are not representatives of those who elected them. They have become representatives of alien racketeers and of foreign Communist parties." These were words steeped in emotive content.

He left no one in any doubt of the PAP government's readiness to strike again, if necessary. He also made plain his contempt and anger for what he termed the "local runner boys of the foreign sponsors of the anti-Malaysia movement". He shook with moral outrage when Barisan leaders threatened that the blood of innocent people would be spilled if Malaysia was pushed through by 31 August. He warned them that "they will not find this Government wanting in resolution and courage to deal with Communist violence and subversion".[11] When Singapore fishermen were shot by Indonesians and the Barisan did not protest at the violence, Raja accused the Barisan of being reduced to the lowest form of treachery, "conniving at and supporting the murder of your own people".[12] His intemperate language was scorching.

As sabres rattled over Southeast Asia, the region was plunged into an unprecedented state of tension. Worried about its impact on the formation of Malaysia, Raja launched a message of unity and solidarity among Malaya, the Borneo States and Singapore, while combating the terror menace at home.

On 16 February 1963, Raja flew to Jesselton for a conference to rally the pro-Malaysia political parties in Malaya and the Borneo territories to stand firm against external interference. Minutes before boarding the plane, Raja said: "This conference will show that nationalist forces are loyal to Malaysia and will stand together, whereas anti-nationalist forces enter into conspiracy against our people by joining forces with alien groups and foreign racketeers."[13]

He made an important distinction between those who disagree with merger, and those who went further to collude with anti-national forces to wreck merger. He made clear that "we do not really mind" if internal and external elements were against Malaysia — as long as they did not take steps to sabotage the formation of Malaysia.[14] The anti-merger and pro-communist elements paid no heed to this warning, determined to cause maximum public disturbance with union strikes and demonstrations.

This would continue even in the months following merger. Michael Fernandez, who was at the time the general secretary of the pro-communist Naval Base Labour Union, would be among those detained under the Internal Security Act in 1964 for being a member of the Communist United Front.[15] Decades after his release in 1973, Fernandez would continue to charge that the PAP leaders, including Raja, "were more interested in safeguarding their political leadership and PAP rule at any cost; hence they took action against their opponents to suppress, neutralise and destroy them".[16]

This would not be the first or last time that such a charge would be levelled at the PAP for its tough actions during that tumultuous period. To such accusations, Raja had this answer: "If we were only interested in preserving the strength of the PAP, both as Government and party, the simple and easy way out would have been to come to terms with the Communists on the issue of merger and carry on for a few more years."[17]

As with most leaders, some values and objectives mattered to Raja more than others. While democratic rights and freedoms were important, more crucial, as always, were the survival and progress of the small, vulnerable country. As he said years later, "freedom is an abstraction. Freedom for what?" He continued: "Once you start translating freedom to specifics, there have to be limits. On that, we were very clear. And the limits had to be based on the specific conditions and problems obtaining in the country at a given time. We made a statement to ourselves that we will not allow the Communists the freedom to use the democratic machinery to win and take over...You can argue in terms of principles, abstractions, that it is wrong, but principles carried to the point where people suffer cannot be allowed."[18]

Furthermore, had the communists been given full freedom and taken over, it would have had grave implications for race relations. "Even though the Communists claim that their ideology is above race, in practice it would have resulted in domination by a particular community under the guise of ideology." Communism in Singapore at the time was an extension of the People's Republic of China. "Victory for them would have meant Singapore becoming a satellite of the People's Republic. With widespread anti-Chinese attitudes of people in Southeast Asia, that would have been the doom of Singapore. There would have been a bloodbath," he asserted.[19]

Raja learnt early that, in politics, moral judgements had to be made. There was no escaping this. In the final analysis, policies and tactics require moral leadership. Decisions based solely on populist pressures or technical details require no leadership at all.

Not long after the arrests, one decision he had to make, which tested his judgment, was whether to hire James Fu who was arrested at Operation Cold Store. Fu, a reporter-translator who had once worked for the pro-communist Chinese newspaper *Sin Pao*, was a voluntary publicity agent for Lim Chin Siong and Fong Swee Suan. Fu had written articles sympathetic to the Chinese-educated student agitators and strikers. He was released four months later after investigations showed that his link with the Anti-British League was broken in 1962.

Towards the end of his detention, Fu expressed to Raja his desire to return to journalism after his release. Fu held Raja in high esteem, having admired his writings in the *Singapore Standard*. Fearing that he now carried a taint as being pro-communist and pro-Barisan, Fu told Raja that he did not mind being a sports writer in *Radio and Television Singapore*. Fu recalled: "Mr Rajaratnam listened to me seriously and carefully. He was trying to ascertain what I was up to. He seemed to be convinced of my intention. I am grateful that he could see me."[20]

A few months after his release, he was hired as a subeditor in the news division. Fu didn't let Raja down. He applied himself to his job diligently. In 1972, he rose to become Lee Kuan Yew's press secretary, a prominent post he held until he retired in 1993. This last posting, which would not have been possible had Raja not first taken the risk by hiring him, was "completely beyond my expectation and imagination", said Fu.[21]

This incident was one of many which underscored how, despite Raja's tough political posture and hectoring, people knew him at base to be a fair-minded and compassionate man. Over the years, as he encountered more people who betrayed the party and his trust, he would become more cautious, and adopt a more pragmatic philosophy that the way to judge people's motives was to look at the result of their actions. But even as he developed a harder exterior, he retained a soft core. Wong Lam Ho, who helped Raja in his Kampong Glam ward for many years from 1967, observed: "He was discerning about people; he didn't want to be played out. But he had a profound understanding of human nature and accepted the failings of humans."[22]

More than placid acceptance, he demonstrated a special grace in reaching out to former political adversaries to mend fences and restore their human dignity after the political tempest had died down. Raja understood that people could in certain circumstances support the communists without supporting communism. Years later, after the communist threat had receded, Raja would invite former opponents such as Woodhull, Chooi Yip and Lee Siew Choh for meals. He would also revive the national public life of Marshall, one of the PAP's harshest critics, and recommend him to become Singapore's ambassador to France in 1978.

Through such actions, Raja revealed his singular ability to transcend personal vendettas, humiliation, or bitterness. President S.R. Nathan, who attended one such dinner at Raja's home in the 1980s when he was permanent secretary of the Foreign Ministry, was astonished at Raja's conviviality towards Lee Siew Choh, the once-nemesis of the PAP. Nathan, who was the permanent secretary for Home Affairs when Operation Cold Store was ordered in 1963, said: "You could not imagine that once, they were political enemies, trying to kill off each other politically."[23]

Raja's motivation in opening his arms to former foes, after the moment of danger had passed, sprang from his ethical world view. Of all the mass leaders during that time, one who had greatly influenced him was Mahatma Gandhi. Here was a man who, despite detesting imperialism, called upon his followers to show love and respect for their imperial masters and his political enemy.

Raja described this as an "act of self-discipline". As he observed: "It is easier and a natural thing to hate your political opponent." By demanding that his followers love their political enemy, Gandhi compelled his people to embark on a measure of self-discipline. Similarly, it required self-discipline to practise the doctrine of non-violence when it was easier to be a demagogue and incite the people to rise up against imperialists using violence and terrorism.

Noting how Gandhi managed to mobilise the masses with his example, Raja said the Indian independence fighter was no dreamy-eyed sage, but a political leader with a shrewd and penetrating grasp and understanding of the mechanics of politics. Revealingly, he said: "If I am asked about Gandhi's contribution to world history, I would say in brief that it showed that you don't have to cheat people or appeal to their baser instincts to mobilise them for political action. Gandhi showed that politics need not be based on cynicism and contempt for the masses."

His words, uttered to mark the 13th anniversary of Gandhi's death in 1962, displayed a certain wistfulness for a different sort of political reality, more dignified and decent, than that he had to contend with every day. It also shines a powerful beam on Raja's own moral values, his cry of conscience for human redemption.

To Raja, the path of non-communal democratic socialism remained hallowed ground. It was more humane and liberal than communism with its call for armed revolution and violence. It was also more just and egalitarian than the communal-based capitalism practised in Malaya, with special rights and privileges for the Malays.

In the abstract, PAP's democratic socialism meant creating a more just and equal society, where there is no exploitation of man by man. This meant creating social wealth that all can share — more schools, free primary education, more clinics, free medical treatment for the poor, more roads, better wages and conditions for workers, more factories to provide jobs for all. Such a system would benefit all races, not only the majority race, and all social classes, not only the capitalist class. Raja regarded these improvements in Singapore as the first phase of peaceful social revolution.[24]

Aware that people could not relate readily to abstract slogans, he exercised all his own communication powers to transform them into something more concrete. Over the decades, he had analysed the ideas of great thinkers and leaders, and concluded that, you could have the greatest vision, but if you could not communicate it effectively, it would fail.

In one notable attempt, he collected facts and figures of the progress in Singapore from June 1959 to June 1963 — the new HDB flats, factories, schools, water standpipes, street lights, electricity for homes, public telephones, and so on — and packaged them all in an easy-to-read booklet *Democratic Socialism in Action*. This was published by his Culture Ministry.

In its pages, he emphasised: "The achievements of the PAP government of the past 47 months indicate what a good democratic government can do even in the limited context of political and economic semi-independence in a little state of 224 square miles." Significantly, he also posed the rhetorical question: In the context of Malaysia, what would the PAP programme mean? He gave a delicious whiff of the possibilities as he highlighted how the PAP's programmes had benefited all sections of the people.

He mounted dramatic exhibitions, drawing curious crowds. One was a mass exhibition on housing held in the National Library. Like most projects conceptualised by Raja, it was spectacular in its imagination and scale. Working with the Museum of Modern Art in New York, the exhibition by the Housing Development Board and the National Library showcased not only public housing in Singapore, but visionary works of some 30 architects and artists of the 20th century from around the world. They included the Japanese architect Kiyonori Kikutake's concept of Marine City, a city floating on the ocean and enclosing farms for the cultivation of seafood, and Italian artist Leonardo Da Vinci's sketches of an imagined underground city. These ideas, which seemed so far-fetched and fanciful in the 1960s, have become reality today.

But what did public housing flats at the time have in common with the celebrated imaginative works of the world's great architects and artists? To Raja, it was vision — the concept of "the ideal city, the ideal environment". It was "an attempt to realise an ideal, how to overcome difficulties, and achieve a reality that is beautiful, imaginative, and practical", he said. The vision had transformed the lives of 70 per cent of the population, providing homes for nearly 300,000 people, he noted.[25]

To give an overview of the island's development, he produced a photograph album *Malaysia Album*, which captured the colourful progress of Singapore in all its aspects. The idea originally came from Goh Keng Swee who was impressed when he saw such a propaganda effort by China.[26] To source for such photos, the Photographic Society of Singapore was asked to hold a competition. When Raja saw the prints, he was not impressed. As he told Goh, they were excellent in the artistic sense of achieving a compositional effect — a balance of light and form — but "few of them reflect the dynamism of our people — their work, their everyday life, the cosmopolitan character of our people, their leisure, sports, etc."[27] The upshot was that the photographic society had to resubmit photos.

Raja knew what he was talking about. A serious amateur photographer, he had accumulated a host of cameras, particularly

Minolta, Mamiya, Leica, and Bronica, covering 35 mm and medium format, and a vast knowledge on photography through self-study and experimentation since his days in London. He kept notebooks devoted to the craft, jotting down carefully the variations of aperture, speed, and lens needed for certain effects.

Raja's superior grasp over the full range of communication tools gave him an unrivalled edge in the cabinet as far as propaganda and presentation were concerned. Using his skills, Raja hounded the Barisan with evidence of the government's ability to bring tangible progress to the people. Advising the Barisan not to underestimate the intelligence of the people, he declared: "The people will judge the Government and forms of government not by oratory, not by promises of a pie in the sky, not by abstract talks of freedom, revolution, anti-colonialism, democracy and other verbal mishmash, but by what the Government does to make the day-to-day life of the people better."

Much of his behaviour and public utterances during this period cannot be comprehended unless it is realised that, from the beginning, he saw it as his duty to explain the government's policies and objectives to the people. To the opposition, which constantly flayed him for using the mass media to conduct PAP propaganda, he held forth in the manner of a long-suffering professor that it was essential for them to understand this: The government was elected on a specific policy. Initially, the policy might have been a party policy. "But once we are elected as a Government, that policy becomes a national policy as long as that Government is the legally and constitutionally elected representative of the people. So it is our duty to put that policy across."[28]

As he reminded them, the PAP was elected essentially on this platform — that it stood for a "non-Communist, democratic socialist Singapore", and "a non-communalist and non-racialist united Malaya and Singapore". That platform became national policy once the PAP was elected. "The people approved of it, and therefore, it is our duty to put across over the radio, TV, and other mass media this policy, because there is the stamp of the people on it," he said. Raja mocked the Barisan's real concern — that his ministry was effectively using radio, and now TV, to win the battle for merger and Malaysia. "We make no bones about it, we make no apology for it," he said.

Indeed, in the booklet *Democratic Socialism in Action*, he had openly stated how radio and TV were used to expose the Barisan as "foreign agents, as people working for foreign powers, who want to sell Singapore to people outside of Malaysia. And we used the radio and television all out". It was no secret.

The fighting talk that characterised his speeches took on an even more aggressive edge as he pointed to the greater propaganda battle that was expected after Malaysia was formed. After merger, "more powerful people would emerge, both in Singapore and outside Singapore, to try to break up Malaysia", he predicted. Singapore would meet "bigger boys, more adept at propaganda". But it would be ready.

Already, he was expanding the island's broadcasting capabilities. This included the purchase of a short-wave transmitter to reach out to a wider audience in the region, another move which was questioned by the Barisan leaders. Raja's bald response: "We are going to ensure that the mass media — radio and television — are up to scratch to fight them."

He was so effective that, in February 1963, Jakarta sent orders to the islanders of Indonesia-held Rhio Islands to get rid of their TV sets because it was a medium of "enemy propaganda". Raja commented laconically that it was their loss, not Singapore's — Rhio (Riau) which was near Singapore, could pick up Singapore's "excellent programmes" for free without having to pay for licence fees.[29]

The Barisan was up in arms over Raja's further plans for television, which Siew Choh slammed as "the new craze".[30] The culture minister replied phlegmatically that he understood why Siew Choh was "more than usually distraught every time he referred to television". "It is one more mass medium — and a very powerful medium — with which to combat and circumscribe the Communists in open encounter," said Raja.

He emphasised that the battle against communism and "anti-national forces" — those opposed to merger — was as much one of restraining their propensity to resort to violence, as it was a battle of ideas. "In the battle of ideas, mass media like radio, television are vital, and the Government intends to use them as effectively as possible to safeguard the democratic system as well as the security of Malaysia," he said.

Despite his confident stance, it was a harrowing time for Raja and the PAP leaders as the open confrontation with the Barisan gained pace on the ground. Raja accompanied Lee on all his constituency visits and rallies. His mind worked like a radar, taking in ground signals, scanning for political threats and opportunities. He made sure the TV captured the political skirmishes which cast a poor light on the Barisan hecklers.

One event which Raja recounted with relish was Lee's clash with Barisan agitators on 14 July 1963. As Lee spoke at a mass rally in Hong Lim park that night, hostile youths jeered at him for the "sell-out" and displayed black banners denouncing the Malaysia Agreement. When Lee drew the crowd's attention to the banners, the lights went off suddenly. The television cameras recorded that, as well as what happened next - the youths running away. Raja declared: "This was seen by the crowds and relayed, I hope, throughout the length and breadth of Singapore. The magic spell of Communist strength and invincibility has been irrevocably broken."[31]

Perfectly aware that more dangers lay in wait, he chose to respond with bravura and defiance. Even as he spoke, a new phalanx of combatants was advancing as the opposition forces massed close and surged to eviscerate the PAP. On 25 July 1963, the opposition sparked a crisis in government when it blocked two vital government bills in the Assembly, and made call after call for the government to resign.[32]

This happened the day Lee and Goh were away in Kuala Lumpur for the merger talks. Raja and Toh had the hardest time trying to beat back their adversaries all baying for blood. Clearly, a new and disturbing cross-current had been added to the endless swirl of political combat. The right-wing Singapore Alliance — made up of UMNO, MCA and MIC — was now joining forces with the Barisan and other opposition parties to block every move by the government.

Immediately after the boisterous sitting that day, Raja and Toh called a press conference to register the PAP government's firmness to lead the country into merger. Raja said: "The opposition is not interested in the future, but to bring down the government." He observed that the defeat of the two government bills marked a new phase in the line-up of political forces. More pointedly, he accused the right-wing Alliance of facilitating the schemes of the "MCA mentors" in the Federation to weaken the PAP.

Raja had reason to suspect that the MCA was keen to displace the PAP and to establish an MCA-UMNO Alliance government in Singapore. For some time now, the MCA had been working hard through its Singapore branch to extend its political influence. Raja could only assume that this had the tacit blessings of UMNO. These were the first ripples of the clash for power that would come.

Amid the myriad dangers and trials, Raja was able to project a voice of confidence to the public that was perhaps less confident than at any time in the country's recent history.

Throughout the campaign with his fiery mien, Raja was in pursuit of something larger, a higher goal which went beyond the immediate task of battling the PAP's political adversaries. He wanted to transform the mind and outlook of the people in Singapore as a whole — to create a people with the courage to stand up to the communists, the conviction to embrace a non-communal way of life, and the toughness to take on the challenges of merger. At this time of anxiety and insecurity among the people, he strode like a lion to the gate of Malaysia and roared, head tilted back, to awaken the lion also lying within them. This was the roar of glorious conviction, of resolute hope. That the Singapore people could discover within themselves the strength and courage to face the future, grab it by the scruff of its neck, and never let go.

His own avid anticipation of the future and passionate faith in his creed were apparent. Despite the rumbling skies darkening the horizon, Raja was alight with ideas on Singapore's place in the region. He imagined Singapore becoming not only New York to the new Malaysia, playing the role of a financial centre as originally conceived by the Tunku, but also the "Paris of the region", a model of creativity and culture.

Part of Raja's motivation for his inventive touches was to change Malaya's perception of Singapore — that it would be a source of strength to the Federation, and not a hotbed of troubles as commonly harped on by the Malayan leaders. He also wanted to prod the Singapore people to reflect on their own image and remould it, to see themselves as more than just money-spinners, and their city as more than just a trading centre.

Despite the grinding pressures he faced day by day, he retained an unflagging faith in his country's potential. Under his watch, Singapore chalked up a number of "firsts" in the cultural field. The city hosted the first Pan-Malayan Writers' Conference on 17 March 1962. It involved some 800 people, including established and budding writers, as well as hordes of schoolchildren.

To the writers, Raja had this message: Produce their own literature that deepen the awareness and understanding of Malayans to the reality of life's problems, that point the way to an integration of the achievements of human ingenuity with the emotional life of a man. This was so that, out of it, "may emerge an enhancement of our values, an enrichment of our perceptions, and a growth in our control both over ourselves and our society".

Singapore also organised the first Malaysia art exhibition at the Victoria Memorial Hall on 23 September 1962. In its opening, Raja said that, as a big city, Singapore had always set the pace for Malayan painting, with Kuala Lumpur a close second. An impressive 220 paintings and sculptures were on display, from the Federation, Singapore, Sabah, Sarawak, and Brunei. Raja said this was merely a prelude to more ambitious exhibitions, and expressed his hope that Singapore would continue to be the pacesetter for art in Malaysia.

Then there was Singapore's first Malaysia Grand Prix in 1963, which attracted more than 100,000 people. Raja's Culture Ministry, being also in charge of tourism, had organised the two-day race which received international status. It served to boost Singapore's standing in the region. Rather than invoke the profit factor for holding the event, Raja dwelt on the people factor: "An international event like our Grand Prix is an opportunity for sportsmen from different nations to match skill and courage, not in a spirit of petty political vindictiveness and animosity, but in a spirit of sportsmanship to learn to understand and respect one another better."[33]

To many outside Singapore, the idea that Singapore could be a cultural jewel in the region must have seemed arrogant. The puny island in pre-colonial times was little more than a swampland for fishermen and pirates. This was in sharp contrast to its larger neighbours with civilisations stretching back centuries, such as Indonesia with its Majapahit empire, or Cambodia with its Khmer (Angkor) empire.

Such an ambition to be the "Paris of the region", of course, was easier to assert than realise. But it had been Raja's consistent goal to take the fortunes and the future of the island out of its geographical and historical confines and into its own hands.

Appropriately, he first gave voice to his ambitious cultural vision for Singapore at a function to raise funds for the performing arts venue National Theatre, one of his most demanding projects.[34] His troubles were aggravated after 1961, when the Barisan emerged and started calling the building of the theatre a waste of money and yet another avenue for PAP propaganda. When it was finally unveiled, the National Theatre was symbolism set in stone. Its five-pointed façade represented the five stars of the Singapore flag. Its outdoor fountain was to represent the crescent moon.

Raja placed special significance on the National Theatre. His hopes for it were revealed at its launch — the first-ever Southeast Asia Cultural Festival. It was a glittering extravaganza involving 11 countries and 1,500 performers in the region. Raja glowed with pride that Singapore was the first country in Southeast Asia to have organised such a large-scale cultural festival. Cambodia's Prince Sihanouk sent not only a contingent of dancers and musicians, but also two of his princesses to perform Cambodian national dances. Not to be outdone, Vietnam sent two of its best film stars to augment its delegation.

His initial plans for it were even more audacious. Earlier, in April that year, he had primed the cabinet of his desire to get internationally acclaimed music conductor Choo Hoey to conduct a concert by the London Philharmonic Orchestra. Choo Hoey had left Singapore for the Royal Academy in London in 1951 to study conducting, after which he made a name for himself conducting many well-known orchestras in Europe. Embracing Choo Hoey as a Singapore prodigy,[35] Raja informed the cabinet that "it will be a great boost to the reputation of Singapore if we can get him to conduct the London Philharmonic Orchestra during the Cultural Festival in August 1963". The cabinet gave its in-principle approval, subject to the cost being cleared by the treasury.[36] A month later, Raja was forced to scrap the idea when the orchestra quoted its cost for flying down for five concerts — about $250,000.[37] Raja did not need to be told this was beyond the pale for the treasury, and withdrew his proposal.

Nevertheless, his attempt reflected his strong desire to showcase Singapore talents, wherever they were in the world, and to use their star power to project Singapore's softer image to the world. When

Raja wanted to promote Choo Hoey in 1963, few had heard of him in Singapore. It would take another 16 years before Choo Hoey became a name in Singapore — that was when he returned to form the Singapore Symphony Orchestra in 1979. He stayed on as music director for 17 years.

At the Southeast Asian festival in 1963, Raja hailed the event as a historic milestone ushering in a "South-East Asian cultural renaissance". He expressed his hope of a Southeast Asian consciousness arising out of the countries' awareness of what they had in common. Seizing the moment, he persuaded the 11 participating countries to issue a joint resolution that the festival would be a regular affair. The implications of his initiative on regional diplomacy were apparent: The countries of Southeast Asia should evolve new ways of cooperation, starting from culture and extending to "fruitful spheres of political and economic co-operation".[38] In his mind, Singapore could play a pivotal role in realising these various modes of regional cooperation.

The iconic theatre clothed some of Raja's most noble ideas and aspirations for Singapore. The building made solid his abstract notions. It was crushed, however, by the pragmatic boots of the later generations in the march of time. More than 20 years later, in 1986, the National Theatre was declared structurally unsafe, with defects in the cantilevered steel roof which would be too costly to rectifty, and demolished.

Not one to stand in the way of the country's progress, Raja made no public fuss about the theatre's destruction. S. Dhanabalan, who became the national development minister in 1987, heard no murmurs of dissent from Raja on the matter. Dhanabalan said: "He was a realist and would not have made an issue over a subject which was overtaken by events."[39] Yet, Raja must have felt more than a twinge of sadness that the National Theatre, and all the symbolism that he had invested in it, was no more. But his toil was not entirely wasted. Although the structure had vanished, it had left a foundation for the arts to develop in Singapore.

Had Raja and his team not tried and persisted in their efforts in those early years, it is doubtful if Singapore would have arrived at where it is today in its cultural development. In 2004, it was the National Library building's turn to be pulled down. The iconic red-bricked structure was replaced by a nondescript road tunnel, to great public dismay. By this time, Raja was enfeebled by his series of strokes.

Of all his heterodox ideas, the ones that prove most enduring were on developing a common national identity and forming a Singaporean Singapore. These ideas were not bound by brick and mortar, only by people's capacity for understanding and imagination. After he stepped down from politics, he would continue to stand guard against any revival of race/ethnic consciousness which might threaten the quest for a common national identity.

While he might stay silent when buildings he treasured were pulled down, he was ready for the attack when it came to moves which encouraged Singaporeans to assert their communal identities, or to trace their roots to their ancestral origins, be it India, China, or any other part of the world. He himself was very clear on this — his loyalty and allegiance were to Singapore, not to his birthplace, Ceylon, or his communal group, Jaffna Tamil. This was a conscious decision, a deliberate act of will.

Today, it seems extraordinary that he had invested so much hope in such ideas. But all those years he preached it, he had great faith in the Singapore people to respond, where necessary, to a call to sacrifice on behalf of a way of life worth building and defending.

On the cusp of merger, Raja had his sights set on Singapore taking a leading role in shaping the politics of the new Malaysia. He declared: "We believe that the people of Singapore, bred in a more cosmopolitan environment and less burdened by provincial and communal way of thinking, can provide leadership and guidance in the evolution of a Malaysian consciousness."[40]

To some Federation leaders, such pious comments no doubt grated. The Federation was apt to think of Singapore as one state out of 14 in Malaysia, but Singapore, and certainly Raja, obviously saw the island as more than that.

His high-octane preaching on educating the Malaysian public on international affairs and on the dangers of communalism, in particular, reflected the messianic role that he had envisaged for himself and for Singapore on the wider Malaysian stage. This self-perception of Singapore was a key factor which was to lie at the base of the disagreements between the central government and the Singapore government after merger.

Raja's unequivocal position on equality, with its intellectual and ideological underpinnings, carried with it a predicament and a paradox. The predicament is: How to be true to his conviction that every citizen is equal and that no one racial group should lord over the others when Singapore was merged with Malaya? It was easy enough to preach equality and race-blind politics in the abstract, and in the context of Singapore. But to carry that over to the Federation, whose politics were communal-based with an entrenched system of Malay political supremacy, was not something that could be achieved by merely believing it. He had to struggle for it.

And the paradox is this: With all his being, he wanted to make merger work. Yet to press for his race-blind ideals would be to risk sabotaging it. Could he be both a practical politician and an idealistic one? Could he exercise the necessary self-restraint to keep out of the politics in the Federation and still be true to his long-held vision of merger? It was the duty of any practical politician, as he had told Siew Choh in the Assembly, to take racial sentiments into consideration — even if these sentiments were, to his mind, mere prejudices and superstitions. But whither then his core ideals?

These dilemmas were resolved to a certain extent in his mind as he found a way of dividing politics into two kinds of realities — the objective reality and the subjective reality. In an unpublished and unfinished article, typed in 1964 during merger, he defined objective reality as that pertaining to events and facts as they really are. "We may like them or we may dislike them."[41] Whatever our own reactions to objective reality, it exists. "It is part and parcel of our political environment and it is of the stuff our politics are made. The most difficult part of politics is to recognise this objective reality and formulate policies in the light of this objective reality," he wrote.

Subjective reality is what people call idealism. "It deals with what we would like the world to be. Where objective reality is harsh, cruel, unfair, then instead of accepting these as in the natural order of things, we aspire to change the world for the better," he wrote. Politics is largely the result of the struggle to bring about some sort of harmony and balance between facts as they are, and facts as we would like them to be, he wrote. His life was a series of such massive struggles.

Raja and his colleagues felt the pressure as the 31 August date of Malaysia Day neared — the negotiations on the economic terms of merger were nowhere near settled. Singapore wanted a common market written into the new Malaysian constitution, while the Federation wanted only agreement in principle, leaving the details to be settled after merger. Another thorny issue was the Federation's control over Singapore's revenue.

Meanwhile, anxious to calm regional tensions, the Tunku met the Indonesian president, Sukarno, and his Filipino counterpart, Macapagal, for a summit conference in Manila from 30 July to 5 August 1963. They discussed the Indonesian and Filipino protest over the inclusion of the Borneo territories. The summit resulted in a shocking decision for Singapore: on 6 August, three weeks before the planned Malaysia Day, the Tunku decided to postpone it indefinitely, to give the United Nations time to ascertain popular support in the Borneo territories for Malaysia.

The Tunku's unilateral decision to delay Malaysia Day was met with disbelief and anxiety in Singapore. The PAP leaders were horrified at how agreements made solemnly to inaugurate Malaysia on 31 August could be discarded so lightly. They were also worried that the prospect of merger being aborted would embolden the Barisan and the confrontationists. Already, the Barisan had been stepping up their agitation. Assembly debates had become mortal political combats with bills defeated and calls for the government to resign at every possible turn.

The British, aware that anti-merger forces from Brunei and Sarawak had already crossed the border for military training in Indonesia, were as furious with the Tunku's decision and pressed the Tunku for a firm date.

In a defiant response which displeased the Tunku, Lee declared that, since Singapore was not party to the Manila Agreement, 31 August was still Malaysia Day.[42] Lee and Raja then flew to Jesselton in a determined attempt to persuade the leaders of Sabah and Sarawak to stick to the 31 August date for Malaysia's inauguration.[43] To Singapore's relief, they concurred.

Lee and Raja next flew to Kuala Lumpur to have discussions with the Tunku and the British Commonwealth and Colonial Secretary Duncan Sandys. The leaders from the Borneo territories were also present. When Lee returned to Singapore for a mass rally on 25 August, Raja stayed behind in Kuala Lumpur to continue talks with the Malayan and Borneo leaders and Sandys.[44] Pressured by the various parties, the Tunku subsequently set a new tentative date — 16 September — for Malaysia.

Raja gave his full-throated support to Lee's decision to declare *de facto* independence on 31 August. In charge of the Malaysia Day celebrations, Raja had for months been planning an elaborate week-long programme to celebrate the historic occasion. He had lined up an air show, a sea carnival, a grand tattoo, and a 90-float procession through the city, capped with two hours of fireworks. Celebrations would continue to 2 September, which would be gazetted as a public holiday. Invitations had been sent out to representatives from the Commonwealth and selected Afro-Asian countries. Not only that, decorations and arches had already gone up all over the city.

When the Tunku decided to postpone Malaysia Day at the last moment, the mood in Raja's Culture Ministry was reminiscent of a family preparing for a grand wedding that had to be delayed because of the groom's sudden attack of nerves.

The practical aspects of Malaysia Day aside, Raja was more worried about the political repercussions. Just recently, he had been taunting the Barisan leaders that 31 August would spell the end for them — that the advent of Malaysia was "always certain as sure as the sun rises, as sure as the red star of the Barisan Sosialis will set".[45] He feared that, with the delay of merger, his bravado would begin to ring false and the Barisan's spirits would be revived.

Of all his fears, his biggest was that something unpredictable could happen to jeopardise merger if postponed even by a few weeks. Despite the referendum results, there were still uncertainties and doubts about merger among the people, especially the Chinese who feared the prospect of Malay rule. "Something could happen where the whole question of Merger would be re-examined. So you pre-empt by declaring independence," related Raja in his oral history years later. Otherwise, there were still 16 days for the Barisan to mount more agitation against merger. Anything could happen. Declaring independence "gave us the finality". Giving an insight into the calculations at the time, Raja related: "We knew at that time, the British did not want independence for Singapore. So once we declared our independence, it would certainly put all the pressure necessary to see that the merger proposals get through."

When Singapore unilaterally declared *de facto* independence on 31 August, Lee announced that all federal powers over defence and external affairs would be reposed in Singapore's *Yang di-Pertuan Negara* until 16 September. The *Yang di-Pertuan Negara* would hold them in trust for the central government. Celebrations that day were muted. The elaborate plans, originally planned for 31 August, were postponed to 16 September.

Despite the churning fears within, Raja managed to project a willed equanimity and confidence at the celebrations at the City Hall grounds on 31 August — designated Malaysia Solidarity Day. With measured ease, he accompanied the prime minister to inspect the Guard of Honour, made up of the state police. The pair then boarded a land rover to inspect the entire parade which had joined up to form the letter 'M' for Malaysia. As Lee waved to the exuberant crowd, Raja wore a relaxed smile. In a message directed at the wider audience, Lee referred to the hard fight for merger and said: "Let no one doubt the resolve of its leaders." At the end of the ceremony, as Raja led Lee to his car in full view of the crowd, their heads leaned towards each other the way good friends would as they exchanged comments and smiles. Their body language demonstrated to all their calm resolve and their close bond.

Raja stayed by Lee's side every step of the way on this uncertain course. On 3 September, Lee dissolved the Legislative Assembly and called for a new election on 21 September, to obtain a new mandate for the PAP government. Several days later, Raja added new significance to Singapore's independence by declaring Singapore would hold *de facto* responsibility over "foreign affairs and defence in trust for the central government until Malaysia is established on terms as outlined in the Malaysia Agreement".[45]

The Straits Times seized on the last 12 words and said: "The Singapore government contends that action in accordance with the Malaysia agreement has not yet been taken in certain matters." This includes the common market, the retention by Singapore of its special powers to suppress secret society gangsters and reciprocal rights to restrict the entry of "undesirables".[46] The newspaper captured the public mood in noting that, with Malaysia only nine days away, the sharp differences of opinion between Singapore and

Federation governments were disconcerting. The atmosphere, it noted, was "chilling".

The mood in Kuala Lumpur was dour. The Federation cabinet bitterly resented Singapore's unilateral act of independence. Raja was aware of this — his newspaper friends in Malaya had in fact told him that this was taken as an indication that "by taking in Singapore, Tunku was going to have uncontrollable, unpredictable Singaporeans".

Behind this episode lies a difficult aspect of the relationship between the Federation and Singapore — Singapore saw itself as a progressive force in the new Malaysia and was not prepared to be pushed around or held down. On its part, the Federation regarded itself as doing Singapore a favour by agreeing to the merger and believed in applying maximum pressure on the island to meet the Federation's demands. It was not a good start to Malaysia.

On 16 September, fireworks lit the sky as Singapore celebrated the historic moment of joining Malaya, Sabah and Sarawak to form an independent Malaysian nation. People packed the streets and crammed the waterfront.

On this momentous day, Raja was away to Kuching in Sarawak as Singapore's representative at the Malaysia celebrations that same day, while Toh attended the festivities in Sabah. The celebrations in Kuching, Sarawak's capital, were marred by a hand grenade blast which injured two people. Raja immediately condemned the violence. In a sombre mood, he said: "The pro-Communists have now resorted to terrorism and intimidation of the people in their futile efforts against Malaysia."[47] In Singapore, Lee was similarly sober as he warned the people: "Communists and anti-national elements within the country, indeed with foreign elements, have expressed their desire to see that Malaysia shall perish."

Malaysia was born of travail. In more than two years of debate, negotiation, and confrontation, there were traumatic moments when failure seemed all too real. For Raja, merger with Malaya was the realisation of a dream which he had longed for, but thought too remote to achieve in his time. The inclusion of the Borneo States to form Malaysia was a "bonus".

Raja's immediate feeling was "one of satisfaction and relief that the pro-Communist threat had been a bit blunted as a result of merger". His dream of merger now realised, he soon woke up to the harsh reality of living it out. "There was considerable anxiety on our part, about how things are going to work out. The communal type of Malay leaders had no particular affection for the PAP leaders or their intentions," Raja related years later. He was clear in his mind that Singapore was not going to be like one of the Malaysian states, such as Penang, Negri Sembilan, or Selangor. "We were going to play a role within Malaysia." He looked forward to the PAP's participation in the wider arena as a pan-Malaysian party.

His analysis all along had been that no party could be truly national without the support of all races, including the Malays. The PAP should extend its influence in Malaysia as a non-communal party, based on democratic socialism. After all, the party had succeeded in proving that this approach could bring about better living standards for the people of all races in Singapore. It could also work for the people of Malaysia.

He was convinced that, to garner support for this, the PAP had to set up branches in Malaysia, just like the other legitimate political parties in Malaysia. He would start one in his hometown Seremban. Raja said: "We genuinely believed that so long as we were loyal Malaysians, non-communal, the Malay leaders would accept that."

With 15 seats in the Federal Parliament, the PAP had become the largest opposition party in the Federal parliament. Lee recalled: "Raja wanted to play the role of outright opposition."[48] Lee was more cautious, preferring to feel his way forward.

Raja was headstrong, and saw it the role of the PAP to convince the moderate leadership of the Malays in Malaya that there was a rational economic method of abolishing rural poverty. This involved a systematic scientific research into the possibilities of profitable crops which could be grown by the Malay peasants, as well as extensive training and education. The emphasis was on education and social programmes, not job or licence quotas. In Raja's book, race-based policies for solving the problem of Malay poverty was an "irrational political solution".

He was under no illusions that it would be a long process to create the sort of Malaysia he had envisioned. As he said, there would need to be a period of peace and harmony for the various communities to readjust themselves to the new situation, and consolidate the existence of Malaysia as a new political entity.

The task of welding many races into a Malaysian nation might seem formidable, but he believed that, with courage and conviction, his dream of a Malaysian nation was possible. This was an ideal which he dedicated himself to as soon as Malaysia was formed.

Raja said: "When we signed and approved the Malaysian Constitution, we were quite clear in our mind what kind of Malaysia we wanted, a Malaysian Malaysia."[50] By 1964, a year after merger, Raja would turn out to be one of the most aggressive advocates of this cause. As Toh would reveal years later, it was Raja who coined the catchy slogan Malaysian Malaysia.[51] The slogan and all it stood for would change the trajectory of Singapore politics in Malaysia.

The battle to achieve merger had been long and tortuous. The seeds of its own destruction had been sown along the route to Malaysia, yet even Raja, with his wisdom, perspicacity, and capacity to dream, did not envisage a time when the PAP's fight for a Malaysian Malaysia could lead to riots, instigated by Malay extremists, and hysterical calls for the arrest of Lee and other PAP leaders. Or that the situation would become so dire that Lee would have to make contingency plans for a base to be set up in Phnom Penh should they be detained.

In 1963, it would have been impossible for Raja to conceive that Lee would, in two years, talk to him about heading a government-in-exile under the protective arm of Prince Sihanouk, if Lee were to be detained. Lee chose him, out of the others, for this leading role because "Raja was a man who will fight to the last, no question of him backing out". Lee added: "He was a man of deep convictions and he would go right to the end."[52] Fight to the end. For his dream of Malaysian Malaysia, the end would come too suddenly and too bitterly with Separation. Then another battle would begin. For the survival of Singapore.

Notes

Chapter 1

1. Raja's private notebook, author's collection. This entry was probably written in 1990, when he was 75.
2. While Raja's mother was known as Annammah to her family and other relatives, her official name, as recorded on Raja's birth certificate, was Annappillai d/o Nagalingam.
3. Ang Swee Suan, ed., *Dialogues with S. Rajaratnam* (Singapore: *Shin Min Daily News*, 1991).
4. *The Straits Times*, "Where Tigers Used to Roam", 6 December 1992.
5. For background and history of the rubber industry in Malaya, see John H. Drabble, *Malayan Rubber: The Interwar Years* (Houndmills, Basingstoke, Hampshire: Macmillan Academic and Professional, 1991); Peter Tamas Bauer, *The Rubber Industry: A Study in Competition and Monopoly* (Cambridge, Massachusetts: Harvard University Press, 1948); and James C. Jackson, *Planters and Speculators; Chinese and European Agricultural Enterprises in Malaya, 1786–1921* (Kuala Lumpur: University of Malaya Press, 1968).
6. Given the complicated relations arising from the pattern of intermarriage, "uncle" was used commonly as a term of address for older male relatives, and "auntie" for female ones.
7. Rajakrishnan Ramasamy. *Sojourners to Citizens, Sri Lankan Tamils in Malaysia, 1885–1965* (Kuala Lumpur: R. Rajakrishnan), p. 96.
8. Speech on 17 August 1975, at the dance debut of Roshni Pillay Kesavan, a relative in Singapore. He said there was no contradiction in being both a Tamil and a Singaporean. Tamils such as Roshni would feel a stranger in India or Ceylon, but she is a Tamil and became one by learning its cultural art forms rooted in Hinduism.
9. *Indian Writing*, Vol. 1, August 1941.
10. The next important milestone was the acquisition of Singapore in 1819 to establish a second fortified trading post for the East India Company.
11. *Asia*, "The Changing Malay People", August 1942.

Chapter 2

1. Unfinished article, "Straight From the Heart", 1991, private papers, author's collection.
2. Chan Heng Chee and Obaid ul Haq, eds., *The Prophetic and the Political* (Singapore: Graham Brash, 1987), p. 481.
3. "My Days at St Paul's", *Pauline Magazine* of St. Paul's Institution, 1993.
4. Ibid.
5. Speech at the official opening of the National Library, 12 November 1960.
6. Interview with Yong Nyuk Lin, 31 August 2005.
7. Singapore's official biography put the date as 1937, but records obtained from King's College showed that he entered the college in October 1935. This was confirmed by his name on the passenger list of the ship, the *Rawalpindi*, in 1935.
8. Interview with C. Sivapragasapillai, 8 September 2006. Many years later, when Raja earned a more stable salary, he would support Siva's daughter through her university education in India. She was not the only one — throughout his adult life, he would help to fund the further education of various relatives.

Chapter 3

1. Rajah, who was seven years older, was also a Seremban boy who had studied in St Paul's in Seremban and Raffles Institution in Singapore before heading off to Britain for his law degree in 1929. His law studies were disrupted by the Great Depression in 1932 during which his family called him back to Malaya. He returned to Oxford in 1937 to complete his studies, which he did in 1939.
2. Interview with V. Kanda Pillay, 9 January 2007.
3. Victor Gollancz, who ran the Left Book Club with John Strachey and Laski, stated that the club's aim was to help "in the terribly urgent struggle for World Peace and against fascism by giving to all who are determined to play their part in this struggle such knowledge as will immensely increase their efficiency". He argued for a peace alliance with Russia as the best means to avert war.
4. Chan Heng Chee and Obaid ul Haq, eds., *The Prophetic and the Political* (Singapore: Graham Brash, 1987), p. 481.
5. Speech at the official opening of the National Library, 12 November 1960.

6. They include *The Problem of Philosophy* (1932), *History of Western Philosophy* (1948), *Authority and the Individual* (1949), *Mysticism and Logic and Other Essays* (1953), *An Inquiry into Meaning and Truth* (1962), and *My Philosophical Development* (1975).
7. Speech at the launch of the book, *Singapore Eurasians: Memories and Hopes*, 18 July 1992.
8. Ibid.
9. He described this experience in his column in *Malaya Tribune*, published on 5 August 1947. In that article, "Europe over Asia", he argued that Asia's impulse for freedom must be understood by Europe, and criticised Europeans for their sense of superiority over Asians.
10. His birth name was Malcolm Ivan Meredith Nurse. It was widespread practice at the time for communist activists to adopt alternative names. In his political capacity, he used the name George Padmore.
11. The Malayan Forum, an anti-colonial group set up by Malayan students in London, such as Lee Kuan Yew and Toh Chin Chye, was formed only after the Second World War.
12. *SPF Police Intelligence Journal*, No. 3/1955, March 1955.
13. *The Straits Times*, 6 December 1992.
14. Padmore knew Krishna Menon of the India League well and, like Raja, was also embraced by the Indian nationalists in London in their activities. As a Marxist at the time, however, Padmore pointed out their limitations and of the Indian National movement, which was under the dominant influence of the Indian bourgeoisie.
15. Padmore believed that the communist struggle would involve a double revolution: first was a racial revolution aimed at white imperialists, during which the Communist Party would collaborate with the local national bourgeoisie; the second was a class-based one after the local rulers had been put in power. For a good account, read James R. Hooker, *Black Revolutionary: George Padmore's Path from Communism to Pan-Africanism* (New York: Praeger, 1967).
16. He established the International African Service Bureau that connected Caribbean political activists, trade unionists, and intellectuals with their African counterparts. He started the journal *The International African Opinion*. His ideas of Pan-Africanism influenced many of the African leaders who subsequently came to power after the war — Nkrumah, Kenyatta, Nyerere. Padmore died in September 1959, without realising his ideal of Pan-Africanism.
17. George Padmore, *Pan-Africanism or Communism? The Coming Struggle for Africa* (London, Dobson,1956).

18. Fenner Brockway, a journalist-turned -politician, later chaired the Movement for Colonial Freedom.
19. Among Lenin's labyrinthine works that Raja had studied carefully was New Data for V.I. Lenin's *Imperialism, the Highest Stage of Capitalism*, which he obtained in April 1939. Over his lifetime, he would collect at least 13 books on Lenin.
20. Lim was president of the Malayan Chinese Association briefly in 1958. Because of severe political differences, he then left MCA to form the United Democratic Party in 1962, and subsequently, Gerakan, in 1968.
21. Interview with Lim Chong Eu, 6 July 2005. Raja was also interacting with Lim's sister, Lim Siew Lan, who was studying at the London School of Economics at the time.
22. Speech at the centenary celebration of the Maghain Aboth Synagogue, 9 April 1978.

Chapter 4

1. Report by A.H. Borthwick, first secretary, Australian Commission in Singapore, to Canberra. 12 June 1959. NAS file no. 3024/2/10 Part 2.
2. Interview with Kiss Istvan, 8 September 2005.
3. King's College records.
4. Ang Swee Suan, ed., *Dialogues with S. Rajaratnam* (Singapore: *Shin Min Daily News*, 1991).
5. Ibid.
6. *SPF Police Intelligence Journal*, No. 3/1955, March 1955.
7. Letter from Jal Dubash to Piroska, 26 June 1989, S. Rajaratnam Papers, ISEAS.

Chapter 5

1. *Indian Writing*, Vol. 1, No. 4, 1941, pp. 211–16.
2. Forster, Edward Morgan, Mary Lago, Linda K. Hughes, Elizabeth MacLeod Walls, P. N. (FRW) Furbank. *The BBC Talks of E. M. Forster, 1929–1960: A Selected Edition* (Columbia, MO: University of Missouri Press, 2008).
3. At the proof stage, Raja's story was apparently named "A Practical Joke", but it was changed to "The Famine" for publication.
4. *Life and Letters and the London Mercury*, 1941. These two stories were also later reprinted in *Life and Letters Today*, Vol. 32, No. 55, March 1942.
5. Reginald, Moore, ed. *Modern Reading*, No. 5, 1942. According to current Singapore literary history, "The Tiger" was first published in the *Span*, edited by L. Wigmore in Melbourne in 1958 (Edwin Thumboo, ed. *The Fiction of Singapore*, Vol. 2, p. 525). This is incorrect.

6. Central Office of Information, London. *Mirror*, Vol. 1, No. 6, 1948.
7. First published in *Life and Letters and the London Mercury*, Robert Herring, ed., *Life and Letters Today*, Vol. 32, No. 55.
8. Hiram, Haydn, and John Cournos, eds. *A World of Great Stories: 115 Stories, the Best of Modern Literature* (New York: Crown, 1947).
9. Sylvia, Tankel, ed., *Short Story International*, Vol. 14, No. 79, April 1990 (New York: International Cultural Exchange, 1990).
10. *The Spectator*, 26 September 1947, p. 410.
11. "Famine", "The Locusts", "What Has To Be".
12. *The Malayan Times*, "Rajaratnam, His Land & Rural Folk Themes", 6 May 1962.
13. More recently, academic Philip Holden discussed some of Raja's stories in terms of laying the foundations for a "national imaginary". *The Journal of Commonwealth Literature*, Vol. 41, No. 1 (2006). "Rajaratnam's Tiger: Race, Gender and the Beginnings of Singapore Nationalism."
14. Denys Val Baker, ed., *Modern International Short Stories*, 1947. Raja's "The Terrorist" was the first of eight stories from writers all over the world featured in this edition. It was the only one categorised under "India".
15. There was some confusion among several scholars when Nigerian poet Christopher Okigbo, a founding figure in modern literature in Africa, acknowledged a certain Raja Ratnam and his story "At Eight-fifteen in the Morning" in the introduction of his collection of poems first published in 1963. An essay in the journal *Research in African Literatures* (Vol. 35, No. 3, Fall 2004) speculated that it was Singapore's Raja, but confessed that that specific short story could not be traced. The scholar was mistaken. It was another man, a T.K. Raja Ratnam. who wrote "At Eight Fifteen in the Morning" which was published in *United Asia: International Magazine of Afro-Asian Affairs* in 1961.
16. *The Tribune*, 19 July 1946, p. 9. Also quoted in *Tribune 40: The First Forty Years of a Socialist Newspaper* (London and New York: Quartet Books, 1977).
17. K.M. Shrivastava, *News Agencies from Pigeon to Internet* (New Delhi: New Dawn Press, 2007).
18. The Ceylonese Trotskyists founded the modern labour movement and set up the Lanka Sama Samaja Party in Ceylon.
19. Special Branch files.
20. All along in his concept of "Malaya", Singapore was in it.
21. Speech at pre-U seminar at the National Junior College, 18 June 1984.
22. The Malayan Union was formally inaugurated on 1 April 1946, with Singapore starting its existence as a separate British colony. Taken aback by the strong Malay protests, the British scrapped the scheme barely three

months later and began negotiations with UMNO leaders in June 1946 to find an acceptable solution to the objections to the Malayan Union. The outcome of these negotiations was the signing of the Federation of Malaya Agreement in 1948.

23. Lim Hong Bee and Wu Tian Wang were the prime movers in forming MDU, which was fronted by Philip Hoalim Sr., a lawyer, who became its chairman. See Philip Hoalim Sr., *The Malayan Democratic Union: Singapore's First Democratic Political Party* (Singapore: Institute of Southeast Asian Studies, 1973).

Chapter 6

1. Interview with Vijayalakshimi Thambiah (or Mrs Seevaratnam), 2 October 2004.
2. Interview with Senathyrajah Kanagasabai, 17 June 2006.
3. Private article by Dennis Bloodworth, dated 5 November 1983, sent to the author.
4. As Hong Bee did not finish his law studies, he returned to London in 1947 to continue them. However, in London, he threw himself into his new duties as the representative of Putera-AMCJA and turned into a communist intellectual, writing for the British Communist Party. He then abandoned his studies altogether.
5. S. Rajaratnam, Oral History, NAS.
6. Eu Chooi Yip, Oral History, NAS.
7. Ibid. Chooi Yip's own account also contradicted another urban myth perpetuated in various news reports — that he never rode a rickshaw on principle.
8. *Malaya Tribune*, 9 May 1947
9. *Malaya Tribune*, 16 May 1947.
10. *Malaya Tribune*, 29 May 1947.
11. Interview with Cecilia Tandoc, 4 October 2005. Cecilia served Raja and Piroska as their domestic help from May 1985 until both passed away.
12. Interview with Tommy Koh, 12 June 2006.
13. Interview with Dennis Bloodworth, 12 February 2005.
14. Raja evoked these vivid images of life in early Singapore in his speech at the pre-university seminar, "*Birth of a Nation: Singapore in the 1950s*", 18 June 1984.
15. Kean Chye left for Christ College in 1935, while Hong Bee went there in 1937.
16. Philip Hoalim Sr., *The Malayan Democratic Union, Singapore's First Democratic Political Party*, 1973. Lim Kean Chye was Hoalim's nephew.

17. Ang Swee Suan, ed., *Dialogues with S. Rajaratnam*, p. 238.
18. Chin Peng, *My Side of the Story*, p. 279.
19. Goh's wife, Alice, then worked at MDU's Cooperative Store, located above the Liberty Cabaret. That provided another reason for Goh to drop by the cabaret and talk politics with the MDU leaders over beer.
20. Ang Swee Suan, ed., *Dialogues with S. Rajaratnam*, p. 239.
21. Ibid., p. 233.
22. In Raja's mind, Malaya included Singapore.
23. Report by A.H. Borthwick, first secretary, Australian Commission in Singapore, to the Department of External Affairs, Canberra. 12 June 1959, NAS.
24. In June 1948, laws were introduced to require federation of unions to be confined to unions catering for workers in similar occupations or industries, and for officials of union, except for the secretary, to have had 3 years' experience in the industry of their union.
25. Interview with Samad Ismail, 3 September 2005.
26. In August 1947, the PMCJA changed its name to the All-Malaya Council of Joint Action (AMCJA) — the Chinese Chambers objected to "Pan-Malayan" as it suggested communist domination, while the Malayan Nationalist Party objected to "Malayan" as it was often used by Malays to refer to only non-Malays.
27. *Malaya Tribune*, 19 July 1947.
28. In another piece on China a year later, headlined "Deeds, not Dollars, will Save China", dated 16 July 1948, Raja pointed out that the Nationalists faced two foes — the Communists and rising inflation. "The inflation has succeeded in 'proletarianising' large sections of the Chinese who have now nothing to fear from the Communists." His warning: The Nationalists must carry out reforms and curb profiteering and graft — if they dither, "they will be handing the future of China into Communist hands in the long run".
29. Exports of Malaya's two greatest raw materials — rubber and tin — depended heavily on the fluctuating American market and provided the sterling area with its greatest source of dollar earnings.
30. *Malaya Tribune*, 10 July 1947.
31. *Malaya Tribune*, 26 July 1947.
32. Ibid.
33. *Malaya Tribune*, 30 August 1947.
34. *Malaya Tribune*, 27 September 1948.
35. In the face of international pressure, the Dutch formally recognised Indonesian independence in December 1949.
36. Chin Peng, *My Side of History*, p. 155.

37. Ibid., p.199.
38. *Malaya Tribune*, 26 April 1949.
39. *Malaya Tribune*, 16 August 1947.
40. *Malaya Tribune*, 9 November 1948.
41. The colonial government invited the British authors over to Malaya for two months to do research for the report.
42. *MSS Political Intelligence Journal*, No. 3/48, 15 February 1948.
43. *The Business Times*, 6 October 1988.
44. Ang Swee Suan, ed., *Dialogues with S. Rajaratnam*, p. 6.
45. As told by his son, Ananda Pereira, in an interview, 26 March 2009.
46. Alex Josey, Oral History, NAS.
47. David Marshall, Oral History, NAS.
48. Ibid.
49. In 1952, Han Suyin married Leon F. Comber, a British officer in the Malayan Special Branch, and moved with him to Johore, Malaya.
50. Emily Hahn, who wrote for *The New Yorker*, was based in New York. She also wrote *Raffles of Singapore*, a biography of Sir Thomas Stamford Raffles (1946).
51. David Marshall's diary, 8 August 1963, ISEAS.
52. Ibid.
53. Alex Josey, Oral History, NAS.
54. Letter from assistant managing editor, Lim Keng Hor, to Raja, dated 24 February 1948. The increases were paid retrospectively.
55. *MSS Political Intelligence Journal*, No. 3/48, 15 February 1948.
56. Also known as the *Singapore Tiger Standard*.

Chapter 7

1. Raja's private papers, author's collection.
2. The rent was $175 for the house and $25 for the furniture.
3. Raja's private papers, author's collection.
4. The communists attacked rubber plantations, factories and warehouses as most were owned by Europeans, a sign of colonial power. In 1950, Malaya's rubber and tin mining industries were the biggest dollar earners in the British Commonwealth. Rubber accounted for 75 per cent of Malaya's income.
5. *Singapore Standard*, 29 July 1950.
6. *Singapore Standard*, 5 December 1950.
7. *Singapore Standard*, 15 December 1950.

8. Ibid.
9. Singapore Legislative Assembly, 19 December 1950.
10. Kean Chye fled to China.
11. S. Rajaratnam, Oral History, NAS.
12. In his Oral History, Chooi Yip recalled that the maid had coincidentally also worked in his elder brother's house previously.
13. Years later, he was arrested and later deported to Hanoi, finally winding up in Beijing in 1967, a year after the Singapore Government issued a ban on his re-entry.
14. *The Straits Times*, 21 November 1990.
15. Ibid.
16. Dennis Bloodworth, "Sinnathamby Rajaratnam: An appreciation by Dennis Bloodworth", 5 November 1983.
17. Interview with Samad Ismail, 3 September 2005.
18. Chin Peng, *My Side of History*, p. 278.
19. *SPF Police Intelligence Journal*, No. 3/1955, March 1955.
20. Eber was subsequently banned from re-entry into the Malayan territories by the governments in Singapore and Kuala Lumpur.
21. *SPF Police Intelligence Journal*, No. 3/1955, March 1955.
22. *Singapore Standard*, 28 March 1952.
23. Ang Swee Suan, ed., *Dialogues with S. Rajaratnam*, p. 40.
24. In this column, headlined "Who Are These Wicked Men of Hatred!", a defiant Raja called on Templer to declare who were the "wicked men" whom he had referred to in a speech at the Legislative Council. Templer had warned of wicked men who fostered hatred against the colonial powers. Raja asked him to clarify if these included people opposed to the official line on the question of Malayan independence.
25. While Raja might disagree with some of Templer's methods and views, he later credited the general for his effective and decisive moves that eventually turned the once seemingly unassailable communist tide.
26. Written communication with James Fu, 11 April 2008.
27. *SPF Police Intelligence Journal*, No. 3/1955, March 1955.
28. *Singapore Standard*, 17 September 1950.
29. As usual, he included Singapore when talking about "Malaya". Hence, these numbers took into account Singapore's population as well.
30. *Asian Horizon*, No. 3, "Malaya: A Nationalism in the Making", New Delhi, 1950–51.
31. *Asian Horizon*, No. 3, "Malaya: A Nationalism in the Making", New Delhi, 1950–51.

32. *Singapore Standard*, 27 August 1950.
33. Interview with Ungku Aziz, 2 September 2005. Ungku Aziz left Singapore in 1961 to head the economics department of the University of Malaya in Kuala Lumpur, and seven years later in 1968, was promoted to its vice-chancellor.
34. Dennis Bloodworth, "Sinnathamby Rajaratnam: An appreciation by Dennis Bloodworth", 5 November 1983.
35. Email interview with Leon Comber, 9 March 2009. Comber was married to Raja's writer friend Han Suyin from 1952 until they divorced in 1959.
36. *SPF Police Intelligence Journal*, No. 3/1955, March 1955.
37. Interview with Othman Wok, 13 June 2005.
38. The SUJ president at the time was D.E. Stewart, a journalist who lacked Raja's high profile.
39. *History of the Labour Movement: Interview with S. Rajaratnam*, 1994.

Chapter 8

1. Tan Siok Sun, *Goh Keng Swee: A Portrait* (Singapore: Editions Didier Millet, 2007).
2. In his oral history, Raja credit Goh as the first person to have planted the seed of Malayan nationalism among the Malayan students in London.
3. Interview with Lee Kuan Yew, 8 July 2005.
4. Ibid.
5. Interview with Ambrose Khaw, 26 May 2008.
6. Lee Kuan Yew, *The Singapore Story*.
7. Interview with Lee Kuan Yew, 8 July 2005.
8. Interview with Ambrose Khaw, 26 May 2008.
9. Interview with Lee Kuan Yew, 8 July 2005.
10. *Malaya Tribune*, 30 May 1952.
11. Interview with Lee Kuan Yew, 8 July 2005.
12. Woodhull, Oral History, NAS.
13. In 1953, Woodhull and other student leaders started the University of Malaya Socialist Club, an alumni which became a hotbed of left-wing politics. By this time, Lee, his hands full with unions, appointed Woodhull to the Naval Base Labour Union as their secretary, while Jamit Singh was posted to the Singapore Harbour Board Staff Association. Lee was adviser to these unions.
14. Melanie Chew, *Leaders of Singapore* (Singapore: Resource Press, 1996).
15. Toh Chin Chye highlighted Raja's role as a leader in the Joint Action Council in a speech at the PAP party conference in 1960.

16. Legislative Assembly Debate, 20 July 1959.
17. Ang Swee Suan, ed., *Dialogues with S. Rajaratnam.*
18. Speech at the working session of the NTUC delegates seminar on "Modernisation of the Labour Movements", 17 November 1969.
19. David Marshall's Diary, 30 December 1953, ISEAS.
20. Melanie Chew, *Leaders of Singapore*, p. 153.
21. Francis Thomas, *Memoirs of a Migrant*, p. 65.
22. David Marshall's Diary, ISEAS.
23. Interview with Victor Savage, 21 June 2006.
24. *The Sunday Tiger Standard*, 11 October 1953.
25. Ang Swee Suan, ed. *Dialogues with S. Rajaratnam.*
26. Ibid.
27. *Singapore Standard*, 16 August 1953.
28. *Singapore Standard*, 19 April 1953.

Chapter 9

1. *Singapore Standard*, 22 November 1953.
2. *Singapore Standard*, 13 September 1953.
3. Ibid.
4. In his column, "There are Limits to Foreign Capital", on 8 November 1953, he cited the example of Russia in bringing together all major enterprises under the strict control of the state. The savings that would have normally been acquired by the capitalists were invested by the government, not on the basis of which enterprises would yield handsome profits to the investor, but according to whether they would accelerate the growth of the national economy.
5. *Singapore Standard*, 29 March 1953.
6. Ibid.
7. *Singapore Standard*, 1 November 1953.
8. *Singapore Standard*, 22 March 1953.
9. *Singapore Standard*, 15 March 1953. Raja wrote this column shortly after the death of Stalin on 5 March that year.
10. *Singapore Standard*, 1 November 1953.
11. *Singapore Standard*, 15 November 1953.
12. Interview with Harry Chan, 28 March 2008. Chan would become Raja's permanent secretary in the Foreign Affairs Ministry in 1968.
13. *Singapore Standard*, 6 December 1963.
14. *Singapore Standard*, 20 September 1953.
15. *Singapore Standard*, 10 January 1954.

16. People's Action Party's 10th Anniversary souvenir, *Our First 10 Years*. 1964, p. 205.
17. Raja's account was that it was Lee who proposed the idea of forming the PAP. This contradicted that of Toh Chin Chye, who later took credit for suggesting the formation of a political party in an interview published in Melanie Chew's "Leaders of Singapore".
18. David Marshall's Diary, ISEAS.
19. Interview with Toh Chin Chye by Sonny Yap, 2002.
20. Special Branch files.
21. Alex Josey, Oral History, NAS.
22. The ASC, which held its first meeting in 1953 in Rangoon, brought together socialists from nine countries of Asia with fraternal delegates from the Socialist International, the League of Communists of Yugoslavia, the Congress of Peoples against Imperialism, and several representatives from African freedom movements, among others. This linkage between socialist parties from Asia and Africa played a fundamental role two years later in the development of the Bandung Conference and the Non-Aligned Movement. The ASC was dissolved in 1960.
23. *SPF Police Intelligence Journal*, No. 3/1955, March 1955 , and Special Branch files.
24. *Fajar*, "Acquisition of Malaya — Peaceful?", June 1954.
25. *SPF Police Intelligence Journal*, No. 8/1954, 31 August 1954.
26. Interview with Lee Kuan Yew, 8 July 2005.
27. Interview with Samad Ismail, 3 September 2005.
28. A survey of the urban incomes and housing between 1953 and 1954, written by Goh Keng Swee, then assistant director of social welfare (social research), found that the average income per household was $168 a month. For the individual, the average earnings was $140 a month. Among the employees, the earnings ranged from $82 by factory workers, to $215 for clerks. Teachers, nurses, and various professions earned an average of $194 a month. As for housing, the survey found that 84 per cent of households in the city limits occupied one room or one cubicle or less. Over half lived in cubicles with an average size of 103 sq ft. Overcrowding was a problem. One third of these cubicles had no window or proper sanitation.
29. Interview with Fong Swee Suan, 4 June 2009.
30. Interview with Lee Kuan Yew, 8 July 2005.
31. Interview with Fong Swee Suan, 4 June 2009.
32. People's Action Party's 10th Anniversary souvenir, *Our First 10 Years*, p. 204.

33. People's Action Party's 10th Anniversary souvenir, *Our First 10 Years*, p. 205.
34. Interview with Lee Kuan Yew, 8 July 2005.

Chapter 10

1. Interview with Yap Chin Kwee, 4 September 2005.
2. Ibid.
3. Anthony Schooling was married to Nalini Nair, sister of S. Devan Nair, another founding member of the PAP.
4. Written communication with Bloodworth, 12 February 2005.
5. Ibid.
6. Interview with Lee Kuan Yew, 8 July 2005.
7. Bloodworth, Oral History, NAS.
8. Louis Heren, *Growing Up on The Times* (London: H. Hamilton, 1978).
9. Written communication with Bloodworth, 12 February 2005.
10. People's Action Party's 10th Anniversary souvenir, *Our First 10 Years*, 1964.
11. *Raayat* is Malay for "citizen" or "the people".
12. Email interview with Lee Kuan Yew, 17 June 2006.
13. *Raayat*, Vol. 1, No. 1, "We believe…" 13 December 1954.
14. *Raayat*, Vol. 1, No. 3. "Beware of Little David". 27 December 1954.
15. *Raayat*, Vol. 1, No. 5. "Malay Capitalists". 10 January 1955.
16. Tan Siew Sin took over as MCA president in November 1961 and became minister of finance from 1959 to 1974.
17. Raja had met Aron in London when the French intellectual fled to London in 1940 to escape German occupation in France. During his exile in London, he edited the newspaper, *France Libre* (Free France).
18. The STU was an open front organisation of the Malayan Communist Party.
19. The S. Rajaratnam Papers, ISEAS.
20. *Raayat*, Vol. 1, No. 7, March 1955.
21. Ibid.
22. *Raayat*, Vol. 1, No. 1, 13 December 1954. It also published an article by Purcell on this issue which echoed Raja's views: "Among those who wish to see Malaya rapidly attain self-government, there is a strong feeling that unless the Emergency regulations are removed or substantially modified together with the present out-of-date sedition laws, the atmosphere necessary for the conduct of free elections is unlikely to exist."
23. Lee discovered later, to his chagrin, that the roaring applause at these rallies was not as spontaneous as it seemed, but orchestrated by the pro-communists for effect. *The Singapore Story*, p. 192.

24. Even prior to this, Raja believed that the communists had conceded defeat in their guerilla campaign and knew the futility of using violence. In 1952, Louis Heren, his friend from *The Times*, had shared notes from a classified document, dated September 1951, which said as much. The directive from the Politburo of the MCP admitted that violence had not won popular support and ordered the state and district committees to end hostilities. But the war was to drag on because the MPAJA did not have radio transmitters, and the directive had to be delivered by messengers. The number of terrorist incidents did fall from 6,100 in 1951 to 1,100 by the end of 1953, leading Heren to conclude that the directive had taken effect. Approvingly, Raja had reproduced Heren's scoop in *The Standard*.
25. *The Singapore Story*, p. 192.
26. Special Branch files.
27. *Raayat*, Vol. 1, No. 7. March 1955. Letter by a "T.S.L.".
28. *Fajar*, 30 December 1954, No. 14.
29. *Raayat*, Vol. 1, No. 5.
30. *Raayat*, Vol. 1, No. 1, 13 December 1954.
31. Ibid.
32. Interview with Lee Kuan Yew, 8 July 2005.
33. *Singapore Standard*, "Growls, Barks and Bites", 25 April 1959.
33. Mary Turnbull, *Dateline Singapore, 150 Years of The Straits Times* (Singapore Press Holdings, 1995).
34. *The Straits Times*, "Repeating the Facts", 15 February 1954.
35. This was confirmed by Mrs Lee Siew Yee in an interview with the author. Although there was another account, mentioned by Raja himself in his later years, that it was David Marshall who was responsible for the job offer, Jean Marshall believed this was highly unlikely given that Marshall's persona was anathema to the *Straits Times*. Jean Marshall's interview with author, 19 March 2008.
36. Interview with Jean Gray, 19 March 2008.
37. Turnbull, C.M., *Dateline Singapore*, p. 179.
38. Interview with Lee Kuan Yew, 8 July 2005.
39. This view was repeated in *Dateline Singapore*.
40. Alex Josey, *Trade Unionism in Malaya* (Singapore: Donald Moore, 1958), p. 61.
41. Email interview with Peter Lim, 21 July 2006.
42. Ibid.
43. Interview with Lee Khoon Choy, 20 June 2005.
44. Interview with Lee Kuan Yew, 8 July 2005.

45. The calculation was that, since the Naval Base workers had the decisive vote, Ahmad would get better support from the Malays and Indian workers, if he was not identified with the radical PAP.
46. *The Straits Times*, 11 April 1955.

Chapter 11

1. 135,000 days in 1954.
2. Lee Kuan Yew, *The Singapore Story*, p. 206.
3. Speech of William Goode, Singapore Legislative Assembly debates, 16 May 1955.
4. Speech of David Marshall, Singapore Legislative Assembly debates, 16 May 1955.
5. The PAP's Tenth Anniversary Celebration souvenir, *PAP's First Ten Years*, 1964.
6. Interview with Fong Swee Suan, 4 June 2009.
7. Interview with Samad Ismail, 3 September 2005.
8. Ibid.
9. *The Straits Times*, 27 October 1955.
10. *The Straits Times*, 27 October 1955.
11. *The Straits Times*, 25 October 1955.
12. *The Straits Times*, 24 October 1955.
13. *The Straits Times*, 25 October 1955.
14. *The Straits Times*, 24 October 1955.
15. David Marshall announced earlier at a Legislative Assembly meeting on 21 November 1955, that an Economic Advisory Unit had been set up, with Sir Sydney Caine as the economic adviser. The purpose of the unit was to give advice to the government on general economic policy, the programme of capital investment, and the broad economic aspects of social policy.
16. The committee also drew from the expertise of G.J. Brocklehurst, a specialist on social security from the International Labour Office, and Walter B. Wilson, from the Department of Labour in Australia.
17. *Petir*, February 1957. (*Petir* is the PAP's newsletter.)
18. Interview with Lim Chong Yah, 3 May 2007.
19. Many unemployed did not register with the Labour Exchange as they lived too far away or had little hope of getting a job through the Exchange, run by the Labour Department.
20. *SPF Police Intelligence Journal*, No. 7/1956, Appendix B, 31 July 1956.
21. Interview with Mahmud Awang, 8 November 2009.

22. The verbatim notes of the meetings of the Malayanisation Commission are available at the NAS.
23. Interview with Lim Chong Yah, 30 June 2006.
24. Singapore Legislative Assembly, 20 July 1959.
25. Interview with Seah Yong, 11 April 2008.
26. *Singapore Standard*, "The News As it Strikes Me", 22 October 1956.
27. Interview with Fong Swee Suan, 4 June 2009.
28. Interview with Othman Wok, 13 June 2005.
29. Interview with Lee Kuan Yew, 8 July 2005.
30. Speech delivered by Goh Keng Swee at the Establishment Dinner on 25 September 1984. Also reproduced in Goh Keng Swee, *Wealth of East Asian Nation*, p. 145.
31. T.T. Rajah, Oral History, NAS.
32. Interview with Samad Ismail, 3 September 2005.
33. Lim Yew Hock had another reason to act — his own mass base at STUC was also on the verge of being captured by the pro-communists.
34. A new class of members — cadres — were introduced, separate from ordinary branch membership. Only they could elect the CEC, and in turn, the CEC selects the cadres.

Chapter 12

1. The radio script can be found in *The S. Rajaratnam Papers*, ISEAS.
2. Interview with Foong Choon Hon, 15 June 2005.
3. Email interview with Wang Gungwu, 23 June 2009.
4. Transmission on 28, 30, and 31 October 1957.
5. *SPF Police Intelligence Journal*, No. 7/1958, 31 July 1958.
6. *SPF Police Intelligence Journal*, No. 4/1957, 30 April 1957.
7. *Petir*, "National Language and Culture", May 1957.
8. Chan became a founder member of the PAP in 1954 and a PAP city councillor in 1957.
9. Interview with Chan Chee Seng, 10 April 2008.
10. Interview with Hoe Puay Choo, 30 May 2008.
11. Interview with Lee Kuan Yew, 8 July 2005.
12. These terms are found in the reports filed by the British and Australian High Commissions during that period.
13. Bloodworth, Oral History, NAS.
14. *Petir*, "Left-Wing Adventurism", October 1957.
15. *Petir*, "An Independent, Democratic, Non-Communist Socialist Malaya", October 1957.

16. Ibid.
17. Interview with Chan Chee Seng, 10 April 2008.
18. Interview with Lee Kuan Yew, 8 July 2005.
19. Rajaratnam, PAP's 10th Anniversary souvenir, *Our First 10 Years*, p. 208.
20. Lim Yew Hock's Labour Front won only four out of the 16 contested. The Liberal Socialist party, which had repeatedly called for the removal of the PAP from the political arena, won seven out of a total of 32 contested.
21. Toh at the PAP meeting on 26 June 1960 which took the decision to expel Ong.
22. Dennis Bloodworth, Oral History, NAS.
23. Lee Kuan Yew, *The Singapore Story*.
24. PAP's 10th Anniversary souvenir, *Our First 10 Years*, p. 209.
25. Interview with Nalini Nair, 28 September 2006.
26. *Asia Magazine*, 15–17 September 1989.
27. *The Straits Times*, "Newsman Quits Job to Work for the PAP", 29 March 1959.

Chapter 13

1. Melanie Chew, *Leaders of Singapore* (Singapore: Resource Press, 1996).
2. This increase was because of the new citizenship laws. The PAP leaders were reasonably confident that they had the support of the working class, having established their credentials with them, but were uncertain of the new Chinese voters who recently came from China, given their instinctive loyalties to their motherland and their pro-communist proclivities.
3. *The Straits Times*, "Lee: Justice for All is PAP Aim", 16 April 1959.
4. *Petir*, "The Rojak Party and the Menace of Real Democracy", February 1959.
5. Fong Sip Chee, *The PAP Story: The Pioneering Years, November 1954–April 1968: A Diary of Events of the People's Action Party: Reminiscences of An Old Cadre* (Singapore: Times Periodicals, 1980), p. 70.
6. *Singapore Standard*, "Lest We Forget", 30 April 1959.
7. *The Straits Times*, "PAP attacks the Straits Times", 16 April 1959.
8. Email interview with Peter Lim, 21 July 2006.
9. *The Straits Times*, 21 April 1959.
10. Email interview with Peter Lim, 21 July 2006.
11. Interview with Ee Boon Lee, 20 May 2008.
12. Interview with Ambrose Khaw, 1 June 2008.
13. *The Straits Times*, "Fancy and Fact", 30 April 1959.
14. Lee Kuan Yew, *The Singapore Story*, p. 298.

15. A.H. Borthwick, first secretary, Australian Commission in Singapore, to the Department of External Affairs,Canberra. 12 June 1959.
16. *The Times* of London, 4 June 1959.
17. Lee Kuan Yew, in his letter to *The Straits Times*, 22 May 1955.
18. *The Straits Times*, 29 May 1959.
19. Interview with Ambrose Khaw, 1 June 2008.
20. Interview with Lee Khoon Choy, 20 June 2005.
21. Email interview with Peter Lim, 21 July 2006.
22. Interview with Boon Yoon Chiang, 4 June 2008.
23. Melanie Chew, *Leaders of Singapore*.
24. Lee Kuan Yew, *The Singapore Story*.
25. Dennis Bloodworth, *The Tiger and the Trojan Horse* (Singapore: Times Books International, 1986), p. 192.
26. The others in the nine-man cabinet were Yong Nyuk Lin as education minister, Ong Pang Boon as home affairs minister, Ahmad Ibrahim as health minister and Ong Eng Guan as national development minister.
27. D.W. McNicol, Australian commissioner in Singapore, to minister for external affairs, R.G. Casey, in Canberra, 12 June 1959.
28. William Goode, the U.K. Commissioner in Singapore, to the secretary of state for the colonies, 26 June 1959.

Chapter 14

1. Singapore Legislative Assembly, 12 December 1959.
2. Singapore Legislative Assembly, 13 December 1959.
3. Dennis Bloodworth, *An Eye for The Dragon*, p. 297.
4. Singapore Legislative Assembly, 29 November 1960.
5. *Sunday Mail*, "Malayan Culture: A Reply to Sceptics", 27 September 1959.
6. Of this amount to the Finance Ministry, $20 million was for setting up the Economic Development Board to create jobs.
7. *The Straits Times*, "Radio: The New Order", *The Standard* "Minister of Culture knocks the rock", 10 June 1959.
8. Notes of discussion held in the office of the minister of culture, 11 June 1959.
9. Ibid.
10. Ibid.
11. Speech on "Malaya's Changing Cultures", at a luncheon hosted by the Junior Chamber of Commerce, 27 February 1960.
12. Email interview with Wang Gungwu, 23 June 2009.

13. Singapore Legislative Assembly, 13 December 1959.
14. Radio broadcast of a talk on Malayan Culture by Raja, 27 February 1960.
15. Email interview with Wang Gungwu, 23 June 2009.
16. Toh was overseas for a conference when the cabinet approved the final design and when Raja took it through the Legislative Assembly. In his oral history, recorded in 1989, Toh said that, in his original recommendation, he was against using red and white — white above red is the flag of Poland while red above white is that of Indonesia.
17. Singapore Legislative Assembly, 13 December 1960.
18. Ang Swee Suan, ed., *Dialogues with S. Rajaratnam.*
19. Ang Swee Suan, ed., *Dialogues with S. Rajaratnam.*
20. Radio broadcast for the series *A Matter of Policy*, 13 June 1960.
21. Singapore Legislative Assembly, 13 December 1959.
22. Speech to Menorah Club, 25 July 1960.
23. Speech to the University Socialist Club, 26 August 1960.
24. V.T. Arasu, Oral History, NAS.
25. Interview with Foong Choon Hon, 15 June 2005.
26. Interview with Gopinath Pillai, 6 November 2008.
27. Speech at the Tamils' festival at the Happy World, 13 January 1960.
28. Speech at the Combined School Variety Show at the Singapore Chinese YMCA, 5 December 1960.
29. Interview with Lee Kuan Yew, 4 May 2009.
30. Ibid.
31. Singapore Legislative Assembly, 12 December 1959.
32. Interview with Lee Khoon Choy, 20 June 2005.
33. V.T. Arasu, Oral History, NAS.
34. Raja referred to the letter in his speech at the opening of the seminar on Malay music, 24 December 1960.
35. Ibid.
36. Speech to establish the National Theatre Trust to manage the National Theatre at the Legislative Assembly, on 16 November 1960.
37. The concert at the Victoria Theatre was in aid of the National Theatre Fund and the Jesuits Foundation fund.
38. *The Straits Times*, "Malaysian Touch — by Minister", 2 May 1963.
39. Speech at the opening of the seminar on Malay Music, Cultural Theatre, 24 December 1960.
40. Ang Swee Suan, ed., *Dialogues with S Rajaratnam.*
41. D.J. Enright, *Memoirs of a Mendicant Professor* (London: Chatto & Windus, 1969).

42. Singapore Legislative Assembly, 29 November 1960.
43. Singapore Legislative Assembly, 11 January 1961.

Chapter 15

1. Interview with Yong Nyuk Lin, 31 August 2005.
2. Interview with Lee Kuan Yew, 4 May 2009.
3. Ibid.
4. Cabinet paper (59) 17, dated 13 June 1959.
5. Radio broadcast on 26 February 1960, translated into Chinese.
6. Minutes of cabinet meeting, 5 October 1959.
7. Cabinet paper (59) 17, dated 13 June 1959.
8. Singapore Legislative Assembly, 15 December 1960.
9. Minutes of the 16th Ministerial Policy Committee meeting on 6 October 1959.
10. Melanie Chew, *Leaders of Singapore*, p. 143.
11. Interview with Lee Kuan Yew, 4 May 2009.
12. Ibid.
13. *Nanyang Siang Pau*, 15 June 1959.
14. *The Straits Times*, "Role of the Press in New Malaya — by Rajaratnam", 27 July 1959.
15. Ibid. See also *The Straits Times*, 13 March 1962, "Journalism for all in Varsity, he urges".
16. Speech at the opening of the seminar on journalism at the University of Singapore, 12 March 1962.
17. Interview with Lee Kuan Yew, 4 May 2009.
18. Singapore Legislative Assembly, 15 December 1961.
19. Singapore Legislative Assembly, 12 December 1959.
20. Interview with Lee Kuan Yew, 4 May 2009.
21. Speech at a dinner hosted by the Foreign Correspondents' Association of Southeast Asia, 17 June 1986.
22. Talk titled "The Cultural Approach to Politics", delivered to the University Socialist Club on 26 August 1960.
23. *Nanyang Siang Pau*, 15 June 1959.
24. Letter from William Goode, the *Yang di-Pertuan Negara* and U.K. commissioner for Singapore, to London, dated 26 July 1959, Public Records Office (PRO), Kew.
25. *The Straits Times*, "Radio: The New Order", 10 June 1959.
26. Ibid.; *Singapore Standard*, 10 June 1959.
27. Interview with S.R. Nathan, 17 September 2009. When Nathan's family turned up on the ship to bid Piroska *bon voyage*, she was surprised that

they knew about her departure and instructed them to keep it a secret. K.M. Byrne, the Minister for Law and Labour, also sent his European wife, Elaine Margaret, abroad during this period.

28. Ibid.
29. Siva Choy, Oral History, NAS.
30. The members of Raja's committee included Puthucheary, Devan Nair, Woodhull, Jek Yuen Thong and Rahim Ishak.
31. Gok Keng Swee revealed this in a Singapore Legislative Assembly debate, on 11 December 1961.
32. Singapore Legislative Assembly, 11 December 1961.
33. Singapore Legislative Assembly, 12 December 1960.
34. Speech delivered at the induction course for the government public relations officers at the Civil Service Institute on 17 May 1982.
35. Ibid.
36. Raj K. Vasil, *Governing Singapore* (St Leonards, N.S.W., Australia: Allen & Unwin, 2000).
37. Interview with Hedwig Anuar, 7 October 2005.
38. Speech at opening of the Southeast Asia room in the National Library on 28 August 1964.
39. Boon Yoon Chiang worked in the Culture Ministry as press officer/reporter from 1960 to 1964, and then as editor (English) Broadcasting Department (*Radio Television Singapura*) until 1967.
40. Interview with Foong Choon Hon, 15 June 2005.
41. Interview with Cecilia Tandoc, 4 October 2005.
42. Lee Kuan Yew's eulogy at Raja's state funeral, 25 February 2006.
43. V.T. Arasu, Oral History, NAS.
44. Inside File PM 049/59 — People's Association General 1959–62.
45. Interview with Ong Kim Leong, 1 June 2005.
46. Singapore Legislative Assembly, 14 June 1963.
47. Singapore Legislative Assembly, 15 June 1963.

Chapter 16

1. Undated and unfinished typewritten article, Raja's private papers, author's collection.
2. The constitution was up for review in 1963.
3. Under the Industrial Relations Ordinance passed in February 1959, an industrial arbitration court was set up with arbitration of industrial disputes made compulsory. A Trade Union Bill was also hurried through to tighten government control of the trade union movement.

4. Woodhull, Oral History, NAS.
5. Bloodworth, *The Tiger and The Trojan Horse.*
6. Telegram from U.K. Commissioner (Singapore) to secretary of state (Colonial Office), 21 June 1960.
7. *The Times* of London, 22 June 1960.
8. Speech at the Anglo-Chinese Junior College pre-University seminar at the Jurong Town Hall, 1978.
9. Interview with Hoe Puay Choo, 30 May 2008.
10. In her letter to Lee Kuan Yew then, Hoe said she wanted to resign because she had not been consulted on important policy decisions.
11. Her exit was a blow to the party which at that time held the majority by just one member. With her departure, PAP members in the House were reduced to 25, against the combined opposition's 26. The party suddenly found itself running a minority government. This happened just three days before the crucial vote on the referendum bill on 6 July which paved the way for merger between Singapore and Malaysia the following year.
12. Melanie Chew, *Leaders of Singapore*, p. 124.
13. The critical articles of Ong were in the 14 July 1960 issue of *Petir*.
14. Singapore Legislative Assembly, 5 August 1960.
15. The motion was to condemn Ong's dishonourable conduct as unbecoming of an elected representative "in that he repeatedly used his privilege in this Assembly as a cloak for spreading malicious falsehoods to unjustly injure innocent persons both inside and outside this Assembly".
16. *Petir*, PAP's 25th anniversary issue.
17. *Petir*, "Double-thinking leads to Double-talking", 14 November 1960.
18. *Sunday Times*, 12 March 1961, "It's PAP v Ong in Hong Lim".
19. *Petir*, Truth and Falsehood, 4 March 1961.
20. Interview with Jek Yuen Thong, 2 September 2005.
21. Bloodworth, Oral History, NAS.
22. Ibid.
23. *The Straits Times*, "Party Told: Analyse setback", 10 May 1951.
24. People's Action Party's 10th Anniversary souvenir, *Our First 10 Years*, 1964
25. *Sunday Times*, 28 May 1961. Tunku's speech was made at the luncheon by the foreign correspondents of South-east Asia at the Adelphi hotel.
26. His reading of the situation would turn out right, as declassified British records later showed, although Selkirk had publicly said at the time that the inclusion of the Borneo territories was Tunku's idea and no one else's. The British knew that any taint of the proposal for merger and Malaysia as being British-inspired at the time would have immediately sunk it as a colonial

plot and opened Tunku and Lee to the debilitating charge of being pro-colonial stooges.
27. Submission from Menzies to Cabinet, Canberra, 11 August 1961.
28. Ibid.
29. *The Straits Times*, 10 July 1961.
30. Toh Chin Chye, "The Ways and Means", *Petir* 25th anniversary issue. The Feedback Unit was renamed Reach in 2007.
31. Cabinet approved Goh's paper on 11 July 1960.

Chapter 17

1. Siao Chang, who was relaying party instructions to senior party cadres in Singapore and Malaya from his base in Peking, would lead the MCP armed struggle at the front line at the Thai-Malaysia border.
2. Chin Peng, *My Side of the Story*, p. 437.
3. Lim Cheng Leng, *Story of a Psy-Warrior* (Batu Caves, Selangor Darul Ehsan, Malaysia: Lim Cheng Leng, 2000), p. 198.
4. Chin Peng, *My Side of the Story*, p. 438.
5. Ibid., p. 409.
6. Interview with Samad Ismail, 3 September 2005.
7. Ibid.
8. Interview with Samad Ismail, 3 September 2005.
9. Chin Peng, *My Side of the Story*, p. 438.
10. Interview with Lee Kuan Yew, 4 May 2009.
11. They were Fong Swee Suan, S. Woodhull, S.T. Bani, Dominic Puthucheary, and Jamit Singh. Together with Lim, they were dubbed the "Big Six".
12. Bloodworth, Oral History, NAS.
13. Singapore Legislative Assembly, 21 July 1961.
14. *Petir*, 17 June 1961.
15. *Petir*, "Democracy On Trial", 13 July 1961.
16. Ibid.
17. The eight were Lee Siew Choh, Wong Soon Fong, Tee Kim Leng, Tan Cheng Tong, Teo Hock Guan, S.T. Bani, Lim You Eng, and Fung Ying Ching.
18. Singapore Legislative Assembly, 21 July 1961.
19. Interview with Fong Swee Suan, 4 June 2009.
20. *The Straits Times*, "Marshall: I don't believe Chin Peng leads Malaya's Reds", 30 December 1955. In his memoirs, Chin Peng gave short shrift to Marshall's powers of analysis.

21. Speech at a students' forum, 14 August 1987.
22. *The Straits Times*, 21 August 1961.
23. Singapore Legislative Assembly, 21 July 1961.
24. Speech on 27 July 1985.
25. The PAP Tenth Anniversary Celebration souvenir, *PAP's First Ten Years*, 1964, p. 214.
26. Ibid.
27. Bloodworth, Oral History, NAS.
28. *The Straits Times*, 22 August 1961.
29. Learning from this experience, they changed the Constitution in 1963 to disallow a person voted into parliament on a party ticket to retain his seat if he ceased to be a member of that party, or was expelled, or resigned from his seat.
30. People's Action Party's 10th Anniversary souvenir, *Our First 10 Years*.
31. Interview with Hoe Puay Choo, 30 May 2008.
32. Ibid.
33. Singapore Legislative Assembly, 23 November 1961.
34. Melanie Chew, *Leaders of Singapore*, p. 124.
35. Interview with Lee Kuan Yew, 8 July 2005.
36. Ibid.
37. Ibid.
38. Ibid.
39. Lee Kuan Yew, *The Singapore Story*.
40. Lee Kuan Yew in his eulogy for Raja, 25 February 2006.
41. Singapore Legislative Assembly, 20 March 1962.
42. Singapore Legislative Assembly, 14 June 1963.
43. Alex Josey, Oral History, NAS.
44. Interview with Chan Chee Seng, 10 April 2008.
45. Interview with Jek Yuen Thong, 2 September 2005.
46. *Petir*, PAP's 25th anniversary issue.
47. Lee Kuan Yew in his eulogy for Raja, 25 February 2006.
48. Goh Keng Swee, *Wealth of East Asian Nation*, p. 147.
49. Speech at the launch of the first National Youth Conference, 16 July 1982.
50. Speech at the 15th anniversary dinner of the Institute of Public Relations, 15 March 1986.
51. Raj Vasil, *Governing Singapore*, p. 42.
52. Interview with Fong Swee Suan, 4 June 2009.
53. Telegram from the Australian High Commission, Singapore, to the Secretary, Department of Foreign Affairs, Canberra, 2 June 1962.

54. David Marshall, Oral History, NAS.
55. Interview with Lee Kuan Yew, 8 July 2005.
56. *Democratic Socialism in Action, June 1959–April 1963.*
57. Malay language issue of *Petir*, August 1961 issue.
58. Said Zahari, *Dark Clouds at Dawn: A Political Memoir* (Kuala Lumpur: Insan, 2001).
59. "Working paper outlines basis for socialism in Malaysia", published in *Petir* on 7 March 1962.
60. *Sunday Mail*, 28 January 1962.
61. Singapore Legislative Assembly, 18 April 1962.
62. Ibid.
63. Singapore Legislative Assembly, 1 December 1961.

Chapter 18

1. Interview with Lee Kuan Yew, 4 May 2009.
2. Ibid.
3. Telegram from the British commissioner in Singapore to the secretary of state for the colonies, dated 25 July 1961.
4. Speech at the business session of the Eighth CPA Regional Conference in Singapore, 22 July 1961.
5. Speech at the business session of the Eighth CPA Regional Conference in Singapore, 24 July 1961
6. The low level of political development in the North Borneo states at the time is well documented. Read especially J.P. Ongkili, *The Borneo Response to Malaysia, 1961–1963* (Donald Moore Press, 1967).
7. The two parties in Sarawak were the Sarawak United People's Party and the Party Negara Sarawak. The Brunei party was the Parti Rakyat. Sabah had its first political party only in August 1961, with Donald Stephen's United National Kadazan Organisation.
8. Speech at the closing session of the CPA Conference, 26 July 1961.
9. Telegram from the British commissioner in Singapore to the secretary of state for the colonies, dated 25 July 1961.
10. Ibid.
11. Lord George Lansdowne, U.K. minister of state for colonial affairs, and chairman of the Inter-Governmental Committee on Malaysia, quoted Razak as telling him this during a long talk alone with him. They were discussing the deteriorating relationship between the Tunku and Lee. Telegram from Lansdowne to secretary of state for commonwealth relations, 17 December 1962.

12. "A Tribute". In tribute to Tunku Abdul Rahman on his 60th birthday, 8 February 1963.
13. Ibid.
14. Interview with Yap Chin Kwee, 4 September 2005.
15. Anthony J. Stockwell, ed., *Malaysia. British Documents on the End of Empire*, Series B, Vol. 8 (London: Stationery Office, 2004), p. xxxvii. Also see Allen M. Healy, *Tunku Abdul Rahman (1957–1970)* (St Lucia: University of Queensland Press, 1982), pp. 20–21.
16. Anthony Shome, *Malay Political Leadership* (Routledge, 2002), p. 78.
17. Interview with Lee Kuan Yew, 4 May 2009.
18. Ibid.
19. Ghazali Shafie, *Memoir on the Formation of Malaysia* (Bangi, Malaysia: Penerbit Universiti Kebangsaan, 1998).
20. Interview with Lee Kuan Yew, 4 May 2009.
21. Singapore Legislative Assembly, 30 July 1963.
22. *The Straits Times*, 24 August 1961.
23. J.P. Ongkili, *The Borneo Response to Malaysia, 1961–1963* (Donald Moore Press, 1967). Ongkili later became Sabah deputy chief minister, among other political appointments.
24. Minutes of the meeting of the Malaysia Solidarity Consultative Committee, 24 August 1961.
25. Cabinet Paper No. (61) 432, 16 October 1961.
26. *The Straits Times*, "$40,000 culture tour by S'pore goodwill mission", 14 April 1962; "Mission to show the identity of culture in Borneo and Singapore", 24 April 1962; "Singapore Culture goes to Borneo — by air", 25 April 1962.
27. Shafie, Ghazali, *Memoir on the Formation of Malaysia* (Bangi, Malaysia: Penerbit Universiti Kebangsaan, 1998).
28. Ibid., p. 159.
29. Memorandum from the British governor of Sarawak to London, 11 December 1961.
30. The radio forum was broadcast over *Radio Singapore* on 10 January 1962, and reported the next day, 11 January 1962, in the newspapers.
31. Denis Warner, "The Second Fall of Singapore", *The Reporter*, 9 September 1965.
32. Singapore Legislative Assembly, 26 April 1961.
33. S.M. Vasagar, Oral History, NAS.
34. Interview with S.R. Nathan, 17 September 2009.
35. S. Subramaniam, Oral History, NAS.

36. Interview with Lee Kuan Yew, 4 May 2009.
37. Denis Warner, "The Second Fall of Singapore", *The Reporter*, 9 September 1965.
38. PAP press statement on 1 November 1961.
39. Singapore Legislative Assembly, 19 March 1962.
40. Statement issued by the Ministry of Culture, 27 April 1962.
41. As reported in a British telegram to London, dated 4 May 1962, Selkirk had asked the Tunku whether it was necessary for him always to refer to Singapore as a headache. The Tunku replied that this was understood by the oriental mind. "If you were nice to people, they got too cocky."
42. The Causeway carries a road and railway between the island of Singapore and the southern tip of the Malayan peninsula, Johor.
43. *The Straits Times*, 28 March 1962.
44. *The Straits Times*, 28 March 1962.
45. Statement issued by the Ministry of Culture, 4 April 1962.
46. Speech at the third convocation of Nanyang University, 30 March 1962.
47. *The Straits Times*, 4 April 1962.
48. The first article, "Three Approaches to Politics", was published in the 31 May 1962 issue of *Petir*, while the second was published in the June–July 1962 edition.
49. Aide-memoire from Toh Chin Chye to Lee Kuan Yew, 30 May 1962. It stated that Raja had been hospitalised since 9 May 1962.
50. Gordon Jockel to secretary, Department of External Affairs, 19 May 1962.
51. This comment was possibly written by the minister or a high-level official at the Department of External Affairs in Canberra upon reading the telegram. The Australian minister for external affairs at the time was Garfield Barwick.

Chapter 19

1. *The Straits Times*, 11 June 1962. His speech was read out by PAP assemblywoman Hoe Puay Choo.
2. U.K. commissioner, Kuala Lumpur, to Commonwealth Relations Office, 17 March 1962.
3. Acting U.K. commissioner, Singapore, to the secretary of state for the colonies, 4 May 1962.
4. Ghazalie Shafie, *Memoir on the Formation of Malaysia*.
5. Bloodworth, Oral History.
6. Interview with Boon Yoon Chiang, 4 June 2008.
7. Raj K. Vasil, *Governing Singapore*, p. 42.

8. British paper presented to the Tunku on 4 May 1962.
9. *The Straits Times*, 6 September 1962.
10. Singapore Legislative Assembly, 10 April 1963.
11. Cablegram to Canberra, 4 September 1962, reproduced in Moreen Dee, ed., *Australia and the Formation of Malaysia, 1961–1966* (Australia: Dept of Foreign Affairs and Trade, 2005).
12. *Petir*, "Verdict of the People", January 1963.
13. Singapore Legislative Assembly, 10 April 1963.
14. Singapore Legislative Assembly, 31 July 1963.
15. Speech at a mass rally organised by the NTUC at the Victoria Memorial Hall on 18 Sept 1962, SR/4/13a.
16. *The Straits Times*, 19 September 1962, "Display of Afro-Asian unity highlights victory rally", p. 20.
17. Singapore Legislative Assembly, 31 July 1963.
18. Singapore Legislative Assembly, 9–10 April 1963.
19. *The Straits Times*, 5 December 1962.
20. *The Straits Times*, 18 March 1988.
21. Interview with Dominic Puthucheary, 23 September 2009.
22. Ibid.
23. Interview with Low Por Tuck, 22 September 2009.
24. Moore's telegram to Ian Wallace in the Colonial Office, 5 December 1962.
25. *The People*, Vol. 5, No. 3, 22 July 1963, p. 1.
26. Interview with Abdullah Ahmad, 7 August 2008.
27. *The Straits Times*, 16 February 1963.
28. Interview with Ananda Pereira, 22 March 2009.
29. *The Straits Times*, 25 March 1963.
30. Speech on 15 January 1964.
31. Singapore Legislative Assembly, 14 June 1963.
32. Speech at the fifth anniversary celebration of Kampong Glam Community Centre, 12 June 1965.

Chapter 20

1. Tory to secretary of state, 16 October 1962.
2. Selkirk to secretary of state, 10 December 1962.
3. Selkirk to secretary of state, 16 December 1962.
4. Note of United Kingdom Delegation meeting on 25 July 1962, under the chairmanship of Lord Landsdowne.
5. Selkirk to secretary of state, 16 December 1962.

6. Landsdowne to secretary of state, 17 December 1962.
7. Chin Peng, *My Side of History*, p. 439.
8. Interview with Samad Ismail, 3 September 2005.
9. Bloodworth, Oral History, NAS.
10. Singapore Legislative Assembly, 10 April 1963.
11. Singapore Legislative Assembly, 10 April 1963.
12. Singapore Legislative Assembly, 25 July 1963.
13. *The Straits Times*, 17 February 1963.
14. Ibid.
15. Among his activities was leading a month-long, 10,000-strong strike at the Singapore Naval Base in October 1963.
16. Email interview with Michael Fernandez, 30 January 2009.
17. Speech at a mass rally on the City Hall Padang on 28 September 1963.
18. Raj Vasil, *Governing Singapore*, p. 7.
19. Ibid., p. 8.
20. Email interview with James Fu, 11 April 2008.
21. Ibid.
22. Interview with Wong Lam Wo, 1 June 2005.
23. Interview with S.R. Nathan, 26 September 2005.
24. The second phase, which he spoke about in 1964, involved more hard work — saving and increasing national wealth. This meant creating "more tools of production, like factories, learn new skills to work the factories, and make more goods for us to use and to export". At the same time, more social assets would be produced. As progress was made, "the individual incomes and standards of life of our people will also begin to rise gradually, especially if there is justice in distribution of the national wealth". Speech at Ponggal Festival at the Tamilian Association, 14 January 1964.
25. Speech at the opening of the Visionary Architecture and Singapore Housing exhibition, broadcast on Radio Singapore, 18 March 1963.
26. Memo from Goh to Raja, dated 27 November 1962.
27. Memo from Raja to Goh, 29 April 1963.
28. Singapore Legislative Assembly, 14 June 1963.
29. *The Straits Times*, 19 February 1963.
30. Singapore Legislative Assembly, 8 April 1963.
31. Singapore Legislative Assembly, 31 July 1963.
32. One was a bill to provide for the elections of 15 representatives for Singapore to the Central Parliament. The other was to raise the limit to borrow money by the issuing of Treasury Bills.
33. *The Straits Times*, 16 April 1963.

34. *The Straits Times*, 10 October 1962.
35. Choo Hoey was born in Indonesia, but was educated in Singapore from the age of 13.
36. Minutes of meeting, 4 April 1963.
37. Minutes of meeting, 7 May 1963.
38. Speech on 8 August 1963.
39. Email interview with S. Dhanabalan, 12 August 2009. Before taking over the National Development Ministry, Dhanabalan was minister for foreign affairs (1980–88), minister for culture (1981–84), and minister for community development (1984–86). When the National Theatre was torn down in 1986, the minister for national development was Teh Cheang Wan.
40. National Day message, June 1963.
41. Unfinished article titled, "Political Trends in Malaysia", private papers, author's collection.
42. *The Straits Times*, 9 August 1963.
43. *Malayan Times*, 23 August 1963.
44. *The Straits Times*, 31 August 1963.
45. Singapore Legislative Assembly, 31 July 1963.
46. *The Straits Times*, 7 September 1963.
47. Ibid.
48. *The Straits Times*, 17 September 1973.
49. Interview with Lee Kuan Yew, 8 July 2005.
50. Speech "Concept and Implementation of a Malaysian Malaysia" at a political forum of the Malaysia Solidarity Convention, 7 June 65.
51. Melanie Chew, *Leaders of Singapore* (Singapore: Resource Press, 1996), p. 95.
52. Interview with Lee Kuan Yew, 4 May 2009.

Interviews

Abdullah Ahmad
Ahmad Rithaudeen
Anuar, Hedwig
Arasu, V.T.
Awang, Mahmud
Bloodworth, Dennis
Boon Yoon Chiang
Chan Chee Seng
Chan, Harry
Chen Man Hin
Cheong, Eric
Chia Keng Hian
Cohen, Nina
Comber, Leon
Conceicao, Joe
Das, S. Chandra
Devan, Janadas
Dhanabalan, S.
Ee Boon Lee
Fernandez, Michael
Fong Swee Suan
Foong Choon Hon
Fu, James
Gray, Jean
Ho Kah Leong
Hoe Puay Choo
Hong, Mark
Istvan, Kiss
Jek Yuen Thong
Jothiratnam, S.
Jumabhoy, A.R.
Kanagasabai, Senathyrajah
Kesavapany, K.
Khaw, Ambrose
Koh, Tommy
Lee Khoon Choy
Lee Kuan Yew
Lee Siew Yee (Puan Sri)
Lim Chong Eu
Lim Chong Yah
Lim Kit Siang
Lim, Peter
Lingam, Anushia
Loh Meng See
Low Por Tuck
Lun Yue Sheong
Mahbubani, Kishore
Menzies, Joe
Mohamed Khir Johari
Mun Chor Seng
Nair, Nalini
Nathan, S.R.
Noordin Sopiee
Ong Kim Leong
Othman Wok
Pereira, Ananda
Pillai, Gopinath
Pillay, V.K.
Puthucheary, Dominic
Rajaratnam, S.
Samad Ismail
Savage, Victor

Seah Yong
Sivapragasapillai, C.
Subramaniam, M.
Tan Boon Chiang
Tan Hwa Luck
Tan Keng Jin
Tan Siok Sun
Tandoc, Cecilia
Teo Ban Hock
Thambiah, Vijayalakshimi
Thumboo, Edwin
Ungku Aziz bin Ungku Abdul Hamid
Vijayaratnam, Ashta
Vijayaratnam, S.
Wang Gungwu
Wong Lam Wo
Yap Chin Kwee
Yap, Sonny
Yong Nyuk Lin

Select Bibliography

Abdul Rahman, Tunku Putra al-Haj. *Looking Back: Monday Musings and Memories*. Kuala Lumpur: Pustaka Antara, 1977.

Anand, Mulk Raj and Iqbal Singh, eds. *Indian Short Stories*. New India Publishing Co., 1946.

Ang Swee Suan, ed. *Dialogues with S. Rajaratnam*. Singapore: *Shin Min Daily News*, 1991.

Baker, Denys Val, ed. *Modern International Short Stories*. London: W.H. Allen, 1947.

Bauer, Peter Tamas. *The Rubber Industry: A Study in Competition and Monopoly*. London: Longmans for London School of Economics and Political Science, 1948.

Bloodworth, Dennis. *The Tiger and the Trojan Horse*. Singapore: Times Books International, 1986.

———. *The Reporter's Notebook*. Singapore: Times Books International, 1988.

Calder, Angus. *The People's War, Britain 1939–1945*. London: Cape, 1969.

Central Office of Information, London. *Mirror*, vol. 1, no. 6 (1948).

Chai Hon-chan. *The Development of British Malaya 1896–1909*. Kuala Lumpur: Oxford University Press, 1967.

Chamberlain, E. R. *Life in Wartime Britain*. London: Batsford, 1972.

Chan Heng Chee. *A Sensation of Independence: A Political Biography of David Marshall*. Singapore: Oxford University Press, 1984.

Chan Heng Chee and Obaid ul Haq, eds. *The Prophetic & the Political: Selected Speeches & Writings of S. Rajaratnam*. Singapore: Graham Brash, 1987.

Cheah Boon Kheng. *The Masked Comrades: A Study of the Communist United Front in Malaya, 1945–48*. Singapore: Times Books International, 1979.

Chew, Melanie. *Leaders of Singapore*. Singapore: Resource Press, 1996.

Chin Peng. *My Side of History*. Singapore: Media Masters, 2003.

Churchill, Winston Spencer. *The Caged Lion*. London: Cardinal, 1989.

Dee, Moreen, ed. *Australia and the Formation of Malaysia, 1961–1966*. Australia: Dept of Foreign Affairs and Trade, 2005.

Drabble, John H. *Malayan Rubber: The Interwar Years*. Basingstoke, Hampshire: Macmillan Academic and Professional, 1991.

Enright, D.J. *Memoirs of a Mendicant Professor*. London: Chatto & Windus, 1969.

Fong Sip Chee. *The PAP Story: The Pioneering Years, November 1954–April 1968: A Diary of Events of the People's Action Party: Reminiscences of An Old Cadre*. Singapore: Times Periodicals, 1980.

Forster, Edward Morgan, Mary Lago, Linda K. Hughes, Elizabeth MacLeod Walls, P. N. (FRW) Furbank. *The BBC Talks of E. M. Forster, 1929–1960: A Selected Edition*. Columbia, MO: University of Missouri Press, 2008.

Gamba, Charles. *The Origins of Trade Unionism in Malaya*. Singapore: Eastern Universities Press, 1962.

Ghazali bin Shafie, Tan Sri Dato. *Memoir on the Formation of Malaysia*. Bangi, Malaysia: Penerbit Universiti Kebangsaan, 1998.

Goh Keng Swee. *The Economics of Modernisation*. Singapore: Federal Publications, 1995.

———. *The Practice of Economic Growth*. Singapore: Federal Publications, 1977.

———. *Wealth of East Asian Nations*. Singapore: Federal Publications, 1995.

Gopinathan, S. and Valerie Barth, eds. *The Need to Read: Essays in Honour of Hedwig Anuar*. Singapore: Festival of Books, 1989.

Harper, Timothy Norman. *The End of Empire and the Making of Malaya*. Cambridge: Cambridge University Press, 2001.

Havighurst, Alfred F. *Twentieth Century Britain*. 2nd ed. New York: Harper & Row, 1962.

Haydn, Hiram and John Cournos, eds. *A World of Great Stories: 115 Stories, the Best of Modern Literature*. New York: Crown, 1947.

Heren, Louis. *Growing Up on The Times*. London: H. Hamilton, 1978.

Herring, Robert. ed. *Life and Letters Today*, vol. 32, no. 55. London: Brendin Publishing Co., 1942.

Hill, Douglas Arthur, ed. *Tribune 40: The First Forty Years of a Socialist Newspaper*. London and New York: Quartet Books, 1977.

Hoalim Snr, Philip. *The Malayan Democratic Union: Singapore's First Democratic Political Party*. Singapore: Institute of Southeast Asian Studies, 1973.

Hooker, James R. *Black Revolutionary*. New York: Praeger, 1967.

Jackson, James C. *Planters and Speculators; Chinese and European Agricultural Enterprises in Malaya, 1786–1921*. Kuala Lumpur: University of Malaya Press, 1968.

Jackson, R.N. *Immigrant Labour and the Development of Malaya, 1786–1920.* Kuala Lumpur: Government Press, 1961.
Josey, Alex. *Labour Laws in a Changing Singapore.* Singapore: Donald Moore, 1966.
———. *Lee Kuan Yew: The Struggle for Singapore.* London: Angus & Robertson, 1980.
———. *Lee Kuan Yew*, vol. 1. Singapore: Times Books International, 1980.
———. *Trade Unionism in Malaya.* Singapore: Donald Moore, 1958.
Kramnick, Isaac and Barry Sheerman. *Harold Laski: A Life on the Left.* New York: Allen Lane, Penguin Press, 1993.
Lam Peng Er and Kevin Y.L. Tan, eds. *Lee's Lieutenants: Singapore's Old Guard.* Sydney: Allen & Unwin, 1999.
Lau, Albert. *A Moment of Anguish: Singapore in Malaysia and the Politics of Disengagement.* Singapore: Times Academic Press, 1998.
Lee Kuan Yew. *The Battle for Merger.* Ministry of Culture series. Singapore: Government Printing Office, 1961.
———. *The Singapore Story: Memoirs of Lee Kuan Yew.* Singapore: Times Editions, Singapore Press Holdings, 1998.
Lee Siow Mong, Tan Sri. *Words Cannot Equal Experience.* Petaling Jaya, Selangor, Malaysia: Pelanduk Publications, 1985.
Lewis, John. *The Left Book Club.* London: Gollancz, 1970.
Lim Cheng Leng. *Story of a Psy-Warrior: Tan Sri Dr C.C. Too.* Batu Caves, Selangor Darul Ehsan, Malaysia: Lim Cheng Leng, 2000.
Ludowyk, E.F.C. *The Story of Ceylon.* London: Faber, 1962.
Martin, Kingsley, ed. *A Volume of Autobiography.* London: Hutchinson, 1968.
Ministry of Culture, Singapore. *Democratic Socialism in Action June 1959–April 1963.*
Moore, Reginald, ed. *Modern Reading, No. 5.* London: Phoenix House Limited, 1942.
Ongkili, J.P. *The Borneo Response to Malaysia, 1961–1963.* Donald Moore Press, 1967.
Pang Cheng Lian. *Singapore's People's Action Party: Its History, Organisation, and Leadership.* Singapore: Oxford University Press, 1971.
Peebles, Gavin and Peter Wilson. *Economic Growth and Development in Singapore.* Northampton, Mass.: Edward Elgar Pub., 2002.
Publicity Division, Ministry of Culture, Singapore. *Malaysian Heritage*, 1962.
Purcell, Victor. *Malaya: Communist or Free?* London: Gollancz, 1954.
———. *The Memoirs of a Malayan Official.* London: Cassell, 1965.

Ramakrishna, Kumar. *Emergency Propaganda: The Winning of Malayan Hearts and Minds 1948–1958*. Richmond, Surrey: Curzon, 2002.

Ramasamy, Rajakrishnan. *Sojourners to Citizens, Sri Lankan Tamils in Malaysia, 1885–1965*. Kuala Lumpur: R. Rajakrishnan, 1988.

Rehman, Rashid and James Wing-On Wong. *Malaysia in Transition: The Battle for the Malay Mind*. Singapore: Institute of Southeast Asian Studies, 2003.

Rolph, C.H. *Kingsley: The Life, Letters and Diaries of Kingsley*. Harmondsworth: Penguin, 1973.

Shafie, Ghazali. *Memoir on the Formation of Malaysia*. Bangi, Malaysia: Penerbit Universiti Kebangsaan, 1998.

Shennan, Margaret. *Out in the Midday Sun: The British in Malaya 1880–1960*. London: John Murray, 2000.

Shrivastava, K.M. *News Agencies from Pigeon to Internet*. New Delhi: New Dawn Press, 2007.

Singh, Iqbal, Ahmed Ali, K.S. Shelvankar, A. Subramaniam, eds. *Indian Writing*, vol. I, no. 4 (August 1941).

Sopiee, Mohamed Noordin. *From Malayan Union to Singapore Separation*. Kuala Lumpur: Penerbit University Malaya Sdn. Bhd., 1974.

Stockwell, A.J., ed. *Malaya: British Documents on the End of Empire, Series B*. London: HMSO, 1995.

Stockwell, A.J. et al., eds. *Malaya: Part III, The Alliance Route to Independence 1953–1957*, edited by A.J. Stockwell et al. London: HMSO, 1995.

Tamney, Joseph B. *The Struggle Over Singapore's Soul: Western Modernization and Asian Culture*. New York: Walter de Gruyter, 1996.

Tan Siok Sun. *Goh Keng Swee: A Portrait*. Singapore: Editions Didier Millet, 2007.

Tan Tai Yong. *Creating "Greater Malaysia": Decolonization and the Politics* of *Merger*. Singapore: Institute of Southeast Asian Studies, 2008.

Tankel, Sylvia, ed. *Short Story International*, vol. 14, no. 79 (April 1990). New York: International Cultural Exchange, 1990.

Thomas, Francis. *Memoirs of a Migrant*. Singapore: University Education Press, 1972.

Thumboo, Edwin et al., eds. *The Fiction of Singapore*, Vol. 2. Anthology of ASEAN Literature. Sponsored by ASEAN Committee on Culture and Information, 1990.

Turnbull, Mary. *Dateline Singapore, 150 Years of The Straits Times*. Singapore: Singapore Press Holdings, 1995.

Vannatta, Dennis P., ed. *The English Short Story, 1945–1980: A Critical History*. Boston, Mass.: Twayne Publishers, 1985.

Vasil, Raj K. *Governing Singapore*. St Leonards, N.S.W.: Allen & Unwin, 2000.

Visram, Rozina. *Asians in Britain: 400 Years of History*. London: Pluto Press, 2002.

Wee, C.J.W. L. *Culture, Empire, and The Question of Being Modern*. Lanham, Maryland: Lexington Books, 2003.

Wignesan, T., ed. *Bunga Emas, An Anthology of Contemporary Malaysian Literature (1930–1963)*. Britain: The Garden City Press, 1964.

Yap, Sonny, Richard Lim and Leong Weng Kam. *Men In White*. Singapore: Singapore Press Holdings, 2009.

Yeo Kim Wah. *Political Development in Singapore, 1945–55*. Singapore: Singapore University Press, 1973.

Zahari, Said. *Dark Clouds at Dawn: A Political Memoir*. Kuala Lumpur: Insan, 2001.

Singapore Parliament: Sessional Papers

Legislative Assembly, Singapore. *Interim Report of the Malayanisation Commission*. Sessional Paper, Cmd. 14 of 1956.

Legislative Assembly, Singapore. *Final Report of the Malayanisation Commission*. Sessional Paper, Cmd. 33 of 1956.

Singapore Parliament Official Report. Vols. 11–22.

Private Papers

The S. Rajaratnam Papers, Singapore: Institute of Southeast Asian Studies (ISEAS).

S. Rajaratnam Papers (in the private possession of Irene Ng).

The David Marshall Papers. Singapore: Institute of Southeast Asian Studies.

History of the Labour Movement: Interview with S. Rajaratnam, 1994. Singapore Institute of Labour Studies, NTUC.

Oral History (National Archives of Singapore)

Arasu, V.T.

Baker, Maurice

Bloodworth, Dennis

Bogaars, George

Choy, Sivanandan

Conceicao, J.F.

Douglas-Hamilton, George Nigel (10th Earl of Selkirk)

Eu Chooi Yip

Josey, Alex

Khoo, T.S.

Lee Khoon Choy
Lim Hock Siew
Marshall, David Saul
Nathan, S.R.
Pillay, V.K.
Rajah, A.P.
Rajah, T.T.
Rajaratnam, S.
Subramaniam, M.
Toh Chin Chye
Vasagar, S.M.
Wok, Othman
Woodhull, S.

Party Publications

People's Action Party. 1st Anniversary Celebration souvenir. 27 November 1955.

People's Action Party's 10th Anniversary souvenir, *Our First 10 Years*.

People's Action Party 1954–1979. *Petir* 25th anniversary issue.

People's Action Party 1954–1984. *Petir* 30th anniversary issue.

"The New Phase After Merdeka — Our Task and Policy". *Petir* (special issue of *Petir* on 22 November 1958). Singapore: People's Action Party.

Index

K

L

ABOUT THE AUTHOR

Born in Penang, Malaysia, Irene Ng came to Singapore to further her studies in 1980. She is now a Singaporean. She studied sociology, English language and philosophy at the National University of Singapore and graduated with a Bachelor of Arts and Social Science in 1986. She later obtained her Master of Science in international relations from the London School of Economics and Political Science. In June 2006, she was awarded an Honorary Professorial Fellowship at the University of Edinburgh. From 1986 to 2001, she worked as a journalist for the Singapore Press Holdings and was the senior political correspondent of *The New Paper* and *The Straits Times*. She has won journalism and writing awards.

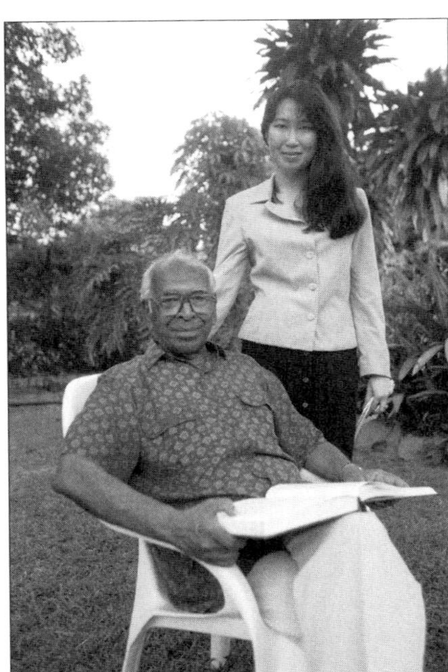

Irene Ng, then a journalist, with S. Rajaratnam at his home, 1997. (*SPH*)

In 2001, she gave up journalism to join politics in Singapore. She currently serves as the Member of Parliament for Tampines GRC. After joining politics, she worked as director of programmes and senior research fellow at the Singapore Institute of International Affairs, and later, as a director at National Trades Union Congress. In 2009, she returned to her passion for writing as a full-time writer. She is currently Writer-in-Residence at the Institute of Southeast Asian Studies, Singapore.